Short Stories
for Students

Short Stories for Students

Presenting Analysis, Context and Criticism on Commonly Studied Short Stories

Volume 4

Kathleen Wilson and Marie Lazzari, Editors

Bonnie J. Newcomer, Beloit Junior - Senior High School, Beloit, Kansas, Advisor
Dorothea M. Susag, Simms High School, Simms, Montana, Advisor

Foreword by Nancy Rosenberger, Conestoga High School, Berwyn, Pennsylvania

GALE

DETROIT · LONDON

55

Short Stories for Students

Staff

Editorial: Kathleen Wilson, Marie Lazzari, *Editors.* Greg Barnhisel, Thomas Bertonneau, Cynthia Bily, Paul Bodine, Julia Burch, Yoonmee Chang, John Chua, Carol Dell'Amico, Catherine Dominic, Mark Elliot, Terry Girard, Rena Korb, Rebecca Laroche, *Sketchwriters.* Suzanne Dewsbury, James Person, *Contributing Editors.* Aarti Stephens, *Managing Editor*

Research: Victoria B. Cariappa, *Research Manager.* Andrew Malonis, *Research Specialist.*

Permissions: Susan M. Trosky, *Permissions Manager.* Kimberly Smilay, *Permissions Specialist.* Kelly Quin, *Permissions Associate.*

Production: Mary Beth Trimper, *Production Director.* Evi Seoud, *Assistant Production Manager.* Shanna Heilveil, *Production Assistant*

Graphic Services: Randy Bassett, *Image Database Supervisor.* Mikal Ansari, Robert Duncan, *Imaging Specialists.* Pamela A. Reed, *Photography Coordinator.*

Copyright Notice

Table of Contents

An Adventure in Reading

Sitting on top of my desk is a Pueblo storytelling doll. Her legs stick straight out before her and around her neck and flowing down into her lap are wide-eyed children. Her mouth is open as though she were telling the Zuni tale of the young husband who followed his wife to the Land of the Dead, a story strangely like the Greek myth of Orpheus and Euridice, as both teach the dangers of youthful impatience.

Although the Pueblo doll was created in New Mexico, she symbolizes a universal human activity. The pharaohs listened intently to tales of the goddess Isis, who traveled to foreign lands to rescue the dismembered body of her husband Osiris. Biblical narratives thrill the reader with stories like that of mortal combat between David and the giant Goliath. Greek and Roman myths immortalize the struggles of the wandering warriors Odysseus and Aeneas. In the Middle Ages, kings, queens and courtiers sat spellbound in drafty halls as troubadours sang of tragic lovers and pious pilgrims.

Around the world and down through the ages, myths, folktales, and legends have spoken to us about the human condition and our place in the world of nature and of spirit. Despite its ancient beginnings, however, there is no rigid criteria to which a story must adhere. It is one of the most protean literary forms. Though many scholars credit the nineteenth-century Romantic writers Edgar Allan Poe and Nathaniel Hawthorne with creating the modern short story, the form refuses to be frozen by a list of essential characteristics. Perhaps this is one of the reasons William Faulkner called it the "most demanding form after poetry." Jack London felt it should be "concrete, to the point, with snap and go and life, crisp and crackling and interesting." Eudora Welty wrote that each story should reveal something new yet also contain something "as old as time."

Below are some of the qualities you may observe as you explore the works discussed in *Short Stories for Students*. These characteristics also demonstrate some of the ways the short story differs from the novel:

1. Because time is compressed or accelerated, **unity** in plot, character development, tone, or mood is essential.

2. The author has chosen to **focus** on one character, event, or conflict within a limited time.

3. Poe wrote that **careful craftsmanship** serves unity by ensuring that every word must contribute to the story's design.

4. Poe also believed that reading should take place in **one sitting** so that the story's unity is not lost.

5. A character is **revealed** through a series of incidents or a conflict. The short story generally stops when it has achieved this purpose. A novel **develops** a character throughout its many chapters.

Now that we have briefly explored the history of the short story and heard from a few of its creators, let us consider the role of the reader. Readers are not empty vessels that wait, lids raised, to receive a teacher's or a critic's interpretation. They bring their unique life experiences to the story. With these associations, the best readers also bring their attention (a word that means "leaning towards"), their reading skills, and, most importantly, their imagination to a reading of a story.

My students always challenged me to discuss, analyze, interpret, and evaluate the stories we read without destroying the thrill of being beamed up into another world. For years I grappled with one response after the other to this challenge. Then one day I read an article by a botanist who had explored the beauty of flowers by x-raying them. His illustrations showed the rose and the lily in their external beauty, and his x-rays presented the wonders of their construction. I brought the article to class, where we discussed the benefits of examining the internal design of flowers, relationships, current events, and short stories.

A short story, however, is not a fossil to admire. Readers must ask questions, guess at the answers, predict what will happen next, then read to discover. They and the author form a partnership that brings the story to life. Awareness of this partnership keeps the original excitement alive through discussion, analysis, interpretation, and evaluation. Literary explorations allow the reader to admire the authors' craftsmanship as well as their artistry. In fact, original appreciation may be enhanced by this x-ray vision. The final step is to appreciate once again the story in its entirety—to put the pieces back together.

Now it is your turn. Form a partnership with your author. During or following your adventure in reading, enter into a dialogue with the published scholars featured in *Short Stories for Students*. Through this dialogue with experts you will revise, enrich, and/or confirm your original observations and interpretations.

During this adventure, I hope you will feel the same awe that illuminates the faces of the listeners that surround the neck of my Pueblo storyteller.

Nancy Rosenberger
Conestoga High School
Berwyn, Pennsylvania

Introduction

Purpose of the Book

The purpose of *Short Stories for Students* (*SSfS*) is to provide readers with a guide to understanding, enjoying, and studying short stories by giving them easy access to information about the work. Part of Gale's "For Students" Literature line, *SSfS* is specifically designed to meet the curricular needs of high school and undergraduate college students and their teachers, as well as the interests of general readers and researchers considering specific short fiction. While each volume contains entries on classic stories frequently studied in classrooms, there are also entries containing hard-to-find information on contemporary stories, including works by multicultural, international, and women writers.

The information covered in each entry includes an introduction to the story and the story's author; a plot summary, to help readers unravel and understand the events in the work; descriptions of important characters, including explanation of a given character's role in the narrative as well as discussion about that character's relationship to other characters in the story; analysis of important themes in the story; and an explanation of important literary techniques and movements as they are demonstrated in the work.

In addition to this material, which helps the readers analyze the story itself, students are also provided with important information on the literary and historical background informing each work.

This includes a historical context essay, a box comparing the time or place the story was written to modern Western culture, a critical overview essay, and excerpts from critical essays on the story or author. A unique feature of *SSfS* is a specially commissioned overview essay on each story by an academic expert, targeted toward the student reader.

To further aid the student in studying and enjoying each story, information on media adaptations is provided, as well as reading suggestions for works of fiction and nonfiction on similar themes and topics. Classroom aids include ideas for research papers and lists of critical sources that provide additional material on the work.

Selection Criteria

The titles for each volume of *SSfS* were selected by surveying numerous sources on teaching literature and analyzing course curricula for various school districts. Some of the sources surveyed include: literature anthologies, *Reading Lists for College-Bound Students: The Books Most Recommended by America's Top Colleges; Teaching the Short Story: A Guide to Using Stories from Around the World,* by the National Council of Teachers of English (NTCE); and "A Study of High School Literature Anthologies," conducted by Arthur Applebee at the Center for the Learning and Teaching of Literature and sponsored by the National Endowment for the Arts and the Office of Educational Research and Improvement.

Input was also solicited from our expert advisory board, as well as educators from various areas. From these discussions, it was determined that each volume should have a mix of "classic" stories (those works commonly taught in literature classes) and contemporary stories for which information is often hard to find. Because of the interest in expanding the canon of literature, an emphasis was also placed on including works by international, multicultural, and women authors. Our advisory board members—current high-school teachers—helped pare down the list for each volume. Works not selected for the present volume were noted as possibilities for future volumes. As always, the editor welcomes suggestions for titles to be included in future volumes.

How Each Entry Is Organized

Each entry, or chapter, in *SSfS* focuses on one story. Each entry heading lists the title of the story, the author's name, and the date of the story's publication. The following elements are contained in each entry:

- **Introduction:** a brief overview of the story which provides information about its first appearance, its literary standing, any controversies surrounding the work, and major conflicts or themes within the work.

- **Author Biography:** this section includes basic facts about the author's life, and focuses on events and times in the author's life that may have inspired the story in question.

- **Plot Summary:** a description of the events in the story, with interpretation of how these events help articulate the story's themes.

- **Characters:** an alphabetical listing of the characters who appear in the story. Each character name is followed by a brief to an extensive description of the character's role in the story, as well as discussion of the character's actions, relationships, and possible motivation.

  Characters are listed alphabetically by last name. If a character is unnamed—for instance, the narrator in "The Eatonville Anthology"—the character is listed as "The Narrator" and alphabetized as "Narrator." If a character's first name is the only one given, the name will appear alphabetically by that name.

- **Themes:** a thorough overview of how the topics, themes, and issues are addressed within the story. Each theme discussed appears in a separate subhead, and is easily accessed through the boldface entries in the Subject/Theme Index.

- **Style:** this section addresses important style elements of the story, such as setting, point of view, and narration; important literary devices used, such as imagery, foreshadowing, symbolism; and, if applicable, genres to which the work might have belonged, such as Gothicism or Romanticism. Literary terms are explained within the entry, but can also be found in the Glossary of Literary Terms.

- **Historical and Cultural Context:** This section outlines the social, political, and cultural climate *in which the author lived and the work was created.* This section may include descriptions of related historical events, pertinent aspects of daily life in the culture, and the artistic and literary sensibilities of the time in which the work was written. If the story is historical in nature, information regarding the time in which the story is set is also included. Long sections are broken down with helpful subheads.

- **Critical Overview:** this section provides background on the critical reputation of the author and the story, including bannings or any other public controversies surrounding the work. For older works, this section may include a history of how story was first received and how perceptions of it may have changed over the years; for more recent works, direct quotes from early reviews may also be included.

- **Sources:** an alphabetical list of critical material quoted in the entry, with bibliographical information.

- **For Further Study:** an alphabetical list of other critical sources which may prove useful for the student. Includes full bibliographical information and a brief annotation.

- **Criticism:** an essay commissioned by *SSfS* which specifically deals with the story and is written specifically for the student audience, as well as excerpts from previously published criticism on the work.

In addition, each entry contains the following highlighted sections, if applicable, set separate from the main text:

- **Media Adaptations:** where applicable, a list of film and television adaptations of the story, including source information. The list also includes stage adaptations, audio recordings, musical adaptations, etc.

- **Compare and Contrast Box:** an "at-a-glance" comparison of the cultural and historical differences between the author's time and culture and late twentieth-century Western culture. This box includes pertinent parallels between the major scientific, political, and cultural movements of the time or place the story was written, the time or place the story was set (if a historical work), and modern Western culture. Works written after the mid-1970s may not have this box.

- **What Do I Read Next?:** a list of works that might complement the featured story or serve as a contrast to it. This includes works by the same author and others, works of fiction and nonfiction, and works from various genres, cultures, and eras.

- **Study Questions:** a list of potential study questions or research topics dealing with the story. This section includes questions related to other disciplines the student may be studying, such as American history, world history, science, math, government, business, geography, economics, psychology, etc.

Other Features

SSfS includes "An Adventure in Reading," a foreword by Nancy Rosenberger, chair of the English department at Conestoga High School in Berwyn, Pennsylvania. This essay provides an enlightening look at how readers interact with literature and how *Short Stories for Students* can help students enrich their own reading experiences.

A Cumulative Author/Title Index lists the authors and titles covered in each volume of the *SSfS* series.

A Cumulative Nationality/Ethnicity Index breaks down the authors and titles covered in each volume of the *SSfS* series by nationality and ethnicity.

A Subject/Theme Index, specific to each volume, provides easy reference for users who may be studying a particular subject or theme rather than a single work. Significant subjects from events to broad themes are included, and the entries pointing to the specific theme discussions in each entry are indicated in **boldface.**

Entries may include illustrations, including an author portrait, stills from film adaptations (when available), maps, and/or photos of key historical events.

Citing Short Stories for Students

When writing papers, students who quote directly from any volume of *SSfS* may use the following general forms to document their source. These examples are based on MLA style; teachers may request that students adhere to a different style, thus, the following examples may be adapted as needed.

When citing text from *SSfS* that is not attributed to a particular author (for example, the Themes, Style, Historical Context sections, etc.) the following format may be used:

> "The Celebrated Jumping Frog of Calaveras County." *Short Stories for Students.* Ed. Kathleen Wilson. Vol. 1. Detroit: Gale, 1997. 19-20.

When quoting the specially commissioned essay from *SSfS* (usually the first essay under the Criticism subhead), the following format may be used:

> Korb, Rena. Essay on "Children of the Sea." *Short Stories for Students.* Ed. Kathleen Wilson. Vol. 1. Detroit: Gale, 1997. 42.

When quoting a journal essay that is reprinted in a volume of *Short Stories for Students,* the following form may be used:

> Schmidt, Paul. "The Deadpan on Simon Wheeler." *The Southwest Review* XLI, No. 3 (Summer, 1956), 270-77; excerpted and reprinted in *Short Stories for Students,* Vol. 1, ed. Kathleen Wilson (Detroit: Gale, 1997), pp. 29-31.

When quoting material from a book that is reprinted in a volume of *SSfS,* the following form may be used:

> Bell-Villada, Gene H. "The Master of Short Forms," in *Garcia Marquez: The Man and His Work* (University of North Carolina Press, 1990); excerpted and reprinted in *Short Stories for Students,* Vol. 1, ed. Kathleen Wilson (Detroit: Gale, 1997), pp. 90-1.

We Welcome Your Suggestions

The editor of *Short Stories for Students* welcomes your comments and ideas. Readers who wish to suggest short stories to appear in future volumes, or who have other suggestions, are cordially invited to contact the editor. You may write to the editor at:

Editor, *Short Stories for Students*
Gale Research
835 Penobscot Bldg.
645 Griswold St.
Detroit, MI 48226-4094

Literary Chronology

1776: The signing of the Declaration of Independence signals the beginning of the American Revolution.

1789: The French Revolution, marked by the violent Reign of Terror, shifts the balance of power in France.

1809: Edgar Allan Poe is born in Boston on January 19.

1843: "The Tell-Tale Heart" by Edgar Allan Poe is published.

1845: *The Raven and Other Poems* by Edgar Allan Poe is published.

1849: Sarah Orne Jewett is born in Maine on September 3.

1849: Edgar Allan Poe dies in Baltimore on October 7.

1850: Guy de Maupassant is born in Normandy, France, on August 5.

1852: Mary Wilkins, later Freeman, is born near Boston, Massachusetts, on October 31.

1861: The U.S. Civil War begins when Confederate forces capture Fort Sumter in South Carolina.

1865: The U.S. Civil War ends; Abraham Lincoln is assassinated.

1865: Sui Sin Far is born Edith Maude Eaton in England.

1871: Stephen Crane is born in Newark, New Jersey, on November 1.

1875: Thomas Mann is born in Germany on June 6.

1876: Sherwood Anderson is born in Ohio on September 13.

1882: Virginia Stephen, later Woolf, is born in London on January 25.

1884: "The Necklace" by Guy de Maupassant is published in the Paris newspaper *Le Gaulois*.

1886: *A White Heron and Other Stories* by Sarah Orne Jewett is published.

1890: "The Revolt of 'Mother'" by Mary Wilkins Freeman is published in *Harper's Bazaar*.

1893: Guy de Maupassant dies in Paris on July 6.

1895: *The Red Badge of Courage,* Stephen Crane's novel of a young soldier who confronts the horrors of war, is published.

1896: F. Scott Fitzgerald is born in St. Paul, Minnesota, on September 24.

1897: "The Open Boat" by Stephen Crane is published.

1899: Jorge Luis Borges is born in Buenos Aires, Argentina, on August 24.

1900: Stephen Crane dies in Germany on June 5.

1902: Langston Hughes is born in Joplin, Missouri, on February 1.

1903: George Orwell is born Eric Blair in India on June 25.

1909: Sarah Orne Jewett dies in Maine on June 24.

1912: The S.S. *Titanic* sinks on her maiden voyage.

1912: *Mrs. Spring Fragrance* by Sui Sin Far is published.

1912: Thomas Mann's novella *Death in Venice* is published.

1913: Albert Camus is born in Algeria on November 7.

1914: World War I begins with the assassination of Archduke Ferdinand of Austria.

1914: Sui Sin Far dies in Montreal, Quebec.

1916: Roald Dahl is born in Wales on September 13.

1917: Arthur C. Clarke is born in England on December 16.

1918: World War I ends with the signing of the Treaty of Versailles.

1919: "Sophistication" by Sherwood Anderson is published in *Winesburg, Ohio.*

1920: The 18th Amendment, outlawing the sale, manufacture, and transportation of alcohol, goes into effect.

1925: "Disorder and Early Sorrow" by Thomas Mann is published in a *festschrift* celebrating the author's fiftieth birthday.

1925: *The Great Gatsby,* F. Scott Fitzgerald's novel of the excesses of the Jazz Age, is published.

1927: "The New Dress" by Virginia Woolf is published in *Forum* magazine.

1929: The stock market crash in October signals the beginning of a worldwide economic depression.

1929: *A Room of One's Own,* Virginia Woolf's landmark essay, is published.

1930: Mary Wilkins Freeman dies on March 15.

1931: "Babylon Revisited" by F. Scott Fitzgerald is published in the *Saturday Evening Post.*

1933: The 18th Amendment, or Prohibition, outlawing alcohol, is repealed.

1936: "Shooting an Elephant" by George Orwell is published.

1939: World War II begins when Nazi Germany, led by Adolf Hitler, invades Poland; England and France declare war in response.

1939: "Pierre Menard, Author of the Quixote" by Jorge Luis Borges is published in the magazine *Sur.*

1939: Toni Cade Bambara is born Miltona Mirkin Cade in New York City on March 25.

1940: Angela Carter is born in London on May 7.

1940: F. Scott Fitzgerald dies in Hollywood on December 21.

1941: Sherwood Anderson dies in the Panama Canal Zone on March 8.

1941: Virginia Woolf dies in Sussex, England, on March 28.

1942: *The Stranger,* Albert Camus's absurdist novel in which a young man commits murder for no apparent reason, is published.

1945: World War II ends in August with the atomic bombing of Hiroshima and Nagasaki, Japan, by the United States.

1945: Tobias Wolff is born in Birmingham, Alabama, on June 19.

1948: *1984,* George Orwell's classic novel of a dystopian society in the near future, is published.

1948: Leslie Marmon Silko is born in Albuquerque, New Mexico.

1950: Senator Joseph McCarthy of Wisconsin sets off the "Red Scare" that leads to government hearings and blacklisting of suspected communists.

1950: George Orwell dies on January 26.

1952: Jayne Anne Phillips is born in Buckhannon, West Virginia, on July 19.

1953: "Lamb to the Slaughter" by Roald Dahl is published in *Collier's* magazine.

1955: "The Star" by Arthur C. Clarke is published. It wins the Hugo Award for best science fiction story published that year.

1955: Thomas Mann dies in Zurich, Switzerland, on August 12.

1957: "The Guest" by Albert Camus is published in his collection *Exile and the Kingdom.*

1960: Albert Camus dies in Paris on January 4.

1963: U.S. President John F. Kennedy is assassinated in Dallas, Texas, on November 22.

1964: *Charlie and the Chocolate Factory,* Roald Dahl's classic children's novel about Willy Wonka's bizarre candy factory, is published.

1967: Langston Hughes dies in New York City on May 22.

1968: *2001: A Space Odyssey,* Arthur C. Clarke's novel about alien intelligence and human evolution, is published concurrent with the release of Stanley Kubrick's film of the same name.

1972: "Blues Ain't No Mockin Bird" by Toni Cade Bambara is published in the collection *Gorilla, My Love.*

1974: President Richard Nixon resigns following the Watergate scandal.

1979: *The Bloody Chamber and Other Stories* by Angela Carter is published.

1979: "Souvenir" by Jayne Anne Phillips is published in her collection *Black Tickets.*

1980: "In the Garden of the North American Martyrs" by Tobias Wolff is published in the journal *Antaeus.*

1981: "Yellow Woman" by Leslie Marmon Silko is published in her collection *Storyteller.*

1986: Jorge Luis Borges dies in Geneva, Switzerland, on June 14.

1989: *This Boy's Life: A Memoir,* Tobias Wolff's tale of a painful childhood, is published.

1990: Soviet leader Mikhail Gorbachev's policy of *glasnost* results in the fracturing of the Iron Curtain. By December the Soviet flag is lowered from the Kremlin.

1990: Roald Dahl dies in Oxford, England, on November 23.

1992: Angela Carter dies on February 16.

1995: Toni Cade Bambara dies on December 9.

Acknowledgments

The editors wish to thank the copyright holders of the excerpted criticism included in this volume and the permissions managers of many book and magazinc publishing companies for assisting us in securing reproduction rights. We are also grateful to the staffs of the Detroit Public Library, the Library of Congress, the University of Detroit Mercy Library, Wayne State University Purdy/Kresge Library Complex, and the University of Michigan Libraries for making their resources available to us. Following is a list of the copyright holders who have granted us permission to reproduce material in this volume of SSfS. Every effort has been made to trace copyright, but if omissions have been made, please let us know.

COPYRIGHTED EXCERPTS IN *SSFS*, VOLUME 4, WERE REPRODUCED FROM THE FOLLOWING PERIODICALS:

America, v. 141, December 8, 1979. © 1979 by America. All rights reserved. Reproduced with permission of America Press, Inc.—*American Indian Quarterly,* © v. 12, Winter, 1988. Copyright © Society for American Indian Studies & Research 1988. Reproduced by permission of the publisher.—*CEA Critic,* v. 57, Fall, 1994. Reproduced by permission.—*CLA Journal,* v. XI, September, 1967. Copyright, 1967 by The College Language Association. Reproduced by permission of The College Language Association—*Colby Library Quarterly,* v. XXI, March, 1985; v. XXII, March, 1986. Both reproduced by permission.—*Contemporary Literature,* v. 22, Spring, 1981. © 1981 by the Regents of the University of Wisconsin. Reproduced by permission of The University of Wisconsin Press.—*The Durham University Journal,* v. LXXXIII, July, 1991. Reproduced by permission.—*English Journal,* v. 55, September, 1966 for "'Shooting an Elephant'—An Essay to Teach" by Kenneth Keskinen. Copyright © 1966 by the National Council of Teachers of English. Reproduced by permission of the publisher and the author.—*The Explicator,* v. XXVII, March, 1969. Copyright © 1969 Helen Dwight Reid Educational Foundation. Reproduced with permission of the Helen Dwight Reid Educational Foundation, published by Heldref Publications.—*Extrapolation,* v. 21, Winter, 1980; v. 24, Fall, 1983; v. 28, Summer, 1987. Copyright © 1980, 1983, 1987 by Kent State University Press. All reproduced by permission.—*The French Review,* v. XLVI, February, 1973 for "The Symbolic Decor of 'The Guest'" by Paul Fortier. Copyright 1973 by the American Association of Teachers of French. Reproduced by permission.—*The Journal of Ethnic Studies,* v. 9, Spring, 1981; v. 13, Winter, 1986. Both reproduced by permission.—*Journal of Modern Literature,* v. 11, July, 1984. © Temple University, 1984. Reproduced by permission.—*Kansas Quarterly,* v. 14, Spring, 1982 for "Structural Metaphors in Fitzgerald's Short Fiction" by William J. Brondell. © copyright 1977 by the *Kansas Quarterly.* Reproduced by permission of the publisher and the author.—

MELUS, v. 8, Spring, 1981. Copyright, *MELUS,* The Society for the Study of Multi-Ethnic Literature of the United States, 1981. Reproduced by permission.—*Modern Fiction Studies,* v. X, Winter, 1964-65; v. XVII, Winter, 1971-72. The Johns Hopkins University Press. All rights reserved. Both reproduced by permission of the Johns Hopkins University Press.—*The New York Review of Books,* v. XXVII, March 6, 1980. Copyright © 1980 NYREV, Inc. Reproduced by permission from *The New York Review of Books.*—*The New York Times Book Review,* November 8, 1953. Copyright 1953, renewed 1981 by The New York Times Company. Reproduced by permission.—*Nineteenth-Century Fiction,* v. 19, March, 1965 for "Poe's 'The Tell-Tale Heart'" by E. Arthur Robinson. © 1965 by The Regents of the University of California. Reproduced by permission of The Regents and the author.—*Publishers Weekly,* v. 225, June 8, 1984. Copyright © 1984 by Xerox Corporation. Reproduced from *Publishers Weekly,* published by R.R. Bowker Company, a Xerox company, by permission.—*The Review of Contemporary Fiction,* v. 14, Fall, 1994. Copyright, 1994, by John O'Brien. Reproduced by permission.—*The Southern Review,* Louisiana State University, v. 22, Winter, 1986 for "Shooting Elephants Right" by D. H. Stewart. Copyright, 1986, by the author. Reproduced by permission of the author.—*Studies in American Indian Literature,* Series 2, v. 1, Fall, 1989 "The Storytellers in Storyteller" by Linda Danielson. Reproduced by permission of the author.—*Studies in Short Fiction,* v. 11, Fall, 1963; v. XII, Spring, 1975; v. 17, Summer, 1980; v. 18, Winter, 1981; v. 19, Winter, 1982; v. 30, Winter, 1993. Copyright 1963, 1975, 1980, 1981, 1982, 1993 by Newberry College. All reproduced by permission.

COPYRIGHTED EXCERPTS IN *SSFS,* VOLUME 4, WERE REPRODUCED FROM THE FOLLOWING BOOKS:

Anderson, David D. From *Sherwood Anderson: An Introduction and Interpretation.* Holt, Rinehart and Winston, Inc., 1967. Copyright © 1967 by Holt, Rinehart and Winston, Inc. All rights reserved. Reproduced by permission of the publisher.—Baker, Carlos. From "When the Story Ends: 'Babylon Revisited'" in *The Short Stories of F. Scott Fitzgerald: New Approaches in Criticism.* Edited by Jackson R. Bryer. The University of Wisconsin Press, 1982. Copyright © 1982 The Board of Regents of the University of Wisconsin System. All rights reserved. Reproduced by permission.—Bell-Villada, Gene H. From *Borges and His Fiction: A Guide to His Mind and Art.* University of North Carolina Press, 1981. Copyright © 1981 The University of North Carolina Press. All rights reserved. Reproduced by permission of the publisher.—Bone, Robert. From *Down Home: Origins of the Afro-American Short Story.* Columbia University Press, 1988. Copyright © 1975 by Robert Bone. All rights reserved. Reproduced by permission of the publisher.—Brooks, Cleanth and Robert Penn Warren. From *Understanding Fiction.* Edited by Cleanth Brooks and Robert Penn Warren. Second edition. Appleton-Century-Crofts, 1959. Copyright 1959, renewed 1987, by Appleton-Century-Crofts, Inc. All rights reserved. Adapted by permission of Prentice-Hall, Inc., Upper Saddle River, NJ—Bruck, Peter. From *The Black American Short Story in the 20th Century: A Collection of Critical Essays.* Edited by Peter Bruck. B.R. Grüner Publishing Co., 1977. Reproduced by permission.—Guy-Sheftall, Beverly. From an interview in *Sturdy Black Bridges.* Roseann P. Bell, Bettye J. Parker, Beverly Guy-Sheftall, eds. Anchor Press/Doubleday, 1979. Copyright © 1979 by Roseann P. Bell, Bettye J. Parker, Beverly Guy-Sheftall. All rights reserved. Reproduced by permission of the author.—Howe, Irving. From *Sherwood Anderson.* Stanford University Press, 1951. Copyright 1951 by the Board of Trustees of the Leland Stanford Junior University. Renewed 1979 by Irving Howe. Reproduced by permission of William Morrow & Co., Inc.—Joselyn, Sister M. (Eileen M. Baldeshwiler). From "Sherwood Anderson and the Lyric Story" in *The Twenties: Poetry and Prose, 20 Critical Essays.* Edited by Richard E. Langford and William E. Taylor. Everett Edwards, Inc., 1966. Copyright © 1966 Everett/Edwards, Inc. Reproduced by permission of Eileen M. Baldeshwiler.—Knapp, Bettina L. From *Stephen Crane.* Ungar Publishing Company, 1987. Copyright © 1987 by The Ungar Publishing Company. All rights reserved. Reproduced by permission.—Lewallen, Avis. From "Wayward Girls but Wicked Women? Female Sexuality in Angela Carter's 'The Bloody Chamber'" in *Perspectives on Pornography: Sexuality in Film and Literature.* Edited by Gary Day and Clive Bloom. Macmillan Press, 1988, St. Martin's Press, 1988. © the Editorial Board, (Co-operative) Press Ltd. 1988. Copyright Gary Day and Clive Bloom. All rights reserved. Reproduced by permission of Macmillan Press Ltd. In North America with permission of St. Martin's Press, Incorporated.—Ling, Amy. From *Between Worlds: Women Writers of Chinese Ancestry.* Pergamon Press, 1990. Copyright © 1990 by

Teachers College, Columbia University. All rights reserved. Reproduced by permission of the publisher.—Marks, Peter. From ''The Ideological Eye-Witness: An Examination of the Eye-Witness in Two Works by George Orwell'' in *Subjectivity and Literature from the Romantics to the Present Day*. Edited by Philip Shaw and Peter Stockwell. Pinter Publishers, 1991. Copyright © The editors and contributors 1991. All rights reserved. Reproduced by permission.—Meyerowitz, Selma. From ''What Is to Console Us? The Politics of Deception in Woolf's Short Stories'' in *New Feminist Essays on Virginia Woolf*. Edited by Jane Marcus. University of Nebraska Press, 1981. © Jane Marcus 1981. All rights reserved. Reproduced by permission of Macmillan Administration (Basingstoke) Ltd. and in the United States by University of Nebraska Press.—Rose, Ellen Cronan. From ''Through the Looking Glass: When Women Tell Fairy Tales'' in *The Voyage In: Fictions of Female Development*. Edited by Elizabeth Abel, Marianne Hirsch and Elizabeth Langland. University Press of New England, 1983. Copyright © 1983 by Trustees of Dartmouth College. All rights reserved. Reproduced by permission of University Press of New England.—Toor, David. From ''Guilt and Retribution in 'Babylon Revisited''' in *Fitzgerald and Hemingway Annual 1973*. Edited by Matthew J. Bruccoli and C. E. Frazer Clark, Jr. Microcard Editions Books, 1974. Copyright © 1974 by Indian Head, Inc. All rights reserved. Reproduced by permission of the author.—Walcutt, Charles Child. From ''Sherwood Anderson: Impressionism and the Buried Life'' in *American Literary Naturalism*. University of Minnesota Press, 1966. Reproduced by permission.—Ward, J. A. From *American Silences: The Realism of James Agee, Walker Evans, and Edward Hopper*. Louisiana State University Press, 1985. Copyright © 1985 by Louisiana State University Press. All rights reserved. Reproduced by permission of the author.—Warren, Alan. From ''Roald Dahl: Nasty, Nasty'' in *Discovering Modern Horror Fiction*. Edited by Darrell Schweitzer. Starmont House, 1985. Reproduced by permission.—White-Parks, Annette. From *Sui Sin Far/Edith Maude Eaton: A Literary Biography*. University of Illinois Press, 1995. Copyright © 1995 by Annette White-Parks. Reproduced by permission.—Wolff, Tobias and Jay Woodruff. From *A Piece of Work: Five Writers Discuss Their Revisions*. University of Iowa Press, 1993. Copyright © 1993 by Jay Woodruff and Tobias Wolff. Reproduced by permission of the publisher.

PHOTOGRAPHS AND ILLUSTRATIONS APPEARING IN *SSFS*, VOLUME 4, WERE RECEIVED FROM THE FOLLOWING SOURCES:

A Chinese procession through turn-of-the-century San Francisco, California, photograph. Archive Photos, Inc. Reproduced by permission.—A farm family, c. 1890, photograph. Ingram Collection/ Archive Photos, Inc. Reproduced by permission.—A great white heron in a Florida swamp, photograph by Buddy Mays. Buddy Mays/Corbis. Reproduced by permission.—Algerian prisoners of the French, photograph. UPI/Corbis-Bettmann. Reproduced by permission.—Anderson, Sherwood, photograph. Corbis-Bettmann. Reproduced by permission.—Toni Cade Bambara, photograph by Sandra L. Swans. Reproduced by permission.—Jorge Luis Borges, photograph. The Library of Congress.—Albert Camus, photograph. AP/Wide World Photos. Reproduced by permission.—Angela Carter, photograph by Jerry Bauer. © Jerry Bauer. Reproduced by permission.—Arthur C. Clarke, photograph. AP/Wide World Photos. Reproduced by permission.—Stephen Crane, photograph. The Library of Congress.—Roald Dahl, photograph by Eli Wallach. The Library of Congress.—F. Scott Fitzgerald, photograph by Carl Van Vechten. The Library of Congress.—Mary E. Wilkins Freeman, photograph. The Library of Congress.—French troops in Algeria, photograph. UPI/Corbis-Bettmann. Reproduced by permission.—Langston Hughes, photograph. AP/Wide World Photos. Reproduced by permission.—Sarah Orne Jewett, photograph. Corbis-Bettmann. Reproduced by permission.—Thomas Mann, photograph. AP/Wide World Photos. Reproduced by permission.—George Orwell, photograph. AP/Wide World Photos. Reproduced by permission.—Jayne Anne Phillips, photograph by Jerry Bauer. © Jerry Bauer. Reproduced by permission.—Edgar Allan Poe, photograph. AP/Wide World Photos. Reproduced by permission.—Leslie Marmon Silko, photograph by Robyn McDaniels. Reproduced by permission.—Dancing a quadrille at a ball, photograph. Corbis-Bettmann. Reproduced by permission.—Sui Sin Far/Edith Maude Eaton, December 1903, photograph. Courtesy of the Southwest Museum, Los Angeles, n.35626. Reproduced by permission.—''The Gulf Stream'' by Winslow Homer. Corbis-Bettmann. Reproduced by permission.—Tranquilized elephant, Kruger National Park, South Africa, photograph by Anthony Bannister. Peter Gallo; ABPL/Corbis. Reproduced by permission.—Tranquilized elephant in close-up, photograph by Anthony Bannister. Peter Gallo; ABPL/Corbis. Reproduced by permission.—Wimbledon crowd, photograph. Archive Photos, Inc. Reproduced by permission.—Tobias Wolff, photograph. AP/Wide World Photos. Reproduced by permission.—Virginia Woolf, photograph. AP/Wide World Photos. Reproduced by permission.—Zellie, a Paris Cabaret, photograph. UPI/Corbis-Bettmann. Reproduced by permission.

Contributors

Greg Barnhisel. Ph.D. in English, instructor of English, University of Texas at Austin. Entry: "Pierre Menard, Author of the Quixote."

Thomas Bertonneau. Assistant professor of English at Central Michigan University, and a senior policy analyst at the Mackinac Center for Public Policy. Entries: "Lamb to the Slaughter," "Shooting an Elephant."

Cynthia Bily. Instructor of literature at Adrian College in Michigan. Contributor to reference works, including *Feminist Writers, Gay and Lesbian Biography,* and *Chronology of Women Worldwide.* Entries: "A White Heron," "Yellow Woman."

Paul Bodine. Graduate of Johns Hopkins University and the University of Chicago. Instructor at the Milwaukee College of Business and a freelance writer, editor, and researcher. Entry: "Babylon Revisited."

Julia Burch. Instructor of literature at Southeastern Louisiana University and the University of Michigan. Entry: "The Guest."

Yoonmee Chang. Ph.D. candidate at the University of Pennsylvania. Entry: "Mrs. Spring Fragrance."

John Chua. Multimedia associate with the National Council of Teachers of English, freelance political writer, and writer for Cliffs Notes. Entry: "The Tell-Tale Heart."

Carol Dell'Amico. Ph.D. candidate in English literature and a Teaching Assistant at Rutgers University. Entry: "Souvenir."

Catherine Dominic. Editor of *Shakespeare's Characters for Students* and freelance writer. Entries: Compare and contrast sections for many entries.

Mark Elliot. Ph.D. candidate in history at New York University. Editor of the section on "New England Puritan Literature" for the *Cambridge History of American Literature.* Entry: "The Open Boat."

Terry Girard. Ph.D. candidate at Wayne State University in Detroit. Instructor of literature at Wayne State University. Entries: "The Star," "Blues Ain't No Mockin Bird."

Rena Korb. Freelance writer and editor specializing in English literature and Education. Entries: "The Revolt of 'Mother'," "Blues Ain't No Mockin Bird."

Rebecca Laroche. Instructor of literature and writing at Bates College, Albertus Magnus College, and Yale University. Entry: "The Bloody Chamber."

Marie Lazzari. Editor and freelance writer. Entries: "The Open Boat," "Shooting an Elephant," "Yellow Woman."

Jean Leverich. Ph.D. in literature from the University of Michigan. instructor of English at the University of Michigan, New York University, and Georgetown University. Entry: "Yellow Woman."

Teresa Lyle. Ph.D candidate at the University of Findlay. Entry: "The New Dress."

Sarah Madsen-Hardy. Ph.D. in English from the University of Michigan, freelance writer. Entry: "Slave on the Block."

Thomas March. Ph.D. candidate at New York University. Entry: "The New Dress."

David Mesher. Ph.D. in English from the University of Washington, professor of English at San Jose State University. Entry: "Souvenir."

Carl Mowery. Ph.D. in rhetoric from Southern Illinois University, instructor in English at Murray State University in Kentucky. Entries: "Disorder and Early Sorrow," "Slave on the Block."

Elisabeth Piedmont-Marton. Ph.D. in English from the University of Texas at Austin, coordinator of the university's writing center. Entries:

"In the Garden of the North American Martyrs," "Lamb to the Slaughter."

Jason Pierce. Ph.D. candidate at the University of South Carolina and an instructor of composition and literature. Entry: "The Necklace."

John S. Reist, Jr. Clergyman and professor of Christianity and literature at Hillsdale College in Michigan. Author of essays on Sherwood Anderson's *Winesburg, Ohio.* Entry: "Sophistication."

William Rouster. Ph.D. in composition from Wayne State University in Detroit, instructor of composition and rhetoric at Wayne State University, Oakland University, and Eastern Michigan University. Entry: "In the Garden of the North American Martyrs."

Anne Trubek. Ph.D. candidate in English at Temple University in Philadelphia, instructor of English literature at Temple University. Entry: "Blues Ain't No Mockin Bird."

Kathleen Wilson. Editor and freelance writer. Entries: "The Bloody Chamber," "Sophistication."

Babylon Revisited

F. Scott Fitzgerald
1931

When ''Babylon Revisited'' was first published in the *Saturday Evening Post* in February, 1931, F. Scott Fitzgerald had already written three of his major novels—*This Side of Paradise, The Beautiful and Damned,* and *The Great Gatsby*—and he was finally making a good living as an author. The story of a recovering alcoholic's return to Paris after the start of the Depression and his attempt to win back custody of his daughter, ''Babylon Revisited'' is a portrait of a man trying to get his life back in order after having made several bad mistakes in the years following his rise to riches during the heyday of the stock market in the 1920s. Fitzgerald came to regard ''Babylon Revisited'' as one of his most important stories. He gave it pride of place as the last story in his 1935 collection *Taps at Reveille;* he called it a ''magnificent story'' in a 1940 letter to his daughter; and to another correspondent he described it as one of the benchmarks in his evolution as a writer: ''You see, I not only announced the birth of my young illusions in *This Side of Paradise,* but pretty much the death of them in some of my last *Post* stories like 'Babylon Revisited'.''

Author Biography

F. Scott Fitzgerald was born in September, 1896, in St. Paul, Minnesota, the son of an entrepreneur and salesman and his wife, a distant cousin of Francis

Scott Key, author of "The Star-Spangled Banner," for whom he was named. He displayed an interest in writing early on and in 1911, he moved to New Jersey to attend the Newman College Preparatory School. Two years later he entered Princeton University, and in 1917 he received a commission as a lieutenant in the U.S. Army. Hoping to eventually see combat in World War I, Fitzgerald was assigned to Camp Sheridan in Montgomery, Alabama, where he met Zelda Sayre, the daughter of an Alabama supreme court justice. He was smitten by Zelda's charm, but was forced to turn his attention fully toward earning a living as a writer. Fitzgerald sold his first short story in 1919, and in September of that year Scribner's accepted his first novel, *This Side of Paradise,* for publication. It immediately became a financial and critical success, and Fitzgerald was suddenly a literary figure of national prominence.

Having achieved success as a writer, Fitzgerald resumed his courtship of Zelda Sayre, and they married in 1920. Their only child, a daughter named Scottie, was born in 1921. That same year, the Fitzgeralds undertook the first of several extended trips to Europe. On one such trip in 1925, Fitzgerald met aspiring novelist Ernest Hemingway, whose career and work he championed until Hemingway's own fame and Fitzgerald's troubled personal life weakened their friendship. Fitzgerald's second novel, *The Beautiful and Damned,* was published to mixed critical reviews in 1922. Three years later, he published *The Great Gatsby,* his most popular and admired work, though it received several disappointing reviews upon publication, which discouraged him deeply. Although Fitzgerald had begun drinking heavily at Princeton, he became severely alcoholic in the mid 1920s, and his drinking, combined with his expensive tastes and Zelda's mental instability, began to seriously affect his health, finances, and productivity. After *Gatsby* in 1925, for example, he did not publish another novel until *Tender Is the Night* in 1934. The bulk of his income came from advances sent by his legendary editor at Scribner's, Maxwell Perkins, and from the sale of his short stories to high-paying magazines such as the *Saturday Evening Post* and *Esquire.* Between 1919 and 1939 he sold 160 stories, primarily to pay his bills and thus buy him small windows of time to work on his novels.

Desperate for income to support his lifestyle and psychologically taxed by Zelda's treatment at mental sanitariums, Fitzgerald moved to Hollywood in 1937 to work as a screenwriter for Metro-Goldwyn-Mayer (MGM) studios. Although he saw only one of his screenplays produced as a finished film, he continued to work on film treatments, short stories, and his last major work, the unfinished novel *The Last Tycoon,* until he died of a heart attack in December of 1940. In a posthumous collection of confessional *Esquire* pieces, *The Crack-Up,* Fitzgerald succinctly offered his own harsh epitaph for his last years: "Then I was drunk for many years, and then I died."

Many autobiographical details shaped the content of "Babylon Revisited." Like Charlie Wale's daughter Honoria, Fitzgerald's only child, Scottie (who was also nicknamed "Pie"), was about nine years old at the time of the story's composition, and, like Charlie, Fitzgerald was confronted with the problem of Scottie's custody after Zelda's mental instability began to accelerate in 1930. Also like Charlie, Fitzgerald was also a prosperous Irish-American expatriate, and, as the evocative description of 1930 Paris in the story suggests, Fitzgerald was also intimately familiar with such Parisian landmarks as the Hotel Ritz, Josephine Baker's nude revue, and the club scene and restaurants of Paris nightlife. Most centrally, however, Fitzgerald, like Charlie, also wrestled painfully with his alcoholism, and his skillful evocation of the self-delusions and strategies Charlie adopts to convince himself of his rehabilitation were drawn directly from Fitzgerald's lifelong struggle with heavy drinking. Charlie's pre-1929 Paris escapades, alluded to throughout "Babylon Revisited"—squandered money, bitter marital disputes, and alcohol-fueled decline—are sharply autobiographical. Fitzgerald biographer Matthew Bruccoli has also pointed out that the baleful Marion Peters, Charlie's sister-in-law, was "obviously" based on Fitzgerald's own sister-in-law, Zelda's older sister Rosalind Smith, who questioned Fitzgerald's ability to raise Scottie properly.

Plot Summary

"Babylon Revisited" is the story of a father's attempt to regain the custody of his daughter after recovering from the death of his wife and his own battle with alcoholism. After having built a fortune in stock investments during the great bull market of the 1920s, American businessman Charlie Wales had quit his job and moved to Paris with his wife, Helen, to enjoy his newfound wealth. Friction within their marriage, his own weakness for alcohol, and the couple's wild lifestyle, however, led to Helen's death and Charlie's admission to a sanitarium to recover from his alcohol dependence. During this time, the couple's young daughter was sent to live with Helen's sister and her husband in Paris. After Charlie was released from the sanitarium, he moved to Prague, Czechoslovakia, where he reestablished himself as a businessman. As the story begins, Charlie sits at his old haunt, the bar at the Ritz Hotel, asking the bartender, Alix, about the whereabouts of some of the people he knew when he was last in Paris a year and a half before. When Alix offers him a drink, Charlie declines, telling him ''I'm going slow these days.''

Out on the Paris streets, Charlie passes places that remind him of his three pre-crash years in Paris and reflects on how his formerly debauched lifestyle has spoiled Paris for him. His cab ride takes him past such Paris landmarks as the Place de la Concorde, the river Seine, and the Left Bank. Charlie arrives at his brother-in-law's apartment and is greeted by his daughter, Honoria. He tells her guardians, Lincoln and Marion Peters, about his newfound success in Prague. When the conversation shifts, Charlie comments nostalgically on the days before the crash, when Paris was overrun by prosperous Americans like himself: ''It was nice while it lasted. . . . We were a sort of royalty, almost infallible, with a sort of magic around us.'' During dinner he feels a great protectiveness toward Honoria, but having decided to let the Peters's bring up the subject of his regaining custody, he leaves for a late-night tour of Paris.

The next day Charlie treats Honoria to lunch at a restaurant and offers to take her to a toy store and then the vaudeville. When Honoria tells Charlie she wants to come live with him, he puts her off in anticipation of his coming conversation with his in-laws about regaining custody of her. As they leave the restaurant, they run into two ''ghosts out of the past,'' Duncan Schaeffer and Lorraine Quarrles. The two still-drunken old friends invite Charlie to join them for lunch, to dine with him later, and ask to accompany him and Honoria to the vaudeville. He evades all their invitations, and when Duncan asks for his address he stalls, telling Duncan he will call him later. Afterward, he views the encounter coolly: ''They wanted to see him, because he was stronger than they were now, because they wanted to draw a certain sustenance from his strength.''

The next day Charlie returns to the Peters's to formally request custody of Honoria. Marion does

F. Scott Fitzgerald

not take kindly to the suggestion. She is still bitter about the death of her sister, which she blames on Charlie, and does not believe that he will remain sober for long. He admits that it is possible that he ''might go wrong at any time.'' Charlie's strategy of assuming ''the chastened attitude of the reformed sinner'' pays off, and Marion eventually sees that Charlie is in control of his life again and resignedly leaves Charlie and Lincoln to make the final decision. As Charlie leaves, Lincoln assures him that Marion now has confidence that Charlie can provide a stable home for Honoria and will agree to his assuming custody of his daughter. That night Charlie is haunted by the memory of Helen, who appears to him in a white dress, sitting on a swing, assuring him that she is happy for him and wants Honoria to return to Prague with him. As he falls asleep, he imagines Helen swinging ''faster and faster all the time,'' until he can no longer understand what she is saying.

Charlie's fourth day in Paris begins with a phone call to Lincoln Peters to finalize his plans for taking Honoria back to Prague with him. Peters assures him that Honoria can return with him but informs him that Marion wants to retain legal guardianship over Honoria for one more year. Charlie agrees, and they arrange to ''settle the details on the spot'' later that evening. Back at his hotel, Charlie finds a note from Lorraine Quarrles forwarded from the Ritz bar in which she reminisces about some of his alcohol-inspired stunts two years before and invites him to meet her ''for old time's sake'' at the Ritz Hotel later that day. Charlie recoils in horror at the memory of the ''utter irresponsibility'' of his pre-crash Paris life and breathes a sigh of relief that Alix at the Ritz has not given her his hotel address. At five, Charlie heads for the Peters's apartment, where he finds that Marion has ''accepted the inevitable.'' Suddenly, a drunken Duncan and Lorraine appear at the door to invite Charlie to dinner. Badly shaken, Marion Peters storms out of the room, and Lincoln tells Charlie that their dinner is off and to call him the next day at his office.

Charlie heads for the Ritz bar hoping to confront Lorraine and Duncan about their drunken appearance at the Peters's. Not finding them, he orders a drink and is greeted by Paul, the head bartender who had presided over Charlie's pre-crash revelries at the Ritz. '' I heard that you lost a lot in the crash,'' Paul inquires. ''I did,'' Charlie answers, ''but I lost everything I wanted in the boom.'' ''Selling short?'' Paul asks, and Charlie answers, ''Something like that.'' He calls Lincoln Peters only to learn that Marion wants him to wait at least six months before they will consider the question of Honoria's custody again. Back in the Ritz bar, he declines the bartender's offer of another drink and resolves to send Honoria some presents the next day—lots of presents. ''He would come back some day; they couldn't make him pay forever. . . . He was absolutely sure Helen wouldn't have wanted him to be so alone.''

Characters

Alix

Alix is the Hotel Ritz bartender who, along with the head barman, Paul, links Charlie Wales to his wild Paris life in the days before the stock market crash of 1929. As the story begins, he is filling Charlie in on the grim fates of Charlie's former Paris compatriots—Mr. Campbell, George Hardt, ''the Snow Bird,'' Duncan Schaeffer, and Claude Fessenden. One is ill, another has returned to the United States after losing everything in the crash, and a third has been banned from the Ritz for trying to pass a bad check.

Alix is the first and last of several characters in the story who test Charlie's resolve to remain an ex-alcoholic. He offers Charlie a drink in the story's opening scene and another in the story's conclusion. Charlie declines both.

Paul

Paul is the head bartender at the Ritz Hotel bar in Paris and one of the witnesses to Charlie's wild lifestyle before his wife's death. He, too, made a killing in the bull market of the 1920s and used the money to buy such luxuries as a country house and a ''custom-built'' car, which he drives to work but scrupulously parks a block from the Ritz so as to maintain his humble image as a barman. He appears only at the end of the story, when Charlie angrily returns to the Ritz to locate Lorraine Quarrles and Duncan Schaeffer, whose drunken arrival at the Peters's has sabotaged Charlie's plans to reclaim custody of his daughter, Honoria. Like his fellow barman Alix at the beginning of the story, Paul fills Charlie in on the post-crash fortunes of Charlie's former Paris social companions. ''I heard that you lost a lot in the crash,'' he tells Charlie. ''I did,'' Charlie answers, ''but I lost everything I wanted in the boom.'' Paul misreads Charlie's reply as a reference to investment blunders. ''Selling short,'' he suggests, referring to the stock market practice of gambling on the future decline of a stock's price. Charlie's answer, ''Something like that,'' continues the financial metaphor, but hints that Charlie's boom-year losses were of a much more personal nature.

Lincoln Peters

Lincoln Peters is the husband of Marion Peters and Charlie's brother–in–law. A fair-minded man, he is devoted to his family and is willing to give Charlie the benefit of the doubt about his apparent reform. His home in Paris is ''warm and comfortably American,'' and, as his first name suggests, Lincoln represents the kind of stolid, traditional American that Charlie had ceased to be during his ''nightmare'' years before the crash. Unlike Charlie, Lincoln had never saved enough money from his job at a Paris bank to invest in the bull market of the 1920s and reap the rewards of the boom's easy money. Charlie describes the Peters's middle-class life succinctly: ''They were not dull people. But they were very much in the grip of life and circumstance.''

Throughout the story, Lincoln is the only adult who expresses a belief that Charlie has reformed himself. When Charlie explains that part of his program for recovery is to have a single drink every day, Lincoln quickly endorses the idea; when Charlie tells the Peters's that his deepest fear is that he will miss Honoria's childhood entirely, Lincoln sympathizes; and when Marion lashes out at Charlie for swearing, Lincoln takes Charlie's side. Finally, when Marion tells Charlie that she holds him partly responsible for Helen's death, Lincoln tells Charlie "I never thought you were responsible for that," he says.

Lincoln is the mediator between Marion and Charlie, translating Marion's emotional words and behavior into terms Charlie can understand: "I think she sees now," he tells Charlie, "that you—can provide for the child, and so we can't very well stand in your way or Honoria's way." But his first loyalty is to his family, even though he agrees that "there was no reason for delay" in letting Charlie take Honoria back to Prague. Lincoln understands his wife's resentment about Charlie's former free-wheeling days: "I think Marion felt there was some kind of injustice in it—you not even working toward the end, and getting richer and richer." It is clear from Lincoln's words that Marion's sense of injustice may be his as well. After Duncan and Lorraine interrupt Charlie's visit to the Peters, it is Lincoln who must tell Charlie that Marion has changed her mind about giving him custody of Honoria. Charlie densely asks Lincoln whether Marion is "angry" with him; the sharpness of Lincoln's reply underscores the new relation between the two men: "'Sort of,' he said, almost roughly."

Marion Peters

Because she retains legal guardianship over Charlie's daughter, Marion Peters represents Charlie's nemesis, the most formidable external obstacle standing between him and his dream of a future with his daughter. The older sister of Charlie's dead wife, Marion is "a tall woman with worried eyes" who once had a "fresh" American attractiveness, but health problems, financial anxieties, and the unexpected death of her sister have left her embittered and frail. She regards Charlie with an "unalterable distrust" and "instinctive antipathy." Though she provides Charlie's daughter with a warm, American-style home—an island of domesticity amidst the pagan wickedness of Paris—for her Charlie represents the ugly undomesticated American, irresponsible, ostentatiously materialistic, and devoid of character. Fitzgerald underscores the contrast Charlie sees between Marion and Helen by describ-

Media Adaptations

- "Babylon Revisited" was adapted as the film *The Last Time I Saw Paris* by director Richard Brooks, starring Elizabeth Taylor, Van Johnson, Walter Pidgeon, Donna Reed, Eva Gabor, and Roger Moore, Metro-Goldwyn-Mayer, 1954; available from Metro-Goldwyn-Mayer.

- "Babylon Revisited" was produced as an audio book, *Babylon Revisited and Other Stories*, read by Alexander Scourby, Listening Library, 1985; distributed by Newman Communications Corporation.

ing Marion as dressed in a "dignified black dinner dress that just faintly suggested mourning" with a necklace of ominous "black stars," while Helen appears to Charlie in a dream as the image of purity in a white dress.

Marion's dislike for Charlie predates his alcoholic collapse and his contribution to Helen's death. She never believed Helen was really happy with him; and, Charlie believes, she needs a "tangible villain" to explain the dissatisfactions of her life. Perhaps most importantly, she resented the fortune that came his was by chance when he played the stock market, and through his own efforts during his period of sobriety and hard work in Prague. Moreover, she has trouble believing that Charlie had overcome his alcoholism. His admission that he had been in the Ritz Hotel bar fuels her suspicions, and the appearance of the snide and inebriated Lorraine and Duncan in confirms her worst fears.

Lorraine Quarrles

Lorraine Quarrles is "a lovely, pale blond of thirty" with whom Charlie socialized in his alcoholic days before the stock market crash. Although she is married, she has left her husband behind in America and is escorted by Duncan Schaeffer (who she familiarly calls "Dunc") throughout the story. She seems to be attracted to Charlie, and though he feels nothing for her now, during his dissipated days

Lorraine was ''very attractive'' to him. Now she is one of the ''ghosts'' from his past: ''blurred, worn away.''

Charlie has severed whatever emotional connection he had to Lorraine, and he dismisses her coolly as ''one of a crowd that had helped them make months into days in the lavish times of three years ago.'' When he escapes Lorraine and Duncan's attempts to renew their friendship, he describes her as a kind of emotional vampire, conscious of Charlie's self-control and sobriety and wishing to pull him back into the alcoholic daze she has not escaped: ''they wanted to see him, because he was stronger than they were now, because they wanted to draw a certain sustenance from his strength.'' Lorraine and Duncan follow Charlie and Honoria to the vaudeville and finally prevail upon him to share a drink with them. Lorraine admits to Charlie that since the crash she and her husband have been ''poor as hell'' and that her husband has given her ''two hundred a month and told me I could do my worst on that.'' At the Peters', as Charlie tries to finalize his future with Honoria, Lorraine appears as a spectral, disembodied ''voice'' that ''develops under the light into . . . Lorraine Quarrles.'' She has appeared to do her ''worst,'' drunkenly disrupting the scene in which Marion Peters is agreeing to let Charlie have custody of his daugher. She teases Charlie for being so ''solemn,'' and when he remains unresponsive to her, she angrily reminds him of a time he sought her out early one morning desperate for a drink.

Duncan Schaeffer

Duncan Schaeffer is a college friend of Charlie's who participated in Charlie's self-destructive life during his three-year Paris debauch before the stock market crash of 1929. Charlie asks the Ritz bartender about him in the story's opening scene. Later, at a Paris restaurant with his daughter, Charlie runs into Duncan, who is escorting another of Charlie's former party chums, Lorraine Quarrles. Duncan repeatedly tries to get Charlie to join them, but Charlie declines, eventually telling him that he and Honoria are headed for the vaudeville show at the Empire.

Charlie views Duncan's dogged sociability with deep suspicion: ''They liked him because he was functioning, because he was serious; they wanted to see him, because he was stronger than they were

now, because they wanted to draw a certain sustenance from his strength.'' Charlie's disclosure that he and Honoria will be at the Empire threatens his resolution to reject his past, for Duncan and Lorraine follow Charlie and Honoria to the Empire, where Duncan offers Charlie a drink. Worn down by Duncan's persistence, Charlie relents.

Later, Duncan and Lorraine, drunkenly burst in on Charlie at the Peters's apartment, seriously damaging Charlie's attempt to reclaim his daughter.

Charlie Wales

Charlie Wales is the protagonist of ''Babylon Revisited'' and serves as the lens through which readers see the events of the story. A thirty-five-year old Irish-American businessman from Vermont, Charlie moved to Paris with his wife, Helen, and daughter, Honoria, to enjoy the windfall from stock investments he made during Wall Street's boom years in the late 1920s. Charlie and his family travel through Europe enjoying their wealth until his drinking, lack of work, quarrels with Helen, the corrupting influence of money, and the couple's new social circle begin to destroy his marriage. One night, after an argument, Charlie locks his wife out of their apartment during a storm. Later, he checks into a sanitarium to treat his alcoholism, learns that most of his money has been lost in the stock market crash, and, as a gesture to his wife, assigns legal custody of Honoria to Helen's sister, Marion. When Helen dies of heart trouble, Charlie moves to Prague to reestablish himself, and a year and a half later, prosperous and apparently sober, he returns to Paris to reclaim Honoria.

During the action of the story, Charlie is described as a devoted, loving father who desperately misses his child and is wracked by guilt and disgust at his earlier actions. He is a garrulous man with many acquaintances, enjoys money and the luxuries it provides, and has a generous streak that leads him to buy his daughter anything she wants and to help his brother-in-law find a better job. He also displays self-control that enables him to control his dormant dependence on alcohol and his natural desire to defend himself when his sister-in-law, Marion, reproaches him for his past mistakes. Once a strict father, he now wants to pamper his daughter. But his new tolerance disguises a moralistic streak that causes him to recoil in alarm at the ''utter irresponsibility'' of his pre-crash life. He affirms his belief in "character" as the "eternally valuable element" and reflects responsibly on his need to give Honoria love, "but not too much love, for he knew the injury that a father can do to a daughter."

If self-control, love, and generosity are Charlie's strengths, alcoholism and guilt are his weaknesses. Under the influence of alcohol, he allowed his marriage to fall apart, locked his wife out in the snow, consorted with Lorraine Quarrles behind his wife's back, and squandered his money in Paris clubs. Now apparently sober, he bears the weight of his previous life and returns repeatedly in his mind to memories of his wife, her death, and his responsibility for it. Charlie's guilt is personified in Marion Peters, who verbalizes every doubt Charlie has about himself. These doubts may be justified: Charlie foolishly gives the Ritz barman the Peters's address to pass on to a "ghost" from his alcoholic past, his generosity suggests that he has the same preoccupation with the power of money he had before the crash, he returns more than once to the decadent Parisian scenes of his pre-crash "nightmare," he seems incapable of shutting Lorraine and Duncan out of his new life, and in his visits to the Peters he displays an ability to self-consciously manipulate his behavior and conversation to win the "points" he needs to get Honoria back. But Charlie's awareness of his weaknesses and his determination to obtain what he wants may help him prevail in the end. "He would come back some day," he tells himself at the story's conclusion, "they couldn't make him pay forever. . . . He was absolutely sure Helen wouldn't have wanted him to be so alone." Though he is temporarily beaten, the tenacity and conviction of Charlie's parting thoughts suggest that he is a survivor.

Helen Wales

Charlie's dead wife, Helen, though physically absent from the story, is the central "ghost out of the past" with whom Charlie struggles to fashion a new future for himself and Honoria. Like Fitzgerald's own relationship with his wife, Zelda, Charlie and Helen's marriage had been an emotionally stormy one. After Charlie makes a fortune in the stock market, he quits his job and moves with Helen and Honoria from Vermont to Paris. They travel throughout Europe "throwing money away." In Paris, they begin to "run around" with a wild, disreputable crowd and to fight with each other. On a February night an argument at a Paris nightclub ends with Helen kisses another man. Charlie storms out alone and angrily locks the door of their apartment behind him. Helen arrives home an hour later and, unable to get inside, wanders through a driving snowstorm to her sister's apartment. Although she avoids pneumonia and she and Charlie half-heartedly attempt a reconciliation, their marriage and her health have been dealt a fatal blow. While Charlie lies in a sanitarium recovering from his alcoholism, he assigns custody of Honoria to Helen's sister as a gesture to Helen, but she dies soon afterward.

As Charlie moves closer to reclaiming Honoria, Helen's ghost continues to haunt him, and on the night Charlie learns that Marion has agreed to let him have Honoria, Helen appears to Charlie in a dream and gives her approval to Honoria's move with him to Prague. After Helen's lone appearance in the story, Charlie's fate begins to change dramatically. The door he locked shutting Helen out in the snow many months before is replaced by the open "door of the world." But as he blissfully contemplates his future with Honoria, sad memories of Helen abruptly interrupt his happiness, and he begins to think gloomily that he must not love Honoria "too much." Later that day, after Lorraine and Duncan's disastrous appearance at the Peters's dashes Charlie's hopes for a life with Honoria, Charlie sits in the Ritz bar, assailed by memories of his trips with Helen and of their debauched lives, and by feelings of self-hatred for locking Helen out months before. For all the disastrous events of the day, however, the story closes with Charlie reassuring himself that Helen "wouldn't have wanted him to be so alone."

Honoria Wales

Honoria Wales is Charlie's nine-year-old daughter, whose custody battle is the central conflict of the story. Honoria adores her father, and she greets his arrival in Paris with shrieks of joy and open arms. She is described as a lovely girl, and though she appears to get along well with the Peters and their children, she is excited by the prospect of going to live with her father in Prague after not having seen him in over ten months. At lunch at Le Grand Vatel, Honoria agreeably eats her vegetables and is pleased that they are going to the vaudeville later on. However, Charlie's offer to buy her anything in the toy store dampens her spirits. Though she likes the doll he has given her, she says "I've got lots of things. And we're not rich anymore, are we?"

Honoria is a good student at school, and when pressed, she admits that she likes Uncle Lincoln more than Aunt Marion. Eager to live with her father, she notes that "I don't really need much taking care of any more. I do everything for myself," and she hypothesizes that the reason she does not live with her father is because "mamma's dead." Though Lorraine and Duncan are condescending towards Honoria, she remains polite to them. At the theater, Charlie notes that she is "already an individual with a code of her own" and he is "absorbed by the desire of putting a little of himself into her before she crystallized utterly." When asked about her mother, Honoria answers that she loved her very much, but now she loves her father "better than anybody." When Charlie suggests that someday she will fall in love, get married, and forget she "ever had a daddy," she replies, "Yes, that's true," a comment which demonstrates her understanding of what adult life is like. Nevertheless, her affection for her father never wanes.

Themes

Change and Transformation

In "Babylon Revisited," a father tries to regain custody of his daughter after the death of his wife, financial disaster in the stock market crash of 1929, and his own battle with alcoholism. A central theme of the story is Charlie's struggle to convince himself and others that he has abandoned the "dissipated" ways of his pre-crash life in Paris. Through telling details, Fitzgerald shows the reader that Charlie has largely reformed, while hinting that his problems may not be entirely behind him.

Throughout the story Charlie is presented with temptations to return to the "utter irresponsibility" of his previous life, which he must overcome to prove he truly understands that personal character is the "eternally valuable element." In the story's opening scene, Charlie appears to demonstrate his new self-discipline by refusing the bartender's offer of a drink. But he then undercuts the reader's

confidence by giving him the Peters's address to pass on to Duncan Schaeffer, a one-time drinking partner. Moreover, the fact that Charlie has found himself in a bar as soon as he reaches Paris, and proceeds to ask the bartender the whereabouts of his old friends, introduces a doubt about Charlie's actual rehabilitation. Similarly, after Charlie's first visit to the warm domesticity of the Peters's home, he avoids returning to his hotel in favor of taking in Paris's decadent nightlife. At the restaurant with Honoria the next day, Charlie successfully avoids the social invitations of old friends from his drinking days, but tells them that he and Honoria are headed to the Empire theater, where Duncan and Lorraine reappear and convince him to have a drink.

Charlie consciously manipulates his conversations with his in-laws to achieve his goal of winning back his daughter. Rather than simply present himself as the reformed man he claims he is, Charlie sees his meetings with his in-laws as contests or performances in which his behavior must be manipulated to win "points." By showing Charlie in the bars and nightclubs he has claimed are no longer a part of his life, drinking with people he claims are part of his past, and viewing his conversations with the Peters's as contests, Fitzgerald introduces an element of doubt that enables the reader to share Marion Peters's suspicion that Charlie's transformation is, at best, incomplete.

Guilt and Innocence

Throughout "Babylon Revisited," Charlie Wales struggles with his sense of guilt over having caused his wife's death, losing custody of his daughter, and squandering the successes of his early years in alcohol and "dissipation." In order to win custody of Honoria, Charlie must convince his sister-in-law, who now has legal guardianship over Honoria, that he has accepted his guilt and turned over a new leaf. Though he admits to her that he has acted badly in the past, he now hopes that his sobriety is permanent, but admits that "it's within human possibilities I might go wrong any time." Marion refuses to interpret his remarks as mature, honest expressions of self-knowledge, and uses them instead to confirm her deepest suspicions about Charlie.

Throughout the story, Charlie's ability to punish himself and make himself feel guilty is every bit as strong as Marion's. "I spoiled this city for

Topics for Further Study

- Research the lives of the American expatriate literary community in Europe in the 1920s, focusing on such figures as Ezra Pound, Ernest Hemingway, F. Scott Fitzgerald, and Gertrude Stein. Explore the factors that compelled these American writers to live overseas.

- On a map of Paris, trace Charlie's travels through Paris in "Babylon Revisited." Try to locate such Parisian landmarks as the Hotel Ritz, Montmartre, the Place de la Concorde, the Place Blanche, the Etoile, and the Left Bank as well as such thoroughfares as the rue Palatine, boulevard des Capucines, rue Pigalle, rue Saint-Honore, avenue de l'Opera, and rue Bonaparte.

- Research the history of the boom years of the American stock market in the 1920s and the crash of October, 1929. Explore the causes and effects of the crash and explain why such a crash could or could not occur again.

- Explore the concept of legal guardianship of children and the laws surrounding child custody. Explore the factors courts weigh when deciding to award or strip parents of legal custody of a child.

- In "Babylon Revisited" Fitzgerald uses several French words and phrases to create a sense of place for the story's setting in Paris. Three of these words, *chasseur, bistro* and *brasserie*, have been assimilated into the English language. Find the definitions for these words in an English dictionary. Find ten other French words used by Fitzgerald in the story that are now part of the English language.

myself," he laments while driving through Paris, "I didn't realize it, but the days came along one after another, and then two years were gone, and everything was gone, and I was gone." Recalling the clubs where he gave away thousand-franc notes as tips, he guiltily makes another donation, this time to a poor woman who accosts him in a *brasserie*. When Marion Peters confronts him directly with the question of his responsibility for Helen's death ("It's something you'll have to square with your own conscience"), her words touch the raw nerve of Charlie's guilt and "an electric current of agony" surges through him. For the remainder of the story, Charlie's sense of responsibility for Helen's death hounds him. Both in his hour of triumph, when Marion agrees to give him custody of Honoria, and later when Lorraine and Duncan's drunken appearance changes her mind, Charlie is haunted by Helen's image, which reminds him that he is one of the heartless "men who locked their wives out in the snow."

Although both Marion and Charlie himself seem to take Charlie's guilt for granted, Fitzgerald leaves the question of Charlie's true guilt open. How guilty was he? After a night of drinking and quarreling, Charlie and Helen create a scene at a Paris nightclub. Charlie tries to take Helen home, but she kisses another man in front of him and his friends, then makes a personal remark that embarrasses Charlie publicly. Angry and perhaps believing that Helen will spend the night with "young Webb," he returns home, locks the apartment door behind him, and goes to bed. Helen returns an hour later in a driving snowstorm, however, and, unable to get in or call a cab, she trudges through the snow in her slippers to her sister's apartment. Though she appears at Marion's "soaked to the skin and shivering," she escapes pneumonia only to die later of "heart trouble." When Charlie later reminds Marion that Helen died not from pneumonia caused by the snowstorm, but from heart trouble, she repeats the phrase *heart trouble* "as if [it] had another meaning for her." This "other meaning" suggests that Marion believes Helen died of a "broken heart." Yet Helen's willingness to kiss another man and embarrass her husband publicly suggests that on that "terrible night" it may have been Charlie rather than Helen who suffered the worst emotional damage.

Wealth and Poverty

The ambiguity that surrounds Charlie's sense of guilt in "Babylon Revisited" is compounded by Fitzgerald's introduction of the theme of money, wealth, and envy. Not only is Charlie riddled with guilt for his wife's death, his alcoholism, and the loss of custody of his daughter, he has also come to feel guilt for his financial success during the boom years before the stock market crash. In "Babylon Revisited" money is seen, in the words of one critic, as a "corrosive power," and though virtually everyone in the story is preoccupied with it, only Charlie has learned that when it comes to matters of the heart, money has no value.

The story opens with Charlie sitting in the bar of the Ritz Hotel, the symbol of opulence in the French capital. Although everyone he asks about is either ill or bankrupt—even his old friend Lorraine tells him, "We're poor as hell"—Charlie has recovered from his financial losses and is doing better in Prague than he was before the crash: "My income last year was bigger than it was when I had money." Although he fondly recalls the pre-crash years when rich Americans abroad "were a sort of royalty, almost infallible," he now feels more guilt than nostalgia for the days of "wildly squandered" cash. Passing a Paris restaurant, he reflects that "he had never eaten at a really cheap restaurant in Paris. Five-course dinner, four francs fifty, eighteen cents, wine included. For some odd reason he wished that he had." Later, when a woman accosts him in a *brasserie,* Charlie guiltily buys her a meal and slips her a twenty-franc note. The next day when Honoria asks him, "we're not rich anymore, are we?" he disingenuously replies, "We never were," but then offers to buy her "anything you want."

The heart of Charlie's guilt over money emerges when he tells the Peterses that his problems did not begin "until I gave up business and came over here with nothing to do. . . . I worked hard for ten years, you know—until I got lucky in the market, like so many people. Terribly lucky. It didn't seem any use working any more, so I quit. It won't happen again." The easy money Charlie won in the boom years of the 1920s was unearned, he now believes, because he acquired it through the stock market rather than through honest work. In his mind, his guilt over Helen's death is linked to his guilt for quitting his job and living off his stock market windfall. Although he has learned his lesson and rebuilt his wealth through hard work in Prague, the Peters do not share Charlie's sense of moral rebirth through good, old-fashioned labor. After telling them that his newfound success in Prague will allow him to give Honoria "certain advantages," including a French governess and a new apartment, Marion lashes out: "I suppose you can give her more luxuries than we can. When you were throwing away money we were living along watching every ten francs." In Marion's mind, Charlie's responsibility for Helen's death is inseparable from his financial success: he should feel guilt for both.

Even Lincoln Peters—who explicitly absolves Charlie of guilt for Helen's death—seems to resent Charlie's knack for prosperity: "While you and Helen were tearing around Europe throwing money away, we were just getting along. . . . there was some kind of injustice in it—you not even working toward the end, and getting richer and richer." And as Charlie himself admits, Lincoln "couldn't be expected to accept with equanimity the fact that his income was again twice as large as their own." When Marion changes her mind about letting Charlie take Honoria back to Prague, Charlie is left alone at the Ritz with only his money, and he reflexively resolves to "send Honoria some things; he would send her a lot of things." But Charlie's emotional losses have taught him that "this was just money" and "nothing was much good" except getting Honoria back. For the Peterses, however, whose circumstances prevented them from enjoying the prosperity of the pre-crash boom years, the guilt Charlie should feel for his alcoholic life and Helen's death are inseparable from the guilt he should feel for his money.

Style

Setting and Symbolism

The setting of "Babylon Revisited" is Paris, France, circa 1930, a year after the U.S. stock market crash that ruined the fortunes of many Americans. In the story's title, Paris is compared to the ancient biblical city of Babylon (on the Euphrates River, near present-day Baghdad, Iraq), which was famous as a hotbed of sin and vice. Like the Babylonian Jews of the Bible who surrendered their Mosaic law to worship Babylon's pagan idols, in his former life Charlie had been corrupted by Paris's licentious ways and had lost touch with his traditional American values. For Charlie, Paris is a beautiful but dangerous place. The Place de la Concorde retains its "pink majesty," and the facade of the Paris opera house remains "magnificent," but the busy allure Paris had when the Americans of the twenties ruled its nightlife is now gone. Paris, like the famous Ritz Hotel where the story begins and ends, "had gone back into France," and Charlie no longer feels "as if he owned it." Seeing Paris with "clearer and more judicious eyes," Charlie is struck by its "provincial," even "bleak and sinister" quality. "Vice and waste" are catered to on an "utterly childish scale," and grim tourist traps snare travelers who are leery of the decadence of Paris's nude revues and prowling prostitutes.

Charlie's attitude toward Paris reflected Fitzgerald's own. In 1927 Fitzgerald wrote, "The best of America drifts to Paris. The American in Paris is the best American. . . . France has the only two things toward which we drift as we grow older—intelligence and good manners." By 1931, however, Fitzgerald saw something alarming in the waves of newly rich Americans who had descended on France before the crash: "With each new shipment of Americans spewed up by the boom the quality fell off, until toward the end there was something sinister about the crazy boatloads." For Fitzgerald, France became merely "a land" while "the best of America was the best of the world." America's "simple pa and ma and son and daughter," he wrote, was "infinitely superior in their qualities of kindness and curiosity to the corresponding class in Europe." Fitzgerald's biographer Matthew J. Bruccoli underscores Fitzgerald's alienation from Paris and France as a whole: he "remained a tourist," Bruccoli maintained, "never felt at home in France," and "found that France intensified his identification with his native land." Moreover, in Fitzgerald's fiction France is depicted, in Bruccoli's words, as "a place where Americans deteriorate or sometimes demonstrate their superiority over the natives." In "Babylon Revisited" Charlie does both: he is briefly part of an infallible "royalty," but he eventually descends into nightmarish "dissipation."

Point of View

Although Charlie does not narrate the story directly, it is through his vantage point that the actions of "Babylon Revisited" are described. The narrator separates himself from Charlie, however, by occasionally telling the reader things that Charlie cannot know or does not himself believe. The narrator, for example, tells readers that Marion Peters "once possessed a fresh American loveliness" but then adds that "Charlie had never been sensitive to it and was always surprised when people spoke of how pretty she had been." Similarly, when Charlie tries to convince Marion that he deserves another chance as Honoria's father, the narrator again separates himself from Charlie by relating Marion's point of view: "part of her saw that Charlie's feet were planted on the earth now, and her own maternal feeling recognized the naturalness of his desire; but she had lived for a long time with a prejudice—a prejudice founded on a curious disbelief in her sister's happiness, and which, in the shock of that one terrible night, had turned to hatred for him. It had all happened at a point in her life where the discouragement of ill health and adverse circumstances made it necessary for her to believe in tangible villainy and a tangible villain."

Throughout "Babylon Revisited," the point of view the narrator adopts is almost always Charlie's. Charlie perceives Paris as a dangerous, decadent place, rather than one of the world's most beautiful cities, and the final judgment about whether Charlie has truly escaped his alcoholic past depends largely on whether readers believe what he tells them about himself. Occasionally, Charlie even seems to turn directly to the reader to plead his case through the narrator. Recalling the night Charlie locked Helen out in the snow, the narrator asks, "How could he know she would arrive an hour later alone, that there would be a snowstorm in which she wandered about in slippers, too confused to find a taxi?" In several passages in the story, the narrator's voice and Charlie's thoughts seem indistinguishable, and the story's narration becomes almost like an interior monologue: "He had never eaten at a really cheap restaurant in Paris. Five-course dinner, four francs fifty, eighteen cents, wine included. For some odd reason he wished that he had"; "He believed in character; he wanted to jump back a whole generation and trust in character again as the eternally valuable element. Everything else wore out"; or, "He would come back some day; they couldn't

Patrons of the Paris nightclub Club Zellie, circa 1929.

make him pay forever. But he wanted his child, and nothing was much good now, beside that fact. . . . He was absolutely sure Helen wouldn't have wanted him to be so alone.'' In passages like these, the third-person narrator and Charlie himself seem to become almost the same voice.

Structure

The structure of a work of fiction is the general organization of the scenes or events that make up the story. In its broadest outline, ''Babylon Revisited'' is divided into five sections. The first and last sections take place in the same location, the bar at the Hotel Ritz in Paris, and thus frame the story. In section 1, Charlie tells the Ritz bartender that he will be spending ''four or five days'' in Paris, and each section of the story narrates the events of each of these days. Only in the story's fifth and last section does Fitzgerald break this pattern, moving not to Charlie's fifth day in Paris, but to the evening of the fourth day, which began in the previous section.

Many critics have praised the structure of ''Babylon Revisited.'' One critic has argued that the story's plot is more minimal than it appears: there is only one real scene—the intrusion of Lorraine and Duncan at the Peters's on the night Charlie hopes to regain custody of his daughter. The rest of the story merely develops or builds up to this moment. Other critics have argued that Fitzgerald unconventionally structured the story with *two* climaxes: one in section 3 when Charlie learns that Marion will grant him custody of Honoria, and one in section 4, when Lorraine and Duncan's sudden appearance changes Marion's mind. Several critics have also noted that the structure of the story consists of alternating scenes, an exterior-interior movement that reflects the struggles occurring in Charlie's mind. Thus, according to one critic, Fitzgerald alternates between interior scenes (the Ritz bar, a restaurant with Honoria, the Peters's home) and exterior scenes (Paris at night) to create the backdrop of ''Babylonian'' corruption against which the story of a man's quest to regain his daughter is played out. This same back-and-forth structure can be seen in the alternation between Charlie's struggles in the real world to regain custody of Honoria and his internal, mental struggle to deal with his past, his sense of guilt, and his confidence in his own rehabilitation and honor.

Other Symbols

Two of the most important symbols in ''Babylon Revisited'' are the swing or pendulum and the door. The image of the swing first appears when Helen appears to Charlie in a dream on the night he seems to have finally regained custody of Honoria. Helen appears on a swing, "swinging faster and faster all the time" and speaking reassuring words until her motion prevents Charlie from making out what she says. Later, after Lorraine and Duncan's appearance at the Peters's has sabotaged Charlie's plans, he turns to see Lincoln Peters "swinging Honoria back and forth like a pendulum from side to side." As symbols, the swing and pendulum not only serve to link Helen and Honoria as the two loves in Charlie's life, they also point to the importance of time in the story. The motion of the swing and the pendulum reflects the quickening movements of the story itself, in which the events of the plot seem to unfold faster and faster. In the span of one day, for example, Charlie's fourth in Paris, he goes from feeling "happy," with "the door of the world" open before him, to unexpected defeat after which he is left alone in a hotel bar to contemplate his guilt and loneliness. As symbols of time, the swing and pendulum also represent the struggle in the story between Charlie's alcoholic past—with its "ghosts" and "nightmare" scenes—and the uncertain present in which he tries to secure a future of happiness, honor, and self-mastery.

Doors appear as symbols of both hope and menace in "Babylon Revisited." Early in the story, Fitzgerald uses doors to symbolize the devouring "mouths" of Paris's decadent nightclubs. After his first visit with the Peters in section 1, Charlie revisits the old haunts of his pre-crash Paris life: "He passed a lighted *door* from which issued music, and stopped with the sense of familiarity. . . . A few *doors* farther on he found another rendezvous and incautiously put his head inside. . . . The Poet's Cave had disappeared but the two great *mouths* of the Cafe of Heaven and the Cafe of Hell still yawned—even devoured, as he watched, the meager contents of a tourist bus." In these scenes the doors of Paris's clubs are virtually the doors of hell, beckoning tourists "with frightened eyes" to squander their money on "drink or drugs" and surrender themselves to the "dissipation" of Paris' temptations. Later, Lorraine, a "ghost " from Charlie's past, will remind him of another similar door, opened to feed his need for alcohol: "I remember once when you hammered on my *door* at four A.M. I was enough of a good sport to give you a drink."

The principal door image in the story, however, is the door Charlie locked behind him a year and a half before the story starts, stranding his wife in the snow and perhaps contributing to her death from heart failure. As Charlie admits, it was the most uncharacteristic act of his life: "Locking out Helen didn't fit in with any other act of his life." The closing of that door signaled the death of his marriage and the death, he now hopes, of his self-indulgent alcoholic life in the days before the crash. Fitzgerald also uses door imagery to represent a metaphorical entranceway to Charlie's hopeful new future with Honoria. The very first door encountered in the story, in fact, opens to reveal "a lovely little girl of nine"—Honoria—who shrieks with joy as she leaps into Charlie's arms. The door as symbol of Charlie's possible future with Honoria is then repeated the morning after Charlie learns that Marion will consent to his regaining custody of his daughter: "He woke up feeling happy. The *door* of the world was open again."

But the next door to open admits Lorraine and Duncan Schaeffer into the Peters's home, shattering Marion's confidence in Charlie's new image: "The *door* opened upon another long ring, and then voices, and the three in the salon looked up expectantly. . . . the voices developed under the light into Duncan Schaeffer and Lorraine Quarrles." Although their appearance separates Charlie from Honoria once again, the last door image of the story returns to the door as a positive symbol, like the open "door of the world" that Charlie first glimpsed when he was reunited with Honoria for the first time in section 1: "Then he opened the *door* of the dining room and said in a strange voice, 'Good night, children.' Honoria rose and ran around the table to hug him."

Perhaps the most obvious symbol in the story, however, is Honoria. Charlie's reason for being in Paris is to regain his honor, which is manifest in his daughter, Honoria.

Lost Generation

Fitzgerald has often been associated with a school of American writers born near the beginning of the twentieth century and who reached maturity around World War I, and, in many cases, lived as expatriates in Europe during the 1920s. Besides Fitzgerald, Gertrude Stein, Ernest Hemingway, poet Hart Crane, and critic Malcolm Cowley are associated with this group of writers rebelling against the no-longer-viable rules of the past. According to

Hemingway, the term *Lost Generation* derived from a remark Stein overheard an auto mechanic make to his younger colleagues as they bungled their attempts to fix Stein's car: "You are all a lost generation." After Hemingway used the remark as the motto for his famous novel *The Sun Also Rises* (1926), the term began to be used to describe his generation's loss of faith in traditional values following the carnage they witnessed in World War I. "Babylon Revisited" is also in some ways an analysis of the consequences of losing touch with these traditional (American) values. Marion and Lincoln Peters represent the sober, prudent, family-oriented values of an earlier America, and the "haunted" Charlie represents the by-product of ignoring these values by surrendering to the temptations of unearned wealth and self-indulgent, immoral behavior. The notion that Charlie's (and Fitzgerald's) generation had perhaps fallen away from the solid values of its predecessors is echoed in the story in Charlie's assertion that "he believed in character; he wanted to jump back *a whole generation* and trust in character again as the eternally valuable element. Everything else wore out."

Historical Context

The Modern Era Arrives

In 1930, the year Fitzgerald wrote "Babylon Revisited," the world was in the midst of profound political, cultural, and economic changes. Political despotism seemed to be on the rise everywhere: the dictatorships of Josef Stalin in the Soviet Union and Benito Mussolini in Italy, both founded in the mid-1920s, were firmly entrenched by 1930; the collapse of Germany's Grand Coalition in March signaled the death of the fragile democratic Weimar Republic; and in September, 1930, Adolf Hitler's Nationalist Socialist Workers Party enjoyed its most dramatic election victory, moving Hitler closer to the complete dictatorial control of Germany he would assume in 1933. In America, Prohibition—which outlawed the manufacture, transportation, and sale of liquor—was entering its eleventh year, and a violent gangster class had emerged to feed the national demand for booze. In 1930, radio entered its golden age, the "talking picture" began to replace the silent film, and experimental television

broadcasts made in the United States and the Soviet Union. In March, construction began in New York City on the Empire State Building; by the end of the year, the number of paid passengers on commercial airlines had increased 300 percent over 1929, and in December, Germany established a rocket program to develop military missiles.

Short-lived Prosperity

Overshadowing all these events, however, was the economic devastation that followed the New York Stock Exchange crash of October, 1929. An investment boom that had begun in late 1924 had by 1927 spiraled into a full-fledged bull market. It was a boom, however, fueled by unprecedented levels of purely speculative money and "margin" stock purchases, in which investors could take out loans to buy stocks for as little as ten percent down. In June, 1929, in what economist John Kenneth Galbraith has called a "mass escape from reality," the ceiling came off the U.S. stock market, and stock prices rose by leaps and bounds to unheard-of levels. "Never before or since," Galbraith wrote, "have so many become so wondrously, so effortlessly, and so quickly rich." Then in September, 1929, the wildly overvalued stocks, the widespread indebtedness caused by banks' loans to speculating investors, and the weaknesses in the U.S. economy set off an extended freefall in stock prices that cleaned out novice and veteran, low-income and well-to-do investors alike. As panicked investors rushed to sell their stocks before their value dropped to zero, the market surrendered, in Galbraith's words, "to blind, relentless fear." The worst carnage was suffered on October 29, 1929, but after a brief stabilization in June of 1930, Wall Street began a further slide that lasted until June, 1932. One thousand U.S. banks closed in 1930 alone, and by the end of the year three million Americans were out of work, and the savings of hundreds of thousands of people had disappeared. By 1933 the U.S. gross national product was fully a third smaller than in 1929, and only the onset of the massive military buildup for World War II managed to pull the world economy out of what came to be called the Great Depression.

From the beginning of his career, Fitzgerald identified himself closely with the American experience. He was fascinated and deeply moved by American history and wove it into the plots and themes of his major works. Although he himself had

Compare
&
Contrast

- **1930s:** On October 28, 1929, the stock market loses 12.8 percent of its value. The event, dubbed ''Black Thursday'' results in widespread panic, numerous bank failures, and precipitates the great depression, which lasts throughout the 1930s.

  1997: On October 27, the stock market loses 7.2 percent of its value, with the biggest one-day point loss in history. Computers automatically shut down the market to prevent panic. Despite the shocking decline, caused by unstable Asian markets, the New York Stock Exchange rebounds significantly in the next day of trading.

- **1930s:** Alcoholism is not a well-understood disease. Individuals deal with the condition to the best of their own ability. Alcoholics Anonymous, the first substantial effort to address the problem, is organized by Bill Wilson in New York City in 1935. The program is a self-help fellowship designed to empower alcoholics to control their drinking habits.

1990s: Alcoholics Anonymous has more than 30,000 local groups in 90 countries and has an estimated membership of more than one million. Spiritual values are emphasized as a means to recovery.

- **1930s:** Josephine Baker is the toast of Paris. After leaving the United States for what she says is a more hospitable culture, she becomes one of the most popular entertainers in France. After starring in the *Folies Bergere*, she opens her own nightclub and continues to perform until her death in 1974.

  1990s: In 1991, Lynn Whitfield stars in the film *The Josephine Baker Story,* which outlines the legend's rise from her impoverished beginnings in St. Louis near the turn of the century to her rise to fame and her involvement with many issues, including children's welfare and the U.S. civil rights movement.

not experienced the overnight riches-to-rags experiences of other Americans in the fall of 1929, he immediately understood its significance and incorporated it into his writing. In his entry for the year 1930 in his personal ledger, for example, he wrote, ''The Crash! Zelda + America.'' While Fitzgerald identified the ''crash'' of his own life—his wife Zelda's first nervous breakdown—with the unraveling of the U.S. economy, he was of two minds about the meaning of the great change in American's fortunes before and after the stock-market crash. On the one hand, he wrote that ''it is the custom now to look back on ourselves of the boom days with a disapproval that approaches horror. But it had its virtues, that old boom: Life was a good deal larger and gayer for most people. . . . There were so many good things.'' On the other hand, in the mid-1930s he wrote that the 1920s were ''the most expensive orgy in history'' and that the youthful happiness he felt during that decade was as ''unnatural as the Boom; and my recent experience parallels the wave of despair that swept the nation when the Boom was over.''

Critical Overview

Throughout the 1930s, Fitzgerald suffered guilt by association for his early identification with the ''flappers and philosophers'' of the so-called Jazz Age. In the years of the Great Depression, Fitzgerald's identification with the comparatively carefree 1920s rendered him irrelevant in the opinion of readers who were now enduring rather hardscrabble lives. Moreover, with ''The Crack-up,'' a series of essays published in *Esquire* magazine in the mid-1930s, readers who were accustomed to seeing Fitzgerald's cleverly phrased romantic entertainments in the ''slick'' magazines now discovered a writer who bluntly described himself as a ''cracked plate,'' an alcoholic has-been whose best days were behind him. With his move to the glitzy, superficial world of Hollywood in the late 1930s, Fitzgerald's critical reputation reached its low tide, and it was not until the decade after his death that his work was seriously reevaluated. From the beginning of the Fitzgerald ''revival'' in the 1950s, ''Babylon Revisited'' was regarded among Fitzgerald's best short stories, and the first critics to analyze it at length focused on the problem of Charlie's character. Some argued that Charlie's failure to regain custody of Honoria was a direct result of his decision to leave the Peters's address with the Ritz bartender. Others maintained that throughout the story, Charlie demonstrated a convincing and even heroic self-mastery and that his ultimate loss of Honoria was therefore the fault of the external world and the unwillingness of Marion, Duncan, and Lorraine to believe that Charlie had truly left his irresponsible past behind.

In more recent criticism, the story's ambiguity has been interpreted as the story's central theme and strength. Recent critics have also begun to more fully explore the story's sophisticated structure. Fitzgerald, for example, successfully used the image of the pendulum and the swing, as well as repeated shifts between present-tense action and references to Charlie's past, to create a sense of back-and-forth movement that perfectly reflects Charlie's own constantly rising and falling hopes. The story's heightened sense of tension or ambiguity and its multiple potential meanings, combined with the sheer emotional pull of Fitzgerald's characters and plot, may account for the critics's continued fascination with ''Babylon Revisited.''

In spite of the disagreements over Charlie's character or the themes or structure of the story, virtually all critics have regarded ''Babylon Revisited'' among Fitzgerald's finest stories. While a few critics have noted traces of pop fiction melodrama in the story, as well as flaws in its structure and point of view, more have described it as nearly perfect, and one has even labeled it ''among finest short stories of the twentieth century.'' Among the aspects of the story that have received the most praise are Fitzgerald's dramatization of the father-daughter relationship; his evocation of Paris as the story's setting and major metaphor ; and his deft use of such metaphors and images as the swing and pendulum

and doors, locks, and bars (in both senses). Above all, Fitzgerald has been praised for balancing depth of theme with economy of plot, creating a richly evocative atmosphere and realistic dialogue, and sustaining a measured tone of restraint and ambiguity.

Many elements of ''Babylon Revisited'' were drawn from Fitzgerald's own life: his knowledge of Paris from his several trips there with his wife Zelda in the 1920s, his lifelong battle with alcoholism, his affection for his daughter, Scottie (the model for Honoria), his preoccupation with money and affluence, his interest in America and its history and identity, and Zelda's absence due to mental illness, which served as a template for the absence in the story of Charlie's wife, Helen. Among the themes explored in the story are freedom and imprisonment, sin, guilt and retribution, alcoholism and self-discipline, self-mastery, responsibility and personal character, greed, envy and money, love, the abandonment of traditional American values, and the irrevocability and burden of the past.

By the time Fitzgerald published ''Babylon Revisited'' in 1931 he had long since established himself as a regular contributor to America's most popular ''slick'' magazine, *The Saturday Evening Post*. By 1929 his per-story fee had climbed to $4,000, and 1931 proved to be his most profitable year ever as a writer. According to critic Morris Dickstein, however, ''Babylon Revisited,'' perhaps because of the seriousness of its themes, was repeatedly rejected by the magazine editors who had previously craved Fitzgerald's more superficial, ''flapper'' stories. When ''Babylon Revisited'' was finally published in the *Post*'s February, 1931 issue, it received a large national readership though no formal reviews from critics. In late 1934 and early 1935, Fitzgerald gave his own critical estimation of the story by choosing it as the last story in his fourth short story collection, *Taps at Reveille*. Critics received the collection positively but urged Fitzgerald to write more serious stories worthy of his talents.

At the time of his death in 1940, few of Fitzgerald's books were popular. In the early 1950s, a Fitzgerald revival began, partly based on word-of-mouth enthusiasm for such works as *The Great Gatsby* that caused critics and scholars to pay his novels new attention. Later, his stories began to spark new critical interest. ''Babylon Revisited'' in particular began to emerge as Fitzgerald's most admired short story, a fact reflected in his publisher's decision in 1960 to reprint some of his stories under the title *Babylon Revisited and Other Stories.* By 1979, ''Babylon Revisited'' had been selected for inclusion in sixty-three short story anthologies—far more than any other Fitzgerald story—and had become the object of much scholarly analysis.

Although the attitude of most critics toward ''Babylon Revisited'' has been reverent, not all have viewed it as a flawless work. In 1962, Arthur Mizener, a Fitzgerald biographer, contrasted Fitzgerald's decision to use the third-person voice for the narrator to Joseph Conrad's more effective first-person style in his classic tale ''Heart of Darkness.'' In 1971, John Higgins claimed that Fitzgerald had ''slightly'' injured his story by deciding to insert two climaxes rather than the one turning point found in most short stories. Two years later, David Toor noted that the story's third-person narration resulted in ''flaws in the technique,'' mainly that the point of view shifts, allowing the narrator to know things that Charlie probably could not know. In 1981, Matthew Bruccoli noted that the story's autobiographical aspect showcased Fitzgerald's ''considerable self-pity,'' and a year later Kenneth Eble, though praising the story's effectiveness, detected ''shades of melodrama '' that detract from its power.

Another group of critics has explored the changes that Fitzgerald made in the story's text between its first publication in 1931 and its appearance in the collection *Taps at Reveille* four years later. In the first version of the story, for example, when Charlie jokes to Alix that, luckily for him, the people in Prague ''don't know about me,'' Fitzgerald has Charlie ''smile faintly'' at his own wit. In the 1935 version, Fitzgerald changes this to ''Alix smiled,'' suggesting that perhaps the joke is really on Charlie. Similarly, in the 1931 version, after Lorraine and Duncan barge in at the Peters's, Lorraine tries to get Charlie to join them for dinner and says, ''Be yourself, Charlie. Come on.'' In 1935 Fitzgerald replaced this with a line that reinforces Lorraine's drunkenness: ''Come and dine. Sure your cousins won' mine. See you so sel'om. Or solemn.'' Likewise, in the earlier version, Fitzgerald had Charlie explain Lorraine and Duncan's sudden appearance by saying they ''wormed'' the Peters's address ''out of Paul at the bar.'' In the 1935 version Fitzgerald made Charlie's explanation more vague and uncertain: ''They wormed your name out of

somebody.'' Finally, in the 1931 version, after Lorraine and Duncan leave, Fitzgerald had inserted a line in which Lincoln is seen ''somewhat uneasily occupying himself by swinging Honoria from side to side with her feet off the ground.'' In the 1935 version, Fitzgerald deleted this passage but failed to cut the word *still* in the subsequent line, ''Lincoln was *still* swinging Honoria back and forth like a pendulum''—introducing a source of possible confusion for later readers.

Several aspects of ''Babylon Revisited'' have received special critical attention. The story's style has been widely praised as demonstrating a masterly, nuanced restraint and its structure has been consistently hailed as tightly balanced and unified. The gravity of its themes has also received special notice. In the span of a twenty-page story, Fitzgerald manages to touch on such themes as time and the inescapableness of the past, money and envy, the abandonment of traditional values, sin and guilt, honor and integrity, freedom and imprisonment, self-delusion, self-pity, parental and romantic love, and emotional bankruptcy and isolation.

Criticism

Paul Bodine

Bodine is a freelance writer, editor, and researcher who has taught at the Milwaukee College of Business. In the following essay, he discusses the characterization of Charlie, touching on several of the story's key themes.

The richness of ''Babylon Revisited'' as a work of fiction lies in Fitzgerald's ability to encompass so many themes while leaving the important questions about Charlie Wales' character unanswered. On the surface, the story is about a father's attempt to regain the custody of his daughter after a series of personal disasters. Critics have consistently praised the story for its authentic and affecting portrayal of the love between Charlie and Honoria, and in discussing a planned film version of the story, Fitzgerald himself later referred to ''the tragedy of the father and the child'' that lies at the heart of the story. Within this basic emotional core, however, Fitzgerald dramatizes a universe of emotional, social, historical, and psychological themes. Charlie's quest to win back Honoria, for example, is also his

Donna Reed and Van Johnson in a still from "The Last Time I Saw Paris," a 1954 MGM film based on "Babylon Revisited."

quest to prove to himself and those who know him that he is a new man. Only a year and half before, he was an unemployed, irresponsible, spendthrift alcoholic with poor taste in friends, a broken marriage, and a malicious streak that allowed him to lock his wife out of their apartment on a winter night. He now presents himself to his sister's family, his former friends, and the reader as a "radically" changed man, once again sober and employed—"a reformed sinner" with a new appreciation of personal character as "the eternally valuable element."

Much of the critical discussion of "Babylon Revisited" has centered on which Charlie is the "real" one. On the one hand, Charlie seems to repeatedly flirt dangerously with his past. He hangs around the Ritz bar, the gathering place for many of his former drinking partners; he leaves the Peters' address with the barman so a former drinking buddy can find him; he waxes nostalgic about the "sort of magic" he felt in his earlier inebriated days; and he returns to the nightclubs and nude revues he frequented in his previous life. On the other hand, he now holds down a well-paying job in Prague, displays a palpable love for his daughter, is clearly

anguished by his wife's death and horrified at his past, breaks firmly with Lorraine Quarrles by failing to meet her at the Ritz Hotel, repeatedly displays self-control by refusing drinks, and maturely controls his anger when Marion accuses him of causing his wife's death. The ambivalence in Charlie's character is also mirrored in the ambivalence of the story's conclusion. Lorraine and Duncan's appearance has changed Marion's mind about surrendering Honoria to Charlie, and he is left alone back at the Ritz bar, replaying his guilty memory of his dissipated former life and the night he locked his wife out in the snow. His final conversation with Lincoln Peters closes the door on Charlie's plans to leave Paris with Honoria, but it also dangles the hope that "six months" from now, he'll get a second chance. The story closes with Charlie ambiguously giving in to self-pity—"He wasn't young anymore, with a lot of nice thoughts and dreams to have by himself"—but also reaffirming his own determination to win in the end: "He would come back some day; they couldn't make him pay forever."

Beyond Charlie's personal drama, "Babylon Revisited" also explores larger social and historical issues: the contrast between Europe's decadent culture and the domesticity of traditional Americans, America's transition from the prosperity of the 1920s to the straitened conditions of the Depression, and the moral value of work versus the "free money" of the speculating investors of the "boom" years. In a scene typical of the story's fusion of narrowly personal and broadly social themes, Fitzgerald compresses Charlie's own history into the history of his generation during the boom years of the twenties. Seated at the Ritz bar after his plans for regaining custody of Honoria have begun to vanish, Charlie converses with Paul the barman about the "great change" wrought by the stock market crash the year before. When Paul mentions that he heard Charlie had lost his money in the crash, Charlie replies, "I did, but I lost everything I wanted in the boom." Paul interprets this as a reference to "selling short," the only sure way to lose money during a boom in the stock market. Short-selling means gambling that the price of a stock bought at a low price will fall to that price, but risking that if the price *rises*—as it does in a booming market— you'll be forced to ante up more money to avoid losing your original investment. Charlie understands Paul's financial allusion but plays on the other meaning of "selling short": selling *oneself* short by surrendering one's principles. In this and other

What Do I Read Next?

- Among the many Fitzgerald biographies, Matthew J. Bruccoli's *Some Sort of Epic Grandeur* (1981) remains the definitive treatment of the author's life. Bruccoli argues that it was Fitzgerald's conflicted attitudes, most notably his love/hate relationship with the rich, as much as his heavy drinking and marriage troubles that prevented him from devoting more of his creative energies to his work.

- *The Great Gatsby* (1925) has proved to be Fitzgerald's most popular novel, and some critics have claimed that it may well be the finest American novel ever written. In it, Fitzgerald lyrically recounts the story of bootlegger and idealist Jay Gatsby's dream of rekindling his relationship with Daisy Fay, his former flame, and the tragic consequences of an automobile accident for which Gatsby takes the blame.

- In his posthumously published memoir *A Moveable Feast* (1964), novelist Ernest Hemingway describes his experiences among the American literary expatriates in Paris during the early 1920s, including Gertrude Stein, Ezra Pound,

Ford Madox Ford, and Fitzgerald. The volume paints a vivid and impressionistic image of the expatriates' Paris of "Babylon Revisited" and includes an extended, if unflattering, portrait of Fitzgerald and his wife Zelda.

- *The Day of the Locust* (1939) by Nathanial West explores the seamy world of the early Hollywood studios, where Fitzgerald wrote screenplays in the 1930s. West explores the vices of all the Californian subcultures of the era, in a book that has come to define misguided attempts to attain the American Dream.

- *The Wild Party* (1928) by Joseph Moncure March is an epic poem about the downfall of a vaudeville dancer. The account epitomizes the Jazz Age.

- *Man Ray's Paris Portraits 1921–1939* is a collection of photographs by artist Man Ray, an American who moved to Paris in the early 1920s and helped found the Dadist and Surrealist art movements. His photographs capture the mood of the artists and writers in residence in Paris during the 1920s and 1930s.

---

scenes, Fitzgerald combines Charlie's personal history with the history of his generation.

As a portrait of the city Paris in the years before World War II, "Babylon Revisited" also captures the glamorous, culturally rich flavor of that city while evoking the darker, morally threatening qualities that distinguish it from the United States in Charlie's eyes. For Charlie, America symbolizes an energy and vitality that Paris now lacks. In the Ritz bar in the story's opening scene, he notes that the "frenzy" and "clamor" the bar had when rich Americans ruled it before the crash has been replaced by an oppressive air of boredom, emptiness, and quiet. With America's fortunes reversed by the stock market crash, the Ritz bar is "not an American bar any more": "It had gone back into France." Although France is once again French, reminders of

America follow Charlie throughout the story: the Peters' home is "warm and comfortably American," Marion Peters possesses the traces of a "fresh American loveliness," a fine fall day reminds Charlie of "football weather," and Lincoln Peters' first name conjures up an image of a simple and decent American far removed from Paris' luxury hotels and prowling prostitutes. This American-less Paris unsettles Charlie: "It seems very funny to see so few Americans around," he tells Marion. When she replies that the absence of her countrymen "delights" her, Charlie nostalgically rushes to their defense, recalling the "sort of magic" he once felt as an American in Paris.

In "Babylon Revisited" Paris is both a heaven and a hell. In two brief early scenes, Fitzgerald presents a snapshot tour of many of Paris's most

> The richness of 'Babylon Revisited' as a work of fiction lies in Fitzgerald's ability to encompass so many themes while leaving the important questions about Charlie Wales' character unanswered."

famous locations, from the Hotel Ritz in the Place Vendome and the Place de la Concorde to the river Seine, the Left Bank, and Montmartre. These glimpses of the "majesty" and "magnificence" of Paris are then contrasted with its seedy tourist traps, licentious nightclubs, loose women, and money-devouring restaurants and nightspots. Against these images of Paris as both splendid icon and threat, Fitzgerald employs images of a familiar America that reminds Charlie of the home he gave up when his ill-gotten stock market windfall separated him from his moral center. Exploring Paris's streets, Charlie catches a glimpse of the effect of Paris's foreign decadence on the American values he claims to have regained: descending into a club appropriately named the Cafe of Hell, "an American couple" glances at him "with frightened eyes." The image of a moral or psychological hell suggested by the nightclub's name conveys the image of Paris as a dark underworld, which Fitzgerald strengthens elsewhere in the story. The "fire-red, gas-blue, ghost- green" signs Charlie sees during his first night in Paris contribute to the city's spectral, otherworldly quality in the story, and Fitzgerald later reinforces this foreboding atmosphere with the images of "bleak sinister cheap hotels," "*cocottes* prowling singly or in pairs," and "women and girls carried screaming with drink or drugs out of public places." By evoking an image of Paris as a Dantean "nightmare," Fitzgerald suggests how far Charlie had fallen in his pre-crash days as well as the dangers that still threaten him. Fitzgerald's ability to broaden Charlie's personal drama into a reflection on the free-spirited times of the twenties, the stock market crash of 1929, the dawning of the Great Depression, the life of American expatriates in Paris, and the contrasts between the American and European ways of life demonstrate the depth of Fitzgerald's accomplishment in "Babylon Revisited."

Most critics of "Babylon Revisited" have agreed with Fitzgerald's own high estimation of the story as "magnificent." The story has been occasionally criticized for its melodramatic touches and imperfect structure, but the majority of critics have regarded it among the very best of the 160-odd stories Fitzgerald wrote during his career. In his 1964 analysis of the story, Thomas Staley focuses on Fitzgerald's exploration of the theme of time. The struggle between Charlie's irrevocable past and his uncertain present leaves him in the end "suspended in time," with only a "future of loneliness" before him. Staley shows that Fitzgerald was "particularly preoccupied" with the theme of time by tracing the story's temporally oriented language, from the title itself, which refers back to the biblical city of ancient Mesopotamia, to the images of movement through time that pervade the story. Charlie's battle with time is reflected in such lines as "he wanted to jump back a whole generation," "a crowd who had helped them make months into days"; "the present was the thing"; or "It's a great change." For Staley, the story's conclusion offers Charlie little real hope; he will remain "suspended" between the past, present, and future—without Honoria.

In his 1973 interpretation of the story, David Toor also argues that the story ends negatively, on a note of "almost total despair." For Toor, "Babylon Revisited" is the unambiguous story of Charlie's "self-destruction" as a result of his "warped" delusion that he has recovered from his past and is deserving of a second chance with Honoria. All Charlie's problems stem from his inability to love, Toor argues, and Charlie repeatedly refuses to confront his guilt for Helen's death, his continuing dependence on alcohol, and his misguided belief that giving money away and giving love are the same thing. For Toor, Charlie's point of view is completely unreliable, self-justifying, and manipulative, and he neither deserves nor will ever win custody of Honoria. In a 1982 discussion of structural metaphors in Fitzgerald's short fiction, William J. Brondell argues that, like all Fitzgerald's better stories, "Babylon Revisited" contains a "deep structure" that illuminates the thoughts and emotions of the characters. In "Babylon Revisited" this deep structure can be understood with the aid of the "structural metaphor" of the swing or pendulum first presented in Charlie's vision of Helen swinging "faster and faster" on a swing. The swing metaphor, with its alternating, back-and-forth movement, pervades the story, which continually shifts between disappointment and exultation, past and present, action and reaction. Because Charlie has proved that he can control his reactions to the forces and events around him, Brondell argues, as a patient realist he will be rewarded with Honoria in the end when the "swing of the past [loses] its momentum."

In his 1982 article, Carlos Baker analyzes the theme of freedom and imprisonment in " Babylon Revisited" by discussing the opposing motifs of Babylon—"the center of luxury and wickedness"—and the "quiet and decent" home Charlie wants to raise Honoria in. Within this opposition, Baker maintains, Fitzgerald uses the imagery of keys, locks, and doors to dramatize Charlie's battle to escape the prison of his past and enter "the door of the world." Noting Fitzgerald's use of alternating interior and exterior scenes to create the threatening "Babylonian" element that lurks behind the action of the entire story, Baker sees Charlie's final fate at the story's end as both a "lock-out" and a "locking-in." Baker also traces Fitzgerald's return to the material of "Babylon Revisited" in the late 1930s when he began work on a screenplay of the story under the name *Cosmopolitan*.

Source: Paul Bodine, "An Overview of 'Babylon Revisited'," in *Short Stories for Students,* Gale, 1998.

Carlos Baker,

In the following excerpt, Baker examines the themes of freedom and imprisonment in "Babylon Revisited," focusing on Charlie's characterization.

> *A kind of change came in my fate,*
> *My keepers grew compassionate,*
> *I know not what had made them so.*
> *They were inured to sights of woe.*
> *And so it was:—my broken chain*
> *With links unfastened did remain*
> *And it was liberty to stride*
> *Along my cell from side to side.*
> *—Byron, "The Prisoner of Chillon"*

Fitzgerald once called "Babylon Revisited" a magnificent short story. The adjective still holds. It is probably his best. Written in December, 1930, it was first published February 21, 1931, in the *Saturday Evening Post,* whose editors must have recognized its superior qualities, well above the norm of the stories from his pen that this magazine had been publishing for the past ten years. Collected in *Taps at Reveille* in 1935, it stood proudly at the end of the volume, a memorable example of well-made short fiction.

The epigraph from Byron bears upon the story for many reasons, not least because "The Prisoner of Chillon" was the first poem that Fitzgerald ever heard, his father having read it aloud to him in his childhood, a circumstance that he recalled in a letter to his mother in June, 1930, when he paid a tourist visit to "Chillon's dungeons deep and old" while staying at Ouchy-Lausanne in order to be near Zelda, who was desperately ill in a nearby sanatorium. The story he wrote six months afterwards might have been called "Chillon Revisited," involving as it does the double theme of freedom and imprisonment, of locking out and locking in. For although Charlie Wales seems to himself to have redeemed his right to parenthood and to have regained his proper freedom, the links of his fetters are still visible when the story ends. And we, the keepers, inured as we are to sights of woe both inside and outside Fitzgerald's life and works, cannot help feeling compassion for this fictive prisoner, who tries so hard to measure up, only to be defeated by a past that he can never shed.

From the triple nadir of the Wall Street crash, months of recuperation from alcoholism in a sanatorium, and the death of his wife, Charlie Wales has now rehabilitated himself as a successful man of business in Prague, Czechoslovakia, and has returned to Paris in the hope of taking custody of his nine-year-old daughter Honoria, who has been living in the care of her aunt and uncle since her mother's death. He feels ready for the responsibility, since he has made another kind of comeback, having staved off drunkenness for a year and a half by the simple expedient of rationing himself to one whisky a day. All those sins of commission which led to the debacle are now, he is sure, behind him. He recognizes that while he was flinging away thousand-franc notes like handfuls of confetti, even the most wildly squandered sum was being given "as an offering to destiny that he might not remember the things most worth remembering, the things that now he would always remember": Honoria taken from him and Helen buried in Vermont.

Two motifs stand opposed in the story. One is that of Babylon, ancient center of luxury and wickedness in the writings of the Fathers of the Church. The other is that of the quiet and decent homelife that Wales wishes to establish for his child. He defines the Babylon motif as a "catering to vice and waste." It is what used to happen every afternoon in the Ritz bar when expatriated Americans like himself systematically hoisted glasses on the way to the ruin, moral or physical or both, that besets so many of them now. More spectacularly, it is places of decadent entertainment like the Casino where the naked Negro dancer Josephine Baker performs ''her chocolate arabesques.'' It is squalidly visible along the streets of Montmartre, the Rue Pigalle and the Place Blanche, where nightclubs like ''the two great mouths of the Cafe of Heaven and the Cafe of Hell'' used to wait, as they still do, to devour busloads of tourists, innocent foreigners eager for a glimpse of Parisian fleshpots.

Fittingly enough, it is in the Ritz bar that the story opens—and closes. The place is nothing like it used to be. A stillness, ''strange and portentous,'' inhabits the handsome room. No longer can it be thought of as an American bar: it has ''gone back into France.'' All the former habitues are absent—Campbell ailing in Switzerland; Hardt back at work in the United States; and Fessenden, who tried to pass a bad check to the management, wrecked at last by shame and obesity. Only Duncan Schaeffer is still around Paris. Swallowing his loneliness, Charlie Wales hands the assistant bartender a note for Schaeffer including the address of his brother-in-law in the Rue Palatine. It is his first mistake. A key clicks in the prison door. Although he does not know it yet, Schaeffer will twice seek Charlie out, only to lock him into loneliness again.

At the outset Fitzgerald alternates interior and exterior scenes, with the obvious intent of providing the Babylonian background against which the principal dramatic scenes are to occur. While Charlie is on his way to the Peters's apartment in the Rue Palatine, he is most impressed by the nocturnal beauty rather than the wickedness of Paris. Bistros gleam like jewels along the boulevards, and the ''fire-red, gas-blue, ghost-green signs'' blur their way ''smokily through the tranquil rain.'' By contrast, the living room at his brother-in-law's place is ''warm and comfortably American,'' with a fire on the hearth and a pleasant domestic bustle in the kitchen. Although Honoria is well, and happy enough with her small cousins, she is plainly overjoyed to see her father again. At dinner he watches her closely, wondering whom she most resembles, himself or her mother. It will be fortunate, he thinks, ''if she didn't combine the traits of both that had brought them to disaster.''

Marion Peters has no doubt as to whose traits must be guarded against. Between Charlie and his sister-in-law an ''instinctive antipathy'' prevails. In her eyes he can do nothing right. When he says how strange it seems that so few Americans are in Paris, she answers that she's delighted: ''Now at least you can go into a store without their assuming you're a millionaire.'' But Charlie replies that it was nice while it lasted. ''We were a sort of royalty, almost infallible, with a sort of magic around us. In the bar this afternoon,''—and here he stumbles, seeing his mistake—''there wasn't a man I knew.'' Marion looks at him keenly: ''I should think you'd have had enough of bars.''

In Marion's mind the reference to bars has no double significance; she means only those places where drinking is done. But to the eyes of the reader, aware of Charlie's prisonlike predicament, the word might well carry an ulterior suggestiveness. For he has had enough of bars in both senses, longing instead for the freedom to live a responsible domestic life and ''more and more absorbed,'' as he thinks next day, ''by the desire of putting a little of himself into [Honoria] before she [has] crystallized utterly'' into maturity.

The bars of his incipient prison move closer on the following afternoon when he takes Honoria to lunch and afterwards to a vaudeville matinee at the Empire. That morning he has awakened to a bright fall day that reminds him, as it so often reminded Fitzgerald, of football games. Charlie is naturally optimistic, sanguine by temperament, at least in the mornings. The gloom closes in when two ghosts from his past—Duncan Schaeffer and Lorraine Quarrles—intrude on the father-daughter colloquy, first at the restaurant and then at the theater. He puts them off as well as he can: they are the counterforce to all he now longs for. Going home in the taxi, Honoria says firmly that she wants to live with him. His heart leaps up. When he has delivered her to the apartment, he waits outside for her to show herself at the window. She appears, warm and glowing like an image of domesticity, and throws him a kiss in the dark street where he stands.

On his return that evening, Marion meets him with ''hard eyes.'' She is wearing a black dinner dress that faintly suggests mourning, possibly for her dead sister. Although he understands that he will ''have to take a beating,'' Charlie supposes that if he assumes ''the chastened attitude of the reformed sinner,'' he may be able to carry the day and win the right to his daughter, despite Marion's legal guardianship. But she remains obdurate. Never in her life, she tells him, can she forget that early morning when Helen knocked at her door, '''soaked to the skin and shivering','' with the news that Charlie, in drunken and jealous anger, had locked her out in the snow, where she had been wandering in slippers, ''too confused to find a taxi.''

Once again the imagery of keys and locks and doors rises into view. Seeing that Marion has ''built up all her fear of life into one wall and faced it toward him,'' Charlie can only swallow his protestations. When he points out in a dull voice that Helen, after all, '''died of heart trouble','' she picks up and echoes the phrase as if—unlike her earlier reference to ''bars''—this one of '''heart trouble''' has ''another meaning for her.'' But she has reached the end of her tether. '''Do what you like!''' she cries, springing from her chair. '''. . . You two decide it. I can't stand this. I'm sick. I'm going to bed'.''

Next day when Charlie lunches with Lincoln Peters, he finds it difficult ''to keep down his exultation.'' The two men agree to a final conference that evening to settle all details. But Charlie's past cannot be shed so easily. Back at his hotel he finds a *pneu* from Lorraine Quarrles, reminding him of their drunken exploit in stealing a butcher's tricycle and pedalling round the etoile until dawn. '''For old time's sake,''' she urges him to meet her at the Ritz that afternoon at five.

Lorraine as temptress has lost her charm for Charlie. At five he leaves instead for the Rue Palatine for what will amount to the obligatory scene of the story. Honoria, who has been told that she is to go with her father, can scarcely contain her delight. Even Marion seems at last to have ''accepted the inevitable.'' Charlie nods to Peters's offer of a drink: ''I'll take my daily whisky.'' The wall that Marion erected against him has fallen now. The apartment is warm—''a home, people together by a fire,'' the ideal of domesticity that Charlie would like to establish on his own for his child.

At this point comes the long peal at the doorbell and the sudden intrusion of Duncan Schaeffer and Lorraine, drunken, word-slurring, ''hilarious . . . roaring with laughter.'' When Charlie introduces his old friends, Marion freezes, drawing back toward the hearth, her arm thrown defensively around her daughter's shoulders. After he has gotten rid of the intruders, Charlie notices that she has not moved from the fire. Both of her children are now standing in the maternal shelter of her arms. Peters is still playfully ''swinging Honoria back and forth like a pendulum from side to side''—a gesture to which Fitzgerald plainly attaches symbolic significance and one that even echoes, though doubtless by chance, the very words of the prisoner of Chillon.

> ''In Marion's mind the reference to bars has no double significance; she means only those places where drinking is done. But to the eyes of the reader, aware of Charlie's prisonlike predicament, the word might well carry an ulterior suggestiveness.''

Once more, in a telling repetition of first effect, Marion rushes from the room. She is in bad shape, as Peters returns to say. Dinner is out of the question and Charlie must go.

> Charlie got up. He took his coat and hat and started down the corridor. Then he opened the door of the dining-room and said in a strange voice, ''Good night, children.''
>
> Honoria rose and ran around the table to hug him.
>
> ''Good night, sweetheart,'' he said vaguely, and then trying to make his voice more tender, trying to conciliate something, ''Good night, dear children.''

The story returns to its opening locale. In the grip of his anger, Charlie hopes to find Lorraine and Duncan at the Ritz bar. But they have done their sorry work and vanished from his life. He orders a whisky and chats idly with the bartender about times past. Once more the memory of those days sweeps over him like a nightmare—the incoherent babbling, the sexual advances, ''the women and girls carried screaming with drink or drugs out of public places,'' or the men like himself ''who locked their wives out in the snow'' on the theory that ''the snow of twenty-nine wasn't real snow. If you didn't want it to be snow, you just paid some money.''

Another lock-out is imminent, which will also amount to a locking-in. When Charlie telephones, Lincoln Peters is compassionate but firm: '''Marion's sick. . . . I know this thing isn't altogether your fault, but I can't have her go to pieces about it. I'm afraid we'll have to let it slide for six months.'''

Charlie returns to his table. Although he tells himself that "they couldn't make him pay forever," he knows he must serve a further sentence in the prison of his days. But he is "absolutely sure that Helen wouldn't have wanted him to be so alone."

Source: Carlos Baker, "When the Story Ends: 'Babylon Revisited'," in *The Short Stories of F. Scott Fitzgerald: New Approaches in Criticism,* edited by Jackson R. Bryer, The University of Wisconsin Press, 1982, pp. 269–77.

William J. Brondell

In the following excerpt, Brondell examines the structure of and the metaphors in "Babylon Revisited."

"Babylon Revisited" has deservedly received more critical attention and praise than any other Fitzgerald short story, with most commentators expressing admiration for its flawless blend of a tight, balanced structure and a significant theme. The only reservation about the story's structural excellence appears in a footnote to Higgins' study of the story [in *F. Scott Fitzgerald: A Study of the Stories,* 1971]: "The story's structure seems slightly flawed in that there are actually two dramatic climaxes, scene four and scene six." One sees a flaw only if one insists on a restricted development in the superstructure; such an emphasis traditionally demands that the climax be followed by a change in the hero's fortunes or in his psychological state. There is obviously a change in Charlie's fortunes and psychological state after Marion relents and yields to Charlie's request for custody of Honoria. But then of course the story continues; and just as his desires are to be fulfilled, the "ghosts" out of the past intervene and turn Charlie into a victim instead of a victor—his fortunes change and his spirit falls. But clearly, Charlie's loneliness at the end of the story is appropriate only if he has been deprived of Honoria, as happened in the climax in Scene six, Section IV.

Even though some disagree with Seymour Gross's interpretation [in *College English,* Nov. 1963] of the ultimate meaning of the story, his reading of "Babylon Revisited" remains the most judicious and detailed appraisal of the relationships between the structure and the theme—so detailed that the following examination of the deep structure and the structural metaphor will be but a fine-tuning of his argument and a moderation of his gloomy interpretation. Gross notices, analyzes, and expands on the structural "maneuvers" Fitzgerald uses to achieve the unity and coherence that raises this story above the others. Since "Babylon Revisited" is

essentially a story of Charlie's character, Gross correctly sees Charlie as having attained the fundamental state of a man of character, a "quiet power over himself." But despite this self mastery, Charlie needs "his daughter back to give shape and direction to his renascence, to redeem his lost honor, and in a sense to recover something of his wife." Charlie's failure to accomplish this "crushes any lingering hopes" that he might have had, and leaves him with nothing to do "but turn for comfort to the dead for whom time has also stopped." Gross's attention is focused primarily on the superstructure and on the action moved along by the extensive parallels between the sections of that structure; as a result, he sees the story as a tightly woven yet simple description of a man cruelly and unjustly denied both his daughter and his honor. A brief analysis of the deep structure of Charlie's internal life and the special metaphor that informs the deep structure suggest that "Babylon Revisited" is indeed a story on two levels: the exterior level which describes Charlie's unsuccessful attempt to reclaim his daughter Honoria; and an interior level which describes Charlie's successful attempt to prove his reformation and thus reclaim his lost honor.

As in "The Freshest Boy," the structural metaphor in "Babylon Revisited" to be found immediately prior to the climax, informs both the superstructure and the deep structure. At the end of Section III, after Marion has agreed to relinquish her custody of Honoria, Charlie returns to his rooms in an "exultant" state of mind. But immediately, he discovers that he cannot sleep, because the "image of Helen haunted him." He begins to review their stormy relationship, and especially the particulars of the night when he, in a pique of jealous anger, locked her out in the snow. He then recalls the aftermath and all its horrors, the superficial "reconciliation," and the eventual death of his wife— "martyrdom," as Marion would have it. The memories are so strong and become so real that Charlie imagines that Helen talks to him. She reassures him that she also wants him to have custody of Honoria, and she praises him for his reformation. Then she says a "lot of other things—friendly things—but she was in a swing in a white dress, and swinging faster and faster all the time, so that at the end he could not hear clearly all that she said." This image of Helen in the swing emanates throughout the story's superstructure. Just as the dream of his dead wife in a white dress (suggestive of the innocent past of long ago) swings into his mind to restrain his "exultation," so the sins of the past, in the shape and form of Lorraine and Duncan, will appear in Section IV to dash his hopes for the custody of Honoria. Similarly, the action of the swing reflects the pacing of the action in the climactic section: its faster and faster movement implies the quick arrival and departure of Lorraine and Duncan, Marion's abrupt change of heart, and the sudden reversal of Charlie's fortunes.

The metaphor with its back and forth motion not only serves to describe and motivate the climax, but also marks the progress of the action which precedes and follows the climax. From the beginning to the end, the plot is characterized by a series of alternating currents from the past to the present. Higgins has suggested that there are three interwoven movements in the story: "A continual reciprocating movement between his old and new world" in a series of seven scenes; "an in-and-out movement among past, present and future"; and the movement of Charlie's "emotional alternations between optimism and pessimism, hope and disillusion." Clearly, every contact with the past seems to dampen Charlie's spirits or to cloud his expectations, or to defeat his hopes. Just as clearly, the swing functions as a metaphor of the intrusion of the past and reinforces the theme of man's inability to escape the consequences of his past behavior. Furthermore, because of its insistent continual motion, the metaphor seems to suggest that as long as Charlie's life continues, he will, like Sisyphus, almost reach the moment of joy; but something out of the past will turn him away. As Thomas Staley has remarked [in *Modern Fiction Studies* 10 (1964–65)], "Time and its ravages have left Charlie suspended in time with a nightmare for a past, an empty whiskey glass for a present, and a future full of loneliness." Or so it seems if only one level of action is examined. But as Gross has suggested, Charlie's attempt to reclaim his daughter implies an attempt to reclaim his lost honor; and the swing metaphor mirrors Charlie's efforts on this level.

According to the physics of swinging, there is a state of near-equivalence between the terminus of the forward motion and the terminus of the rearward motion. But if the swing must rely on its own momentum, the laws of gravity demand that the terminus of the succeeding motion be lower than the terminus of the preceding motion. There is a similar "balance" in the heights and depths of Charlie's emotional responses to the actions that elicit these responses. In a sense, the physical laws that control the swing are transformed into the metaphysical and

ethical laws that govern Charlie's feelings. Thus for every action in the plot, there is Charlie's less-than-equal reaction—and never any overreaction. Unlike the reactions of every other character in the story, Charlie's are always under control. He may not be able to control the events of his life, but he can and does control his reactions. As he states in Section III while justifying his daily drink, "It's a sort of stunt I set myself. It keeps the matter in proportion."

Throughout the difficult inquisition in Section III, Charlie consciously restrains his natural desires to match the venom of Marion's accusations. "Keep your temper," he tells himself after discovering that he "would take a beating." When Marion recalls the morning after he had locked his wife out in the snow, Charlie "wanted to launch out into a long expostulation," but he doesn't. Later, he becomes "increasingly alarmed" because he feared for Honoria if she remained in the "atmosphere" of Marion's hostility. But "he pulled his temper down out of his face and shut it up inside him. . . ." Near the end of Section III, Marion, eaten up by her prejudice against him and her inescapable memories of her sister's death, cries out, "How much you were responsible for Helen's death I don't know." Even in this desperate moment, as he feels a "current of agony" surge through him, he "hung on to himself" and restrained his emotions—he kept "the matter in proportion." Even Marion realizes the extent of his mastery over himself: "She saw him plainly and she knew he had somehow arrived at control over the situation." In essence, by restraining his reactions, Charlie makes Marion's actions seem all the more out of control. Thus, by being more controlled and reasonable, Charlie proves his reformation and achieves a victory over Marion. For every swing of Marion's argument, Charlie swings back with a controlled response.

In the climactic fourth section the swing begins to move faster and faster, and Charlie's interior world moves in the same rhythm. The first paragraph clearly suggests this motion: "He made plans, vistas, futures for Honoria and himself, but suddenly he grew sad. . . ." In the next breath, he says, "The present was the thing; work to do and someone to love"; and then, "But not to love too much." His mind is swinging back and forth in rapid succession: the hopes for the future are controlled by his thoughts of the past; the sadness of the past is restrained by the needs of the present; and over all, a sense of control, of moderation.

> "By being more controlled and reasonable, Charlie proves his reformation and achieves a victory over Marion. For every swing of Marion's argument, Charlie swings back with a controlled response."

It is this moderation and control that characterizes Charlie's response to the devastating swing of the past that squashes his hopes for reunion with Honoria. The climax brings into clear focus the essential nature of his "character," and his mastery over his emotions. After Lorraine and Duncan materialize, Charlie's attempts to control the situation prove fruitless. At first he was "astounded," then "anxious and at a loss." Later he approaches them "as if to force them backward down the corridor," back into the past. But the momentum of their untimely visit can't be stopped; and in their swinging, they figuratively knock him out of the way: Marion changes her mind and therefore Charlie's future. His last lines in the section show the completeness of his self-control. They are peculiarly measured and restrained, not at all the farewell speech of a man who feels that he has lost everything he has ever wanted. His farewell to his daughter, "Good night, sweetheart," echoes Horatio's farewell to Hamlet; but Charlie broadens his farewell in order to lessen the possible tragic overtones: "Trying to make his voice more tender, trying to conciliate something, 'Good night, dear children.'" Undeniably, the action of the climax proves that even a man of strong character cannot control the actions and feelings of others, nor the strange, almost accidental swing of fortune; but, Charlie's reactions prove that a man who has mastery over his emotions and can control himself has a sense of integrity and honor that cannot be made hostage to the quirks of fate and the meanness of others.

In the first three sections of the story, Charlie's tactics of control and his measured responses to the actions of others accomplished their purpose. As Marion realized in Section III, Charlie is in control of the situation, and is on the point of reclaiming his daughter and redeeming his honor. But as the events of the climax show, Charlie's tactics are not enough. But by this time, his self-control is no longer just a tactic; it is clearly a habitual ethical strategy based on a strong belief in the "eternally valuable element," character. By the end of the story, he realizes that "there was nothing he could do" about the remote and recent past, nor about the future: he is neither a pessimist nor an optimist, but a realist. From the beginning, he has known that he wanted Honoria, and in Section III, "He was sure now that Lincoln Peters wanted him to have his child." Looking back on his experience he also realizes that Marion has yielded before, and may very well yield again. Finally, as he sits in the Ritz bar considering his victories and defeats, he becomes "absolutely sure Helen wouldn't have wanted him to be so alone." All of his experiences during the last few days in Paris suggest to him that it is only a matter of time, perhaps Lincoln's "six months," before the swing of the past will have lost its momentum.

A large measure of the success of "Absolution," "The Freshest Boy," and "Babylon Revisited" depends on Fitzgerald's ability to portray accurately and convincingly the inner life of the characters who inhabit the stories. He has drawn, as it were, a believable picture of souls in motion. To control this motion, he has created a deep structure which traces the characters' most profound thoughts and emotions; and in these stories, he has provided a map, the structural metaphor, so that the reader may follow the motion of these souls. Using this map, the careful reader will be able to discover and feel that "special emotion" and "special experience" that is at the heart of the stories and at the center of Fitzgerald's art.

Source: William J. Brondell, "Structural Metaphors in Fitzgerald's Short Fiction," in *Kansas Quarterly,* Vol. 14, No. 2, Spring, 1982, pp. 107–11.

David Toor

In the following essay, Toor offers his view of Fitzgerald's handling of the theme of guilt and self-destructiveness, focusing on the character of Charlie.

Roy R. Male's perceptive article on "Babylon Revisited", [*Studies in Short Fiction* II (1965)] goes far in clearing up many of the unresolved problems that have recently been discussed in relation to the story. Male has pointed out, as James Harrison had shown in an earlier note [*Explicator* 16, (January, 1958)], that Charlie Wales is in a sense responsible for the appearance of Duncan and Lorraine at the Peters's house at precisely the wrong moment. Male has further called into serious question the general interpretation of the story, most specifically Seymour Gross' contention that Charlie has been renovated and that the punishment he suffers is brought upon him from external sources. Gross says: "That moral renovation may not be enough is the injustice that lies at the center of the story" [*College English* XXV (November, 1963)]. Both Male and Harrison point out that had Charlie not given the bartender the Peters' address at the opening of the story, Duncan and Lorraine would not have shown up there and given Marion Peters a real reason to refuse to return Honoria to Charlie.

Gross' further statement, "Nor is there anything here of that troubled ambivalence which characterizes our response to that fantastic ambiguity, Jay Gatsby," seems quite wrong, because it is precisely in the troubled ambivalence of Charlie Wales that the meaning of the story is found. But Charlie's ambivalence is not the result of the fact that, as Male argues, "his is a story of suspension between two worlds," although to a great extent the story is structured on the contrasts between the past, as represented by Lorraine and Duncan, and the present, in the persons of Marion and Lincoln, but in a deeper awareness of Charlie's own guilt and his inability to work it out. It is in a kind of personal psychological morality that the meaning of the story is found.

It is convenient for Charlie to blame the errors of his past for the pains of his present—and future. But Fitzgerald's world is not a world of external retribution—you are not made to pay for what you've done—not at least by a God, or in Hemingway's words, "what we have instead of God," a code, or even by a deterministic fate. The payment is self-punishment, and the ironically disastrous result of such punishment is the intensification of the feelings of guilt. There is no expiation, only the further degeneration of the mind—neurotic reinforcement of behavior that leads eventually to total insanity or a form of suicide.

Charlie Wales is not torn between the poles of two opposing worlds so much as he is torn by his own inner sense of guilt and his inability to expiate it. He is not morally renovated, only sicker and less able to cope with the guilt. In one part of him he wants his Honoria (honor) back, but in the deeper man, the guilt-ridden one, he knows he doesn't deserve her. He has exiled himself to a dream world

free of past responsibilities—Prague—where he creates the fresh image of himself as a successful businessman. Of course the image cannot hold, and his distorted view of the real world leads him into delusion and jealousy: "He wondered if he couldn't do something to get Lincoln out of his rut at the bank." What kind of rut is Lincoln really in? A warm homelife that Charlie envies, children who love him, a neurotic wife, yes, but a reasonable contentment.

There are many hints through the story which point to these conclusions, and one of the most significant may be viewed as flaws in the technique of the tale. Fitzgerald chose a third-person limited point of view to tell the story, and the lapses, few as they are, are telling. All of the lapses—the shifts from limited to omniscient—are concerned with the Peters. The three most important ones directly involve Marion:

> She had built up all her fear of life into one wall and faced it toward him.

> Marion shuddered suddenly; part of her saw that Charlie's feet were planted on the earth now, and her own maternal feeling recognized the naturalness of his desire; but she had lived for a long time with a prejudice—a prejudice founded on a curious disbelief in her sister's happiness, and which, in the shock of one terrible night, had turned to hatred for him. It had all happened at a point in her life where the discouragement of ill health and adverse circumstances made it necessary for her to believe in tangible villainy and a tangible villain.

> Then, in the flatness that followed her outburst, she saw him plainly and she knew he had somehow arrived at control over the situation. Glancing at her husband, she found no help from him, and as abruptly as if it were a matter of no importance, she threw up the sponge.

In a way these passages are indeed flaws. Certainly a craftsman like Henry James, whose meanings so much depend on careful control of point of view, would not have allowed them to pass. But Fitzgerald, as much a conscious artist as he was, as in the excellent handling of such matters in *The Great Gatsby,* for instance, did let them pass because, I think, perhaps he might have been too involved in the problems of this tale, as he was not in *Gatsby.* There is the possibility that these few passages can be read as consistent with a limited third-person point of view and that these were indeed Charlie's reactions to the situation.

But what these flaws may represent is Charlie's attempt to somehow put himself in a position to account for the (subconscious) terrors that were

> " Charlie Wales is not torn between the poles of two opposing worlds so much as he is torn by his own inner sense of guilt and his inability to expiate it."

plaguing him on this return to Babylon. All three of these cited passages are explanations of the sources of Marion's hostility and her resignation in the face of Charlie's apparent renovation. Charlie is convinced that Marion has seen that he is a changed man. But it becomes more and more clear as we examine the story that he himself was by no means convinced.

Aside from the early action of leaving the Peters' address for Duncan Schaeffer at the bar—and Charlie's subsequent denial of any knowledge of how Duncan could have found it out—we need examine in some detail what Charlie does and says through the story to understand just how completely he is caught between the psychologically necessary self-delusion that he is somehow blameless and changed, and the deeper recognition of his own guilt.

Charlie's pose, once again, is that of the reformed alcoholic, allowing himself one drink a day to prove to himself he doesn't need it. "I'm going slow these days," he tells Alix at the beginning. "I've stuck to it for over a year and a half now." The reassurance seems to ring true—it has been a long time. But in the way that he tells himself he can face and beat alcohol, he hasn't allowed himself to try to face and beat the deeper problems. He lives in Prague, adding to Alix, "They don't know about me down there." The dream world of escape, a foreign land where maybe Charlie too, doesn't know about himself. He is cooling it—going slow these days—even the taxi horns play the opening bars of *Le Plus que Lent*.

The Peters' home reminds Charlie of what he has lost. It "was warm and comfortably American." He responds inwardly to the intimacy and comfort of the children in the house, but his outward reaction, while holding his daughter close to him, is to boast to the Peters about how well he himself is

doing. He has more money than he'd ever had before. But he cuts it off when he sees "a faint restiveness in Lincoln's eye." His defensive opening had been wrong, he sees, but still he persists. He boasts also about the past: "We were a sort of royalty, almost infallible, with a sort of magic around us."' And twice in three lines he repeats, "'I take one drink every afternoon. . . .'"

In one way Charlie is ready to admit to himself—and others—that he has a large burden of blame to carry, but too often this admission is qualified with either a denial, a shifting, or a sharing of the blame. As he looks at his daughter he silently hopes that she doesn't "combine the traits of both [Charlie and Helen] that had brought them to disaster." In his lyrical reminiscences of the past in Paris, especially about the money squandered, he tries to convince and justify himself: "But it hadn't been given for nothing." Hadn't it? The next passage is really quite confused, and although it sounds meaningful, in reality it is a pastiche of attempted self-justification and escape from responsibility:

> It had been given, even the most wildly squandered sum, as an offering to destiny that he might not remember the things most worth remembering, the things that now he would always remember—his child taken from his control, his wife escaped to a grave in Vermont.

He thinks about Honoria being "taken from his control," not that "he had lost the right to her control." His wife has not "died," but has "escaped." The last part of the sentence essentially contradicts and yet reinforces the first part.

His encounters with Duncan and Lorraine demonstrate much the same kind of ineffectual self-justification: "As always, he felt Lorraine's passionate, provocative attraction, but his own rhythm was different now." After they leave the restaurant where he had been dining with Honoria, Charlie tries to separate himself from Duncan and Lorraine:

> They liked him because he was functioning, because he was serious; they wanted to see him, because he was stronger than they were now, because they wanted to draw a certain sustenance from his strength.

How do we understand this in terms of his later desire to get "Lincoln out of his rut at the bank?" We can't because of Charlie's inability to admit consciously the distorted state of his mind. Once again, it is not a conflict between the past and present, between Charlie Wales and Charles J. Wales of Prague, but between Charlie and his guilt. Charles J. Wales does not really exist, except in Charlie's limited perception.

Back at the Peters' on the evening of that first encounter with these spectres from the past, he proposes that he take Honoria back with him to Prague. He again boasts about his position and how well he is prepared to care for the girl, but he knows what he is in for—and in a way he is demanding to be punished, but he will put on an act for the Peters': "if he modulated his inevitable resentment to the chastened attitude of the reformed sinner, he might win his point in the end." But Charlie doesn't really know what his point is.

Marion, hurt and ill herself, pushes him to further self-justification: "You know I never did drink heavily until I gave up business and came over here with nothing to do. Then Helen and I began to run around with—." He is cut short, but he can't help but bring Helen into it. When Marion blames him for being in a sanitarium while Helen was dying, "He had no answer." Marion pushed him further. "Charlie gripped the sides of the chair. This was more difficult than he expected; he wanted to launch out into a long expostulation and explanation, but he only said: "The night I locked her out—.""

When Marion asks him why he hadn't thought about what he had done before, and the damage he had caused to Honoria and himself, he again refuses to admit to the full blame:

> "I suppose I did, from time to time, but Helen and I were getting along badly. When I consented to the guardianship, I was flat on my back in a sanitarium and the market had cleaned me out. I knew I'd acted badly, and I thought if it would bring any peace to Helen, I'd agree to anything. But now it's different. I'm functioning, I'm behaving damn well, so far as—."

His guilt at the damage he'd done to Helen is further reflected in the fear of what his daughter might learn about him: "sooner or later it would come out, in a word here, a shake of the head there, and some of that distrust would be irrevocably implanted in Honoria."

Marion hits Charlie hardest when she verbalizes the real and deepest source of Charlie's guilt: "How much you were responsible for Helen's death, I don't know. It's something you'll have to square with your own conscience." And this is just what Charlie can't do. "An electric current of agony surged through him. . . ." But his only outward response, after Lincoln's attempt to defend him, is, "Helen died of heart trouble." There is no other answer Charlie can give, for to admit consciously, even for an instant that he might really have been to blame for Helen's death might permit him to face his guilt and thus enable him to start the cleansing process that might lead back towards balance.

In the reverie of Helen that follows the bitter scene ending with Marion's agreeing to return Honoria, we find evidence of his inability to admit to his blame. "The image of Helen haunted him. Helen whom he had loved so until they had senselessly begun to abuse each other's love, tear it into shreds." He excuses himself again for the events of the night he had locked her out. "When he arrived home alone he turned the key in the lock in wild anger. How could he know she would arrive an hour later alone, that there would be a snowstorm in which she wandered about in slippers, too confused to find a taxi?" The final scene of the vision of Helen that night is again part of his ambivalent attempt and refusal to find expiation. Helen seems to comfort him with tenderness and forgiveness, except that as she swings faster and faster the forgiveness is not complete: "at the end he could not hear clearly all that she said," leaving him to delude himself into half-believing the closing words of the story about Helen forgiving him.

The remaining two sections of the story, IV and V, reinforce what has gone before. Further self-delusions of himself as cured, even a garbled version of how best to raise a daughter:

> The present was the thing—work to do, and someone to love. But not to love too much, for he knew the injury that a father can do to a daughter or a mother to a son by attaching them too closely: afterward, out in the world, the child would seek in the marriage partner the same blind tenderness and, failing probably to find it, turn against love and life.

This is just the kind of distortion that Charlie's mind would drive him to. Certainly there is a base in Freudian psychology for what he says, but only in his conscious rationalization of "not to love too much," can Charlie make sense out of his own inability to love fully and completely. He is too warped to see that the only love worth having or giving is one without reservations and limits.

Reference has been made in footnotes to some of the changes in the above passages between the 1931 and 1935 versions of the story. Two of the most significant changes between the two printed versions of the story occur in part IV. Both versions open with Charlie leaving the address of the Peters' with the bartender to give to Duncan Schaeffer. Lorraine's later message reaches Charlie by different means in the two stories. In the 1931 version:

Back at his hotel, Charlie took from his pocket a *pneumatique* that Lincoln had given him at luncheon. It had been redirected by Paul from the hotel bar.

In the final version:

Back at his hotel, Charlie found a *pneumatique* that had been redirected from the Ritz bar where Charlie had left his address for the purpose of finding a certain man.

It's likely that part of the confusion results from an oversight of Fitzgerald's in revising the manuscript. But the confusion here may also be the result of Fitzgerald's intention to emphasize that Charlie was responsible for the appearance of Duncan and Lorraine at the Peters'. The "certain man" in 1935 is still Duncan at the beginning of the story. And further, that if Lincoln had given him the message, as in the earlier version, Lincoln also would have known that Charlie had given out the address, and Charlie's denial would have been seen immediately as a lie. It was important that Charlie be able to continue his self-delusion without any real fear that Lincoln would know that Charlie was responsible.

Another important change is in Lorraine's invitation to Charlie after she and Duncan have barged in at the Peters': "Come on out to dinner. Be yourself, Charlie. Come on," reads the 1931 version. The final draft: "Come and dine. Sure your cousins won' mine. See you so sel'om. Or solemn." In the *TAR* version Lorraine is quite drunk, obviously intended to make Marion even angrier than in the magazine version. But Fitzgerald has cut the line, "Be yourself, Charlie." It is too obvious to Lorraine in that early version that Charlie is still Charlie, but more important, it is too obvious to Charlie that he is still what he was.

The ghastly scene at the Peters' ends with Charlie getting what he was begging for subconsciously all along—Marion's rejection of his plea for Honoria. Before Charlie leaves he lies—consciously or not—to Lincoln: "I wish you'd explain to her [Marion] I never dreamed these people would come here. I'm just as sore as you are."

Charlie cannot make amends, cannot "conciliate something," as he puts it, and the story ends on a note of almost total despair. It is not by accident that his thoughts turn back to money and his imagination of the power of money. He reflects that "the snow of twenty-nine wasn't real snow. If you didn't want it to be snow, you just paid some money." Charlie hasn't been able to deal in love, but he has been able to handle money and the things money can produce. He still isn't convinced that the two are not equal,

nor can he admit to himself the possibility that the main source of his troubles was his inability to love and that his present guilt feelings stem directly from that source. So he will turn back to the new old ways and instead of dealing with people, deal with things. "There wasn't much he could do now except send Honoria some things; he would send her a lot of things tomorrow. He thought rather angrily that this was just money—he had given so many people money. . . ." And that's all he had given.

In the tormented inner world of Charlie Wales, the world where God could not exist and therefore not punish, and where the individual retains, if not a sense of sin, at least a sense of guilt, we find the real conflict. "Babylon Revisited" is not a story about the inability of the world to forgive and forget, or even about a man drawn back to the past and therefore unable to come to terms with the present. It is a story about self destruction, about the human mind's ability to delude itself into thinking that what it does is based on logic and reason. The story ends with only the promise of emptiness to come in Charlie's life; it ends with the lie that may lead Charlie to destruction: "He was absolutely sure Helen wouldn't have wanted him to be so alone."

Source: David Toor, "Guilt and Retribution in 'Babylon Revisited'," in *Fitzgerald/Hemingway Annual 1973,* edited by Matthew J. Bruccoli and C. E. Frazer Clark, Jr., Microcard Editions Books, 1974, pp. 155–64.

Thomas F. Staley

In the following essay, Staley presents his interpretation of the motif of time in the story, focusing on the way the past constantly impinges upon present events.

[Immanuel] Kant wrote that time is the most characteristic mode of our experience, and, as Hans Myerhoff has pointed out [in *Time and Literature,* 1955], "It is more general than space, because it applies to the inner world of impressions, emotions and ideas for which no spatial order can be given." Modern fiction is preoccupied with the concept of time; [Henri] Bergson's concept of *la duree realle* and [Marcel] Proust's *la memoire involontaire* have of course, exerted a large influence on fiction; in fact their indirect influence has been enormous. Modern writers since Bergson and Proust have become increasingly aware of the implications of time in the structure of their fiction. F. Scott Fitzgerald was particularly preoccupied with the forces of time. His personal life, together with his reading, gave him a profound sense of the importance of time with regard to self.

Fitzgerald felt the ravages of time especially in his own life, and a great deal of his fiction touches on this theme. He was less inward in his treatment of time than either Joyce or Thomas Wolfe, but there is in his fiction a sense of the unity of past and present; the past is irrevocable because it brings about the reality of the present. An understanding of how Fitzgerald's concept of time informs his fiction can be illustrated by an analysis of his famous short story "Babylon Revisited." The plot of this story moves directly through time and space, and its movement conveys its theme.

The theme of "Babylon Revisited" suggests that the past and the future meet in the present; moreover, Fitzgerald also dramatically expresses Bergson's idea that duration is the continuous progress of the past which forces into the future. In the story, Charlie Wales relives the disastrous events of his past in a few days, and he realizes in the brilliant final scene in the Ritz Bar that time is irreversible, that the empty glass in front of him is the emptiness of his whole life, past, present, and future. At the beginning of the story, Charlie intends to shuck away the memory of his past through the recovery of his lost child, but the actuality of the past has nullified this prospect from the first.

The very title of the story suggests the movement of time and space. The scene is set in the modern city along the Seine, but we are intended to recall the ancient city on the banks of the Euphrates. Charlie Wales returns to Paris in order to claim his daughter and thus give meaning and purpose to his life. But just as Charlie has changed in the three years since he left Paris, so, too, has the world he left. In the opening scene in the Ritz Bar he inquires about his former friends, but finds they have scattered, to Switzerland, to America. He notices a group of "strident queens" in the corner and is depressed because he realizes that ". . . they go on forever" and are not affected by time.

Throughout Part I of the story Charlie is continually trying to turn back the clock. During dinner at the Peters' he looks across at Honoria and feels that ". . . he wanted to jump back a whole generation." As he walks through the Montmartre district after dinner, he recalls his dissipated life in Paris, and he realizes that his bar hopping was "an increase of paying for the privilege of slower and slower motion." As he wanders the streets of Paris, Charlie Wales' attitude toward time is that of some-

> " The theme of 'Babylon Revisited' suggests that the past and the future meet in the present."

thing lost. Throughout Part I all the references to time are to the past; the hope for the future remains in the background.

There is a shift of emphasis in time as Part II opens. Charlie wants to forget the horrors of the past as he has lunch with Honoria. He deliberately chooses a restaurant that is "not reminiscent of champagne dinners and long luncheons that began at two and ended in a blurred vague twilight." Today is to be a special day; today is to be isolated into the present; but this is impossible, for out of that twilight world of the past "sudden ghosts" emerge. Two of the people who helped him to "make months into days" confront him in the restaurant, and the past impinges on the present, and also foreshadows its impingement on the future.

In this scene present, past and future fuse. Both past and future collide as Honoria, a symbol of the future, meets Lorraine and Duncan, symbols of the lurking past. This scene in which the past and future meet in the present also foreshadows the climax of the story in Part IV, when Lorraine and Duncan invade the Peters' home and in so doing both symbolically and literally destroy the future.

Part II opens at noon when the sun is high in the air and the day is full of expectation for Charlie, but it ends as Charlie stands outside in the dark street and looks up at Honoria as she blows him a kiss ". . . out into the night." This scene also recalls the impossibility of Gatsby's dream illustrated as he stands outside in the darkness waiting for Daisy following the automobile accident in *The Great Gatsby*.

In Part III Charlie is aware that he will have to submit to Marion's verbal beating in order to get Honoria back. "It would last an hour or two hours. . . ." But what is two hours in relation to a lifetime? The scene with Marion and Lincoln begins with Charlie's confidence quite high, but the desperateness of his situation shows through the conversation. He says to Marion: "'But if we wait much longer I'll lose Honoria's childhood and my chance for a home.'" Charlie leaves the Peters' home and crosses through the Paris streets. With the question of Honoria's coming with him still unresolved he recalls again his past and is haunted by the image of his dead wife as he crosses the Seine, the same Seine that he crossed many times three years before with his wife Helen. His spirits rise and the Seine seems fresh and new to him. The opposition of present and past is visually reinforced by the black dress that Marion wears in the present and by the white dress that Helen has on as she swings ". . . faster and faster all the time." But this is the Helen that emerges in a dream, out of relation with time. But even in the dream, time is present in the symbol of the pendulum swinging and swinging; Helen becomes the pendulum of time herself. Dreams momentarily take the burdens of time from Charlie; they offer him an escape from the present, distort the past, and belie the future.

Charlie wakes up to another "bright, crisp day" as Part IV of the story opens. Separating past and present for a moment, Charlie looks to the future, believing for an instant that the past doesn't determine the future: "He made plans, vistas, futures for Honoria and himself." But this glimpse into the future is quickly thwarted by a glance backward at past visions: "Suddenly he grew sad, remembering all the plans he and Helen had made." Seeing the future as not quite real and the past as a crushed dream, Charlie thinks of the present: "The present was the thing—work to do and someone to love."

Each time Charlie's future with Honoria seems temporarily possible the past quickly snuffs out the hope. After having lunch with Lincoln, he returns to his hotel room to find a note from Lorraine. In the note Lorraine recalls that "crazy spring" when she and Charlie stole a butcher's tricycle. This incident again brings Charlie back to that past which in retrospect was a nightmare. Out of his feeling of repugnance for the past, symbolized in Lorraine, he quickly turns to thoughts of the future, symbolized by Honoria.

At five o'clock Charlie arrives at the Peters' and his dreams of the future seem realized; he seems to have finally defeated the past. But the final tension of past and present in the story comes to a climax. Duncan and Lorraine suddenly interrupt the discussion of plans concerning Honoria. These "blurred, angry faces" from the past emerge to destroy the future forever. "Charlie came closer to them, as if to force them backward down the corri-

dor." It was impossible for Charlie to blot out the past. After Lorraine and Duncan leave, Charlie returns to the salon to see Lincoln "swinging Honoria back and forth like a pendulum from side to side." Whether Charlie realizes it or not, this action is visual testimony that time has placed Honoria in the hands of the Peters. Charlie leaves the house knowing full well that he is not to get Honoria; the past has spoiled the present and determined the future.

The final irony of Charlie's life is brought out in the final section of the story, Part V, which is set again in the Ritz Bar where the story opened. Paul, the bartender, points out the irony unknowingly when he says, "'It's a great change. . .' ." Charlie's mind goes back to the past again, but now he sees himself in the eternal present, alone. He thinks back to a fixed period of time, the Wall Street crash, and then to the time just before that when the snow wasn't real snow. "If you didn't want it to be snow, you just paid some money." To escape from the past Charlie tried to make a life for himself and Honoria, but now he must be concerned with only the hollow thought of buying her something. As the story ends, he must escape time and reality and dream again of Helen, who he is sure "wouldn't have wanted him to be so alone." Time and its ravages have left Charlie suspended in time with a nightmare for a past, an empty whiskey glass for a present, and a future full of loneliness.

Source: Thomas F. Staley, "Time and Structure in Fitzgerald's 'Babylon Revisited'," in *Modern Fiction Studies,* Vol. X, No. 1, Winter, 1964–65, pp. 386–88.

Sources

Baker, Carlos. "When the Story Ends: 'Babylon Revisited.'" In *The Short Stories of F. Scott Fitzgerald: New Approaches in Criticism,* edited by Jackson R. Bryer, pp. 269-77. Madison: University of Wisconsin Press, 1982.

Bruccoli, Matthew J. *Some Sort of Epic Grandeur,* Harcourt Brace Jovanovich, 1981, pp. 308-09.

Eble, Kenneth E. "Touches of Disaster: Alcoholism and Mental Illness in Fitzgerald's Short Stories," in *The Short Stories of F. Scott Fitzgerald: New Approaches in Criticism,* edited by Jackson R. Bryer, University of Wisconsin Press, 1982, pp. 39- 52.

Galbraith, John Kenneth. *The Great Crash: 1929,* Houghton Mifflin, 1961.

Toor, David. "Guilt and Retribution in 'Babylon Revisited.'" In *Fitzgerald/Hemingway Annual 1973,* edited by Matthew J. Bruccoli and C. E. Frazer Clark, Jr., pp. 155-64. Washington, D.C.: Microcard Editions Books, 1974.

Further Reading

Gallo, Rose Adrienne. *F. Scott Fitzgerald,* Modern Literature Monographs, Frederick Ungar Publishing, 1978, pp. 101-5.
    Gallo argues that Fitzgerald hints that Charlie has not completely rejected his past alcoholic life and praises Fitzgerald's "brilliant evocation of place."

Lehan, Richard. "The Romantic Self and the Uses of Place in the Stories of F. Scott Fitzgerald," in *The Short Stories of F. Scott Fitzgerald: New Approaches in Criticism,* edited by Jackson R. Bryer, University of Wisconsin Press, 1982, pp. 3-21.
    Lehan emphasizes Fitzgerald's fusion of individual experience and the larger "spirit of the times" in the story. Charlie's dissipation is dramatized as being inseparable from the dissipation of his age, and the "note of loss" that surrounds Charlie's predicament at the story's conclusion reflects Fitzgerald's theme throughout his fiction that his protagonists' tragedies reflect the larger events of society around them.

Mangum, Bryant. "F. Scott Fitzgerald," in *Critical Survey of Short Fiction,* pp. 858-66.

Mangum argues that in "Babylon Revisited" Fitzgerald strikes a compromise between the reader's feeling that Marion unfairly persecuted Charlie and the reader's sense that Charlie should not escape the consequences of his pre-crash irresponsibility. Fitzgerald's compromise is to have Marion retain Honoria, but give Charlie the hope that at some point in the future he can make another attempt to regain custody of his daughter. Mangum sees the story as a workshop for *Tender Is the Night,* because it successfully dramatizes the father-daughter relationship and creates a "mythic level" in which everything conspires to drive Charlie into "exile" from the "fallen" city of Paris.

Prigozi, Ruth. "Fitzgerald's Short Stories and the Depression: An Artistic Crisis," in *The Short Stories of F. Scott Fitzgerald: New Approaches in Criticism,* edited by Jackson R. Bryer, University of Wisconsin Press, 1982, pp. 111-26.
    Prigozi claims that "Babylon Revisited" showcases the "nuanced and elliptical" style of Fitzgerald's "masterpieces," in which he employs a sophisticated approach to scene and atmosphere to explore the themes of struggle, responsibility for others, professionalism, and "above all . . . that elusive trait, character."

Staley, Thomas F. "Time and Structure in Fitzgerald's 'Babylon Revisited.'" *Modern Fiction Studies,* Vol. 10, No. 1, Winter, 1964-65, pp. 386-88.
    Analyzes the construction of the story.

The Bloody Chamber

Angela Carter

1979

Published in 1979, *The Bloody Chamber and Other Stories,* which received the Cheltenham Festival Literary Prize, retells classic fairy tales. Angela Carter revises Puss-in-Boots and Sleeping Beauty, for example, from an adult, twentieth-century perspective. Her renditions are intended to disturb and titillate her audience, instead of lulling it to sleep. The title story recasts the legend of Bluebeard, the mysterious French nobleman who murders his many wives. The legend, as recorded by the seventeenth-century author Charles Perrault, begins with the marriage of a girl to an eccentric, wealthy man. Called away on business, the newlywed husband leaves his wife the keys to every room and cabinet in the house. This keyring includes one key that she must not use: the one to the "room at the end of the great gallery." Of course, she eventually enters the room forbidden to her. In it she finds the corpses of her husband's previous wives, all with their throats cut. Startled, the girl drops the key, which is enchanted and permanently stained by the blood on the floor. From this stain, Bluebeard discovers her disobedience. He raises his scimitar, but just in time, her brothers arrive to slay the murderer.

Though it follows the original tale in basic structure, "The Bloody Chamber" adds details of character and setting that raise issues of sexual awakening and sexual depravity, of the will to live, and of life in hell. In having the young bride be the one to tell her story and in having her courageous

mother come to the rescue, moreover, Carter revisits an age-old tale with her feminist viewpoint.

Author Biography

When Angela Carter died of cancer on February 16, 1992, she was only 51 years old. In her relatively short lifetime, she wrote nine novels, dozens of short stories, a volume of poetry, and numerous essays on cultural and literary themes. Her work is known for its lush, imagistic prose, gothic themes, violence, and an undercurrent of eroticism. Critics have considered her a female Edgar Allan Poe and compared her to the English decadent artist Aubrey Beardsley.

She was born Angela Olive Stalker in London, England, on May 7, 1940. In 1960 she married Paul Carter (the couple divorced in 1972). In 1962, she began her studies in medieval English literature at Bristol University in England, where she also developed an interest in anthropology and French literature. In 1966 her first novel, *Shadow Dance,* was published. Set in an antiques shop, it concerned a pathological love triangle and exhibited elements of the fantastic that bloomed fully in her later novels. Her next two novels, *The Magic Toyshop* and *Several Perceptions,* experimented with elements of science fiction and magic realism. They were well-received by critics and were awarded the John Llewllyn Rhys Memorial Prize and the Somerset Maugham Award, respectively.

In 1979, Carter published *The Sadeian Woman and the Ideology of Pornography,* a nonfiction work in which she took a feminist view of the Marquis de Sade, an eighteenth-century French nobleman and author known for his sexually explicit novels. She argued that in his female characters, either passionate sex objects or dominant tyrants, the Marquis de Sade was "claiming rights of free sexuality for women." *The Bloody Chamber,* published the same year, combined Carter's interests in feminism, fairy tales, pornography, and anthropology (the study of human beings and their environment) into adaptations of cultural legends. Reworkings of fairy tales became one of Carter's dominant themes in the next two decades. Two of Carter's last published works were scholarly collections of fairy tales: *The Old Wives' Fairy Tale Book* (1990) and *Strange Things Sometimes Still Happen* (1992).

Angela Carter

Plot Summary

"The Bloody Chamber" begins with the narrator on her wedding night, traveling by train from Paris to her new home. Her husband is asleep near her, and she, a young pianist, lies sleepless, not knowing what to expect of her married life. She recounts their speedy courtship. Her husband, a marquis who is much older than she and much richer than she, had three wives before her—an opera diva, an artist's model, and a countess—all of whom died under mysterious circumstances.

The couple disembarks the train at dawn and are taken to the Marquis's castle, which is on an island. However, the husband must attend to some business before they can commence their honeymoon. While he is gone, she discovers an out-of-tune piano in the conservatory and a library that includes many volumes of pornography. Her husband returns to find her perusing these volumes and brings her back to the "maternal bed." He puts his grandmother's ruby choker around her neck and they consummate the marriage.

Later, they are awakened by the telephone, and her husband is called away to New York on urgent business. Against her protests, he prepares to depart. He leaves her the keys to every cabinet and room in the castle. He tells her of the treasures that await her viewing, but also informs her that there is one small key that she must not use. ''Every man must have one secret,'' he explains and makes her promise not to enter the room ''at the foot of the west tower.''

After he leaves, the narrator has a restless night alone. She spends the next day practicing the piano and wandering through various rooms. An hour before dinner, she realizes that she has nothing to do all evening. She calls her mother and but is unable to articulate her misery and breaks into tears. In order to distract herself, she decides to open the doors to all the rooms and starts with the Marquis's office. She searches through his business files and desk drawers, searching for clues to his character. In a secret compartment, she discovers a file marked ''Personal.'' In this file are three love notes from his past wives. In these short notes, the Marquis's fourth wife catches a glimpse of the personalities of these women and some ''traces of the heart'' of their husband. She decides to go to the forbidden room, where she hopes to find out about his soul.

There she finds her husband's first three wives, all murdered. The opera singer has been strangled, and the model is hanging from a wall. The most recent wife, the countess, has been penetrated by the spikes of the Iron Maiden. Startled, the narrator drops the key to the torture chamber, and it falls into a pool of blood. She quickly picks it up and flees the gruesome scene.

In her bedroom, she tries to think of a way to escape the castle. She tries to call her mother, but the phone is dead. She tries to comfort herself by turning to her music. Suddenly, she hears a thump in the hallway. It is Jean-Yves, the blind piano-tuner, who has been listening outside the door. She tells him everything. In turn, he tells her that local legends have hinted at these horrors.

At dawn, they hear a car approaching. It is the Marquis. They try to wash the blood from the key, but it is enchanted and permanently stained. Jean-Yves submits to her entreaties to be left alone to face her husband. After exposing her futile attempt to hide the key, the Marquis seizes it and presses the key to her forehead, leaving a mark indicating that she will be sacrificed.

Having dismissed the servants, he intends to behead her. He calls her down to the courtyard. She stalls because, in the distance, she can hear a horse

approaching. Its rider, she later finds out, is her courageous mother whose instincts had told her that her daughter was in danger. Just as the Marquis raises his sword, the mother shoots him dead. ''The Bloody Chamber'' ends with the mother, daughter, and piano tuner living happily ever after. They convert the castle into a school for the blind, and the narrator runs a music school. She is forever thankful that her companion, the piano tuner, cannot see the mark left on her forehead because she views it as a mark of shame.

Characters

Bluebeard
See Marquis

Bride
See Narrator

Heroine
See Narrator

Jean-Yves
Jean-Yves, the blind piano tuner, befriends the narrator when she first marries the Marquis and learns the fate of his previous wives. Through him, readers learn of the long history in the area of the Marquis's family and their violent nature. After her mother kills the Marquis, the narrator establishes a music school and is ''busily engaged in setting up house'' with the piano tuner, who loves her for who she is and cannot see the mark of shame that brands her forehead. His role as the man with whom the protagonist lives happily ever after is a subversion of the typical fairy-tale ending, in which the woman falls in love with a handsome prince or other dashing hero.

Marquis
Modeled after the legendary figure of Bluebeard, the wife-murderer of legend and lore, much of the Marquis's character remains a mystery. He is ''much older'' than his seventeen-year-old bride, but his exact age is not given. He is as ''rich as Croesus,'' the ancient Lydian king, and lives in a forbidding castle surrounded by a moat. A Marquis, he comes

from a long line of French aristocrats, but seems to have no family. This large, leonine man has been married three times, but each of his wives has died mysteriously, though he shows no grief. Because the Marquis is such an enigma, his new bride is overwhelmed with curiosity and seeks to discover something about him as she rifles through his personal belongings while he disappears mysteriously on business during their honeymoon. She discovers a few clues to his character: evidence that he is a "connoisseur" of pornography and is involved in an opium-dealing ring in Laos. All these discoveries, including a cryptic love note from his third wife, the countess, leads her to disobey his ultimatum—that she not enter the locked room in the west wing—where she discovers his true nature as a murderer. Her broken promise is all the reason he needs to murder her as well, proving that he puts his love for violence and his need for the complete obedience and submission of women above all else.

Mother

The mother, who saves her daughter at the end of the story, has a history of adventure and sacrifice. The daughter of a wealthy tea planter who spent her girlhood in Indo-China, she married a soldier of modest means, and when he dies, she is left with nothing. She has sold all her jewelry, "even her wedding ring," so that her daughter could attend a music conservatory. The close connection she has to her daughter explains her instinct in knowing something is wrong when her daughter calls from the castle on her honeymoon, even though the daughter herself cannot even explain what is wrong. But it is the warrior in her—that part of her that fought tigers and pirates as a girl—who kills the Marquis just as he is preparing to kill her daughter. The mother, then, becomes the hero of the story, instead of the girl's brothers, as in the original version of Bluebeard. This turnabout gives Carter's adaptation of the legend a feminist meaning.

Narrator

The narrator of "The Bloody Chamber" is a young pianist who has grown up in Paris with her mother and nanny. Her father died in battle when she was young, but her fondest memory of him is attending the opera *Tristan and Isolde;* these strong memories helped form her love for music, upon which she relies when isolated in the Marquis's castle. She is seventeen when she meets the Marquis, and she is still slender, delicate, and sexually

naive. She is a child who does not know how to answer her mother truthfully when she is asked if she loves the Marquis, and who orders avocado, shrimp, and ice cream for dinner. All she knows is that the Marquis stirs her in some way, but she is unfamiliar with what these feelings mean. When confronted with the horrors of her husband's past, she gains maturity: "Until that moment, this spoiled child did not know that she had inherited nerves and a will from the mother who had defied the yellow outlaws of Indo-China. My mother's spirit drove me on." Facing disaster, she calls on her mother for help and strength. In the end, she finds true love in a blind piano tuner, who does not undress her with his gaze as does the Marquis, but who instead appreciates her for her music. Still, she is scarred with the imprint of the bloody key, a mark she equates with shame, an inevitable result of her maturation that began when she was seduced in a room full of white lilies and mirrors.

Narrator's Husband
See Marquis

Themes

Coming of Age

From the beginning, the seventeen-year-old protagonist describes in her own words the story's movement from her mother's hearth to her husband's castle. The train ride at the beginning of the story may be viewed as a symbol of this transition. Throughout the narrative, the narrator refers to herself as a child. As evidence of the child in her, for her first formal dinner at the castle, she orders avocado, shrimp, and ice cream. Though she is a child in many ways, her situation is that of an adult.

Moral Corruption

The mark she bears on her forehead at the end of the story signifies her moral corruption, which was initiated in the consummation of her marriage. The loss of her virginity, symbolized by the blood-stained sheets, along with the scar on her forehead, indicate the corrupting knowledge—sexual and moral—that the Marquis offers her. He has chosen her because he saw in her "thin white face . . . [a] promise of debauchery only a connoisseur could

Topics for Further Study

- Critics have noted the influence of Carter's interest in anthropology in *The Bloody Chamber*. Explain.

- Research Richard Wagner's opera *Tristan and Isolde*. How is it similar in plot and mood to ''The Bloody Chamber''?

- Read Charles Perrault's version of ''Beauty and the Beast'' and compare it to Carter's version, ''The Courtship of Mr. Lyon,'' which appears in *The Bloody Chamber*. How do these ''literary'' versions of the story compare to another rendition of the tale, for example, Disney's film version of *Beauty and the Beast*? What is the significance of these differences?

- Investigate the life and death of St. Cecilia. How does this saint's life resemble that of the narrator in ''The Bloody Chamber''?

detect.'' In recognition of this fact, the narrator blushes ''to think he might have chosen me, because, in my innocence, he sensed a rare talent for corruption.'' However, her corruption is largely brought about by her own curiosity. Having been warned not to enter the tower in which she found the dead wives, her decision to do so indicates that she needed no help from her husband to initiate her fall from grace. Upon the return of the Marquis, she is faced with the possibility of her own death. At this point, she realizes that she ''must pay the price for her new knowledge.''

Sex

The narrator's descent into moral corruption parallels her sexual initiation. After the consummation of her marriage on her first night at the castle, which she uses the word ''impale'' to describe, she finds a ''dark newborn curiosity'' stirring in her. This curiosity is fueled by the pornographic books she finds in the library, the contents of which ''make her gasp.'' This curiosity also leads her to

the torture chamber, where the connection between sex and death is made explicit, for the third wife has been killed by being impaled by the sharp spikes of the Iron Maiden.

Victim and Victimization

In the social world of ''The Bloody Chamber,'' women are born into the position of passive victim and men are the aggressive victimizers. The marquis impales; his wives are impaled. The marquis chooses the narrator because of her vulnerability, her poverty, and fragility. For him, she resembles the martyr St. Cecilia, and she is to be martyred by him. But the Marquis does not count on the warrior-mother, who breaks the cycle of victimization perpetuated within the castle.

Sex Roles

Carter confronts the paradigm of the male aggressor and the female victim through her feminist re-telling of the Bluebeard myth. She subverts the original tale's traditional sex roles when she substitutes the mother for the brothers of the bride as the rescuer. This switch calls to attention the stereotypes of the traditional fairy tale's male-as-savior and female-as-victim roles. A woman is the hero this time instead of a white knight. And instead of relying on the evil mother/stepmother motif common to fairy tales, the bride's mother wants only what is best for her daughter. In addition, Carter adds the unusual character of Jean-Ives, a man who comforts and empathizes with the female protagonist, but does not save her.

Flesh/Animal vs. Spirit/Divine

The husband's moral corruption is indicated by imagery that compares him to an animal. He is described as heavy, ''fleshy,'' his features ''leonine,'' and his hair a ''mane.'' When ''the beast waver[s] in his stroke'' and is shot in the end, he becomes another version of the tiger slain by the mother in her girlhood. The Marquis is also figured as the god-head of his enclosed world because he determines the destiny of its inhabitants. Upon her discovery by the Marquis, the narrator says: ''I had played a game in which every move was governed by a destiny as oppressive and omnipotent as himself, since that destiny was himself.'' The mother's intervention, ''like a miracle,'' delivers a deadly blow to this ''man as god,'' as well as to the figure of ''man as beast.''

Style

Point of View

One of the most striking changes Carter makes to her version of Bluebeard is the point of view. Whereas the traditional fairy tale has an omniscient, detached narrator, Carter's first-person narrator lends more psychological suspense to the story, since readers learn of her fear through her own thoughts, something that would not be possible with an impartial, third-person narrator. Though the events in ''The Bloody Chamber'' are similar to those in Bluebeard, that they are witnessed through the eyes of the female narrator gives the story a more feminist sensibility. Furthermore, the story is told in the past tense, hinting that the narrator has survived her ordeal. The tension, then, stems from wondering how she survives, rather than if she will or not.

Setting

The traditional legend of Bluebeard is set, as are most fairy tales, in the indistinct era of ''long, long ago.'' In contrast, ''The Bloody Chamber'' is set in a modern era, though the story retains much of a traditional fairy tale setting. Trains, telephones, guns, and automobiles figure prominently in the story. Though no specific year is given, it can be assumed that the story takes place sometime in the twentieth century in France. Still, the familiar trappings of fairy tales are present: an evil Marquis, an opulent castle with a moat, a dungeon-like torture chamber, and a blind piano-tuner who speaks of ''strange tales up and down the coast.'' This mix of contemporary life with the timeless conventions of fairy tales provides a unique setting. Carter updates a classic story, illustrating how traditional themes are still relevant and pervasive to modern life and literature.

Symbolism

Carter embellishes the fairy-tale plot with symbols. One of the most obvious symbols is the white lilies that surround the marriage bed. In Christian iconography, the white lily represents virgin purity and innocence. But they remind the young bride of a funeral, especially when they begin decay. Another symbol is the mark left on the narrator's forehead by the bloody key, a scar the narrator equates with ''the caste mark of a Brahmin woman. Or the mark of Cain.'' ''The mark of Cain'' is a Biblical reference to the brandishment of the first murderer as an outcast. The mark is also thematically linked to the stain on the sheets when she loses her virginity; the narrator considers both unremovable emblems of shame.

Folklore

Based on the legend of Bluebeard, ''The Bloody Chamber'' not only retells the tale, it also comments on it. By basing her story on such a well-known fairy tale, Carter acknowledges the power of such tales and provides modern touches that underscore the themes she is most concerned with. The original story is mostly a frightening tale about a murderous man. Though ''The Bloody Chamber'' still contains the same acts of violence, Carter tells her version from the bride's perspective, adding a female viewpoint. And though the damsel is still saved in the end, she is rescued by her mother, not her brothers. This plot twist underscores Carter's intention to highlight the strong bonds between mothers and daughters, a bond that rarely exists in traditional fairy tales, in which most saviors are male.

Gothicism

Gothicism is a literary genre characterized by elements of horror, supernatural occurrences, gloom, and violence. An isolated castle, a feeling of terror created by a mysterious and vengeful husband, and the discovery of the narrator's three butchered predecessors are all emblematic of a gothic story. Much of Carter's writing is cast in this vein, in which the protagonist's dread is an essential element. The author's detailed, flowery descriptions of the castle and its mysterious rooms and the psychological terror instilled in the young bride, an innocent trapped in a situation she cannot control, also contribute to the gothic mode of the story.

Historical Context

Feminism in Literature

The year 1979 marked the end of a decade known as the feminist movement's ''second wave.'' The phrase, coined by the Australian writer Germaine Greer in her book *The Female Eunuch,* referred to the resurgence of feminist activity in the decades after the suffragist movement had succeeded in most of the Western world. The 1970s brought about big changes with regard to women's political, economic, and social power.

Several works published in the early 1970s have become landmarks in the history of feminist thought. Greer's work discussed the "eunuch-like" condition of the socially constructed "ideal woman," a being without sex drives whose "sexual organs are shrouded in mystery." Kate Millet's *Sexual Politics* examined the male domination promulgated in most literature written by men. Meanwhile in France, Luce Irigaray was struggling with the inability of women to achieve their own voice in a language that reflected gendered power structures. These works asked why, with the proper legislation in place, women still held few positions of command in the world and controlled little of the world's resources.

Along with these works of nonfiction came similarly minded works of fiction. Though first published in 1963, Sylvia Plath's *The Bell Jar,* an account of a young woman's battle with mental illness, which resulted in part from the lack of support for her creative talents, became popular as women sought more integration in their lives between their roles as students, employees, mothers, and wives. Other writers who gained popularity during the 1970s for their probings of the female psyche were Marge Piercy, Margaret Atwood, Doris Lessing, and Erica Jong.

The changes in these social roles were driven in part by the availability of the birth control pill, which was legalized in the United States in the 1970s. In 1973, the Supreme Court ruling in Roe vs. Wade meant that women had more choices when faced with an unwanted pregnancy. Women now had more control than ever over when and if to have children. This freedom affected many aspects of women's lives, from their career opportunities, to their marital status, to their economic power. From the first edition of *Our Bodies, Ourselves* in 1973, a volume devoted to empowering women by explaining how to take control of their own health, rather than entrusting their well-being to the male-dominated medical profession, to Shere Hite's 1976 report on female sexuality, the discussion of the female body became an integral part of the women's movement, and issues were brought to the forefront that had once been shrouded in mystery, tradition, and repression. The politics between men and women, which had previously been contained within the home, were now matters of public debate.

Critical Overview

Carter's short story collection *The Bloody Chamber* was published in 1979, at the height of the women's movement, an era in which women sought greater political and social equity than they had been afforded in previous decades. In the realm of literature, many authors were concerned with creating strong female characters in their work, and Carter was on the forefront of this trend. Her adaptations of traditional fairy tales sought to subvert the patriarchal leanings of the stories by inserting strong women in the roles of Little Red Riding Hood and Sleeping Beauty, among others. Ellen Cronan Rose celebrates the "strong bond between mother and daughter " depicted in "The Bloody Chamber" as an example of what can happen when "a female fiction writer" takes on "male cultural myths." Indeed, the image of the mother, who knows by instinct that her daughter is in danger, riding in on horseback to slay the serial killer, seems unequivocally feminist. However, some reviewers felt that her characterizations of the brutal, murderous husband and the vulnerable, fragile heroine who *almost* becomes a passive victim, seem to follow the traditional paradigm of victim and victimizer. Some feminists questioned whether Carter's revision of the ending is enough to overcome this paradigm.

Critics such as Avis Lewallan, agreeing with Patricia Duncker, Robert Clark, and others, take issue with Carter's feminism, stating that this revision is *not* enough. The opposition of passive and aggressive found in sadomasochism still dominates Carter's fictional and polemical world, even if some of her female characters take on the role of aggressor. To these critics, the revisionist ending seems backhanded in view of Carter's polemic. Carter's prose is simply too seductive, as is the Marquis's castle, and too aligned with pornography, as is the narrator's position as sexually-awakened potential victim, for the stories to be considered stalwartly feminist. Throughout the late 1980s, Carter's detractors seemed to be winning the debate.

The 1990s have seen a re-emergence of Carter's defenders, or, at the very least, a recognition that the debate demonstrates the complexities of Carter's work. Hers is not an easy feminism, as Elaine Jordan argues, nor a feminism that can be generalized or quickly summarized. Mary Kaiser recognizes this complexity when she argues that Carter's *The Bloody Chamber* is anti-universalist, in that each story presents a different context for male-female relations. For example, the context of the title story is "fin-de-siecle" French decadence, a context that necessarily raises sadomasochistic specters. Novelist Margaret Atwood, in her analysis of the tiger and lamb imagery in Carter's fiction, reads *The Bloody Chamber* as "'writing against' de Sade . . . as an exploration of the possibilities for the kind of synthesis de Sade himself could never find." One can see how this kind of criticism uses the short story as something other than evidence in a debate; it looks to it as a work of art commenting upon a wider cultural moment.

Criticism

Rebecca Laroche

Laroche has taught literature and writing at Bates College, Albertus Magnus College, and Yale University. In the following essay, she discusses how Carter's story interweaves elements of three literary genres.

In "The Bloody Chamber," Angela Carter incorporates the elements of three genres, or categories, of literature in her writing, creating a distinct style that could be called "Carterian." This long story subtly links the fairy tale, Gothic literature, and pornographic literature. The thread that connects these three kinds of writing is the theme of curiosity, the human impulse that motivates an individual to uncover what is hidden or unknown.

Fairy tales not only entertain the children to whom they are told, but they also teach them the behavior a particular culture considers proper. The teller of the tales, usually a maternal figure, presents these stories to children as examples of how to act or how not to act. Many such stories end with morals, adages to live by, such as "Slow and steady wins the race," "Don't talk to strangers," or "Curiosity killed the cat." The last of these could feasibly be the moral attached to the fairy tale "Bluebeard," recorded by the seventeenth-century Frenchman Charles Perrault and adapted by Angela Carter in "The Bloody Chamber." Perrault ends his story with the rhyme: "Curiosity has its lure / But all the same / It's a paltry kind of pleasure / And a risky game. / The thrill of peeping is soon over / And then the cost is to discover." Certainly, this adage

seems inadequate for Carter's version of the story of a serial killer. Furthermore, it does not ring entirely true. The reader has no evidence that the other wives had died because of their curiosity, or that if the current wife had not opened the forbidden door, she and her wealthy husband would have lived happily ever after. What, then, is this story's moral?

In her compilations of fairy tales from around the world, Carter has contributed to our understanding of fairy tales and their function. Like many compilers before her, she recognized the existence of an oral tradition that predates the Brothers Grimm in Germany and Charles Perrault in France. Carter revived the term "old wives' tales" in order to emphasize that many of these storytellers were women (even though those who achieved literary fame were men). This fact tells us something about the function of the fairy tales: the stories are meant, among other things, to tell boys and girls about their respective places in the world. With this function in mind, Perrault's admonition against curiosity in the Bluebeard legend can be seen as warning against the specific curiosity young women may have about the world of men. The gender of the protagonist is no accident.

Carter places her own story in line with these "old wives' tales." After he has heard of the horrors seen by the narrator, the blind piano-tuner, Jean-Ives, tells her of "all manner of strange tales" told "up and down the coast" about a Marquis who lived before the current one and hunted young girls "as though they were foxes." "Oh madame," he cries, "I thought these were old wives' tales." And later, the narrator is afraid that if she were to tell her story to the inhabitants of "this distant coast," "who . . . would believe . . . a shuddering tale of blood, of fear, of the ogre murmuring in the shadows." In calling her husband "an ogre," the narrator signals that her story would not be believed because of its fairy tale nature. In positioning the Marquis as a descendent of the evil characters in an "old wives's tales," Carter creates a literary genealogy for her own work. That is, her Marquis belongs to a latter-day generation of Bluebeard's progeny.

In addition to including references to the oral fairy-tale tradition within her story, Carter embeds another type of fiction within her text, that of the Gothic novel. Gothic novels, which typically include remote castles and damsels in distress, were the popular literature of the nineteenth-century. The narrator goes into the Marquis's library looking

What Do I Read Next?

- Carter's collection of folklore from different cultures, *Old Wives' Fairy Tale Book* (1990), examines the common themes of the genre and includes an introduction by the author.

- *The Uses of Enchantment: The Meaning and Importance of Fairy Tales* (1976) by Austrian-born psychologist Bruno Bettelheim is a classic nonfiction account of the sociological and psychological need for fairy tales and their effect on children and culture in general.

- Germaine Greer, a contemporary of Carter, demystifies female sexuality in *The Female Eunuch* (1971) and demonstrates how the socially constructed "ideal woman," a person without a discernible sexuality, needs to be undone for the benefit of women.

- Published in 1697, Charles Perrault's *Fairy Tales* is a collection of stories from many cultures, including "Little Red Riding Hood," "Sleeping Beauty," and "Puss in Boots." The versions penned by this French author are the ones with which most readers are familiar.

- Poet Anne Sexton published *Transformations* in 1971, a volume of poems that rewrites the tales of the Brothers Grimm.

---

for an escape, wanting "to curl up on the rug before the blazing fire, lose myself in a cheap novel, munch on sticky liqueur chocolates." But instead of reading such a novel, she finds herself living a version of it.

Consider for a moment the stylistic and structural similarities between Carter's story, which is set in turn-of-the-century France, and a Gothic nineteenth-century novel, Charlotte Bronte's *Jane Eyre*. This comparison will help illustrate the general characteristics of the Gothic tale and how they compare to "The Bloody Chamber." Bronte's protagonist, like Carter's, is an inexperienced, poor young virgin who finds herself alone in a remote estate house with a dark, brooding, and rich owner, Mr. Rochester. As in Carter's story, Mr. Rochester's huge house contains a room which the heroine is forbidden to enter, and which contains a secret of the owner's past. But in *Jane Eyre* the discovery is not half so grisly as that in *The Bloody Chamber*: the room houses Mr. Rochester's insane Caribbean wife. The elements of an isolated, cold house; an agitated owner; an innocent visitor; and a horrible mystery all constitute the main attributes of the Gothic novel, a form of literature that flourished in the eighteenth and nineteenth centuries. That the secret in *Jane Eyre* is not half so grisly perhaps proves that Bronte's novel is not half so Gothic as Carter's story. Another difference is that, although Jane Eyre is curious, she obeys Mr. Rochester's edict and never goes into the room forbidden to her. A true Gothic heroine, like Carter's, goes where she should not.

In the afterword to her first volume of short stories, *Fireworks,* Carter positions her tales in the tradition of Edgar Allan Poe and E. T. A. Hoffmann, rather than with Bronte and her eighteenth-century predecessor, Ann Radcliffe, who is best known for *The Mysteries of Udolpho*. In that same afterword, Carter writes that the Gothic tale's "great themes are incest and cannibalism." *Jane Eyre* addresses neither of these themes; Poe's "The Fall of the House of Usher" embraces one, that of incest; Carter's story arguably has a hint of both— in the Marquis' fondness for pornography and brutality.

More than one commentator has noted, like Mario Praz, that "Radcliffe and Sade belong to the same mental climate, the climate which produced so many incarnations of the theme of the persecuted maiden." Sade is the eighteenth-century French pornographer whose name is the root of our word "sadistic" and whose fictions established the whips-and-chains practices of "sadomasochism." Indeed, Carter herself writes that ''the tale has relations with the subliterary forms of pornography.'' The Marquis de Sade, like Bluebeard and Mr. Rochester, is a forefather of Carter's Marquis.

It is this connection between folklore, Gothic, and pornography that allows Carter, as Patricia Duncker writes, to make ''the mystery sexually explicit.'' Duncker refers directly to the mystery at the center of the fairy tale, but it can be applied to the Gothic novel, for example, Radcliffe's *Udolpho,* as well. Both *Bluebeard* and *Jane Eyre* imply the sexual awakening of the heroines in the presence of their dark, brooding lovers. Behind locked doors, the former wives bear the marks of their violated virginity.

In making the sexuality of the tale's mystery explicit, Carter makes the curiosity explicit as well. When her narrator looks for a cheap novel in the library, she instead finds the Marquis's pornography collection. Among these volumes, she finds a detailed picture of a sadomasochistic scene entitled ''Reproof of Curiosity.'' The Marquis's tortures and murders can be read as more extreme versions of these reproofs. Other titles in this collection, ''The Key of Mysteries'' and ''The Secret of Pandora's Box,'' link the mysteries of the castle with the secrets of female sexuality. The presence of these volumes in his library add sexual innuendo to the narrator's observation that the Marquis hands her the keyring ''as if he were giving a child a great, mysterious treat.'' And when he comes back to kill her, she says that ''I must pay the price of my new knowledge. The secret of Pandora's box; but he had given me the box.'' As the Marquis awakens in her a ''dark newborn curiosity,'' the desire to know more about her sexuality, he hands her the keys to his house and to the bloody chamber. The secret that the heroine discovers is the sadomasochistic paradigm, her husband's position as torturer and hers as victim, which lies behind her newly awakened sexuality.

Examining the elements of folklore, Gothicism, and pornography in Carter's ''The Bloody Chamber'' helps give the heroine's predicament a historical perspective. The narrator bears the weight of centuries of literary history when she describes her position, ''I had played the game in which every move was governed by a destiny as oppressive and omnipotent as himself, since that destiny was himself; and I had lost.'' The narrator feels that her ''destiny'' is written in the stories told before she writes her own. But Carter's story implies that

> The reader has no evidence that the other wives had died because of their curiosity, or that if the current wife had not opened the forbidden door, she and her wealthy husband would have lived happily ever after."

writing within predetermined genres does not mean submitting to a destiny that is already written. Perhaps Carter's answer appears to be too simple when she revises the end of the fairy tale so that the mother instead of the brothers rescue the narrator; when she creates a Gothic heroine who has an involved and rich relationship with a mother; and when she has her Sadeian heroine survive and open a music school. But Carter's fiction is predetermined. It critiques and revises the thematic similarities of three types of writing with one ingenious narrative: a truly ''Carterian'' feat.

Source: Rebecca Laroche, ''Overview of 'The Bloody Chamber','' in *Short Stories for Students,* Gale, 1998.

Mary Kaiser

Kaiser teaches English at Jefferson State Community College in Birmingham, Alabama. In the following excerpt, she examines Carter's use of intertextuality and the sexual symbolism in ''The Bloody Chamber.''

As Carter suggests in her introduction to *The Old Wives' Fairy Tale Book,* intertextuality was embedded into the history of the fairy tale when Charles Perrault, the Grimm Brothers, and other compilers of the eighteenth and nineteenth centuries transposed oral folk tales into fairy tales. This transfer involved what [Julia] Kristeva refers to as ''a new articulation of the thetic,'' as the politics, economics, fashions, and prejudices of a sophisticated culture replaced the values of rural culture that form the context of oral folklore [*Revolution in Poetic*

Language, 1990]. Part of this transfer, Carter argues, was the transposing of an essentially feminine form, the ''old wives' tale,'' onto a masculine one, the published text. Referring to the tradition of ''Mother Goose,'' Carter asserts that oral folktales record the ''strategies, plots, and hard work'' with which women have coped with the conditions of their lives but that in their oral form these narratives are considered ''Old wives' tales—that is, worthless stories, untruths, trivial gossip, a derisive label that allots the art of storytelling to women at the exact same time as it takes all value from it'' [*The Old Wives' Fairy Tale Book,* 1990]. In her 1979 collection of retold fairy tales, *The Bloody Chamber,* Carter shows an acute awareness of the changes that result from an oral to written transposition and calls attention to them by heightening the intertexuality of her narratives, making them into allegories that explore how sexual behavior and gender roles are not universal, but are, like other forms of social interaction, culturally determined. This theme is closely related to that of Carter's 1978 study of the writings of the Marquis de Sade, *The Sadeian Woman,* where she attacks what she calls the false universalizing of sexuality, which, tending to enforce the archetype of male aggression and female passivity, merely confuses ''the main issue, that relationships between the sexes are determined by history and by the historical fact of the economic dependence of women upon men.''

I wish to argue that Carter's use of intertextuality in *The Bloody Chamber* moves the tales from the mythic timelessness of the fairy tale to specific cultural moments, each of which presents a different problem in gender relations and sexuality. Although she recounts the plots of the same fairy tales—''Beauty and the Beast'' twice, ''Little Red Riding Hood'' three times—Carter changes the cultural context from tale to tale, and, as a result, each retelling generates a different narrative. The outcomes for her protagonists can be tragic or triumphant, the tone can be serious or farcical, depending on the historic and cultural circumstances. To demonstrate the range of the collection, I will consider two tales with the same scenario, a young, powerless woman under the domination of an older, powerful male figure who is not only a threat to her virginity but a threat to her life. ''The Bloody Chamber,'' a retelling of ''Bluebeard,'' is set in the world of decadent turn-of-the-century French culture, among the operas of Wagner and the fashions of Paul Poiret. ''The Snow Child'' is set in medieval Europe, deep in a forest, and is based

much more closely on its original, a version of ''Snow White.'' ''The Bloody Chamber'' is a tale of feminine courage triumphant, while ''The Snow Child,'' as its chilling title suggests, is a stark, uncompromising tale of sexuality as a function of overwhelming male power.

The lengthiest and perhaps the paradigmatic story of the collection, ''The Bloody Chamber'' explores the sexual symbolism of the secret room, making explicit the Freudian interpretation given by Bruno Bettelheim in *The Uses of Enchantment* that the ''bloody chamber'' is the womb. In addition to making the tale's latent sexual symbolism manifest, Carter also addresses in this story what she calls in *The Sadeian Woman* the ''mystification'' associated with the womb. The ''bankrupt enchantments of the womb'' led, she writes, to the segregation and punishment of women; in ''The Bloody Chamber,'' Bluebeard, the connoisseur of women, makes his womblike secret chamber into a museum of tortured and murdered women.

Following the tradition recorded by Iona and Peter Opie [in *The Classical Fairy Tales,* 1974], that the original of Bluebeard was a notorious Breton nobleman, Carter places her version of the tale in a castle on the coast of Brittany but makes its owner a wealthy aesthete who is as much at home at a performance of *Tristan* at the Paris Opera as he is within his ancestral hall. If the secret room containing the corpses of his dead wives is likened to a womb, Bluebeard's castle is a metaphor for his sexuality. A phallic tower, it floats upon the ''amniotic salinity of the ocean,'' reminding Bluebeard's bride of an ''anchored, castellated ocean liner,'' and becomes the stage for a symbolist version of the battle of the sexes. The fin de siècle time period is critical to Carter's interpretation of ''Bluebeard,'' because she sees the bride's fate as possible only at the moment in history when images of female victimization and of female aggression converged.

Combining, like J. K. Huysmans, a taste for Catholic ritual and for sensual experimentation, Carter's Bluebeard displays an edition of Huysmans's *La-bas* ''bound like a missal'' among an extensive collection of eighteenth- and nineteenth-century pornography. Like Huysmans also, Bluebeard has discovered a group of symbolist painters whose imagery accords with his temperament. Among these images of young, attenuated, passive women, Carter includes some imaginary symbolist paintings, such as Moreau's "famous *Sacrificial Victim* with the imprint of the lacelike chains on her pellucid skin" and "Two or three late Gauguins, his special favourite the one of the tranced brown girl in the deserted house." A willowy young music student, living in poverty with her widowed mother, the bride becomes a vehicle for Bluebeard's attempt to realize the decadent image of the dependent, virginal child-woman, ripe for tragedy.

Avis Lewallen has commented that she finds "The Bloody Chamber" the most disturbing of the tales in the collection, because of its lush, seductive descriptions of sexual exploitation and victimization. Carter, however, uses the language of the story not to lull the reader into ignoring the dangers posed by Bluebeard but instead to heighten the reader's awareness of the threat posed by the sadomasochistic underpinnings of much of decadent culture, which created a dangerously passive and readily victimized feminine ideal. In *The Sadeian Woman,* describing the ideal presented by Sade's victimized Justine, she writes, "She is obscene to the extent to which she is beautiful. Her beauty, her submissiveness and false expectations that these qualities will do her some good are what make her obscene." The decadent sign system that surrounds this version of Bluebeard brings the sadomasochistic subtext of the original to the foreground by giving its murderous episodes the lush refinement of Beardsley's illustrations of *Salome.*

Bluebeard, like his historical precursor the Marquis de Sade, is a producer of theatrical effects. His rooms are deliberately planned as stages for symbolic action, the bloody chamber a kind of wax museum of his previous wives, preserved in their last moments of agony, the mirrored bedroom with its "grand, hereditary, matrimonial bed" a set for "a formal disrobing of the bride." Clothing, in this theatrical context, becomes costume, in which, as in theater and religious ritual, the individual is subsumed by a role. The bride's dress (designed by Poiret, the inventor of the "hobble" skirt) and her wedding gift, "A choker of rubies, two inches wide, like an extraordinarily precious slit throat," not only situate her in fin de siècle France but also reflect the image of innocence, vulnerability, and victimization that Bluebeard desires. Nakedness becomes a kind of costume as well, in the overdetermined imagery of Bluebeard's bedroom. Watching herself being disrobed by him, the bride perceives herself as a pornographic object: "He in his London tailoring; she, bare as a lamb chop. Most

> The fin de siecle time period is critical to Carter's interpretation of 'Bluebeard,' because she sees the bride's fate as possible only at the moment in history when images of female victimization and of female aggression converged."

pornographic of all confrontations." In this scene the bride has been reduced to an unaccommodated body, while Bluebeard retains all the accoutrements of power, wealth, and taste.

However, Bluebeard has conveniently excised from his collection of fin de siècle imagery the era's complement to the woman-as-victim, the avatar of the New Woman, "She-who-must-be-obeyed." Sandra Gilbert and Susan Gubar point out that these complementary images appeared almost simultaneously in the late 1880s, when the harrowing mutilations and murders of women by Jack the Ripper took place at the same time as Rider Haggard's enormously popular novel *She* introduced a heroine who, by combining virtue with authority, represented "an entirely New Woman." Gilbert and Gubar suggest that the emergence of female aggression in the suffrage movement generated a backlash of images of suffering, victimized women. Carter, in *The Sadeian Woman,* shares this interpretation when she argues that the real threat posed by the emancipation of women was the removal of "the fraudulent magic from the idea of women." If Bluebeard's murders mirror those of Jack the Ripper, who was also obsessed with the womb, then Bluebeard's murders are avenged by a figure who also seems to have stepped out of the zeitgeist of the 1880s. The bride's mother rides onto the scene just as Bluebeard is preparing to dispatch his latest wife and kills him with a single shot from her dead husband's service revolver. Like Haggard's fearsome heroine, she is woman-as-avenger on a grand scale. At the tale's opening the bride calls her mother "eagle-featured, indomitable," recalling that she "had outfaced a junkful of Chinese pirates, nursed a village through a visitation of the plague, shot a man-eating tiger with her own hand and all before she was as old as I.'' Appropriately, she reappears at the conclusion as a complement to her daughter's masochistic passivity, just at the point when the bride herself has begun to act in her own behalf and emancipate herself from Bluebeard's pornographic scenario.

Patricia Duncker reads the ending of ''The Bloody Chamber'' as carrying ''an uncompromisingly feminist message'' [*Literature and History,* Vol. 10, 1984], while all of the other tales in the collection, she feels, merely recapitulate patriarchal patterns of behavior. What Duncker perceives as an inconsistent application of feminist principles is, I believe, merely a reflection of Carter's project in this collection, to portray sexuality as a culturally relative phenomenon. The feminism, as well as the masochism of ''The Bloody Chamber,'' is a feature of its turn-of-the-century setting. . . .

In *The Sadeian Woman* Carter writes, ''the notion of a universality of female experience is a clever confidence trick,'' a statement that neatly sums up her deuniversalizing of fairy tale plots in *The Bloody Chamber.* Situating her tales within carefully defined cultural moments, Carter employs a wide-ranging intertextuality to link each tale to the zeitgeist of its moment and to call attention to the literary fairy tale as a product, not of a collective unconscious but of specific cultural, political, and economic positions. In addition, focusing on the ''strategies, plots, and hard work'' of women allows Carter to reappropriate the ''old wives' tale'' as feminine narrative. In *The Bloody Chamber,* then, Carter deconstructs the underlying assumptions of the ''official'' fairy tale: that fairy tales are universal, timeless myths, that fairy tales are meant exclusively for an audience of children, and that fairy tales present an idealized, fantastic world unrelated to the contingencies of real life. Instead, Carter pushes Bruno Bettelheim's reading of fairy tales as Freudian fables even further and presents them as studies in the history of imagining sexuality and gender.

Source: Mary Kaiser, ''Fairy Tale as Sexual Allegory: Intertextuality in Angela Carter's 'The Bloody Chamber','' in *The Review of Contemporary Fiction,* Vol. 14, no. 3, Fall, 1994, pp. 30–6.

Avis Lewallen

In the following excerpt, Lewallen offers her interpretation of Carter's ''The Bloody Chamber,'' *particularly in regard to the themes of gender roles and sexuality. Lewallen also examines Carter's use of symbolism and irony.*

The Bloody Chamber is mostly a collection of fairy tales rewritten to incorporate props of the Gothic and elements of a style designated 'magic realism', in which a realistic consciousness operates within a surrealistic context. The characters are at once both abstractions and 'real'. The heroine in 'The Tiger's Bride', for example, bemused by surreal events, comments, 'what democracy of magic held this palace and fir forest in common? Or, should I be prepared to accept it as proof of the axiom my father had drummed into me: that, if you have enough money, anything is possible?' Symbolism is prevalent: white roses for sexual purity; lilies for sex and death; lions, tigers and wolves for male sexual aggression. Throughout the collection, specific attention is often drawn to the meaning of fairy tales themselves, and this has implications for the reading of Carter's stories.

In a perceptive but highly critical essay Patricia Duncker argues that the form of the fairy tale, along with all its ideological ramifications, proves intractable to attempted revision:

> Carter is rewriting the tales within the strait-jacket of their original structures. The characters she re-creates must, to some extent, continue to exist as abstractions. Identity continues to be defined by role, so that shifting the perspective from the impersonal voice to the inner confessional narrative, as she does in several of the tales, merely explains, amplifies and reproduces rather than alters the original, deeply, rigidly sexist psychology of the erotic. [*Literature and History,* Spring 1984]

While I agree with Duncker's overall analysis, I think she significantly overlooks the use of irony, particularly the effect produced by the 'inner confessional narrative', which both acknowledges patriarchal structure and provides a form of critique against it. The ultimate position taken up may be politically untenable, but at the same time the ironic voice does not wholeheartedly endorse the patriarchal view. . . . The question of choice, or lack of it, is echoed throughout the tales. . . . As Patricia Duncker puts it, 'we are watching . . . the ritual disrobing of the willing victim of pornography'.

This comment is particularly applicable to the tale 'The Bloody Chamber', which begins,

> I remember how, that night, I lay awake in the wagon—lit in a tender, delicious ecstasy of excite-

ment, my burning cheek pressed against the impeccable linen of the pillow and the pounding of my heart mimicking that of the great pistons ceaselessly thrusting the train that bore me through the night, away from Paris, away from girlhood, away from the white enclosed quietude of my mother's apartment, into the unguessable country of marriage.

The rhythm and language of this long sentence directly associates the movement of the train with the sexual anticipation of the adolescent heroine, with an imagination perhaps bred on Gothic horror stories. It is a tale full of Gothic motifs, and it plays with desire and danger, placing the reader, through the first-person narrative, in the heroine-victim position. This is the tale of one of Bluebeard's wives, and the heroine, seduced by wealth, power and mystery, skirts death in the quest for sexual knowledge. The narrative strategy, therefore, puts us the readers imaginatively within this ambivalent willing-victim position, and the tale attempts to illustrate not only the dangers of seduction, but also the workings of pleasure and danger seemingly implicit in sexuality for women. Again the narrative draws attention to the connection between material wealth and marriage. The heroine's mother has 'beggared herself for love' and thus tries to ensure her daughter's economic security by getting her a musical education. The heroine's corruption is threefold: material, as she is seduced by wealth; sexual, as she discovers her own sexual appetite; and moral, in the sense that 'like Eve' she disobeys her master-husband's command.

But this is a victim who is not only willing but also recognises that she has been bought:

> This ring, the bloody bandage of rubies, the wardrobe of clothes from Poiret and Worth, his scent of Russian leather—all had conspired to seduce me so utterly that I could not say I felt one single twinge of regret for the world of tartines and maman that now receded from me as if drawn away on string, like a child's toy. . . .

And, when she comes to pay the price, 'I guessed it might be so—that we should have a formal disrobing of the bride, a ritual from the brothels . . . my purchaser unwrapped his bargain'. Her slow recognition of the real essence of the bargain she has struck is ironically underlined by the associations with death: 'A choker of rubies, two inches wide, like an extraordinarily precious slit throat'; 'funereal lilies'; and a husband with eyes 'dark and motionless as those eyes the ancient Egyptians painted upon their sarcophagi'.

Her own sexual potential is another form of corruption. Again this is conveyed through contra-

> **"This is the tale of one of Bluebeard's wives, and the heroine, seduced by wealth, power and mystery, skirts death in the quest for sexual knowledge."**

dictory impulses, and there is a sensual, physical detail in the writing:

> The perfume of the lilies weighed on my senses; when I thought that, henceforth, I would always share these sheets with a man whose skin, as theirs did, contained that toad-like, clammy hint of moisture, I felt a vague desolation that within me, now my female wound had healed, there had awoken a certain queasy craving like the cravings of pregnant women for the taste of coal or chalk or tainted food, for the renewal of his caresses. . . . I lay in bed alone. And I longed for him. And he disgusted me.

The intermingling of disgust and desire is not so much fear of the husband as for the sexuality in herself:

> I seemed reborn in his unreflective eyes, reborn in unfamiliar shapes. I hardly recognised myself from his descriptions of me and yet, and yet—might there not be a grain of beastly truth in them? And, in the red firelight, I blushed again, unnoticed, to think he might have chosen me because, in my innocence, he sensed a rare talent for corruption.

The 'talent for corruption' is not only a willingness to be bought but also perhaps a willingness to participate in 'the thousand, thousand baroque intersections of flesh upon flesh', amply detailed in a connoisseur's collection of sado-masochistic volumes found in the library.

Of all the tales in the volume I found 'The Bloody Chamber' most troubling in terms of female sexuality, largely because of the very seductive quality of the writing itself. As readers we are asked to place ourselves imaginatively as masochistic victims in a pornographic scenario and to sympathise in some way with the ambivalent feelings this produces. The heroine's own subsequent recognition of total manipulation does not allay my unease at being manipulated by the narrative to sympathise with masochism. The writing playfully equivocates between explanation of the victims position and condemnation of the sadistic perpetrator of atrocities.

The husband puts the heroine to the test. He ostensibly goes away on business leaving her the keys to the castle with strict instructions not to enter his private room, which of course she does. There she discovers not only the mutilated bodies of his three former wives, but also the fate that awaits her. It seems, however, that the moral of the tale—that wives should not disobey their husbands—gets lost on the way, since as this quotation shows she had no choice in the matter anyway:

> The secret of Pandora's box; but he had given the box, himself, knowing I must learn the secret. I had played a game in which every move was governed by a destiny as oppressive and omnipotent as himself, since that destiny was himself; and I had lost. Lost at that charade of innocence and vice in which he had engaged me. Lost, as the victim loses to the executioner.

The husband promptly returns to claim his victim and what saves her is not the presence of the blind piano-tuner—he is merely a comfort—but her mother's prescience. Puzzled at her newly-wed daughter crying during a telephone call, she has intuitively recognised danger and flown to her rescue. Thus the *denouement* gives us female revenge against male tyranny, but the heroine must wear the mark of her 'shame' on her forehead for ever. To be branded as guilty, despite recognition of the manipulation to which she has been subject, seems somewhat unfair. This is the only tale where the mother figure plays an important and positive role. In the others, as in their fairy-tale originals, mothers are either absent, insignificant or bad. . . .

The problem with Carter's attempts to foreground the relationship between fairy tales and reality, a productive exercise, is that the action for the heroines is contained within the same ideological parameters. So the actual constructedness of reality and the ideological premises of fairy tales remain intact. The tiger's bride, like the other heroines, realises the 'truth' of the 'nursery fears' and chooses a non-materialistic, animal sexuality, but she does not have the option of *not* choosing it. Within the framework of the tale her choice appears to be a liberating one, but in reality it is not, despite Carter's Sadean proposition that misogyny can be undermined by women's refusal to be sexual victims and by their adoption of a more sexually aggressive role.

Although there are dangers in comparing theoretical and fictional writing, I feel it is perfectly justifiable to argue that many of the ideas in *The Bloody Chamber* rest on Carter's interpretation of Sade, even if they do not fulfil her own analysis of the mechanisms of the historical process. It is possible to say that some of the tales 'render explicit the nature of social relations' as outlined in Carter's definition of the 'moral pornographer', but explanation is not always enough. Indeed, 'The Bloody Chamber' tale, through its equivocation, borders on the reactionary. We do have to address questions of binary thinking as it affects gender and sexuality, but Carter's prescribed action for her heroines within stereotypical options is ultimately politically untenable. Her use of irony might blur the boundaries at times but it does not significantly attack deeprooted ways of thinking or feeling.

Source: Avis Lewallen, ''Wayward Girls but Wicked Women? Female Sexuality in Angela Carter's 'The Bloody Chamber','' in *Perspectives in Pornography: Sexuality in Film and Literature,* edited by Gary Day and Clive Bloom, Macmillan Press, 1988, pp. 144–57.

Ellen Cronan Rose

In the following excerpt, Rose comments on the significance of the narrator's mother in ''The Bloody Chamber.''

When we turn to the fairy tales we are most familiar with, preserved and transmitted by Perrault and the Grimm brothers, what we see is that in our culture there are different developmental paradigms for boys and girls. In fairy tales, boys are clever, resourceful, and brave. They leave home to slay giants, outwit ogres, solve riddles, find fortunes. Girls, on the other hand, stay home and sweep hearths, are patient, enduring, self-sacrificing. They are picked on by wicked step-mothers, enchanted by evil fairies. If they go out, they get lost in the woods. They are rescued from their plights by kind woodsmen, good fairies, and handsome princes. They marry and live happily ever after. . . .

What Adrienne Rich calls ''the great unwritten story'' of the ''cathexis between mother and daughter'' [*Of Woman Born,* 1976] can be written many ways. . . . [A] mother is not only her daughter's first love object. She is also her first and therefore most impressive image of adult womanhood. It is this aspect of the mother/daughter relationship that Angela Carter emphasizes in her retelling of ''Bluebeard,'' the first and title story of *The Bloody Chamber.* Here the strong bond between mother and daughter figures as a kind of "maternal telepathy" that sends not her brothers (as in the original) but her mother to the curious bride's rescue. As Bluebeard's sword ascends for the fatal blow, his young bride's mother bursts through the gate like a Valkyrie—or an Amazon—and fires "a single, irreproachable bullet" through his head.

It is significant that this fighting mother appears in the first story of *The Bloody Chamber*. "What do we mean by the nurture of daughters?" Adrienne Rich asks. Since "women growing into a world so hostile to us need a very profound kind of loving in order to learn to love ourselves," she concludes that "the most important thing one woman [a mother] can do for another [her daughter] is to illuminate and expand her sense of actual possibilities." A mother "who is a fighter" gives her daughter a sense of life's possibilities. Following her example, Bluebeard's widow and her "sisters" in the stories that follow are enabled to explore life's possibilities, to develop into adult women by learning to love themselves.

Source: Ellen Cronan Rose, "Through the Looking Glass: When Women Tell Fairy Tales," in *The Voyage In: Fictions of Female Development*, edited by Elizabeth Abel, Marianne Hirsch, Elizabeth Langland, eds., University Press of New England, 1983, pp. 209–27.

Sources

Carter, Angela. *The Sadeian Woman*. New York: Pantheon Books, 1978, 154 p.

Carter, Angela. Introduction to *The Old Wives' Fairy Tale Book*. New York: Pantheon Books, 1990, pp. ix-xxii.

Clark, Robert. "Angela Carter's Desire Machine," in *Women's Studies*, Vol. 14, no. 1, 1987, pp. 147- 59.

Further Reading

Atwood, Margaret. "Running with the Tigers," in *Flesh and the Mirror*, Virago Press, 1994, pp. 117-35.
    Analyzes Carter's "talking back to" the Marquis de Sade in *The Bloody Chamber* by looking at images of the tiger and the lamb, the eater and the eaten.

Duncker, Patricia. "Re-imagining the Fairy Tales: Angela Carter's Bloody Chambers," *Literature and History*, Vol. 10, 1984, pp. 3-14.
    This "anti-pornography " critique of Carter's collection discusses how "The Bloody Chamber" delivers a "perhaps unwitting . . . feminist message."

Jordan, Elaine, "The Dangers of Angela Carter," in *New Feminist Discourses*, edited by Isobel Armstrong, Routledge, 1992, pp. 119-32.
    Defends Carter's feminism and sees "The Bloody Chamber" as a re-working of the stories of the French author Colette.

Rushdie, Salman. Introduction to *Burning Your Boats: The Collected Short Stories of Angela Carter*, Holt, 1995, pp. ix-xiv.
    Carter's career as a short-story writer as communicated through a friend's testimony.

Sage, Lorna. "Angela Carter," in *Dictionary of Literary Biography*, Vol. 14, Gale, 1983, pp. 205-12.
    The critic outlines Carter's life and work.

Warner, Marina. Introduction to *Strange Things Sometimes Still Happen*, by Angela Carter, Faber, 1993, pp. ix-xvi.
    A history and analysis of Carter's interest in fairy tales.

Blues Ain't No Mockin Bird

Toni Cade Bambara

1972

First published in 1971, "Blues Ain't No Mockin Bird" was included the following year in Toni Cade Bambara's highly acclaimed first collection of short stories, *Gorilla, My Love*. Like most of Bambara's stories, "Blues Ain't No Mockin Bird" features strong African-American female characters and reflects social and political issues of particular concern to the contemporary African-American community. In the story, the young female narrator is playing with her neighbors and cousin at her grandmother's house. Two white filmmakers, shooting a film "about food stamps" for the county, lurk near their yard. The narrator's grandmother asks them to leave: not heeding her request, they simply move farther away. When Granddaddy Cain returns from hunting a chicken hawk, he takes the camera from the men and smashes it. Cathy, the distant cousin of the narrator, displays a precocious ability to interpret other people's actions and words as well as an interest in storytelling and writing. Her intelligence and ambition echo Bambara's own accomplishments as well as the larger African-American storytelling tradition.

Author Biography

Toni Cade Bambara, writer, filmmaker, and political activist, says she has known "the power of the word'' since she was a child on the streets of Harlem. Born Miltona Mirkin Cade in 1939 in New York City, she adopted the African name ''Bambara'' in 1970. Upon her death in 1995, the *New York Times* called her a ''major contributor to the emerging of black women's literature, along with the writers Toni Morrison and Alice Walker.'' She grew up in Harlem, Queens, and Jersey City. In 1959, at the age of twenty, she received her B.A. in Theatre Arts and English from Queens College and won the John Golden award for short fiction. While enrolled as a graduate student of American fiction at the City College of New York, she worked in both civic and local neighborhood programs in education and drama and studied theater in Europe. After receiving her Masters degree, Bambara taught at City College from 1965 to 1969. Immersed in the social and political activism of the 1960s and early 1970s, Bambara sometimes saw her writing of fiction as ''rather frivolous,'' yet this period of her life produced some of her most popular works.

Bambara participated in the Black Arts Movement of the 1960s and 1970s and was active in the civil rights, Black Power, anti-war, and feminist movements that characterized this period. Along with other members of the black intelligentsia, Bambara sought to challenge traditional representations of blacks, recuperate significant African-American events and personages of the past, and explore black vernacular English. Bambara's writings also explore themes of women's lives and social and political activism.

In 1970 Bambara (writing as Toni Cade) was one of the first authors to bring together issues of feminism and race with her *The Black Woman*. In the anthology *Tales and Short Stories for Black Folk* (1971), Bambara collected stories by other published authors as well as fiction written by herself and her students. In 1972, Bambara's short stories were collected in *Gorilla, My Love*. Celebrated for its focus on the voice and experience of young black women and its compassionate view of African-American communities, this collection has remained her most widely read work.

Before publishing her second collection of stories, *The Sea Birds Are Still Alive* (1977), Bambara travelled to both Cuba and Vietnam, where she saw the effectiveness of women's organizations and ''the power of the word'' in these countries as a legitimate tool for social change. During this time,

Bambara moved with her daughter to Atlanta, Georgia, where she took the post of writer-in-residence at Spelman College from 1974 to 1977 and helped found a number of black writers' and cultural associations. In 1980, Bambara published *The Salt Eaters*, which is set in Georgia and focuses on the mental and emotional crisis of a community organizer, Velma Jackson.

In the 1980s and 1990s Bambara concentrated on film, another medium for ''the power of the voice,'' working as scriptwriter, filmmaker, critic, and teacher. She collaborated on several television documentaries, such as the award-winning *The Bombing of Osage Avenue* (1986), a documentary about the bombing of a black separatist's organization's headquarters in Philadelphia. A selection of her writings, *Deep Sightings and Rescue Missions,* was published posthumously in 1996.

Plot Summary

Children are playing in a front yard. The twin boys from next door, Tyrone and Terry, are on the tire swing, while the narrator and her cousin, Cathy, jump and dance on a frozen puddle. The narrator's grandmother is on the back porch, ladling rum over the Christmas cakes she has baked. Near the house, in a meadow, are two men who have been there all morning shooting film with their movie camera; they claim they are from the county and are making a film that has to do with food stamps. Granny has asked them to get off the property and has protested their filming, but although they have moved father away they have continued to film.

Granddaddy Cain returns home from the woods where he has shot a chicken hawk. The two filmmakers film his approach. Granny asks him to get the men out of her flower bed.

Granddaddy Cain holds out his hand for the camera. Without arguing, the men give it to him. They explain they are filming for the county. One of the man asks for the camera back, using the word ''please.'' Granddaddy smashes the camera. The camera man gathers up the pieces. Granddaddy tells the men that he and Granny own this place and they are standing in her flower bed. The men back away.

Toni Cade Bambara

Characters

Camera

"Camera" is how the narrator refers to the cameraman who is filming for a county project on food stamps. The camera on his shoulder is so much a part of him that when he hands it to Granddaddy Cain he keeps his shoulder "high like the camera was still there or needed to be." When Granddaddy deliberately damages the camera, Camera gathers up the pieces and holds them "like he's protectin a kitten from the cold."

Cameraman

See Camera

Cain

Granddaddy Cain is Granny's husband, whom she always refers to as "Mister Cain" in keeping with rural Southern protocols. Although he speaks only a few lines in the story, he performs its most dramatic action. When he returns from hunting, carrying a bloody chicken hawk over his shoulder, Granny asks him to get the cameramen to leave. First, however, he dispatches the hawk's attacking mate by throwing a hammer at the swooping bird. Although he displays no anger, greeting the filmmakers calmly with a simple, "Good day, gentlemen," Granddaddy Cain is a forceful presence. Cathy observes that he unnerves people because he is "tall and silent and like a king," and the narrator reports that when he worked as a waiter on trains he was always referred to as "The Waiter," while his colleagues were just "waiters." Granddaddy gestures for the camera, and the cameraman, flustered, gives it to him. Granddaddy's hand is huge and skilled, "a person in itself"—holding the camera in one hand, he tears the top off of it with the other. He offers no explanation beyond the statement, "'You standing in the misses' flower bed . . . This is our own place,'" and the filmmakers leave without further protest.

Cathy

Cathy is the most perceptive of the four children in the story. The narrator is impressed by her ability to understand the workings of the adult world and of the family, such as "how come we move so much," even though she is a relative newcomer. The narrator's third cousin, Cathy became a part of the family during a visit one Thanksgiving. Although no more information about her origin is offered, this suggests that Cathy may have a troubled past or a disrupted family life. Her statement that one day she will write a story situates her as the heir of the storytelling Granny and, perhaps, the predecessor of the storywriting Bambara.

Filmmaker

See Smilin

Granny

The narrator's grandmother, Granny occupies a central position in the family. Her displeasure at the intrusive behavior of the filmmakers is at the root of the story's theme and conflict, and her behavior towards the children, both in the story and in the recollections of the narrator, makes manifest her dominant role as teacher, caretaker, and guardian of the community. Granny also has an explosive temper and a low tolerance for patronizing and demeaning behavior; the family has moved many times "on account of people drivin Granny crazy till she'd get up in the night and start packin." Her anger at the presence of the filmmakers causes her to mumble menacingly in the kitchen, and the narrator fears she might "bust through that screen with somethin in her hand and murder on her mind." Granny is fiercely protective—as protective as the chicken hawk who squawks and attacks her slain mate's killer—yet caring and perceptive as well, teaching the children "steady with no let-up" and cautioning them against in-fighting.

Narrator

The narrator is a young girl through whose curious and engaged eyes the reader absorbs the events of the story. The narrator looks up to her cousin Cathy, whose perceptiveness outstrips the narrator's own. She also is in awe of her grandparents, whose strength and love provide the core of the family. Although the narrator does not fully understand everything that she observes, her youthful point of view engages the reader and allows the reader to gain the insights that she herself only partly grasps.

Smilin

"Smilin," as the narrator calls him, does most of the talking for the two filmmakers, smiling constantly as he explains that they are filming for a county project on food stamps.

Terry

With Tyrone, Terry is one of the twins who lives next door to the narrator. Terry mimics Tyrone, leading Cathy to observe that he "don't never have anything original to say." Terry and Tyrone exhibit none of the perceptiveness of Cathy and the narrator; instead, they wrestle with each other and ask eager questions.

Tyrone

Tyrone is the twin brother of Terry and lives next door to the narrator. Terry mimics his brother, but neither boy displays the insight or perceptiveness of the narrator or her cousin Cathy.

Themes

The central conflict in "Blues Ain't No Mockin Bird" is between the white filmmakers and Granny, who is offended by their presence and wants them to leave.

Race and Racism

The story's conflict is really a conflict over race and representation: Granny believes that the filmmakers have no right, uninvited, to shoot footage of her, her family, and her home; the filmmakers, meanwhile, are attempting to use her life to make a political and social statement, sponsored by the state government, about the black rural poor. The filmmakers, then, want to see the family as "representative" or "typical"; Granny sees herself and her family as individuals. This difference in attitude is demonstrated in the first dialogue between the filmmakers and Granny. When they first approach Granny, they fail to greet her. She interrupts them with an ironic "Good mornin." They respond sheepishly, with a guilty, hangdog expression. They continue, though, referring to Granny as "aunty," a condescending, stereotypical term used for older black women. Later in the story, when Camera repeats the appellation, Granny snaps backs: "'Your mama and I are not related.'" The filmmakers also offend Granny when they praise her place: "'Nice things here,' said the man, buzzin his camera over the yard. The pecan barrels, the sled, me and Cathy, the flowers, the painted stones along the driveway, the trees, the twins, the toolshed." The filmmakers, referring to the narrator and Cathy as "things" and regarding children as little different than driveways or flowers, objectify people. Granny is aware of this: her first line in the story is a request to "'Go tell that man we ain't a bunch of trees.'" She responds to their appraisal of her place by stating, "'I don't know about the thing, the it, and the stuff, . . . Just people here is what I tend to consider.'"

Social Class

The filmmakers from the county are filming about food stamps; specifically, they appear to be making a film arguing against the food stamp program, a federal program instituted to aid the poor. We know this from Smilin's comment to Granny: "'I see you grow your own vegetables. . . . If more folks did that, see, there'd be no need—'" Thus the issue of class is intertwined with the question of race: the filmmakers want to portray Granny as self-sufficient, not needing government assistance, and therefore "nice." While we do not know the views of Granny or the others on this issue, the crass and demeaning behavior of the filmmakers leads us to question rhetoric about poverty and entitlements that depend upon uninformed, general representations and has little to do with the actual lives of people.

Responsibility toward Others

A final, related issue of representation can be traced by considering the stories-within-the-story. Granny and Cathy are the storytellers in the family, and their stories revolve around the harmful intru-

Topics for Further Study

- The filmmakers in the story, who say they are doing a film for the county on food stamps, note favorably that Granny grows her own vegetables. Research the history of food stamps in the United States, from their institution to the present. Consider the debates on this issue, and use this information to consider why Granny has such a negative reaction to the men's intrusive filming and, perhaps, to their objective in making the film.

- Bambara is known for her use of dialect. Read the story, paying close attention to how Bambara denotes the speech patterns of her characters. Consider what dialects you speak or hear spoken in daily life. Attempt, like Bambara, to transcribe these speech patterns into writing.

- "Blues Ain't No Mockin Bird" examines the question of stereotyping. The filmmakers and some previous landlords or employers have stereotyped Granny, her family, and home. Discuss these stereotypes and how Bambara counters them. Consider, also, whether Bambara might herself be accused of stereotyping in her fiction.

- While "Blues Ain't No Mockin Bird" is not set in any particular place or time, it does seem to take place in the rural South during the 1960s or 1970s. Research conditions of rural poverty in the South during the period, particularly for African Americans. Compare your findings with conditions today.

---

siveness of looking at and representing the plights of others. Granny tells a story about a man who was going to jump off a bridge. A crowd gathered; the minister and the man's girlfriend tried to talk him out of it. Then a man with a camera arrived and took pictures of the man. She notes that he saved a few pictures, implying that he wanted to photograph the man as and after he jumped (and, by extension, that he wanted the man to jump). The twins want to know whether the man jumped or not: Granny stares at them, saying nothing until they realize that there is something wrong with their question, although they may not recognize the similarity between their curiosity and the callous and prurient attitude of the cameraman. Cathy then tells the story of Goldilocks and the Three Bears. While the story is usually seen as harmless and cute, Cathy retells it to emphasize Goldilocks's rude behavior: she "barged" into a stranger's house, "messed over the people's groceries and broke up the people's furniture." The twins want to know if she was forced to pay for the mess she made. Both stories are left unfinished, but both point to the same theme: the indignity of invading the lives of strangers for sensational or selfish reasons. In addition, these stories-within-the-story, in which third-person narrators represent others, are in contrast with the overall story, which is narrated in first person and constitutes an example of self-expression, the telling of one's own story.

Style

In "Blues Ain't No Mockin Bird," a young black girl recounts an incident in which two white filmmakers attempted to film her home and family over the protests of her grandmother.

Dialect

Toni Cade Bambara's use of dialect has been highly praised by readers and critics. Her ability to capture the cadences and languages of rural Southern black speech has been equated with Mark Twain's ability to capture the dialects of nineteenth-century American speech.

The informal and conversational tone of "Blues Ain't No Mockin Bird" allows the narrator to "talk" to us in her own voice, and her figurative language conveys as much of the story's themes as any action of the plot. When the twins ask Granny what happened to the man who was going to jump off the bridge, the narrator reports: ''And Granny just stared at the twins till their faces swallow up the eager and they don't even care any more about the man jumpin.'' The image of the faces of the young boys ''swallow[ing] up the eager'' brilliantly conveys a complex psychological process in a few words. Similarly, Bambara renders dialogue so competently that the reader can ''hear'' the words of her characters and, by so doing, better understand their motivations and values. When Granny responds to the filmmakers's praise of her ''nice things,'' she says: '''I don't know about the thing, the it, and the stuff. . . . Just people here is what I tend to consider.''' The syntax of Granny's words conveys the cadences in her speech, and the narrator's comment that she ''speaks with her eyebrows'' helps the reader to visualize her. Bambara's adept ability to capture the language of her characters in its specificity and fullness enables the reader to gather the story's themes almost entirely through the words of the characters.

Point of View

''Blues Ain't No Mockin Bird'' is told from the point of view of a young child. In the fifteen short stories which comprise the short story collection *Gorilla, My Love,* in which ''Blues Ain't No Mockin Bird'' appears, ten are told from the perspective of young, female narrators. Most of the narrators are imaginative and intelligent, but many also display a considerable vulnerability and insecurity. The narrator of ''Blues Ain't No Mockin Bird'' is aware that both her grandmother and Cathy are more perceptive than she is and have a better understanding of the world. Yet the use of the point of view of a child whose language reflects her age, race, and rural Southern background allows the reader a particular advantage. We understand the events through her consciousness, and her unsophisticated yet insightful narration allows us to consider the complex issues present in the story through her subtle, questioning, and poignantly innocent eyes.

Historical Context

The Black Power Movement

When ''Blues Ain't No Mockin Bird'' was published in 1971, the influence of the Black Power Movement was widely felt among African-Ameri-

can artists and writers. While the Black Power movement, extending through the decade from 1965 to 1975, grew out of the Civil Rights movement for the dignity and equality of black people in the United States, the Black Power movement stressed the importance of self-definition rather than integration and demanded economic and political power as well as equality. The movement was fuelled by protest against such incidents as the shooting of Civil Rights leader James Meredith in 1966 while he led a protest march across Mississippi. Shortly afterward, Civil Rights leader Stokely Carmichael initiated the call for Black Power and the first National Conference on Black Power was held in Washington, D.C. in 1966. In the same year, the Black Panther Party was founded in Oakland, California by Bobby Seale and Huey P. Newton, taking a militant stand against police brutality and the appalling conditions of black urban ghettoes, which lacked adequate municipal services and suffered crime rates up to 35 times higher than white neighborhoods.

While the unemployment, crime and lack of facilities in black urban communities were denounced, black communities were also seen as the source of a vibrant culture. By the early 1970s, Black Power had become a widespread demand for black people to control their own destinies through various means: political activism, community control and development, cultural awareness and the development of black studies and ''Black Arts.'' Pride in both African heritage and in the cultural distinctiveness of black communities in the United States, often summed up in the word ''soul'' was reflected in a variety of forms from ''Afro'' hairstyles to soul music and soul food. In the arena of sports, heavyweight champion Muhammed Ali embodied the self-confident attitudes of black pride. In the arts, black writers saw themselves as both inheritors and creators of a black aesthetic tradition. African-American writers like Toni Cade Bambara played an important part in developing awareness of a distinct African-American culture and folk tradition which emphasized the collective and maintained oral forms of expression. Bambara's sympathetic portrayal of Granny's resistance of efforts to patronize her and to exploit her family is typical of the concerns of the time, as is the emphasis Bambara places on the storytelling roles of Granny, Cathy, and the narrator.

By the mid-1970s organizations like the Black Panthers, targets for police persecution and FBI

Compare & Contrast

- **1970s:** The Equal Rights Amendment, a proposal to change the constitution to guarantee women's rights, particularly equal pay for equal work, becomes a central issue of political debate.

  1990s: Women continue to struggle for political, social, and especially financial equality with men in the United States. Comparably educated and experienced women still earn, on average, only 75% of what men earn for performing the same work.

- **1970s:** The broad-based civil rights movement of the early '60s gave way, in the wake of the deaths of Malcolm X (1967), and Dr. Martin Luther King, Jr. (1968) to more the radicalized racial politics of a younger generation of activists, including the Black Power movement, Angela Davis and the Black Panther Party founded by Huey Newton and Bobby Seale. The more militant Black Power organizations were targeted for investigation and infiltration by the government and quickly faded from prominence.

  1990s: The Black Power tradition continues with the public prominence of Louis Farrakhan and the Nation of Islam. Alternative strategies for social integration and minority advancement are visible in the popularity of multicultural education.

- **1970s:** A full range of government guaranteed services to the poor, known as entitlements, are instituted to guarantee a minimum standard of living for all American citizens, continuing reforms of the 1960s.

  1996: President Bill Clinton signs the Welfare Reform Bill, limiting recipients to five years of benefits and ending a federal guarantee of a sustainable income through the use of food stamps, medical assistance and cash grants.

- **1970s:** Judges begin interpreting Civil Rights legislation as requiring full racial integration of public school systems. Many efforts to integrate schools result in violence, for instance Boston in 1974, or the abandonment of public schools and mixed-race districts by middle-class whites.

  1990s: Debates over the quality and equity of education continue. Many school districts remain segregated, despite twenty years of efforts at integration. New proposals for education reform include school choice, school vouchers, home schooling, charter schools, and a federal guarantee of access to higher education.

---

surveillance, were decimated. In 1976, the 4,000 black officials elected represented a larger number than had ever held office, but were still only 0.5% of all American elected officials. In the 1990s, African-Americans constitute less than 2 percent of all elected officials. Economic conditions for African-Americans suffered in the 1980s: the recessions in the early 1980s reduced black family income to only 56% of white family income, less than in 1952, and the gap remains the about same in the 1990s. Nevertheless, the cultural heritage of the Black Power movement—black self-awareness and the celebration of an African-American culture and identity—has remained.

Black Women and the Women's Movement

The Women's Movement developed in the late 1960s in North America partly in response to the radicalizing processes of the Civil Rights and Black Power movements and the antiwar movement. At the same time, many women were radicalized by their realization that they were treated as second-class participants in these movements. Women analyzed their situation and advocated radical change, forming their own local organizations and national networks for women's equality and women's rights. Consciousness groups were formed and women's centers established, concerned about issues such as sexual discrimination and harassment, spousal abuse, rape, and freedom of choice concerning abortion. Bambara's portrayal of strong, capable, and independent-minded female characters in stories like "Blues Ain't No Mockin Bird" challenged conventional assumptions about female roles. In particular, her emphasis on the story-telling abilities of Cathy, Granny, and the narrator insists on the ability of women to interpret reality effectively and their right to do so.

Black women, however, did not necessarily embrace the same ideology as the mainly white, middle-class women who dominated mainstream women's groups. As Toni Cade Bambara did in her anthology, *The Black Woman,* black women tended to connect issues of sexual equality with those of race and class. The struggle for welfare rights and decent housing was also seen by women in the black community as a woman's issue. As well, many black women felt that taking on the education and socialization of the young was an important role for them to play in order to strengthen their communities and empower future generations. "Blues Ain't No Mockin Bird" emphasizes the nurturing and teaching roles of both Granny and Cathy, whose stories impart lessons about personal and community values. Moreover, while many feminist writers white and black have been accused of vilifying men, Bambara in this story portrays a strong, positive black male character.

Critical Overview

When *Gorilla, My Love,* the collection of short stories which includes "Blues Ain't No Mockin Bird," was published in 1972, it was hailed by critics as a powerful portrayal of the experience of blacks in America. A writer in the *Saturday Review* remarked that the book was "among the best portraits of black life to appear in some time."

No full-length study of "Blues Ain't No Mockin Bird" has been completed, but critical discussion of Bambara as a short story writer generally concur on one point: Bambara is exemplary for her ability to capture the dialects and speech patterns of the characters she portrays. In an essay, "Youth in Toni Cade Bambara's *Gorilla, My Love,*" Nancy D. Hargrove writes that Bambara's narrators speak "conversationally and authentically." Anne Tyler,

herself a fiction writer, praises "the language of her characters, which is so startlingly beautiful without once striking a false note." In an essay in *Black Women Writers,* Ruth Elizabeth Burks comments of Bambara's range and dexterity in portraying languages. According to Burks, all of Bambara's works "uses language to particularize and individualize the voices of the people wherever they are—on a New York City street, crossing the waters of the Pacific, amid the red salt clay of the Louisiana earth. . ." One critic, Caren Dybek, claims that Bambara "possesses one of the finest ears for the nuances of black English." In her ability to capture the particular cadences and rhythms of her character's speech, Bambara has been compared to Mark Twain and Zora Neale Hurston.

Critics also consider Bambara's representations of black communities and concern with the formation of black identities. Burks argues that Bambara is less concerned with issues of race and class than many other black women writers: "Bambara appears less concerned with mirroring the black existence in American than in chronicling 'the movement' intended to improve and change that existence." Burks argues that Bambara's role is comparable to that of the griot, an African term for one who preserves history through story-telling. Bambara, Burk claims, "perpetuates the struggle of her people by literally recording it in their own voices." Burk also notes that Bambara considers the limits of language as a way to gain independence. An "innate spirituality" must accompany an awareness of the power of words if blacks are to succeed in their quest for freedom. In a study of American women writers, *American Women Writing Fiction,* Martha M. Vertreace examines Bambara's definitions of identity and community. According to Vertreace, Bambara's sense of identity, defined as "personal definition within the context of community," is one of her consuming interests. The strength of her female characters stems from the "lessons women learn from communal interaction," not from an essential "feminine" trait they are born with. Thus, Vertreace claims, identity "is achieved, not bestowed." Bambara's concern with pedagogy and teaching, the centrality of community in her stories and her portrayal of the struggle to achieve despite seemingly overwhelming situations are all evidence of this definition of identity. While other writers "paint a picture of black life in contemporary black settings," Bambara's stories "portray women who struggle with issues and learn from them."

Criticism

Rena Korb

> *Korb is a writer and editor from Austin, Texas. In the following essay, she looks at ways in which language and dialect are used in "Blues Ain't No Mockin Bird" to support the theme of respect for oneself and others.*

Toni Cade Bambara, the possessor of "one of the finest ears for the nuances of black English," may have revolutionized the use of contemporary African American dialect in literature, introducing it to non-African American audiences in much the same way that Mark Twain brought the dialect of middle America to people of the mid-nineteenth century through his character Huckleberry Finn. Like Zora Neale Hurston in her works of the 1920s and 1930s, Bambara uses language to capture what is unique about her characters' experiences and voices. Through Bambara's fiction, people around the world have come to better appreciate the richness of African-American language, mythology, and history and the strength of the African-American commitment to community. Bambara's work mirrors the lives of African Americans and strives to chronicle the civil rights movement which sought to improve the quality of those lives.

After earning a reputation as a worker in the civil rights movement, a college teacher, and an editor, essayist, and collector of writings by African Americans, Bambara published her first book in 1972, a collection of short stories. *Gorilla, My Love* was immediately and enthusiastically welcomed. In a review in *Washington Post Book World,* Anne Tyler remarked on "the language of her characters, which is so startlingly beautiful without once striking a false note"; the *Saturday Review* placed it "among the best portraits of black life to have appeared in some time," and the *New Yorker* noted the "inspirational angle" of the stories. Readers admired and learned from the view of African American life presented in the stories, while critics exclaimed over the "bold, political angle" of Bambara's language. Of the collection and public and critical reaction to it, Bambara once wrote, "It didn't have anything to do with a political stance. I just thought people lived and moved around in this particular language system. It is also the language system I tend to remember childhood in" (in her *Deep Sightings and Rescue Missions,* 1996). Because Bambara was so familiar with the culture she represented in the book, because she wrote in "the language many of us speak," she would need other people to teach her just "what was so different and distinct" about her work.

In an article in *Black Women Writers: A Critical Evaluation* (ed. Mari Evans, 1984), Ruth Elizabeth Burks describes Bambara as a *griot,* an African who preserves history by retelling it; she "perpetuates the struggle of her people by literally recording it in their own voices." When looked at as a unit, her three major works trace the history of the civil rights movement in America and African Americans' struggle for freedom. *Gorilla, My Love* preceded the principal flowering of the movement, but it demonstrated a need for equality and a willingness to take it when it is not offered. For Bambara, a spiritual communion, one that is based on a shared sense of community and purpose, is necessary for African Americans to achieve freedom. The type of communion found in "Blues Ain't No Mockin Bird," one of the stories that appeared in *Gorilla, My Love,,* is unique in the collection, for it portrays a harmonious, cooperative relationship between a man and woman; the other stories in the collection all depict close ties among women. In the story, Granny is feeling threatened by outsiders, two men who claim to have been sent by the county to make a film about the food stamp program. Granddaddy Cain responds to her outrage and forces the men to leave the property. The old couple's granddaughter, grandniece, and young neighbors all witness, and learn from, the interaction.

At the time of *Gorilla, My Love*'s publication, many commentators associated its breezy style of speech with African American street dialect. But even when the stories take place in a non-urban environment, as does "Blues Ain't No Mockin Bird," Bambara's characters exhibit the same ease. The narrator tells the story using a rural Southern tone and language that unconsciously convey a distinct sense of the place and atmosphere in which she and her family live. While it twists and breaks the rules of standard English, the language of Bambara's narrator and the other African American characters is concise and expressive, from the narrator's description of a "tall man with a huge camera lassoed to his shoulder. . . buzzin our way," to the screeching hawk "reckless with crazy," to Granny about to "bust through that screen with somethin in her hand and murder on her mind." But most importantly, their speech is true to who they are, and even when they are threatened by the presumably white strangers, the characters' voices do not waver; they do not alter their speech to make it seem

What Do I Read Next?

- "Blues Ain't No Mockin Bird" was published in Toni Cade Bambara's critically acclaimed collection of short stories, *Gorilla, My Love* (1972).

- Toni Morrison's novel *Sula* (1973) recounts the struggle of Nel Wright and Sula Peace, who live in the black community of Medallion, Ohio. The novel recounts the decline of the community after World War I, the ostracism of Sula by the townspeople, and the friendship between Sula and Nel.

- William Faulkner's novel *The Sound and the Fury* (1929), one of the most important and influential novels of modern American literature, recounts the decline of a wealthy Southern white family and explores issues of race relations in the South through an experimental style, shifting narration, and use of dialect.

- Zora Neale Hurston's novel *Their Eyes Were Watching God* (1937) is an insightful portrayal of rural black life in the early twentieth century. Trained in anthropology, Hurston, in both her fictional and nonfiction works, explores the folk culture of black Southerners and contrasts its complexity with the superficial understanding generally available to outsiders.

more dignified or formal. The two filmmakers are the only people who change their speech patterns. When they first are called upon to explain their presence, they say, "*We're* [italics mine] filmin for the county," but after they are challenged by Granddaddy Cain, they say, "*We* [italics mine] filmin for the county. . . *We* [italics mine] puttin together a movie." Commenting on their behavior, the narrator observes that they talk to each other "like they was in the jungle or somethin and come upon a native that don't speak the language." They change their way of communication to try to reach Granddaddy Cain by using what they perceive to be his own language.

It is interesting that, despite Bambara's powerful use of dialect, Granddaddy and Granny communicate primarily through "nonlanguage." Granny indicates her great displeasure with the filmmakers by the sounds she makes, such as moans and hums. Without even looking at Granny, Granddaddy and the children know, simply from her "low groanin music," that "any minute now, [she] gonna bust through that screen with somethin in her hand and murder on her mind." The filmmakers, on the other hand, are insensitive to this careful and intuitive transmission of feelings, and continue to try to smile and talk their way past the family's hostility until Granddaddy Cain's quiet dissection of their camera makes their maneuvering pointless.

The filmmakers are at least able to recognize the dignity and self-assurance of Granddaddy Cain, even asking politely for the return of the camera with the words, " Please, sir.'" The outsiders do not notice or individuate the other African Americans, however, categorizing pecan barrels, a sled, stones, trees, and a tool shed along with the children as some of the "[N]ice things here," whereas Granny sees "[J]ust people here." They call Granny "aunty," exposing their view of her as a person who fits into their stereotype of a nonthreatening, submissive black woman whom they can overlook and overrun. Far from being submissive, however, Granny stands up to the men and refuses to give them permission to film on her property. When they continue to address her as "aunty," she retorts, "'Your mama and I are not related'." The narrator's cousin, Cathy, also emerges as a strong and capable character. Cathy understands the unspoken and has the ability to interpret events. Unlike the narrator, Cathy "knew how come we move so much and [she] ain't but a third cousin we picked up on the way last Thanksgivin visit." When Granny tells of photographers taking pictures of a man about to jump off a bridge "[b]ut savin a few [shots], of

> It is interesting that, despite Bambara's powerful use of dialect, Granddaddy and Granny communicate primarily through 'nonlanguage.'"

course," Cathy immediately repeats "of course," while the narrator is left "standin there wonderin how Cathy knew it was 'of course' when I didn't and it was *my* grandmother." Cathy's wisdom that extends beyond her years brings hope for the future of African Americans—she is the one who points out the nobility of Granddaddy Cain, who is "tall and silent and like a king" and she makes sure others perceive this quality as well by bringing their attention to it. She also expresses a desire to chronicle her experiences, and thus, the lives of African Americans in general. The story she's "goin to write one day" about "the proper use of the hammer" will presumably also convey the perceptions she has gleaned about the community in which she grew up and the people whom she cared for and who supported her. Like Bambara, Cathy will become a griot, and in retelling the past, she will inspire future generations.

If Cathy has the power to transform the future, the relationship between the grandfather and the grandmother in "Blues Ain't No Mockin Bird" provides the courage to impose bold changes. The grandparents provide the children with models of African Americans who demand to be treated with respect. Even though Granny, by herself, cannot induce the intruders to leave, she continues to show her displeasure at their presence and does manage to get them to move some distance away. Moreover, she has a history of educating the children in the sort of behavior that commands respect. Granny "teaches steady with no let-up," the narrator comments; and when the twins get into a tussle with each other, the narrator expects Granny to come off the porch and tell them "about how we can't afford to be fightin amongst ourselves." Granddaddy Cain functions as what Toni Morrison calls the "ancestor" of the family, a parent or other adult who is an "advisor with a strong connection to the past" [*Literature*

and the Urban Experience, edited by Michael C. Jaye and Ann Chalmers Watts, 1981]. In "Blues Ain't No Mockin Bird," Granddaddy fulfills his role as the "competent protector," and in keeping with this duty, he demands and receives respect from outsiders. Unlike most of Bambara's stories, "Blues Ain't No Mockin Bird" takes place in a rural area, but the city and its lack of values still are highlighted—"'How come your grandmother calls her husband "Mister Cain" all the time?' Tyrone whispers all loud and noisy and from the city and don't know no better." These values of respect learned from the ancestor will aid African-Americans because, in showing respect for each other, they will command respect from outsiders.

The importance that Bambara places on the younger generation may be one reason why she is able to portray children with sensitivity and compassion. Like other great writers of literature about youth—Mark Twain with Huckleberry Finn or J. D. Salinger with Holden Caulfield—Bambara takes her young characters, their experiences, and their perceptions of the world seriously. She captures that time of life extraordinarily well and shows, even during the course of just one story, the maturation and growth of her characters. Her depiction of children learning to come to terms with a world that is not always welcoming, and doing it with grace and anticipation, shows her faith in a more positive future for African Americans and in the drive to make it happen.

Source: Rena Korb, "Dialect and Story-telling in 'Blues Ain't No Mockin Bird'," for *Short Stories for Students,* Gale, 1997.

Theresa M. Girard

Girard is a Ph.D candidate at Wayne State University who has taught many introduction-to-literature classes. In the essay below, she offers an introduction to "Blues Ain't No Mockin Bird," focusing on its qualities as a told story grounded in the African-American oral tradition.

The short story as a literary form is unique in that it "does what it does in a hurry," as Toni Cade Bambara said in an interview with Beverly Guy-Sheftall in 1979. Bambara also commented that "it's quick, it makes a modest appeal for attention, it can creep up on you on your blind side." Those are a few of the reasons that Bambara prefers to write short stories as well as read them. The short story "Blues Ain't No Mockin Bird" was written in

1971 and, as Bambara says, manages to take you by surprise and blindside you. Toni Cade Bambara accomplishes many things in focusing on short stories in her writing. She is able to, among other things, tell stories of experience which hold interest; teach the young and/or ill-informed about the pride of a people; and, carries on the story-telling oral tradition of blacks, while transposing it into the written form. Above all, she spins a story in ''Blues Ain't No Mockin Bird'' which seems to be lifted right out of someone's life.

Conventional story lines do not inhabit Bambara's writing. She fails to define her characters in comfortable, recognizable ways. Martha M. Vertreace says that she does ''do more than paint a picture of black life and contemporary black settings. . . . Her stories portray women who struggle with issues and learn from them.'' Elliot Butler-Evans notes that Bambara primarily uses girls or women as narrators.

The story begins by depicting some children playing. The narrator and one of the other children, identified as Cathy, are jumping on a frozen puddle. The fact that the puddle is frozen and Granny is ladling rum onto tinned Christmas cakes leads to the conclusion that Christmas is near. The mention of the nearby meadow and the cameraman cutting across the neighbor's yard places the scene in a semi-rural area. The pecan barrels, as well as the pecan grove, indicate that the setting is southern because pecans are a major crop of the South.

The action centers around the grandmother of the narrator and how she interacts with a variety of people, some of whom are characters in the story and some who are only referred to as past experiences. Initial introductions to Granny, by the narrator, reveals a complex woman. She owns and likes nice things. As the children crack the ice in the puddle, the narrator (whose name is never known), lets us know that it resembles the crystal paperweight Granny has in her parlor. That the paperweight is crystal is significant, as is merely having something as frivolous as a paperweight.

The other important bits of information revealed about Granny is that she has moved a great deal: from the Judson's woods, to the Cooper place, at the dairy, to where they are now residing. Cathy, the narrator's cousin, knows that Granny's dignity and sense of privacy are the reasons they moved so often. For example, Mr. Cooper insulted Granny by bringing her boxes of old clothes and magazines.

> **By duplicating the story telling within the story, Bambara reinforces the value of oral tradition and its place in the culture of the black community."**

Mrs. Cooper infuriated Granny by touching all of Granny's things and remarking ''how clean it all was.'' The times lived at the other locations also reveals that they had not lived at any single place very long, as indicated by the use of the ladle. ''The old ladle dripping rum into the Christmas tins, like it used to drip maple syrup into the pails when we lived in the Judson's woods, like it poured cider into the vats when we were on the Cooper place, like it used to scoop buttermilk and soft cheese when we lived at the dairy.'' The use of the ladle also indicates the passage of the seasons: spring, ladling maple syrup; summer, ladling buttermilk and soft cheese; autumn, ladling cider; winter, ladling rum.

When two men begin to film Granny's yard without her permission, Granny becomes quite upset. After filming the yard, they say that they ''thought we'd get a shot or two of the house and everything and then—'' and are cut off by Granny. She simply says, ''Good mornin,'' and in those two words, she teaches the men, the children, and the readers about proper manners. After an exchange that forces the men to realize that they had made several errors in etiquette. When one man condescendingly calls her ''aunty,'' she responds: ''Your mama and I are not related.''

Through Granny, Bambara also instructs young blacks in the black story-telling tradition. While the men finally back out of the yard, the children all wait ''cause Granny always got somethin to say. She teaches steady with no let-up.'' She tells a story of a man who was going to jump off of a bridge and how an unfeeling person with a camera could be. She tells the children how awful it was that the camera person took nearly a whole roll of film of the poor man—''saving a few, of course.'' Cathy is the only one of the children to understand, immediately, why the person saved a few pictures. The other children waited for an answer which never came. They are left to figure it out, as is the reader.

The filmmakers make another mistake when they encounter Granny's husband, Grandaddy Cain. Granny asks him to ''Get them persons out of my flower bed.'' Granddaddy Cain simply puts out his hand to the cameraman and says ''Good day, gentlemen.'' The man unquestioningly hands Granddaddy his camera, and after destroying the film, returns the camera when the man asks for it, adding a polite, ''Please, sir.''

Bambara does not waste an opportunity to instruct her characters or her readers. She tells stories to that end and embedded in her written stories are the oral stories. She gives clues to indicate features, but encourages readers to figure it out on their own. By duplicating the story telling within the story, she reinforces the value of oral tradition and its place in the culture of the black community.

Source: Theresa M. Girard,''Overview of 'Blues Ain't No Mockin Bird','' for *Short Stories for Students,* Gale, 1998.

Beverly Guy-Sheftall

An American educator, editor, nonfiction writer, and critic, Guy-Sheftall has served as director of the Women's Research and Resource Center at Spelman College. In the following excerpt from a longer interview, Bambara comments on her literary influences and her approach to writing fiction.

[*Guy-Sheftall*]: *Have women writers influenced you as much as male writers?*

[Bambara]: I have no clear ideas about literary influence. I would say that my mother was a great influence, since mother is usually the first map maker in life. She encouraged me to explore and express. And, too, the fact that people of my household were big on privacy helped. And I would say that people that I ran into helped, and I ran into a great many people because we moved a lot and I was always a nosey kid running up and down the street, getting into everything. Particular kinds of women influenced the work. For example, in every neighborhood I lived in there were always two types of women that somehow pulled me and sort of got their wagons in a circle around me. I call them Miss

Naomi and Miss Gladys, although I'm sure they came under various names. The Miss Naomi types were usually barmaids or life-women, nighttime people with lots of clothes in the closet and a very particular philosophy of life, who would give me advice like, ''When you meet a man, have a birthday, demand a present that's hockable, and be careful.'' Stuff like that. Had no idea what they were talking about. Just as well. The Miss Naomis usually gave me a great deal of advice about beautification, how to take care of your health and not get too fat. The Miss Gladyses were usually the type that hung out the window in Apartment 1-A leaning on the pillow giving single-action advice on numbers or giving you advice about how to get your homework done or telling you to stay away from those cruising cars that moved through the neighborhood patrolling little girls. I would say that those two types of women, as well as the women who hung out in the beauty parlors (and the beauty parlors in those days were perhaps the only womanhood institutes we had—it was there in the beauty parlors that young girls came of age and developed some sense of sexual standards and some sense of what it means to be a woman growing up)—it was those women who had the most influence on the writing.

I think that most of my work tends to come off the street rather than from other books. Which is not to say I haven't learned a lot as an avid reader. I devour pulp and print. And of course I'm part of the tradition. That is to say, it is quite apparent to the reader that I appreciated Langston Hughes, Zora Hurston, and am a product of the sixties spirit. But I'd be hard pressed to discuss literary influences in any kind of intelligent way. . . .

[Have] your travels revealed to you how American black and other Third World women can link up in their struggles to liberate themselves from the various kinds of oppression they face as a result of their sexual identity?

Yes, I would say that two particular places I visited yielded up a lot of lessons along those lines. I was in Cuba in 1973 and had the occasion not only to meet with the Federation of Cuban Women but sisters in the factories, on the land, in the street, in the parks, in lines, or whatever, and the fact that they were able to resolve a great many class conflicts as well as color conflicts and organize a mass organization says a great deal about the possibilities here. I was in Vietnam in the summer of 1975 as a guest of the Women's Union and again was very much struck by the women's ability to break through traditional roles, traditional expectations, reactionary agenda for women, and come together again in a mass organization that is programmatic and takes on a great deal of responsibility for the running of the nation.

We missed a moment in the early sixties. We missed two things. One, at a time when we were beginning to lay the foundations for a national black women's union and for a national strategy for organizing, we did not have enough heart nor a solid enough analysis that would equip us to respond in a positive and constructive way to the fear in the community from black men as well as others who said that women organizing as women is divisive. We did not respond to that in a courageous and principled way. We fell back. The other moment that we missed was that we had an opportunity to hook up with Puerto Rican women and Chicano women who shared not only a common condition but also I think a common vision about the future and we missed that moment because of the language trap. When people talked about multicultural or multiethnic organizing, a lot of us translated that to mean white folks and backed off. I think that was an error. We should have known what was meant by multicultural. Namely, people of color. Afro-American, Afro-Hispanic, Indo-Hispanic, Asian-Hispanic, and so forth. Not that those errors necessarily doom us. Errors may result in lessons learned. I think we have the opportunity again in this last quarter of the twentieth century to begin forging those critical ties with other communities. It will be done. That is a certainty. . . .

You are one of the few black literary artists who could be considered a short story writer primarily. Is this a deliberate choice on your part or coincidental?

It's deliberate, coincidental, accidental, and regretful! Regretful, commercially. That is to say, it is financially stupid to be a short story writer and to spend two years putting together eight or ten stories and receiving maybe half the amount of money you would had you taken one of those short stories and produced a novel. The publishing companies, reviewers, critics, are all geared to promoting and pushing the novel rather than any other form.

I prefer the short story genre because it's quick, it makes a modest appeal for attention, it can creep up on you on your blind side. The reader comes to the short story with a mind-set different than that with which he approaches the big book, and a different set of controls operating, which is why I think the short story is far more effective in term of teaching us lessons.

Temperamentally, I move toward the short story because I'm a sprinter rather than a long-distance runner. I cannot sustain characters over a long period of time. Walking around, frying eggs, being a mother, shopping—I cannot have those characters living in my house with me for more than a couple of weeks. In terms of craft, I don't have the kinds of skills *yet* that it takes to stay with a large panorama of folks and issues and landscapes and moods. That requires a set of skills that I don't know anything about yet, but I'm learning.

I prefer the short story as a reader, as well, because it does what it does in a hurry. For the writer and the reader make instructive demands in terms of language precision. It deals with economy, gets it said, and gets out of the way. As a teacher, I also prefer the short story for all the reasons given. And yes, I consider myself primarily a short story writer. . . .

That leads me into the next question which is about the process involved in your writing a story. Do you have the whole idea of it before sitting down to write, or does it unfold as you're writing?

It depends on how much time you have. There are periods in my life when I know that I will not be able to get to the desk until summer, until months later, in which case I walk around composing while washing dishes and may jot down little definitive notes on pieces of paper which I stick under the phone, in the mirror, and all over the house. At other times, a story mobilizes itself around a single line you've heard that resonates. There's a truth there, something usable. Sometimes a story revolves around a character that I'm interested in. For example, "The Organizer's Wife" in the new collection. I've always been very curious about silent people because most people I know are like myself—very big-mouthed, verbally energetic, and generally clear as to what they're about because their *mouth* is always announcing what they're doing. That story came out of a curiosity. What do I know about people like that? Could I delve into her? The story took shape around that effort.

There are other times when a story is absolutely clear in the head. All of it may not be clear—who's going to say what and where it's taking place or what year it is—but the story frequently comes together at one moment in the head. At other times, stories, like any other kind of writing, and certainly anybody who's writing anything—freshman compositions, press releases, or whatever—has experienced this, that frequently writing is an act of discovery. Writing is very much like dreaming, in that sense. When you dream, you dialogue with aspects of yourself that normally are not with you in the daytime and you discover that you know a great deal more than you thought you did. So there are various kinds of ways that writing comes.

Then, too, there is a kind of—some people call it automatic writing—I call it inspiration. There are times when you have to put aside what you intended to write, what got you to the desk in the first place, and just go with the story that is coming out of you, which may or may not have anything to do with what you planned at all. In fact, a lot of stories (I haven't published any of these because I'm not sure they are mine) and poems have come out on the page that I know do not belong to me. They do not have my sense of vision, my sense of language, my sense of reality, but they're complete. Each of us has experienced this in various ways, in church, or fasting, or in some other kind of state, times when we are available to intelligences that we are not particularly prone to acknowledge, given our Western scientific training, which have filled us with so much fear that we cannot make ourselves available to other channels of information. I think most of us have experienced, though we don't talk about it very much, an inspiration, that is to say, an inbreathing that then becomes ''enthusiasm,'' a possession, a living-with, an informing spirit. So some stories come off like that.

Do you make many revisions before the story is finished and ready for publication?

Oh yes. I edit mercilessly. Generally, my editing takes the form of cutting. Very frequently, a story will try to get away from me and become a novel. I don't have the staying power for a novel, so

when I find it getting to be about thirty or forty pages I immediately start cutting back to six. To my mind, the six-page short story is the gem. If it takes more than six pages to say it, something is the matter. So I'm not too pleased in that respect with the new collection, *The Sea Birds Are Still Alive.* Most of those stories are too sprawling and hairy for my taste, although I'm very pleased, feel perfectly fine about them as pieces. But as stories, they're too damn long and dense. . . .

One of the characteristics of your fiction which is apparent in Gorilla, My Love, *an older collection of short stories, as well as in* The Sea Birds *is the extent to which—though one knows you're there— you can remove yourself from the narrative voice. You don't intrude. Is that deliberate?*

Well, I'm frequently there. You see, one of the reasons that it seems that the author is not there has to do with language. It has to do with the whole tradition of dialect. In the old days, writers might have their characters talking dialect or slang but the narrator, that is to say, the author, maintained a distance and a ''superiority'' by speaking a more premiumed language. I tend to speak on the same level as my characters, so it seems as though I am not there, because, possibly, you're looking for another voice.

I rarely get the impression that your fiction comes directly out of your personal experience, even though it's obvious that what you have written about has been filtered through your consciousness. I don't have the impression that these particular characters or that particular incident are very close to what you may have actually experienced. Is that correct?

Yes, that's correct. I think it's very rude to write autobiographically, unless you label it autobiography. And I think it's very rude to use friends and relatives as though they were occasions for getting your whole thing off. It's not making your mama a still life. And it's very abusive to your developing craft, to your own growth, not to convert and transform what has come to you in one way into another way. The more you convert the more you grow, it seems to me. Through conversion we recognize again the basic oneness, the connections, or as some blood coined it: ''Everything is Everything.'' So, it's kind of *lazy* (I think that's the better word) to simply record. Also, it's terribly boring to the reader frequently, and, too, it's dodgy. You can't tell to what extent things are fascinating to you because they're yours and to what extent they're useful, unless you do some conversion.

What can we expect from you in the future?

I'm working on several things—some children's books, a new collection of short stories, a novel, some film scripts.

"Children of Struggle" is a series I've been working on that dramatizes the role children and youth have played in the struggle for liberation—children of the Underground Railroad, children of Frelimo, children of the Long March, of Granma, of El Grito de Lares, The Trail of Tears, and so forth. . . .

Source: Toni Cade Bambara with Beverly Guy-Sheftall, "Commitment: Toni Cade Bambara Speaks," in *Sturdy Black Bridges,* Roseann P. Bell, Bettye J. Parker, Beverly Guy-Sheftall, eds., Anchor Press/Doubleday, 1978, pp. 230–49.

Sources

Hargrove, Nancy D. "Youth in Toni Cade Bambara's *Gorilla, My Love,*" in *Southern Quarterly,* Vol. 22, No. 1, 1983, pp. 81-99.

Vertreace, Martha M. "Toni Cade Bambara," in *American Women Writing Fiction,* edited by Mickey Pearlman, University Press of Kentucky, 1989, pp. 155–7.

Further Reading

Bambara, Toni Cade. "How She Came by Her Name," in her *Deep Sightings and Rescue Missions,* Pantheon Books, 1996, pp. 201-45.
    In this collection of Bambara's later writings is included an interview with the author, discussing her early career as a writer and essayist.

Burks, Ruth Elizabeth. "From Baptism to Resurrection; Toni Cade Bambara and the Incongruity of Language," in *Black Women Writers,* edited by Mari Evans, Doubleday, 1984, pp. 48–57.
    Burks discusses what she sees as the spiritual power of Bambara's use of language.

Morrison, Toni. "City Limits, Village Values: Concepts of the Neighborhood in Black Fiction," in *Literature and the Urban Experience,* edited by Michael C. Jaye and Ann Chalmers Watts, Rutgers University Press, 1981, pp. 35-43.
    Morrison discusses the role of the city in the works of many African-American writers, including Bambara.

Robinson, Lillian S., ed. *Modern Women Writers.* Continuum, 1996.
    A compilation of critical writings on modern women writers, including an extensive section on Toni Cade Bambara.

Disorder and Early Sorrow

Thomas Mann

1925

Thomas Mann is one of the most important German novelists of the twentieth century. But not to be overlooked are his contributions to the genre of the short story, among which "Disorder and Early Sorrow" is one of his best. It first appeared in 1925 in a publication celebrating his fiftieth birthday. Regarding the story, he said, "For the first time in my life I wrote something literary, one might say to order: the editorship of the Fischer *Neue Rundschau* published a *Festschrift* for my 50th birthday and they wanted it to contain a narrative contribution by the birthday child. So emerged 'Disorder and Early Sorrow,' a story which I like so much that I am tempted to count it among my very best."

The story examines the life of the Cornelius family as they prepare for a party at their home. Through their simple preparations, the reader is given a glimpse into daily life of 1920s Germany during the last years of the Weimar Republic. Frustrations over the country's economic instability and social upheaval constitute the undercurrent of his tale. Professor Cornelius, the patriarch of the family and a professor of history, finds safety and stability in his profession. He says that "the past is immortalized; that is to say, it is dead; and death is the root of all godliness and all abiding significance." It is that dead significance that he finds comforting in contrast to the revolution going on about him. Professor Cornelius also comes into quiet conflict with the modern art forms that so attract his children and their friends. He sees these new styles as

fraudulent and phony. These two thematic issues, social upheaval and the role of art and the artist in society, are basic to most of Mann's writings, and such is the case in this story. Additionally, the theme of the search for self-identity plays an important part in the unfolding of the story.

Author Biography

Thomas Mann was born on June 6, 1875 in Luebeck, Germany, to Thomas Johann Heinrich Mann, a government official and small business owner, and his wife, Julia. He started writing at a young age, and had his first story published when he was fifteen. He married Katja Pringsheim on February 11, 1905, and they eventually had six children. Mann was a devoted father and husband, and on those occasions when he was separated from Katja he would become depressed and would question his artistic and creative processes.

As he began his literary career he acquainted himself with many other writers, philosophers, musicians, and thinkers of Germany. He was particularly captivated by the music of German opera composer Richard Wagner. Wagner's use of leitmotiv, a melody that becomes associated with a particular character or idea in a musical work, was a feature that Mann would adapt to his literature. Mann is most widely known for his novels, which often examined the degeneration of society and the conflict between art, the artist, and society. Critics have said that Mann had become suspicious of the role of the artist, because he believed that self-expression could lapse into self-indulgence.

Mann's success as a writer was established from his very first publications, and he maintained this prominence throughout his entire career. In 1929 he won the Nobel Prize for Literature, which established him as one of the most important literary figures of the twentieth century. His most famous works include *Buddenbrooks, The Magic Mountain,* and *Doctor Faustus.* Almost overshadowed by these monumental novels are his contributions to short fiction, which include *Death in Venice, Tristan, Tonio Kroger,* and "Disorder and Early Sorrow."

Mann's writings also included many essays and speeches on a variety of topics, notably his opposition to Nazism and the mistreatment of the Jews. His continuing concern about the plight of the Jews was the impetus for the four novels published as

Thomas Mann

Joseph and His Brothers. Because of his outspoken opposition to the Nazis, he was exiled to Switzerland in 1933 and lost his German citizenship in 1936. That year he became a Czech citizen. He eventually immigrated to the United States and became a naturalized citizen in 1944. He lectured widely at universities and was a consultant in German literature for the Library of Congress. After World War II, he returned to Switzerland and died of phlebitis in Zurich in 1955.

Plot Summary

"Disorder and Early Sorrow" is a novella that examines the life of Professor Cornelius's family during one day in post-World War I Germany. The scene opens with a discussion between the members of the family and how they interact. Members of the family are identified by their generation: Ingrid and Bert, both teenagers, are "the big folk"; Professor Cornelius and his wife are "the old folk"; Ellie and Snapper, the youngest of the Professor's children, are "the little folk"; and Professor Cornelius's parents, who are only mentioned and have no part in the action of the story, are referred to as "'the ancients." Other members of the household include the servants, Xaver, the Nurse, and the Hinterhofer sisters. Several friends of Ingrid and Bert also appear in the story at the party.

The setting for the tale is Munich in the mid-1920s. It takes place during one day in which Ingrid and Bert plan and give a party for their friends. During the afternoon, there are occasional digressions that reveal incidents from the "big folks" recent past which serve to expand the scope of this tale and give the reader a more complete understanding of the nature of the characters in the story and the times in which they live. The point of view for the story is the Professor's. He thinks about his children, his profession, and his concerns about the modern art forms. The third-person limited narrator allows the reader to witness the action of the story through the Professor's eyes only.

After the opening section, there is the first digression: the incident on the bus. Bert and Ingrid pretend to be people from another part of the country, adopting exotic accents and mannerisms. They "delight in misleading and mystifying their fellow-men" by "impersonating fictitious characters." They talk in loud voices, making up their stories about events that never happened, each one more outrageous than the last. Finally, an old man on the bus has had enough and tells them so. Bert then pretends to want to strike him but holds back his temper. The man gets off the bus at the next stop. This episode is followed by a discussion of Bert and Ingrid's other diversion, to use the telephone to carry on additional pretenses. They call anyone they please (opera singers or government officials), pretending to be a shopkeeper or a Lord or Lady, and spinning tales that annoy those on the other end of the phone.

Ellie and Snapper are children who are dependent on their parents, spending as much time as possible sitting in their laps, getting caressed and cuddled. However, the Professor becomes more attached to Ellie than he believes is natural. He is uncomfortable with the thought and worries that his affection for his daughter might not be "perfectly good and right." In this same passage, he links his love for her to his love for history. He believes that "only the most fanatical . . . could be capable . . . of tearing this purest and most precious feeling out of his heart."

The reader later learns that Ellie is very concerned with her appearance. Her father often reminds her that one of her ears is larger than the other, a defect that she covers with her hair. Snapper also worries about himself, but his concerns are moral rather than physical. He believes that he is a sinner and that he will go to "the bad place." Snapper also is given to fits, tantrums, and "berserker rages." Because of this he gets extra attention from the Nurse and from his mother. During one of these outbursts he is made to stand in the corner, weeping. The nurse observes his face turning blue and alerts others in the family. As it turns out, the blue is merely a stain from the wall paint that had come off onto his wet face. Nursy teaches the children their nursery rhymes and songs. Ellie is much better at this than Snapper. The children also engage in teacher/student play during which times Ellie instructs Snapper on the pronunciation of bird names and diseases. If he does not do this correctly, she makes him stand in the corner.

As the household prepares for the evening's party, Professor Cornelius withdraws to his study to prepare for his next day's lecture. Soon he falls asleep until he is awakened by the arrival of the guests. He does not like the thought of the party, seeing it as a disruption of his orderly routines. But he tries to accept it and to take part in some small way. He carefully plans the words he will speak as he enters the party for the first time. After he walks through the party, he again retreats to his study. Later he offers the guests a pack of cigarettes.

While in the room he notices the dress of several of the guests. Herr Hergesell is wearing shoes that are too tight; another male guest is wearing make-up, including rouge. Professor Cornelius finds the actor repugnant because he sees a falseness and an affectation in his manners and behaviors, "a perfect illustration of the abnormality of the artist soul-form." Professor Cornelius again retreats to his den.

Later in the evening, as Max dances with Ellie, Cornelius feels a pang of jealousy at the sight of them dancing. He worries about the party's "power to intoxicate and estrange his darling child." He leaves the house and walks the streets for a while. When he returns, Xaver tells him that Ellie is "in a bad way." He finds her in her bed weeping uncontrollably, surrounded by all the women of the household. She sobs, "Why—isn't Max—my brother." Despite attempts by the Professor and others, she is inconsolable. Finally, Max enters in an attempt to calm her down. He talks to her in literary snippets, designed more to impress her father than her. Once she is calm, he leaves her and the professor alone. Ellie falls asleep as Cornelius watches. He believes that by the morning all this will be forgotten and everything will be back to normal once again.

Characters

Aladdin

Aladdin is a party guest who is known for his gift-giving and for treating his friends to parties and meals, despite the deteriorating economic situation.

Blue-faced Ann

See Nursy

Abel Cornelius

Professor Abel Cornelius is the 47–year-old patriarch of the family, and the story is revealed through his perspective. He is a history professor who finds great personal satisfaction in preparing lectures. He is a devoted father to his four children, especially Ellie, whom he calls "Eleonorchen" and "childie." Contrasted to this is his appraisal of his older son, Bert, who he believes lacks motivation and intellect in comparison to some of Bert's friends. The Professor dislikes the party but makes a stilted appearance, addressing the guests with a well rehearsed sentence and showing a "mechanical smile." Despite his fascination with history and its "truth," he is himself a phony and puts up a facade to conceal his feelings. He is judgmental of artists and dislikes modern art.

Bert Cornelius

Bert, the Professor's 17-year-old son, wears an elaborate hair style and trendy clothing like the house servant, Xaver. He wants to be a dancer or actor at the local club, the Cairo, much to his father's displeasure. Like Ingrid, he delights in deceiving people by loudly telling false stories on the bus or making prank telephone calls.

Ellie Cornelius

Ellie is the Professor's five-year-old daughter, who has captured his full attention and affection. She calls her father by his first name, Abel. She likes to play games with the kitchen staff and her father. At the party she becomes infatuated with Max and throws a crying tantrum because Max is not her brother. She knows her nursery rhymes and songs

Media Adaptations

- "Disorder and Early Sorrow" was adapted by Franz Seitz for the film *"Disorder and Early Torment,"* Jugendfilm, 1977.

better than her brother Snapper; she often plays the teacher to Snapper's student and instructs him in the names of birds and diseases. If he gets things wrong, she makes him stand in the corner or she hits him. She is described as frail and birdlike. She is concerned with her appearance and does not like the way she looks. Her father teases her about her asymmetrical ears, which she tries to keep covered with her hair.

Ingrid Cornelius

Ingrid is the Professor's 18-year-old daughter. She is a student preparing for exams for a certificate that she will never use. She is manipulative "because she knows how to wind masters, and even headmasters, round her finger," and deceptive. She likes to make harassing phone calls and tell loud, obnoxious stories with her brother while riding the bus.

Mother Cornelius

Mother Cornelius has been "broken and worn" by her housekeeping chores, but still maintains her control over the daily routines of the house. She agonizes over the mundane things in their lives: the price of eggs and the devaluation of the currency, but from a practical rather than a philosophic standpoint. She attends to Snapper, especially trying to calm his tantrums.

Snapper Cornelius

Snapper is the Professor's four-year-old son and Ellie's brother, who often tries to make himself look older and more masculine. He throws angry fits in order to get attention from his mother and Nursy. He worries about his moral imperfections and believes that he will go to "the bad place."

Max Hergesell

Max Hergesell is a friend of Bert and Ingrid's who is invited to the party. He is a student of engineering, a profession that the Professor regards highly. He has a nasal twang in his voice, a dark complexion, and no beard. He comes to the party wearing ill-fitting shoes, which gains him sympathy from the Professor. After he dances with Ellie and she becomes disappointed that he is not her brother, he goes to her room in an effort to calm her crying. His words, though, are meant as much to impress the Professor as they are to soothe the crying little girl.

Ivan Herzl

Ivan Herzl, also called Wanja, is acting in a production of *Don Carlos* at the Stadttheatre. He comes to the party wearing make-up, including rouge. The Professor believes that Herzl's appearance and actions "ring false" and that Ivan is aware of this. He is a revolutionary artist and a proponent of the modern arts.

Cecelia Hinterhofer

Cecelia Hinterhofer and her older sister have fallen upon hard times and have had to take on the role of servants for the Cornelius family. They play games with the children but otherwise are only seen on the edges of the story. They take abuse from Xaver over their fall from middle-class status.

Moeller

Moeller is a party guest who plays the guitar and sings several popular songs. He is a bank clerk, and the Professor believes that he is very good at his work.

Nursy

Nursy is a sleek-haired, owl-eyed servant who tends to the young children. Also called Blue-faced Ann, she has a dignified look but is worried that everyone is talking about her new set of teeth. She teaches the children nursery rhymes and songs.

Fraulein Plaichinger

Fraulein Plaichinger is a blonde, plump, snub-nosed party guest who dances with Max, to Ellie's great disappointment.

Wanja

See Ivan Herzl

Herr Zuber

Herr Zuber is Ingrid's golfing partner and a guest at the party. He works in his uncle's brewery. The Professor asks him if anything can be done about the watery beer.

Themes

Degeneration of Society

Several prominent themes run though Mann's writing. One is the theme of the degeneration of society and its impact on the people in the society. From his first major work, *Buddenbrooks* (1901), to his last completed work, *Felix Krull* (1954), Mann lived in and wrote about a society that was undergoing major changes. At the beginning of the twentieth century, the effects of the Industrial Revolution were still being felt all across Europe. People were displaced because of the increasing centralization of industry. Workers were losing their individual identity as industrial centers grew larger and more impersonal. Small family businesses and occupations were lost. Human beings were being turned into parts of a greater machine.

In "Disorder and Early Sorrow," the degeneration of society was brought about by the Great War (World War I). Once again, the war displaced people; businesses, towns, and communities were destroyed and abandoned, leaving the people to collect in larger cities to compete for the meager support they could find there. The people were stripped of individuality and thrust into a chaotic society not of their own making, and not to their liking. The Cornelius family is representative of that situation. The Professor has maintained his position as a university history teacher, but his salary, though very high, is consumed by rampant inflation. Food prices and availability are a daily concern for the family. The mother must make special trips to buy eggs before the money loses its value. Others in the family use false names to secure more eggs than the rationing legally allows. These routines, as Mann includes them in this tale, are representative of the broader issues common to Germany at the time.

Art and Artists in Society

A second thematic consideration in Mann's fiction is the role of art and the artist in society. As the story unfolds, Professor Cornelius expresses his disapproval of many of contemporary art forms and society's attitudes towards them. He takes issue with the way Herzl comes to the party wearing make-up. The Professor also takes offense at Herzl's interactions with "the little folk," when Herzl rolls his eyes up and puts his hand over his mouth and blesses them when he first meets the children. The Professor believes "he is so addicted to theatrical methods of making an impression and getting an affect that both words and behaviors ring frightfully false." As with Mann's representation of society by one small family, here too he represents his concerns about the artist in one character. Mann's primary concern is that art and the artist have become too self-indulgent to be taken seriously. The party guests are preoccupied with posturing and looks. He looked at this theme in many other works, most notably in *Tonio Kroger.*

Past versus the Present

The Professor's infatuation with history establishes another of Mann's themes, the conflict between the past and the present. The Professor says on several occasions that he believes that only the past is worthwhile; the present is not as important. He believes that the past is stable and the present is unstable because it is constantly changing, and he dislikes instability.

Search for Self-Identity

Yet another theme that is found in this story is the search for self-identity. Most of the characters in the tale take on false identities or desire to be someone other than who they are. The Professor struggles throughout the story with his loss of prestige due to the country's economic downturn and with the loss of Ellie's affection as she becomes interested in people other than her parents. As a result, he searches for a way to identify himself. Bert tries to look and behave like Xaver; Ingrid and her brother both adopt false identities on the bus and during their telephone pranks. Even Ellie wants to be Max's sister.

Style

Point of View and Setting

In "Disorder and Early Sorrow," the story is narrated in a limited third-person point of view, in which the events are seen from the vantage point of Professor Cornelius. Because it is a limited point of view, the narration does not relate the unobservable

thoughts of the other characters. The Professor is not telling the story, but the narrator does recount what the Professor thinks about the events going on around him. The use of limited third-person narration allows the author to reveal insights into activities only from the Professor's perspective.

Setting

"Disorder and Early Sorrow" is set in Munich, Germany, in the middle 1920s, after Germany lost World War I and the country was suffering from the chaos and economic insecurity that would soon give rise to the Nazi party. The action takes place specifically in the home of the Cornelius family, which was once securely upper-middle class. Though the Cornelius's still have servants and modern conveniences like a telephone, their existence is more of a struggle than it used to be. The Professor's wife worries about the price of eggs rising during the day, and it is clear that both parents are weary of the instability of the future. Ingrid and Bert, in contrast, have come of age during this hardship and are much more comfortable with the uncertainty of things. They are willing to accept the class divisions between themselves and their working-class friends; they think of obtaining more eggs than their ration allows as a game, and they are less likely than their parents to judge their friends by what they wear or how they look. The war has broken down the former rules of conduct, particularly as they relate to art and the theater (both once considered the realm of the morally corrupt or the unrespectable), and Professor Cornelius finds the resultant relaxing of mores and decorum (in public especially) disconcerting, hence his tendency to want to stay in his study or take a walk by himself.

Symbolism

Symbolism is the literary technique by which an author uses an item, issue, or situation in a story to represent something quite different. In this story, the Professor's bifocals are symbolic of his dualistic view of the world about him. He sees the past as "true" and the present as "repugnant." They also represent his twofold life, as a member of the family and as one who withdraws from the family into his study. Additionally these symbolize his twofold manner of regarding his children. He idolizes Ellie but has little regard for Bert. In the final scene, Ellie's eyes are swollen from weeping. She wants Max to be her brother but cannot see clearly. Symbolically, her tear-filled, swollen eyes represent her inability to see the impossibility of her wishes. Situations can also be symbolic. The unsettled nature of the afternoon's preparations for the party is symbolic of the unsettled nature of the society in the country now that the war is over. Contained within both are economic concerns, worry about food, and social problems. The interaction between the party guests and the household is symbolic of the interaction of various facets of society.

Style

Mann's style is understated and detached. These characteristics are readily seen in "Disorder and Early Sorrow." Throughout the tale, Mann never raises his voice to get the reader's attention. While some may find this detachment too inactive, it is this very quality that has attracted many to his writings. An example of Mann's detached style is the calm and collected tone of the final scene. While another writer might spend more time on the overt emotional aspects of the scene, Mann focuses on the Professor's quiet demeanor, the sleeping Snapper, the withdrawn Hinterhofer sisters, and Max's calming interaction with the crying Ellie, all of which contribute to this reserved atmosphere.

Throughout the story, events and situations that might warrant more intense scrutiny are quietly reviewed and discussed. The rampant inflation, the deteriorating house, the rationing of food are all critical events, but Mann presents them in understated matter-of-fact ways. The reader learns about them by accident, not through the direct comment of any of the characters. In this way, Mann avoids being didactic–too moralizing—in his fiction. He leaves that to the Professor in his history lectures.

Irony

Irony is a technique that lets a writer or character say or do one thing, while believing something quite different. The Professor, who likes the predictability of history, is a deep thinker and an intellectual, but is unable to see that the daily problems and situations facing his family are similar to those in the lectures he is preparing. The irony is in this is his failure to make the connections between the events of the sixteenth and seventeenth centuries and those of his own time.

Historical Context

Germany of the Post War Period

"Disorder and Early Sorrow" was first published in 1925, midway between the end of World War I and the beginning of the Great Depression. This was a time of high hopes and expectations for better life to come in both Europe and the United States, especially for those who had suffered the incredible ravages of the war. But there were still many reminders of the war throughout Europe, and in Germany in particular. The physical devastation of many buildings, the social dislocation of refugees fleeing from war zones, and the economic upheaval that resulted from these disruptions all combined to create a very unstable condition in Germany. Monetary inflation was rampant; eventually money was worth only as much as the paper it was printed on. It was a combination of these circumstances, plus Mann's lingering misgivings about the justification for the beginning of the war in the first place, that contributed to his state of mind. In this situation, he wrote "Disorder and Early Sorrow."

Mann had not expected the war. Writing to his brother Heinrich on July 30, 1914, he said, "one must be ashamed not to have considered this possible, and not to have seen that the catastrophe had to come." Men on both sides of the conflict eagerly took up arms to fight in the war, assuming that it would be brief and victory would be easy and sweet. Mann was depressed over the fact that he did not qualify for wartime service. Within months, however, with both sides bogged down in the trenches and suffering massive casualties inflicted by new technologies, including poison gas and more effective guns, bayonets, and cannons, it became clear that the ramifications of the Great War would be severe.

The shock of the German surrender in 1918 had a negative effect on Mann and his fellow countrymen. Like others, his financial status suffered and he was baffled by the change in the leadership from an imperial government to a Western-style democracy. Henry Hatfield remarked that "to a large extent his development seems to have been determined by political factors. The salutary shock of the German defeat of 1918 . . . had (its) effect" on Mann.

"Disorder and Early Sorrow" was written during the time he was also working on *The Magic Mountain,* even though the novel was published a year before the short story. As Leser says, it is a story "that contains postwar autobiographical references, such as the home, the atmosphere, the language and the characters themselves." Bolkosky notes that, "The war had brought Germans impoverishment, austerity, debt, a collection of revolutions and Putsch, unbelievable inflation, malaise, cynicism, imbalance, loss of values, and a

Compare & Contrast

- **1924:** To curb inflation, Germany issues a new Reichmark. Each new Reichmark is worth one billion of the old marks, which are withdrawn from circulation.

  1997: Germany of the 1990s has one of the strongest economic systems in the Western world. Even after absorbing the former country of East Germany, it is a leader among all European nations. But this has not come without some difficulties. The industrial output of the eastern parts of the country was far below that of the western section.

- **1925:** Adolf Hitler publishes the first volume of *Mein Kampf,* which he dictates to Rudolph Hess while he is in prison. In it, he outlines his ideas for social reform, commenting that "The great masses of the people . . . will more easily fall victims to a great lie than to a small one."

  1998: Nazi hate groups, in both Germany and the United States, come under attack from the Jewish Anti-Defamation League for their Internet Web sites devoted to Holocaust-denial propaganda.

- **1920s:** Cabaret theater is popular entertainment in the big cities of Germany, especially Berlin. Young people are attracted by the relaxed moral atmosphere of the 1920s, and nightclub stage shows often push the boundaries of decorum and obscenity.

  1998: A new version of the stage play *The Diary of Anne Frank* opens on Broadway, coming under fire for its revisionist interpretation of *The Diary of Anne Frank,* the story of a teenager's life in hiding from the Nazis during World War II. Cynthia Ozick, a noted Jewish critic and writer, objects to the optimism and universality of the production.

rejection of history. Both the nation and families were wracked by generational conflict and rebellion." These kinds of situations find their way into "Disorder and Early Sorrow" in varying degrees. It has been noted that one of Mann's constant themes, the degeneration of society, is found in this story. The price of eggs goes up daily as the value of money goes down. The Professor's wife must "dash into town on her bicycle, to turn into provisions a sum of money she has in hand, which she dares not keep lest it lose all value."

The effects of the war had an impact on all aspects of German life. The Weimar Republic, despite its heroic efforts, was unable to control the staggering inflation rate, and as a result there was increasing discontent among the people. Political undercurrents, including the rise of Nazism, were threatening the stability of law and order in the country. This culminated in the 1923 Beer Hall Putsch, staged by Adolf Hitler, in Munich, Mann's home town and the setting of the story. Hitler seizes control of the city government as the German mark falls to one trillion to the dollar; he is eventually arrested and sentenced to jail, where he outlines his political manifesto in *Mein Kampf.*

Despite the dramatic nature of these socioeconomic issues, Mann presented them in this story with understated style and tone and lightness of language. According to Henry Hatfield, "the ideological element is kept tactfully in the background." His people are "good and evil, perceptive and blind; extraordinarily real" according to Hatfield. In his way, Mann's contemporary audience saw themselves in his writings and his later audiences saw the society in which Mann lived and wrote.

Critical Overview

"Disorder and Early Sorrow" is often overlooked in the discussions of Mann's literary output. After its first publication in 1925, it was reissued in 1934 with ''Marion the Magician'' and then in 1936 in the collection *Stories of Three Decades.* It has been included in several short story anthologies, including *The Norton Anthology of Short Fiction* (1977) and *The Norton Introduction to Literature: Fiction* (1973). It has received limited attention from reviewers, but perhaps its most impressive appraisal came from Mann himself. On the occasion of his fiftieth birthday, his publisher asked for a special piece to be included in a commemorative collection. He submitted ''Disorder and Early Sorrow.'' He remarked at the time that it is ''a story which I like so much that I am tempted to count it among my very best.'' This praise is noteworthy since Mann was a very severe critic of his own work. About his *The Magic Mountain,* generally highly regarded among critics, he said that it was ''a triumph of stubbornness, even if nothing more.''

Noted critic Malcolm Cowley remarked that in ''Disorder and Early Sorrow,'' ''all the hysteria of the German inflation is distilled into the tears of a six-year-old girl.'' Agnes E. Meyer, recognizing the story as what Mann once called ''little finger-exercises,'' regards the work as something that allowed the author to clear his head before he moved on to write a longer novel, and calls the story a tale of ''impeccable beauty.'' Franklin E. Court summarized the symbolism of the title in an essay for *Studies in Short Fiction:* The disorder of the world is manifest in the workings of the Cornelius family, and ''the revelers . . . seem to have come to terms with the 'disorder'—they ignore it or find happiness in spite of it. Ellie's 'early sorrow' is destined to intensify as long as she believes so firmly in 'swan knights' and 'fairy princes' like Hergesell.''

Critical opinion on Mann's writing as a whole has been consistently favorable. Though some critics have suggested that his stories suffer from pretentiousness and that his characters are cold and distant, most praise him for the depth of his vision and the vastness of his intellect. He has been called a master of style, and his works, through their realism and symbolism, have appealed to a wide audience.

Criticism

Carl Mowery

Mowery has a doctorate in rhetoric/composition and literature from Southern Illinois Universi- ty. *He has taught at SIU and Murray State University. In the following essay he examines the theme of the search for personal identity in ''Disorder and Early Sorrow.''*

During the tumultuous years following World War I, most of the nations of Europe struggled to rebuild the homes, businesses, and towns destroyed by the fighting. Individuals also struggled to rebuild their personal lives and identities. In Germany much of this effort found an outlet in newly formed political parties, which offered the defeated people promises of hope and new opportunities. But for many, daily survival was their only concern. The search for personal identity amid the ruins of war is one of the themes of Thomas Mann's story ''Disorder and Early Sorrow.'' In it, the Cornelius family strives to maintain its middle-class status in the midst of a deteriorating social structure, while at the same time dealing with questions of individual identity.

Professor Abel Cornelius struggles the most with his self-image. He has been a respected college history professor. But now his position is less valued because of the instability of a society that has more dire issues to worry about than education. ''The Professor shaved his pointed beard and goes smooth faced. The pointed beard had become impossible—even professors must make some concession to the changing times,'' Mann wrote in an example that illustrates the necessity for people to keep up with the times. The concessions are deeper than having to shave every morning. His beard was once ''the symbol of his academic individuality,'' but now it is gone, and his position at the university has been diminished, according to critic Franklin E. Court. His professorship had been awarded because he had ''written a valuable work on'' the Counter-Reformation. But his stature is dwindling because he has not written equally worthy papers recently. His cigar burns down, just as his status and career symbolically burn down.

In the face of his decreasing status, the professor tries to maintain his academic identity. He continues to retreat to his den to prepare class lectures on old topics. In an act of meditation on his past academic glory, ''He savors his sentences; keeps on polishing them while he puts back the books he has been using.'' He takes long walks by the river, during which he ruminates on ''scientific preoccupations,'' especially as they relate to his

What Do I Read Next?

- *A Man and his Dog* (1919) by Mann. This is an autobiographical story about life in Munich. This story, a "depiction of idyllic domesticity," forms a kind of triptych with "Disorder and Early Sorrow" and "Song of the Child," according to Henry Hatfield.

- *Tonio Kroger* by Mann (1925). This is one of Mann's best known short stories. It is about the development of a young artist; many critics believe it is Mann's personal statement about art and artists.

- *Mein Kampf,* 1925-27, by Adolf Hitler. This two-volume work was the basis for Hitler's rise to power. Written while he was in prison, it formulates economic and social programs that he believed would bring the country back from disgrace at the end of World War I. This work is instructive from a rhetorical standpoint, showing how he was able to captivate his audience and to lead them into thinking the way he did. It is useful as an historical document, coming out of the same time period as "Disorder and Early Sorrow," and showing some of the same socioeconomic difficulties that Mann addressed in his writing.

- *Metamorphosis* by Franz Kafka (1915). This tale is often included in reading lists because of its rather unusual subject: an office worker wakes up one morning to find that he has turned into a large cockroach. However, it is more a tale of interpersonal abuse, intolerance, and isolation.

- *The Berlin Stories* (1946) by Christopher Isherwood, a compilation that explores the decadence of 1930s Berlin through the eyes of a young narrator, just as the Nazi party is gaining political power in Germany.

---

historical specialty. He "communes with himself." But just as he "puts back the books," he is symbolically put back on the shelf while the river moves on.

Despite these ironic withdrawals to the den, which separate him from his family and the difficulties of daily life, he wants to be a good father to his children. He wants to be seen as an important person in the life of the household. He dotes on Ellie, cuddling her in his lap and sitting by her side as she cries herself to sleep. But he has misgivings about the attention he lavishes on her, believing that "something (is) not perfectly right and good in his love." He draws himself up by thinking that the questions he has just asked himself are merely scientific in nature. These thoughts reinforce his combined needs to be the professor and good father without fault or bad judgment.

On other occasions he is a critic, raising another of Mann's major themes: the role of art and the artist in society. He makes remarks and judgments about the behaviors of the party guests "that ring frightfully false" and about their occupations as "artist(s) of the modern school." He is offended by their "mad modern dances." He condemns Herzl for wearing rouge. But then, in contrast, he flatters him by calling him a "Court actor" as an "atonement for his previous hard thoughts about the rouge." After hearing Moeller sing several songs, in a moment of over reaction he "applauds with ostentation. It warms his heart and does him good, this outcropping of artistic, historic, and cultural elements all amongst the shimmying." In this one moment he has let down his critical guard and has combined the arts that he dislikes with disciplines he admires, revealing an ambivalence in his attitude.

Bert is not immune from his barbed judgments. "And here is my poor Bert, who knows nothing and can do nothing and thinks of nothing except playing the clown, without even talent for that!" Even his positive remarks about Bert are tinged with sarcasm and pessimism. Comparing Bert to Moeller, the Professor says that "his dancing and table-waiting are due to mere boyish folly and the distraught times.'' He denies his son the right to choose his own career.

In spite of his antipathy to his children's friends, he still feels attracted to the party and the guests. His carefully rehearsed first entry stands in ironic contrast to his disdain for actors and their role playing. He acts out the role of gracious host, and later recreates and adds to it by giving the party guests a package of cigarettes. After putting the package on the mantel with a flourish and a smile, he looks around the room to see if anyone noticed. He is looking for recognition, just as an actor does at the end of a drama.

As Ellie dances with Max, the professor "feels an involuntary twinge." At first this is jealousy, but it also becomes a desire to participate in the party activities. The Professor is not averse to fun and games, often playing "four gentlemen taking a walk" with Ellie and the kitchen staff. But as Ellie and Max dance, he becomes more agitated and finally leaves the house for a brief walk in the evening air.

He escapes into illusion at the end of the story, according to Bolkosky. And because of this, the Professor never really finds himself. After Ellie goes to sleep in her crib, he sits and thinks that things in the morning will return to the way they used to be. Hergesell has noted that "she's beginning young," echoing an earlier remark by blue-faced Ann: "It's pretty young for the female instincts to be showing up." The comment caused the Professor to snap back at Ann, hiding his agony at the realization that despite Ellie's youth she was growing up. Yet, in his mind, he returns to the past and to his past self, the history professor who reveres history and things dead. He wants Ellie to return to his vision of the past. But this act of self-deception conceals the reality that Ellie will not forget and things will not return to the way they were.

The Professor is not the only one searching for a personal identity. Both Bert and Ingrid struggle continually to find their identity, much of which is focused on mimicking and mocking others. They assume phony *personae* on the bus and tell tall tales about nonexistent lives, using exotic accents. They call dignitaries and make up false identities while they harass the unsuspecting listeners.

Bert seems most insecure in his attempts to find himself. He struggles with his school work but "intends to get done with school somehow." Then he plans to "fling himself into the arms of life. He

will be a dancer or a cabaret actor.'' His goals for his future are not well planned. As Court notes, "Bert is forced to mimic others." He adopts the mannerisms and dress of Xaver, wearing his "hair very long on top, with a cursory parting in the middle," just as Xaver does. When he is seen from behind while leaving the house, "Dr. Cornelius from his bedroom window cannot, for the life of him, tell whether he is looking at his son or his servant." Bert even tries to emulate Xaver by smoking, but comes up short because he "has not the means to compete with Xaver, who smokes as many as thirty a day." In his attempts to be like Xaver, Bert is not up to the task.

Ingrid has her own difficulties with self-identity. She will soon take an exam for a certificate that she does not plan to use. In the process, she winds the "masters, even the headmaster, round her finger." She becomes a kind of vamp who can manipulate others and who has "a marked and irresistible talent for burlesque." In her manipulation of the masters, she has lost the sense of the difference between her real life and the stage life to which she aspires. By failing to make these distinctions, as well as by her phone and bus behaviors, she is acting even as she lives. Her sense of personal identity has been lost in the false characters she has created for herself.

Even Ellie is not content with her identity. She fusses at her appearance, aggravated by her father's constant reminders about her ears. Perhaps the most telling incident is her reaction to the dance with Max. Afterwards, she is not content with being the daughter of the Professor; in her youthful naivete, she has defined herself in terms of being the sister to Max.

The guests at the evening party also seem to be on a quest for their own personal identities. Some of them come wearing make-up. These artists "find their identity in artifice, in a self-created world," according to Court. The guests, however, do not hide behind the conventions of the older generations. They talk to each other "offensively to an older ear; of social forms, of hospitable warmth, there is no faintest trace. They call each other by their first names." These deviations amuse and irritate the Professor because they violate his sense of order. To the guests, these behaviors establish themselves as equals among their own age groups. The theme of disorder and disruption is also found in the identity searches of the party guests. As Bolkosky says, Mann "captures not only the personal disorder and sorrow of a family . . . but . . . the confusion of generations.''

Xaver stands out among the characters in this tale because of his individuality, self-assurance, and personal strengths. He is unmoved by others and makes no attempts to assume any other identity. He leads a ''free and untrammeled existence,'' satisfied with himself as he is. He ''is not a puppet,'' according to Court. He has ''quite distinct traits of character of his own,'' which his employers have conceded. He lives at his own pace, being willing to get out of bed at any time of the night for his own reasons, but ''to get up before eight in the morning, he cannot do it'' when schedules require it. He has demonstrated in this way that he will work for the Cornelius family, but he will not become one of them. He will ''not be trained to the performance of the daily round.'' He does not obey the family rules; ''he will not jump over the stick'' as though he were a trained dog.

Xaver is the object of Bert's attentions and the Professor's quiet praise, despite being called ''a thorough-paced good-for-nothing and a windbag'' because he speaks his mind and is a ''follower of the revolution, Bolshevist sympathizer.'' The Professor also calls him the ''minute man'' because he responds to crises quickly and without hesitation. He gets gratification from the egg-buying enterprise as he dons ''civilian garb and attends his young master and mistress.'' They all ''delight in misleading and mystifying their fellow-men.'' But he does not make this experience the major focus of his life. It serves him as a diversion, not as way of living.

The search for individual identity is an experience shared by characters in fictional tales and by real people. But the manner and success of this journey depends on the circumstances that accompany the individuals, as well as the depth and strength of character of the individual doing the seeking. In this story the two most insecure people, the Professor and his son, Bert, have the most difficulty in finding themselves. The Professor hides in the well-known past, and Bert hides in an unknown future. But hiding does not complete their searches. At the end of the tale both are still looking for themselves. They still have someone to find.

Source: Carl Mowery, for *Short Stories for Students,* Gale, 1998.

Sidney Bolkosky

In the following essay, Bolkosky discusses ''Disorder and Early Sorrow'' as not only the story of a

> "Xaver stands out among the characters in this tale because of his individuality, self-assurance, and personal strengths."

family, but also as an illustration of ''national disorder and sorrow, the confusion of generations.''

. . . . ''Disorder and Early Sorrow'' is a ''realistic'' description of a day in the life of an upper middle-class family in the Munich of 1924. It has, however, deeper significance, suggesting an analysis of the time more pointed than any of Mann's previous aesthetic undertakings. He seems almost off his guard, somehow at ease, with a keen if relaxed eye for historical results. Written in 1925 at and about a time when the turbulent circumstances of people's lives were indisputably attributable to such a monumental political event as World War I, the narrative makes a political statement and embodies Mann's evolving feelings about life in the Weimar Republic and the future of Germany.

The war had brought Germans impoverishment, austerity, debt, a collection of revolutions and *Putsch,* unbelievable inflation, malaise, cynicism, imbalance, loss of values, and a rejection of history. Both the nation and families were wracked by generational conflict and rebellion. Instead of *Kultur,* ''dedication to a basic order of things and its lasting values,'' there was disorder, which Mann addressed here, from its midst, in every conceivable aspect. In ''Disorder and Early Sorrow'' he satirized what one critic has dubbed his ''seismographic neutrality'' through a poignant self-accusation, and he expressed moral, historical, social, and political opinions—unequivocally.

Abel Cornelius, the head of the family in ''Disorder and Early Sorrow,'' is a university professor. He and his wife are referred to by their children as the ''Old Folk''; the grandparents, ''The Ancients,'' are never seen. The two older children, teenagers Bert and Ingrid, are the ''Big Folk''; and the younger ones, Ellie and Snapper, ages five and six, the ''Little Folk.'' The household includes servants, the most important of whom is Xaver Kleinsgutl, a

> Mann captures not only the personal disorder and sorrow of a family and a child, but the national disorder and sorrow, the confusion of generations."

proletarian contemporary of the Big Folk. The day is a special one because of an informal party the Big Folk are giving for their friends. During the party Ellie becomes enchanted by a young man, Max Hergesell, who playfully dances with her. She is heartbroken when she must leave the party with her brother and go to bed; she weeps bitterly as she watches Max dance with a plump, Germanic girl, and cries out that she wishes he were her brother. Professor Cornelius, profoundly, ineffably attached to his daughter, is helpless and anguished. Xaver fetches Max who appears like a fairy-tale prince, dashingly competent, to soothe Ellie, who, with her father, is astonished at his heroic appearance and magnanimity. She drifts off to sleep peacefully, Cornelius thanks Hergesell gratefully yet with some inexplicable resentment, and the story concludes with the professor pondering the prospect of a normal tomorrow filled with games.

The apparent straightforwardness of the novella is, of course, deceptive. Mann captures not only the personal disorder and sorrow of a family and a child, but the national disorder and sorrow, the confusion of generations. There are more or less standard types: Xaver, the "child of his time," Max, the "new man," Cornelius, the representative of older traditions and institutions, Ellie and Snapper, the new life born at around the same time as the Weimar Republic and, like it, troubled, disturbing, and problematic. But Mann's genius for humanizing stereotypes is perhaps more evident here than in the major works. Through deft and subtle descriptions he begins to express a sociopolitical stand regarding Germany's future—this before the anti-Fascist statement in "Mario," before the clear and present danger of Nazism, before his open, if ambiguous, defenses of the Republic. It is a position in many ways consistent with his earlier attitudes, but more concrete, overtly critical of both the new and

the old choices. It is a political statement because any consideration of German society after World War I was forced to deal with politics; the economy, the social structure, the educational institutions, as well as ideologies were all directly traceable to political experience. In a sense, then, "Disorder and Early Sorrow" marks a significant turning point in Mann's career because it bridges his earlier and later work. More than that, it discloses continuity along with discontinuity, consistency along with contradiction, commitment and engagement along with apparent aloofness and detachment.

"Disorder and Early Sorrow" presents a surprisingly detailed account of daily life in the Weimar Republic. The economic plight of Germans during the inflation reveals itself in the first sentence as the Cornelius family dines on croquettes made not of meat but of turnip greens and a trifle made from "those dessert powders we use nowadays": unnatural food suitable for unnatural times. Frau Cornelius is no more than a shadow in the story, but Mann relates simply yet fully that the "fantastic difficulties of the housekeeping have broken and worn her" to whom "everything seems upside down." She is frantic over the need to buy the rationed, one-thousand mark eggs as soon as possible before the price rises. The task rests with the Big Folk and Xaver—the resourceful "moujik."

For this egg escapade the Big Folk must use assumed names in order to exceed the family egg quota. Xaver dons "civilian clothing" to assist, and dressed in outgrown clothes similar to those of his master's son, he is virtually indistinguishable from Bert. Indeed, Cornelius has intimations that this fellow of the lower classes is somehow superior to his own son. The younger children add to the confusion by addressing their father by his first name, Abel, and the disturbing, painfully descriptive initial paragraphs become explicitly sarcastic in the mocking conduct of Ingrid as she reminds Abel of the forthcoming party, calling him "Darling old thing." The unnatural, strained, and comic tone of the scene is heightened by the contrast between the children and Abel who, despite the discontinuity of life, still "presides in proper middle class style."

We are immediately aware of a generational conflict and that children lack respect for parents and ghostly grandparents. They lack more; their goals either are not defined or flaunt traditional aspirations. Eighteen-year-old Ingrid, on the eve of her exams, having ingratiated herself with teachers and headmasters through guile and deviousness, leans toward stage burlesque. Seventeen-year-old Bert plans to finish school ''somehow, anyhow, and fling himself into the arms of life,'' perhaps as a dancer or a waiter. Seeking diversion in Weimar's notorious underground, they are shocking and publicly irreverent toward the older generation and its values. Apparently addicted to the telephone, they call anyone—government officials, operatic celebrities, Church authorities, any representative of the old establishment—to play tricks; Mann labels these verbal vandals ''wanton and impish.'' From the perspective of the father's generation, their lives are aimless, their goals unanchored and ephemeral.

In the center of the activity, a bit confused and frazzled by the commotion, a bit absent-minded, is Professor Abel Cornelius. His name suits him: ''Cornelius'' evokes a portrait of a classical and patriotic outlook and ''Abel,'' the obedient servant of authority, formal, precise and faithful—but doomed. He is the ''*geistiger Mensch*,'' akin in some respects to Aschenbach, but more to Mann himself. As historian, he is faithful to the past, obsessed with time, watching clocks and calendars, losing track of the days, trying to hold time back and to become history. He is old Germany: the historian as state bureaucrat, pedantic civil servant, teacher and authority figure who, before World War I, was conformist, unquestioning, and, most importantly, apolitical. Because of his love for the past, for the ''timeless,'' the ''eternal,'' and ''infinity,'' he hates the revolution. But as an apolitical man by scholarly principle and commitment, he does not confront it actively. Abel has made compromises: he has shaved his pointed beard (probably reminiscent of the Kaiser), for example, and silently tolerated the laziness and near-insolence of the servants and children.

When the present confronts him, Cornelius ''withdraws to his study.'' Mann does not have him ''go,'' ''retire,'' or ''move,'' but ''withdraw'' (*Zuruckziehen*), a word that increasingly implies retreat. And there he reads. Is reading perhaps an escape from disorder? A way to combat it? Words seem to control past events in the historian's ''art,'' to order them clearly and to define and explain rationally the flow of history. Unchanging words provide unchanging significance and meaning for him, while perfectly ordered syntax provides perfectly ordered history; both disappear in the world of the party. What attracts the historian, Abel thinks, is the certainty and order of the past—certain, even immortal, because it is dead ''and death is the root

of all godliness and abiding significance.'' Such pious Hegelian ruminations sound not profound, but foolish, irrelevant, almost quaint in the historical context of this story. Dutiful Abel withdraws to his inner sanctum and escapes the living present and its hostile insecurities by reading of ''genuine history,'' the dead past. The washbasin, broken for two years, remains unfixed, the quest for eggs not his worry, the myriad of minor and major crises remote from him. And the language of the young remains unintelligible to him, alienating him from his children, from the party, from real life and action.

Professor Cornelius is simultaneously a realistic figure and a rich literary symbol of a way of life that was fast fading from existence in 1924. He encapsulates more than the ''preoccupation with death of a typical bourgeois of the pre-war period'' in Lukacs' limiting description of him. Life in his study is the life of the mind, replete with words separated from action and reality. He reads backwards in time: first of England in the seventeenth century, the origin of the English public debt; then of Spain's enormous debt at the close of the sixteenth century. Here is food for a lecture comparing the prosperity of England despite its debt with the catastrophic failure of Spain under similar circumstances. A wealth of material rests in the English and French texts from which the professor will form an ethical and psychological analysis. All this provides a means of discussing his specialty, Philip II of Spain and the Counter-Reformation. (Cornelius has already written a monograph on the subject.) In his self-contained refuge, Abel makes no connection whatsoever between these historical crises and that of Germany in 1924, between the end of Spain's Empire and the collapse of Germany's in wars against England. His failure to do so is breathtaking in its blindness. This boundary between mind and matter, this divorce from reality testifies to a fatal flaw in those of Abel's class, profession, and ethos. And Mann does not justify it, sympathize with it, or pity it. We feel the pathos of Abel's situation, but no sympathy for his separation; no meditative, artistic excuses for disengagement insinuate themselves.

Abel's scholarly specialty conveys his own essence, symbolizes his most hidden nature. He has written on Philip II, son of Emperor Charles V, defender of the Church against the revolutions of Protestantism. With his ''conservative instinct'' Abel identifies with Philip to some extent, much as Mann had earlier identified with Frederick the Great, whom he had characterized as waging hopeless wars to test himself. To Abel, Philip is a tragic figure engaged in a "practically hopeless struggle . . . against the whole trend of history." With idealistic aplomb and abstraction he conceives Philip's fight to have been against the "Germanic revolution," never consciously acknowledging his own opposition, as futile as Philip's, to another Germanic revolution. Even as he ponders the dramatic impact of the well-formed sentences he writes for tomorrow's lecture on "black-clad Philip," past and present "mingle with a confused consciousness." His thoughts circle back to the party—from Philip to the party—and he dozes, escaping.

Abel's historical interpretation of his hero illuminates his own character. Philip seems to him to cling gallantly, if tragically, to his ideal of Right as it is rigidly defined by the past. He represents order, obedience, traditional standards, duty and authority: all the qualities of life that Abel honors and embraces. Historically, however, Philip II was perhaps the man most directly responsible for the decline of Spain, having assumed the throne at the apogee of its imperial glory and leaving it with only shadows of greatness glimpsed in subsequent artistic and intellectual flowering. One historian describes him as "narrow, despotic and cruel." And Mann's description of Frederick's temperament, "as vicious as it is melancholy," may be applied to Philip. Determined at all costs to force strict conformity, Philip instituted the worst aspects of the Spanish Inquisition and initiated the war for suppression of the revolt in the Netherlands—a rebellion led by his son, Don Carlos. His portraits suggest his character: austere, black-clad, bookish, deceptively serene, and efficiently bureaucratic. Unlike Schiller in *Don Carlos,* northern historians have painted him as the secret murderer of his son, dark and foreboding. His enormous kingdom was in turmoil, disunited, almost as polyglot as the eastern Hapsburg Empire, and as divided as Germany—while he, inactive, tried to rule from his desk by written decree. His shadow hung over the generation of fathers in Weimar Germany, manifested in the image of authority created by post-World War I intellectuals and personified in historians and teachers: an unfeeling figure, the betrayer of the lost generation of sons as well as the lost empire. Abel has unwittingly assumed the qualities—all of them—of Philip. . . .

Abel faces this new world of intensified pragmatism and, like his model Philip II, cannot accept it. Whereas the aesthetic man of the *Reflections* voluntarily disengaged himself and loftily observed politics and history at a distance, isolated because he refused to take sides or abide by totalizing definitions and dogmas, Abel flees to illusion, to the past, as confused by the needs of life (Ellie) as Aschenbach was by the ecstasies he experienced when he too confronted youth and real life. In "Disorder and Early Sorrow" Mann declares that change is imminent, inescapable—declares, too, that the viability of the apolitical isolation of the phlegmatic thinker is superannuated—lamentably, perhaps, but necessarily. This testimony simultaneously reaffirms the condemnation of *Gesellschaft* or *Zivilisation* and rejects the virtue of the apolitical or disengaged man of mind. Erich Heller suggested that Mann attributed the isolation of the artist to the nature of art and that he could not yet see, in 1918, another possible basis for isolation: "the misdemeanour of society." Mann felt it, and saw it by 1925. Bourgeois society and values had been terrifyingly, depressingly transformed beyond radical and conservative labels to confusing mixtures of both, to apolitical stances by uncultured and unscrupulous new young men.

This new phenomenon, a decline of *Kultur* worse even than nineteenth century mediocrity, was not the Dionysian witch's brew that some critics have claimed prefigured Nazism in Mann's early stories. For all the discussion of the famous tension between Dionysian frenzy and bureaucratic control, it was the latter that would prove the greater threat. Historians have discerned the deadliest aspects of Nazism in its cold, technological, bureaucratic amorality: a "logical" product of a bourgeois spirit devoted to order, administration, and success that facilitated the routine execution of "civilized" terror. This other side of Nazism had its roots in the nineteenth century but found fertile soil in the Weimar Republic of 1925–1930. Who better than the dispassionate, unfeeling, and rational engineer—antithesis of irrationality and passion—to represent the new man? Despite his apolitical stance, Max is political, plastic, and practical. He is not the mystifying, artistic tyrant of "Mario," but he would certainly fall under the tyrant's spell—logically. Abel will be displaced by this Cain/Max who has no past to hinder or bind him in any way. Ronald Gray has described Mann's narrator in "Mario" as "unattached, calmly setting down the catastrophe." In "Disorder and Early Sorrow" Mann described an impending social catastrophe that involved him, and judged it. His writing reveals a political and social consciousness that predated the rise of Fascism. Bertolt Brecht would argue years later that for all the unspeakable horror, Hitler was nevertheless a comic fool. It is ironic, then, that Mann described Max Hergesell as "the fairy clown."

Source: Sidney Bolkosky, "Thomas Mann's 'Disorder and Early Sorrow': The Writer as Social Critic," in *Contemporary Literature*, Vol. 22, No. 2, Spring, 1981, pp. 218–233.

Franklin E. Court

In the following essay, Court examines deception and irony in "Disorder and Early Sorrow."

Professor Cornelius's loss of his young daughter, Ellie, and Ellie's loss of Max Hergesell, the "fairy prince" who captures her tiny heart at the "big folks'" party in Mann's "Disorder and Early Sorrow," are but the final movements in a narrative that suggests fraud and hopelessness from beginning to end. The opening paragraph, for example, quite appropriately begins with a reference to one of the most deceptive of all foods—croquettes—deceptive because the ingredients are disguised. The Corneliuses, a very "proper" middle class family, living in an illusory house outwardly appearing elegant but actually badly in need of repair, a house in which "they themselves look odd . . . with their worn and turned clothing and altered way of life," sit to eat a dinner of "croquettes made of turnip greens" followed by a trifle that is "concocted out of those dessert powders" that the reader learns really taste like something else—soap.

Here we have a small example at the outset of how Mann uses a stylistic device called "parody of externals" to create irony, a subject that John G. Root discusses in an enlightening article on Mann's style, but one which has never been successfully applied to an analysis of "Disorder and Early Sorrow." This brief study will attempt to explain how the *leitmotiv* of deception in this unusual tale is re-inforced through the description of physical externals. We will find that in each character considered, except one, outer traits complement inner peculiarities. The one exception is the servant, Xaver, who has the ironic last name of Kleinsgutl, ironic because he is without doubt the only character in the story who is "his own man."

In contrast to Xaver, the other characters are poseurs, bearing more resemblance to puppets or mannequins than to real beings. The "big folks" (Bert and Ingrid), for instance, seem to lack integrity. They are much like the telephone that plays such

> The one external feature associated with the Professor, his glasses, suggests the essential weakness in his character. They are bifocals . . . and are symbolic of his divided personality which adjusts his view according to the circumstances."

a prominent part in their lives: expressionless, capable only of audible contact, an artificial sound device. Bert, the Professor's seventeen year old son, having succumbed to Ivor Herzl's influence, "blackens the lower rim of his eyelids" and assumes the unnatural pose of a performer. Like Oscar Wilde's Dorian Gray, who is a creation of the artistic imagination of Lord Henry Wotton, Bert is Herzl's creation. From a distance, Bert is said to resemble Xaver, but there the resemblance ends; the doubles are inconsonant—Xaver is not a puppet. He toys with the idea of being engaged by a cinema director, but he is, as the Professor envisions, too much of a "good-for-nothing . . . with quite distinct traits of character of his own" ever to take the cinema dream seriously. He must be taken "as he is." Xaver does what he has the urge to do (he smokes thirty cigarettes a day, for instance); Bert, because he lacks "the means to compete with Xaver," or, for that matter, with anyone else, is forced to mimic others. Bert's deficiency manifests itself by the paternal envy his father experiences when comparing Bert's failures with the accomplishments of a number of male guests at the party. Bert's fraudulent, showy outward behavior mirrors his inner failure: "'poor Bert, who knows nothing and can do nothing . . . except playing the clown'." His external appearance parodies his hollow, self-deception.

Ingrid, the Professor's older daughter, is also a markedly deceptive character whose entire life appears to have been comprised of sham and impersonation. She is said to know how to "wind masters, and even headmasters, round her finger," and she is in school working for a certificate that she never plans to use. The performance that she and Bert put on in the bus, at the expense of the unhappy old gentleman sitting opposite them, and the delight she takes in ridiculing Max Hergesell's nasal drawl reflect a bizarre and sadistic inner quality. Both she and Bert foreshadow through their outward behavior the pose and affectation which will later distinguish the many painted figures who turn up for the party.

What the Professor observes of Herzl the actor seems to encompass the entire guest list: "'Queer,' thinks the Professor, 'You would think a man would be one thing or the other—not melancholic and use face paint at the same time. . . . But here we have a perfect illustration of the abnormality of the artist soul-form'." "The artist soul-form"—shades of Aschenbach, Cipolla, and Tonio Kröger are conjured up by the professor's comment; no doubt the painted, artificial host of guests at the party share with them the soul-form of the artist. The artist-figures who attend the party emphasize by contrast the commonplace, rather mediocre nature of the professor's entire family; the extent of their mediocrity is emphasized finally by the professor himself—who is as self-deceived as his children.

The Professor sees something abnormal in the artist's soul. Unlike the "big folks," he does nothing or wears nothing that gives one the impression that he is self-deceived. Ironically, however, the professor appears less and less attractive as the party progresses. The revelers are artist-figures living devoid of class awareness; the same cannot be said for the "big folks" and the Professor. The artists seem to find their identity in artifice, in a self-created world. They must, because the generation of the "old folks" has given them nothing with which they can identify. And whatever else these art seekers might be, they are not hypocrites. Like the "madmen" and the "immortals" in Hesse's *Steppenwolf,* whom they resemble, their strange outward behavior does not conceal inner deformities. They are surrealistic externalizations of a total acceptance of life's absurdity, and they do not take themselves seriously. The same, however, cannot be said for the "big folks" or for the Professor himself.

The one external feature associated with the Professor, his glasses, suggests the essential weakness in his character. They are bifocals with lenses "divided for reading and distance" and are symbolic of his divided personality which adjusts his view according to the circumstances. Mann explains that being a history professor, Professor Cornelius's heart belongs "to the coherent, disciplined, historic past." We are also told that inwardly the Professor dislikes the pose and artificiality of the artists and resents the party "with its power to intoxicate and estrange his darling child." Yet all of his inward resentment and opinions are hidden by an exterior far more deceitful than the rouged cheeks of Herzl the actor. The Professor laughs at the sick humor of the "big folks," not because he really wants to, but because "in these times when something funny happens people have to laugh." Although he attacks the changing times in his lectures, he, nevertheless, has shaved his beard, the symbol of his once academic individuality, and now smooth-faced—his "concession to the changing times"—he outwardly embraces the society and world view he detests. He seems to associate the "big folks'" party with the tone of the new society that he attacks in his lectures, yet his mind wanders during the very process of formulating his argument to a pleasurable anticipation of the coming festivities. And when the time does arrive, we see him polishing his glasses (it is time to readjust his perspective to suit the circumstances) and practicing "appropriate" phrases to impress the guests whom he will flatter with undue approval and unnecessary praise. The Professor is a hypocrite.

The devastating irony that Mann achieves mainly through the parody of externals in this story reaches its culmination in the characterization of the Professor. The *leitmotiv* of deception, that pervades the story, ends with the lie that appears at the end of the narrative—the lie that the professor forces himself to believe: that tomorrow the glittering Hergesell will be, for Ellie, "a pale shadow." The story, however, suggests otherwise. His prayers to heaven that Ellie will forget Hergesell and the festive world he symbolizes is the professor's final act of self-deception. She will not forget.

The title of the story is appropriate: the world out of joint, the "disordered" world, is viewed in microcosm in the lives of the Cornelius family; the revelers, at least, seem to have come to terms with the "disorder"—they ignore it or find happiness in spite of it. Ellie's "early sorrow" is destined to intensify as long as she believes so firmly in "swan knights" and "fairy princes" like Hergesell. As Hergesell uncannily seems to know, "'she's beginning young'."

Source: Franklin E. Court, ''Deception and the 'Parody of Externals' in Thomas Mann's 'Disorder and Early Sorrow','' in *Studies in Short Fiction,* Vol. XII, No. 2, Spring, 1975, pp. 186–89.

Mann, Thomas. *Stories of Three Decades,* translated by H. T. Lowe-Parker, Knopf, 1936, pp. v-ix.

Meyer, Agnes E. ''Thomas Mann's Fable for Today,'' in *The New York Times Book Review,* June 8, 1941, pp. 1, 15-16.

Sources

Bolkosky, Sidney. ''Thomas Mann's 'Disorder and Early Sorrow': The Writer as Social Critic,'' in *Contemporary Literature,* Vol. XXII, No. 2, Spring 1981, pp. 218-33.

Court, Franklin E. ''Deception and the Parody of Externals' in Thomas Mann's 'Disorder and Early Sorrow','' in *Studies in Short Fiction,* Vol. XII, No. 2, Spring 1975, pp. 186-89.

Cowley, Malcolm. ''The Last Great European: Thomas Mann,'' in his *Think Back on Us: A Contemporary Chronicle of the 1930's,* edited by Henry Dan Piper, Southern Illinois University Press, 1967, pp. 291–94.

Hatfield, Henry. *Thomas Mann,* revised edition, Knopf, 1962.

Leser, Esther H. ''New Humanism: Fading of Formal Genre Limitations,'' in *Thomas Mann's Short Fiction: An Intellectual Biography,* edited by Mitzi Brunsdale, Fairleigh Dickinson University Press, 1989, pp. 181-92.

Further Reading

Critical Essays on Thomas Mann, edited by Inta Ezergailis, G. K. Hall, 1988, 270 p.
    Reprinted essays on many of Mann's works.

Heilbut, Anthony. *Thomas Mann: Eros and Literature,* University of California Press, 1997, 638 p.
    A biography of Mann, in which the author compares Mann to other great writers, including Goethe, Melville, and Kafka.

Prater, Donald A. *Thomas Mann: A Life,* Oxford University Press, 1995, 554 p.
    A biography of Mann.

''Thomas Mann,'' in *Short Story Criticism,* Volume 5, edited by Thomas Votteler, Gale, 1990, pp. 305–60.
    Reprinted critical essays on Mann's short fiction.

The Guest

Albert Camus

1957

Perhaps the best known and most popular of Camus's short stories, "L'Hote" ("The Guest") was published in 1957 in his first and only story collection, *L'exil et le royaume* (1957; *Exile and the Kingdom*). *Exile and the Kingdom* received a mixed reception from critics. Some saw the collection as revitalizing his career and laying the groundwork for future works after the writer had gone for several years without publishing. Others found that it did not live up to expectations. Many felt that there was an unresolved tension between the stories as fiction and as explorations of philosophical ideas. Evoking numerous and sometimes contradictory interpretations, "The Guest" has endured as one of Camus's more important works, with recent critics delving more deeply into the colonial context of the story. It remains a compelling exploration of Camus's moral and philosophical themes and a powerful evocation of colonial relationships. Camus worked on the story mainly from 1952 to 1954, revising it many times, most particularly as the crisis leading to the Algerian War deepened and he wanted to avoid worsening the tensions between French and Arab Algerians with his portrayals. Some of these modifications heightened the ambiguities in the story, particularly with respect to the character and motivations of the prisoner.

"The Guest" tells of an encounter between a French Algerian schoolteacher and an Arab prisoner on the eve of the Algerian uprising. The story emphasizes many of Camus's most characteristic

themes: individual alienation, freedom, the value of human life, responsibility, the difficulty of moral choice, and the ambiguity of actions. It gains additional layers of meaning through its incisive portrait of colonial life and the psyches of colonizer and colonized alike.

Author Biography

Albert Camus was born in 1913 in Mondavi, Algeria. His father died in World War I and he was raised in poverty by his mother and grandmother. As a scholarship student he completed secondary school and planned to begin university studies before falling seriously ill at seventeen with tuberculosis, an experience which shaped his understanding of human vulnerability to disease and death. He worked in Algeria as a journalist, co-founded a theater group, and in general became part of the intellectual community in Algeria before World War II. In 1934 he joined the Communist Party, but broke with it a year or two later over the issue of Algerian nationalism. During much of World War II he was in Paris as an active member of the French resistance. He published some of his most important novels, including *L'Etranger* (1942; *The Stranger*) and *La Peste* (1947; *The Plague*) in the 1940s, when his reputation as a writer and an intellectual was at its peak. He remained in Paris after the War and worked as a reader at the publishing company Gallimard.

In 1952 his close friendship with Jean-Paul Sartre was broken when the two men disagreed over the legitimacy of communism in the face of the Soviet purges and labor camps. Camus bore the brunt of Sartre's bitter personal attacks in the public press. His refusal to back any political movement which called for violence or which restricted human freedom drew more criticism from both the Left and the Right political factions in Paris during the Algerian conflict. French government officials and Algerian nationalist leaders both looked to him for support and were frustrated by his refusal to make public endorsements of either side. To some extent, the schoolmaster's reluctance to take sides in "The Guest" may reflect some of Camus' own sense of frustration with the polarized and violent Algerian conflict.

For much of the 1950s Camus suffered writer's block, depression, and ill health. In 1956 he pub-

Albert Camus

lished *La Chute* (1956; *The Fall*) and shortly thereafter, the collection of stories *L'exil et le royaume* (1957; *Exile and the Kingdom*) from which "The Guest" is taken. That same year he won the Nobel Prize for literature.

Plot Summary

Arrival

"The Guest" is a spare tale of Daru, a French Algerian schoolmaster, who is assigned against his will to deliver an Arab prisoner to the nearest city on the eve of the Algerian uprising. Daru was born in the rural area where the schoolhouse and the attached room in which he lives are located. His students come from poor villages nearby and have been suffering from a severe drought. To aid them, Daru has been distributing government-provided food rations. The story takes place just after an unseasonable snowstorm, when classes are suspended and the schoolmaster has spent the last three days alone. Daru first notices two men in the distance, one on horseback, one on foot, approaching the steep hill on which the schoolhouse is situated.

Given the distance, the snow, and the rocky terrain, he knows it will take them a while to reach him.

When the two men are closer, Daru recognizes the horseman as Balducci, a policeman whom he knows. The other, with hands bound, being led by a rope, is marked by his clothing as an Arab. Daru brings them inside to get warm and makes tea for both. After asking Balducci's permission, he unties the prisoner's hands. Once his guests are settled, Daru asks about their destination. When Balducci indicates the schoolhouse, Daru is puzzled and asks if they are staying the night. Balducci replies that he will be leaving and that Daru is to escort the prisoner on the remainder of the journey to Tinguit, the nearest town. Daru at first thinks it is a joke, then protests that it is not his job to transport prisoners. Balducci argues that with the growing unrest, people must be willing to take on additional civic responsibilities. Moreover, he maintains that staff at his headquarters is too small already, and cannot spare him any longer.

Daru shifts the discussion to the prisoner, asking about his crime. Balducci explains that the Arab killed his cousin in some sort of dispute over grain. He had been hidden for a month by his villagers before finally being captured. His immediate transfer to Tinguit is partly owing to the fact that the villagers want to take him back. Daru is disgusted at the petty violence represented by the Arab's crime. He also asks if the Arab is against the French. Balducci doubts it, but comments that one can never be sure.

After some more tea, Balducci prepares to depart. He moves to retie the prisoner, but Daru stops him. Then, disconcerted at the schoolmaster's nonchalance in the face of a possible enemy, he asks if Daru is armed, and insists that he take a pistol, since his only other weapon is a shotgun in storage. Daru begins to argue about his assignment again. While the Arab and his violent crime repel him, he is unwilling to turn him in to the French authorities. Balducci acknowledges Daru's feelings, but reminds him that an order is an order. Daru insists he will not do it. Eventually Balducci decides that he will complete his task of delivering the prisoner to Daru and say nothing more about Daru's refusal to his superiors. Continuing to resist his role in the transfer, Daru initially refuses to sign the paper acknowledging receipt of the prisoner. Balducci cites the rules once more, and this time Daru gives in and signs. Balducci is insulted by Daru's refusals and leaves gruffly.

Night

Daru orders the prisoner to wait in the schoolroom and goes to his room for a nap. When he gets up, he is half hoping the prisoner will simply have left. Instead, he finds him where he left him. It is now evening, so Daru prepares a meal and a bed for the Arab and they converse for the first time. The Arab asks if Daru is the judge, and why he eats with him. Daru is uncomfortable in the presence of the prisoner. After they eat, they both prepare to sleep, but Daru does not sleep well. During the night, he hears the prisoner get up and leave the room; he hopes it is to make an escape. But the prisoner merely relieves himself and then returns.

Departure

Daru orders the Arab out ahead of him, but the prisoner does not move until Daru insists that he is coming, too. Daru prepares a package of food and they start off. Daru turns back once, again thinking he heard something around the building. They walk for two hours to a fork in the path. Daru gives the package of food and some money to the Arab and offers him two choices. To the east, it is a two hours' walk to the police station in Tinguit. To the south, it is a day's walk to nomadic tribes who will take him in and protect him. The Arab looks panicky and starts to respond, but Daru silences him and turns back toward the schoolhouse. The Arab doesn't move. Daru looks back once, and then again a few minutes later. The Arab still has not moved. Impatient, Daru gives a half wave and continues on his way. Some time later he turns back one more time to see what the Arab has done, and he spots him in the distance, on the road toward the police. When he finally returns to the schoolhouse, there is a message scrawled on the chalkboard: "You handed over our brother. You will pay for this."

Characters

Arab

The Arab, who is never given a name in the story, has been arrested in his village by the French police for killing his cousin during a dispute. He is being transferred to police headquarters in a nearby town, Tinguit. Though he is treated reasonably well by Balducci, the Arab is sullen and unresponsive. He does not utter a word until after Balducci has left and Daru offers him a meal and a bed. The Arab's motivation for killing his cousin is unclear. His explanation that "He ran away. . . I ran after him" baffles Daru. Daru's questions about fear and remorse both embarrass and astound the Arab, and as a result he develops a kind of attachment to Daru. The Arab then requests that Daru accompany him and Balducci to Tinguit. He is reluctant to leave the schoolhouse without Daru and appears panicked at having to choose whether or not to escape. In the end, the Arab remains largely an enigma to Daru and, to some extent, the reader.

Balducci

Balducci is the gendarme, or policeman, who delivers the Arab prisoner to Daru before returning to his post. He is brusque but not vicious; he is careful, for example, not to walk his horse too fast when the prisoner is tied behind him. He twice expresses regret or distaste for the harsher aspects of his job. Balducci is truly a man of law and order. He strictly obeys the rules, and is neither unnecessarily cruel nor ambivalent towards prisoners. Balducci is a longtime acquaintance of Daru, but their relationship is strained by their conflicting views toward their responsibility for the Prisoner.

Daru

Daru is the schoolmaster of a rural schoolhouse and is commissioned to escort an Arab prisoner on the second half of his journey to Tinguit. Daru is a native of the region who lives an isolated and monastic existence. He is compassionate toward the poor villagers, especially during this time of famine, and he treats the prisoner as his "guest," with compassion and respect. He is annoyed and frustrated, however, with the prisoner's apparent passivity, and disgusted by the violence of his crime. Ordered to transfer the prisoner to the authorities in Tinguit, Daru resists at every turn. He announces to Balducci that he will not turn the prisoner over to the authorities, and hopes that the prisoner will escape. Daru later attempts to pass the choice on to the prisoner himself by leaving him abruptly at a crossroads with the means to either escape or turn himself in. This decision is an emotional one for Daru and it is misunderstood by the Arab's compatriots, who leave a threatening message for him on the chalkboard at the schoolhouse. The entire experience leaves Daru with a sense of bitterness and isolation.

Gendarme

See Balducci

Prisoner

See Arab

Schoolmaster

See Daru

Themes

"The Guest" tells of an encounter between a French Algerian schoolteacher and an Arab prisoner on the eve of the Algerian uprising. The story emphasizes many of Camus's most characteristic themes: individual alienation, freedom, the value of human life, responsibility, the difficulty of moral choice, and the ambiguity of actions. It gains additional layers of meaning through its incisive portrait of colonial life and the psyches of colonizer and colonized alike.

Choices

Daru, the rural schoolmaster, is charged, against his will, to take responsibility for an Arab prisoner and transport him to the nearest town. This situation sets up the most powerful theme in the story, that of the difficulty and inevitability of moral choice. Daru would like to remain neutral in a worsening political climate. He acknowledges his French allegiance and suggests that a declared war would make his position clear—he would fight for France. In any case, there is no declared war at the present moment. Moved by his compassion for and knowledge of the Arab villagers of the region, Daru believes that it is wrong and dishonorable to turn the prisoner over to the French authorities. At the same time, he is unwilling or unable to consider either a defense or a challenge to the system. He simply wishes to be relieved of responsibility or participation. He first tries to refuse to accept the Arab from the gendarme who brings him to the schoolhouse. Later he leaves the prisoner untied and hopes more than once that the Arab will simply escape, eliminating his dilemma. In the end, angry and frustrated, he tries to pass the choice along to the Arab by showing him two roads—one to the police headquarters, and one to ostensible freedom and safety among nomadic tribes. In the end, the Arab chooses the road to prison, and Daru is held accountable by the Arab's compatriots. Had the prisoner escaped, Daru would have been held accountable by the

Topics for Further Study

- Outline the history of the Algerian War and connect that history to allusions in the story. What kinds of events would have led to Balducci's and Daru's questions about the Prisoner's loyalties and talk of impending war? Who might have written the threatening note on the chalkboard?

- Research the basic principles of Islamic law. Under what circumstances would the Prisoner have been guilty of a crime for killing his cousin? Under what circumstances might the action have been justifiable? Use your knowledge to prepare a defense of the Prisoner in the French legal system.

- Study the geography of Algeria and match it to places and events described in the story. What does the area Camus described look like on a map? What kind of climate conditions lead to severe drought? What kinds of government policies have contributed to, or prevented droughts like the one described in the story?

French authorities. The ultimate result of Daru's decision is misunderstanding and a profound alienation from the world.

Honor

Underneath Daru's difficulty in deciding what to do about his conflicting responsibilities toward the Arab is his strong sense of honor. In his final exchange with Balducci, Daru makes this explicit: "All this disgusts me, beginning with your fellow here. But I won't hand him over. Fight, yes, if I have to. But not that." Balducci understands and concedes the point, allowing that he feels ashamed of "putting a rope on another man." But he sees it as his unavoidable, if distasteful, duty. Later Daru declares to himself that to turn the prisoner in would be contrary to honor. These European concepts of honor are placed next to the unstated and unexplored concepts of honor in the Arab culture. Honor may have played a role in the killing of the Arab's

cousin. It is certainly not honorable to be afraid, and the notion of remorse makes no sense to the Arab, possibly because he views his action as appropriate. The fact that the people of his village protected him may indicate that his action was legitimate according to their moral code.

Absurdism

Another fundamental motif of Camus's is the idea of the Absurd. Generally speaking, absurdism is based on the belief that the universe is irrational and meaningless and that attempts to find order or meaning will bring the individual into conflict with that absurd universe. For Camus, there is no resolution to this conflict. According to Camus's early writings, each person is like the Greek hero Sisyphus, who must struggle stubbornly to live as if there were a purpose and sense to individual actions. Acceptance of this fundamental condition can militate against nihilism. This is in contrast to many Existentialist thinkers who hold that meaning is created by each individual who has the freedom and, indeed, the responsibility to do so. In his later writings, Camus introduced the idea of revolt against inhumane and unjust conditions or systems: each person must act as an individual in opposition to a common fate or a tyrannical system by refusing to participate. The theme of Absurdism is evoked in many of the descriptions of the natural landscape in the story, which express powerfully what Camus once called the "benign indifference of the world." Daru's attempt to maintain an outsider status in the developing conflict and with respect to the prisoner's crime is an example of an individual rebellion in the style of Camus.

Hospitality

Hospitality is a fundamental part of virtually all cultures. In this story the theme is invoked in the French title: "l'Hote" means both "guest" and "host" in French. Thus the word captures both sides of the hospitality relationship and the reciprocal obligations it traditionally produces. In the story, Daru treats the Arab less like a prisoner and more like a guest. The Arab calls attention to this unexpected behavior in asking why Daru eats with him. Daru's response is somewhat evasive; he states merely that he is hungry. Some critics have suggested that the Arab's unwillingness to escape is a response to the hospitality he has received; having accepted Daru's gesture, he "owes" him, and cannot insult him by escaping. The title is also ironic.

While Daru is ostensibly the host and the prisoner the guest, as a descendent of colonial conquerors, Daru is, in effect, a guest in the prisoner's country. There is a final reference to the well-known hospitality of the Berber nomads, who traditionally take in and protect other wanderers in their hostile desert climate.

Style

"The Guest" tells of an encounter between a French Algerian schoolteacher and an Arab prisoner on the eve of the Algerian uprisings. The story emphasizes many of Camus's most characteristic themes: individual alienation, freedom, the value of human life, responsibility, the difficulty of moral choice, and the ambiguity of actions. It gains additional layers of meaning through its incisive portrait of colonial life and the psyches of colonizer and colonized alike.

Point of View

The narrative style in "The Guest" is a classic example of the use of free indirect discourse—essentially an interior monologue told in the third person rather than the first. In contrast to the objective and external viewpoint of the traditional third person narrator, or the clearly subjective viewpoint of a first person narrative, this technique places the character between the author and the reader, diminishing authorial independence and authority. At the same time, the thoughts and feelings of the character may be selectively expressed to serve the purpose of the narrative. In Camus's story, much of the background information about the setting and about Daru is provided through his extended reflections.

Setting

The rich descriptions of the Algerian landscape are weighted with symbolic importance. To begin with, the schoolhouse is located in the desert on a high plateau—an intermediate area that belongs to neither the plains nor the mountains. It is described as being part-way up a steep rise. The physical location of Daru's school and his home comes to symbolize the moral space that Daru wants to find between the French and the Arabs, the "us" and the "them." The unpredictable weather helps to further mark the time and place of the story as unusual. The

action of the story takes place between two states of weather. Under normal conditions, the landscape is hot, dry, and harsh. Daru describes it as an "expanse where nothing had any connection with man." The violent storm changes that landscape; it is "cruel" in its suddenness, but it has the effect of softening the landscape. The storm has passed, but the effects of the snow linger. The landscape that Daru knows so well is transformed. There is more light, but it is "dirty" and the snow on the ground moistens it and muffles footsteps that normally sound sharp on the hard soil. Throughout the walk toward Tinguit Daru notices the landscape shifting back as the snow melts and puddles gradually dry up; by the end of their walk to where Daru leaves the Arab, once again "the ground rang under their feet." When Daru has returned to the schoolhouse, the harsh sun bathes the entire plateau in clear light.

Foreshadowing

Like the storm that disrupted the normal routines of classes and grain distribution, the arrival of the prisoner breaks the placid rhythm of Daru's life. It is Balducci who makes this explicit, promising Daru that once he has delivered the prisoner to Tinguit, ". . . all will be over. You'll come back to your pupils and your comfortable life." This claim is ironic, since the experience of meeting the prisoner and the moral choices it forces on him will transform Daru's relationships with Balducci, his fellow Frenchman, the Arabs he lives among, and even the place to which he is so attached. Balducci leaves angrily, questioning Daru's loyalty, the Arabs hold him responsible for handing over the prisoner, and Daru's connection to the landscape has been ruptured. In the closing line of the story, he uses the past tense, describing the view from his window as the "vast landscape he had loved so much" but from which he is now alienated.

Another instance of ironic foreshadowing draws attention to the ambiguous and ambivalent relationship between the schoolmaster and the prisoner. In response to Daru's kindness and hospitality, the Arab has requested strongly and repeatedly that Daru accompany him to Tinguit. When they are ready to leave the schoolhouse, Daru orders the prisoner out ahead of him, but the Arab does not move. Daru shows an implicit understanding of the prisoner's reluctance, not repeating the order, but assuring him, "I'm coming." This scene is echoed in the final parting. This time the Arab is visibly distressed, and once again he does not move. Daru looks back once, then again to find that the prisoner has not moved. It is only after Daru has definitively left him, waving good-bye, that the Arab makes his choice.

Historical Context

The Algerian War

The encounter depicted in "The Guest" takes place in "mid-October," on the eve of the outbreak of the Algerian War. The revolt, led by the National Liberation Front (FLN) began on October 31, 1954, and lasted until July, 1962, when Algeria achieved independence. There had been scattered uprisings and nationalist movements in Algeria since the first French colonial presence in Africa in 1830. But the nationalist movement had gained considerable strength after World War II. By the time the story takes place, the revolt was imminent, so when Balducci talks of war, he is describing a realistic fear. Likewise, the positions of "us" and "them" refer not just to cultural differences, but to the now clear battle line between settlers of European origin and the Arab rebels and sympathizers. While the events and characters in the story are fictional, Camus drew on his early experience as a court and police reporter for some of the details and context of the story. The devastating effects of the drought, the crushing poverty of the villagers, the monotony of the schoolteacher's life, and the collision between Arab culture and the European justice system were all phenomena he had witnessed at close hand.

Many people describe the Algerian War as "France's Vietnam" and certainly it was as politically controversial and divisive for the French as the Vietnam War was for many people in the United States. As one of France's most distinguished writers, a man who had been active in the French Resistance, and a native Algerian, Camus was looked to for moral and political guidance. He was vehemently criticized by both the Left and the Right political factions in France, and denounced by both officials of the French government and the nationalist leaders for his refusal to take either side in the conflict. Camus believed strongly in the need for democratic reforms and greater rights for the Arab population, but he could not support a break with France and held dearly to the notion of a unified country in which both European and Arab Algerians could hold full citizenship. In connection with the war, his only clear statements sought to protect civilian lives on both sides and supported efforts to achieve a cease fire. While the story is by no means a direct reflection of Camus's views about the Algerian situation, the character of Daru captures Camus's discomfort with the idea of having to choose sides in a violent conflict and his profound humanism and sympathy for any suffering human being.

Colonialism

The Algerian War was the outcome of many years' resistance to French colonial rule. There were similar, if less violent, conflicts in French Tunisia and Morocco as well. And the pattern was repeated for other European powers. In the years following World War II there was a mass movement in Africa, the Caribbean, and Asia to de-colonize territories that had been ruled by European countries since the eighteenth and nineteenth centuries. Dozens of these former colonies sought democratic reforms and national independence. Because colonial rule had extended over several centuries, both Arabs, like the prisoner, and many European Algerians, like Daru, were natives of the country. (Balducci is a more recent immigrant from Corsica, a French territory in the Mediterranean.) Camus makes ironic reference to the colonial situation in the opening paragraphs of the story where "the four rivers of France" are drawn on the chalkboard. This geographic knowledge would have been of little use to rural Algerian students and is symbolic of a well developed system of colonial education that endeavored to disseminate European culture and traditions throughout the colonial possessions.

Critical Overview

The Guest appeared in Camus's 1957 collection of stories entitled *Exile and the Kingdom.* The stories received a mixed but generally positive reception. Camus's writing career had been largely stalled for many years owing to writer's block and personal difficulties. Thus some critics saw in the stories a renewed energy that bode well for his next major work of fiction. Some specifically saw these stories as short explorations of themes and situations that he would explore at novel length. Many found,

Compare
&
Contrast

- **1950s:** Revolt against French rule in Algeria begins in 1954 and is led by the Front de Liberation (FLN).

  1990s: After the FLN separates from the government in the late 1980s, Algerian voters approve a multiparty political system. The first multiparty elections are held in 1991. In 1992, government authorities cancel a general election in which radical Muslims were gaining a strong lead. In 1996, a referendum approves reforms which prevent the use of Islam as a political platform. In 1997, more than 1,000 civilians are killed by Muslim rebels. A cease-fire is declared in October. In November, Algeria implements an international civil and political rights treaty.

- **1950s:** With FLN terrorist activity on the rise,

the French Parliament votes Premier Bourges-Mannoury special powers in 1956 to suppress the group. Charles de Gaulle is voted Premier in 1957 as the Algerian crisis threatens civil war.

1990s: Algerian President Chadli Benejedid resigns in January of 1991 after Islamic fundamentalists triumph in national elections. Former FLN rebel Mohammed Boudiaf returns from 27 years of exile and is sworn in as President. He is assassinated in June of 1991.

- **1950s:** Muslims comprise approximately 88 percent of the population of French Algeria.

  1990s: About 99 percent of Algeria's population is Muslim.

---

however, that Camus had not successfully mastered the distinction between philosophy and fiction. As Irving Howe wrote in *The New Republic:* "Camus still seems torn between the impulse to offer testimony (which means to reduce his fiction to mere examples) and the impulse to tell stories and create characters. . . . The result is a curious mixture of the threadbare and the obscure. . .". His untimely death three years later foreclosed the possibility of further development and "The Guest" became his last published work. In general, while they were not regarded as on a level with his best previous fiction, his short stories were understood as an important contribution to his oeuvre. Camus himself had been reluctant to declare them finished, revising them throughout 1956 and 1957 and extending the publication date until late that year. "The Guest" is often regarded as one of the strongest stories in the collection and it has been widely anthologized.

Early interpretations placed the story easily within a philosophical framework similar to that of Camus, finding in Daru's action his self-realization as a moral human being, with the necessary sense of alienation that comes from acting in an absurd

world. Others noted and analyzed the ambiguity the story forces on its readers. Balducci's uncertainty about the prisoner's crime, Daru's inability to understand the Arab's explanation, and, at their parting, Daru's unwillingness to listen to the prisoner's plea, or to fully examine his own feelings, all ensure that the story will be read as a bit of a puzzle. More recently critics have been influenced by a growing awareness of different cultural perspectives and have paid more detailed attention to the Arab. Often critical of those who judge the Arab too quickly as slow or evil, they have pointed to unexamined aspects of Arab culture and Islamic law that can make the prisoner a fuller, more comprehensible character, and have suggested that European cultural biases made it easy for critics to perceive the Arab as primitive or animalistic.

Camus's story stands as a masterful example of the short story genre and the use of free indirect discourse. In addition, it illuminates some of the profound literary and cultural ideas of the mid-twentieth century (such as existentialism and absurdism) and it offers a powerful representation of colonialism and colonial relationships.

French troops detain Algerian nationals circa 1957.

Criticism

Julia Burch

Burch has taught at Southeastern Louisiana University and at the University of Michigan. In the following essay, she examines "The Guest" in relation to Camus's philosophical ideas and with reference to postcolonial criticism.

Camus best-known short story, "The Guest" is also notoriously subject to conflicting interpretations. Virtually all critics recognize the tale as obscure and enigmatic. Some of this is certainly part of Camus' artistic intent. He worked on the story for at least two years, and continued to revise it right up until the publication date. Some, including perhaps Camus himself have regarded the stories in *Exile and the Kingdom* as transitional works, or explorations of themes to be treated more fully in novels to come. Certainly Camus' philosophy and political thought were still developing, and he never lived to see or make sense of the end of the Algerian War and the establishment of an independent Algeria. While *Exile and the Kingdom* was completed in his lifetime and stands as Camus' last published work, part of the interpretive difficulty a story like "The

Guest" poses may be due to the fact that Camus' life and thought were works in progress, interrupted and unfinished by his untimely death. However, there are a number of established frameworks which can go a long way to grounding different interpretations. The first is Camus' own philosophy as he had articulated it. The second is the related philosophy of existentialism, which Camus steadfastly disavowed. Finally, there is the discourse of postcolonialism, which would not have been fully available to Camus in his lifetime, but which now seems essential to understanding the world which he described.

If we try to make sense of "The Guest" in terms of Camus' own philosophy, we can see Daru as a moral man confronting an absurd and indifferent world, symbolized especially by the landscape. He manages his existential feelings of alienation by living near the place where he was born and carrying out his duties with compassion. Like Sisyphus in Camus' early essay "The Myth of Sisyphus," Daru lives stubbornly "as if" existence were not meaningless and the world not absurd. The arrival of Balducci and his prisoner presents a moral quandary. Daru must confront the fact that his world is not just absurd—meaningless—but also unjust and violent. His basic position is clear from the start; while he cannot condone, and indeed is disgusted by, the Prisoner's internecine violence, to turn him in to face French law would be dishonorable and unjust. Moreover, his conversations with Balducci make it clear that the transporting of the Prisoner takes place in and depends on a context of "us" and "them." With a rebellion brewing, this divide represents not just a cultural conflict, but two extreme political positions, both willing to back their beliefs with violence and force. Daru's heroism then, comes from being a rebel of the sort Camus described in *L'Homme Revolte* (*The Rebel*), the individual who acts against unjust ideologies–in this case, of both the French colonial government and the Arab nationalists. His solution is both a refusal to take sides and a humanist stand against extremism and violence. For Camus, to make the right moral choice, is a necessarily isolating act. It is staking out a position as an individual, and while it is the appropriate decision and the route to Camusian self-realization, there is no expectation that it will provide a coherence or sense of meaning in an absurd universe. As Alfred Noyer-Weidner puts it: "Daru's final loneliness is a loneliness of tragedy and not of human weakness. . . . For Daru . . . to have remained true to the absolute respect for that

French soldiers in Algeria circa 1957.

which is human, up until the final moment of isolation, seems to be a condition of the Camusian 'kingdom'.'' If such a conclusion seems hard to accept, it indicates perhaps less a misreading of the story than an argument with the Camusian philosophy on which this interpretation depends.

One major position from which to argue with Camus is that of Existentialism, since Existentialism was fundamental to the political and philosophical milieu in Paris when Camus came to prominence, and because existentialist were among his sharpest philosophical critics. Not everyone sees Daru as successful or a hero. Many do indeed see Daru's isolation at the end as a "loneliness of weakness" or a predictable result of his failure to fully accept his responsibility for the Prisoner. One doesn't have to be an Existentialist to offer such interpretations, but they can certainly be grounded and elucidated in an Existentialist framework. While Camus insisted that there was no way to make sense of the absurd, many existentialists saw this activity as a fundamental responsibility and freedom of each individual. Each person must constantly make him or herself through and in actions, striving for an authentic existence; this is not an easy path; at best, people will struggle with reactions such as despair (at the meaninglessness of the universe) and anxiety

(over the choices which must be made in an authentic existence), at worst, they will avoid this responsibility, living passively, letting others determine choices and actions, and living unauthentically with what Sartre called "bad faith" or self-deception. This second course leads to progressively worsening estrangement from what one can be, and ultimately a profound sense of nothingness, an existential crisis.

It's not hard to see how some of this might apply to Daru. While it has been convincingly argued that it is too simple to say that Daru fails to act or make a decision, there are any number of problems with both the decision he makes, and the way he makes it. His refusal to turn the Arab in is clear from the start. But in taking charge of the Prisoner, he hedges. One authentic choice might have been to refuse to accept the Prisoner altogether, and, more importantly, refuse to sign for him, accepting fully and freely Balducci's anger and whatever reprisals came after. Once Daru has made the decision to honor his friendship with Balducci by signing the receipt, he struggles with unwanted responsibility. Daru's repeated hope that the Prisoner will simply escape, thereby freeing him of his dilemma, points to a certain level of self-deception and an unwillingness to face the implications of his

What Do I Read Next?

- *The Stranger,* Camus's first novel from 1942. Mersault, the protagonist, is on trial for the senseless shooting of an Arab. He is condemned as much for his social alienation and indifference as for his crime. Provides an introduction to Camus's themes of absurdism and alienation.

- *The Plague,* Camus's second novel, published in 1947. It tells the story of several men confronting a plague in the Algerian city of Oran. Introduces the theme of revolt.

- Jean-Paul Sartre's existentialist novel *Nausea,* published in 1938, treats a number of Sartre's philosophical themes, including meaninglessness and the responsibility of each individual to achieve an authentic existence.

- ''Zaabalawi'' is a well known story by the Nobel Prize winning Egyptian writer Naguib Mahfouz. Published in 1963, the story tells of a quest to find a holy man who will provide a physical cure and spiritual salvation for the ailing narrator. Mahfouz uses some Absurdist techniques and focuses on individual experience in a social rather than alienated context.

---

accepting responsibility for the Prisoner. Similarly, the plan to escort the Prisoner halfway and then invite him to make his own choice reveals a desire on Daru's part to have it both ways—i.e. at some level not to choose. In Existentialist terms this can only be a kind of bad faith, a self-deception about one's motives and actions, and an unwillingness to shoulder the responsibility of one's freedom to forge an authentic existence. From this perspective, Daru's bitter estrangement form the world and landscape he had felt connected to is a predictable result of his bad faith and lapse into unauthentic existence. One can read some bad faith in Daru's interactions with the Prisoner as well. On the one hand Daru offers him compassion and hospitality, yet he rejects the ''strange brotherhood'' he feels forming and can scarcely bring himself to look at the Arab. When finally leaving the Arab, Daru behaves brusquely and ignores his own mixed feelings.

Part of the complexity of Daru's relationship with the Arab cannot be fully examined without considering the colonial context which has brought them together. Thus far, in interpreting the story in terms of Camus' ideas or the competing philosophy of existentialism the characters and conflicts have been treated as universal. While the events take place in a specific location and at a specific time, the philosophical themes of moral or individual choice in a meaningless universe are not limited in their significance to that setting. But many critics would argue with the very notion of universal themes or representative characters and events. In particular, critics adopting a postcolonial perspective would look at the way in which Algeria in the 1950s created a very particular set of experiences that need to be understood and analyzed on their own. While there were certainly critics of the colonial empires during their heyday, the term postcolonial refers generally to the period since independence was gained by many former colonies; thus it is post (after) the end of colonialism as a widespread political system. As a critical orientation, postcolonialism can encompass many modes of analysis. But central to all postcolonial critiques is a tendency to reveal the ''universal'' as specific to a European or Western cultural viewpoint, and to pay much more attention to heretofore ignored cultures and philosophies from outside the Western tradition. To analyze ''The Guest'' from this perspective raises new questions, especially about the portrayal and traditional interpretations of the Arab. The basic portrait of the Arab draws on two traditional colonial perceptions of non-Europeans. The first has been called Orientalist, in which the non-European is seen as silent, mysterious, and often alluring. The second views indigenous peoples as uncivilized and animalistic. Both of these views are at work in Daru's descriptions of the Prisoner. His lips and mouth are described as "Negroid" and "animal"; he is seen as "feverish" and "vacant and listless." At the same time, he speaks and interacts little, and what he does say is largely incomprehensible to Daru. Certainly his choice of the road to prison is an enigma.

Daru may be sensitive and humane enough to care about the poverty and hunger of the his students and their families and to treat the Arab prisoner gently and hospitably, but he remains clearly allied with the French and the colonial system: he is a civil servant and he knows that in a war he would defend the French. His position as a colonizer creates a blind spot for him in his perception of and relation to the Arab. He feels disgust at the Arab's killing on two counts—its violence and the apparent weakness that let him be captured. But certainly such internecine violence is not limited to Arabs or indigenous peoples, and the Arab did hide in his village for a month before he was finally captured and taken away. In the central conversation between the two men, Daru maintains his position of power by deflecting or refusing to respond to the Arab's questions, and when they part in the desert, Daru refuses to listen at all to the Arab's protest. Part of this is to protect himself from knowledge or intimacy that would deepen his conflicted feelings; part of it is an exercise of his authority; part of it comes from a colonial expectation that the Arab will have little to say—ultimately he is not and cannot be an equal. The result of this is that Daru, and hence the reader, knows very little of what the Arab believes and feels. Many recent critics have tried to close this knowledge gap by drawing on ethnography and trying to understand the Prisoner from the perspective of Arab culture and law. A number of salient points arise in these kinds of analyses. To begin with, the details of the Prisoner's crime are fuzzy at best. Balducci relates the little he knows with a series of tentative and speculative statements. From within Arab culture, the Prisoner may have been acting appropriately, defending a point of honor. The fact that his village was willing to protect and defend him suggests strongly that from their perspective he had not committed a crime. Similarly, the fact that he makes no effort to escape or choose the road to freedom may be a point of honor for him; having been charged, he must face his accusers. What he wants from Daru is that he accompany him, as he recognizes Daru's fairness and believes that he

> **"** If we try to make sense of 'The Guest' in terms of Camus' own philosophy, we can see Daru as a moral man confronting an absurd and indifferent world, symbolized especially by the landscape."

can aid him in the alien French legal system. There are other reasons he might choose not to escape, the most powerful being that he comes from a strong village culture. His entire life and sense of identity are connected to his village and tribe. Freedom among the Berbers could well be meaningless for him. Finally, with a rebellion about to break out, he could well fear that his escape could bring reprisals to his village, again making escape a dishonorable and unconscionable action.

Source: Julia Burch, "Overview of 'The Guest'," for *Short Stories for Students,* Gale, 1997.

Eberhard Griem

In the following excerpt, Griem examines the Arab's character in Camus's "The Guest," and contends that he is acting in accordance with his own cultural norms and codes.

Interpretations of Albert Camus's short story "The Guest" so far have had a tendency to make rather little of the prisoner, typically treating him as a primitive, brutalized, somewhat dull or even dim-witted character. In an influential early reading, Laurence Perrine helped establish this view, claiming that "his incomprehension . . . is emphasized" [*Studies in Short Fiction*, 1, 1963–64]. His comments in the *Instructor's Manual* accompanying his widely used textbook *Story and Structure* [1988] reinforce the view: "From the beginning the Arab is pictured as passive, uncomprehending, a little stupid." Nor does John K. Simon's reply to the original article in [*Studies in Short Fiction*] contradict this general view when he states, for example, "Having always lived under French law and authority, with no education or independence, the Arab can follow only the negative dictate of inertia and passivity'' [*Studies in Short Fiction,* 1, 1963–64]. More recently, Elwyn F. Sterling, while allowing the Arab some measure of moral awareness (''aware that the act of murder has set him apart from men'' [*French Review,* 54, 1981]), again endorses the view that he doesn't know very clearly why he committed the murder: ''As a reason for killing his cousin, he can only answer, 'il s'est sauve. J'ai couru derrière lui'.'' And again, as recently as 1988, Diana Festa-McCormick repeats the claim that the Arab ''hardly knows why he had killed ('He ran away, I ran after him').'' [*Critical Essays on Albert Camus,* 1988].

A close study of the way in which the story deals with the Arab's act of killing his cousin will throw a different light on his character. The question of his motives arises twice. First, in the course of the discussion between Daru and Balducci, the policeman offers this information: ''A family squabble, I think. One owed grain to the other, it seems. It's not at all clear.'' What is remarkable here is Balducci's great uncertainty, emphasized in each of the three short successive sentences. Obviously his is not a very definitive version of the story; the reader is alerted to watch out for further clues. For the time being, Daru's response is not very helpful in that it merely expresses strong feelings against a barbaric deed: ''Daru felt a sudden wrath against the man, against all men with their rotten spite, their tireless hates, their blood lust.'' He generalizes and is clearly not aware of a need to investigate further and to penetrate Balducci's uncertainties.

The question comes up again when Daru and the prisoner are alone and have shared a meal, i.e., Daru's kindness has earned him the Arab's deep respect. Struggling with his own feelings of hostility, possibly in the hope of finding the prisoner a contrite sinner, Daru asks him: ''Why did you kill him?,'' only to elicit the response that so many critics have construed as being less than clear or plausible: ''He ran away. I ran after him.'' But what can we make of this reply if we try to take it seriously? Could it be that the cousin's act of running away, instead of taking full responsibility in the family squabble over a debt of grain, constitutes the complete loss of his honor, and a severe injury to the family honor as well, in his own indigenous culture? And could it be that the prisoner, in running after him (possibly because he was the first to notice, or the one with the best starting position as pursuer), and then killing him, was

merely acting in accordance with his own tribal custom?

The assumption that the prisoner's own cultural norms play a crucial part in the matter has a number of interesting ramifications. It certainly helps to explain his body language in the passage in question. The fact that he ''looked away'' in giving his reply may well indicate some doubt as to whether Daru the French colonist will be able to appreciate what he says. His wordless response to Daru's next question, ''Are you afraid?'' is to stiffen, which strongly suggests a proud rejection of such an insinuation; at the same time he repeats the gesture of ''turning his eyes away,'' as if once again appealing to those who could appreciate him better. Finally, and perhaps most importantly, when Daru asks, ''Are you sorry?'' the prisoner ''stared at him open-mouthed. Obviously he did not understand.'' Surely he is not being stupid; rather, he does not see the relevance of the question. Why, indeed, should he feel sorry about the killing if it was the honorable thing to do? To him, under the circumstances, regret is a perfectly incongruous, meaningless kind of response.

Yet, in spite of such signals of Daru's limited understanding of his plight, the Arab has developed an almost compulsive trust in Daru, in response, no doubt, to Daru's earlier kindness, the significance of which lies not merely in Daru's humane and compassionate behavior, but in his acceptance of the Arab as an honorable man who deserves all the privileges of a guest. That is not easy for the Arab to grasp, so that he asks, ''Why do you eat with me?'' Encouraged by such honorable treatment, he hopefully asks next, ''Are you the judge?'' And upon hearing the negative reply, he still urges Daru twice to come with him to Tinguit, presumably in the hope that Daru will secure him a fair and honorable trial.

The view that the Arab's indigenous culture plays a key role in the story finds additional support in certain historical and systematic features of Islamic law. In pre-revolutionary Algeria, the substitution of the French legal system for Islamic law, extending even to the local level and to rural areas, was particularly offensive to the Arabs because of the religious foundation of their traditional system, and was one of the motives behind the incipient rebellion. The two legal conflicts the prisoner is involved in, the family squabble over a debt of grain and even the homicide, are matters that can both, under Islamic law, be settled privately, unless one of the parties seeks a trial before the local judge, the *kadi*. In either case, enforcement of the terms of the settlement or judgment is left up to the plaintiff, for ''No sharp distinction is made between execution and self-help'' [Joseph Schacht, *An Introduction to Islamic Law,* 1964]. On the basis of these observations it seems understandable (a) that the Arab man ''punished'' his cousin through self-help, (b) that his community hid him for a month from the French authorities, as someone who was not culpable unless a complaint was raised against him in his own tribe, and (c) that he worries in ''woeful interrogation'' about what the French authorities will do to him.

An interesting consequence of this view of the Arab's motivation for the killing is the light it throws on his behavior when Daru, toward the end of the story, provides him with the means to regain his freedom instead of handing him over to the authorities. The fact that he chooses to face his trial is perfectly consistent with the notion, presumably a part of his cultural identity, that one cannot run away from an accusation without losing one's honor. In spite of the hostility between the Arabs and their French colonial oppressors in general, Daru's hospitable, honorable treatment of the prisoner seems to have struck a chord in him so that his indigenous code of honor asserts itself in an automatic response, despite Daru's lack of understanding of other parts of his cultural identity.

A further interesting consequence of this view of the prisoner lies in the fact that his final choice, to face his trial, creates an ironic existentialist impasse very similar to that of Daru. Both men have acted according to the dictates of their different moral codes, and yet both are threatened with annihilation, in a system that does not recognize their respective merits. Daru has given the prisoner his freedom of choice, but is threatened by the man's Arab brothers with punishment for allegedly handing him over to the authorities. The prisoner, following his moral code, chooses to face his trial; yet he will most certainly not be judged on the basis of that code, but must expect lifetime imprisonment or, worse, a death sentence. That the French intellectual and the Arab tribesman are aligned in this existentialist dilemma seems to me to add significantly to the poignancy of the story's resolution.

Source: Eberhard Griem, ''Albert Camus's 'The Guest': A New Look at the Prisoner,'' in *Studies in Short Fiction,* Vol. 30, no. 1, Winter, 1993, pp. 95–8.

> **"The fact that the Arab chooses to face his trial is perfectly consistent with the notion, presumably a part of his cultural identity, that one cannot run away from an accusation without losing one's honor."**

Susan Tarrow

In the following excerpt, Tarrow offers an interpretation of Camus' ''The Guest,'' particularly in regard to the motifs of Colonialism and the character of Daru. Tarrow also examines Camus' use of imagery.

Daru, the protagonist of ''The Guest'' [is a misfit in the landscape]. The ambiguity of the title word, *l'hote,* meaning both ''guest'' and ''host,'' and of which meaning should be applied to which character, is resolved by the landscape. Paul Fortier has shown how the landscape and its changing aspects offer an interpretation of historical events and of moral values (''Decor,'' pp. 535–42). Daru believes himself in harmony with the natural world around him. But it is an illusion. The sun is dominant during the drought, ''the plateaus charred month after month, the earth gradually shrivelling, literally scorched.'' The snowfall represents a brief reprieve, a temporary truce before hostility is renewed. When the sun shines again, Daru feels a kind of exaltation, but it is as if the sun were in league with the rocks against him, quickly drying out the puddles of melting snow and returning the landscape to its former rockiness. Now the sun becomes destructive, and ''began to devour his brow . . . sweat trickled down it.''

The physical attack portends the human violence with which the teacher is threatened on his return to the school. The wind ''lurking'' around the school building parallels the activities of the rebels who are following his movements. And the precise location of Daru's school, on an isolated plateau, an intermediate stage between the coastal plain and the

> "Camus stresses Daru's roots in this harsh landscape; yet his origins continue to separate him from the indigenous population."

mountains, reflects the moral stance of neutrality and isolation maintained by the schoolteacher (Fortier, *Une Lecture*, p. 29). The Arab prisoner, as Fortier points out, resembles the desert, "his skin sunburnt but slightly discolored by the cold." He fears what the Frenchmen may do to him, but he does not fear the desert. Of course in reality the natural world is hostile to the Arabs too: Daru is well aware that "in the desert, all men, both he and his guest, were nothing." But Camus's landscapes are never innocent. A welcoming environment can become inimical and can inflict pain and even death on the unwary individual. . . .

The opinions Camus expressed in a political context are apparently contradicted by the fictional worlds of these short stories. Camus opposed independence because it would lead to the expulsion of his own people. Yet the European characters he places in an Algerian setting are uncomfortable strangers in a country they regard as theirs. In "The Guest," for example, despite the sympathetic portrayal of characters, it is clear that Daru's position is untenable. Warm human bonds between individuals are not enough to assure a peaceful settlement of struggle in the political arena.

Daru fits in with Albert Memmi's portrait of the left-wing colonizer. He "refuses to become a part of his group of fellow citizens. At the same time it is impossible for him to identify his future with that of the colonized. Politically, who is he? Is he not an expression of himself, of a negligible force in the varied conflicts within colonialism?" (*The Colonizer*, p. 41). Daru has isolated himself from his fellow Europeans, and lives alone on a barren plateau in the foothills. As a schoolteacher he is obviously committed to the welfare and education of his pupils, and sympathetic towards their impoverished and ill-nourished condition. He feels at home: "Daru had been born there. Anywhere else he felt an exile." In earlier versions of the manuscript, Daru was a disenchanted businessman from the coast, who had given up his old life and become a teacher. In the final version, Camus stresses Daru's roots in this harsh landscape; yet his origins continue to separate him from the indigenous population: "Faced with this wretchedness [Daru], who lived almost like a monk in this isolated school, yet was happy with the little he had and with this simple life, had felt like a lord." Colonialist rule is symbolized by the drawing on the school blackboard of the four rivers of France: the local schoolchildren follow the same curriculum as children in metropolitan France, even though it may be irrelevant to their culture and their needs. The colonial administration uses the schools as distribution centers for emergency supplies of food during the drought, so that children have to come to school to receive their allocation. Daru is thus placed in the position of an overlord, separate from "that army of ragged ghosts." The word *army* evokes a sense of hostility and violence which runs through the whole narrative and explodes across the map of France at the end of the story.

The advent of Balducci and his Arab prisoner brings the reality of the current situation into Daru's monastic retreat, brings movement into a static world, and forces him to take a position. "Commitment comes like a guest who does not want to leave" (Cryle, *Bilan critique*, p. 142). It is his failure to choose in a positive way that leaves him helpless to affect the course of events. His attitude toward Balducci and the Arab is entirely laudable: Balducci is a tough but sympathetic Corsican who dislikes mistreating an Arab, but who believes in discipline, while the Arab, despite his act of violence, is nevertheless a man who deserves to be treated with human dignity. By refusing to take the Arab to prison, Daru offends Balducci personally; by allowing the Arab a choice he does not understand, he alienates himself from the local people. His actions are misunderstood by the groups represented by the two individuals, just as Daru fails to recognize the political reality behind those two people.

On a personal level, ambiguity and humanitarian instincts are possible; but on a political level, actions cannot bear any nuance without being misconstrued. Thus the colonial administration will view Daru's refusal as a treacherous act, while the Arabs interpret the result of his inaction as a betrayal too: "You have handed over our brother. You will pay." The words "hand over" recall mockingly Daru's thrice-repeated "I will not hand him over"; Camus obviously had some biblical references in mind, for in an earlier version of the story, the teacher's name is Pierre (Peter), and at one time he considered "Cain" as a title. Daru's future in Algeria is precarious, and the use of the pluperfect in the final sentence bears out this sense of finality. "Daru looked at the sky, the plateau, and beyond it the invisible landscape that stretched out to the sea. In this vast country he had loved so much, he was alone." The reference to the sea indicates the direction in which Daru will now have to travel, into his exile.

The individual's viewpoint cannot be reduced to a single vision, and yet circumstances often demand it. By refusing to commit himself to one side or the other, Daru loses all. He deplores the Arab's resigned decision to accept his fate, and yet his own indecisiveness allows him also to be swept away by events; he is no better than the Arab at choosing his own future. The text clearly shows that Daru's behavior is understandable but sterile. In a polarized situation, one must choose between black and white and put aside all the shades of gray that intervene, if one is to have any impact on the situation. . . .

The stories of *Exile and the Kingdom* reveal the impasse in which Camus found himself with regard to the Algerian situation. His existence as a writer depended on his identity as a Frenchman, yet his experience as an Algerian made liberty his foremost social ideal. There was no political solution to his personal dilemma. Had he lived, he would doubtless have accepted the inevitable tide of events, just as Daru did. But his vision of the trends in society, of the triumph of violence over dialogue, of the state over the individual, is now generally recognized as a relevant indictment of the modern world.

Source: Susan Tarrow, in *Exile from the Kingdom: A Political Rereading of Albert Camus,* The University of Alabama Press, 1985, pp. 173–93.

Paul Fortier

In the following excerpt, which originally appeared in the French Review in February 1973, Fortier assesses the symbolic value of Camus's descriptions of nature in "The Guest."

Camus situates this short story in the North African desert at a time when revolutionary violence is about to break out. There are three characters: the schoolmaster Daru, a policeman, and an Arab. Because of the extraordinary circumstances, the policeman hands the Arab prisoner over to Daru, telling him that he is to take the prisoner to the jail in the neighboring town. Finding this task odious, Daru takes the prisoner to a crossroads, gives him food and money, then leaves him, after showing him the road that leads to prison, and the one that will permit him to escape. This gesture is misunderstood by the Arab, who goes off docilely to prison, and by his compatriots who announce that they will take vengeance on the man who has turned in their brother. This story is of interest especially because of the moral and political questions that it raises. This article will attempt to define the role of the numerous descriptions of nature which are also an important element in the story.

In this third person narrative, everything is presented from the point of view of the protagonist. Certain passages allow us to see how, in general, he perceives the country in which he lives, while others deal with the precise settings for the action. These two series of descriptions constitute the essential elements in the creation of a decor which, in our opinion, produces an additional level of meaning and suggests an interpretation which, perhaps, goes beyond the strictly historical framework. In order to identify this level of meaning and arrive at this interpretation, a careful reading of the descriptive passages is essential.

Daru is meditating on the normal appearance of the desert where his school is located: "In the beginning, the solitude and the silence had been hard for him on these wastelands peopled only by stones." . . . Man has little place in this "ungrateful" and completely mineral country. The "silence" characteristic of an uninhabited region prolongs the notion of "solitude" reinforced by the word "only." However harsh the country may be, Daru affirms that it is the only place where he can "really live."

The evocations of the seasons associate several new themes with these dominant traits of the countryside:

> It would be hard to forget that poverty, that army of ragged ghosts wandering in the sunlight, the plateaux burned to a cinder month after month, the earth shriveled up little by little, literally scorched, every stone bursting into dust under one's foot. The sheep had died then by thousands and even a few men, here and there, sometimes without anyone's knowing. . . . And suddenly this snow, without warning, without the foretaste of rain. This is the way the region was, cruel to live in, even without men—who didn't help matters either. But Daru had been born here. Everywhere else he felt exiled.

> The descriptions of the school's location, of the weather and of the snow all point out the moral situation of the protagonist."

Snow had suddenly fallen in mid-October after eight months of drought without the transition of rain. . . . [One had to wait for fair weather.]

When all the snow was melted, the sun would take over again and once more would burn the fields of stone. For days, still, the unchanging sky would shed its dry light on the solitary expanse where nothing had any connection with man. . . .

"Stone," "dust" and "dry" recall the mineral aspect of the countryside. "Army," "bursting," "died," blow, "without warning," without . . . respite, "cruel," brutally, "without . . . transition" and "would burn" introduce the theme of violence; in summer as in winter, the desert is a country of violence.

The image of the sun is surrounded by a constellation of secondary themes. "Burned to a cinder," "shriveled up . . . literally scorched," "would burn," would pour: a violent entity, the sun, moreover, acts with an excessive force on the countryside. It "takes over," and makes the sky "unchanging." The text underscores the persistence of the sun's domination: "again," "once more," "still," "for days," "month after month." The sun creates a type of eternity. The countryside appears like a limitless expanse; the domination of the sun also evokes, it seems, the theme of immensity. The vision of thousands of sheep during the period of intense heat, and the metaphorical transformation of men into "ragged ghosts wandering in the sunlight" associate the desert under the sun with a world of death. Although he evokes a countryside which is not only "solitary," but actively hostile to man, Daru insists for a second time that he loves this world.

The descriptions of the desert create a decor characterized by the following elements: mineral countryside, silence, solitude, inhumanity, violence, sun, excess, eternity, immensity, death. Daru feels bound to this inhuman desert by strong sentimental

attachments. When he describes the Arab—"his weathered skin now rather discolored by the cold"— the schoolmaster establishes, probably without being aware of it, a parallel between his guest and the desert, which is also being weathered and discolored by the cold snow.

Daru is plunged into a very particular environment when the policeman arrives with the prisoner:

The schoolmaster was watching the two men climb toward him. . . . They had not yet tackled the abrupt rise leading to the schoolhouse built on the hillside. They were toiling onward, making slow progress in the snow, among the stones, on the vast expanse of the high, deserted plateau. . . . They were following the trail although it had disappeared days ago under a layer of dirty white snow. The schoolmaster calculated that it would take them half an hour to get onto the hill.

They were no longer visible. Hence they must have tackled the rise. The sky was not so dark, for the snow had stopped falling during the night. The morning had opened with a dirty light which had scarcely become brighter as the ceiling of clouds lifted. At two in the afternoon it seemed as if the day was merely beginning. But still this was better than those three days when the thick snow was falling amidst unbroken darkness.

He stepped out onto the terrace in front of the schoolhouse. The two men were now halfway up the slope. . . . He watched them climb. . . . "Hello," said Daru when they got up onto the terrace. "Come in and warm up."

Daru was looking out the window. Decidedly, the weather was clearing and light was increasing over the snowy plateau. When all the snow was melted, the sun would take over again and once more burn the fields of stone. . . .

Daru is on the "high plateau" of the Sahara. The word "plateau" appears sixteen times in the twelve pages of this short story. A plateau, flat like a plain and raised like a mountain is however neither one nor the other: it is an intermediate region. A series of verbs underscores the position of the schoolmaster relative to the plateau: "[to] climb," "had not yet tackled the abrupt rise," "tackled the rise," "were now halfway up the slope," "got up onto." The school where he lives, although "on the plateau itself" is located on a "hill," not on the summit, but on the "hillside." The schoolmaster finds himself in an intermediate position on the hill which separates him from yet another intermediate position, the plateau. The school itself is built on a "terrace," i.e. on a little plateau. In the text, then, two closely related notions describe the geographical situation of the protagonist: separation, intermediate zone.

The description of the weather contributes to the creation of a particular atmosphere. The sky is less dark, the light is dirty, the ceiling of clouds lifts, the weather is clearing, the light is increasing, the snow will be melted: the protagonist is between two climatic conditions. The scene is linked, in Daru's mind, to the past as well as to the future. The evocation of this moment of detente between two extreme types of weather recalls for a second time the themes of separation and of intermediate zone already implicit in the description of the school's location. The violence normally associated with the decor has been suspended during the period of transition: the only allusion to this theme—attacked—relates to the men and not the countryside.

The snow which hides the trail is described as a "dirty white layer" neither perfectly clean nor completely transformed by the desert. It is present but about to disappear. The snow changes the nature of the countryside; for example: "His steps were muffled by the snow. . . . A big stone could be heard rolling softly." The snow mutes the sharp sound of boots on rocky ground as it attenuates the harshness of the stone which, because of it, rolls "softly." For the moment, the snow neutralizes the countryside's mineral hardness, a fundamental element of the universe of the desert.

The descriptions of the school's location, of the weather and of the snow all point out the moral situation of the protagonist. An unwilling guardian of the Arab prisoner, Daru is caught between two loyalties. He must decide between solidarity with the threatened European community, or with the broader human fraternity which motivates him to free the Arab. The themes of neutrality and of separation inherent in the description of the setting, and reinforced by the evocation of ambivalent weather, reflect the neutrality and isolation of a mind which has not yet made a decision. The snow softens the hardness of the countryside; the violence of the blizzard is now at an end, and the sun's has not yet begun again. Everything is undecided.

The schoolmaster daydreams a little during the day without deciding anything. Then the night comes:

> When Daru turned out the light, the darkness seemed to coagulate all of a sudden. Little by little, the night came back to life in the window where the starless sky was stirring gently. . . . A faint wind was prowling around the schoolhouse. Perhaps it would drive away the clouds. . . . During the night, the wind increased. . . .

Blow, "was prowling" and "would drive away" suggest violence; but "little by little" and "gently"

are opposed to this suggestion. Each evocation of violence is attenuated: "*seemed* to coagulate all of a sudden," "a *faint* wind was prowling," "*perhaps* . . . would drive away." The night's atmosphere, like the day's, is neutral. However, the wind, associated with violence, is increasing. The neutrality and indecision are not permanent.

The next morning, Daru is contemplating the countryside before leaving with the Arab:

> When he awoke, the sky was clear; the loose window let in a cold, pure air. . . . Then he went through the classroom and out onto the terrace. The sun was already riding in the blue sky; a soft, bright light was bathing the deserted plateau. On the ridge the snow was melting in spots. The stones were about to reappear. . . .

"Terrace," "plateau," "ridge" and "snow" evoke the neutral decor of the preceding night. But the sky is not "clear." The light floods the scene: it is already excessive. The snow is melting in a short while, dominated by the rising sun, the countryside will be completely mineral once again. Daru is contemplating a world which is in the process of returning to its normal state: mineral, dominated by the sun, excessive and implicitly— thanks to the associations already established— violent and human. The time of transition is coming to an end. But the air is "pure," the sky "blue," the light "soft and bright." The countryside that is reappearing is the one Daru loves; he sees no threat in it.

At this point, the protagonist decides to refuse all solidarity, both with the Europeans and with the Arab. But the latter has been integrated into the desert by means of two characteristics they have in common: both are weathered and discolored. At the moment that Daru makes his decision, he "threw a pebble that whistled through the air before sinking into the snow." . . . The plateau is composed exclusively of stone. Symbolically, and certainly without being aware of the meaning implicit in his action, Daru thus rejects the countryside he loves.

Daru leaves the school with the prisoner, then, resting after an hour's walk, glances at the surrounding countryside:

> The snow was melting faster and faster and the sun was drinking up the puddles at once, rapidly cleaning the plateau, which gradually dried and vibrated like the air itself. When they resumed walking, the ground rang under their feet. From time to time a bird rent the space in front of them with a joyful cry. Daru breathed in deeply the fresh morning light. He felt a sort of rapture before the vast, familiar expanse, now almost entirely yellow under its dome of blue sky. . . .

The sun—which is melting the snow, drinking up the puddles, and spreading its light—is beginning to dominate again. The snow is no longer masking the mineral countryside, which is once again "yellow," "dry" and hard—suggested by "vibrated" and "rang." The air too is hard: it "vibrate[s]"; the birds "ren[d]" it. The countryside is assuming "faster and faster," "rapidly," "at once" the appearance of the inhuman desert.

Daru recognizes that this mineral and solar decor is "familiar." He breathes in the light; he unites himself by deep breaths with the countryside that he loves. From this union comes his "rapture." When he describes the bird's cry as joyful," he is probably expressing his own feeling. But he has already noted that the countryside is indifferent to men. Now, it seems to him that a gratuitous happiness in the natural world corresponds to his own joy. Daru believes that he is being united with the countryside without anything in the text suggesting that the countryside is being united with him. The two joys are essentially parallel; the union between Daru and the decor thus established could well be the product of the schoolmaster's imagination.

The two men finally stop on a flat hill. There, Daru shows the Arab the road leading to prison, then the one leading to freedom. Leaving the choice up to the prisoner, he starts to return to the school:

> Daru hesitated. The sun was rather high in the sky and was beginning to beat down on his head. The schoolmaster retraced his steps, at first somewhat uncertainly, then with decision. When he reached the little hill, he was bathed in sweat. He climbed it as fast as he could and stopped, out of breath, at the top. The rockfields to the south stood out sharply against the blue sky, but on the plain to the east a steamy heat was already rising. And in that slight haze, Daru, with heavy heart, made out the Arab walking slowly on the road to prison. . . .

"Rock," "sun" and "heat" point out that the desert has become mineral and inhuman again. The violence of the decor is now directed against Daru: the sun "beat[s] down on his head" and makes him sweat profusely. The unevenness of the terrain impedes his movements: when he arrives at the top of the hill, he is "out of breath." At the moment when he sees that the Arab has misunderstood him, Daru finds himself in a world which is both familiar and hostile.

When, a little later, the protagonist learns that he is threatened with revenge, the countryside takes on another aspect:

> The schoolmaster was watching the clear light bathing the whole surface of the plateau, but he hardly saw it. . . . Daru looked at the sky, the plateau, and, beyond, the invisible lands stretching all the way to the sea. In this vast landscape he had loved so much, he was alone. . . .

This countryside is the normal decor of the protagonist. All the elements are there: the sun suggested by "light," the mineral landscape evoked by "plateau." Heights, "sky" . . . , "the whole surface," "stretching out" and "vast" underscore the immensity of the decor. The image of a "young light" which "leaps" evokes joy. But Daru, who is looking at the countryside without seeing it, does not share in this joy nor in the immense panorama which stretches out before him. The countryside is no longer hostile; it is indifferent. Henceforth, Daru will be an exile in it.

Daru, who loved the desert, identified it with life: only there "could [he] have really lived." . . . He believed, it seems, that the countryside could resolve the problem which confronted him. The freedom that he gives the Arab is presented in the form of a choice between two human solidarities which intervene between him and the countryside. Daru manifests a tendency which Camus had noted in his *Notebooks* in May, 1937: "In our youth, we attach ourselves better to a landscape than to a man."

Attached to the desert, Daru was not able to see his situation clearly. The descriptions of the school's location, of the weather and of the snow have a symbolic value. They show that, as long as the Arab remained with him, the schoolmaster enjoyed a certain freedom of action. But that indecision could not continue. A choice was necessary: Daru had to join with either his threatened community or with a broader and more wretched humanity, represented by the Arab. He refuses to choose, daydreams about the countryside that he loves, and does nothing. Finally, the next morning, he rejects both the European community and the Arab. The similarity between his guest and the countryside plays a prophetic role; because of his refusal to join with the Arab, Daru loses the countryside. Even the gesture which accompanies the decision, the throwing of the stone, indicates that he has set in motion a mechanism which, in the end, exiles him from the country he loves.

The choice imposed on Daru orients the short story toward an underlying theme, the necessity for action. His indecision, when confronted with the need for action, exiles Daru from the comforting state of harmony with an indifferent nature which had satisfied him to that point. In all probability, he will be a victim of the quite human conflict which he could not escape. Whatever the outcome, Daru, a human being, a moral being, could not, without serious consequences for himself, deny his responsibility by identifying himself with a countryside.

The structure of the short story increases the value of the motif of inhumanity inherent in the presentation of the decor. Joy emanates from nature when Daru is joyful, but it also emanates from it when he is profoundly unhappy, overwhelmed by solitude. Daru has gambled on nature instead of on men. He has lost the help which human solidarity offers. The feeling of perfect union with the desert, a countryside after his own heart, has proven to be an illusion. From a certain point of view, this short story, published in 1957, states in esthetic terms one of the essential ideas concerning Camus's vision of nature, an idea which he formulated as early as 1937 in *The Wrong Side and the Right Side:* nature, an independent entity, does not lend itself to the schemes of man.

Source: Paul Fortier, ''The Symbolic Decor of 'The Guest','' translated by Joseph G. Morello, in *Essays on Camus's Exile and the Kingdom,* Romance Monographs, Inc., 1980, pp. 203–15.

Laurence Perrine

In the following excerpt, Perrine gives an overview of Camus' ''The Guest'' and discusses common misinterpretations of the story.

When I entered the classroom that morning, I was just in time to catch the class wag writing some ''clumsily chalked up words'' on the blackboard: ''You have handed us a difficult assignment. You will pay for this.'' She was absolutely right. When I read the papers my students had written defining the theme of Camus' short story ''The Guest,'' I found that, though they had sped their arrows bravely, none, in my opinion, had nicked the center of the target. The assignment was more difficult than I had anticipated. I paid by having to write lengthy notes in margins. Yet they were bright students, a selected group, not the usual cross-section of mediocrity.

Although there were scattered unique mistakes (e.g. Daru is an Arab schoolmaster), the misreadings clustered in four areas. I wish to examine these major misinterpretations. But first I must shoot my own arrow.

The protagonist of ''The Guest'' is Daru, a French Algerian who teaches a one-room school for

> ''A sensitive, humane, and compassionate man, Daru treats his hostage as a human being rather than as a member of a subject race, as a guest rather than as a prisoner.''

Arab children in the middle of the bleak Algerian plateau where he was born and which he loves. Into his solitude during a spell of bad weather comes the gendarme Balducci, leading an Arab who has killed his cousin in a dispute over some grain. Balducci insists on handing the prisoner over to Daru for delivery to police headquarters at a village some four hours distant. Daru protests that this is not his job; but Balducci, citing police shorthandedness in the face of an incipient Arab revolt, makes Daru sign for receipt of the prisoner, and departs.

A sensitive, humane, and compassionate man, Daru treats his hostage as a human being rather than as a member of a subject race, as a guest rather than as a prisoner. He unties the Arab's wrists so that he can drink his hot tea; he refuses to put the rope back on him afterwards; he eats his supper beside the Arab, much to the latter's surprise, for the Arab is not used to being treated as an equal by a Frenchman; he neglects to keep a pistol near his bed that night, though he has given the Arab a cot in the same room. Even though he is a French civil servant, he rebels against the notion of handing the Arab over to French authorities for trial.

The story centers around Daru's dilemma. Should he do what Balducci would consider his duty, obey orders, and deliver the prisoner? Or should he follow his own human impulse and give the Arab his freedom? On the one hand, Daru is responsible for the prisoner; he has been given an order; he has signed a receipt. In addition, he is a Frenchman; he will fight against the Arabs if war is declared; for him, as for Balducci, the French are ''us'' and the Arabs are ''they.'' Moreover, the Arab is a murderer; and Daru, a peaceable man, cannot repress his wrath against all men who wantonly kill, motivated by hate, spite, or blood lust. But then, on the other hand, the Arab is a human being, and it offends Daru's "honor" to treat him, however guilty, with anything less than human dignity. Such treatment demands that the Arab should be judged by his own people, not by alien French masters. It also demands that the Arab shall be treated as a "guest" while under Daru's roof. But this very treatment introduces an additional complication into Daru's dilemma, and one that is morally irrelevant. The stranger's presence in his room that night

> imposed on him a sort of brotherhood he refused to accept in the present circumstances; yet he was familiar with it. Men who share the same rooms, soldiers or prisoners, develop a strange alliance as if, having cast off their armor with their clothing, they fraternized every evening, over and above their differences, in the ancient community of dream and fatigue.

A guest, even an unwanted guest, exercises a rationally unjustifiable claim on one's loyalties.

The necessity of moral choice can be an almost intolerable burden, and Daru several times wishes he were free of it. In the afternoon, when he awakes from his nap, Daru is "amazed at the unmixed joy he derived from the mere thought the Arab might have fled and that he would be alone with no decision to make." During the night, when the Arab gets up to urinate, Daru at first thinks, "He is running away. Good riddance!" In the morning the Arab's continued presence irks him. "He simultaneously cursed his own people who had sent him this Arab and the Arab who had dared to kill and not managed to get away." But the decision must be made.

Daru solves his dilemma by taking the Arab a two hours' journey across the plateau to where two ways divide. Giving him a thousand francs and enough food to last for two days, he first points out the way to prison, a two-hour walk, and then the way to freedom, a day's journey to the pastures where the nomads will take him in and shelter him according to their law. When Daru looks back, later, he sees "with heavy heart" the Arab walking slowly on the road to prison. Still later, back in the classroom, he finds "clumsily chalked up" on the blackboard the words, "You have handed over our brother. You will pay for this."

Camus' story is about the difficulty, the agony, the complexity, the necessity, the worth, and the thanklessness of moral choice. It tells us that moral choice may be difficult and complex, with no clear distinction between good and evil, and with both rational and irrational, selfish and unselfish claims justifying each course of conduct. It tells us that

moral choice is a burden which man would willingly avoid if he could, but also that it is part of the human condition which man cannot evade and remain man. It shows us that man defines himself by moral choice, for Daru makes the choice which the reader wants him to make, and establishes his moral worth thereby. But the story also shows that moral decision has no ulterior meaning, for the universe does not reward it. Not only does the Arab fail to take the freedom offered him, but ironically the Arab's tribesmen misinterpret Daru's action and threaten revenge.

In large terms, Daru is representative of moral man, and the desert is representative of the world. Daru is essentially alone in this world, which is "cruel to live in," and life in it has no overarching or transcendental meaning.

> This is the way it was: bare rock covered three quarters of the region. Towns sprang up, flourished, then disappeared; men came by, loved one another or fought bitterly, then died. No one in this desert, neither he nor his guest, mattered.

In Camus' world man lives alone, makes his moral decisions alone, suffers alone, and dies alone. At the end of the story, in consequence of the very action by which Daru has affirmed his selfhood, he has cut himself off from those he had tried to aid. "In this vast landscape he had loved so much, he was alone." His loneliness is both literal and symbolic.

This account is doubtless incomplete, but it provides a context for discussing the major misinterpretations to which the story seems peculiarly subject. These are as follows:

1. *The main conflict is between conscience and society.* Daru must choose between doing what he himself believes right and what is expected of him. He must decide between his own standards and society's.

This interpretation is not so much wrong as it is an oversimplification. It is true that Balducci, the gendarme, is the voice of society, and that by Balducci's standards Daru's duty is clear and unequivocal. It is true also that Daru's immediate human impulse, his individual inner direction, is opposed to Balducci's concept. But the story is not a fictional counterpart of Emerson's *Self-Reliance* or Thoreau's *Civil Disobedience,* with individual right opposed to social wrong. Actually Daru's conscience is divided: it is on both sides of this conflict, and so are his loyalties. He does consider it contrary to honor and humanity to hand the prisoner over; but he is also revolted by the Arab's "stupid crime," which deserves trial and punishment. He does feel loyalty to the Arab as a member of the human race, but he also feels loyalty to his countrymen, with whom he will fight if war breaks out. What is required of Daru is not simply the courage to resist the pressures of society and do what is right, it is the courage to make a moral decision between alternatives neither of which is right. Balducci is not the representative of shallow social convention, nor is his request unreasonable: it makes sense in terms of ordinary "justice" and in terms of the national danger. Balducci, it must be noticed, is not portrayed unsympathetically. Though not so quickly sensitive as Daru, he is a fundamentally decent and kindly man, careful not to ride too fast and hurt the Arab, quick to approve of removing the bonds from the Arab's wrists, still ashamed, when he thinks of it, of putting a rope on another man. Fond of Daru as he is of his own son, he will not denounce Daru and he trusts Daru to tell the truth. He is representative, moreover, as is Daru, of a government which has tried to educate the Arabs and which provides wheat in times of drought. Daru is reluctant to hurt such a man, and feels remorse when he has done so. Conscience, that is, is on Balducci's side as well as on the Arab's.

2. *The story concerns the impossibility of isolating oneself from society and from human responsibility.* Though a man cannot accept the world, he is inevitably a part of the world. However hard he tries to escape it, the world will break in upon him and compel him to acknowledge its claims.

If my students had not made occasional references to the characters and plot, I would have sworn that some of them were describing Conrad's *Victory.* According to this interpretation Daru, like Conrad's Heyst, disgusted by mankind, feeling wrath "against all men with their rotten spite, their tireless hates, their blood lust," has disclaimed human involvements. He thus lives "almost like a monk" in the middle of a bleak plain far from humanity.

Again, this statement of theme is not so much wrong as it is an oversimplification. The story does show the impossibility of escaping human involvement. But Daru has fled neither responsibility nor mankind. He is an employee of the French government. He is engaged in the responsible task of education. In times of drought he distributes wheat, and deals not only with his pupils but with their fathers. If war comes, he will be a soldier, as he has been before, not a deserter. He has chosen this

isolated region to live in because he loves it, not because he hates mankind. "Daru had been born here. Everywhere else, he felt exiled." This is the place where he is rooted, not one that he has fled to. If his schoolhouse is remote from human habitation, it is probably so in order to serve all the neighboring villages equally. Moreover, he "had requested a post in the little town at the base of the foothills"; it was not his own choice that had assigned him to this more isolated spot, where at first he had found "the solitude and the silence" hard to bear.

3. *Daru evades making a decision.* Taking the easy way out, he shifts the entire responsibility for decision to the Arab. By thus refusing to become involved in the affairs of men, he rejects their brotherhood, and the consequences of his failure to act are worse than either of the alternative choices would have been.

It is true that Daru several times wishes he might be relieved of the necessity of choice. It is true also, as one perceptive student wrote, that Daru in pointing out the two ways to the Arab, "was trying to transfer some of the weight of decision from himself to the Arab." *Some* of the weight—precisely. For Daru is not paralyzed by inaction. He does not simply wait in indecision till the authorities or the Arabs crash in on him. By putting the Arab two hours on his way, by giving him a thousand francs and enough food to last two days, Daru takes positive action. The decision to let the Arab make his own decision is itself a decision. In effect, moreover, Daru is presenting the Arab with his freedom, if he will only take it. That the Arab does not take it leaves Daru with a "heavy heart," and is an ironical reward for all his trouble and agitation. He needn't have troubled himself. Except that, by troubling himself, he defines himself as a man, however little the action means to the total cosmos. He has not, like Pilate, washed his hands of evil; rather, in allowing the Arab to make his own choice, he has given the Arab the ultimate freedom—the only real freedom, Camus might say, that men have.

4. *The Arab chooses the road to prison* because *of Daru's kindness.* Responding to Daru's humane treatment, he feels that it would be dishonorable to violate Daru's trust. Like Daru he has a moral decision to make for right or wrong, and, like Daru, he chooses right. This decision is a point of honor to him.

If this interpretation is correct, then Daru's decision has indeed made some impact on the outer world, has meaning, however ironical, beyond a meaning for Daru himself. For this reason the reader who is repulsed by Camus' bleak portrayal of life is tempted to accept it. But it rests on too little evidence. From the beginning the Arab is pictured as passive, uncomprehending, a little stupid. Though his face has "a restless and rebellious look," he at no point makes any motion toward attempting to escape. When Daru asks Balducci, "Is he against us?" Balducci replies, "I don't think so." A prior attempt to escape, or an act of rebellion, would be necessary to establish a change of attitude on the Arab's part after Daru's decision. Instead, his passivity is stressed from the beginning of the story. He first appears, following Balducci, hands bound and head lowered, and the point is made that he not once raises his head. In the schoolroom he squats "motionless in the same spot" and "without stirring." During the night he makes no attempt to get away or to seize Daru's pistol, though he might easily have done so. His incomprehension also is emphasized. When Daru asks him why he killed the cousin, he gives an almost inconsequential answer. When Daru asks, "Are you sorry?" the Arab stares at him openmouthed. "Obviously he did not understand." He sleeps with "his mouth open"; the next morning his expression is "vacant and listless"; when Daru returns, after the journey has begun, to investigate a noise, the Arab watches "without seeming to understand"; when Daru gives him the food and money, he acts "as if he didn't know what to do with what was being given him." The Arab *is,* of course, anxious about his fate at the same time that he seems resigned to it. He wants to know whether Daru is the judge, and whether the gendarme is coming back the next day. He is also warmed by Daru's humanity; but his response is that he wants Daru to accompany him and Balducci to the police headquarters. Exactly what he is trying to communicate to Daru when Daru finally leaves him is of course a matter of speculation.

> The Arab had now turned toward Daru, and a sort of panic was visible in his expression. "Listen," he said.

But a good guess is that he is trying to repeat his earlier request, "Come with us." He doesn't want to be left alone in a hostile world. He wants the man to come with him who has treated him as a human being.

Camus' "The Guest" is a subtle and complex story. At one level it tells us about the French situation in Algeria between World War II and the Algerian War, a situation as difficult as Daru's, where also no choices were right ones. But primarily it is less about a political situation than about the human situation. It is about the difficulty, the complexity, the futility, and the glory of human choice.

Source: Laurence Perrine, "Camus' 'The Guest': A Subtle and Difficult Story," in *Studies in Short Fiction,* Vol. 11, no. 1, Fall, 1963, pp. 52–8.

Sources

Greim, Eberhard. "Albert Camus's 'The Guest': A New Look at the Prisoner." *Studies in Short Fiction* 30, No. 1 (Winter 1993): 95-8.

Hurley, D. F. "Looking for the Arab: Reading the Readings of Camus's 'The Guest.'" *Studies in Short Fiction* 30, No. 1 (Winter 1993): 79-93.

Noyer-Weidner, Alfred. "Albert Camus in His Short Story Phase." In *Essays on Camus's "Exile and the Kingdom,"* translated by Ernest Allen, ed. Judith Suther. University of Mississippi: Romance Monographs, Inc., 1980, pp. 45-87.

Perrine, Laurence. "Camus's 'The Guest': A Subtle and Difficult Story." *Studies in Short Fiction* 11, No. 1 (Fall 1963): 52-8.

Tarrow, Susan. In her *Exile from the Kingdom: A Political Rereading of Albert Camus,* pp. 173-93. Alabama: University of Alabama Press, 1985.

Further Reading

Howe, Irving. "Between Fact and Fable" Review in *The New Republic,* March 31, 1958, pp. 17-18.
   Early, mostly favorable review that discusses the tension between Camus as a man of ideas and a creative artist.

Hurley, D. F. "Looking for the Arab: Reading the Readings of Camus's 'The Guest.'" *Studies in Short Fiction* 30, No. 1, (Winter 1993): 79-93.
   An analysis of why many critics have been quick accept or further the negative portrayal of the Arab. Examines the use of early (unpublished) drafts of the story and biases on the part of critics.

In the Garden of the North American Martyrs

Tobias Wolff

1980

First published in the journal *Antaeus* in the spring of 1980, "In the Garden of the North American Martyrs" was later revised and became the title story of Tobias Wolff's first collection of short stories, published in 1981. This collection of fiction helped Wolff earn a reputation as one of the most promising writers of his generation. In this and the other stories in the book, Wolff probes the details of everyday life and ordinary characters in an effort to discern the aesthetic and moral patterns beneath the surface. In this story, Mary, a college professor who has carved out a safe career for herself by never risking originality, gets an offer to interview for an opening at a prestigious college. When she realizes that her interview has been arranged "just to satisfy a rule" about considering female candidates, she must choose how to react. Her final performance is a speech in which she finally recovers her power to speak in her true voice.

Author Biography

The widely respected author Tobias Wolff followed an unlikely and meandering path to such a position. As his memoir *This Boy's Life* chronicles, Wolff's childhood and adolescence were unconventional and unpromising. Wolff was born in 1945 in Birmingham, Alabama, the second son of Arthur Wolff, an aeronautical engineer, and his wife, Rosemary.

When Wolff was four his parents separated. His brother Geoffrey stayed with his father, and Wolff moved on with his mother.

Wolff and his mother moved from Florida to Utah, to Seattle, before settling in the remote Washington town of Chinook. His adolescence was characterized by loneliness, delinquency, and abuse from his stepfather. Finally fed up with his own dead-end life in high school, Wolff reestablished contact with his brother. Geoffrey Wolff, then a student at Princeton University, encouraged his younger brother to make more of himself and helped him channel his imagination into writing. Not completely reformed, however, Wolff forged both his transcript and letters of recommendation so that he would be admitted to and offered a scholarship by the elite boarding school, the Hill School. Though he was successful in getting in, he was eventually expelled because, as he says in *This Boy's Life,* he "knew nothing."

After his expulsion, Wolff joined the army and served in Vietnam. He then legitimately passed the entrance exams at England's Oxford University where he earned a B.A. degree in 1972. After failing as a journalist, he won one of the coveted fellowships to study creative writing at Stanford University in California. Having at last found his true calling, Wolff published his first story in 1976 and his first collection, *In the Garden of the North American Martyrs,* in 1981. He is a member of the English department at Syracuse University in New York and is the author of two additional volumes of stories, two memoirs, and a novella. According to an article in *Time* magazine in 1993, "a couple of years ago, the Hill School invited him back and, on the unanimous vote of his former classmates, gave him his high school diploma. Michael Caton-Jones' film version of *This Boy's Life,* starring Leonardo DiCaprio, Ellen Barkin, and Robert De Niro, was released in 1993.

Plot Summary

The story begins with a distant, omniscient narrator describing Mary, the main character. She is a history professor who has made a career of avoiding controversy and expressing only safe, approved views. After fifteen years of teaching at Brandon College she is forced to look for a new job when the college suddenly closes in the wake of an administrator's reckless and disastrous mishandling of its funds. Mary's belief in the rewards of prudence and caution is shaken by the evidence that anyone "could gamble a college."

Mary's mid-career job search yields only one offer: at a "new experimental college in Oregon." The narrator's description of the place makes it seem more like a high school than a college: "Bells rang all the time, lockers lined the hallways, and at every corner stood a buzzing water fountain." Mary dislikes Oregon and continues to look for other positions. After three years she receives an unexpected offer from a former colleague in the history department at Brandon, identified only as Louise. Louise, whose career and work on Benedict Arnold have been more high-profile than Mary's, wants to know if Mary is interested in applying for an opening at "the famous college in upstate New York" where she teaches. The offer surprises Mary, who remembers Louise as self-absorbed and indifferent to other people, but she sends off a resume. Louise calls to tell her she will be interviewed for the job.

Mary researches the area and feels comfortable when she arrives and is picked up at the airport by Louise. On the drive to the college, Louise demands certain responses from Mary—"how do I look?" and "Don't get serious on me." She abruptly tells Mary that she has a lover and complains that her husband and children have not been very understanding about it. Louise offhandedly mentions that Mary will have to give a class lecture as part of her interview. When Mary protests that she does not have anything prepared, Louise offers her a paper of her own on the Marshall Plan. She leaves Mary at the college visitor's center, saying she has to hurry off for a night with her lover.

After only a few hours, Mary is awakened by Louise, "snuffling loudly" and demanding to know if Mary thinks she is "womanly." She paces, cursing an unnamed "son of a bitch" who can be assumed to be her lover Jonathan, and then demanding "Let's suppose someone said I have no sense of humor. Would you agree or disagree?" Mary placates Louise with the compliments and praise she expects. Louise delivers a demeaning remark about Mary's own appearance before settling down to pass the rest of the night chain-smoking on the couch. She leaves at daybreak. Mary has had no further sleep.

Mary spends the morning touring the campus with a student guide named Roger. The campus is an exact duplicate of a college in England, and college-themed movies have been filmed there. Mary notes that the college's motto, "God helps those who help themselves" takes on an entirely new meaning considering how many of the school's "illustrious graduates" had "helped themselves to railroads, mines, armies, states; to empires of finance with outposts all over the world."

Roger is especially reverent when he shows Mary the power plant that runs the college. Mary gets the impression that the machine is the soul of the place. While they are contemplating it, Roger brags that the college has become much more progressive, even letting "girls come here now, and some of the teachers are women." In fact, a new policy requires that at least one woman be interviewed for each opening.

The interview begins badly and gets progressively worse. Arriving twenty minutes after the scheduled time, Louise and her male colleagues do not even pretend to take Mary seriously. They chat inanely about the weather and the other differences between Oregon and upstate New York and then pronounce that they are out of time. When Dr. Howells, the department chair, asks if there is anything she wants to tell them, Mary laughs and says "I think you should give me the job." When nobody else laughs, Mary understands that "they were not really considering her for the position." She confronts Louise about bringing her there on false pretenses, but Louise's characteristically self-centered response is that she thought a visit from Mary might cheer her up. "I deserve some love and friendship but I don't get any."

Mary still has to go through the charade of delivering her lecture. In front of a room full of students and faculty, Mary for once in her professional life does not take the safe path. Rather than reading Louise's article, Mary tells the gruesome story of the capture and torture of French Jesuits by the Iroquois, one of the tribes native to the region. When Dr. Howells tries to stop her, she begins to preach in the guise of recounting one of the priest's last words: "Mend your lives. . . . You have deceived yourselves in the pride of your hearts. . . . Turn from power to love. Be kind. Do justice. Walk humbly." Mary turns off her hearing aid so that she can continue to talk without the distractions of those trying to silence her.

Tobias Wolff

Characters

Dr. Howells

Dr. Howells is the chairman of the department of history at the prestigious college where Louise works and where Mary is led to believe she is a job candidate. He is arrogant, detached, and pretentious. The air of entitlement and superiority with which he presents himself is undermined, however, by his appearance. Mary is able to remember his name in part because he is so strikingly ugly, with a "porous blue nose and terrible teeth."

Jonathan

Louise describes Jonathan as her lover. He never appears in the story. Because Louise barges in on Mary late on a night she said she would be spending with Jonathan, demanding to know if Mary thinks she is "womanly" or has a sense of humor, readers can guess that he has expressed dissatisfaction with her in regard to those qualities.

Louise

Louise, a former colleague of Mary's at Brandon College, is now a professor of history at an unnamed "prestigious college in upstate New York." At first glance she is everything Mary is not: married and

Media Adaptations

- "In the Garden of the North American Martyrs" was recorded on audiotape by Symphony Space Literary publishers with Jane Curtin narrating. The story appears on Volume VII of *Selected Shorts: A Celebration of the Short Story*.

outgoing, but self-centered and pretentious. It becomes evident that she is desperately insecure and has no scruples about using other people to fulfil her own needs: she talks incessantly about herself, complains about her husband and children's negative reactions to her having taken a lover, and frankly admits, when confronted, that she knew Mary did not have a chance at the job, but arranged for her interview because she remembered Mary as "funny," saying "I've been unhappy and I thought you might cheer me up."

Mary

Mary, whose last name is not revealed, is the protagonist of the story. She has based her career as an academic on saying, writing, and teaching nothing with which anyone could reasonably disagree. As a result she practically loses the capacity for original thought, and has managed to survive fifteen years on the faculty of Brandon College, teaching and writing the blandest of ideas. When she eventually loses her job due to the closing of the college, she is forced to trade her dull credentials on a fiercely competitive job market. An interview at a prestigious college finally gives her the opportunity to take stock of her life and career. At the conclusion of the story she recovers the voice she had lost in a lifetime of listening too closely to the words of others.

Roger

Roger is the college student whose job it is to show Mary around the campus before her interview and lecture. He is cheerful and shallow as he uncritically points out the emblems of the college's elitism and privilege.

Ted

Ted is Louise's husband and the father of her children. Though he never appears in the story, he is a sympathetic character because readers understand that his intolerance of Louise's behavior is completely reasonable and understandable.

Themes

Moral Corruption

The inclusion of the word *martyr* in the title invites readers to consider the themes of moral corruption and sin. Martyrs are those who are willing to die for their beliefs, usually at the hands of unbelievers or sinners. Because their deaths live on in legend and story, the martyrs serve as examples to others of the ultimate triumph of their purity over corruption, good over evil.

Though no one actually dies in Wolff's short story, the author does ask readers to compare the martyrdom of Mary by Louise and the members of her department to the Jesuit missionaries at the hands of the Iroquois. Mary's experience during her campus visit and interview reveals the total moral corruption of the members of the history department, if not of the entire college, and the culture to which it belongs. They have come to believe that their social and intellectual superiority grants them permission to take advantage of and manipulate other people in order to serve their own ends. Mary herself is prepared to behave in the same morally corrupt fashion when she agrees to present Louise's paper as her own. In the end, though, Mary chooses the martyr's path, sacrificing her personal success and reputation in order to reveal the corruption of her tormentors.

Betrayal

The theme of betrayal dominates the narrative of "In the Garden of the North American Martyrs." Mary's betrayal by Louise and the rest of her department at the upstate New York college is foreshadowed by Mary's own lifetime of betraying herself. Readers learn early in th story that Mary has betrayed her own inner compass by making a habit of suppressing her true feelngs and practising dull, safe scholarship. The costs of this betrayal are physical as well as intellectual. She loses her ability to speak freely and spontaneously, wryly attributes a premature hearing loss to her tendency to hang on the words of others, and contracts a mysterious illness in her lungs.

Louise betrays Mary by luring her to interview for a job she has no chance of getting. Unlike Mary, though, Louise is arrogantly unaware that there are or will be any consequences for her actions. She does not see, for example, as readers do, that her research into famous traitor Benedict Arnold has taught her history lessons of a more practical variety. She betrays her husband and children by taking a lover and then faults them for being unsupportive of her. Although the story ends before we know what the future holds for Louise, her nervousness, heavy smoking, and evidently unsatisfactory experience with her lover give some indication that her world is fraying around the edges.

In all these instances betrayal is a source of pain and confusion, but "In the Garden of the North American Martyrs" challenges readers to consider another definition of the word. In some instances, *betray* can mean to give away, disclose, or unconsciously reveal. So when Roger brags about the college's new recruiting policy for female faculty, he betrays the real reason that Mary has been brought to campus. Dr. Howells and the other committee members betray their true intentions by spending only a few minutes with Mary, chatting inanely about the weather in different parts of the country, clearly not conducting a serious interview for the open position.

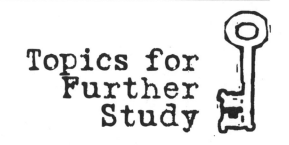

Topics for Further Study

- Why would a college have a rule that requires interviewing at least one female candidate for each job opening? What laws or court decisions have helped shape such policies?

- Critics often mention Flannery O'Connor when talking about Wolff. How does Wolff's exploration of morality and prophecy differ from O'Connor's as illustrated in her story "A Good Man Is Hard to Find"?

- Research the history of the French Jesuits in the Great Lakes region during colonial times. How did their religious views influence their behavior, and what effects did their presence have on the culture?

- What are Louise's motivations for using Mary as she does? What theories of psychology might explain her behavior?

goes on to say that this shift in point of view was necessary because her voice needs to dominate the narrative by the time she gets to her dramatic concluding speech.

Style

Point of View and Narration

"In the Garden of the North American Martyrs" is presented to readers in third-person omniscient narration. The narrator describes Mary's past in order to clarify her present situation. In the first part of the story, the narrator appears to regard Mary indifferently or even negatively. As the narrative progresses, however, Mary is presented more sympathetically and—importantly—Louise and some other characters are shown in a very bad light. Wolff subtly shifts the point of view. He explained in an interview with Jay Woodruff in 1991 that he always intended to let Mary take over the narration, that his "aim was to hand the story over to her." He

Tone

"In the Garden of the North American Martyrs" contains some significant tone variations that help contribute to the meaning of the story and parallel the shifts in point of view. Tone is the dominant attitude that the reader hears in the story. It can be ironic, genial, or objective, for example. The beginning of the story is characterized by the neutral and objective tone of the narrator, but by the end the tone is prophetic, resembling the language of the Old Testament. The success of the story hinges on this dramatic shift in tone, so that Mary's voice shatters the aura of smug and false objectivity that dominates both the auditorium and the story. Wolff describes Mary's speech in the interview with Jay Woodruff as language that "bursts the bounds of traditional realistic fiction."

Imagery

Careful readers will notice that "In the Garden of the North American Martyrs" begins and ends with images of birds. Mary likens her diminishing capacity for original thought to the sight of "birds flying away." In the final scene, when she delivers her prophecy to her stunned audience, one of the last things Mary hears before she turns off her hearing aid is "someone whistling in the hallway outside, trilling the notes like a bird, like many birds." According to Wolff's explanation in his interview with Jay Woodruff, "Language, especially the language which she speaks at the end, her own language, is freedom, is flight." In an earlier interview with Bonnie Lyons and Bill Oliver, Wolff explains that the sound of the bird in the hallway is "a sign of her own voice coming back to her. An image of the words she has lost, like birds flying away."

Historical Context

The Iroquois and the Jesuits

The Iroquois are the original inhabitants of the land on which the prestigious college now sits. The League of the Iroquois became a powerful force in colonial America because of the military prowess of its member nations, the Mohawk, Cayuga, Oneida, Seneca, and Onandaga. Although they once presided over most of what is now upstate New York, the remaining 11,000 Iroquois now own less than 80,000 acres.

The Iroquois are also remembered for their savage treatment of Jean de Brebeuf and Gabriel Lalemant. The two French Jesuit missionaries were captured near their mission in March of 1649 and tortured before being executed. They are known as the North American Martyrs and were canonized, or declared saints, in the Catholic church in 1930.

Academia

During the 1970s the job market for college and university professors began a steep decline. There were many more highly educated candidates than there were positions available. Following a trend that continues today, hiring departments can make whatever demands they wish on job candidates and have occasionally regarded applicants with disdain and condescension. Furthermore, the increased competition for jobs among recent Ph.D.s has inflated the importance of scholarly production, of books and articles, in other words. For example, Mary has had to produce a second book in order to be considered for other positions, but nobody cares, not even Mary, that it is not very good. During this period, institutions of higher education were also experiencing the effects of the women's movement. Elite colleges saw the economic, if not the ethical, advantages of admitting female students and administrators under pressure to hire female faculty launched initiatives to at least create the appearance of fair hiring practices.

Critical Overview

When the collection of which "In the Garden of the North American Martyrs" is the title story was published in 1981, it received almost universal critical praise. The twelve pieces in this collection included the first story Wolff ever published, "Smokers," which had first appeared in *Atlantic Monthly*. In 1986 Bantam Books reissued six of the twelve stories in a single volume together with Wolff's award-winning novella set on a Georgia Army base during the Vietnam War, *The Barracks Thief*.

Though Wolff published a second volume of short stories, *Back in the World* in 1985, his first volume remains a favorite with critics. Offering backhanded praise for *In the Garden of the North American Martyrs* while criticizing Wolff's newest book, Russell Banks wrote in the *New York Times Book Review* that "this book is a considerable falling off for Mr. Wolff." Writing in *The Nation*, reviewer Brain Kaplan has high praise for Wolff's first collection, singling out the title story as an exceptional example of Wolff's ability to "use words to test lives against accidental and self-selected conditions."

Criticism

Elisabeth Piedmont-Marton

Piedmont-Marton holds a Ph.D. in English and teaches American literature and administers

What Do I Read Next?

- *This Boy's Life* (1989) by Tobias Wolff is an account of Wolff's adolescence and early adulthood. The memoir is told through the eyes of the boy, leaving the reader free to draw conclusions and make judgements about events the child could not have fully understood at the time.

- *The Adventures of Huckleberry Finn* is the classic novel about another boy whose coming of age is characterized by a tendency to stretch the truth and who must make difficult decisions without much adult guidance.

- *Wise Blood*, Flannery O'Connor's darkly comic novella about a misguided preacher's search for meaning and moral certainty.

- *Dubliners* is the collection of short stories by Irish author James Joyce that Wolff often mentions as having a major influence on his writing.

- *Ellen Foster* (1989) by Kaye Gibbons is a novel about a female character whose lonely and unparented childhood resembles Huck Finn's and the young Toby Wolff's.

- *The Duke of Deception* (1979) is Geoffrey Wolff's memoir of growing up with his father, a con artist.

---

the Writing Center at the University of Texas. In this essay she discusses the symbolic and moral dimensions of "In the Garden of the North American Martyrs."

"In the Garden of the North American Martyrs" belongs to the category, or genre, of literature known as modern realism. Tobias Wolff has often expressed his admiration for the stories of John Cheever and is a particular fan of James Joyce's collection of stories *Dubliners*. Despite his canny eye for detail and his gift for dialog, however, Wolff seems to work against the constraints of realism. "In the Garden of the North American Martyrs" in particular dramatizes the tension between the realistic and symbolic ways of looking at the world. The story, in Wolff's own words, "bursts the bounds of traditional realistic fiction." Reviewer Brian Kaplan writes in the *Nation* that Wolff "scrutinizes the disorders of daily living to find significant order underneath the surface." "In the Garden of the North American Martyrs" suggests that this order, or meaning, may be found on both the symbolic and moral levels.

The symbolic strands that will be woven together at the story's conclusion are introduced at the beginning. The narrator likens Mary's failure to pursue original thought to birds shrinking away to "remote, nervous points, like birds flying away." Mary even takes on some physical characteristics of birds, even cocking her head to one side in an effort to "catch everything everyone said."

Another cluster of images whose symbolic significance unfolds as the story develops is that of the wilderness and that most immutable force of nature, the weather. During the three years she spends at the experimental college in Oregon, Mary feels as if she is being besieged by rain and its consequences. "There was water in Mary's basement. Her walls sweated, and she had found toadstools growing behind the refrigerator. She felt as though she were rusting out, like one of those old cars people thereabouts kept in their front yards, on pieces of wood. Mary knew that everyone was dying, but it seemed to her that she was dying faster than most." She develops a lung disorder and her hearing problem is exacerbated by the dampness, almost as though she were trapped underwater.

The climate and scenery in New York at first seem to invigorate Mary, but soon the landscape takes on more ominous features. Louise prattles on

> "A cluster of images whose symbolic significance unfolds as the story develops is that of the wilderness and that most immutable force of nature, the weather."

about her love life as she drives Mary to her guest cabin, oblivious to the persistent and vaguely menacing presence of the world outside her window. Mary, however, notices "the forest all around, deep black under a plum colored sky. There were few lights and these made the darkness seem even greater." Though it will not become clear until Mary invokes the spirits of the Iroquois and the martyred Jesuits at the conclusion of the story, the landscape represents the dark and violent history of the place from which, ironically, Louise and her fellow historians are completely disconnected. Mary, whose habit of listening closely serves her well in this instance, is almost able to hear the voices of those who have gone before.

The next day when Mary visits the college she sees that Louise is not alone in her arrogant dismissal of the history of the place. The college, as the student guide Roger explains, is "an exact copy of a college in England, right down to the gargoyles and stained glass windows." The symbolic heart of the place, as it turns out, is not the library or the chapel, but the power plant, which represents the power that those with wealth and privilege use to grind up those without it. The machine puts its mark on the landscape and appropriates the earth's resources in order to keep itself running. Wolff is suggesting in this image that Louise and her colleagues have become so obsessed with feeding the machine and so deafened by its noise that they cannot recognize *history*—even their own—when they are surrounded by it. Ironically, it is the machine that finally reveals the truth to Mary. While watching it hum, Mary comes to understand that "she had been brought there to satisfy a rule," that the overwhelming mechanisms of power have manipulated her. But the machine also offers her a choice. She can be a smoothly compliant cog, or she can be a stray bolt

that brings the whole thing to a grinding halt. Though the machine is a morally neutral object, its symbolic presence offers Mary a moral choice.

Knowing that she has been betrayed by Louise and used by the "machinery" of the prestigious college, Mary must decide whether she should stick to the safe course she has followed all her career, or strike out into the wilderness of the unknown. To do only what is expected—blandly read Louise's lecture on the Marshall Plan—is to give in. When she comes to the podium Mary is "unsure of what she would say; only that she would rather die than read Louise's article." She decides to "wing it," and all the words that had long ago flown away into "remote, nervous points" return to her, giving her the power not just of speech but of prophecy. In the end, she address the group directly, speaking in the tradition of the stern New England preacher, imploring them to mend their ways and "turn from power to love."

In invoking the story of Brebeuf and Lalement's torture and capture by the Iroquois, Mary proves herself the superior historian and defeats the machine reasoning of Louise, Dr. Howells and the rest of the faculty. Her "pronouncements on justice and love disorder the machinery of expectation," as critic Brina Caplan puts it. Her sense of history is so profound that when she looks around the lecture hall it has been almost transformed to the mission where the French priests were held in 1649: "The sun poured through the stained glass onto the people around her, painting their faces. Thick streams of smoke from the young professor's pipe drifted through a circle of red light at Mary's feet, turning crimson and twisting like flames." Like the North American martyrs, Mary regards her "captors," or audience, as savages with painted faces. Also like Brebeuf and Lalement, Mary knows that there is nothing she can do to change their minds or alter the inevitable course of action. Her only choice is to make her final moments morally instructive.

While readers appreciate the dramatic and symbolic effect of the comparison between Mary's ill treatment and that of the North Americans martyred by the Iroquois, and may recognize that Mary's performance is an act of moral courage, the story poses an even larger moral question that lingers long after reading. Readers must ask themselves whether, by any standards of right and wrong, Mary's ordeal is even remotely comparable to the hideous torture and execution of Brebeuf and

Lalement. While Mary's speech can be understood as ironic, or even farcical, as Brina Caplan suggests, some readers may still be left with the troubling sense that the tortures and death that Mary so vividly describes have been trivialized in order to serve Mary's (nonlife-threatening) ends, making her just as morally corrupt as Louise and her colleagues.

Source: Elisabeth Piedmont-Marton, for *Short Stories for Students,* Gale, 1998.

William Rouster

Rouster has a Ph.D. in rhetoric and composition and has published in a number of composition journals. In the following essay he discusses symbolism in "In the Garden of the North American Martyrs."

Tobias Wolff's "In the Garden of the North American Martyrs" was published in his book of short stories, *In the Garden of the North American Martyrs: A Collection of Short Stories* in 1981. As the title indicates, the story deals with images of martyrdom on this continent. Of the literary devices used in this short story, the dominant one is that of symbolism, which refers to the use of people, objects, creatures, places, and events to represent more than just themselves. Symbolism is one of the most widely used and effective literary devices of all, since many authors wish to give their work greater relevance than just the story that is being told. Therefore, Mary in this story symbolizes more than just this one person, Mary, and the university in the East is meant to represent more than that one university. In "In the Garden of the North American Martyrs," nearly all of the characters, events, and places have symbolic significance, and the meaning of the story is to be found therein.

Of the characters presented, the most significant is Mary, no last name given, and we are told the story of her academic career. Mary appears to symbolize those members of the academy, or university system, who lose their identity to the power of that system. Mary, in itself, is a very common name, thus the main character could represent almost anyone, and, indeed, she works very hard to not be someone who stands out from the academic crowd in any important way.

Mary particularly strives to remain anonymous after witnessing the dismissal of an intelligent and

> " In 'In the Garden of the North American Martyrs,' nearly all of the characters, events, and places have symbolic significance, and the meaning of the story is to be found therein."

insightful colleague who had offended powerful members of their college with his ideas. She writes her history lectures out in total and uses not her own ideas, but only those of others who have been judged by the academy to be noncontroversial. In doing this she begins to lose her own ideas: "her own thoughts she kept to herself, and the words for them grew faint as time went on; without quite disappearing they shrank to remote nervous points, like birds flying away." To avoid being thought too boring, Mary cultivates an image of eccentricity by committing to memory comedy routines and jokes.

Mostly, Mary listens to others. Her image of herself as a listener comes to her from a reflection that she spots in a window as she is listening to a senior member of her department. "She was leaning toward him and had her head turned so that her right ear was right in front of his moving mouth." This image symbolizes her loss of self to the power of the academy, an academy to which she only listens and does not speak. Eventually, Mary develops hearing problems from, she guesses, listening too much to others.

Fifteen years after Mary's arrival at Brandon University, it closes its doors. She eventually finds work at an experimental college in Oregon where she is most unhappy in the persistent rain. Mary, however, appears to be rescued from the rust and rain of Oregon when a former colleague, Louise, contacts her to tell her of a job opening at her college in upstate New York, for which Mary applies and gets an interview. She is determined to get this job, mainly by not offending anyone. On the plane trip she begins to feel that she is going home, a feeling which grows stronger during the flight eastward. She describes this feeling to Louise as "deja vu."

What she is going home to is her own martyrdom at the hands of the machine itself. In this story, the machine symbolizes the almighty, unappeasable, unfeeling force of the university system which feeds on people such as Mary. The student showing her around the campus takes her to view the power plant: "They were standing on an iron catwalk above the biggest machine Mary had ever beheld. . . . Where before he had been gabby Roger now became reverent. It was clear that for him this machine was the soul of the college, that the purpose of the college was to provide outlets for the machine."

The college served the machine and this college is meant to symbolize all colleges: "Roger, the student assigned to show Mary around, explained that it was an exact copy of a college in England, right down to the gargoyles and stained-glass windows. It looked so much like a college that moviemakers sometimes used it as a set." The motto of the college, written above the door of the Founder's Building read "God helps those who help themselves" and listed among the most prominent graduates of the college were men who took a great deal from society in terms of riches, but gave very little in return.

Louise is an interesting example of an individual who takes without giving at this college. She likely represents one of the feeding tentacles of the college machine. Louise is totally self-absorbed, and although she is wreaking havoc on the lives of those around her, she is concerned only with herself. She invites Mary to be sacrificed because Mary cheers her up. She takes a lover in spite of the pain it causes her husband and family because of the positive influence she thinks it has on her: "My concentration has improved, my energy level is up, and I've lost ten pounds. I'm also getting some color in my cheeks." She says about her family's negative reaction: "there is no reasoning with any of them. In fact, they refuse to discuss the matter at all, which is very ironical because over the years I have tried to instill in them a willingness to see things from the other person's point of view." Indeed, Louise is as incapable of feeling for others as the marauding Iroquois had been, and the writer makes it clear that Louise is a modern-day Iroquois: Louise "reminded Mary of a description in the book she'd been reading of how Iroquois warriors gave themselves visions by fasting" because "she had seemed gaunt and pale and intense" at the airport.

It becomes clear throughout the latter half of the story that Mary is to become a North American martyr in this college garden, the sacrificial offering. Fire and smoke play prominently in the story's imagery. Louise, a chain smoker, asks Mary to light her a cigarette soon after Mary arrives. Smoke drifts from two of the cabins in the visitor's quarters and, as soon as Mary and Louise step through the door of Mary's cabin, Louise states "Look . . . . they've laid a fire for you. All you have to do is light it." One of the men interviewing Mary smokes a pipe. As Mary beings to give the lecture part of the interview, "thick streams of smoke from the young professor's pipe drifted through a circle of red light at Mary's feet, turning crimson and twisting like flames." Mary is being symbolically burned at the stake, by an audience of savages who are painted by the sunlight streaming through the windows.

It is in Mary's lecture that we learn about the North American martyrs and their garden, two Jesuit priests who were tortured and killed by the Iroquois on the site of the college. Originally, Mary is going to read one of Louise's papers, thereby giving her own voice and identity up completely, but when she learns that she has no chance at the position, she decides to do something she never before would have dared—to "wing it"—and quit playing it safe. The place she is giving the speech is in the Long House of the Five Nations of the Iroquois, a pitiless tribe of torturers and murderers who became powerful through their lack of mercy, much as the members and graduates of this college had done to others. Of the two Jesuit martyrs, one was burned to death and the other tortured and eaten alive as he preached to them. The Iroquois ate strips of his skin and cut off his lips and then drank his blood, all while he was still alive. In much the same way the academy has eaten Mary alive: she has almost nothing left of herself, and cannot even speak her own ideas.

Mary continues to speak through the silence of those listening once she runs out of facts about the Iroquois, and rebuffs the professors much as she imagined the dying Jesuit had rebuffed the Iroquois as they were killing him:

> Mend your lives, she said. You have deceived yourselves in the pride of your hearts, and the strength of your arms. Though you soar aloft like the eagle, though your nest is set among the stars, thence I will bring you down, says the Lord. Turn from power to love. Be kind. Do justice. Walk humbly.

Mary is not done talking after this, winging it as she goes. She shuts off her hearing aid so that no one can interrupt her and continues talking. At the moment of her martyrdom, Mary has found her own voice.

Source: William Rouster, for *Short Stories for Students,* Gale, 1998.

Tobias Wolff with Jay Woodruff

In the following excerpt from a longer interview, Wolff describes his writing process and how the story "In the Garden of the North American Martyrs" evolved.

[Jay Woodruff] How did this story get started? What was its genesis?

[Tobias Wolff] Well, there are a few things that I can trace it to. One is a job interview I had several years ago which was not, it turned out, a serious interview. That is, I had been brought across the country in order to fulfill a requirement of the college that so many people be interviewed for each position. And when I found this out it really burned me up. I tried writing the story a couple of times from a personal point of view, my own point of view. This never really took. It sounded whiny, "poor me." After all, I live a rarified life, one that's lucky compared to almost everybody else's. This didn't seem to be the stuff of tragedy.

I'd had the experience of watching my mother struggle and have a harder time of it than she would have had if she were a man. It occurred to me that this was the kind of experience women have a lot more often than men. And once I was able to make that leap, get out of my own case and see the whole question of injustice in a larger way, then this story began to take. I began to feel its possibilities. I went back to it and worked on it for several months. And this is what I came up with. I was ransacking my files here, hoping to find some remnants of that original draft. But I couldn't find it, so I must have thrown it away. Anyway, I put it through many different versions. That's the genesis of the story.

How long did you struggle with those first attempts before you put the story aside?

I'm a very slow writer. If people knew how hard it was for me they'd think I was crazy to be a writer. I suppose a couple of months, anyway. It usually takes me that long to give up. I'll usually even finish a bad story and then not send it off rather than not finish it, because I'm terrified of developing the habit of giving up on stories as I write them. I've had trouble with even my best stories along the way, and I've been tempted to quit on them. So I

> "Language, especially the language which Mary speaks at the end, her own language, is freedom, is flight. It's why I use the image of birds there."

know from experience that if I see it through I might end up with a good story. Then again I might not. But it's the only chance I've got to finish the thing. I did finish a story—it just wasn't a story that I liked, that's all. But that took me a couple, three months to write. And then I went back and worked another three months on the version you're reading now.

Once you'd made that leap and knew this was going to be in the third person with a female point-of-view character, how much at that point did you know about the story?

Well, by no means everything. I was surprised, as I often am in writing a story, by many of the things that came up. For example, the appearance of the Jesuit martyrs in the story was a late thought in the process. You ask, what's the genesis of a story? Almost everything a writer is doing at a given time can be part of the genesis of a story. I was reading Parkman's wonderful book, *The Jesuits in North America,* and I was riveted by his description of the martyrdom of Brebeuf and Lalement. I dreamt about it a couple of nights. It exerted itself on the story I was writing in a strange way, because it helped me to see that much of what the story was about had to do with power. It illuminated that for me. There are so many forces at play in the writing of a story. Take "The Dead," Joyce's story. Why did he write that story in the first place? Because somebody scolded him about *Dubliners,* told him he'd left out something essential to the people of Dublin, their great sense of hospitality. And he agreed. He went back and he wrote, I think, the greatest thing he ever wrote. Somebody said something that illuminated his own work for him.

When I made the peculiar juxtaposition that allowed the Jesuits to spill into the story, I knew that there was something right and even necessary about it. I wrote this story thirteen or fourteen years ago now, and it's hard to recover all the stages of its evolution because I don't keep rough drafts.

Why don't you keep drafts?

They embarrass me, to tell you the truth. Many writers seem to have a tremendous confidence in their futures and a certain assumption that generations to come are going to be interested in what they've written at every stage. I guess I really don't have that feeling. I only want people to see my work at its very best. I don't even let my wife look at things I'm writing until I'm done with them, or at least until I've brought them as far as I can. I come very slowly to the ends of my stories, and the work I do to get there is rough. It's often very false. It's awkward. It's not interesting to me. It might be interesting, I suppose, to somebody who wanted to see just how dramatic a difference revision can make to a hopeless writer, to give everyone else hope. But I think part of my reluctance is that people would think I was crazy, really, to be a writer, if they could see my early drafts and see how hard it is for me to get from one place to another.

Do you get terribly discouraged?

Less and less so because I know now that it will finally work out. It used to be much harder for me because it seems such a strange way to write. And I knew that other people weren't writing that way. I thought there must be something wrong with me. But now I've learned that this is the way I write. And I can't imagine doing anything else. I love finishing a good story. Or finishing what I think is a good book. No feeling can compare. And then it's all been worth it. But it's hard as it goes, sometimes. Once I get a first draft down, once I really know where I'm going and what the story is about, and what I'm trying to do, then a kind of playfulness enters in to my writing that I absolutely live for. It's getting that first draft out that's very, very hard for me.

Do you ever get a draft out and get stuck with it? Like not know—

How to crack it?

Yeah.

Once in a while that happens to me. It does happen sometimes. And then I just throw the story away. I'll fool with it for a while and then throw it away. Once in a while I'll finish something that I like but don't really think is a serious story. That

happened to me last year. I'm going to let the story be published, but I'm probably not going to include it in a collection. I think it's a funny story, and it's an odd story. I like it. But in the end it really doesn't really earn its keep for me, so I probably won't collect it.

So you have a good number of uncollected stories?

Oh yes, I have enough uncollected stories to make a couple of collections, probably. At least one. But I won't collect them. Now and then I'll go back and reread them, wondering if I was just being too hard on myself. And I'll say no, I wasn't.

It must be a difficult position to negotiate. I mean to be at a point in your writing life where you could, I would assume, get a story published just about anywhere you want.

I wish.

Am I completely naive about that? I would assume that most magazines would be very happy to publish your work.

I've been very lucky. But there's a lot of competition. Don't forget, Saul Bellow had won the Nobel Prize before he was ever able to place a story in the *New Yorker*. ''The Silver Dish'' was the first story he ever had in the *New Yorker*. Magazines are run by editors with tastes of their own. And that's the way it ought to be. What other way could it be? Some editors seem hospitable to my fiction; others don't. It isn't a question, though, of my being able to finish a story and send it out and be sure of selling it, because that really isn't the case. I've got a story right now I really like that I'm sending to quarterlies, because I know I can't place it with large-circulation magazines because of the things that go on in it. Andre Dubus has an essay on being a writer, in which he says that there's a moment when something happens in a story he's writing, something untoward or violent, and he thinks to himself, Well, there goes the *New Yorker*. And the moment he has that thought, a wonderful sense of release and freedom comes over him—that it is no longer even possible to think about responding to some editor's taste. He's beyond the pale already and it gives him freedom. And I think that's exactly where you start becoming interesting as a writer, when you give up trying to second-guess some editor somewhere into taking a story, which you can never count on anyway. It doesn't do to try to figure it out. You just write the best you can and hope that somebody out there is going to hear you. . . .

Getting back to "In the Garden of the North American Martyrs": that was not the first story that you wrote in this collection.

No, by no means. The first published story in there came out in '76. That is the story called "Smokers." Actually, there's another story in here that predates it, called "Face to Face." That was written in '73 or so, though it wasn't actually published until '78.

Do you always have to be sure you've found the right first sentence in order to find the rest of a story?

I simply need a place to begin. Later on, when I revise, I often think of a better first line, especially, of course, if I've decided to change point of view, as I did in this story. Once in a while I'm lucky enough to find the right first sentence in the very beginning. For example, the tone I struck in the first line of "The Poor Are Always with Us" was right and helped me find the rest of the story. I also liked the first sentence I wrote for "The Rich Brother." But that doesn't always happen. I try to be as open to chance as possible when I'm writing. If I have things too firmly in mind I lose a certain fluidity and ability to be surprised, which is very important to me. In this story I realized I needed to begin with the image of this woman making herself a completely accommodated creature.

What particular passages gave you special trouble? Do you recall any in the story?

Her speech, at the end. I didn't know how far to go with it. To some extent it bursts the bounds of traditional realistic fiction. The voice becomes prophetic. In fact, I think some of those passages are from the Psalms and the Prophets. Jeremiah is the source of a couple of lines. They're all jumbled together in my mind, but they came out, I think, coherently. But she's definitely speaking in a heightened voice there. It isn't a realistic story of the kind, say, in *Dubliners*. And the decision whether to allow that to happen in the story was a tough one to make because it then became a different kind of story—a parable, almost, rather than the kind of story I think of myself as writing.

That ending seems to work very well on a realistic level, though. I guess partly that might be because she's at a podium giving a lecture to an audience.

It lends itself to that, it does. I tried to hold it as close as I could to the possible. I didn't want to lose the story's authority by becoming just clever, or facile. . . .

Did you know much about Louise when you started this version of the story?

By the time I got this far along, in this draft, yes, of course I did. But I had to explore her. And the way I explore my characters is by writing them. I'm not very good at sitting down and thinking a whole story out before I write it. I don't seem to have that gift. I really have to sit down and write the story out, and write my way into the story, and just keep going at it again and again and again, sinking farther and farther into it just by spending more time with it. In that way I get to know the characters. The main character was very, very different in different drafts.

In what ways?

Well, in one draft I had her niece living with her, who'd had to leave home because she was pregnant. So there was an additional onus on Mary and a necessity to work. But that felt cluttered. It was another character to develop, another situation. Once I made the decision to allow the prophetic voice to enter the story, I thought it should have the cleanness of line that a parable has, that it shouldn't have those jagged edges and little tributaries that I'm somehow quite willing and happy to have in a more realistic short story.

There seems to be such a fine line between those slightly tangential moments that add a real texture and verisimilitude, and more unrelated asides that can get you sidetracked. I'm thinking of the moment with the deer, when Mary and Louise are in the car. Aside from its immediate vividness, that moment has clear symbolic resonance. But it's not a moment that would have occurred to everybody to include. You then even emphasize the moment by having Mary say "Deer," which adds the slight irony and humor of the double entendre. Was that something that came to you in an earlier draft or something you added later?

That was something that came to me as I wrote my way into the story. I was imagining myself going along the road, and the sense of the old country asserted itself in the great wilderness that underlies the veneer we live in. That percolated up from a later sense of the story. So that wasn't in an earlier draft, no. I know what you mean. There's a passage in a John Cheever story that I really love, "The Sorrows of Gin," when a man is driving to get his runaway daughter at the railway station, and a flurry of leaves blows across his headlight. Why that breaks my heart, that image, it's hard to say, but it does. And it's not anything you can thematically explain. You could make an argument for it, but really I think it's irreducible. The image works on the nerves more than in the mind. It's a wonderful moment, Cheever at his very best, I think. . . .

There's another moment like that at the very end of your story, when Mary realizes she doesn't know what Brebeuf's last words were. And the silence of her audience is beginning to well up, a silence we already know she equates with water and drowning. At that moment she hears someone "whistling in the hallway outside, trilling the notes like a bird, like many birds." That line recalls the beautiful image at the very beginning, at the end of the second paragraph about her thoughts that she kept to herself: "and the words for them grew faint as time went on; without quite disappearing they shrank to remote nervous points, like birds flying away." That relates both to the wilderness theme and also her struggle to reemerge. Was that something that you were aware of right away?

It's an image. Language, especially the language which she speaks at the end, her own language, is freedom, is flight. It's why I use the image of birds there. It's song too.

Was that something that you wrote and then discovered, the connection with the image at the beginning? Or did you have to work that in later?

I'm not exactly sure which came first, whether the image at the end came and then I went back to the beginning and found a way of preparing for it, or the other way. I have a feeling, though, that the image at the beginning was antecedent to the one at the end. That was a right, natural way to describe someone's language deserting them. Then it was a natural thing to pick it up again at the end.

I wish you could have talked to me when I was writing the final drafts, because then you would know everything about the story. I'd been living with it for four or five months, thinking about it day and night. And I knew literally why every pause was there. I had a reason for it. Now I have to go back

and second-guess myself, which is one of the problems with not keeping drafts.

At what point did the ending become clear to you? At what point did you start to get a sense where things might be leading, that there might be this sort of prophetic moment at the end? Did you have a strong sense of direction early on as you were writing it?

That ending became possible through my reading the Parkman book. I wonder if a writer is able to identify the motion in his mind that suddenly delivers up a possibility. I can't do that in retrospect. Because the mind surprises you. I'll bet that Cheever was surprised by the image of those leaves blowing across the headlights of the car when he was writing "The Sorrows of Gin." I'll bet that in the first draft anyway he was taken aback by it. Startled and frightened. I know that when I had the idea of doing what I did in this story, I was surprised by it. Obviously that couldn't have come to me if I had not been reading that book, and even had a couple of dreams about it. But beyond saying that, who knows? The mind works even when we're not aware of it working or thinking of it working. Certainly when I'm up here "writing," what I'm really doing much of the time is walking around. I walk a lot. I don't even know what I'm doing half the time up here. But something is happening. . . .

Those moments of surprise that occur when you're, writing: are those moments the things that really sustain you?

Yes, they are. That's what I live for. They sustain me even if I don't have very many of them. I live with the expectation that I will have more, the faith that I will have more. What I could predict I will do when I sit down to write is not what I want to end up with. I want to end up with what surprises me along the way, what jumps out at me from the potential of my work and not from what I've already realized about it before I've even started. If I'm simply writing down what I already know, it is of no earthly interest to me. And not only that, everyone else will know it anyway. Simply obvious stuff. I'm not subtle. When I sit down to write, I discover things that I have, for one reason or another, not admitted, not seen, not reflected on sufficiently. And those are the things that I live for in other people's fiction as well as my own.

At one point in this story, you offer this description of Louise: "Enthusiasm for other people's causes did not come easily to Louise, who had a way of sucking in her breath when familiar names were mentioned, as though she knew things that friendship kept her from disclosing." This strikes me as a good example of what we're talking about.

That's an important moment for me in the story because in writing that sentence I came to know something about that character. I didn't start off knowing that about Louise. I discovered it by writing that sentence. You know, language leads you to these discoveries. Until you start practicing the language of the story, start hearing the music of the story, you can't learn what the story has to tell you. That's why it's so important for me to learn from the writing. Writing is not just a process of getting out what I've already thought, what's already in my head. Though it can be for very good writers exactly that. A writer of my acquaintance had a blackboard that ran all around his office, and he would keep detailed notes on the blackboard of everything that was going to happen in the novel he was writing. That worked for him; it wouldn't work for me. . . .

At what point did you know that Louise had to be a scholar, a Benedict Arnold scholar?

That was one of those little flashes. I remember writing it. I was getting on toward the end of the story. I had never mentioned what her scholarship was. And I thought that would be perfect. She would have written the book on Benedict Arnold.

I guess this is an example of what my English teachers would have called foreshadowing, but at its best: you sense it's a fact without realizing its full significance. I only noticed it when I was rereading.

Right. You don't know what's going to happen when you first come across it, so it has no meaning then. It's a neutral fact, except that it can color your sense of her a little bit, without your quite knowing it.

A similar moment occurs when Louise says to Mary on the phone "Now don't get your hopes too high."

Exactly. It all means something. You just don't know what it means at the time.

In retrospect, the reader can also appreciate the cumulative significance of Mary's physical problems, too—the hearing aid, the lung disorder, and maybe especially the disappearing eyebrows. Have you ever sensed that any of your academic colleagues have been offended by this story?

Oddly enough they seem to like it. None of them seem to think that this applies to them.

They just know jerks. . . .

One particular line in the story captures perfectly a kind of pompous fatuousness—during the interview, when Dr. Howells is ruminating on precipitation and says "But it's a dry rain."

Well, that's the kind of thing you only hear in interviews, isn't it?

How come the Marshall Plan?

That was a misstep, I think, because an Arnold Scholar wouldn't have been writing about the Marshall Plan in the first place.

Maybe that's why she didn't do anything with this particular paper—tried something new without success. I like that line, "I can't get enough of the Marshall Plan," because you can't tell for sure whether Dr. Howells is being snide or sincere.

Right. I think that line had a lot to do with it. I think I actually once heard somebody say that, and it went into my bank.

What about the title of the story? Was that from the Parkman book?

No. There's a church up in northern Vermont called the Church of the North American Martyrs. A writer named Roger Weingarten, a poet, had a book of poems called *Ethan Benjamin Bolt* published in the late '70s. And there's a line in there which goes, "Near the garden of the North American Martyrs." I was writing the story at the time and it just lashed out at me, so I asked him if I could use it. There's no way I could quote it as an epigraph because it had nothing to do with what I was writing about. He wasn't writing about any of these things. I asked him if I could use that phrase as the title of the book, and he was pleased to have me do that. . . .

Reading it ["In the Garden of the North American Martyrs"] again the other day, did you see anything else you'd change now?

Not really. The kind of stories I mostly prefer to read these days are not of this kind, to tell you the truth. It has a lot of symbolic machinery, this story. It has an almost mathematical logic. It leads very purposefully to where it's going. It has a very clear ending, almost a triumphal ending. It's a well-made story. It's written with a great deal of irony. And those are all things that I'm not particularly interested in doing myself right now. I prefer to write a story that doesn't have any obvious symbolic machinery, that is essentially unironic. The voice that tells it might be, but the conception is not. And a story in which the ending is not quite so clean and well pronounced as in this story.

Source: Tobias Wolff with Jay Woodruff, in an interview for his *A Piece of Work: Five Writers Discuss Their Revisions,* University of Iowa Press, 1993, pp. 22–40.

Sources

Banks, Russell. Review in *New York Times Book Review,* October 20, 1985, p. 9.

Current Biography Yearbook 1996, H.W. Wilson Company, 1996, pp. 631-34.

Lyons, Bonnie and Bill Oliver. "An Interview with Tobias Wolff," in *Contemporary Literarure,* Vol. 31, No.1, Spring 1990, pp. 1-16.

Skow, John. "Memory, Too, Is an Actor," in *Time,* April 19, 1993, p. 62.

Further Reading

Prose, Francine. "The Brothers Wolff" in *New York Times Book Magazine,* February 5, 1989, p. 23.
    An interesting interview with both Geoffrey Wolff and Tobias Wolff that covers topics ranging from their childhoods to their current successes as writers.

Parkman, Francis. *The Jesuits in North America in the Seventeenth Century,* University of Nebraska Press, 1997.
    A narrative account of the Jesuit experience with the indigenous people of the region.

Lamb to the Slaughter

Roald Dahl

1953

Initially rejected, along with four other stories, by *The New Yorker,* "Lamb to the Slaughter" eventually appeared in *Collier's* in 1953, after Knopf published its first collection of Dahl's short stories and established his American reputation. Dahl had been making headway as a professional writer with a spate of tales which, like "Lamb to the Slaughter," reflect aspects of human perversity, cruelty, and violence. "Lamb to the Slaughter" opens with Mary Maloney, the pregnant, doting wife of a policeman waiting for her husband to come home from work. When he does so, he makes an abrupt but unspecified statement to Mary, the upshot of which is that he intends to leave her. Her connubial complacency shattered by this revelation, Mary crushes her husband's skull with a frozen leg of lamb and then arranges an alibi. The laconic suddenness of the events, as Dahl tells them, creates an experience of shock for the reader, an effect which no doubt accounts for the popularity of this frequently anthologized and reprinted story. Dahl, who is also the author of popular childrens' fiction, appears here as an adult student of adult evil, as a cynically detached narrator, and as an advocate of a grisly form of black comedy. Yet "Lamb to the Slaughter" prefigures the grotesqueness in even his work for children: in both *James and the Giant Peach* and *Charlie and the Chocolate Factory* "bad" children meet with bizarre and horrific but appropriate fates.

Author Biography

Roald Dahl was born in Wales to Norwegian parents. His father died the year he was born, and his mother remained in Great Britain. He attended the prestigious Repton public preparatory school, where he was a quiet, bookish student, but never went on to college. After graduation, Dahl went to work for the Dutch Shell Oil company, and was posted overseas in Africa. At the outbreak of World War I in 1939, he joined the Royal Air Force and became a fighter pilot. Shot down during a sortie over Greece, Dahl was injured and spent the rest of the war in Washington DC, as a spy. Among his colleagues in the United States at the time was another future writer, the creator of James Bond, Ian Fleming.

Dahl published a highly embellished account of his war escapades in *Colliers* magazine in 1942, and started writing regularly after that, gradually gaining success. By the end of the 1950s, he was a successful and well-known author. With *James and the Giant Peach* (1961) and *Charlie and the Chocolate Factory* (1964) he also established himself as a writer for young people. In 1954 he married the film actress Patricia Neal. In part through Neal, he made acquaintances in the film industry and worked in Hollywood as a screen writer. His most famous screenplay may have been his adaptation of Fleming's James Bond novel *You Only Live Twice* (1967). He also adapted his own work for motion pictures, writing the screenplay for *Willy Wonka & the Chocolate Factory* (1971). Dahl died in 1990.

Plot Summary

Dahl commences with a picture of static coziness in a middle-class, domestic setting. Mary Maloney, six months pregnant, waits for her policeman husband Patrick Maloney to come home from work. The scene emphasizes domesticity: ''The room was warm and clean, the curtains drawn.'' Matching chairs, lamps, glasses, and whisky, soda, and ice cubes await.Mary watches the clock, smiling quietly to herself as each minute brings her husband closer to home. When he arrives, she takes his coat and hangs it in the closet. The couple sits and drinks in silence—Mary comfortable with the knowledge that Patrick does not like to talk much until after the first drink. So by deliberate design, everything seems normal until Mary notices that Patrick drains most of his drink in a single swallow, and then pours

himself another, very strong drink. Mary offers to fix dinner and serve it to him so that he does not have to leave his chair, although they usually dine out on Thursdays. She also offers to prepare a snack. Patrick declines all her offers of food. The reader becomes aware of a tension which escapes Mary's full notice.

Patrick confronts Mary and makes a speech, only the upshot of which is given explicitly: ''So there it is. . . . And I know it's a kind of bad time to be telling you, but there simply wasn't any other way. Of course, I'll give you money and see you're looked after. But there needn't really be any fuss.'' For reasons which Dahl does not make explicit, Patrick has decided to leave his pregnant wife.

Mary goes into shock. At first she wonders if she imagined the whole thing. She moves automatically to retrieve something from the basement freezer and prepare supper. She returns with a frozen leg of lamb to find Patrick standing by a window with his back to her. Hearing her come in, he tells her not to make supper for him, that he is going out. With no narrative notice of any emotional transformation, Mary walks up to him and brings the frozen joint of meat down ''as hard as she could'' on his head. Patrick falls dead.

She emerges from her shock to feel panic. Do the courts sentence pregnant women to death? Do they execute both mother and child? Do they wait until the tenth month? Not wanting to take a chance on her child's life, she immediately begins setting up an alibi. She puts the lamb in the oven to cook, washes her hands, and tidies her hair and makeup. She hurries to her usual grocery store, telling the grocer, Sam, that she needed potatoes and peas because Patrick did not want to eat out and she was ''caught . . . without any vegetables in the house.'' In a moment of truly black comedy, the grocer asks about dessert: ''How about afterwards? What are you going to give him for afterwards?'' and she agrees to a slice of cheesecake. On her way home, she mentally prepares herself to be shocked by anything tragic or terrible she might find.

When she sees her husband's corpse again, she remembers how much she once loved him, and her tears of loss are genuine. She is sincerely distraught when she calls the local police station—the one where Patrick has worked—to report what she has found. Mary knows the policemen who report to the crime scene, and she casts Sergeant Jack Noonan in the role of her comforter. A doctor, police photographer, fingerprint expert, and two detectives join the investigation, while Noonan periodically checks on Mary. She tells her story again, from the beginning: Patrick came home, was too tired to go out for supper, so she left him relaxing at home while she started the lamb cooking and then ran out for vegetables. One detective checks with the grocer, who confirms Mary's account. No one seems to seriously consider her a suspect. The focus of the investigation in on finding the murder weapon—which must be a large, heavy blunt instrument. The detectives ask Mary about tools, and she professes ignorance but says that there may be some out in the garage. She remains in a chair while the house is searched.

Noonan tries to persuade Mary to stay somewhere else for the night, but she refuses. She asks him to bring her a drink and suggests that he have one too. Eventually all of the police investigators are standing around, sipping drinks, tired from their fruitless search. Noonan notices that the oven is still on and the lamb has finished cooking. Mary thanks him for turning the oven off and then asks her dead husband's gathered colleagues–knowing that they have worked long past their own mealtimes—to eat the dinner she had fixed for Patrick. She could not eat a thing, she tells them, but Patrick would want her to offer them "decent hospitality," especially as they are the men who will catch her husband's killer.

The final scene of the story concerns the policemen eating in the kitchen and discussing the case while Mary listens from the living room. The men agree that the killer probably discarded the massive murder weapon almost immediately, and predict that they will find it on the premises. Another theorizes that the weapon is probably "right under our very noses."

Characters

Mary Maloney

Mary Maloney, the story's protagonist, is six months pregnant and satisfied with her (from an external perspective) rather banal life with her policeman-husband Patrick, whom she adores. She had "a slow smiling air about her" and was "curiously tranquil." Mary keeps a neat home, and busies herself with preparations for the baby. When Patrick unexpectedly announces that he is ending their marriage, Mary enters a state of shock. She automatically goes to the basement to remove some-

Roald Dahl

thing from the freezer for supper. She takes the first thing she finds—a leg of lamb—carries it back up the stairs, approaches her husband from behind, and strikes him on the head with the frozen leg of lamb. He falls to the floor dead. "The violence of the crash, the noise, the small table overturning, helped bring her out of the shock." Concern for the well-being of her coming child leads her to act quickly and efficiently to establish an alibi. She starts cooking the leg of lamb, rehearses a normal conversation with the grocer, and then goes to the store to buy vegetables. She hurries home, thinking that if "she happened to find anything unusual, or tragic, or terrible, then naturally it would be a shock and she'd become frantic with grief and horror." In fact, when she sees her husband's lifeless body again, she remembers her "love and longing for him" and cries over him quite sincerely. She then telephones her husband's police colleagues and collapses in a chair while they search the house for the "heavy blunt instrument, almost certainly a large piece of metal," that is believed to be the missing murder weapon. When a sergeant points out that the oven is still on and the leg of lamb is done, Mary urges the policemen—"good friends of dear Patrick's . . . helping to catch the man who killed him"—to eat it because she knows they have missed their own suppers. The policemen consume the murder weapon while speculating about the case. "And in the other room, Mary Maloney began to giggle."

Patrick Maloney

Patrick Maloney is a policeman still walking a beat. The reader learns that it is unusual for him to drain most of his evening cocktail in one swallow, as he does when he first comes home. He replies in short sentences or monosyllables as Mary watches him intently, trying to anticipate and fulfil his desires by offering to fix him another drink, bring his slippers, fix him a snack. He does not answer at all when Mary expresses her displeasure that "a policeman as senior as you" is still walking a beat—a suggestion that Patrick may not be especially successful at his job. On the evening of the story, Patrick abruptly announces that he is leaving Mary, although he will continue to provide for her financially. His only acknowlegement of her pregnancy is that he says he knows "it's kind of a bad time to be telling you." He hopes that there will be no fuss about it. Although the reader is told little outright about Patrick's character, the narrative implicitly indicates that he dislikes her worshipful adoration of him, her constant catering, and her tactless reminder about his lack of advancement in his profession.

Sergeant Jack Noonan

Noonan is one of the policemen at Patrick Maloney's precinct who responds to her frantic telephone call that she found her husband lying on the floor, apparently dead. He and Mary know one another, and he helps the weeping woman gently into a chair before joining another policeman in examining the body and scene and calling for other investigators. He is solicitous of Mary's well-being, asking if she would like to go and stay with a relative or with his own wife, or be helped up to bed. At one point she asks him to bring her a drink. He, and the remaining officers and detectives, also help themselves to whisky at her urging. It is the sergeant who notices that the oven is still on and the leg of lamb done cooking. Mary begs him and the others to eat the meal that she cannot bring herself to touch, and after some demurral, all the policemen sit down in the kitchen and completely devour the murder weapon.

O'Malley

O'Malley is Sergeant Noonan's partner. Dahl is having fun with stereotypes, for O'Malley, like Maloney and Noonan, is an Irish name, and "the

Irish cop" was a sociological phenomenon in American big cities in the late nineteenth and early twentieth centuries. O'Malley's words and actions are not specified in the story: he is just one of the policemen on the scene, discussing the case and, eventually, unwittingly consuming a portion of the tasty murder weapon.

Sam

Sam, the grocer, appears in the middle of the story. After Mary has killed Patrick, she constructs an alibi by making a hasty visit to the grocery store to buy vegetables to go with the meal she tells Sam she is cooking because Patrick does not want to eat out, as they usually do on Thursday nights. Mary later overhears a policeman reporting that Sam found her behavior at the store "quite normal."

Themes

Betrayal

"Lamb to the Slaughter" tells of at least one betrayal: Patrick Maloney's unexplained decision to leave his pregnant wife. This violation of the marriage-vow is obviously not the only betrayal in the story, however. Mary's killing of her husband is perhaps the ultimate betrayal. Her elaborately planned alibi and convincing lies to the detectives also constitute betrayal.

Identity

Dahl plays with the notion of identity both at the level of popular psychology and at a somewhat more philosophical, or perhaps anthropological, level. At the level of popular psychology, Dahl makes it clear through his description of the Maloney household that Mary has internalized the bourgeois, or middle class, ideal of a young mid-twentieth-century housewife, maintaining a tidy home and catering to her husband; pouring drinks when the man finishes his day is a gesture that comes from movies and magazines of the day. Mary's sudden murderous action shatters the image that we have of her and that she seems to have of herself. Dahl demonstrates, in the deadly fall of the frozen joint, that "identity" can be fragile. (Once she shatters her own identity, Mary must carefully reconstruct it for protective purposes, as when she sets up an alibi by feigning a normal conversation with the grocer.)

Topics for Further Study

- Examine the elements of the story that make it a black comedy. How does Dahl use irony to bring humor to the plot?

- "Lamb to the Slaughter" can be considered a revenge fantasy. Think of some other revenge fantasies you have read or seen in movies and on television shows. Write about how such stories can function as a catharsis. Think of a revenge fantasy you have had yourself and write it as a fictional story.

- What percentage of murders are instances of domestic abuse? Does the unpremeditated nature of Mary's crime make it seem less horrible than if it had been planned? Do you think a person like Mary could really kill someone so suddenly?

- An old saying hold that "Revenge is a dish best served cold," meaning that if you want to take vengeance, you should wait and plan carefully and not act impulsively against the person who has wronged you. If Mary had consciously decided to avenge herself on her husband for deserting her, and waited and planned, do you think she would have killed him? What else might she have done to pay him back for his treatment of her?

In the anthropological sense, Dahl appears to suggest that, in essence, human beings are fundamentally nasty and brutish creatures capable of precipitate and bloody acts. Then there are the police detectives, who pride themslves on their ability to solve a crime, but whom Mary sweetly tricks into consuming the main exhibit. Their identity, or at least their compctency, is thrown into doubt.

Love and Passion

At the beginning of "Lamb to the Slaughter," Mary Maloney feels love and physical passion for her husband Patrick. She luxuriates in his presence, in the "warm male glow that came out of him to her," and adores the way he sits, walks, and behaves. Even far along into her pregnancy, she hurries to greet him, and waits on him hand and foot—much more attentively, it appears from his reactions, than he would like. Patrick is presumably motivated to leave his wife by an overriding passion for something or someone else. Mary's mention of his failure to advance at work, and his own wish that she not make a "fuss" about their separation because "It wouldn't be very good for my job" indicate that it may be professional success that he desires. His treatment of his wife does not suggest that he loves her.

Passivity

The concept of passivity figures in the story. The first pages of the story portray Mary's existence as almost mindlessly passive: she sits and watches the clock, thinking that each minute brings her husband closer to her. She is content to watch him closely and try to anticipate his moods and needs. Patrick's predictability up to this point is part of this passivity. The two are living a clockwork life against which, in some way, each ultimately rebels. Passivity appears as the repression of passion, and passion finds a way to reassert itself.

Justice and Injustice

The question of justice and injustice is directly related to the question of revenge. "Lamb to the Slaughter" narrates a train of injustices, beginning with Patrick's betrayal of Mary and their marriage, peaking with Mary's killing of Patrick, and finding its denouement in Mary's deception of the investigating officers. Patrick acts unjustly (or so it must be assumed on the basis of the evidence) in announcing his abandonment of Mary, for this breaks the wedding oath; Mary acts unustly, in a way far exceeding her husband's injustice, in killing Patrick, and she compounds the injustice by concealing it from the authorities.

Style

Black Humor

Black humor is the use of the grotesque, morbid, or absurd for darkly comic purposes. Black humor became widespread in popular culture, especially in literature and film, beginning in the 1950s; it remains popular toward the end of the twentieth century. Joseph Heller's novel *Catch-22* (1961) is one of the best-known examples in American fiction. The short stories of James Thurber and the stories and novels of Kurt Vonnegut, Jr. also offer examples. The image of the cheerful housewife suddenly smashing her husband's skull with the frozen joint of meat intended for his dinner is itself blackly humorous for its unexpectedness and the grotesque incongruity of the murder weapon. There is a morbid but funny double meaning, too, in Mary's response to her grocer's question about meat: "I've got meat, thanks. I got a nice leg of lamb from the freezer." She did indeed get a leg of lamb from the freezer, and after she used it as a club, she found herself with a rather large portion of dead meat on her living-room floor. Also darkly funny is the grocer's question about what she plans to give her husband "afterwards," that is, for dessert. From Mary's point of view, Patrick has already gotten his "just desserts," and there will be no more "afterwards" for him! The ultimate example of black humor in "Lamb to the Slaughter" is, of course, the spectacle of the policemen and detectives sitting around the Maloney kitchen table, speculating about the murder weapon while they unwittingly devour it.

Point of View

Dahl grants the point of view to Mary, the protagonist. Right away, readers see the scene through Mary's eyes. The warmth and cleanliness, the punctilious ordiliness, of the living room where Mary awaits Patrick reflect Mary's conviction, soon to be shattered, that she has built a comfortable and even beautiful life. In Patrick's case, Dahl communicates indirectly by gesture. Mary greets Patrick with a "Hullo, Darling," while Patrick responds with a "hullo" only, omitting the endearment. He drinks his evening scotch and soda more quickly than usual and resists Mary's efforts to wait on him; he fails to respond to Mary's conversation. Readers see these things more or less as Mary sees them, although they likely interpret them more quickly than she does as signs of his dissatisfaction with his marriage. After the killing, Mary changes. No longer the ornament of a contented setting, she becomes

the calculator of her own survival, and that of her unborn child. As Dahl writes, Mary's mind suddenly clears; she begins to dispose of evidence, and she sits in front of her dresser-mirror rehearsing a normal conversation with her grocer. When she returns home, having founded her alibi, she views the body of her husband as if for the first time, and readers, too, get a newish view of it, described much more grotesquely, with greater and more poignant detail, than previously. In these two contrasting scenes of the death, Dahl completes the transformation of his central character.

Symbols

The setting is symbolic: Its domestic primness implies Mary's having bought into a rather banal version of middle class happiness. The frozen leg of lamb is also symbolic and indeed constitutes the central symbol of the story. The piece of meat is already a token of violence: an animal traditionally viewed as meek and gentle slaughtered for carnivorous consumption. The notion of a lamb, moreover, resonates with biblical symbols, such as the scapegoat mentioned in Leviticus, the ram that substitutes for Isaac in the tale of Abraham and Isaac, or Jesus himself, "the Lamb of God." But Dahl's story reverses the connotation of these biblical images.

Historical Context

The Post-War Decade

Dahl began his writing career in 1942 with a story about being shot down while fighting in North Africa. Violence, whether associated with warfare or with crime, continued to fascinate Dahl and figures prominently even in his childrens' stories. "Lamb to the Slaughter" belongs to the first full decade of Dahl's writing career and to the first decade of what historians call the Post-War period. This period witnessed the sociological and cultural transformation of the Western world and took hold as strongly in the United States, where Dahl had come to live, as in Europe. Among the features of the Post-War period may be tallied the growth of cities and the attendant rise in urban tension, the incipient liberation of women, young people, and minorities, the sense that the normative, agriculturally based America that had existed up until the nation's involvement in World War II was in radical dissolution. It is significant with respect to Dahl's story that divorce, formerly rare in the statistics of

Compare & Contrast

- 1950s: Precisely because the traditional social norms had begun to come under the pressures that would lead to change, American society in the 1950s tended to reaffirm the norms of religion, family, self-reliance, law and order, and strongly defined gender roles.

  1990s: Certain social trends only barely visible in 1950 now present themselves glaringly: the statistical likelihood that many marriages will fail, for example, and the ubiquitousness of violent crime. Restrictive gender roles are one of the most frequently attacked social mores in the late twentieth century. Murder is commonplace and horrific domestic violence abounds. For example, in the mid-1980s, a suburban Detroit, Michigan man killed his wife and kept her body in a locked freezer for several years, until one of the couple's daughters discovered it.

- 1953: Simone de Beauvoir's nonfiction study of 1949 denouncing the unequal position of women in most public and private arenas is published in translation in the United States as *The Second Sex.*

  1990s: Women still earn, on average, only 75% of what similarly educated men earn in comparable positions.

- 1950s: The English and American populations, recovering from two wars (World War II and the Korean War), responded enthusiastically to economic trends, embracing the new standard of cheap housing and abundant material goods within the price-range of middle-class "consumers."

  1990s: The "baby boom" generation (those born in the post-World War II years) is the first in English and American history to be measurably worse off financially than their parents generation.

American life, began to rise in the aftermath of the war.

Popular Fiction

The same decade was also the heyday of popular fiction in the United States, with dozens of weekly and monthly journals featuring short fiction and serialized novels, and with paperback publishing getting under way. Dahl began his career in the "weeklies" before breaking into print in commercial book form. The wave of popular fiction, emphasizing the short story, saw the differentiation of genres. Police and detective fiction, war fiction, science fiction, romance, even the business story, all represent distinct genres which appealed to well-defined groups of readers.

Television Culture

The year of "Lamb to the Slaughter," 1953, puts the story in the glory days of American television, on which at the time gimmicky dramas of a slightly grotesque character frequently appeared. (Rod Serling's *Twilight Zone,* which would come along in 1957, represented the zenith of the trend.) With its two-setting structure (the Maloney household and the counter of a grocery store) and its limited dramatis personae, "Lamb to the Slaughter" has the feel of a teleplay scenario. The black comedy and the opportunity for potential viewers to be in the know while certain characters (the detectives) remain ignorant of the facts, also conform to the nature of the one-act, half-hour TV drama interrupted by commercial messages.

Critical Overview

The critical reception of Dahl's story "Lamb to the Slaughter" needs to be put in the context of his critical reception generally. First of all, Dahl achieved commercial success, and after a period of struggle, became wealthy on the basis of his writing. For this to happen, a writer must have talent and he must have a sense of how to make that talent appeal to large numbers of ordinary readers. There is, moreover, often a difference between what a large segment of the literate public wants and what academically trained editors, who stand between authors and the public, think that the public wants or what the public ought to want. Once his writing reached its audience, Dahl never experienced any difficulty; before reaching his audience, at the editorial level, however, Dahl often confronted obstacles. "Lamb to the Slaughter" was originally rejected by *The New Yorker* in 1951. In the meantime, Dahl had established contact with the publishing firm of Knopf, which brought out a collection of his previously published stories called *Someone Like You* in 1953. This collection was successful with the American reading public. Unpublished Dahl stories were now sought by magazines, and *Colliers* ran the stories that *The New Yorker* had rejected, including "Lamb to the Slaughter."

Critical reaction to Dahl's first published collection, summarized by Jeremy Treglown in a biography of the author, makes the case. *Someone Like You* received a good number of reviews, the majority favorable, a few condescending; but even the favorable ones tended to categorize Dahl as a strictly popular writer. Treglown quotes *New York Times* critic James Kelly praising Dahl as "the *compleat* short-story writer." Yet Kelly went on to differentiate classes of short-story specialists. On the one hand there are writers like Chekhov, the Russian, an indubitable artist and explorer of human psychological depth; on the other hand, there are "solid plotters like Saki, O. Henry, Maupassant and Maugham" to which latter category he assigns Dahl. "The reader looking for sweetness, light, and subtle characterization will have to try another address," Kelly wrote. Among the negative reviews, one from the *Buffalo News* opined that even though he was a beginning author, Dahl was unlikely to achieve much in the way of a higher level of artistic expression; the same reviewer disliked Dahl's stories for their unrelievedly sardonic attitude and for their lack of social significance. Nevertheless, as Treglown notes, "by Christmas [1953], 7500 hundred copies had been sold."

"Lamb to the Slaughter" benefited from the success of *Someone Like You,* and Dahl quickly marketed it to *Colliers.* The story has been widely reprinted ever since. As Treglown writes, the story of Mary Maloney's murder of her husband constitutes "a comic crime thriller in miniature which was

to become one of [Dahl's] best-known stories and whose plot must be among the first to depend on a domestic freezer." Notice that Treglown refers to the story as "comic," stressing its black humor. Treglown makes a virtue of what other critics of Dahl have seen as a vice, namely a penchant for the grotesque and a nasty vision of human existence. This divergence of opinion sums up the critical reaction to Dahl rather neatly.

As he gradually deemphasized "adult" fiction in favor of "children's stories" in the late 1950s and early 1960s, Dahl found that, despite the popularity of such items as *Charlie and the Chocolate Factory,* some academic students of "children's stories" did not approve of him. It was thought that an amoral viciousness undermined the moral order in Dahl's chilcren's fiction. In its elements of savagery and rejection of the rules of behavior, "Lamb to the Slaughter" might be described as a "childrens' story for adults."

Criticism

Thomas Bertonneau

Bertonneau holds a Ph.D. in comparative literature from UCLA and has published over thirty scholarly articles on aspects of modern literature. He is particularly interested in the anthropological implications of narrative, an interest which he explores in the following essay on "Lamb to the Slaughter".

In his short story "Lamb to the Slaughter" Roald Dahl offers his readers a tale so grotesque, so darkly comic, so hilarious in some of its incidental details (the fourth line from the end features a belch), that one can easily fail to take it seriously. "Lamb to the Slaughter" seems a kind of literary joke, a morbid toss-off, which the author luckily convinced some editor to buy. Yet part of Dahl's cleverness in this slick tale of domestic comfort disrupted, of marriage betrayed, and of a life taken, is that he tricks his readers into complicity with a murder, just as the murderer tricks the investigators into complicity by getting them to consume the evidence.

If readers feel sympathetic to Mary Maloney (as well they might) because her husband Patrick has abrogated their marriage and rejected her love without prelude, they must nevertheless not forget that Mary's act, her escalated turnabout against

What Do I Read Next?

- Dahl's first published story, "Shot Down over Libya," appeared in *Saturday Evening Post* in August 1942. As Dahl's earliest work, it merits the attention of anyone interested in the remainder of his stories. The story stems from Dahl's experience in the Royal Air Force, heavily fictionalized, and introduces the element of violence which threads through his oeuvre. A pilot, a British flying his Hurricane in support of ground troops, meets up with an aerial ambush by Italian aircraft, which shoot him into the ground. He survives the crash, but is injured. Despite its slightness, "Shot Down" prefigures much of the later writing.

- The short stories of Kurt Vonnegut, Jr., collected in *Welcome to the Monkey House*, have been cited in comparison with those of Dahl for their darkly comic nature and often bleak assessments of human nature.

- In Dahl's story "The Way Up To Heaven," a woman is infuriated by her husband's chronic lateness. She begins to suspect that he is late deliberately to torment her. She siezes a chance opportunity to leave him stranded in a disabled elevator where he will almost certainly die.

- For many years, Dahl was married to the actress Patricia Neal, whose autobiography *As I Am* (1988) contains a frank depiction of their life together and of the factors that drove them apart.

- In James Thurber's short story "Mr. Preble Gets Rid of His Wife," a typically mild-mannered, married Thurber protagonist had an ongoing joke with a female colleague about running away together. One day she varies her standard response by saying that first he will have to "get rid of" his wife. That night Mr. Preble lures his wife into the cellar of their home, planning to kill her and bury the body under the earthen floor. She is reluctant to enter the cellar, but once she does, she realizes what he plans to do. She belittles his plan, criticizes his choice of a murder weapon, and mocks his general ineptitude as a prospective murderer. The story ends with Mrs. Preble sending him away to find a more suitable weapon and screaming after him to "close the door . . . were you born in a barn?"

- *A Modest Proposal* by Jonathan Swift is an early and famous example of literary irony and grotesque humor. Under its full title: *A Modest Proposal for Preventing the Children of the Poor People from Being a Burthen to Their Parents, or the Country, and for Making them Beneficial to the Publick*, the essay shocked some members of the public when it appeared in 1729, advocating that problems of famine, poverty, and overpopulation be addressed by eating the children of the poor.

Patrick, violates a much deeper tabu than that against the unilateral dissolution of marriage; it violates the tabu against murder. Rather like an authorial devil, Dahl tempts readers to join with Mary's "giggle" at the end of the tale, when her self-exculpating plan has prevailed. Attentive students of Dahl's text will understand, however, that the comedy conceals an eruption of ugly vengefulness and that such vengefulness potentially entangles all people, actual and fictional. The law, represented in the story by the unfaithful Patrick and the bumbling detectives, serves in real life, under coercive threat, to defer just this type of personal score-settling. "Lamb to the Slaughter," perhaps surprisingly, turns out to be a story about the fundamental—and fragile—devices of civilization, and about the ease with which the seemingly law-abiding citizen lapses back into the murderous brute.

Consider the murder itself and its immediate effects. Approaching Patrick from behind, with the frozen leg of lamb hefted as a club, Mary swings

> " Part of Dahl's cleverness in this slick tale of domestic comfort disrupted, of marriage betrayed, and of a life taken, is that he tricks his readers into complicity with a murder."

high and directs the full weight of it on Patrick's head "as hard as she could." As Dahl affirms, a frozen joint smashes as well as cold steel. (The detectives will suspect something like "a heavy metal vase.") Grotesquely, Patrick "remained standing there for at least four or five seconds, gently swaying." The adverbial qualification constitutes a neat, and telling, bit of narrative irony on Dahl's part, for the act is anything but gentle. Patrick crashes to the carpet. When Sergeant Jack Noonan arrives, he finds "a small patch of congealed blood on the dead man's head." Over the sinister repast, one investigating detective remarks that the police doctor had found Patrick's head to be "smashed all to pieces just like from a sledgehammer." In the story, these details lie dispersed at different stages of the telling. Putting them together serves as a reminder that Patrick's death is quite brutal, and that Mary, seemingly out of character, has summoned the grim strength of a Neanderthal. To Patrick, it seems, falls the role of sacrificial lamb to which the story's title refers, the one who goes unwittingly to his own pathetic slaughter. Yet whatever his offense, no matter how much he corresponds to stereotype of the male betrayer of women, Patrick does not deserve to die.

One might imagine a feminist reading of "Lamb to the Slaughter" in which the interpreter focuses on Patrick's betrayal of Mary, his casual sacrifice of the marriage to his career, to his ambition, to his very own withdrawn intentness. Perhaps one does not even have to be a feminist to succumb to the urge to defend Mary on just such suppositional grounds. Patrick's piggishness—if that is what it is—after all seems to confirm the worst things that contemporary (especially academic) convention ascribes to the naturally reprobate male character. The

plight of abandoned, and at least emotionally abused, women circulates widely and is well known to many. Why should readers therefore not side with Mary and even delight in her revenge against patriarchal oppression? All the more so because the events take place in a story, not in real life. Are not stories, after all, precisely the locus in which our impractical wishes may be carried imaginatively to fruition, thereby sublimating dangerous thoughts and urges? A close reading of the details ought to dampen this urge. The scene in which Patrick announces his intention to leave Mary looms as particularly interesting.

Patrick begins his tense speech to Mary with the assertion that "this is going to be a bit of a shock to you." Mary, whom Dahl has previously characterized as being "without anxiety," exhibiting "a slow smiling air," and being "curiously tranquil," has already "begun to get frightened," now infuses her eye with a "bewildered look." Patrick says that he has thought about what he is planning to say "a good deal" and that he hopes that Mary will not lay too much "blame" on him. So far, Dahl has employed direct discourse. Now, however, he switches to indirect discourse and to a purposefully vague vocabulary: "And he told her. It didn't take long, four or five minutes at the most, and she sat very still through it all, watching him with a kind of dazed horror as he went further and further away from her with each word." Switching back to direct discourse, Dahl makes Patrick conclude his speech with remarks about how "there needn't be any fuss" and how a fuss "wouldn't be very good for my job." It sounds selfish. What else can it be? But the important thing to note is what Dahl premeditatedly declines to divulge, what he quite deliberately conceals through elision. Readers never learn from Dahl's carefully elided narrative precisely what Patrick's line of reasoning, his case, is. (Or even what his line of unreasonable self-justification, his non-case, is, for it could be one as easily as the other.) While a strong tendency to put the worst light on such matters no doubt afflicts every reader, the fact remains that Patrick's motive hovers outside any reader's ken. To fill in the blank, no matter how certain one is about an assignable motive, would be to collaborate unbidden in the storytelling, a violation of critical principles.

What happens to the instinctive reading of the story (namely that Mary is primitively justified) immediately the reader's lack of knowledge about Patrick's motive makes itself known? In the first place, what Dahl casually calls Mary's "instinct," her "instinct . . . not to believe any of it, to reject it all," becomes suspicious, the more so since, having dispatched Patrick with the convenient and fatal mutton-joint, she herself experiences clarity: "It was extraordinary, now, how clear her mind became all of a sudden." In the light of this clarity, Mary carefully rehearses her alibi. She sits in front of her vanity mirror and practices saying normal things to Sam the grocer. Her talent for lying rises, here, to the superb. It shows itself superb again when, returning from Sam's, she convinces herself to act naturally, as though she did not know the fact of her own criminal deed. It expands into the superlative when she skillfully lies to Sergeant Noonan and O'Malley, on their arrival, feigning the distressed survivor, mocking herself up as the discoverer of a grisly crime perpetrated by an unknown assailant. Now if, in the unrecorded blank of his speech, Patrick said to Mary, I've taken up with someone else more helpful to me in my career, younger and more beautiful, so I'm abandoning you, one might say that Mary was, indeed, primitively justified. But of course Patrick might just as well have said, I've discovered that the child is not mine and that you are not what you seem, in which case the reader's sympathy with Mary would be considerably undermined. A purely speculative interpretation which insisted on this could point to Mary's adeptness at manipulation and deception, her acquaintance with "nearly all the men at the precinct," as clues that she might be capable of such duplicity. The point is that Dahl leaves us entirely without knowledge. And it is therefore without knowledge of Patrick's motive that readers must assess Mary's act.

Of course, "Lamb to the Slaughter" belongs to the genre of comedy, as well as to the genre of crime fiction. Dahl exaggerates everything, selects morbid details, transforms mere domestic facts, like the existence of a meat-freezer in the basement, into the occasion for criminal enormity. Mary hefting the lamb-joint is a moment of dark comedy as well as a nasty little scene. Even the title, with its multiple if rather simple ironies, contributes to the comedy. For who exactly is the lamb on the way to the slaughter? At first it is Mary, about to be rejected by her husband, then her husband, fatally stunned with a leg of lamb, and then the police investigators, tricked fiendishly by Mary into consuming the very murder weapon which would enable them to solve the case. In this last detail, one might even sense a hint of ritual cannibalism, since in eating the lamb the men are participating, unwittingly of course, in the immolation of Patrick. At one point, one of the

men belches. Seen this way, the placid little postmortem meal takes on a higher degree of morbidity. But it also points to the "moral," so to speak, of Dahl's amoral tale.

Civilization calls on its members to renounce primitive justification in favor of rational justice; it requires them to renounce personal vengeance, that is, in favor of established institutions which depersonalize the assignment of guilt and the administration of punishment. Even though it feels slightly absurd to invoke ideas like due process and the assumption of innocence in the case of a story which probably does not take itself altogether seriously, emphasizing these philosophical points is nevertheless imperative.

Modern middle class domesticity, represented by the living room where Dahl first reveals Mary in the story's opening paragraphs, is an instance of civilization. Taken for granted and even reviled, such homely banality nevertheless amounts to the culmination of an age-old battle by human beings against their base nature, their tendency to act out of selfish motives without regard for others. For one thing, domesticity has a wider context beyond itself, the public order of which the policeman are the putative caretakers. Dahl shows us that the caretakers of order are always less than perfect, but that is merely to underline the fragility of the achievement. Not a material, but a spiritual achievement, the triumph of trust and cooperation over selfishness, as in marriage, requires continuous maintenance. The parties must cherish one another and hold vigil each over himself. When one party breaks the trust, or breaks the law, or otherwise disrupts the peace, the almost inevitable natural reaction of others is to reply in kind, or to escalate their response above kind. The whole fabric of trust now verges on unraveling. Dahl shows us, in sardonic fashion, just this unraveling, and in transforming the sweetly pregnant wife into the calculating killer, he reminds his audience that angelhood is a rare achievement and that revenge, especially, is an appetite which only faith and morality enable us to suppress.

In Mary's concluding "giggle," then, the comedy ends and the serious discussion must begin. Readers caught up in the fantasy of vengeance, made palatable by the comedic elements in Dahl's story, will be sorely tempted to chuckle quietly along with the clever killer, but this temptation reveals something about the primitive being in every reader. To be sure, that primitive lurks in every individual, and seeks any justification, any chink in the moral framework, to manifest itself. The lamb of our best nature must always keep a wary eye on the slaughtering beast.

Source: Thomas Bertonneau, for *Short Stories for Students*, Gale, 1998.

Elisabeth Piedmont-Marton

Piedmont-Marton is the coordinator of the undergraduate writing center at the University of Texas at Austin. In the following essay, she analyzes the irony behind the title of Dahl's "Lamb to the Slaughter."

"Lamb to the Slaughter" is representative of Dahl's economical style and dry, dark sense of humor. Like all of his short fiction, the narrative in this story is driven by plot, not by character or mood. Readers find themselves dropped into the middle of the action with no knowledge of the background or history of the characters to establish tone or motive. Starting with the double meaning of its title, however, "Lamb to the Slaughter" offers readers a number of opportunities to explore the complexities and possibilities beneath the taut and matter-of-fact surface of the story. Alert and curious readers will find themselves opening narrative trap doors and rummaging through Mary's psyche in search of reasons why an ordinary evening ended in murder.

The expression "lamb to the slaughter" is used to describe an innocent or naive person being led into danger or failure. Unprepared political candidates, or woefully outmatched sports teams are often described as lambs being led to the slaughter. Dahl's use of the expression is surprising and effective for two reasons. First, it reminds us that the slaughter that the lamb is led to is a real, not a metaphorical, killing. Second, in this story, readers discover later, the lamb is not the victim of the slaughter, but the instrument. When we first encounter meek Mary Maloney, bent over her sewing and awaiting her husband's arrival, we think she will be the lamb. As it turns out, her husband Patrick is literally the lamb led to slaughter, Mary brings her little leg of lamb to the slaughter as weapon, and in the metaphorical sense of the expression, the investigating officers are lambs, that is, naive followers, led to the slaughter, first to the scene of the crime, and second to the dinner table to consume the evidence. When readers last see Mary Maloney she is giggling to herself at the unwitting joke one of the officers makes when he claims that the weapon is "probably right under our very noses."

Mary Maloney is hardly the lamb she seems to be. As critic Mark West has noted, seemingly ordinary and respectable characters who "are confronted with peculiar problems or opportunities and respond by committing, or at least contemplating, cruel or self-destructive acts," are a feature of Dahl's stories of this period. Unlike the characters in the war stories, however, characters like Mary "do not behave nobly under pressure." When they find themselves in extreme circumstances they "lose their moral bearings." In "Lamb to the Slaughter" Mary, in West's words, "so easily makes the transition from housewife to murderer that one wonders about her mental state prior to the day she killed her husband." A close reading of the story suggests that she may have possessed the traits of a killer all along, and by extension, so do we all.

Upon re-reading, "Lamb to the Slaughter" offers some provocative insights into Mary's character and her relationship to her husband. Because on the first reading we are predisposed to think of her as the "lamb," the innocent who is about to get hurt, we do not notice how her composure that evening seems put on, or at least strained. Dahl describes her as having a "slow smiling air about her." She is "curiously tranquil" as she waits for the clock to tick off the minutes until her husband comes home. When he finally does come home, he becomes the center of her universe, the "sun" around which her world revolves. Her desire to please him seems edgy and frantic, more an act of control than affection.

Patrick's news that he is leaving her threatens the control she has over him, and thus over her own impulses. She seems to make a last-ditch effort to remain in his orbit by insisting that he let her make him supper. Patrick does not respond when she whispers "I'll get the supper," after hearing his devastating announcement, and she takes that as acceptance of her offer. As it turns out, though, he simply is not listening to her and lashes out when she enters the room with the frozen leg of lamb: "For God's sake . . . Don't make supper for me. I'm going out." When her offer of service is rebuffed, Mary perceives it as a loss of control and literally hits her husband over the head with the meal he rejected. Readers are left with several questions. At what point does Mary decide that she'll use the meal first figuratively and then literally as a weapon? If she has no intention of attacking him why does she unwrap and inspect the meat in the cellar? If she were really planning to make supper then surely she would have selected something smaller, like the lamb chops she has suggested earlier. A whole frozen leg of lamb will—and does—take hours to cook. And why does she grasp it like a weapon rather than a piece of food, "holding the thin bone-end of it with both hands"? What seems most calculated about her behavior is the fact that after he rebuffs her final offer she comes up behind him "without any pause," as if to get a running start.

After she brings lamb to the slaughter of her husband, Mary sets about gathering the rest of the lambs into her circle of influence. Mary's behavior after she kills Patrick asks readers to consider some difficult questions about her true nature. This is unnerving because, as West points out, Dahl asks that readers see something of themselves in the apparently ordinary Mary who finds herself in ex-traordinary circumstances: pregnant and facing the death penalty for killing her husband. Her deliberate behavior to cover her guilt is explainable as the natural instincts for a woman trying to protect her unborn child. But the explanation is less than con-vincing, however, since the welfare of the child occurs to her almost as an afterthought, "on the other hand, what about the child," never to be mentioned again. Furthermore, Mary seems much more calculating than instinctive in the hours that follow her husband's murder.

Mary's actions immediately after the murder are a chilling mirror image of her behavior in the first scene of the story. Earlier that evening she had carefully set the ideal domestic scene while she waited for Patrick to come home, arranging their two chairs and the "two tall glasses, soda water, whiskey." After the murder Mary puts the lamb in the oven and then "sat down before the mirror, tidied her hair, touched up her lips and face." Then she begins to rehearse the appropriate emotional reactions to the situation. First, she feigns noncha-lance for her visit to the store that will establish her alibi. Later on her way back from the store she practices how she will be overcome with shock and grief at discovering her murdered husband's body. Mary's performance is so convincing that she quickly diverts attention from herself as a suspect. While she sits quietly playing the distraught widow the officers scour the house and grounds looking for the weapon.

Mary ultimately uses the same means of control over the investigating officers that she had used with Patrick: food, drink, and the illusion of uncom-prehending innocence. It is because Patrick finally rejected her offers that he ended up dead. Because

> Mary ultimately uses the same means of control over the investigating officers that she had used with Patrick: food, drink, and the illusion of uncomprehending innocence."

the officers can only perceive her as a helpless victim, they cannot see how they are being led astray. First she tempts them with a little whiskey. Then finally, using Patrick's sense of duty and their loyalty to him as reasons, she convinces them to abandon the trail of the murderer and sit down to eat the weapon that she used to kill her husband and their colleague.

"Lamb to the Slaughter" is unusual for a Dahl story in that the murderer seems to face no conse-quences for her actions. But by drawing readers into Mary Maloney's psyche, Dahl demands that readers ask themselves some difficult moral questions. Seen as a crime of passion, an emotionally distraught woman's single impulsive act that ends in tragedy, Mary's crime does not seem to require punishment other than her own lifelong remorse and knowledge that she has caused her child to be fatherless. But a woman in the throes of passion and jealous rage could not have behaved with the forethought and self-control that Mary displays in the hours follow-ing the murder. Her orchestration of the investiga-tion goes far beyond the knowledge she would have gained as "the detective's wife." She appears to be a master manipulator who killed her husband be-cause he was no longer willing to submit to her control. Dahl's chilling conclusion seems to be that as long as there are lambs, people willing to ma-nipulated, there will be slaughters.

Source: Elisabeth Piedmont-Marton, for *Short Stories for Students,* Gale, 1998.

Alan Warren

In the following essay, Warren gives some background on Dahl's life and analyzes Dahl's position as a writer of horror stories. He likens

Dahl's style to that of James Thurber and Saki, other notable twentieth-century humorists who possessed a satiric and sometimes morbid bent.

Roald Dahl is a short story writer of highly unusual gifts whose specialty is what the French term *contes cruel,* but minus the bloodshed. He is one horror writer who rarely spills blood. His short stories have earned him great distinction not only in the field of horror, but among the great short story writers of the twentieth century, an assemblage that includes James Joyce, Frank O'Connor, John Collier, Saki, Katherine Mansfield, John Cheever, and Ernest Hemingway (who was a personal friend of Dahl's and whose advice on storytelling and the value of economy Dahl took to heart).

Dahl was born in Llandaff, South Wales, in 1916. His parents were Norwegian. After education at Repton School he went to work for Shell Oil Company and was sent to Dar-es-Salaam in Tanzania, East Africa. The next year, with the outbreak of war, he enlisted in the R.A.F. at Nairobi. He was severely wounded in the Libyan desert, but later served as a fighter pilot in Syria and Greece and became wing commander, but recurrent headaches made him unable to fly. He was invalided back to England, then sent to Washington, D.C. as assistant air attache in January 1942. At this point he still had no thought of becoming a writer.

While stationed in Washington he made the acquaintance of a small man with steel-rimmed spectacles who was looking for an account of flying with the R.A.F. This man turned out to be C. S. Forester, author of the Horatio Hornblower adventures. Dahl wrote up his experiences and sent them on to Forester, who, bowled over by Dahl's natural writing ability, sold it to the *Saturday Evening Post* without Dahl's knowledge. The *Post* paid Dahl nine hundred dollars, which he promptly lost playing poker with Harry S. Truman. They also asked for more pieces by the same writer. Dahl wrote a second, fictional, piece. That too was accepted for publication. Dahl continued writing, and in 1945 these pieces were issued together in a slim volume entitled *Over To You.* All on flying themes, these are unlike Dahl's later work though they are just as vivid and economical. (One amusing incident occurred when Hemingway borrowed the volume: he returned it after two days, and when Dahl asked how he'd liked the stories, Hemingway, striding off along the corridor, replied: "I didn't understand them.")

The short stories for which Dahl is best known and most highly regarded began to appear in *The New Yorker* and other publications in 1948. They were collected in three volumes, *Someone Like You,* published in 1953, *Kiss Kiss,* in 1959, and *Switch Bitch,* in 1974.

Dahl married actress Patricia Neal in 1953, and in between writing short stories became a bestselling children's author. Among his more popular children's books are *Charlie and the Chocolate Factory, James and the Giant Peach,* and *The Enormous Crocodile.* He has also written *The Gremlins,* a children's book, *Sometime Never,* a novel, and several screenplays, including *You Only Live Twice,* a James Bond film, and *The Night Digger,* a suspense thriller. He also found time to host two television series featuring adaptations of his works, *Way Out* in 1961, and *Tales of the Unexpected* in the late seventies. His more recent books include *The Wonderful World of Henry Sugar and Six More,* his first collection of stories designed for both juvenile and adult readers, and *My Uncle Oswald,* a novel featuring more overtly sexual themes than he'd previously dealt with.

It is, however, as a short story writer that Dahl is most renowned. His stories are not horrific in the usual sense. They have been likened to those of Saki, John Collier and James Thurber, and to the whimsically macabre cartoons of Charles Addams. The comparison is judicious. Praised for the "grinning skull" quality of the narration, and the technical excellence of their construction, his short stories have been well received by critics, though they disagree on whether Dahl is, at heart, a moralist. Although his evildoers are usually punished, the form that retribution takes is usually so outlandishly unexpected that opinions differ. Naomi Lewis of *New Statesman* believes "these really are moral tales. Go wrong and you get some very peculiar desserts." Whether there is an unsuspected vein of profundity in Dahl's work, or whether Dahl is simply an entertainer "a master of horror—an intellectual Hitchcock of the writing world," says a reviewer for *Books and Bookmen* who writes supremely well, one can hardly fault the originality of his plots, the economy of his storytelling, or his craftsmanship.

Dahl himself, in interviews, has stressed the importance of plot above all else, not only in his own work but in that of his contemporaries. "After having done my twenty-five years of short stories," he told Lisa Tuttle in a *Twilight Zone* interview,

I think I probably ran out of plots, and that's the hardest thing in the world. If you write the sort of short stories I write, which are real short stories, with a beginning, a middle, and an end, instead of the modern trend, which is mood pieces . . . found about thirty-five plots, and then I probably ran out of them. I don't know many now. I don't know *any,* I don't think. I couldn't sit down and write a short story now—it's very hard. And these people who are writing them now, they don't have any plots, they don't bloody well have them. Maupassant had them. Salinger had them. That's why they were so sparing. Salinger found eleven. . . .

''Lamb to the Slaughter'' is one of Dahl's most memorable tales, frequently anthologized and dramatized on *Alfred Hitchcock Presents,* as were several of Dahl's stories. As directed by Hitchcock himself, it remains probably the most famous of the half-hour segments. The plot concerns a policeman's wife who, upon learning her husband is leaving her, hits him over the head with an enormous leg of lamb, killing him, then serves the lamb up to the investigating policemen who sit around eating it while complaining they cannot lay their hands on the murder weapon. This is typical of Dahl in its mixing of humor and horror. The plot is just outrageous enough to be plausible, and his deadpan style sustains it to the last line. As always with Dahl, one is conscious of a master stylist at work, polishing every line, every phrase. This impression is not mistaken: Dahl estimates it took him six hundred hours over five months to complete his story, ''Mrs. Bixby and the Colonel's Coat.'' . . .

Some of Dahl's other stories are less horrific and more like well-told jokes, elaborate leg-pulls by an amused, self-assured, sardonic and somewhat sadistic storyteller. ''Vengeance Is Mine, Inc.'' concerns two entrepreneurs who set up a service that offers punching the nose, or blacking the eye, of a prominent vitriolic newspaper columnist. Their charges: five hundred dollars for the first, six hundred for the second, or one thousand dollars for both. . . .

Roald Dahl's position in the field of horror is difficult to judge, for he has always stood apart from other practitioners of the genre. One reason for this is the slimness of the volume of his published work. A contemporary of Dahl's, Robert Bloch, has for example published some five hundred stories over fifty years. Dahl, although he got a later start as a writer, has published perhaps one tenth as many. While it is arguably easier to produce first-rate work if you publish only two stories a year, as Dahl was doing in the late forties and early fifties, the consistent excellence of his work would not be

> **With Dahl, one is conscious of a master stylist at work, polishing every line, every phrase."**

possible otherwise. It is hardly fair to fault Dahl for remaining true to his ideal and never sacrificing quality for quantity. More horror writers, as well as ''mainstream'' short story writers, should follow his example. . . .

Source: Alan Warren, ''Roald Dahl: Nasty, Nasty,'' in *Discovering Modern Horror Fiction,* edited by Darrell Schweitzer, Starmont House, 1985, pp. 120–28.

James Kelly

In the following review, Kelly examines the use of suspense in the short story collection Someone Like You, *in which ''Lamb to the Slaughter'' appeared.*

At disconcertingly long intervals, the *compleat* short-story writer comes along who knows exactly how to blend and season four notable talents: an antic imagination, an eye for the anecdotal predicament with a twist at the end, a savage sense of humor suitable for stabbing or cutting, and an economical, precise writing style. No worshiper of Chekhov, he. You'll find him marching with solid plotters like Saki and O. Henry, Maupassant and Maugham. He doesn't really like people, but he is interested in them (to paraphrase the author of ''Cakes and Ale''); the reader looking for sweetness, light and subtle characterization will have to try another address. Tension is his business; give him a surprise denouement and he'll give you a story leading up to it. His name in this instance is Roald Dahl, here represented by *Someone Like You* (a collection of eighteen short stories, quite a few of which have appeared in *The New Yorker* and other magazines); and a more imperturbable young Englishman would be hard to find.

Mr. Dahl must bring off a tour de force every time out, since credibility seldom plays much part in the situations that interest him. His stories are like a fast game of badminton in which there's never a positive answer to the big question: Where's the bird? Honed dialogue, a masterful hand with nuance and an ability to keep the reader off balance through sheer astonishment are usually enough to see him through. Not always, though. For some observers (including this one) the spell will not extend to four or five of the stories where the humor is too ghoulish and the originality too intrusive. But it is safe to predict that anybody who responds to one entry will respond to all; Mr. Dahl is never, never dull.

For satirical burlesque, not many recent stories coming from either side of the Atlantic can compete with the outrageous ''Nunc Dimittis,'' an intricate tale of a man of culture and his resourceful revenge upon a young woman who had indiscreetly allowed her full-length portrait to be painted from the skin out. In a similar vein, '' The Great Automatic Grammatisator'' gravely explains what happens when an electronic genius named Adolph Knipe (who wants to be a man of letters) converts an electronic computing machine into a device for writing short stories and novels. The idea, of course, is to buy up all practicing writers and produce the world's creative output by Knipe's Grammatisator, which, Mr. Dahl estimates, must already be responsible for at least half the novels and stories published in the English language during the past year.

A short one—maybe the best one—called ''Taste'' captures the high drama and gourmet flavor of a dinner party where an expert wine-bibber backs his judgment of breed and vintage with a fraudulent bet and almost gets away with it. There's a story about a dubious host and hostess who put a microphone in the guest room and open up new horizons on cheating at bridge; another concerns a man who invents a sound machine which picks up cries of anguish from flowers and trees.

There's a wonderfully underplayed murder story in which the murderess gets off scotfree, thanks to a truly perfect crime. There's a pure horror story with muted sadism at its heart—and a last line guaranteed to raise most readers' hackles. There's one about a genteel commuter who mistakes his

companion for a boyhood bully and falls into a ''Stalky and Co.'' reverie. For many readers the final scarifying story about greyhound racing and the cheating men and willing dogs who share it will live as long as any in the book.

Someone Like You was made to be read—but tough-minded people who don't care which way the cat jumps will probably get the most fun out of it. Mr. Dahl could be a cult without half trying, and he deserves the warm welcome he'll get. No electronic machine will ever turn out *his* stuff.

Source: James Kelly, ''With Waves of Tension,'' in *The New York Times Book Review,* November 8, 1953, p. 5.

Sources

Treglown, Jeremy. *Roald Dahl: A Biography.* New York: Farrar Strauss & Giroux, 1994, p. 105.

Further Reading

Raphael, Frederic. ''Stories from the Source of Heartlessness.'' *The Times Literary Supplement,* No. 4618, October 4, 1991, p. 28.
     An assessment of Dahl's career, noting that he was a mass-market writer but comparing him to some of the finest prose stylists of the twentieth century. Raphael theorizes that Dahl's war experiences as a fighter pilot, which he wrote about in the stories collected in Over to You, are responsible for the bitterness and cruelty of much of his later fiction.

Warren, Alan. *Roald Dahl.* Mercer Island, Wash.: Starmont, 1988, 105 p.
     Critical study of Dahl's fiction, including a chapter on filmed adaptations of his stories.

West, Mark I. *Roald Dahl.* N.Y.: Twayne, 1992, 148 p.
     Biographical and critical study, covering Dahl's life and literary career.

Mrs. Spring Fragrance

Sui Sin Far

1912

"Mrs. Spring Fragrance" is the title story in Sui Sin Far's first and only collection of short stories, *Mrs. Spring Fragrance,* published in 1912. The collection also contains twenty stories about children, collectively known as "Tales of Chinese Children." As a whole, the collection discusses issues of racism, assimilation, and the alienation of Chinese Americans in North America. The title story describes the matchmaking tendencies of a recent arrival to the United States, who eagerly assimilates American customs and language and meddles in the lives of her neighbors. Through this character sketch of a young married Chinese woman, Far also subtly satirizes the patronizing attitude of the policies of the United States government and its citizens towards Asian immigrants. Mrs. Spring Fragrance's wry and insightful observations of the incidents in her neighborhood are heavily ironic.

The other stories in *Mrs. Spring Fragrance* also express the struggle of Chinese Americans to find identity in an oppressive society, particularly from a woman's point of view. Sui Sin Far, a pseudonym of Edith Maude Eaton, was born of a Chinese mother and a British father and moved to the United States at a young age, eventually becoming a journalist in the Pacific Northwest and in Canada. Keenly aware of her heritage, Far embraced her Chinese roots in an era when many were quick to become as American as possible. Writing under the pseudonym Sui Sin Far instantly identified her as an immigrant, and lent credence to her

writings, which were often social commentaries on the state of immigrant life in the still-growing United States.

Author Biography

Sui Sin Far was born in England in 1865 as Edith Maude Eaton. She was the eldest of fourteen children born to an English shipping merchant, Edward Eaton, and Grace Trefusis Eaton, a Chinese woman whom Edward met on his frequent business trips to Shanghai. Proud of her Chinese heritage, Far's mother often went by the name Lotus Blossom. Far's father had studied art in France, and her mother was an orphan raised by Christian missionaries in China. The Eaton family lived primarily in England and Canada, where Far went to school. Even though her given name was British, and her appearance was not markedly Chinese, Far she proudly claimed her Chinese identity. She recounts the painful anxiety of being a Eurasian in her 1909 autobiographical sketch, *Leaves from the Mental Portfolio of an Eurasian,* first published in the New York newspaper *The Independent :*

> The question of nationality perplexes my little [childhood] brain. Why are we what we are? I and my brothers and sisters? Why did God make us to be hooted and stared at? Papa is English, Mamma is Chinese. Why couldn't we have been either one thing or the other? Why is my mother's race despised. I look into the faces of my father and mother. Is she not every bit as dear and good as he? Why? Why? . . . I do not confide in my father and mother. They would not understand. How could they? He is English, she is Chinese. I am different to both of them—a stranger, tho their own child.

Living in Canada, her family suffered several financial setbacks and Far had to leave school at the age of ten to work. Though her formal education had ended, she spent several hours a day with Mrs. William Darling, a family friend, who tutored her in French and music. In a 1912 article in *The Boston Globe,* entitled, ''Sui Sin Far the Half Chinese Writer, Tells of Her Career,'' Far recalled: ''I, now in my 11th year, entered into two lives, one devoted entirely to family concerns; the other, a withdrawn life of thought and musing.'' She spent her adolescence occupied in odd jobs like crocheting lace and selling her father's paintings. She suffered a debilitating illness at age 14 that required a lengthy period of bedrest and which she describes as, ''affect[ing]

both head and heart and retard[ing] development both mentally and physically.'' This illness made her prone to attacks of fever for the rest of her life and exacerbated her later development of inflammatory rheumatism.

At age eighteen, Far got a job at *The Montreal Star* as a typesetter and later worked in several law offices as a stenographer. She traveled to Jamaica as a reporter and lived in San Francisco, Seattle, Los Angeles, and Boston, returning often to Montreal to visit her family. All the while, Far was writing short stories and nurturing her ambition to write a book about the Chinese-American experience. She met many influential figures in the various offices in which she worked, and they encouraged her to publish her stories in local papers. Her early fiction was published in newspapers such as *The Montreal Daily Witness, The Montreal Daily Star, The Dominion Illustrated, Texas Liftings,* and *The Detroit Free Press.* Not all of these stories dealt with the Chinese immigrant experience, but the few that did often expressed controversial opinions such as ''The Land of the Free,'' which later became an entry in *Mrs. Spring Fragrance.* Far was able to express her opinions because she often did not sign her newspaper submissions. In her later writing career, Far, who had been writing under the name Edith Maude Eaton, took on her pen name and definitive identity as a Chinese-American woman and dedicated her works to exploring—and vindicating—the Chinese American experience.

In San Francisco, Far immersed herself in Chinatown, the largest concentration of Chinese people outside of China. Far commented in her *Boston Globe* article that life in San Francisco nearly cured her weak health: ''I fell in love with the City of the Golden Gate . . . the place in which all the old ache in my bones fell away from them, never to return again.'' She moved to Seattle where she worked in a Chinese mission school, to Los Angeles, and then finally to Boston where she hoped to work on her book. Far commented in the *Boston Globe* on her final conviction to dedicate herself to writing her book on Chinese Americans: ''a shock of sudden grief so unfitted me for mechanical work [stenography, typesetting etc.] that I determined to emancipate myself from the torture of writing other people's thoughts and words with a heart full of my own.'' She wrote this article in May of 1912 and was anticipating the publication of *Mrs. Spring Fragrance* as well as the forthcoming *The Dream of a Lifetime,* which was never published. Far died in

1914, two years after the article was printed. Of her sojourn to Boston, Far wrote: "I came here with the intention of publishing a book and planting a few Eurasian thoughts in Western literature."

Plot Summary

Although Mrs. Spring Fragrance has lived in Seattle for only five years, her husband says "There are no more American words for her learning." Having quickly become skilled at the English language and American customs, Mrs. Spring Fragrance has become friendly with a young woman who lives next door, Laura, who is the eighteen-year-old daughter of Chinese immigrants. Laura's parents, the Chin Yuens, have decided to adhere to Chinese tradition and have their daughter marry a man she has never met. Laura confides in Mrs. Spring Fragrance that she does not want to marry the young man, the son of a Chinese schoolteacher, because she is in love with Kai Tzu, an American who likes to play baseball and sing popular songs. Giving advice to a young lovelorn friend, Mrs. Spring Fragrance quotes Tennyson: "'Tis better to have loved and lost. Than never to have loved at all."

Puzzled upon overhearing these lines of poetry, Mr. Spring Fragrance, who has been eavesdropping on his wife, seeks an interpretation from his white American neighbor, a student at the University of Washington. Mr. Spring Fragrance is even more confused at the student's careless interpretation and declares angrily: "The truth of the teaching! . . . There is no truth in it whatever. It is disobedient to reason. Is it not better to have what you do not love than to love what you do not have?" Mr. Spring Fragrance decides that American logic is plagued with "unwisdom."

Shortly thereafter, Mrs. Spring Fragrance travels to San Francisco to visit her cousin. While there, she arranges for Laura's finance, the man she does not want to marry, to meet Ah Oi, who is known as the most beautiful girl in San Francisco. Just as Mrs. Spring Fragrance has intended, Ah Oi and the schoolmaster's son fall in love and get married. Mrs. Spring Fragrance writes an exuberant letter to Laura telling her the good news. Now, Laura is free to marry her true love, Kai Tzu. She also writes a letter to Mr. Spring Fragrance, ingratiatingly asking

Sui Sin Far (born Edith Maude Eaton)

him if she can stay in San Francisco another week so she can make fudge for a festival. She also adds a few details about a lecture she has attended, called "America—the Protector of China!" Sarcastically, she asks her husband to forget that the barber charges him a dollar for what he charges an American only fifteen cents, and for the government detaining his brother rather than letting him stay with the Spring Fragrances; "he is protected under the wing of the Eagle, the Emblem of Liberty."

Still pondering the "unwise" poetry, Mr. Spring Fragrance begins to worry when his wife extends her stay in San Francisco. He has received a letter from a friend who writes that he has seen Mrs. Spring Fragrance many times together with Man You, the schoolmaster's handsome son. Unaware that his wife is matchmaking Man You and Ah Oi on Laura's behalf, Mr. Spring Fragrance suspects that his wife is having an affair. He questions the university student again about the mysterious lines of poetry, and comes to the conclusion that Mrs. Spring Fragrance has gone to San Francisco to find the "love that she has lost." Angrily, he plans to invite some men over for a party to get his mind off his seemingly unfaithful wife.

When Mrs. Spring Fragrance at last returns, her husband is rude and gruff. He barely speaks to her and pretends that he must rush off to take care of business. Mrs. Spring Fragrance is surprised at his behavior, but hides her hurt emotions. Laura, having seen Mrs. Spring Fragrance arrive, runs over to hug and thank her for her efforts on her behalf. While the women are talking, Mr. Spring Fragrance overhears their conversation and realizes that he has been mistaken about his wife's infidelity. After Laura leaves, Mr. Spring Fragrance sheepishly tells his wife that he is very happy about Laura and Kai Tzu. Surprised at her usually business-minded husband's interest in romance, Mrs. Spring Fragrance happily declares: ''You must have been reading my American poetry books!'' At this remark, Mr. Spring Fragrance exclaims: ''American poetry is detestable, *abhorrable!*'' Confused, Mrs. Spring Fragrance asks why he has formed a hatred for American poetry, but he only answers by giving her as an anniversary present a beautiful jade pendant that she once admired in a jewelry store window.

Characters

Ah Oi

Ah Oi is described as the prettiest young woman in San Francisco. She is quite popular and Mrs. Spring Fragrance introduces her to Man You knowing that he will easily fall in love with her beauty and charm. When Ah Oi and Man You decide to marry, Laura is no longer obligated to Man You and is free to marry Kai Tzu.

Carman

See University Student

Laura Chin Yuen

Laura is the young Chinese-American woman whom Mrs. Spring Fragrance is trying to help. She has been in love with Kai Tzu for some time, but because of her parents's insistence that she marry the man they have chosen for her, Laura believes she will have to live her life in misery. Laura represents the more Americanized second generation of Asian Americans who often struggle with their parents conservative and traditional lifestyles. As Laura's Chinese name in the story, Mai Gwi Far, meaning ''rose,'' is similar to the author's own name, Sui Sin Far, meaning ''Chinese lily,'' the

author may be asserting an identification with this young woman who is trapped between two cultures.

Kai Tzu

Kai Tzu is the man Laura loves but cannot marry. In addition to not having been selected by Laura's parents, he was born and raised in the United States and is described as ''as ruddy and stalwart as any young Westerner, [and] was noted amongst baseball players as one of the finest pitchers on the Coast.'' As Laura's parents are interested in retaining their Chinese culture, the Chin Yuens's objection to Kai Tzu may be linked to his American upbringing.

Mai Gwi Far

See Laura Chin Yuen

Man You

The son of a Chinese government schoolmaster, Man You has most likely been selected as Laura's husband for his good family and educational background. It is implied that perhaps he is not enthusiastic about an arranged marriage, as he seizes the opportunity to date a young woman who is introduced to him by Mrs. Spring Fragrance.

Mrs. Jade Spring Fragrance

Mrs. Spring Fragrance is the main character of the story, as well as the namesake of the story collection. She is a young Chinese woman living in Seattle who interacts with her multi-racial neighbors. Mrs. Spring Fragrance often serves as the cultural bridge between characters who are in conflict due to their cultural differences. In ''Mrs. Spring Fragrance,'' she cleverly arranges for her Chinese-American friend, Laura, to marry her true love without offending Laura's parents, who have already pre-arranged a match for their daughter. In this case, Mrs. Spring Fragrance facilities harmony between the older generation of Chinese immigrants and their more Americanized children. In a later story, ''The Inferior Woman,'' Mrs. Spring Fragrance similarly convinces an American woman to allow her son to marry his true love rather than the snooty upper-class woman the mother hopes he will choose instead. Mrs. Spring Fragrance is often described as a ''trickster'' figure, that is, an entertaining figure that can subtly charm and persuade people. The ''trickster'' often speaks and acts with humor and irony, thus while she is telling funny stories or acting silly, she utters deep truths about her society, functioning much like the fools and clowns in Shakespeare's plays.

Mr. Sing Yook Spring Fragrance

Mr. Spring Fragrance is a curio merchant in Seattle's Chinatown. He is portrayed as somewhat hot-tempered and conservative in his politics. The plot and humor of "Mrs. Spring Fragrance" is primarily based on Mr. Spring Fragrance's misunderstanding of Western poetry and his subsequent doubts about his wife's fidelity. Though Mr. Spring Fragrance tries to be a stern and domineering husband, he is not so in actuality. Although he momentarily doubts his wife's faithfulness, he loves Mrs. Spring Fragrance very much and when he learns that he is mistaken, he offers his wife the peace offering of a jade necklace that she once admired.

University Student

The Spring Fragrances' next door neighbor, the university student, is the impetus for Mr. Spring Fragrance's misunderstanding of Western poetry. When Mr. Spring Fragrance asks him to explain the meaning of, "'Tis better to have loved and lost, than not to have loved at all," the student drifts off into his own daydreams of the many girls he has dated. In their second conversation, Mr. Spring Fragrance asks him why he thinks America claims to be "noble" yet insists on holding his older brother in a detention center, the student again skirts the question and replies that sometimes Americans have to act against their "principles." The student is portrayed as self-absorbed and arrogant and is described as "not [having] the slightest doubt that he could explain the meaning of all things in the universe." Of course, it is his inability to explain anything to Mr. Spring Fragrance that causes Mr. Spring Fragrance so much anxiety. When Mr. Spring Fragrance decides to hold a "smoking party" to get his mind off his wife, the student suggests that Mr. Spring Fragrance only invite other Chinese Americans so that he can get an insider's look into Chinese-American life. The student later uses this information to write a newspaper article, exploiting and exoticizing the Chinese culture. Though Far gives the student a name, Carman, she only mentions it in passing and chooses to describe him primarily as the American student. By keeping his identity vague and generic, Far may be implying that the student's insensitive and unethical behavior

towards Chinese Americans is representative of America's attitude as a whole.

Themes

Culture Clash

The most prevalent theme in "Mrs. Spring Fragrance" is the culture clash between the Spring Frangrances' Chinese customs and those of their adopted country. The conflicts in the story arise from the misunderstandings between people and their cultures. Mr. Spring Fragrance worries that since his wife is learning Western poetry, she is becoming more American than Chinese. In fact, Mr. Spring Fragrance thinks she is so Americanized that he remarks: "There are no more American words for her learning." This remark underscores how quickly Mrs. Spring Fragrance has assimilated American culture. Though he may admire his wife for her quick learning, her quotations of Western poetry confuse him, especially in regard to American ideas about love. (A subtle joke in the story is that Tennyson, whom Mrs. Spring Fragrance quotes, is not American at all; he is British.) The American university student who lives next door further confuses Mr. Spring Fragrance, as he can only explain the poetry from the point of view of a modern American bachelor who is free to choose his girlfriends. Since his marriage was pre-arranged, Mr. Spring Fragrance begins to fear that his wife may be taking this "American" advice to seek out her true love. This leads Mr. Spring Fragrance to decide that American values are not so desirable after all.

Laura Chin Yuen's life is also complicated by the differences between Chinese culture, which her parents would like to adhere to, and the American culture in which she has been raised. Though her parents quite Americanized, they would like to retain the Chinese customs regarding marriage, and have Laura marry a man she has not yet met. As a result, Laura lives in misery, expecting that she must renounce her true love out of obedience to her parents.

As the only white American who figures prominently in the story, the University of Washington student represents dominant American culture. His

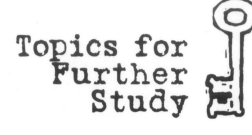

Topics for Further Study

- Investigate discrimination against Chinese immigrants to the United States in the early twentieth century, and select two or three factors that express American discrimination against the immigrants. Considering this environment, select two stories other than "Mrs. Spring Fragrance" from Far's collection and discuss the ways she may be critiquing American treatment of Chinese Americans.

- Do some research about Chinatown. Besides San Francisco and New York, what are some other cities that have Chinatowns? Given that laws restricting Asians are not as oppressive as they were a hundred years ago, why do you think Chinatowns still thrive? What other ethnic groups have "towns" of their own; what groups do not?

- Find out about some cultures that still practice arranged marriages. How do these marriages usually turn out? How do the bride and groom feel about the situation? What might be some of the benefits of such an arrangement? What might some drawbacks be?

- Think of a contemporary or historical event where groups of people have been oppressed or killed because of their race or political affiliations. How have these groups enacted resistance? Is literature an effective way to challenge oppressive political systems?

culture "clashes" with Chinese-American culture when he unsuccessfully interprets Tennyson for Mr. Spring Fragrance. In the exchange between Mr. Spring Fragrance and the student, the student drifts off into a reverie about his numerous girlfriends, the women he has "loved and lost," ignoring Mr. Spring Fragrance's desperate attempts to understand the poetry. On their second meeting, Mr. Spring Fragrance is enraged that his wife might be having an affair and calls together a "smoking party." The student opportunistically asks him to only invite Chinese-Americans so that he can do a

write-up about "authentic Chinese life" for the college newspaper.

The university student's culture "clashes" with Mr. Spring Fragrance's insofar as the student is uninterested in communicating with Mr. Spring Fragrance as a fellow American. Absorbed by thoughts of his complacent bachelor life, the student takes little time to help Mr. Spring Fragrance understand his mistaken notion of Western poetry. The student is only interested in Chinese-American culture as a "scoop" for a newspaper article.

Bridging Cultural Gaps

Mrs. Spring Fragrance acts as a bridge between Chinese and American cultures by maintaining characteristics of both cultures. While the story describes her as so American "that there are no more words for her learning," Mrs. Spring Fragrance never gives up her Chinese culture. Respecting Chinese customs, she does not tell Laura to disobey her parents, but instead plans a subtle scheme that ultimately satisfies the parties involved. She maintains some of the submissiveness of women in ancient Asian cultures, evidenced in the letter she sends to her husband, which she addresses to "Great and Honored Man." When she wants to extend her stay in San Francisco, she asks her husband's "permission" first. Perhaps adhering to an Asian tradition of modesty, she mixes praise with phrases of great humility: "there is much feasting and merry making under the lanterns in honor of your Stupid Thorn." Finally, she signs her letter: "Your ever loving and obedient woman."

On the other hand, Mrs. Spring Fragrance is a very Americanized woman. Not only does she quote Western poetry, but she is an expert in making fudge. In San Francisco she attends lectures in English given by prominent political figures and instead of forcing Laura to obey her parents in blind adherence to tradition, she cleverly helps her marry the man she loves.

Most importantly, Mrs. Spring Fragrance is neither entirely American or entirely Chinese. She utilizes positive aspects of both cultures to create a balanced identity as well as help others, like Laura, who may be trapped in between cultures. She is a direct contrast to her husband who rejects American culture because of a few lines of poetry he does not understand and to the university student who is not interested in truly getting to know Chinese immigrants.

Gender Roles

On the surface, Mr. and Mrs. Spring Fragrance abide by traditional gender roles, but subtle incidents in the story show a more complicated relationship. For example, while Mrs. Spring Fragrance asks her husband for ''permission'' to stay in San Francisco, she intends to stay regardless of her husband's approval. She writes in the letter: ''Waiting, by the wonderful wire of the telegram message, your gracious permission to remain for the celebration of the Fifth Moon.'' Her husband never writes back, but Mrs. Spring Fragrance is not at all concerned and enjoys the rest of her vacation. Embarrassed by her independence, Mr. Spring Fragrance tells his friends that he is the one who asked her to stay away longer so that he can give an all-male ''smoking party.'' Mrs. Spring Fragrance apparently has much control over her husband domestically and emotionally.

Race and Racism

The exploration of racism in this story is subtle. The university student considers the Chinese culture of his neighbors as something foreign and exotic, and he plans to exploit it for the purpose of a sensational newspaper article. The student also has no answer for Mr. Spring Fragrance's queries about the illogic of American society. When the student asserts that everyone who comes to America is treated like royalty, Mr. Spring Fragrance asks him why his brother is still held up in an immigration detention pen. The student's response is that sometimes the American government must act against their noble principles. This facile answer does not explain *why* in the case of Chinese immigration the American government is acting against their ''principles'' and merely condones this unjust treatment of Chinese immigrants. Perhaps American ''principles'' are not so noble after all.

In her letter to her husband, Mrs. Spring Fragrance cleverly lists the case of discrimination against Chinese Americans while pretending to tolerate it. She remarks that she has been to a lecture called, ''America, the Protector of China!'' The lecture was so eloquent that Mrs. Spring Fragrance urges her husband to ''forget to remember that the barber charges you one dollar for a shave while he humbly submits to the American man a bill of fifteen cents. And murmur no more because your honored elder brother . . . is detained under the roof-tree of this great Government instead of under your own humble roof. Console him with the reflection that he is protected under the wing of the Eagle, the Emblem of Liberty. What is the loss of ten hundred years or ten thousand times ten dollars compared with the happiness of knowing oneself so securely sheltered?'' The heavy irony is this passage denotes that Mrs. Spring Fragrance and other Chinese Americans will not ''forget to remember'' the legalized discrimination imposed on them.

Prejudice and Tolerance

White Americans are not the only racist figures in ''Mrs. Spring Fragrance.'' When he does not readily understand Western poetry, Mr. Spring Fragrance jumps to the conclusion that American logic is flawed and ''unwise.'' He does bring up the hypocrisy of America claiming to be benevolent while consistently discriminating against Chinese immigrants, but from his limited experience with Western poetry, Mr. Spring Fragrance decides that everything else about America must be deplorable too. The way Mr. Spring Fragrance forms his hasty negative opinion about America is analogous to the way dominant American culture forms quick and irrational judgments about minority groups without fully understanding them. Like the dominant American culture, Mr. Spring Fragrance is guilty of stereotyping.

Politics

In addition to the humorous romances between Laura and Kai Tzu, and Mr. and Mrs. Spring Fragrance, ''Mrs. Spring Fragrance'' provides a political critique of legalized discrimination against the Chinese. The detention of Mr. Spring Fragrance's brother evokes America's history of legalized racism against the Chinese. The Chinese Exclusion Act of 1882 barred further entry of any Chinese citizens into the United States and previous to this law, Chinese were allowed to immigrate primarily as laborers for the building of the Transcontinental Railroad (for which labor they were grossly underpaid). Any immigrant not planning to work on the railroad was charged a head tax of $500, an exorbitant sum at the turn of the century, often making it impossible for the wives and families of the laborers to come to the country. Even if a Chinese citizen met all the conditions to immigrate, he/she was often detained unjustifiably for indefinite periods of time at immigration detention centers to prevent rapid increases in the Chinese American population. In addition to these legalized forms of racism, Chinese in America were discriminated against in everyday society as exhibited in the attitude of the university student.

Style

Point of View and Narration

"Mrs. Spring Fragrance" uses "author omniscient" narration, meaning that an outside voice describes the incidents of the story and is privy to the thoughts and feelings of each of the characters. By knowing the inner thoughts of the major characters of the story, the reader can form an opinion about them. For example, knowing the university student's motives in attending the "smoking party," and Mr. Spring Fragrance's mistake in prematurely judging American culture, helps the reader understand that they are both enacting racial prejudice.

Dramatic Irony

Much of the plot of "Mrs. Spring Fragrance" depends on characters being misinformed or ignorant of others's actions while the reader is fully aware of all the situations going on at one time. This is called "dramatic irony." Mr. Spring Fragrance's anger and anxiety hinges on his ignorance of his wife's real motives for visiting San Francisco. This misunderstanding leads to the climax of the plot and also introduces much humor into the story.

Irony and Hyperbole

The political critique in "Mrs. Spring Fragrance" is expressed through irony, saying or doing one thing while meaning another. Instead of directly stating her views on American racism, Mrs. Spring Fragrance pretends that she is praising America and its benevolence. In the letter to her husband, she speaks in hyperbole, exaggerated praise or criticism

to prove a point. By excessively praising America's so-called altruistic treatment of Chinese immigrants, Mrs. Spring Fragrance hints to the reader that her praise is ironic. What she is expressing beneath the surface of her words is an attack on American racism. Both Mr. and Mrs. Spring Fragrance call attention to the ironic situation of America claiming to be the "protector of China" while overcharging them for haircuts and detaining their relatives at immigration centers. There is also irony in Mrs. Spring Fragrance believing that Tennyson was an American poet. Not only was he British, but he held the title of baron, indicating his position within the British aristocracy. Perhaps Far was subtly commenting that Asians who do not distinguish between various Caucasian nationalities are like Americans who often have difficulty distinguishing between various Asian cultures.

Rhetoric

Rhetoric is the persuasive use of speech to gain personal or political advantage. Rhetorical speech often utilizes hyperbole and irony. "Mrs. Spring Fragrance" challenges the American rhetoric that the United States treats its immigrants fairly. Public speakers and politicians often use rhetoric to gain votes and public approval. Mrs. Spring Fragrance attends such a political speech in San Francisco, entitled, "America, the Protector China!" that hopes to lead Americans to believe that Chinese in the United States are treated fairly. On a smaller scale, the university student uses this kind of racist rhetoric to deflect Mr. Spring Fragrance's accusatory query regarding his brother's detention. The student replies: "Well, that is a shame—'a beastly shame,' as the Englishman says. But understand, old fellow, we that are real Americans are up against that [holding immigrants unjustifiably at detention centers]—even more than you. It is against our principles." As in this example, rhetorical speech is often manipulative and insincere, intended to mask unpleasant realities. "Rhetorical questions" are questions posed to prove a point and do not expect an answer. Mrs. Spring Fragrance uses rhetorical questions herself in her letter to her husband regarding his brother: "What is the loss of ten hundred years or ten thousand times ten dollars compared with the happiness of knowing oneself so securely sheltered?" Charged with irony, this rhetorical question is meant to uncover the unfair treatment of Chinese immigrants.

Historical Context

The "Chinese Problem"

Far wrote about the experience of Chinese immigrants in a politically sensitive environment. In the mid-nineteenth century, the United States encouraged mass immigration of young Chinese men to Hawaii to work on sugar plantations and to California to build the first transcontinental railroad. Any immigrant who did not plan to labor in these projects was often charged an exorbitant entry tax. Thus, the early Chinese immigrants were mostly bachelors or young men who left their wives and families overseas. Once in the United States, the laborers were legally forbidden to live in white communities or marry outside of their race. After the completion of the railroad, strict hiring regulations, as well as employers's personal discrimination against minorities, left only menial jobs like food service or laundering available to Chinese Americans. In *Asian Americans: An Interpretive History,* Sucheng Chan quotes an interview with a Chinese laundry owner: "White customers were prepared to patronize [a Chinese man] as a laundryman because as such his status was low and constituted no competitive threat. If you stop to think about it, there's a very real difference between the person who washes your soiled clothing and the one who fills your prescription. As a laundryman [the Chinese man] occupied a status which was in accordance with the social definition of the place in the economic hierarchy suitable for a member of an 'inferior race.'" These discriminatory laws and practices helped form the early Chinatowns in large cities across the country, where Chinese Americans fostered and developed their own rich culture.

Discomfited by this new population of a people of color, Chinese immigration was effectively halted in 1882 for a period of ten years with the Chinese Exclusion Act, which was renewed in 1902. Absolutely no more Chinese were allowed into the United States. White Americans compared the presence of Chinese to a disease, calling them the "Yellow Peril." Jacob Riis, a pre-eminent social commentator at the time wrote in his study of tenement life in New York: "The Chinese are in no sense a desirable element of the population . . . they serve no useful purpose here [New York], whatever they may have done elsewhere in other days." To paraphrase, Riis was saying that while in the past they were useful on the sugar plantations and in building the transconti-

nental railroad, Chinese Americans no longer served a purpose in the United States and therefore no longer deserved to be here. Others agreed that the Chinese should be shipped back. As Roger Daniel quoted one politician: "The health, wealth, prosperity and happiness of our State demand their [the Chinese] expulsion from our shores."

In this environment of legalized racism, writers exploring the unequal treatment of Chinese in America would find it difficult to publish overt criticism of the United States government. Most Asian-American writers wrote non-threatening "orientalized" books that represented Asian and Asian Americans as happy, carefree, and exotically interesting. Modern critics accuse these books of accommodating a racist American sensibility while erasing the legislated injustices enacted on Asian Americans. Far's stories seem to fall into this category of "accommodation," but beneath the surface of harmless words, Far's use of irony and implication subtly criticize American racism.

Critical Overview

Working in the heavily Sinophobic environment of the turn-of-the-century, Far had to carefully choose her words. Any explicit criticism of the Chinese-American situation might have been considered subversive and unfit for publication. As a result, Far disguised her critique of American society under a surface of charming, "harmless" stories about Chinese-American life. White Americans were indeed curious about the Asian Americans, and a number of books were published during this time that were intended to "inform" the dominant culture about the immigrants' exotic lifestyles. The D. Lothrop Publishing Company in Boston published a group of works entitled "When I Was a Boy in . . ." that included Lee Yan Phou's *When I Was a Boy in China* (1887), New Il-Han's *When I Was a Boy in Korea* (1928), and Sakae Shioya's *When I Was a Boy in Japan* (1906). The books in this series rarely touched on the struggles the authors may have had in adjusting to life in the United States. Because the American publishers were not interested in publishing indictments of their own country, they ensured that these books provided interesting, enlightening,

Compare & Contrast

- **1852:** 195 Chinese contract laborers are sent to Hawaii to work on sugar plantations. Over 20,000 Chinese live in California; many of them have immigrated to work in gold mines. California is commonly referred to by the Chinese as the "Gold Mountain."

  1982: A Chinese American named Vincent Chin is beaten death in Detroit for being "Japanese."

- **1907:** The "Gentleman's Agreement" is formed between the United States and Japan and prohibits the entry of Japanese into America.

  1987: The U.S. House of Representative votes to make an official apology to Japanese Americans and their families affected by the World War II internment. Plans are made to pay each surviving internee $20,000. The action is supported by the Senate in 1987, and by President George Bush in 1989.

- **1882:** Chinese Exclusion Act is passed. Terms of the law effectively prohibit entry of Chinese immigrants into the United States for 10 years. In 1892, Chinese immigration is barred for another 10 years as Geary Law renews terms of the Chinese Exclusion Act.

  1997: The University of Pennsylvania proposes the Minority Permanence Act, deeming certain minority groups as "over-represented." If the act passes, Asian Americans will no longer be considered as minority groups in admissions procedures. This adversely affects Southeast Asian immigrants and other new Asian immigrant groups who may not have the economic and educational advantage of the larger Asian sub-groups (Chinese, Japanese, Korean) that have been in the country longer.

---

and *harmless* information about the authors' Asian homelands. For now, this satisfied and accommodated Americans' desire for a lively and non-threatening account of Asian lifestyles.

With her verbose and flowery style, use of Chinese dialect and pidgin English (often for comical effect), and "insider" details of Chinatown, Far did not readily appear to be different from the other "Oriental" writers of her time. The author's power lies not in overt and sermonizing racial accusations, but in subtlety and suggestiveness that American readers of the time were likely to overlook. Even contemporary critics miss her irony and sarcasm; Lorraine Dong and Marlon K. Hom claim that while Far's work may be sympathetic to the Chinese-American experience, it perpetuates stereotypes. This glossing over of the transgressive potential of works like *Mrs. Spring Fragrance* unmasks readers' willful erasure of attempts at Chinese cultural empowerment. Denying the work's moments of sarcasm, subtle or blatant, the book's audience reveals that it is more comfortable placing and

reading the work as a fanciful. oriental, and harmless group of tales in any time period. Through *Mrs. Spring Fragrance* Far has created an ingenious form of political resistance while working within the limits of dominant culture. It is the readers' choice to be satisfied with a facile, surface reading of her works or to recognize its deeper, political interpretation.

Far's sister, Winnifred Eaton, was also a writer and published under the Japanese pseudonym Onoto Watanna. The Japanese in America were considered at this time more elegant and refined than the Chinese. Eaton capitalized on this perception and created a "fan and slipper image" that catered to curious white Americans. Watanna wrote and published with great success with Rand McNally in New York, publishing numerous romances, a cookbook, and a preface to a volume of American poetry over a period of twenty-five years. Watanna's romances are uncomplicated love stories in which, typically, a white American traveler goes to Japan, falls in love with a Japanese woman and teaches her

A Chinese procession in turn-of-the-century San Francisco.

how to love. The content of these stories pander to white America's fantasy that the coy and cowering Orient waits in anticipation of a more educated and more passionate American figure to enlighten it.

Should Winnifred Eaton be reproached for abjuring her Chinese heritage for an easier, more profitable Japanese one? Or, was she, like her sister, playing a trick on American readers by expressing critical subtexts beneath the enchanting and seemingly harmless surface of her stories? A translation of the ideograms that represent Winnifred's pseudonym reveal that "wata (ru)" means "to cross," and "na" means "to name." Perhaps then, Winnifred's

name that "crosses names" is playing a joke on the reader who believes that these stories are nothing but sincere representations of Japanese life written by an actual Japanese woman.

As a half-Chinese, half-British woman, Far was keenly aware of the racist pressures surrounding literary production. Knowing that negative portrayals of Chinese-American life would not be published, she masked her often bitter feelings about America in the blithe and carefree collection of stories *Mrs. Spring Fragrance*. Some of the more lighthearted titles in the collection are: "In the Land of the Free," "The Chinese Lily," and "The Prize

China Baby.'' Of course, there was the second part of her collection, ''Tales of Chinese Children'' that promised adorable depictions of Asian babies. Like ''Mrs. Spring Fragrance,'' the content of many of these stories was subversive and serious. For example, ''In the Land of the Free'' is not about achieving the American dream as it as it seems to be. It ends with the tragedy of a toddler forgetting his mother after having been detained in an immigration center for a number of years. ''The Chinese Lily'' is not about a beautiful Chinese maiden, but about a crippled Chinese-American woman living alone in a Chinatown garret. Initially, 2,500 copies of *Mrs. Spring Fragrance* were published in 1912. The collection was not widely reviewed at the time, though a review in the *Independent* stated that ''The conflict between occidental and oriental ideals and the hardships of the American immigration laws furnish the theme for most of the tales and the reader is not only interested but has his mind widened by becoming acquainted with novel points of view.'' The book was out of print for decades before it was republished in 1995, along with a biography on Far, by Amy Ling and Annette White-Parks. This recent resurgence of interest in her life and writing is part of a larger trend in which women writers from the early twentieth-century are being re-evaluated as important voices in literature and feminism in an era that was almost completely devoid of a woman's perspective in the arts and sciences.

Criticism

Yoonmee Chang

Yoonmee Chang has a master's degree in English and American literature from the University of Pennsylvania where she is currently a Ph.D. candidate. She works on contemporary Asian-American literature and in the following essay she discusses the subtexts of Sui Sin Far's ''Mrs. Spring Fragrance'' that critique America's history of often legalized oppression of Asian-American immigrants.

As a writer of Chinese ancestry writing about the Chinese-American experience, Sui Sin Far, pseudonym of Edith Maude Eaton (1865-1914), would have found it easier at the turn-of-the-

century to write about anything else. Her first and only collection of short stories, *Mrs. Spring Fragrance,* was published in 1912, just thirty years after the Chinese Exclusion Act and twenty years after its 1902 renewal. Once their labor was no longer needed on the first transcontinental railroad or the Hawaiian sugar plantations, the Chinese in America were considered undesirable by politicians who wanted to preserve the white face of America. Literary critic Susan Lanser in *Feminist Studies* recalls the pejorative epithets used to describe the Chinese immigrants: ''The Yellow Peril,'' and ''hirsute, low-browed, big-faced, ox-like men of obviously low mentality.'' On the other end of the spectrum was the stereotype that the Chinese were enchanting, mysterious, and exotic. This was an era when the dominant culture's interest in Chinese-American culture extended only insofar as it was charming and interesting, not angry or politically threatening. The Asian-American literature of this time attests to this, for example, D. Lothrop Publishing Company's ''When I Was a Boy'' series (*When I Was a Boy in China,* (1887) *When I Was Boy in Japan,* (1906), *When I Was a Boy in Korea,* (1928), and Onoto Watanna's saccharine but best-selling Japanese romances (published between 1899-1925). Onoto Watanna (Winnifred Eaton) was Sui Sin Far's sister, and her adoption of a Japanese writing identity indicates how flexible the Eaton children's identity as Eurasians was. Both sisters resembled white Americans more than Asian Americans, but nonetheless, Sui Sin Far took on a Chinese American persona, despite the social adversity it ensured. In this intensely Sinophobic environment, Far challenged America's racist treatment of Chinese Americans, but aware that overt criticism would hardly be published, she wove her critique with subtly and irony into a surface of seemingly harmless words. In this essay, I will explore Sui Sin Far's technique in her short story, ''Mrs. Spring Fragrance.''

As the title character of the collection, Mrs. Spring Fragrance figures in several of Far's stories as a delightful ''busy-body.'' She is introduced in the first lines of ''Mrs. Spring Fragrance'' as being so fully Americanized that ''there are no more American words for her learning.'' Ostensibly, this is the reason for her popularity among her white American and Chinese-American neighbors alike. She has become a favorite for her delicious American fudge and attends the popular social lectures of the day such as ''America, the Protector of China.''

What Do I Read Next?

- *Leaves from the Mental Portfolio of an Eurasian* (1909) by Sui Sin Far is the author's memoir of growing up in Canada and the United States as a half-Chinese and half-British woman.

- *Mrs. Spring Fragrance and Other Writings* (1995) edited by Amy Ling and Annette White-Parks. The most comprehensive collection of Sui Sin Far's written works, including her early newspaper articles, to date.

- *Tama* by Onoto Watanna. A romance about an American professor who travels to the Japanese countryside and meets Tama, a half-Japanese, half-American woman who is blind. Tama has been rejected by the people of her village for her odd appearance and is considered an evil "fox-woman" until the American professor teaches them otherwise.

- *Asian Americans: An Interpretive History* (1991) by Sucheng Chan. A historical account of how Asian immigrants in the United States were *really* treated. Chan brings to the forefront the discrimination and legalized racism against Asian Americans that frequently is omitted from American history books.

- *The Joy Luck Club* (1989) by Amy Tan. Four American-born women of Chinese immigrants try to bridge the cultural differences between themselves and their mothers, who met during the Japanese occupation of China during World War II.

- *Nisei Daughter* by (1953) Monica Sone. A Japanese American woman's account of life in United States in the years surrounding World War II. Sone discusses the outrage of the internment of all Japanese in America, particularly the *nisei,* meaning "second generation," who were born in America and were legal American citizens.

- *The Woman Warrior* (1975) by Maxine Hong Kingston. Kingston's fictionalized autobiography explores her complicated position as a Chinese American born in the United States. She explores her alienation as a young girl trapped between Chinese and American cultures, neither of which she belongs to fully.

- *Clay Walls* (1987) by Ronyoung Kim. The story of a young Korean-American woman whose impoverished immigrant life contrasts sharply to the life of wealth and leisure she led in Korea. It is set in the first two decades of this century, when many Koreans were fleeing persecution from Imperial Japan and immigrating to the United States.

- *Charlie Chan Is Dead,* edited by Jessica Hagedorn. An anthology of recent Asian-American short stories exploring the racism, oppression, and alienation that Asian Americans still face today.

But beneath her happily Americanized exterior, Mrs. Spring Fragrance harbors resentment against America's racist treatment of Chinese immigrants. To express her resentment overtly in sermons against racism might make Mrs. Spring Fragrance and her creator, Sui Sin Far, unpopular or ignored, thus, she thinly conceals her real sentiments under a surface of irony.

For example, as Mrs. Spring Fragrance travels to San Francisco from her hometown of Seattle, she writes a letter to her husband praising a lecture she attended, entitled, "America, the Protector of China." She writes:

> I am enjoying a most agreeable visit, and American friends, as also our own, strive benevolently for the accomplishment of my pleasure. Mrs. Samuel Smith, an American lady, known to my cousin, asked for my accompaniment to a magniloquent lecture the other evening. The subject was "America, the Protector of China!" It was most exhilarating, and the effect of so much expression of benevolence leads me to beg of you to forget to remember that the barber charges you one dollar for a shave while he humbly submits to the American man a bill of fifteen cents. And murmur no

> "Mrs. Spring Fragrance has been described by literary critics as a 'trickster' figure. The privilege of a 'trickster' is to move in and out of social boundaries, criticizing those boundaries without reproach."

more because your honored elder brother, on a visit to this country, is detained under the roof-tree of this great Government instead of under you own humble roof. Console him with the reflection that he is protected under the wing of the Eagle, the Emblem of Liberty. What is the loss of ten hundred years or ten thousand times ten dollars compared with the happiness of knowing oneself so securely sheltered? All of this I have learned from Mrs. Samuel Smith, who is as brilliant and great of mind as one of your own superior sex.

The heavily ironic tone of this passage implies that Mrs. Spring Fragrance may not be entirely pleased with her life in America. She has recorded here a list of grievances and unfair treatment, but by couching it in praise of America, however insincere, Mrs. Spring Fragrance appears to be innocent of subversive sentiments. By encouraging her husband to "forget to remember" the discriminations he has experienced, she is charging Chinese Americans to *always* remember them. Incidentally, this letter also enacts a reversal of gender roles. She addresses her husband with the honorific, "Great and Honored Man," signs off with the submissive, "Your ever loving and obedient woman," in this letter asking permission to stay in San Francisco a little while longer. But though she says she will humbly await her husband's "gracious permission," Mrs. Spring Fragrance does not wait at all and continues her trip according to her own plans. Later in the story, Mr. Spring Fragrance is embarrassed by his wife's independent behavior and tells his neighbor that he she is staying away longer at his request, so that he can give a party for his male friends.

While Mr. Spring Fragrance may not be as clever as his wife, he expresses his own discontent about life in America. In a discussion with his white American neighbor, a student at the University of Washington, Mr. Spring Fragrance is puzzled by the student's comment that "everyone" is royalty in America. The student says: "all Americans are princes and princesses, and just as soon as a foreigner puts his foot upon our shores, he also becomes one the nobility—I mean, the royal family." This statement rings untrue for Mr. Spring Fragrance who wonders aloud why then his brother is detained at the immigration center if he is supposed to be part of the "nobility." The student's answer is evasive and rhetorical. According to him, sometimes Americans must act against their "principles." Though this answer does not satisfy Mr. Spring Fragrance, the conversation moves on to other topics. While this passage may not offer any concrete answers to Mr. Spring Fragrance's general question regarding discrimination against Chinese immigrants, Sui Sin Far at least allows this bit of historical information to be articulated. By placing it in a casual and seemingly harmless conversation, Far calls attention to the hypocrisy of American rhetoric. By not dwelling on its implications and putting the words in the mouth of a befuddled, generally harmless man, Far deflects criticism that her work may be threatening to the American government. In this way, Sui Sin Far briefly speaks the unspeakable, subtly instigating the careful reader's mind.

Structured around Mr. Spring Fragrance's rash conclusions regarding his wife's fidelity, the story as a whole is a critique of making irrational and unjustified judgments about any group of people. Mr. Spring Fragrance bases his entire opinion about American culture on a trivial misunderstanding of Western poetry. The university student's inattention aggravates Mr. Spring Fragrance's confusion, and he concludes that the mysterious lines of poetry, "'Tis better to have loved and lost, than never to have loved at all," indicates his wife's desire for seek her true love. In his anger, he decides that his wife's Americanization is going to ruin his marriage, and he concludes that the poetry as well as American culture in general is "detestable, *abhorrable!*" Mr. Spring Fragrance is guilty of stereotyping. By taking one small piece of information, Mr. Spring Fragrance makes a wholesale negative judgment about the entire culture, which results in confusion and misunderstanding. In this way, Far warns against stereotyping and prejudice from any angle, whether it be the majority against a minority or vice versa.

Through "Mrs. Spring Fragrance," Far offers a partial reconciliation to the disparate cultures. The heroine of the story is Mrs. Spring Fragrance, who is neither entirely Chinese, and despite her early description, entirely American. She is a bridge figure who emerges triumphantly from the story precisely because she achieves a balance between cultures. For example, when her friend Laura Chin Yuen is despondent over her pre-arranged marriage, Mrs. Spring Fragrance respects both Chinese and American views of marriage. While she believes that Laura should indeed be permitted to marry her true love, she does not directly challenge Laura's conservative Chinese parents. Instead, she manipulates events so that Laura's betrothed will fall in love with someone else, freeing Laura and her family from the marriage arrangement. In this way, the Chin Yuen's desire to retain Chinese customs is not directly challenged while Laura's more "American" notion of marrying her childhood sweetheart can be fulfilled. Mrs. Spring Fragrance's strategy is much like Far's. By working subtly and indirectly, she enables social changes without inciting public opposition.

Mrs. Spring Fragrance has been described by literary critics as a "trickster" figure. The privilege of a "trickster" is to move in and out of social boundaries, criticizing those boundaries without reproach. The "trickster" might be compared to the fool or clown in Shakespeare's plays who often speaks the unspoken, or what others will not articulate for fear of punishment. Because of the fool's low social standing and his reputation for uttering harmless and entertaining nonsense, his often insightful criticism of the social apparatus, for instance criticism of the King, goes unpunished. Mrs. Spring Fragrance travels through Far's stories uttering such insights, but her charming reputation, excessive, though ironic, praise of America, and her real efforts at helping those around her, buffer her from blame. Even when she is criticizing Americans, they often thank and support her. In the second story of the collection, "The Inferior Woman," Mrs. Spring Fragrance visits her American neighbors for the purpose of writing a book. In a clever reversal of the stereotype that Chinese are mysterious and exotic, Mrs. Spring Fragrance declares: "Ah, these Americans! These mysterious, inscrutable, incomprehensible Americans! Had I the divine right of learning I would put them into an immortal book!" In this quote Mrs. Spring Fragrance reverses who is "them" and places white Americans as the culturally different outsider. But the characters of the story do not readily realize this and encourage her to sit in on their conversations so that she can garner cultural information from them. In this story, Far conjures up the image of Mrs. Spring Fragrance as a silent but persistent observer lurking behind the routine goings-on of the white American woman's life. The absurdity of this situation belies the very real observation and scrutiny that the Chinese in America experience every day and the negative stereotypes and discriminatory treatment that result from them. The American women in "The Inferior Woman" let Mrs. Spring Fragrance sit in on their lives because they perceive her as harmless. Far was also perceived as harmless to the literary and political world and was permitted to publish her collection, *Mrs. Spring Fragrance*. It is only within the last ten years or so, nearly a century later, that Far's trenchant criticism of America's racism against Chinese has been properly unearthed and dominant culture has come to realize that she has been playing a trick on us all.

Source: Yoonmee Chang, for *Short Stories for Students*, Gale, 1998.

Annette White-Parks

In the following excerpt from a longer essay, White-Parks compares the stories "Mrs. Spring Fragrance" and "The Inferior Woman" in an effort to highlight the various cultural influences on the character of Mrs. Spring Fragrance.

. . . Printed four months apart in *Hampton's Magazine* (January and May 1910), "Mrs. Spring Fragrance" and "The Inferior Woman" deal with many of Sui Sin Far's central themes and develop her most obvious trickster figure. Mrs. Spring Fragrance is the main character in both stories. "Mrs. Spring Fragrance" presents a comic fantasy world, ruled over by the "quaint, dainty" Mrs. Spring Fragrance, or "Jade," a young immigrant wife who, when she "first arrived in Seattle . . . was unacquainted with even one word of the American language"; "five years later, her husband speaking of her, says: 'There are no more American words for her learning.'" Unlike Chinese Americans in other Sui Sin Far stories, the Spring Fragrances live not in a Chinatown but in an integrated middle-class Seattle suburb with white neighbors on one side and Chinese on the other. Mr. Spring Fragrance, "a young curio merchant," is what westerners call "Americanized," and "Mrs. Spring Fragrance [is] even more so." Appropriately pluralistic, Mr. Spring Fragrance, when he gets home from his commute, sits in a bamboo settee on the verandah reading the *Chinese World* and feeding pigeons lichis out of his pocket. At the center of their blend of "East" and "West" life-styles is a marriage that combines elements of "arranged" and "romantic": "He had fallen in love with her picture before ever he had seen her, just as she had fallen in love with his! And when the marriage veil was lifted and each saw the other for the first time in the flesh, there had been no disillusion, no lessening of respect and affection, which those who had brought about the marriage had inspired in each young heart."

Desiring this same goal for others, Mrs. Spring Fragrance assumes the role of arranging marriages in both stories. She thus evokes a traditional figure out of Chinese culture, the matchmaker, who traditionally worked for the parents of the bride and groom to arrange marriages in which romantic love played no part. In this instance, however, the matchmaker becomes a catalyst to the Western romantic convention by helping young, second-generation Chinese American lovers outwit their more traditional immigrant parents. In "Mrs. Spring Fragrance," she conspires with the young woman Mai Gwi Far (Laura) to help her marry her "sweetheart" Kai Tzu, a young man whose Western ways are represented by his being "one of the finest [baseball] pitchers on the Coast" and his singing the British classic "Drink to Me Only with Thine Eyes" to Mai Gwi Far/Laura's piano accompaniment.

In the midst of Mai Gwi Far and Kai Tzu's romance, Mrs. Spring Fragrance takes on another romance when she travels to San Francisco and introduces Ah Oi—"who had the reputation of being the prettiest Chinese girl in San Francisco and, according to Chinese gossip, the naughtiest"— to the son of a Chinese American schoolteacher and then accompanies the couple on their impromptu elopement. Ironically, the San Francisco matchmaking visit puts Mrs. Spring Fragrance's own marriage in jeopardy, because her husband misinterprets her absence and thinks she is having an affair. In a comedy of errors, however, Mr. Spring Fragrance's fears are allayed, and all three matches are happily resolved. When Mai Gwi Far's father, Mr. Chin Yuen, who has been adamantly opposed to his daughter's marriage to Kai Tzu, suddenly accepts her romantic choice with scarcely a hint of dissension, the story's verisimilitude is strongly tested. The metaphor Mai Gwi Far's father voices in consent to the marriage is, however, overtly thematic: "'the old order is passing away and the new order is taking its place, even with us who are Chinese'.". . .

As in "Mrs. Spring Fragrance," the verisimilitude of "The Inferior Woman" also is challenged by a too facile ending. When Mary Carman visits Alice and begs her to "'return home with me. . . . for the prettiest wedding of the season'," she changes her point of view as readily as Mr. Chin Yuen did in "Mrs. Spring Fragrance." Moreover, the "inferior woman's" superiority is proven by a classic Victorian test—Alice gets the man. As in so many stories about Chinese American women, Sui Sin Far slips her characters' lives into a groove she herself has rejected, that of a fairy-tale marriage. With Mrs. Spring Fragrance as catalyst, the dynamics involved in such marriages are virtually the same for both Chinese and white Americans.

On a deeper level, this storyteller figure plays "tricks" with political as well as romantic messages. For example, an anecdote in Mrs. Spring Fragrance's letter to her husband in "Mrs. Spring Fragrance" subverts the story's surface concern with the arrangement of marriages. This letter highlights Mrs. Samuel Smith, whom Mrs. Spring Fragrance has heard lecture on "America, the Protector of China" and describes "'as brilliant and [as] great of mind as one of your own superior sex.'" This satirical overstatement spoofs both Mrs. Smith's arrogance and the patriarchal assumptions to which white women in Sui Sin Far's fiction are so frequently handmaidens. The letter satirizes Mrs. Smith's claims about the protection offered to Chinese Americans by "'the wing of the Eagle, the Emblem of Liberty,'" "protection" that should make Mr. Spring Fragrance "'forget to remember that the barber charges you one dollar for a shave [and] . . . the American man . . . fifteen cents'" and that "'your honored elder brother, on a visit to this country, is detained under the rooftree of this great Government'." Clearly Mrs. Samuel Smith, like Ethel Evebrook, exemplifies the "new" woman, who goes beyond breaking silence and steps up to the public lectern in the public arena previously reserved for men, one that Alice Winthrop shuns. While Sui Sin Far herself takes up a public voice as a writer of fiction and journalism, she seems to distinguish between her own role and that of this breed of "new" woman, perhaps because she feels that—unlike the privileged Ethel Evebrook or Mrs. Smith but like Alice Winthrop—she has earned her voice through long and painful experience.

Mrs. Spring Fragrance's border position—between cultures and individuals, as matchmaker and trickster—mirrors Sui Sin Far's role as author, especially when Mrs. Spring Fragrance turns writer.

"'I listen to what is said, I apprehend, I write it down,'" Mrs. Spring Fragrance says in "The Inferior Woman." Both Sui Sin Far and Mrs. Spring Fragrance arrange marriages, and both do it through fiction. The character's desire to put "'these mysterious, inscrutable, and incomprehensible Americans . . . into an immortal book'" for "her Chinese women friends" because "many American women wrote books" about the Chinese recalls the author's desire to write about Chinese for Americans and the irony with which she did so. The interplay of author/ character identity is deftly revealed in one line in the text, when Mrs. Spring Fragrance imagines Lae-Choo reading her book to Fei and Sie and Mai Gwi Far—all names of characters from various Sui Sin Far stories.

Motifs in the two Mrs. Spring Fragrance stories comically present topics we have found in the *Westerner* pieces. Both are concerned with the redistribution of power between races, sexes, classes, and generations, redistributions acted out on the threshold of change from old orders—Victorian England and Imperialist China—as an immigrant people found ways of adapting to new conditions. "Mrs. Spring Frangrance" in particular presents some major problems for interpreting these topics. At several points the story's narrator does not seem aware of the obvious cultural ironies that Mrs. Spring Fragrance's character raises. For instance, the title character is apparently serious in her use of the verse from Alfred Lord Tennyson's "In Memorium" as her refrain throughout— "'It is better to have loved and lost than never to have loved at all.'" Both Mrs. and Mr. Spring Fragrance call Tennyson "an American poet." Sui Sin Far, reared on British literature when Tennyson was laureate, certainly knew the difference, however, and could be suggesting, satirically, that to her fictional couple—as white Americans say about Chinese in both the United States and China—poets in the United States and England all sound the same. As Ammons observes, "She is forcing us to think about American literature and sentimentality from a place outside white western consciousness." Comments such as Mr. Spring Fragrance's "'American poetry is detestable, abhorrible!'" certainly recall Sui Sin Far's satiric treatment of romantic fiction in "Albemarle's Secret." But the reader is given no guide to such irony; the narrator neither corrects nor comments on the Spring Fragrance's erroneous reference to Tennyson as "an American poet."

There are other problems with the Mrs. Spring Fragrance stories. Complex and timely questions that these texts as a whole raise—How does one deal with cultural obedience, filial piety, respect for old customs in this new environment? How does a woman's freedom to do low-paying secretarial labor for a man really speak to problems of class or to the tenets of woman suffrage?—are resolved simplistically. Mr. Chin Yuen readily accepts the "new order," and Mary Carson readily accepts the "inferior woman." Both involve changes in their basic cultural assumptions about marriage and class that take place during a few minutes' chat, which violates the reader's sense of believability. "Mrs. Spring Fragrance" and "The Inferior Woman" solve the problems of living on intercultural borders too easily. They turn comic and cute, and the examination of important issues they open fades back into silence. Is Sui Sin Far caricaturing this "quaint, dainty" woman and the fantasy world she manipulates? Or is she presenting the character she created—one like her authorial self in many ways— as a serious model for negotiating the cultural borders faced by her Chinese American and female characters?. . .

Source: Annette White-Parks, in her *Sui Sin Far/Edith Maude Eaton: A Literary Biography,* University of Illinois Press, 1995, pp. 164–69.

Amy Ling

In the following essay, Ling discusses Sui Sin Far's fiction and her primacy in representing the concerns of Asian-American women at the turn of the century.

The personal story of what life was like for the Chinese and Eurasians in America at the turn of the century is Sui Sin Far's special contribution to American letters, for she was the first person of any Chinese ancestry to take up this subject. And she took up the subject as a woman warrior takes up her sword: to right/write wrongs and to uplift the downtrodden. Her major purpose in writing was to right wrongs done the Chinese in America, but her minor themes were to give credit due to working class women and to acknowledge the strength of the bond between women.

Sui Sin Far, translated literally, is "water fragrant flower," or narcissus; also called Chinese lily. A story that appeared in the September 19, 1891 issue of the *Dominion Illustrated* may be the origin of Edith's choice of a pseudonym. The legend of the Chinese lily appeared in an article, "Episodes of Chinese Life in British Columbia," by James P. MacIntyre.

> **❝❞** Far's major purpose in writing was to right wrongs done the Chinese in America, but her minor themes were to give credit due to working class women and to acknowledge the strength of the bond between women.❞

It is said a farmer left half each of his estate to two sons, the eldest receiving good land in which he planted tea, and prospered; the younger son having only land of a swampy character, nothing would grow in it, and he was sorely moved to grief. But a white elephant presented him with a bulbous root which he placed in water and the result was, through time, grief changed to joy and a paradise of flowers. Through the outcome of this incident which brought him great wealth, he became a mandarin, and attained to the third degree of state in the kingdom, the Emperor planting the yellow flag with golden dragon on his horse.

Certainly, the transformation of grief into joy, handicap into glory, failure into success would have appealed to Edith Eaton, who, "carried the burden of the Eurasian" upon her slight shoulders throughout her life. Great, too, was the appeal of the humble beauty of these small bulbs that needed only a shallow bowl of water and rewarded little effort with a cluster of highly perfumed, modest white flowers, becoming in the dead of winter a symbol of the persistence of life and beauty, and a particular favorite in Chinese homes.

Mrs. Spring Fragrance, her collected stories, is an attractive book. Its vermillion cover is embossed in gold letters and decorated with lotus flowers, a dragonfly and the moon. Like Winnifred's novels, which had appeared before this, the physical appearance of the book attests to the publisher's attempt to promote sales by appealing to a particular notion of things "oriental" as exotic, delicate, and lovely. The book is printed on decorated paper, each page imprinted in a pastel "oriental" design: a crested bird on branches of plum blossoms and bamboo with the Chinese characters for Happiness, Prosperity, and Longevity vertically descending along the right margin. Some of Sui Sin Far's stories are appropriately delicate, charming, and lovely; however, the more serious ones strike ironic, tragic, and even somewhat bitter notes very much at odds with their physical presentation. The medium and the message thus engage in a tug of war.

The reviews for *Mrs. Spring Fragrance* were generally favorable, with the progressive New York *Independent* praising the book thus:

> The conflict between occidental and oriental ideals and the hardships of American immigration laws furnish the theme for most of the tales and the reader is not only interested but has his mind widened by becoming acquainted with novel points of view.

Though *The New York Times* recognized that "Miss Eaton has struck a new note in American fiction," its reviewer did not think that she had "struck it very surely, or with surpassing skill." But he did recognize that "it has taken courage to strike it at all." This reviewer goes on to elucidate her purpose and makes a puzzling judgment on her task:

> The thing she has tried to do is to portray for readers of the white race the lives, feelings, sentiments of the Americanized Chinese on the Pacific coast, of those who have intermarried with them, and of the children who have sprung from such unions. It is a task whose adequate doing would require well-nigh superhuman insight and the subtlest of methods.

Why should it be a "superhuman" task to render the Chinese understandably human to white readers? Is it because the Chinese are so far from being human or that white readers are so far from being willing to accept them as such?

> In some of the stories . . . she has seen far and deep, and has made her account keenly interesting. Especially is this true of the analysis she makes occasionally of the character of an Americanized Chinese, of the glimpses of the Chinese women who refuse to be anything but intensely Chinese, and into the characters of the half-breed children.

In style and tone, Sui Sin Far's stories, like her characters, are unpretentious, gentle, sometimes sentimental. Like other late nineteenth century American women writers, she also wrote stories for children, which make up nearly half of this collection. Through basic human themes—love of men and women, parents and children, brothers and sisters, she draws forth the reader's empathy. What sets her stories apart is her sympathetic portrayal of the Chinese characters living in the United States. Bret Harte had used Chinese characters in his Western stories, but he always presented them from the white man's perspective. Sui Sin Far gave to American letters the Chinese perspective on racial prejudice, economic harassment, and discriminatory immigration regulations. A strident or militant tone was hardly necessary, for she had only to show the situation as it was for the injustice to be apparent; instead, she employed irony.

One of the best examples of Sui Sin Far's ironic tone may be found in the title story of the collection. Lively, unconventional Mrs. Spring Fragrance, while visiting in San Francisco, writes a letter home to her husband in Seattle after attending a "magniloquent lecture" entitled "America the Protector of China" to which a white friend had taken her:

> It was most exhilarating, and the effect of so much expression of benevolence leads me to beg of you to forget to remember that the barber charges you one dollar for a shave while he humbly submits to the American man a bill of fifteen cents. And murmur no more because your honored elder brother, on a visit to this country, is detained under the roof-tree of this great Government instead of under your own humble roof. Console him with the reflection that he is protected under the wing of the Eagle, the Emblem of Liberty. What is the loss of ten hundred years or ten thousand times ten dollars compared with the happiness of knowing oneself so securely sheltered? All of this I have learned from Mrs. Samuel Smith, who is as brilliant and great of mind as one of your own superior sex.

Mrs. Spring Fragrance first reaches out a sympathetic hand to her husband, who would immediately understand the emptiness of the patriotic rhetoric, given the prejudicial treatment he has received from his barber and the indignities his brother has suffered at the hands of immigration officials. Then she uses this opportunity to her own advantage by drawing a parallel between her well-meaning but misguided friend, who thought she would find this lecture edifying, and her self-righteous husband, who is always critical of her actions. In other words, racism and sexism are rooted in the same error: the belief that one is innately superior to another. As a Chinese American woman, Mrs. Spring Fragrance must endure the superior attitudes of both white people and of Chinese American men. Though thinly veiled in apparent good humor, the ironic force of this passage, with its double-pronged attack, is strong and uncompromising, and the barb at the end unexpected.

Humor is another of Sui Sin Far's weapons, as in the following exclamations by Mrs. Spring Fragrance to her husband, when their Caucasian neighbor's lovelorn son fails to give them his usual greeting: "Ah, these Americans! These mysterious, inscrutable, incomprehensible Americans! Had I the divine right of learning I would put them into an immortal book." Sui Sin Far is obviously taking delight in the inversion of her Chinese character's appropriating the adjectives commonly used to describe "Orientals" and applying them to whites. The author is also commenting subtly on the supposed superiority—"the divine right of learning"—of those who pass such judgments on other people; the implication here is that the Chinese are not "inscrutable" because of qualities inherent in themselves but because of blind spots in those doing the scrutinizing. Furthermore, Sui Sin Far is taking delight in inverting the character/reader relationship, for a character, who has been made most scrutable, is expressing a desire to write a book about the "inscrutable" white Americans, the reader. We are all comprehensible, of course, to ourselves; it is only the other who is incomprehensible.

Sui Sin Far attempted to reproduce the speech rhythms and patterns of ordinary Chinese Americans in her stories. But her use of literal translations from the Chinese—as in proper names, honorific titles, and axioms—results in a flowery, exotic language somewhat at odds with her purpose of rendering the Chinese familiar to whites, as in the title of the book and in this letter from Mrs. Spring Fragrance to her protege:

> My Precious Laura,—May the bamboo ever wave. Next week I accompany Ah Oi to the beauteous town of San Jose. There we will be met by the son of the Illustrious Teacher, and, in a little Mission, presided over by the benevolent American priest, the little Ah Oi and the son of the Illustrious Teacher will be joined together in love and harmony—two pieces of music made to complete each other.

At other times, the syntax more realistically reproduces Chinese English, as when Lae Choo urges the white lawyer to go to Washington to procure the papers releasing her toddler son from immigration authorities in "In the Land of the Free":

> "Then you go get paper. If Hom Hing not can give you five hundred dollars—I give you perhaps what more that much."

Though Edith Eaton's linguistic portraits may seem at times quaint or strained, her purpose is unfailing: to dramatize the humanness of the Chinese, to draw the reader into their lives, their tragedies, their triumphs. As critic Florence Howe recently noted in a different context, "their view is generic not individualistic; their ideology is explicit"; so is Sui Sin Far's work also the "literature of social documentary—and unabashedly partisan." Her fiction is comparable to the early stories by Black women, which Carole McAlpine Watson described as "purpose fiction . . . [employing] moral suasion . . . as a conscious strategy of racial self-defense.''

Watson's description of the fiction of late nineteenth century Black American women writers, in fact, can very easily be applied to the fiction and purpose of Sui Sin Far:

> . . . black women novelists, beginning in the 1890s, produced works of social protest and racial appeal based upon Christian and democratic principles. During the final decade of the nineteenth century, their stories challenged the social order then being established in portrayals that refuted the black stereotype, exposed injustice in both the North and South, and, in curious tales about tragic mulattoes, focused attention on the irony and irrationality of the color line.

Sui Sin Far faced with the same irrational color line also wrote stories about mulattoes or Eurasians, who were not only victims of racial discrimination but were figures ''with whom white readers could identify.'' In such stories as ''Its Wavering Image,'' in which a Eurasian, living in Chinatown with her Chinese father, finds her trust betrayed by a white newspaper reporter, and ''The Story of a White Woman Who Married a Chinese'' and ''Her Chinese Husband.'' Sui Sin Far is highly successful in personifying and personalizing her cause by embodying it in characters caught in the between-world condition. These characters may be Eurasians wavering between the cultures and peoples of their parents; whites adopted by or married to Chinese; or Chinese who have assimilated Western ways but still are tied by Old World bonds.

In ''The Wisdom of the New,'' tragedy results when an Americanized Chinese immigrant, Wou Sankwei, does not realize the extent of his Chinese wife's fear of American ways. Pau Lin, the wife, a Chinese villager suddenly brought to America by a husband she has not seen in seven years, is unhinged by jealousy and culture shock and comes to believe, literally, that the Americanization of their son is a fate worse than death. The night before the boy is to start American school, the mother kills him to save him from impending doom. To his credit, the husband, Wou Sankwei, shows great solicitation for his deranged wife and takes her back to China. Sui Sin Far maintains a balanced perspective in the narration of this story, neither condemning the husband for insensitivity nor the wife for rigidity. Instead, her purpose is to show the tragedy of being between worlds. As Wou Sankwei's American friends observe,

> ''Yes, I admit Sankwei has some puzzles to solve. Naturally, when he tries to live two lives—that of a Chinese and that of an American.''

> ''Is it not what we teach these Chinese boys—to become Americans? And yet, they are Chinese, and must, in a sense, remain so.''

Nor can the blame of the tragedy be laid at the feet of these kind white women who helped a Chinese student adjust to American life. The fault lies in the situation itself, in the clash between cultures and the fragility of the people caught in this clash.

In ''Pat and Pan,'' a white orphan boy, reared by a Chinese family until the intervention of a white missionary, learns, after spending some time with whites, to be contemptuous of his Chinese family. In the ''Story of One White Woman Who Married a Chinese'' and its sequel, ''Her Chinese Husband,'' Eaton writes a moving tale of an interracial marriage from the perspective of a white woman. Abandoned by her first husband, a Caucasian, who found her too unsophisticated in politics and, ironically, too ignorant of women's rights to hold his interest, a white woman eventually marries the Chinese man who rescued her from an attempted suicide and gave her a means of employment. For herself, she does not mind the contempt of other whites, but she does worry about the future of their little son in a racially biased world:

> . . . as he stands between his father and myself, like yet unlike us both, so will he stand in after years between his father's and his mother's people. And if there is no kindliness nor understanding between them, what will my boy's fate be?

Undoubtedly, Edith Eaton is here writing out of a deeply felt personal experience. She expressed the same anxiety in her autobiographical essay by concluding it with these words:

> After all I have no nationality and am not anxious to claim any. Individuality is more than nationality. . . . I give my right hand to the Occidentals and my left to the Orientals, hoping that between them they will not utterly destroy the insignificant ''connecting link.''

In ''Her Chinese Husband,'' the white wife gives a fuller picture of her Chinese husband and of the life she led with him. On finding her weeping over the future of their child, her husband asks her pointedly:

> What is there to weep about? The child is beautiful: the feeling heart, the understanding mind is his. And we will bring him up to be proud that he is of Chinese blood; he will fear none and, after him, the name of half-breed will no longer be one of contempt.

But the father with these idealistic visions is brought home one night with a bullet through his head and, in his pockets are the presents his children had requested: two red rubber balls, an image with undeniable sexual implications. Since race was the only motivation for the murder, the story would seem to indicate a despair at society's ever arriving at a time when different races can live in mutual respect. However, the very writing of the story itself moves us in that direction.

In addition to her major cause—rendering the Chinese human—Sui Sin Far's stories plead two additional causes: acceptance of the working class woman and of friendship between women. In "The Inferior Woman" her sympathy lies with the hard-working, self-made woman as opposed to the wealthy, privileged suffragette. Alice Winthrop, who began working at the age of 14 as an "office boy" in a law office and is now private secretary to the most influential man in Washington, is at first rejected by the mother of the man she loves and called the "inferior woman" because of her family's poverty. She is given her rightful due, however, when her more privileged but generous friend says of her:

> It is women such as Alice Winthrop who, in spite of every drawback, have raised themselves to the level of those who have had every advantage, who are the pride and glory of America. There are thousands of them, all over this land: women who have been of service to others all their years and who have graduated from the university of life with honor. Women such as I, who are called the Superior Women of America, are after all nothing but schoolgirls in comparison.

This story courageously criticizes the Suffragettes for class discrimination, and praises the self-made working-class woman.

Of friendship between women, Sui Sin Far wrote explicitly in several stories in *Mrs. Spring Fragrance.* In "The Inferior Woman," it is the "superior woman," the well-educated, upper-class Ethel Evebrook, who recognizes the actual superiority of the so-called "inferior woman," as demonstrated in the quote above. In a story called "The Chinese Lily," a character transparently named Sin Far sacrifices her life for another woman, a cripple. The cripple, Mermei, had been used to evening visits from her brother. When he fails to come one evening, Sin Far, her neighbor, pays her a visit which both enjoy immensely. Comparing this visit to those from her brother, Mermei concludes, "Lin John is dear, but one can't talk to a man, even if he is a brother, as one can to one the same as oneself," To which Sin Far replies, "Yes, indeed. The woman must be the friend of the woman, and the man the friend of the man." One night a fire breaks out in the rooming house; the brother arrives in time to save only one person. Though he has fallen in love with Sin Far, at her request, Lin John saves his sister, and Sin Far perishes in the flames.

Here we find not only the woman-bonding theme, but the ideal of self-sacrifice, or martyrdom, as the ultimate expression of love. Using the transparent non-artifice of her own name, Sui Sin Far declares her willingness to make the ultimate sacrifice for others. In "Leaves" she had revealed a childhood Joan-of-Arc fantasy that foreshadows the theme of this story: "I dream dreams of being great and noble . . . I glory in the idea of dying at the stake and a great genie arising from the flames and declaring to those who have scorned us: 'Behold, how great and glorious and noble are the Chinese people!'. On another level, since Edith Eaton herself had a limp and was sickly throughout her life, the two characters may be a doubling of herself, with Sin Far, her active assertive self, coming to the rescue of *Mermei,* (little sister in Chinese) her weak victimized self. What is sacrificed, then, is sexual love embodied in the person of Lin John.

"The Heart's Desire" is a parable about a Chinese princess surrounded by all that wealth and tender care can provide her but who is nonetheless unhappy. Her attendants attempt to cheer her by bringing her successively a father, a mother, and a brother, but all fail to make her happy. The princess then takes the matter into her own hands and sends a note to a poor girl who lives outside the palace walls. When this girl arrives, the princess announces to all the palace: "Behold, I have found my heart's desire—a little sister" And the two girls "forever after . . . lived happily together in a glad, beautiful old palace, surrounded by a glad, beautiful old garden, on a charming little island in the middle of a lake." The tale has a symmetrical shape since the ending is identical to a sentence in the opening paragraph, with the exception of one significant change, the replacement of the word *sad* by *glad.* However, the language of the conventional fairy tale ending is so little changed as to draw attention to the bold inversion of this tale's ending. This princess does not ride off to live happily ever after with a handsome prince, but finds her "heart's desire" and life-long happiness in a relationship with "another like herself."

In an early essay, "Spring Impressions: A Medley of Poetry and Prose" in the June 7, 1890 issue of *Dominion Illustrated* Edith Eaton announced her chosen career, for "the communicativeness of our nature will no longer be repressed" and set forth her causes as a writer:

> We can suffer with those who have suffered wrongs, we can weep for those whose hearts unnoticed broke amidst this world's great traffic; we can mourn for

those whom the grave hath robbed of all that was dear to them, and can sympathize with those remorse-tortured ones, who, gifted with utmost divine wisdom, yet wilfully turned from the guiding light and with eyes that saw all the horror and shame before them walked into the arms of sin.

Her Christian upbringing is apparent in the rhetoric: ''divine wisdom,'' ''guiding light,'' ''arms of sin.'' She would be the great empathizer, and she did indeed make it her life's work to ''suffer with those who have suffered wrongs.'' But perhaps part of her empathy and melancholy had roots in a deep sense of guilt over what she may have perceived as her own sexual deviance. It is pure speculation on my part, but ''Heart's Desire'' and ''The Chinese Lily'' are suggestive of a lesbian sensibility, which the author herself would not have approved and would have striven to repress.

Sui Sin Far's major theme, of course, was the plight of the Chinese in America. The full extent of her accomplishment in this area stands out when contrasted to contemporaneous works about the Chinese in the so-called Chinatown fiction written by Caucasian authors, examined ably and thoroughly by William Wu in *The Yellow Peril: Chinese Americans in American Fiction 1850–1940* (Hamden, Connecticut: Archon Books, 1982). That so many negative images of the Chinese appeared in white American writing of the late nineteenth and early twentieth centuries, Wu traces to the European memory of Mongol invasions and the subsequent fear of history repeating itself in the New World. This fear gave rise to the stereotypes of Chinese as opium addicts, prostitutes, cheaters, cleaver wielders, and clever villains. Even the sympathetic white writer ''envisions the Chinese as subhuman pets incapable of morality until they are converted into the Christianity of the West.''

Such missionary zeal is much in evidence in Helen Clark's *The Lady of the Lily Feet and Other Tales of Chinatown* (Philadelphia: Griffth and Rowland Press under the imprint of the American Baptist Publication Society, 1900). Published a dozen years before *Mrs. Spring Fragrance*, Clark's book was a collection of short stories focused entirely on the atrocities of foot-binding, wife beating and selling, the literal enslavement of Chinese women by their men, showing the Chinese to be in desperate need of Christian salvation. The characters are flat, the plots repetitious, the author's perspective outside of and obviously superior to the Chinese community. Christian zeal so overrides artistry that finally only the rare photographs of

nineteenth century Chinese women and children in their elaborate Manchu clothing and formal poses remain as the most interesting aspect of the book.

Though the plight of some Chinese women was a cause comparable to Negro slavery, an entire book focused exclusively on the peculiar, horrifying aspects of Chinese culture would give readers additional proof of the ''heathenness'' of the Chinese, serving to increase the rift between the two races. By contrast, Sui Sin Far, with her stories of ordinary family life, of love triumphing over or thwarted by obstacles, of characters with three-dimensional depth, did much more to bridge the gap between Chinese and whites.

Finally, Edith Eaton fully recognized the pioneer quality of her work and accepted the fact that as a bridge between two worlds, she had to expect to be stepped on. Martyrdom, as she expressed in her stories ''A Chinese Lily'' and ''The Smuggling of Tie Co,'' and as Jane Tompkins explained in her analysis of *Uncle Tom's Cabin,* is a strategy of the powerless. The major purpose of both Sui Sin Far's life and her writing may be summed up in this passage from ''Leaves'':

> Only when the whole world becomes as one family will human beings be able to see clearly and hear distinctly. I believe that some day a great part of the world will be Eurasian. I cheer myself with the thought that I am but a pioneer. A pioneer should glory in suffering. . . .

Source: Amy Ling, in her *Between Worlds: Women Writers of Chinese Ancestry,* Pergamon Press, 1990, pp. 40–49.

S. E. Solberg

In the following essay, Solberg traces Far's writing career, paying particular attention to her status as a Chinese-European writer.

Both her photographs and her own testimony seem to indicate that Edith Maud Eaton (1867–1914) could have ''passed'' into the majority society with little trouble. Moreover, although her mother was Chinese, Edith was unacquainted with her mother's native language, except for a few phrases, during her early years; in fact, she had very little contact with Asians or Eurasians, except for her own large group of siblings. Yet when she began to publish stories and articles, she chose to write chiefly about China and Chinese-Americans, and she wrote under the *nom de plume* of Sui Sin Far (occasionally Sui Seen or Sin Fah). . . .

William Purviance Fenn, in a basic study of attitudes towards Chinese in American literature, suggested that [attitudes towards the Chinese in America] might be summed up in four periods, the first three falling into what he somewhat wryly labeled the era of the "Chinese 'Invasion'"—"1) that of toleration, from 1849 to 1853; 2) that of growing antagonism, from 1853 to 1882; and 3) that of restriction, from 1882 on." The San Francisco fire of 1906 marked the end of that "era," he says, and "the Chinese question dropped into discard as a real issue, making way . . . for the Japanese question of more recent times."

In terms of that periodization, Edith succeeded during the time of restriction in having five publications, one of them in the prestigious *Century* magazine. She had no model to follow; the public taste was for the exotic or for the stereotype. The "funny people" who wanted her to trade on her nationality told her:

> if I wanted to succeed in literature in America I should dress in Chinese costume, carry a fan in my hand, wear a pair of scarlet beaded slippers, live in New York, and come of high birth.

Not only did she repudiate all this; she saw it as ineffectual. She knew that Americans definitely preferred Japanese to Chinese:

> The Americans having for many years manifested a much higher regard for the Japanese than the Chinese, several half-Chinese young men and women, thinking to advance themselves, both in a social and business sense, pass as Japanese. They continue to be known as Eurasian, but a Japanese Eurasian does not appear in the same light as a Chinese Eurasian.

Immediately after this she adds:

> The unfortunate Chinese Eurasians! Are not those who compel them to thus cringe more to be blamed than they?

The question of choice, of being true to one's heritage and family, of selling a birthright for momentary peace in an uncomfortable society are the same questions that have plagued Asian-American writers down to the present.

Further comprehension of her situation, as a Chinese person as well as a writer, can be found in American cultural history and in mainstream literature of her time. Howard Mumford Jones, in an extended discussion of the taste for the exotic in what he calls the "cosmopolitan spirit," makes the provocative suggestion that while the American response to Japan was derived from a taste for the exotic the same was not true of China. "American taste for Chinoiserie descends from the eighteenth

> " The question of choice, of being true to one's heritage and family, of selling a birthright for momentary peace in an uncomfortable society are the same questions that have plagued Asian-American writers down to the present."

century, and aside from vulgar notions about Chinese sexuality, joss houses, and opium dens, it is problematical whether things Chinese served greatly to quench any thirst for the exotic." While the reasons for this are no doubt complex, central to them would seem to be the simple fact that the Chinese were already present in the United States and most of the popular images derived from that direct contact. The Japanese had, for the most part, the added attraction of being across the Pacific without much danger of the facts of their presence damaging whatever fantasies might be evoked.

While this contrast could be illustrated from many sources, it is suggested in even the works of those great champions of Anglo-Saxon supremacy, Jack London and Frank Norris. Note, for example, London's description of Captain West in *The Mutiny of the Elsinore* as a "samurai," or the evocation of a remembered woman in *Martin Eden:* "Japanese women, doll-like, stepping mincingly on wooden clogs" as contrasted with his treatment of the Chinese in the short story "Yellow Handkerchief": "What was to happen next I could not imagine, for the Chinese were a different race from mine, and from what I knew I was confident that fair play was no part of their make-up" or, further on, "I was familiar enough with the Chinese character to know that fear alone restrained them."

Frank Norris, in describing Vanamee's vision in *The Octopus,* has the spectre "dressed in a gown of scarlet silk, with flowing sleeves, such as Japanese wear, embroidered with flowers and figures of birds worked in gold threads," while in *Moran of the Lady Letty,* the Chinese crew of the *Bertha Millner* is described in these terms: "the absolute indifference of these brown-suited Mongols, the blankness of their flat, fat faces, the dullness of their slanting, fishlike eyes that never met his own or even wandered in his direction was uncanny, disquieting."

A general pattern had been established, much as in these examples, of the Chinese as mysterious, evil, nearby, and threatening, while the Japanese were exotic, quaint, delicate (or manly, as the samurai), and distant. A verbal equivalent appears in a curious article in the *Bookman* in 1923, entitled "Chinese Characters in American Fiction": "The Chinese resent the popular term *Chinaman.* They prefer to be referred to as *Chinese,* just as natives of Japan are termed *Japanese.* Would anyone ever use the expression Japanman?" While this is not the place to go into the specific stereotypes of Japanese and Chinese that existed at the turn of the century, it is necessary to note the curious way in which the general fascination with the exotic (Japan) was able to transcend racist ideas so long as distance was a part of the formula.

As a Chinese-American writer, then, Far had to find a mode that would enable her to deal with her own experience (as the classic editorial injunction has it), but to do that meant to fall outside the boundaries of any of the "maincurrents" of American writing. She was not a regionalist nor nationalist. If anything, she was an internationalist, but hardly of the Henry James school, though some of what is interesting in her work lies in the subtleties that are apt to be lost on the untrained casual reader. She is not naturalist or local colorist, and her essays at humor, which tend to fall short of the mark in any case, can hardly be looked upon as falling in the Mr. Dooley or Mark Twain "native American" styles. She was trapped by experience and inclination into working within a sub-genre of American prose: what, for lack of a better term, we might call Chinatown Tales. Such classification by subject matter (Chinatown, or more broadly, the Chinese in America) breaks down an established literary form, the novel, into sub-genres defined by content, not form or stylistic skill. Eaton, by choosing to identify with and write about the Chinese, found herself alone in an essentially formless field. There had been fifty years of writing about the Chinese in America, but out of that writing no clear literary form had evolved. As William Purviance Fenn sums it up:

> The impress of Chinese immigration on American literature . . . is hard to evaluate. . . . Its influence has been two-fold: first, as a problem the discussion of which has resulted in literature; second, as a source of subject matter for the literature of local color. In the first place, the half century of economic and political discussion resulted in an immense amount of material which is still preserved for us in newspaper, magazine, pamphlet, and book. Of this, a larger proportion, of course, is of value only to the economist, historian, or sociologist; but the heated emotions of that struggle occasionally found expression in fiction, drama, and verse. Party prejudices and passions, however, are poor inspiration for anything but cheap propaganda, and it is in the appeal of the subject to the sense of justice that we have an approach to the fundamental inspirational problems of literature.

> In the second place, the existence of a large number of this alien race offered an unusual opportunity for devotees of the local-color movement; and in the glorious process of exploding old myths and of creating new ones, the Chinamen were bound to suffer in many a poem, story, and play. . . . They were strange and they were enigmatical; their appearance and ways added color to already too colorful backgrounds, and the difficulty of understanding them piqued the curiosity of American readers. The result was a body of fiction, drama, and verse exploiting the Chinese as a rich source of local color.

> But even of this small body of creative literature, by far the greater part was written by amateurs in the field of letters, and only a handful of efforts even approach greatness.

Fiction, drama, and verse, each with a sub-genre which exploits the "Chinese as a rich source of color." This gave Eaton little enough to build on, for her intent was certainly not to exploit, but rather to record, explain, and somehow give meaning to the experience of the Chinese in America. Fenn's 1933 summing up is interesting, for he had considered two of Eaton's stories in his summary, though his bibliography does not list her collection, *Mrs. Spring Fragrance.*

> Such, then, is the literature of Chinatown—no poems, no plays, but possibly half a dozen short stories worth remembering. And Chinatown will never be adequately described by anyone who fails to see in it something more fundamental than the superficial barbarity and high coloring which have been almost the only appeal so far. . . . The real Chinatown that is worth preserving lies beneath the surface color, among the deeper currents.

I would argue that Edith Eaton as Sui Sin Far did manage to dip into those deeper currents beneath the surface color, but no matter what she saw and understood, there was no acceptable form to shape it to. Had she been physically stronger and had a more sophisticated literary apprenticeship, she might have been able to create that new form. As it was, she was defeated, for in that "glorious process of exploding old myths and of creating new ones," as Fenn puts it, "the Chinamen were bound to suffer." ·

Fictional stereotypes for the Chinatown tales had been established, and it was difficult for anyone, even of a strongly independent mind, to ignore them. No matter how frank and open Eaton might have been in a memoir such as "Leaves from the Mental Portfolio of an Eurasian," when she turned her hand to fiction the possible was limited by the acceptable. She was modest about her work. In acknowledging permissions to reprint previously published stories in *Mrs. Spring Fragrance* she writes: "I wish to thank the Editors . . . who were kind enough to care for my children when I sent them out into the world, for permitting the dear ones to return to me to be grouped together within this volume."

Even at the outset there were those who appreciated her difficulties and her attempts to create authentic characters. Said the editor of *Land of Sunshine,* a California magazine, in 1887:

> [Her stories are] all of Chinese characters in California or on the Pacific Coast; and they have an insight and sympathy which are probably unique. To others the alien Celestial is at best mere "literary material": in these stories, he (or she) is a human being.

That her contemporaries saw Sui Sin Far's writing as an attempt to speak for Chinese-Americans is borne out by the review of *Mrs. Spring Fragrance*

> Miss Eaton has struck a new note in American fiction. She has not struck it very surely, or with surpassing skill, but it has taken courage to strike it all, and, to some extent, she atones for lack of artistic skill with the unusual knowledge she undoubtedly has of her theme. The thing she has tried to do is to portray for readers of the white race the lives, feelings, sentiments of the Americanized Chinese of the Pacific Coast, of those who have intermarried with them and of the children who have sprung from such unions. It is a task whose adequate doing would require well nigh superhuman insight and the subtlest of methods.

The review had more insight that the publisher who inserted an advertisement on the same page; the advertisement reads in part: "Quaint, lovable characters are the Chinese who appear in these unusual and exquisite stories of our Western Coast. . . . Altogether they make as desirable reading as the title suggests." Taken out of context,

what does the title suggest? Perhaps the exotic, that could be traded on, at worst, the quaint, but hardly the struggle toward realism that is found in the pages.

The title story of *Mrs. Spring Fragrance* deals with the difficulties of Mr. Spring Fragrance in understanding and coming to grips with his very Americanized wife. While the story is slight, it does allow Eaton to create passages such as the following exchange between Mr. Spring Fragrance and an American friend:

> "Everything is 'high class'' in America," he [Mr. Spring Fragrance] observed.
>
> "Sure!" cheerfully assented the young man. "Haven't you ever heard that all Americans are princes and princesses, and just as soon as a foreigner puts his foot upon our shores, he also becomes of the nobility—I mean, the royal family."
>
> "What about my brother in the Detention Pen?" dryly inquired Mr. Spring Fragrance.
>
> "Now, you've got me," said the young man, rubbing his head. "Well, that is a shame—'a beastly shame,' as the Englishman says. But understand, old fellow, we that are real Americans are up against that—even more than you. It is against our principles."
>
> "I offer the real Americans my consolations that they should be compelled to do that which is against their principles."

In the story "The Inferior Woman" an interesting possibility is suggested, then dropped. But the suggestion shows that Eaton knew what she was up against and was somehow trying to warn her readers. The story describes Mrs. Spring Fragrance's interference in the love life of her American neighbor's son, and she helps him to marry the "inferior woman" he prefers rather than the "superior woman" chosen by his mother. As the story opens, Mrs. Spring Fragrance is walking in the garden reflecting upon the possibilities of "a book which she had some notion of writing. Many American women wrote books. Why should not a Chinese? She would write a book about Americans for her Chinese women friends. The American people were so interesting and mysterious." Unfortunately Mrs. Spring Fragrance never writes her book, and we never see her develop the stereotypes of the "mysterious Americans."

"Particularly interesting," says the *New York Times* reviewer, "are two stories in which an American woman is made to contrast her experiences as the wife of an American and afterward of a Chinese." In 1952 the same stories caught the attention of John Burt Foster, and impressed him so much that he speculated: "So intimately does the author write of mixed marriage that one is tempted to believe that she herself married a Chinese and was enabled in this way to get firsthand information."

Yet despite the fascination of many of the stories and their subjects—the problems with Angel Island, the self-protective aspects of the Chinese community, the Eurasians who in the crunch throw in their lot with the Chinese—the most impressive aspect of the writing is the conviction that environment is more important than heredity, that race is an accident, and, when, as with the Eurasian, there is a question of choice, the individual has the power to make that choice.

The most dramatic statement of the theme of choice is in "Pat and Pan," the story of two children, the boy Caucasian-American, the girl Chinese-American, being raised together in a Chinese household; the Chinese couple has raised the boy from a baby as their own. He speaks only Chinese, has only Chinese playmates, is inseparable from his little "Chinese" sister. Enter the meddling mission school teacher who cannot allow a "white boy" to be brought up Chinese. The child is removed from his Chinese home and adopted by a white family. Slowly he grows away from his Chinese background. On his next meeting his little Chinese sister, he is friendly, but in their second encounter after their separation, egged on by his new playmates, he rejects her completely, shouting at her to get away from him. "But when she reached the foot of the hill, she looked up and shook her little head sorrowfully. 'Poor Pat!' said she. 'He Chinese no more; he Chinese no more!'"

While Eaton wrote well, she never acquired the control of style necessary to deal with her subjects in depth or at length. What she wrote were chiefly sketches, vignettes. The task she had set herself was nearly impossible at that time. Trapped in the stylistic conventions of the time, including dialogue in a forced and artificial dialect, she could only try, by selection of her story material, to tell about the real Chinese-Americans she knew. . . .

What she left was a unique public record of the difficulty of being an individual without racial, national, or group claims. "After all I have no nationality and am not anxious to claim any," she wrote. "Individuality is more than nationality. 'You are you and I am I,' says Confucius." And then she

goes on to the bitter heart of her dilemma. "I give my right hand to the Occidentals and my left to the Orientals, hoping that between them they will not utterly destroy the insignificant 'connecting link.' And that's all."

Source: S. E. Solberg, "Sui Sin Far/Edith Eaton: First Chinese-American Fictionist," in *MELUS*, Vol. 8, No. 1, Spring, 1981, pp. 27–39.

Sources

A review of *Mrs. Spring Fragrance* in the *Independent,* August 15, 1912.

Chan, Sucheng. *Asian Americans: An Interpretive History.* New York: Simon & Schuster, 1991.

Daniels, Roger. *Asian America: Chinese and Japanese in the United States since 1850,* Seattle: University of Washington Press, 1998.

Lanser, Susan C. "*The Yellow Wallpaper* and the Politics of Color in America," in *Feminist Studies,* Vol. 15, No. 3, Fall, 1989, pp. 415-41.

Matsukawa, Yuko. "Cross-Dressing and Cross-naming: Decoding Onoto Watanna," in *Tricksterism in Turn-of-the-Century American Literature,* Hanover: New England University Press, 1994.

Riis, Jacob. *How the Other Half Lives: Studies among the Tenements of New York,* New York: Hill and Wang, 1957.

Sui Sin Far. *Mrs. Spring Fragrance and Other Writings,* ed. Amy Ling and Annette White-Parks, Chicago: University of Illinois Press, 1995.

Further Reading

Ammons, Elizabeth. "Audacious Words: Sui Sin Far's Mrs. Spring Fragrance," from *Conflicting Stories.* New York: Oxford University Press, 1991.
    Feminist reading of Sui Sin Far's collected short stories.

Chang, Yoonmee. *Tama On-line* http:// www.eng-lish.upenn.edu/~yoonmeec.

An on-line ''re-version'' of Onoto Watanna's *Tama.* Includes biography of Watanna and Sui Sin Far. This project is still in development.

Ling, Amy. ''Writers with a Cause: Sui Sin Far and Han Suyin,'' from *Women's Studies International Forum,* Vol. 9 (1986): 411-419.

Revisionist historical of Sui Sin Far's and Korean writer Han Suyin.

Ling, Amy. ''Edith Eaton: Pioneer Chinamerican Writer and Feminist,'' in *American Literary Realism,* Vol. 16, Autumn, 1983, pp. 287-98.

Discussion of Sui Sin Far as the first Chinese-American writer.

Ling, Amy. ''Pioneers and Paradigms: The Eaton Sisters,'' in *Between Worlds: Women Writers of Chinese Ancestry,* New York: Pergamon, 1990.

Detailed study of the first Asian American women writers, Sui Sin Far and Onoto Watanna from feminist viewpoint.

White-Parks, Annette. *Sui Sin Far/Edith Maude Eaton: A Literary Biography.* Chicago: University of Illinois Press, 1995.

A biographical study of Sui Sin Far and the social pressures surrounding her writing.

The Necklace

Guy de Maupassant
1884

Guy de Maupassant's short story "The Necklace" ("La parure") was first published in the Paris newspaper *Le Gaulois* on February 17, 1884, and was subsequently included in his 1885 collection of short stories *Tales of Day and Night* (*Contes de jour et de la nuit*). Like most of Maupassant's short fiction, it was an instant success, and it has become his most widely read and anthologized story. In addition to its well-rounded characters, tight plotting, wealth of detail, and keen social commentary, "The Necklace" is conspicuous for its use of the "whip-crack" or "O. Henry" ending, in which a plot twist at the end of the story completely changes the story's meaning. Although Maupassant rarely made use of the device, its presence in this work has tied him to it irrevocably. Although it is not known where Maupassant got the idea for his story, certain connections may be made between "The Necklace" and the novel *Madame Bovary,* written by Maupassant's mentor and friend, Gustave Flaubert. Both stories feature a young, beautiful woman in a social situation that she finds distasteful. Like Madame Bovary, Mathilde Loisel attempts to escape her social station in life, but her scheming actions ultimately doom her.

Author Biography

Henri-Rene-Albert Guy de Maupassant was born on August 5, 1850, near Tourville-sur-Arques in

Normandy, France, where he spent most of his early life. The oldest child of wealthy parents who eventually separated, Maupassant was not allowed to attend school until he was thirteen years old. Before then, the local parish priest acted as his tutor.

After being expelled from a Catholic seminary school, Maupassant finished his schooling at a Rouen boarding school before studying law at the University of Paris. His studies were soon interrupted by the 1870 Franco-Prussian War, and Maupassant became a soldier in Normandy. After the war, Maupassant did not return to the university and instead entered the civil service, working as a clerk in the Naval and Education Ministries.

Resigning from the Ministry of Education in 1880, Maupassant became a full-time writer. He began by imitating the style of Gustave Flaubert, a prominent French novelist who had been a close friend of Maupassant's mother for decades. Unsubstantiated rumors circulated at the time that Flaubert was Maupassant's true father; both parties always vehemently denied the allegations. Taken under Flaubert's wing, Maupassant became acquainted with some of the most prominent authors of his time, including Emile Zola, Ivan Turgenev, and Alphonse Daudet.

Following the publication of his first story, "Boule de suif" ("ball of fat" or "ball of suet"), in an 1880 collection of stories by several authors, Maupassant established himself as a prominent writer of both short stories and novels. During the next decade, he published six novels and nearly three hundred short stories, many of them in the Paris newspapers *Gil-Blas* and *Le Gaulois*. He also wrote plays, poetry, travel essays, and newspaper articles. "The Necklace" ("La parure") appeared in *Le Gaulois* on February 17, 1884, and was included in Maupassant's 1885 collection *Stories of Night and Day* (*Contes du jour et de la nuit*).

During the 1880s, Maupassant's health declined, largely as a result of syphilis, which he had contracted in the 1870s but which physicians had not diagnosed. Following an unsuccessful suicide attempt on January 2, 1892, Maupassant was placed in a sanitarium. He died a year and a half later of complications from the disease.

Plot Summary

"The Necklace" begins with a description of Madame Mathilde Loisel. Though she is "pretty and

Guy de Maupassant

charming," she and her husband, a clerk in the Ministry of Education, are not well off financially. She has always dreamed of a life of leisure, with attentive servants and a large home, but her lifestyle is decidedly more modest. Ashamed of her social standing, she no longer visits Madame Forestier, an old school friend who has become rich.

When the Loisels are invited to a ball, Madame Loisel becomes very upset, insisting that she has nothing appropriate to wear to such an event. Hoping to make his wife feel better, Monsieur Loisel offers to buy her a new dress. As the ball approaches, Madame Loisel again becomes anxious because she has no jewels to wear. Her husband suggests she borrow jewels from Madame Forestier. Madame Loisel pays her old friend a visit the next day. She is welcomed and encouraged to borrow any piece of jewelry that she desires. She selects a beautiful diamond necklace.

At the ball, Madame Loisel enjoys herself immensely and many men notice her. She dances until 4:00 in the morning, and then she and her husband return home in a decrepit cab. Not until they are back in their humble house does Madame Loisel realize that she has lost the diamond necklace. Her husband spends several hours retracing their steps but finds nothing. They decide to replace the necklace without telling Madame Forestier, and they go heavily in debt.

Years of toil and grueling work in an effort to repay their debt ages Madame Loisel so she looks quite older than her years. After ten long years of poverty, however, they finally pay off their entire debt. Still, Madame Loisel wistfully and fondly remembers the evening of the ball. One day shortly thereafter, Madame Loisel runs into Madame Forestier, who still looks young and beautiful. Madame Loisel tells her friend the whole story. Madame Forestier, who had not realized that her necklace had been replaced with another, reveals that the original, made of imitation diamonds, was not valuable.

Characters

Madame Jeanne Forestier

Madame Forestier is a school friend of Mathilde Loisel, and she lends her the necklace that Madame Loisel wears to the ball. Madame Forestier's wealth has intimidated Madame Loisel, preventing her from keeping in touch with her old friend. When Madame Loisel does visit, Madame Forestier is as friendly as ever, generously offering to lend her friend a piece of her jewelry for the ball. When the diamond necklace is returned more than a week late, however, Madame Forestier is cold and reproachful. She does not know that the borrowed necklace was lost and that the Loisels have pledged themselves to years of debt to buy a costly replacement. Years later, the two meet on the street. Madame Loisel has aged prematurely by toil and hardship, while Madame Forestier is "still young, still beautiful, still attractive." She does not recognize her old friend when they meet and is "deeply moved" when she learns that the Loisels had spent the last decade in debt to replace her necklace.

Madame Mathilde Loisel

It is Madame Loisel's desire to be part of the upper class which sets the story's events in motion. She is a beautiful woman who feels herself "born for every delicacy and luxury." Her belief that she is meant for better things than middle-class drudgery forms the core of her personality. She believes that superficial things—a ball gown, better furniture, a large house—will make her happy, and an invitation to a ball makes her miserable because it reminds her of her dowdy wardrobe and lack of

jewels. After securing these trappings of luxury, she has the time of her life at the ball, for one evening living the lifestyle she believes herself entitled to. After losing a borrowed necklace, she is not able to admit the error to the friend who lent it. While spending many years in poverty, toiling to repay the debt of replacing the necklace, Madame Loisel prematurely loses her physical beauty.

Monsieur Loisel

Monsieur Loisel's complacency and contentment with his social situation contrasts markedly with his wife's desire to experience life among the social elite. Whereas Madame Loisel dreams of magnificent multi-course meals, her husband is satisfied with simple fare: "Scotch broth! What could be better?" He is attentive to his wife's desires, however, procuring tickets to a ball so that she can see "all the really big people." He gives his wife the four hundred francs that he had set aside for a gun so that she can buy a dress, and spends several early morning hours searching the streets for the lost necklace even though he must go to work that day. Seeking to protect his wife's honor, he suggests that they tell Madame Forestier that the necklace is being fixed rather than that it has been lost.

Themes

Appearances and Reality

In his poem "Ode on a Grecian Urn," John Keats pronounced that "beauty is truth, truth beauty." While subsequent generations have appreciated this Romantic assertion, Maupassant's story aptly demonstrates that it is not always correct. Madame Loisel is beautiful, but she is not content. She has the appearance of beauty but not the reality (or truth) of beauty. She is pretty and charming, but she is also unhappy with her lot in life and believes that she deserves more. Living modestly with her husband before the ball, Madame Loisel believes she is suffering a terrible injustice by having few luxuries. In fact, she does not experience the reality of poverty until she and her husband go into debt to pay off the necklace. The necklace itself represents the theme of appearances versus reality. While sufficiently beautiful to make Madame Loisel feel comfortable during the ministerial ball, the necklace is actually nothing more than paste and gilt. Thus, it is not the reality of wealth or high social class that is important for Madame Loisel, just the appearance of it.

Class Conflict

The theme of class conflict is closely tied to that of appearance and reality. The Loisels are members of the lower bourgeoisie, a class that stands above tradesmen and laborers (and above Madame Loisel's artisan family) but significantly below the class that has a hand in running things. Madame Loisel's dreams of ''delicacy and luxury'' are beyond her social reach. She has only one opportunity to attend a ball, but for the dignitaries and under-secretaries of state she meets there, such occasions are commonplace. She desperately wants to be part of this world, and remembers the affair fondly for many years. Her childhood friend, the upper-class Madame Forestier, is the target of Madame Loisel's envy before the ball, and the target of her blame afterwards as she descends into poverty to repay the necklace. Madame Loisel's focus on social climbing is unbecoming and in opposition to her outward beauty. Her belief that beautiful things and luxury are essential to her happiness is the fallacy that mars her physical beauty. Monsieur Loisel does not suffer the same obsession with class conflict as his wife does. He realizes that his wife would like to go to a ball, and he thinks that presenting the invitation to her will make her happy. He is surprised to learn that she will only be happy if she can give the illusion at the ball that she belongs to the upper class.

Generosity and Greed

Although she does not have a lot of money, Madame Loisel may be justly characterized as greedy. Her life is comfortable enough to afford one servant, but she wishes for several. She has plenty of food, but she dreams of ''delicate meals.'' Her husband can barely afford to buy her a ball gown, but she insists on having jewelry to go with it. When she first sees her friend's diamond necklace, ''her heart [beats] covetously.'' Her greed stands in marked contrast to the generosity of her husband and Madame Forestier. Monsieur Loisel forgoes both the purchase of a gun and plans for a shooting holiday with friends so that his wife can have an appropriate dress. Later, when his wife discovers that she has lost the necklace, he voluntarily spends several late hours scouring the streets for it even though he must go to work that morning. Similarly, Madame Forestier does not hesitate to offer her old friend the use of any of her jewelry, answering Madame Loisel's

Media Adaptations

- There are at least three film versions of Maupassant's story available in English. The first, a silent film from 1909, was directed by D. W. Griffith and runs eleven minutes. A 1980 version runs twenty minutes and is distributed by Britannica Films. A 1981 production runs twenty-two minutes and is distributed by Barr Entertainment.

- Another film version of ''The Necklace,'' which followed the French title of ''La parure,'' appeared on American television on January 21, 1949. The famous conclusion was changed to a happy ending, which was apparently more to the producing advertiser's liking.

- In addition, there are several audio recordings of ''The Necklace,'' most available on both cassette and compact disc: *Maupassant's Best-Known Stories* (two volumes), distributed by Cassette Works; *De Maupassant Short Stories* (one volume), distributed by Listening Library; *Favorite Stories of Guy de Maupassant* (two volumes), distributed by Jimcin Recordings; and the French-language *"La parure,'' ''Deux amix,'' ''Le bapte"* (one volume, abridged), distributed by Olivia & Hall.

entreaty to let her wear the necklace with a simple ''Yes, of course.'' Although the necklace is made of imitation diamonds, it is still worth five hundred francs—more than Madame Loisel's gown.

Style

Narration and Point of View

Like most of Maupassant's short stories, ''The Necklace'' is told by an omniscient third-person narrator, who refrains from judging the characters or their actions. The narrator does have access to the

Topics for Further Study

- Research the development of France's Third Republic and examine how the society depicted in this story reflects the aspirations and apprehensions of the French nation in the 1880s.

- Explore the literary circles of which Maupassant was a part and explain how their theories about the role of literature in society affected the development of French, European, and Western fiction.

- Read several versions of the Cinderella fable and compare them with this story.

- Compare this and other translations of the story with the French original and account for differences between the English versions.

---

characters' thoughts, and mentions that Madame Loisel is unhappy because she feels that she married beneath her. But for the most part, the narrator simply describes the events of the story, leaving it up to the reader to determine the nature of the characters through their actions. Most of all, the narrator is concerned with Madame Loisel. Though most of the story concerns the events surrounding the ball, the narrator recounts her birth into a humble family, her marriage, and also the many years of poverty they suffer afterward as a result of losing the necklace. This deft narration allows Maupassant to tell a story that stretches many years in the space of only a few pages.

Symbolism

The necklace is the central symbol of the story. Madame Loisel "had no clothes, no jewels, nothing," and while her husband can buy her a dress, they cannot afford jewelry. The necklace thus represents Madame Loisel's greed and also her artificiality. She judges herself by the things that she has, and believes others will too. The necklace of artificial diamonds symbolizes the insincerity of her character. Those who admire the necklace only for its supposed worth have been fooled. Just because it looks real does not mean that it is real. This symbol-

ism can be extended to Madame Loisel: Just because she looks like an upper-class lady in her ball gown and jewels does not mean that she is one. The men at the ball who admire her and succumb to her charms and wits can also be said to value appearance over reality, since they have been beguiled by a woman whose charms have been brought out by such artificial means.

Fable

Many critics have read "The Necklace" as a Cinderella tale in reverse. Like Cinderella, Madame Loisel lives a humble life of drudgery (or so she believes) and cannot attend the ball until a fairy godmother figure—Madame Forestier—provides her with a dazzling necklace that will make her one of the most beautiful women at the dance. As Madame Loisel leaves the ball, the illusion of her refinement begins to crumble. Just as Cinderella's gown turns into a servant's frock, so must Madame Loisel put on "modest everyday clothes" to protect herself from the cold of the night air. Ashamed, she "rapidly descend[s] the staircase," likely losing the necklace then—just as Cinderella loses her glass shoe as she hurries to beat the stroke of midnight. The wagon that takes the Loisels home is old and shabby, more like a pumpkin than a grand carriage. Whereas Cinderella eventually wins her prince and thus gains admission to elite society, Madame Loisel's fortunes progress in the opposite direction from "happily ever after." In Cinderella, truth and beauty go hand-in-hand, but in "The Necklace," Madame Loisel is not truthful to Madame Forestier about the fate of the necklace, and she loses her beauty during the years of hard labor she suffers as a result of her insincerity and greed.

Irony

Concerned with the disparity between appearance and reality, "The Necklace" deals with issues arising from ironic situations. In a society that so highly values appearance, it is ironic that the beautiful Madame Loisel is excluded from society because of her class standing. The story's greatest irony, however, is embodied in the necklace itself; while it appears to be a piece of jewelry of great value, it is really an imitation. The Loisels sacrifice their humble but sufficient home to buy an expensive replacement for a cheap original. The reader may also discover irony in the main character's name. "Madame Loisel" sounds much like "mademoiselle," the French term for a young, unmarried girl, which is what Mathilde wishes she could be.

Couples dancing a quadrille at a nineteenth-century ball.

Hamartia

In tragic stories, *hamartia* is an error in action or judgment that causes the protagonist to experience a reversal of fortune. In "The Necklace," this is not when Madame Loisel borrows her friend's jewelry, but when she fails to tell Madame Forestier the truth about what has happened to it. Because she does not tell the truth, Madame Loisel does not learn that the necklace is a fake. She and her husband are forced into lives of poverty as a direct result of their dishonesty.

Historical Context

The Third Republic

Following the Franco-Prussian War of 1870-71 and the expulsion of Napoleon III as emperor, the remains of the French government reestablished itself as a republic. Peace with the Germans had been dearly bought; the French paid a five billion franc indemnity and surrendered valuable land along the eastern frontier. While the Prussian victory helped establish the modern German state, France was demoted to a somewhat secondary role in European affairs. Civil war erupted in Paris between Republicans and Monarchists, threatening to

tear apart the French state, but a peaceful settlement was eventually reached. By 1879, with the resignation of its Monarchist president, the Third Republic had become the firmly established government, and the French began to look beyond their domestic troubles. During the 1880s, France reinstated itself as a primary force in the geopolitical arena, establishing protectorates in China and Southeast Asia and reasserting its control over areas of Africa. The mood of the French following their defeat by the Prussians in 1871 was somber, but a decade later the nation was buoyant, even though certain factional conflicts still remained.

The Ministry of Education

While most English-language translations of "The Necklace" declare that Monsieur Loisel is a civil servant under the Minister of Education, technically this is not true. The French term is actually "ministre de l'Instruction publique," or Minister of Public Instruction. During the early 1880s, there was considerable debate over the relationship between religion and education. Predominantly Catholic France had relied upon parochial education, particularly at the primary school level, for generations. As the Republicans gained power, however, laws governing the separation of church and state were more actively enforced. Unauthorized congre-

Compare
&
Contrast

- **1880s:** During the 1880s, as a republican government solidified following the Franco-Prussian War of 1870–71, France entered into a period of expansionism. In part, their imperialistic attitude was fueled by a desire to restore the national pride that was wounded in the war. During this time, a distorted view of social Darwinism took hold of many Europeans, infusing them with the belief that they were naturally superior to "lesser" races and should therefore rule over them.

  1998: French President Jacques Chirac and his Prime Minister Alain Juppe are concerned with reducing government spending and lowering taxes. In 1995, Chirac won the presidential election in part because of his promise to address the disparity between the rich and the poor in his country, but within two years growing labor unrest attests to the public's dissatisfaction with his policies.

- **1880s:** Loisel attempts to pay for the lost necklace in a variety of ways. He borrows money from usurers and incurs enormous debts in the process. Usury is the practice of charging more than the legal rate of interest for lending money. Since the sixteenth century, the practice of usury has been the subject of ethical debate, but it is a common practice in Europe.

  1990s: Borrowers are protected against usurious rates in the United States by various state and federal laws. Nevertheless, credit card debt reaches record highs as many consumers buy on credit and pay high interest rates for the privilege. High credit card balances keep millions in debt for years.

---

gations such as the Jesuits were forbidden to offer instruction, creating considerable discord. Free, non-religious elementary schooling was established by law and became obligatory in 1881. It is worth noting that, like Monsieur Loisel, Maupassant was a clerk in the Ministry of Education from 1878 to 1880.

Literary Movements

During the second half of the nineteenth century, French fiction was dominated by two literary movements: realism and naturalism. Prior to 1850, French novels—including those written by such famous authors as Victor Hugo, Honore de Balzac, and Alexandre Dumas—had been highly imaginative and romantic, filled with admirable protagonists, dire conflicts, and exciting scenes. Following the uprising of 1848, however, a new generation of French writers led by Gustave Flaubert actively promoted a different approach to fiction that emphasized the realistic depiction of the human condition rather than romanticized tales of heroes and villains. These realists were soon joined by the naturalists, a group of writers, of whom Emile Zola was the most prominent, who portrayed civilization as a thin veneer that barely separated human beings from their natural (and sometimes animal) instincts. In was within this literary environment that Maupassant began his writing career. Many of his stories, including "The Necklace," demonstrate his affinity to both the realist and naturalist movements. Following the realist tenet, his characters are not types but individuals whose motives are understandable if not always agreeable. In the naturalist vein, Maupassant's stories are often attentive to the failings of society, demonstrating that humankind's inherent instincts do not always conform to social values.

Critical Overview

By the time "The Necklace" was first published, Maupassant had already established his reputation as one of France's foremost short story writers.

Boule de suif, which appeared in an 1880 collection of stories by several authors, made him an instant member of the literary elite. ''The Necklace,'' however, was considerably different from Maupassant's previous stories; its trick ending surprised many of his readers who were not used to such a jarring reversal of meaning at the end of a story. Other readers of Maupassant thought that the short story format was beneath him, and they would have preferred that he write novels instead.

American readers of the time, however, were fascinated by the author. The first English translation of Maupassant's stories, an 1888 collection entitled *The Odd Number* because it contained thirteen tales, included ''The Necklace.'' In the book's introduction, Henry James, a prominent American writer and advocate of literary realism, praised the stories as ''wonderfully concise and direct.'' Other critics were similarly enthusiastic, comparing Maupassant favorably with such American short story writers as Bret Harte and Sarah Orne Jewett.

Some critics, however, doubted that Maupassant's popularity would last. In an essay for the January 16, 1892, edition of the *Illustrated London News,* Irish novelist and critic George Moore insisted that Maupassant would be forgotten by the middle of the twentieth century. On the contrary, his popularity in the English-speaking world has never faltered, due in large part to frequent anthologizing of ''The Necklace.'' In a 1939 survey of seventy-four authors by the journal *Books Abroad,* Maupassant tied with Homer and Walt Whitman for sixth place among the most influential writers of all time.

The continued popularity of ''The Necklace'' in the United States, however, eventually resulted in a skewed view of Maupassant's writing. Because, as some critics had predicted, many of his works were no longer well-known, he became associated with the surprise ending, even though he did not use it often. Although critics devoted to the short story genre continued to praise Maupassant for his mastery of style and plotting, those whose experience of Maupassant's works was limited to ''The Necklace'' began to dismiss him as a literary trickster. Indeed, despite renewed attention between World Wars I and II, Maupassant's reputation slipped considerably during the 1950s and 1960s, and his name was rarely mentioned outside of passing references in texts devoted to criticism of short story or realist fiction.

Interest in Maupassant was renewed in 1969 following a special publication of the journal *Europe* devoted to critical analyses of his works. A host of books, essays, and articles followed, but few paid significant attention to ''The Necklace.'' Indeed, since 1980, only two articles have appeared that have focused primarily on ''The Necklace''— a 1982 essay by Gerald Prince that examined the relationship between the characters and their names, and a 1985 article by Mary Donaldson-Evans that compared the story with Maupassant's 1883 tale ''Les bijoux.''

For a story that continues to be included often in modern anthologies, ''The Necklace'' has received little attention in recent decades, possibly because, as Edward Sullivan wrote in his 1974 presentation *Maupassant et la nouvelle,* it is ''too accessible to the public at large.'' Instead, modern critics tend to pay more attention to the works of Maupassant that were passed over during his lifetime, particularly his novels. Thus, a strange permutation of priorities has come about in Maupassant criticism; those texts that made his reputation, save a few select stories, are today largely ignored while those that were overlooked by his contemporaries are central to modern critical discussions.

Criticism

Jason Pierce

Pierce is a Ph.D. candidate at the University of South Carolina. In the following essay, he comments upon the surprise ending in ''The Necklace'' and its correlation to the mystery genre.

Discussions of ''The Necklace'' almost invariably begin with its famous (or, by some accounts, infamous) ending. Much, if not most, of Maupassant's modern reputation in English-speaking countries rests on Madame Forestier's revelation that the original necklace that Madame Loisel borrowed was in fact a fake. Because ''The Necklace'' has been so often anthologized and so few of the author's other works have been translated into English, the surprise ending is often what the modern reader associates with Maupassant. It is important to understand, however, that the trick ending was not commonly associated with Maupassant during his lifetime, nor was Maupassant its originator. In fact, the surprise ending had existed for some

What Do I Read Next?

- The other short story that competes with "The Necklace" for the title of "Maupassant's masterpiece" is his first published story, "Boule de suif" (1880). Based on Maupassant's experiences as a soldier during the Franco-Prussian War, the story depicts the ravages of war on society and illustrates the hypocrisy of patriotism.

- Another of Maupassant's stories, "The Jewels" ("Les bijoux," 1883), offers a plot that is the reverse of that of "The Necklace," with a character discovering that his deceased wife's supposedly imitation jewelry is in fact real.

- The American novelist and critic Henry James, who considered Maupassant's story a "little perfection," wrote a short story entitled "Paste" based on "The Necklace." Its plot is remarkably similar to that of "The Jewels."

- Gustave Flaubert's 1857 novel *Madame Bovary,* originally condemned as obscene, is today rec-ognized as one of the classic novels of nineteenth-century French literature. Not only was Flaubert Maupassant's mentor, but there are also certain interesting parallels between the novel's title character and Madame Loisel.

- Francis Steegmuller's *Maupassant: A Lion in the Path,* published in 1949, presents a good overview of Maupassant's life, his career as a writer, and his relationship with Flaubert.

- For another example of the surprise ending by one of Maupassant's contemporaries, read "The Gift of the Magi" by O. Henry. It was collected in his 1906 book *The Four Million* and has been reprinted many times since.

- In his 1819 poem "Ode on a Grecian Urn," John Keats examined the relationship between truth and beauty. His conclusion contrasts markedly with Maupassant's.

---

time, although not necessarily in the form used by Maupassant.

In the mid- to late-nineteenth century during which Maupassant was writing, the mystery story was gaining in popularity as a genre unto itself. Earlier, police "procedurals" and true crime stories—the latter reputedly but not always reliably based on actual events—had been popular, but suspense rarely played any part in these tales. Through the innovations of such notable authors as Edgar Allan Poe and Arthur Conan Doyle, the mystery genre began to emerge. At its heart was the surprise ending; the solution, the key that unlocked the story's puzzle, was reserved for the ending. Without it, the mystery story would have been just another procedural, following the actions of the characters to their inevitable and foreseeable conclusion. To give their stories suspense, writers delayed revealing all the pertinent "facts of the case," saving certain significant pieces of information for the end.

Even today, mystery stories are very rarely true "whodunits" that the reader can solve; instead, the narrative is woven around certain gaps that are only filled in when the true culprit is revealed. The writer teases the audience by mixing tidbits of useful information with enough "red herrings" to make solving the mystery almost impossible. After all, it is the detective's role to solve the mystery; were the reader to solve the mystery, the story's attempt at building tension would be a failure.

With this in mind, it is possible to read "The Necklace" as a sort of mystery story without the traditional trappings of detectives, criminals, and crimes. The mystery here regards what will happen to Madame Loisel. From the outset it is her wants—a want of prestige, of station, of wealth, of material objects—that gives the narrative its tension and suspense. Madame Loisel is defined by what she lacks and what she is not, rather than by what she has and is. She is not a well-rounded character, but

Maupassant did not intend for her to be one. Instead, she is a type—a figure whose motivation is to fill in the gaps in her own character, in the same way that the detective fills in the gaps in the mystery narrative.

In "The Necklace," the mystery comes into play when the main character's gaps are temporarily filled by the ball, the gown, and, most importantly, Madame Forestier's jewels. Although the event and the dress are prerequisites for Madame Loisel's happiness, she is "utterly miserable" and seriously contemplates not going to the Ministry because she lacks jewelry and the appearance of elegance and wealth. It is thus not the accumulated finery that appeases Madame Loisel's feelings of inadequacy but rather the necklace in particular. Whereas before she was filled with "grief, regret, despair, and misery," with Madame Forestier's jewels about her neck Madame Loisel is "elegant, graceful, smiling, and quite above herself with happiness." It is the necklace that transforms Madame Loisel into such a success. Her possession of the necklace, however, is temporary—unlike her dress or her memories of the ball, she cannot hold onto it—and from this arises the story's mystery. What, the reader asks, will happen when Madame Loisel must return the necklace? How will its return affect her? What sort of person will she be when she no longer has the necklace to make her content?

Before these questions can be answered, "The Necklace" undergoes a plot twist—a common element in the mystery genre. Madame Forestier's jewels are somehow lost between the Ministry and the Loisels's home, prompting Monsieur Loisel to search the streets of Paris looking for them, much as a detective from Scotland Yard might track down a criminal in the back alleys of London. Facing the embarrassment of telling Madame Forestier that her jewels have been lost, Madame Loisel is persuaded by her husband to lie to her old friend—to tell her that the clasp has been broken and is being mended so that they will have time to look for the necklace. When they finally give up their search, Madame Loisel declares that they must "see about replacing the diamonds." With this it would seem that the mystery has been solved. The introduction of the necklace into Madame Loisel's life has made her temporarily content, but more importantly, it has produced in her the tendency to lie, even to one of her oldest friends. The incident has revealed that she lacks the moral fiber to admit the truth about Madame Forestier's jewels. As a result of this ethical stumble, the Loisels must learn to cope with hardship and true poverty to a degree that they had never

> "Madame Loisel is defined by what she lacks and what she is not, rather than by what she has and is."

known before. The formerly beautiful Madame Loisel becomes "like all the other strong, hard, coarse women of poor households." This is the effect of the loss of the necklace. With it, she is a grand success, literally the "belle of the ball"; without it, she is a hollow woman, bereft of morals and burdened by poverty.

With the mystery apparently solved, the reader might think that the story should end at this point. Indeed, several critics have argued that its surprise conclusion is unnecessary. In his 1974 book *The Short Story,* Sean O'Faolain argued that "the real merits of the tale as read, do not lie in the cleverness of that ending." O'Faolain believes that Maupassant's genius lies in his characterization of the Loisels and his depiction of the hardships that they encounter. He is partially supported in this position by Francis Steegmuller, the author of an influential Maupassant biography, who regarded "The Necklace" as "inherently inferior" to Maupassant's other works because it is "flawed by improbabilities," by which he meant all of the story's unlikely coincidences, particularly the revelation of the necklace's true value. Despite these critics' wishes to the contrary, the ending is an integral part of Maupassant's story.

If one reads "The Necklace" as a mystery story, then the true trick is not the fact that the diamonds are actually paste but that the mystery with which the story is concerned is itself a deception. The reader is led to believe that the story's central conflict is based on Madame Loisel's social situation and her desire to become a member of a higher class. In fact, however, that conflict is only the basis for the story's true conflict—the disparity between appearances and reality. At the Ministry ball, Madame Loisel's success is a direct result of her appearance of wealth and high social standing, whereas, in reality, she is relatively poor. And yet the key to her success, the symbol of her social prosperity, is itself not what it appears to be. Whereas the reader thinks that the mystery is how the necklace will affect Madame Loisel's character, in truth the mystery centers on how symbols of wealth and power affect social interaction. Maupassant's story is less the tale of Madame Loisel's rise and fall than a work of social commentary. The reader does not recognize his or her role as "detective" until the story's final line, at which point Maupassant's purpose is laid bare. The effects on Madame Loisel of Madame Forestier's jewels and her experiences at the ball are irrelevant; she is little more than a tool for Maupassant's commentary upon the superficiality of 1880s Parisian society.

The story's ending was necessary for Maupassant to attain his goal. Having achieved the reputation of being France's foremost short story writer, he hardly could have switched to nonfiction social commentary and hoped to reach as great an audience as he garnered with his fiction. In order to ensure that his message would be received by the greatest possible number of readers, it had to be imbedded in a short story, the genre with which he was most closely associated. The story needed to have believable characters, realistic situations (whether or not it has these is a matter of critical debate), and a strong plot in order to disguise its true mission. The ending had to be a surprise because it is where Maupassant chose to insert his social commentary. Had this criticism of French society and its preference for appearance over substance emerged earlier in the text, Maupassant's point would have been lost. He allows the readers to get caught up in appearances before revealing the reality of the situation. This tactic allows the full weight of the plot to be felt by the reader as well as Madame Loisel. By saving his revelation for the end, Maupassant is able to shock his readers, who are just as caught up in appearances as Madame Loisel, and reveal the story's true purpose as a social criticism.

Source: Jason Pierce, "Overview of 'The Necklace'," for *Short Stories for Students,* Gale, 1998.

Robert Penn Warren and Cleanth Brooks

In the following excerpt, the critics examine Maupassant's treatment of time in "The Necklace," in which he alternates between dramatic action and narrative summary.

["The Necklace"] gives us a good chance to consider the problem of the treatment of time in fiction. The story takes Madame Loisel from youth to middle age. Her girlhood is passed over in one sentence in the first paragraph, and the early years

of marriage are treated in the second to the fifth paragraphs. Then the time of the ball is treated at considerable length in five direct scenes, the conversation about the dress, the conversation about the jewels, the visit to Madame Forestier, the ball itself, the search for the lost necklace. Then the time of deprivation and payment, ten years, occupies a page or so. Then comes the denouement, the encounter with Madame Forestier in the park.

There is, we see, a sort of balance between the long periods of time treated by summary, and the short periods, treated more or less dramatically by direct rendering. In treating the long periods, in which the eye sweeps, as it were, over a panorama, the writer needs to hit on the important fact, or the essential feeling of the period. He needs to distill out the thing fundamental to the story—the character of the young Madame Loisel, or the way she lived through the ten years of deprivation. In the dramatic—or scenic—treatment the need, however, is to show the process of the movement through the time involved, how there is, step by step, a development; how, for example, Madame Loisel decides to speak to her old friend in the park, how she accosts her, how she discovers the unexpected joy in the thought that the necklace she had bought had successfully deceived Madame Forestier, how Madame Forestier makes the revelation which, for us, will carry the burden of meaning. The scene, in other words, gives the "close-ups" of time, and the summary gives the "long shots."

Often in a summary a writer must give more than mere summary. After all, he is writing fiction, and fiction wants to give the feeling of life, not merely the bare facts. Let us notice how even in the relatively bare summary in which Maupassant presents the years of hardship, he manages by a few specific touches to make us sense the quality of the life of the Loisels. Madame Loisel scraped "her rosy nails on the greasy pots and pans." When she carried up her household water every morning, she had to stop "for breath at every landing." She had become, Maupassant tells us, strong, hard, and rough. Then he writes: "With frowsy hair, skirts askew, and red hands, she talked loud while washing the floor with great swishes of water." It all comes alive with the phrase "great swishes of water." We *see* that.

Some pieces of fiction, even some novels, can proceed almost entirely by scenes, by direct presentation. For instance, "De Mortuis" gives us a single little segment of time, as does "The Girls in Their

Summer Dresses,'' with only a minimum of summarized exposition from the past. In fact, both of these stories, in treating the present time, depend almost entirely on conversation and direct action—more so, for instance, than even ''The Lottery,'' which, also, occupies a single short section of continuing time.

Many stories and almost all novels, however, must swing back and forth between more or less direct treatments and narrative summary with more or less of description and analysis thrown in. It is well to begin to notice how these two basic kinds of treatment (with the various shadings and combinations) are related. We must ask ourselves how much the feeling of a particular story, the logic of its telling, the effect it has on us, are related to the writer's handling of this question of time. Again, there is no rule. We must try to inspect our own reactions as carefully and candidly as possible, and try to imagine what would be the effect, in instance after instance, if a different method were used.

Source: Cleanth Brooks and Robert Penn Warren, ''The Necklace,'' in *Understanding Fiction,* second edition, edited by Cleanth Brooks and Robert Penn Warren, 1959, pp. 106–15.

Sean O'Faolain

In the following excerpt, O'Faolain asserts that the cleverness of ''The Necklace'' lies not in the surprise ending but in its realistic portrayal of human relationships and society.

[In ''La Parure''] we have a civil-servant, with a pretty little wife. They are poor, as, no doubt, civil servants occasionally are. And being pretty and young she wants to go to dances, and receptions, and mix with people from the Legations and so on, as even poor folk do. One day they get an invitation to an important function, a dance—and for the occasion she naturally wants to look her very best. She can make do with her best frock, but she has no jewels, and she fears that without them she will look just as poor as she is. So she borrows a diamond necklace from a rich school-friend, and delighted, off she goes to the dance and has a thoroughly happy time. When it is all over she has to wake up her husband—who has gone to sleep in an anteroom, as husbands will—they go out, get a cab, and off they go, back to their home.

But when she puts her hand to her throat to remove the necklace it is gone! She has lost those priceless diamonds. They go back; they search: they put advertisements in the paper. All in vain. She

> ''Notice how even in the relatively bare summary in which Maupassant presents the years of hardship, he manages by a few specific touches to make us sense the quality of the life of the Loisels.''

dare not face her rich friend without them, so what does she do? She goes to the best jeweller in the city and she buys, on the instalment system, an identical necklace. So, that one really happy night of all her life becomes thereby the last happy night of her life; for, now, their poverty is ten times worse than before: they are sunk under this load of debt; and for years and years the two poor creatures slave to pay for those diamonds. Her pretty looks go. Her hair dries up. The wrinkles come. And, then, after about ten years of this penury she meets her old school-friend once again and when her friend commiserates with her on her changed appearance, the once-pretty, still-plucky little woman says, proudly: 'It was all because of you.' And she recounts the sad tale. 'O, my dear child!' says her friend, in agony. 'But how unnecessary! Those diamonds were paste. I bought them for a few francs.'

Now, that is probably the most famous example in literature of what is known as the 'whip-crack ending.' Those who like Chekov do not like it—it is so hard and so cruel. Personally, I do not particularly like it, but that, I realise, is a mere matter of taste and not of judgment. But the essential point is that this story would still be an excellent story, and some have even held that it would be a better story, if the thing stopped short with the slavery of the little wife and if there were no revelation about the diamonds being paste, no whip-crack ending at all. Those critics maintain that the whip-crack ending is too artificial, too unlikely, too ingenious. In any case, the real merits of the tale as read, do not lie in the cleverness of that ending. The tale has won its spurs long, long before we come to the ending. It has revealed a segment of society in which life is cruelly compressed and wounded. Those two people, man and wife, are real; their surroundings are real—real, perhaps, in a large typical way rather than in the individualised way which is Chekov's way. They evoke our pity. In short, the story makes its comment on human relationships; though in this case the relationship is social rather than personal. And . . . every story that is a story will, unconsciously, do that.

Source: Sean O'Faolain, "The Technical Struggle: On Subject," in *The Short Story,* The Devin-Adair Co., 1951, pp. 171–92.

Francis Steegmuller

In the following excerpt, Steegmuller maintains that the shock ending of "The Necklace" is the highlight of the story, condemning Maupassant's portrayal of relationships as "vague and unconvincing" and his plot as improbable. Steegmuller also asserts that while Maupassant has a reputation as a specialist in surprise endings, only a few of his stories actually conclude in this manner.

At the smiling moment of his life when he was thirty-four, had built his house at Etretat, hired François, and begun to enjoy his *amours plus elegants,* Maupassant did some of his best and his best-known work. In both these categories can be placed "La Parure" ("The Necklace"), one of the most famous short stories in the world, described by Henry James when it was new as "a little perfection."

Although everyone knows the plot, not everyone knows James's resume of it:

> In "La Parure" a poor young woman, under "social" stress, the need of making an appearance on an important occasion, borrows from an old school friend, now much richer than herself, a pearl [sic] necklace which she has the appalling misfortune to lose by some mischance never afterwards cleared up. Her life and her pride, as well as her husband's with them, become subject, from the hour of the awful accident, to the redemption of this debt; which, effort by effort, sacrifice by sacrifice, franc by franc, with specious pretexts, excuses, a rage of desperate explanation of their failure to restore the missing object, they finally obliterate—all to find that their whole consciousness and life have been convulsed and deformed in vain, that the pearls were but highly artful "imitation" and that their passionate penance has ruined them for nothing.

The particular brilliance with which "La Parure" is written triumphs over a number of improbabilities. (The lack of insurance on the necklace, sometimes mentioned by critics, is not among them: insurance of jewelry in France began to be common only a few years later.) But even a halfway careful reading of the famous tale shows the relationships between the two women and between the heroine and her husband to be vague and unconvincing; and the purchase and successful substitution of the new necklace are of dubious verisimilitude. But the shock of the shattering, crushing end has always endeared the story to the multitude. The common tribute of nonliterary readers of "La Parure"—"It shouldn't have been written! It makes you feel too bad!"—is phrased as a reproach; but actually it is an expression of the intensest pleasure, the ability to be made to "feel bad" by a story being prized by most readers beyond rubies.

Maupassant would have enjoyed that tribute. For he liked very much to make people "feel bad"—to give them, at least, a few bad moments, to shock them and surprise them. The perpetration of what the French call *farces* and we call practical jokes was one of his favorite forms of amusement, and the memoirs of François and of Maupassant's friends are full of examples of the elaborate lengths to which he was willing to go to secure a victim's momentary discomfiture. In addition to "Farce Normande", the story about wedding-night horseplay, he wrote another, "La Farce", which contains two practical jokes, one of them involving an old lady's chamber-pot, and innumerable other tales about victimizations; and in life he enjoyed inviting people to dinner under false pretenses (pretending to be launching an investment scheme, to furnish a needy courtesan of his acquaintance with a wealthy protector in the form of a "Spanish marquis," actually a friend in disguise, to introduce to a group of ladies a charming college boy whom they allow to take certain precocious liberties, not realizing that he is a woman); having François deliver to a lady in her salon a basket full of live frogs, making his dinner guests at Chatou, when he took an apartment there one spring, miss the last train back to Paris; turning mice loose on his boat among lady guests; using filthy language in the hearing of stuffy people; assuring acquaintances that he had once eaten "roast shoulder of woman" and so enjoyed it that he had taken a second portion, and so on. This rather infantile love to shock is a mild expression of the sadism which finds further outlet in his frequent and usually artistically superfluous descriptions of blood—such as the hideous abortion in "L'Enfant", and, in his travel sketches, a sanguinary fight among Mediterranean fishes and a description of the red flesh of watermelons. A brutal, shocking ending like that of "La Parure" is another expression of the tendency.

Maupassant has an immense reputation as a specialist in stories that end in this way—stories with "trick" or "twist" endings. Considering how deeply engrained in his nature was the desire to shock, he might be expected to have written numerous such stories; but the fact is that he did not. It is impossible to mention a precise figure, since between shock and non-shock there is no clear demarking line, but of Maupassant's more than two hundred short stories a mere handful have endings that can properly be called trick or shocking.

The legend of his being a specialist in this kind of story did not exist during his lifetime. His work was repeatedly and rigorously analyzed by such contemporary critics as Jules Lemaître and Anatole France, men who despite the differences in their approach to literature from that of present-day critics were keenly discriminating and perceptive; and they would without mercy have pointed out the aesthetic inferiority—the drastically diminished pleasure of re-reading—inherent in a large body of Maupassant stories with trick endings, had such a body existed. Present-day critics who make the charge reveal that they are repeating what they have heard or read, that they are not well acquainted with Maupassant. Indeed, the statement that Maupassant's work is generally characterized by trickery can usually be considered a warning: a warning that other inaccuracies are hovering near. When a critic [Edmund Wilson, *The New Yorker,* Dec. 13, 1947] reviewing Henry James's notebooks, for example, says, "One sees that the example of Maupassant—more frequently invoked, I think, than that of any other writer—with his plots that depend on pure trickery, has had much more influence on Henry James than one would ever have expected," he betrays not only a faulty memory of Maupassant, but also a careless reading or interpretation of the work in hand: examination of James's notebooks shows that it is not Maupassant's trickery or plots that Henry James keeps invoking, but Maupassant's enviable ability to write with brevity and compactness.

In exactly one recorded instance Maupassant's "trickery" did influence Henry James and influence him concretely; and on this unique occasion the trickery was that of "La Parure." The origin of his short story "Paste," James tells us, "was to consist but of the ingenious thought of transposing

> " Even a halfway careful reading of the famous tale shows the relationships between the two women and between the heroine and her husband to be vague and unconvincing."

the terms of one of Guy de Maupassant's admirable *contes*—"La Parure."

It seemed harmless sport simply to turn that situation round—to shift, in other words, the ground of the horrid mistake, making this a matter not of a false treasure supposed to be true and precious, but of a real treasure supposed to be false and hollow: though a new little "drama," a new setting for *my* pearls—and as different as possible from the other—had of course withal to be found.

Source: Francis Steegmuller, "'The Necklace'," in *Maupassant: A Lion in the Path,* Random House, 1949, pp. 203–10.

H. E. Bates

In the following excerpt, Bates discusses Maupassant's ability to combine trick and tragedy into one, asserting that in "The Necklace" it is clear that the author was completely aware of the limitations of the surprise ending.

[To] Maupassant . . . still belongs that supreme *tour de force* of surprise endings, "The Necklace," in which the excellence and the limitation of the method can be perfectly seen. Maupassant's story of the woman who borrows a diamond necklace from a friend, loses it, buys another to replace it, and is condemned to ten years' suffering and poverty by the task of paying off the money, only to make the awful discovery at last that the original necklace was not diamond but paste—this story, dependent though it is for effect on the shock of the last line, differs in one extremely important respect from anything O. Henry ever did. For here, in "The Necklace," trick and tragedy are one. By placing a certain strain on the credulity of the reader (why, one asks, was it not explained in the first place that the necklace was paste? or why, later, did not Madame Loisel make a clean breast of everything to a friend who had so much trusted her?), by the skilful elimination of probabilities, Maupassant is left holding a shocking and surprising card of which the reader is entirely ignorant. He is entirely ignorant, that is, *the first time*. Like a child who is frightened by the first sudden boo! from round the corner, but knows all about it next time, the reader of ''The Necklace'' can never be tricked again. For Maupassant is bound to play that card, which is his only by a process of cheating, and having played it can never again repeat its devastating effect. In story-telling, as in parlour games, you can never hope to hoodwink the same person twice. It is only because of Maupassant's skilful delineation of Madame Loisel's tragedy that ''The Necklace'' survives as a credible piece of realism. Maupassant, the artist, was well aware that the trick alone is its own limitation.

Source: H. E. Bates, ''American Writers after Poe,'' in *The Modern Short Story: A Critical Survey,* The Writer, Inc., 1941, pp. 46–71.

Douglas Bement

In the following excerpt, Bement offers an interpretation of Maupassant's development of the plot of ''The Necklace,'' believing he may have considered the implications of both greed and innocence to form his story.

We have no clue as to where the idea for [''The Necklace''] originated; it might have sprung from the sight of a paste necklace in a shop window. The keen eye of the storyteller, lighting on it, might have been arrested with the germ of an idea, upon which his imagination set to work. Suppose a person were to buy a necklace at a fabulous price, believing it to be genuine? As the writer played with this idea, some objections must have offered themselves. ''What of it?'' Maupassant might well have asked himself. ''What would it mean? What significance does it have? How is it related to my experience, or to the experience of my fellows? What sort of a person would be apt to buy a paste necklace, thinking it real?''

The last query might well raise the ever-present problem of *probability*. Would it be probable that an average person would buy a paste necklace for a fabulous sum without making an investigation of its true worth? And even if he were duped after having investigated, should we really feel sorry for him; would he stir our emotions; shouldn't we feel him to be something of a fool? And if a person could afford to buy such an expensive trinket, should we feel his loss very much?

But suppose he couldn't afford to buy it? Suppose he were buying it to win the favor of a girl? But neither should we sympathize with a girl who could be so bought, nor with a man who wanted to buy her. Still, he might have his side of the story; that is a possibility.

Eventually, we may suppose, Maupassant hit on the idea of a woman's borrowing the necklace from another, supposing it to be real. She loses the necklace and replaces it with a valuable one. If the borrower were rich, the whole proceeding would be a joke. If she were poor, it would be tragic. If her poverty were shared by another, an innocent victim, it would be still more tragic. The innocent victim might be her husband.

Here Maupassant might well have stopped to take stock. The *idea* is unfolding, but what are its *implications* ? By means of the necklace there is personified all the greed, all the shallow love of costly ornaments, all the striving of so many people to impress others by appearance. Such people are the Biblical whited sepulchres, symbolic of the sham and pretense of society. Here is the oft-recurring human trait of seeming to be what one is not, the desire to appear better than one is.

Here, in this philosophic reflection, enters the observation of life which forms part of the warp of the fabric. Here is the theme which translates the imaginary into the real, ''which gives to airy nothing a local habitation and a name,'' which brings the imaginative out of nowhere, imbues it with the spirit of reality, and translates it into terms of life.

Her husband, then, shall be the innocent victim, for she herself, because of her vanity, may not be innocent in our eyes. We are willing that the guilty should suffer; but our emotion is aroused when we see the innocent pay the penalty.

Then, let us suppose, came the question of the characters of the principals of the story. What sort of woman would want to borrow a necklace? She must be vain, but even behind a mask of vanity are hidden human foibles with which we can sympathize. We pity the woman who would be vain just once, if the whole background of her life, like Cinderella's, were a succession of gray days filled with endless dreary routine. Perhaps the woman wanted just one fling in the world; she shall not be blameless, but at least we may understand.

Then what of the husband? He must be poor, hardworking; he must love his wife enough to give her things even beyond his means; he must be weak enough to be prevailed upon.

And who is the center of the story? On whom shall the spot-light focus? Who is to arouse our most profound emotions? It must be the husband. They will both suffer, but we must be sorrier for him, the innocent victim, than we are for her. . . .

And so we might speculate endlessly and in much greater detail regarding Maupassant and his story. Even without any guidance from the author himself the speculation would be profitable. We are helped to see ultimately through his eyes, and while, in some cases, we may not care for the author's point of view, attitude, interpretation, or material, we can at least see genius at work, shaping to its ends the materials that lie about us daily.

But fortunately there are sources available for us to study with some exactness the germination of story ideas. There are the notebooks of Hawthorne, Chekhov, Katherine Mansfield, and others, which tell the struggles which each had with the stories that we have been accustomed to read as finished artistic achievements. And here we are helped to realize that the germination of a story idea is a long and devious process, which calls into play not only the ability to seize upon the idea, but also the faculty for feeling out its significance and its implications. . . .

Source: Douglas Bement, "The Woof—Plot," in *Weaving the Short Story,* Farrar & Rinehart, Inc., 1931, pp. 65–87.

Sources

James, Henry. "Guy de Maupassant," reprinted in his *Partial Portraits,* Macmillan, 1888, pp. 243-87.

Prince, Gerald. "Nom et destin dans 'La Parure'," in *The French Review,* Vol. 55, 1982, pp. 267-71.

Sullivan, Edward D. "Maupassant et la nouvelle," in *Cahiers de l'association internationale des etudes francais,* Vol. 27, pp. 223-36.

Further Reading

Artinian, Artine. "Introduction" in *The Complete Short Stories of Guy de Maupassant,* Hanover House, 1955, pp. ix-xvii.
An introduction to Maupassant's literary reputation, particularly in the United States.

Donaldson-Evans, Mary. "The Last Laugh: Maupassant's 'Les bijoux' and 'La parure'," in *French Forum,* Vol. 10, 1985, pp. 163-73.
Compares "The Necklace" to "Les bijoux," another Maupassant story with similar themes, arguing for the superiority of the former based on its greater complexity.

Europe, no. 482, 1969.
A collection of essays in French on Maupassant and his works, which helped reestablish his literary reputation.

James, Henry. "Guy de Maupassant," in Maupassant's *The Odd Number,* Harper & Brothers, 1889, pp. vii- xvii.
Also published in the October 19, 1889, edition of the influential periodical *Harper's Weekly,* this piece served as an introduction to American readers to the works of Maupassant.

O'Faolain, Sean. *The Short Story,* Devin-Adair, 1974.
In a section entitled "The Technical Struggle: On Subject," O'Faolain addresses "The Necklace," among other works, and argues that the story's merit lies not in its "whip-crack ending" but in Maupassant's portrayal of characters and society.

Steegmuller, Francis. *Maupassant: A Lion in the Path,* Collins, 1949.
Primarily a biography, this work relates much of Maupassant's fiction to his life through the device of psychoanalysis.

Sullivan, Edward D. *Maupassant: The Short Stories,* Barron's, 1962.
An introduction to Maupassant's *contes* and *nouvelles,* with some useful commentary on "The Necklace."

Thibaudet, Albert. "The Generation of 1850," in his *French Literature from 1795 to Our Era,* Funk & Wagnalls, 1968, pp. 263-359.
Offers an overview of the major figures and movements in French literature and contextualizes Maupassant's writings in terms of his contributions to literary development and his relationships with other authors.

The New Dress

Virginia Woolf

1927

Virginia Woolf's short story "The New Dress" was written in 1924 while she was writing the novel *Mrs. Dalloway,* published in 1925. Critics have entertained the possibility that the story may originally have been a chapter of the novel because some of the same characters and events appear in both works. The story was published in the May 1927 issue of the monthly New York magazine the *Forum.* In the story, a deeply insecure and painfully self-conscious guest at a party is convinced that she is the target of mockery.

Leonard Woolf later republished "The New Dress" in the collection *A Haunted House* in 1944, three years after Virginia Woolf's death. It was republished in 1973 in the collection *Mrs. Dalloway's Party,* with other stories by Woolf that focus on the guests and events of the day leading up to Clarissa Dalloway's party.

Author Biography

Virginia Woolf was born Adeline Virginia Stephen in London on January 25, 1882, the third of four children of Julia Duckworth and Sir Leslie Stephen, a noted historian and biographer. As a child, Woolf received no formal education but made use of her father's library and literary friendships to educate herself. After her mother's death in 1895, Woolf experienced a nervous breakdown, the first in a

series of four debilitating emotional traumas. When her father died nine years later, Woolf had her second mental breakdown. Upon her recovery, she moved with her sister, Vanessa, and her brothers, Thoby and Adrian, to the Bloomsbury district of London.

She, her siblings, and their friends made up the famous Bloomsbury Group, which included such notable figures as E. M. Forster, Lytton Strachey, Roger Fry, and John Maynard Keynes. As the group's reputation spread among London art and literary circles, Woolf grew intellectually within her group of friends, which included Leonard Woolf, whom she married on August 10, 1912.

Amidst the nurturing and intellectual atmosphere of the Bloomsbury Group, Woolf began writing book reviews and critical essays for publication. Her early works appeared in such periodicals as the *Times Literary Supplement,* the *Forum,* the *Guardian,* and the *National Review,* among others. It was also during this time that Woolf completed her first novel, *The Voyage Out,* and suffered another emotional breakdown.

Woolf began keeping a diary in 1915, the same year that *The Voyage Out* was published. Two years later, she and Leonard started the Hogarth Press. Significantly, they began publication with her short story "The Mark on the Wall" and later "Kew Gardens" and "An Unwritten Novel." They also published *Monday or Tuesday,* a volume of short fiction which was the only collection of Woolf's stories published during her lifetime. Woolf never prioritized this genre, although she wrote short stories throughout her career. For her they were projects to sustain her between novels. Leonard Woolf explains that she "used at intervals to write short stories. It was her custom, whenever an idea for one occurred to her, to sketch it out in a very rough form and then to put it away in a drawer. Later, if an editor asked her for a short story, and she felt in the mood to write one (which was not frequent), she would take a sketch out of her drawer and rewrite it, sometimes a great many times. Or if she felt, as she often did, while writing a novel that she required to rest her mind by working on something else for a time, she would either write a critical essay or work upon one of her sketches for short stories."

Woolf wrote "The New Dress" in 1924 while she was revising her fourth novel, *Mrs. Dalloway.*

The story was not published until 1927, when it appeared in the *Forum,* a monthly New York magazine read primarily by the intelligentsia. This was the first story in a group that was collected by Stella McNichol in 1973 and published as *Mrs. Dalloway's Party.* Each of these stories explores the perspective a different guest at the Dalloway party.

Woolf continued to write novels and in 1929 completed *A Room of One's Own,* which has been hailed as a feminist manifesto of the twentieth century. In 1941 Woolf published her last novel, *Between the Acts.* She suffered another emotional breakdown in February 1941, but this time she did not recover. Woolf committed suicide by drowning on March 28, 1941.

Plot Summary

In Woolf's 1924 short story "The New Dress," Mabel Waring arrives at Clarissa Dalloway's party and is instantly consumed by feelings of inadequacy and inferiority. These negative feelings are set off by concerns that her new dress in not appropriate for the occasion. Immediately after greeting her hostess, she goes straight to a mirror at the far of the room to look at herself and is filled with misery at the conviction that "It was not *right.*" She imagines the other guests exclaiming to themselves over "what a fright she looks! What a hideous new dress!" She begins to berate herself for trying to appear "original": since a dress in the latest fashion was out of her financial reach, she had a yellow silk dress made from an outdated pattern. Her self-condemnation verges on self-torture, as she torments herself with obsessive thoughts of her foolishness "which deserved to be chastised." She thinks of the new dress as a "horror . . . idiotically old-fashioned." When the stylishly dressed Rose Shaw tells her the dress is "perfectly charming," Mabel is sure she is being mocked.

She tries to think of some way "to annul this pain, to make this agony endurable." The extremes of language and the obvious torment Mabel is experiencing may be intended to give the reader some indication that perhaps she is not entirely mentally or emotionally stable. It may also, however, be intended to underscore the discomfort that shy or socially unskilled individuals can experience in social settings.

Virginia Woolf

Mabel tries to envision the partygoers as ''flies, trying to crawl over the edge of the saucer,'' all looking alike and with the same goals. But she cannot make herself see the others in this light. She tells another guest that *she* feels like ''some dowdy, decrepit, horribly dingy old fly,'' and then is mortified to realize that he must have interpreted her remark as a ploy for the insincere compliment that he hastily delivers.

Mabel remembers how happy and comfortable she felt at the dressmaker's, as Miss Milan pinned her hem, asked her about the length, and tended her pet canary. This image vanishes quickly, however, as she is catapulted back to the present, ''suffering tortures, woken wide awake to reality.'' She berates herself for caring what others think of her, but drifts into thoughts about her own ''odious, weak, vacillating character.''

Mabel thinks about her unremarkable family and upbringing, her dreams of romance in far-away lands, and the reality of her marriage to a man with ''a safe, permanent underling's job.'' She thinks about isolated moments in her life—characterized as ''delicious'' and ''divine''—when she feels happy and fulfilled, connected with all of the earth and everything in it, ''on the crest of a wave.'' She wonders if those moments will come to her less and

less often, and determines to pursue personal transformation through ''some wonderful, helpful, astonishing book'' or an inspirational public speaker. She gets up to leave the party, assuring Mrs. Dalloway that she has enjoyed herself.

Characters

Mrs. Barnet

Mrs. Barnet is a maidservant in the Dalloway household. Her behavior in greeting Mabel Waring and taking her coat seem unremarkable to the reader, but sets off great waves of insecurity in the party guest about her appearance and social role.

Clarissa Dalloway

Clarissa Dalloway is the hostess of the party that Mabel attends. Clarissa is affable and courteous to her guests, and her presence lingers, though the reader only hears her speak once in the story—to encourage Mabel not to leave the party early.

Mrs. Dalloway

See Clarissa Dalloway

Mabel Waring

Mabel Waring is a middle-aged woman who reflects constantly and, some might say, obsessively, about her alienation from the members of the elevated level of society she wants to join. When she is invited to a party given by the wealthy and socially prominent Clarissa Dalloway, she is overwhelmed with worry about her inability to dress fashionably because of the cost. She has an old-fashioned dress made from a book of dress patterns that had belonged to her mother, then spends much of her time at the party fretting over its inappropriateness and drawing the attention of other partygoers to it. She also engages in perfunctory conversations that provide further evidence of her dissociation from this strata of society.

Rose Shaw

Rose Shaw is a guest at Clarissa Dalloway's party. Mabel Waring characterizes her as being dressed ''in the height of fashion, precisely like everybody else, always.'' Rose compliments Mabel on her new dress, but Mabel is convinced that she is being subtly mocked.

Themes

Alienation and Loneliness

Mabel Waring's feelings of alienation surface when she attends a party given by Clarissa Dalloway. The reader first sees her insecurity when the Dalloways's servant, Mrs. Barnet, immediately recognizes Mabel's humble origins from the new dress that she has had made for the party. The servant's behavior affirms Mabel's belief that she is an outsider and does not belong in this society. Social interactions at the party further verify her estrangement. Although the other guests engage Mabel in conversation, an acute self-consciousness about her appearance and manners makes her unable to communicate on anything other than a superficial level. Mabel's self-absorption and self-centeredness isolate her from the other party guests and make any communication impossible. Wrapped up in her own world, she never carefully considers what others say; instead, Mabel assumes that everything at the party somehow involves her. In the story, she imagines the guests making fun of her new dress: "Oh these men, oh these women, all were thinking—'What's Mabel wearing? What a fright she looks! What a hideous new dress!'" What Mabel does not realize is her own complicity in the alienation and isolation that she feels.

Human Condition

Closely connected to the theme of alienation in the story is the desperation of the party guests, whose inauthentic lives make them incapable of real communication. According to Mabel, they are all flies in a saucer, trying desperately to escape. But while everyone around her appears to be a butterfly or dragonfly, Mabel alone remains trapped. Lamenting her banal life and the superficiality of the conversations which "bored her unutterably," Mabel lingers in the saucer, amidst her own hypocrisy, unable to change her condition.

Class Conflict

Throughout "The New Dress," the disparity between Mabel's class status and that of the other

guests is underscored as Mabel compares her clothes, furniture, and manners to those at the party. She concludes that she cannot be fashionable because she is not rich. Her husband, Hubert, is not the empire builder she had dreamed of but a safe, unthreatening underling employed at the law court.

Wealth and Poverty

The upper middle-class guests at the Dalloway party have their share of financial resources, but Mabel is a woman of limited means, and her lower middle-class status makes her feel inferior to the Dalloways and their friends. Throughout "The New Dress," she focuses on the power of wealth and the debilitation of poverty: "She could not be fashionable. It was absurd to pretend it even—fashion meant cut, meant style, meant thirty guineas at least." Mabel's intense envy of Rose Shaw, whose green gown makes her yellow dress pale in comparison, makes her unable to accept her financial limitations and make the best of her situation. She instead blames her parents and their poverty for her inadequateness at the party: "But it was not her fault altogether, after all. It was being one of a family of ten; never having money enough, always skimping and paring. . . and one sordid little domestic tragedy after another." Had her family had greater financial resources, Mabel might have married better, and her life might have turned out differently. She might have had a fashionable dress, and she might have been a Rose Shaw.

Style

Stream of Consciousness

Woolf's short story "The New Dress" is related through a stream-of-consciousness narrative in which the thoughts and feelings of Mabel Waring are central to the narrative. In fact, Woolf is commonly regarded, together with Edouard Dujardin and James Joyce, as one of the creators and early practitioners of stream-of-consciousness narrative. The focus is more on character than plot; actually, the plot is revealed as the reader learns about the protagonist. The story emerges from Mabel's thoughts as she perfunctorily addresses the other guests and her unconscious associations are evoked by a look or gesture. There is no logical progression of ideas in the story; they occur randomly, as Mabel's thoughts drift to and from the party.

Topics for Further Study

- Many of Woolf's works highlight gender and class oppression. Research the decade of the 1920s in English history to discover why these were pertinent themes for Woolf and her contemporaries.

- Woolf has become a cultural icon for feminists across the world. Read her essay *A Room of One's Own* and explore the extent to which her ideas are useful for feminists today.

- After some preliminary research into Sigmund Freud's theories of various mental conditions, offer a partial ''diagnosis'' of what might be troubling Mabel Waring and how she might best approach attaining good mental health.

- Mabel Waring suffers from feelings of inadequacy, unworthiness, and personal failure. Identify a work of fiction—a short story, novel, play, or poem—in which a man feels inadequate, unworthy, or incapable of performing as he thinks he should. Some suggestions: ''The Beast in the Jungle,'' by Henry James; ''The Door in the Wall,'' by H. G. Wells; ''Paul's Case,'' by Willa Cather, ''The Short, Happy Life of Francis Macomber,'' by Ernest Hemingway; ''Babylon Revisited,'' by F. Scott Fitzgerald; *An American Tragedy*, by Theodore Dreiser; *The Wild Duck*, by Henrik Ibsen; *Hamlet*, by William Shakespeare; ''Richard Cory,'' by E. A. Robinson. Do women and men experience these feelings in the same ways? Discuss what you see as similarities or differences.

Point of View

The story is told from an anonymous, third-person perspective. In a stream-of-consciousness narrative, the narrator knows the inner thoughts of the protagonist and takes advantage of the privilege of omniscience by presenting Mabel's feelings as they unfold.

Interior Monologue

The reader learns about Mabel's life through an indirect interior monologue that occurs during the party. Her thoughts are presented by an unknown, third-person narrator and reveal events from Mabel's past, her daydreams, and her feelings about the people she encounters at the party.

Setting

The setting of ''The New Dress'' is a party hosted by Clarissa Dalloway. The reader never learns the occasion for this gathering, but the party functions as a microcosm of the larger society from which Mabel Waring is alienated. The ubiquitous but unseen presence of Clarissa Dalloway, the un-canny intuition of the servant who recognizes Mabel's class status, the undescribed drawing room where the party occurs, and the party guests all contribute to Mabel's sense of her ''appalling inadequacy.''

Symbolism

As the title suggests, Mabel's new dress functions as an important symbol throughout the narrative. Its old-fashioned cut and material stand as everpresent reminders to the party guests and, more importantly, to Mabel that she does not belong. This enormously self-absorbed woman sees her dress each time that she passes a mirror, and Mabel mentions it to everyone she meets. Paradoxically, the dress, which ''marks'' Mabel as inferior, is what she uses to begin conversations: '''It's so old-fashioned,' she says to Charles Burt, making him stop on his way to talk to someone else.'' She gets his attention, if not the response she wanted, when he exclaims, ''Mabel's got a new dress!''

The fly is another important symbol in the story. Mabel repeatedly refers to herself as a fly in a saucer. She cannot escape from it, as the milk has covered her wings. The other guests are butterflies

Fashionably dressed Londoners at Wimbledon in the 1920s.

and dragonflies, able to dance and fly; she alone remains in the saucer. The fly thus signifies Mabel's estrangement and isolation from her contemporaries.

Historical Context

Although World War I had ended nearly nine years before the publication of Virginia Woolf's short story "The New Dress," in 1927, the lingering effects of the war resonate throughout the work. Many commentators have remarked that much of Woolf's fiction has little connection to events taking place in the world. This may seem to be true of "The New Dress." It records one woman's impressions and experiences at a party. The disillusionment and despair that Mabel Waring exhibits during the party, however, may be seem to mirror the anguish that touched much of English society after the war.

Britain in the 1920s was characterized by contradiction and paradox. It was a time of celebration—Britain and its allies had won the war—yet postwar elation quickly faded as war debts and loss of markets threatened to destabilize the English economy. Unemployment figures rose sharply, and prices fell concurrently. By 1929, 2.5% owned two-thirds of the nation's wealth and 1.5% received 23% of its income.

In spite of such disparities, however, the country as a whole prospered. People were healthier; infant mortality decreased and longevity increased. Literacy rates increased. There was an improvement in the quality of life, particularly for women. The 1918 Act gave all men over 21 the right to vote and all women over 30 the same privilege. These steps toward equality led to an increased democratization of British society. Moreover, the Matrimonial Act of 1922 allowed women to sue for divorce on the same grounds used by men.

It was within this landscape that Virginia Woolf wrote. Growing up at the turn of the century, she had witnessed enormous societal changes. Increased communication, social mobility, and affordable commodities dramatically changed how people lived. Estimates show that 9 of 10 homes owned radios; easy access to news events occurring throughout the world forged new links between members of all classes of society. Movies also helped unite people; 45% of the population went to the cinema at least once per week. Finally, electrical appliances changed life in unprecedented ways. Although many appliances had been available even before the war, their

Compare
&
Contrast

- **1920s:** Most items of womens' apparel are home-made or custom-made. Apart from basics such as stockings, underclothing, and nightgowns, most women have dresses made for them during once-yearly or seasonal sessions with dressmakers.

  1990s: Most clothing is bought off-the-rack. Only a fractional percentage of the world's population regularly buys couture, or custom-made clothing.

- **1920s:** Very little is known about different kinds of mental illness, despite widespread familiarity with the theories of pioneering psychoanalyist Sigmund Freud. Woolf's mental breakdowns are

variously diagnosed and treated primarily with "rest cures."

  1990s: The number of recognized mental illnesses codified by the medical profession has grown from several dozen to several hundred. A combination of drug and psychiatric therapies are recommended for most mental illnesses.

- **1920s:** Britain offers unemployment insurance for the first time; it does not cover domestic servants or farm workers.

  1990s: Few households continue to employ domestic servants. Most household employees work for agencies rather than individuals.

---

wide-scale use was not realized until the 1920s. For example, the invention of electricity promoted the development of refrigerators. Better storage meant food lasted longer, and this revolutionized food production, distribution, and consumption. This led to another change in behavior patters: daily marketing became less necessary.

Such technological advances and material gains radically transformed people's lives. Intellectual and scientific advances also contributed to a change in how people viewed themselves. Darwinian evolutionary theory, Einstein's theory of relativity, and Freud's concept of the unconscious, to name only three contemporary social and scientific hypotheses, diminished the sense of certainty that had previously characterized the British Empire. These ideas helped undermine what the war had not destroyed. They suggested that humankind could not with any certitude assume that it enjoyed a privileged place in the universe.

Working within this atmosphere of skepticism was James Joyce, whose publication of *Ulysses* in 1922 was a watershed in literary history. Woolf's own *Mrs. Dalloway* in 1923 and T.S. Eliot's *The Waste Land* in the same year contributed to the passing of Victorian sensibilities. D. H. Lawrence's

frank and unabashed characterizations of human sexuality and Aldous Huxley's satirical novels also helped make the 1920s a time of radical and far-reaching consequences for the development of new literary styles and trends.

Critical Overview

The publication of the short story, "The New Dress" in *A Haunted House and Other Short Stories* suggests that the story had been well-received when Woolf initially published it in 1927 in the New York monthly magazine the *Forum*. Woolf chose this story, one of eighteen, for a collection she planned to publish in 1942, but her suicide in 1941 postponed the edition's publication until Leonard Woolf edited the stories in 1944.

Most Woolf scholars have focused on her novels, essays, and diaries. Consequently, the significance of the short stories in Woolf's canon has been largely overlooked. Leonard Woolf's comments in the foreword to *A Haunted House* may have contributed to this. He explains that Woolf considered short fiction an interlude, a form of writing that enabled her to relax during or in between writing her novels.

Only a few of her stories ("Kew Gardens," "The Mark on the Wall," and "Monday or Tuesday") have generated much critical work. There has, however, been some attention given to "The New Dress," though generally in its relationship to Woolf's novel, *Mrs. Dalloway.* For example, Jean Guiguet organizes Woolf's stories into three periods: 1917–1921, 1927–1929, and 1938–1940 and explores the connectons between these "experiments" and the development of Woolf's novelistic technique. However, while he convincingly establishes connections between the short fiction and novels, he reminds us that many of the stories, particularly "The New Dress," are also "self-contained narratives."

Although "The New Dress" can stand as an autonomous narrative, Stella McNichol encouraged reading it alongside six other thematically-related stories. Their "simple narrative and chronological unity "prompted McNichol to publish them as a collection, which she called *Mrs. Dalloway's Party: A Short Story Sequence.* While the editor states that one need not read the novels to understand the stories, she cautions that if one wants a thorough understanding of the novels, especially *Mrs. Dalloway,* the short stories are a good place to begin. Other critics have specifically emphasized the political vision Woolf presents in her short fiction. In Selma Meyerowitz's 1981 essay, she reads "The New Dress" as a statement of the vulnerability of female characters to class and social discrimination in English society. The short stories, she cautions, not only demonstrate the stream-of-consciousness narration so familiar to Woolf readers but also show Woolf's censure of social institutions that deny women access to education and the means to affect social change.

Criticism

Teresa Lyle

In the following essay, Lyle examines the changing social and cultural conditions in England following World War I and their influence on such Woolf short stories as "The New Dress."

Virginia Woolf had seen the devastating effects of social unrest and war, but she also understood that small events in a single life had enormous conse-

quences. A gesture or nod might radically change a person's thoughts or course of action. In an essay published in *Modern Fiction,* therefore, she encouraged writers to "record the atoms as they fall upon the mind in the order in which they fall . . . let us trace the pattern, however disconnected and incoherent in appearance, which each sight or incident scores upon the consciousness. Let us not take it for granted that life exists more fully in what is commonly thought big than in what is commonly thought small."

We see this attention to gesture in most of Woolf's fiction, including her short stories. In "The New Dress," published in 1927, Woolf traces Mabel Waring's thoughts as she attends a party hosted by Clarissa Dalloway. A forty-year-old wife of a minor official and the mother of two, Mabel has a yellow dress made for the party. Far from being insignificant, Mabel's dress prompts a series of reflections on her life. Its material and old-fashioned cut remind Mabel of her humble origins and low social status. Mabel's acute self-consciousness leads her to despair and hopelessness. She sees herself moving through the Dalloway drawing room suffering immense tortures, as "if spears were thrown at her yellow dress from all sides." This paranoia, however, is not without justification. The enemies may appear less tangible than those on the war front, but even without guns and tanks the guests exact colossal harm by their insincerity and inauthenticity. They become unyielding opponents, and trench warfare gives way to drawing-room campaigns; battles are fought through polite but insincere conversations.

Even though Mabel realizes the vacuousness of the party guests, she longs to be one of them. Rose Shaw, Charles Burt, and Mrs. Holman, in particular, represent the best and worst of the world Mabel envies. The ease with which Rose Shaw would have responded to insults, the delight with which Charles Burt had withheld his praise, and the ability with which Mrs. Holman had risen above the mundane are qualities Mabel desperately desires.

Instead, however, Mabel sees herself as a fly in a saucer. Although she tries to picture the other guests similarly, they appear as dragonflies, or butterflies, or "beautiful insects, dancing, fluttering, skimming, while she alone dragged herself up out of the saucer." Later in the evening, when one guest calls attention to Mabel's new dress, she again refers to herself as "the poor fly [that] was absolutely shoved into the middle of the saucer." As Mabel

What Do I Read Next?

- *Mrs. Dalloway*, Virginia Woolf's fourth novel, was published in 1925 and uses interior monologue from Dalloway's point of view to describe the events leading up to her party.

- Dean R. Baldwin's *Virginia Woolf: A Study of the Short Fiction* (1989) traces three periods of Woolf short-story writing and provides an overview of all of Woolf's short fiction. He uses a strong biographical focus to explore the stories, and the study contains a collection of critical essays on selected works.

- Avrom Fleishman's essay "Forms of the Woolfian Short Story," included in *Virginia Woolf: Revaluation and Continuity*, considers the extent to which Woolf's stories contribute to the development of the modernist short story.

- Stella McNichol's edition of *Mrs. Dalloway's Party: A Short Story Sequence*, published in 1973, offers a useful introduction to the seven Woolf short stories that are thematically related to *Mrs. Dalloway*.

- T.S. Eliot's *The Waste Land* was published in 1923 by Hogarth Press, which was owned and operated by Woolf and her husband. It provides a useful social critique of postwar society and emphasizes the sense of despair and hopelessness of Mabel Waring's generation.

- Aldous Huxley's 1923 novel *Antic Hay* is interesting for its depiction of postwar London's bohemian district.

- F. Scott Fitzgerald's short stories collected in *Flappers and Philosophers* (1920) and *Tales of the Jazz Age* (1922) chronicle the values and behavior of the United States in the decade before the Great Depression.

---

moves from conversation to conversation, her distress increases as she imagines herself trapped in the saucer.

"The New Dress" thus supports Marjorie Brace's claim that for Woolf the "unknowableness of people and the impossibilities of communion were ... terrifying." This belief is underscored each time Mabel tries to connect with the other guests. For example, when she turns to Rose Shaw for assurance about her dress, Rose responds, "It's perfectly charming," but Mabel watches her "looking her up and down with that little satirical pucker of the lips which she expected," and this look belies all assurances. Mabel then turns to Robert Haydon and laments, "'I feel like some dowdy, decrepit, horribly dingy old fly.'" But Haydon's polite response cannot fool Mabel, who recognizes that he is "quite insincere." A final and particularly telling example occurs during her conversation with Mrs. Holman, a matronly figure who, according to Mabel, "could never get enough sympathy and snatched what little there was greedily, as if it were her right." She cannot understand Mabel's need, but what Mabel does not yet realize is that her self-absorption makes her equally unresponsive to Mrs. Holman's needs. Thus, no real connection occurs between the women. As Mabel engages in a perfunctory conversation with the matron, her thoughts drift and wander to her past.

Mabel's regret that she had not married an "empire builder" is clear here. Her description of her marriage to Hubert, "with his safe, permanent underling's job in the Law Courts," reveals her dissatisfaction. Yet she admits that in her life with Hubert she had had "divine moments" when she would say, "This is it. This has happened. This is it!" These epiphanies, or moments of insight, occur during ordinary moments and are inspired by nothing out of the ordinary. Her memory of them temporarily assuages Mabel's stress and loneliness, and in a short-lived instant of hope she determines to escape from the saucer and her meaningless life.

Mabel's escape fails, however, when she leaves the party and tells Clarissa Dalloway, ''I have enjoyed myself enormously.'' Whatever flicker of inspiration those earlier moments had sparked is extinguished as Mabel finally recognizes her own complicity in the affair. She exclaims to herself: ''Lies, lies, lies! . . . Right in the saucer!'' In this instance, the reader realizes that although Mabel has always lived on the fringe, such a position ironically affords her a small degree of comfort. As she thanks Mrs. Barnet for ''helping her and wrapped herself, round and round and round, in the Chinese cloak she had worn these twenty years,'' we understand that Mabel has chosen this life, this marginal status, because she lacks the courage to change.

Selma Meyerowitz has commented that the female characters in Woolf's short stories feel inferior and inadequate. They are dissatisfied with their existence and cannot achieve fulfillment because of the deceptive nature of the class-bound society in which they live. This scenario is seen in ''The New Dress,'' in which the reader witnesses Mabel's alienation and detachment from the upper-class world of the party. Yet Mabel's heightened self-consciousness and self-loathing arise as much from the banality of existence as from class inequality. Mabel's ruminations are as much about boredom as impoverishment. When Mabel exclaims that ''a party makes things either much more real, or much less real,'' she may be referring either to class differences or the realization that we are all ultimately trapped in the saucer.

In ''The New Dress,'' Woolf presents the Dalloway party as a microcosm of English society. Mrs. Dalloway, the elusive but controlling presence of the party, represents the unseen but all-powerful forces that propel society forward; Rose Shaw, the charming and always appropriately dressed guest, represents the successful player of the game; Mrs. Holman, with an overwhelming sense of domestic responsibility, represents women of a past age. Similarly, Robert Haydon, the polite, old-fashioned man, is a throwback to an earlier time, whereas Charles Burt represents the witty, urbane young man of the postwar era. Mrs. Barnet, the servant who recognizes the guests' status and rank, represents a threat to the class-conscious women who aspire to the affluence of the Dalloways. Finally, Mabel represents a group of alienated and estranged women so wrapped up in social conventions that she chooses the masquerade rather than exclusion, despite its enormous burden and sense of dissatisfaction. The story's tragedy centers on Mabel's com-

> " Mabel's dress prompts a series of reflections on her life. Its material and old-fashioned cut remind Mabel of her humble origins and low social status."

plete self-absorption and incapacity for action, which make her as unauthentic as the other guests. Like them, she cannot comprehend a life outside; the rules of the game may not be those that she wants to follow, but she never works to change them. Social prestige and its trappings leave Mabel empty, and there is no hope of emotional fulfillment. Although Mabel questions the values of this society, she ultimately embraces them. Such scenarios occur in most of Woolf's short fiction; ''The New Dress'' is the rule, not the exception.

In a diary entry from April 27, 1925, shortly before the publication of *Mrs. Dalloway,* Virginia Woolf wrote:

> ''[My] present reflection is that people have any number of states of consciousness: and I should like to investigate the* party consciousness, the frock consciousness, etc. The fashion world of the Becks . . . is certainly one: where people secrete an envelope which connects them and protects them from others, like myself, who am outside the envelope, foreign bodies.''

Mabel's source of anguish stems from her position in between. She can neither secure herself within an envelope nor remain outside of it: ''Her odious, weak, vacillating character'' prevents her from choosing a side, so she remains hopelessly suspended between two worlds—or, as she might imagine, she is a fly trapped in a saucer.

Source: Teresa Lyle, ''Overview of 'The New Dress','' for *Short Stories for Students,* Gale, 1998.

Thomas March
In the following essay, March examines the insecurity and self-ridicule demonstrated by the protagonist of ''The New Dress.''

Virginia Woolf's short story "The New Dress" is often overshadowed by her more popular stories, such as "The Duchess and the Jeweler," "The Mark on the Wall," and "Kew Gardens." Stella McNichol includes "The New Dress in *Mrs Dalloway's Party,*" a volume of short stories by Woolf that centers around the experiences of guests at the party Mrs. Dalloway throws in Woolf's novel *Mrs Dalloway.* McNichol writes that "The New Dress" "was written in 1924 when Virginia Woolf was revising *Mrs Dalloway* for publication." Here, though, as in the other stories in that volume, Woolf gives us not Clarissa Dalloway's experience of her own party but the experiences of other guests at that party. Mabel, the protagonist of "The New Dress" is one of those guests, and she feels out of place, insecure about her new dress, unable to see herself as anything but ridiculed, unable to take a compliment, yet critical of those that she receives. She cannot enjoy the party because she will not *let* herself enjoy the party. The party, for Mabel, is a self-inflicted torture—an exercise in masochism and, ironically, vanity, from the moment she receives the invitation.

As soon as Mabel walks in the door of the Dalloway home, she has reservations about her dress. When Mrs. Barnet greets her in the foyer and helps her to arrange herself before entering the party, "Mabel had her first serious suspicion that something was wrong as she took her cloak off and Mrs Barnet, while handing her the mirror and touching the brushes and thus drawing her attention . . . to all the appliances for tidying and improving hair, complexion, clothes, which existed on the dressing-table, confirmed the suspicion—that it was not right, not quite right." But, as will become evident shortly, it is not Mrs. Barnet or her innocent actions here that have caused Mabel to be so self-conscious and insecure about her appearance. Shortly thereafter, Mrs. Dalloway herself comes to greet Mabel. Mabel's reaction is to reflect that "It was not *right.* And at once the misery which she had always tried to hide, the profound dissatisfaction—the sense she had had, ever since she was a child, of being inferior to other people—set upon her, relentlessly, remorselessly, with an intensity which she could not beat off." Thus it is clear that Mabel is insecure before she ever sets foot in the party. In short, she has a chip on her shoulder.

She goes on, as she is entering the party, to recall the arrival of Mrs. Dalloway's invitation. She remembers that her reaction was that "she could not be fashionable. It was absurd to pretend it even—

fashion meant cut, meant style, meant thirty guineas at least—but why not be original? . . . And . . . she had taken that old fashion book of her mother's, a Paris fashion book of the time of the Empire . . . , and so set herself . . . trying to be like them . . . an orgy of self-love, which deserved to be chastised, and so rigged herself out like this." It would seem, then, that Mabel is undaunted by her limited financial means and determined to make the best of them by procuring for herself a dress that is "original." She busies herself with the determination of just what sort of dress it will be, raiding the fashions of the past in "an orgy of self-love." This, she concludes, deserves "to be chastised, and so rigged herself out like this." That is, the dress, which begins as a statement of originality and vanity—indicators of self-confidence—ends as the means by which she will bring ridicule on herself to punish herself for her vanity and frivolity. She cannot indulge herself without guilt.

Neither can she accept a compliment. Mabel's entire stay at the party consists of her encountering other partygoers whose compliments she either dismisses as lies or whom she secretly chastises for failing to compliment her. The dress is convenient to her larger goal of allowing herself to be ridiculed. As she enters the party, "she dared not look in the glass," an indicator of how truly insecure Mabel is. Furthermore, she "felt like a dressmaker's dummy standing there, for young people to stick pins into." But the choice to wear such a dress is Mabel's, and this response is not unexpected. Although Rose Shaw calls Mabel's dress "perfectly charming," Mabel is skeptical of the compliment and bitterly begins her metaphor of the flies: "We are all like flies trying to crawl over the edge of the saucer." Just as she asserts this, however, she changes her mind abruptly and notes that "she could not see them like that, not other people. She saw herself like that." So insecure is she that she ultimately turns even her criticism of others around on herself. In the following exchange, however, she tries to have someone compliment her and mean it. "'I feel like some dowdy, decrepit, horribly dingy old fly,' she said, making Robert Haydon stop just to hear her say that, just to reassure herself by furbishing up a poor weak-kneed phrase and so showing how detached she was, how witty, that she did not feel in the least out of anything. And, of course, Robert Haydon answered something, quite polite, quite insincere, which she saw through instantly, and said to herself, directly he went . . . 'Lies, lies lies!'." She has provoked the compliment, and once she has it, she cannot believe it. She *will* not believe it, perhaps because she *has* to provoke it. Whether provoked or unprovoked, however, the compliments Mabel receives are invariably rejected.

After the exchange with Haydon, Mabel turns to another flashback. She recalls the scene in Miss Milan's shop as the dress was being made. "Rid of cares and wrinkles, what she had dreamed of herself was there—a beautiful woman. Just for a second (she had not dared look longer . . .), there looked at her . . . , a grey-white, mysteriously smiling, charming girl, the core of herself, the soul of herself; and it was not vanity only, not only self-love that made her think it good, tender and true." At the fitting, she sees herself as beautiful, the dress as wonderful, and she concludes that this assessment is the result not of "vanity" but of something else, which goes unnamed. Yet she only watches herself in the mirror "for a second," indicating that she cannot sustain the illusion of her own beauty. She is fundamentally insecure and can believe the contrary only in brief and fleeting moments. When she returns her attention to the present again, to the party, "the whole thing had vanished." It had vanished long before, however, if indeed the belief in her own beauty has *ever* been present.

The remainder of Mabel's experiences at the party consist of more rejection of compliments. Mabel lures Charles Burt to herself by exclaiming "It's so old fashioned." Mabel tries "to make herself think that she meant, that it was the picture and not her dress, that was old-fashioned." Of course, she is hoping that Charles will think that she is referring to her dress and stop to contradict her. She thinks that "one word of praise, one word of affection from Charles would have made all the difference to her at the moment." It is clear, though, from the way in which Mabel has reacted to previous compliments, that this is not true. She would only have accused him of lying, have said "Lies! Lies! Lies!" to herself once again. Mabel is, of course, unaware of what she is doing: "'Why,' she asked herself, 'can't I feel one thing always, feel quite sure that Miss Milan is right, and Charles wrong and stick to it'." After her conversation with Mrs. Holman, Mabel assumes that "Mrs. Holman . . . [thought] her the most dried-up, unsympathetic twig she had ever met, absurdly dressed, too, and would tell everyone about Mabel's fantastic appearance." Yet Mrs. Holman has said no such thing.

The party, for Mabel, is a failure before she ever arrives or receives an invitation. In "Worship-

> **"The party, for Mabel, is a self-inflicted torture—an exercise in masochism and, ironically, vanity, from the moment she receives the invitation."**

ping Solid Objects: The Pagan World of Virginia Woolf," Marjorie Brace writes that Mabel's dress, "designed to be exotic, appears only laughably eccentric to her once she arrives at a party where she is doomed to be either snubbed or bored because—we grasp the point only too quickly—her own unreflecting egotism turns all dresses and parties drab." However, Mabel is not an egotist. She does not have an exaggeratedly high opinion of herself; quite the opposite. She cannot believe in her own fantasies of her own beauty, and she cannot believe in others' assertions, whether requested or spontaneous, of her beauty. In *Virginia Woolf and Her Works,* Jean Guiguet writes that "Mabel, having gone through the hell of her shame and loneliness, reaches the safe shore of happy memories, which reconcile her to herself and her life; she acquires new strength and resolution; but is it through having looked in the mirror, having once again encountered the same Mabel that the others see? She can merely mumble a conventional falsehood, and goes back to her own truth." Her "own truth," however, has not been left at the door upon her entering the party. It infects and affects every event of the party as Mabel experiences it. The "truth" of her being unattractive prevents her from enjoying the party, and she has created these circumstances herself, using the dress as punishment for a vanity that never truly existed. For Mabel, insecurity is primary and confidence is secondary and fleeting. Mabel tells Mrs Dalloway, as she is leaving, that she has "enjoyed" herself, and then thinks "'Lies, lies, lies!'. . . and 'Right in the saucer!'" She has applied this phrase to others previously and now applies it to herself; they have "lied" about her appearance, and she has "lied" about having a good time. Or has she? After all, this is precisely the result that Mabel's actions have encouraged—the result that, for whatever reason, Mabel has needed to punish herself, to verify her own insecurities. In Mabel's world, everyone is a liar.

Source: Thomas March, ''Overview of 'The New Dress','' in *Short Stories for Students,* Gale, 1998.

Selma Meyerowitz

In the following excerpt, Meyerowitz provides a thematic interpretation of ''The New Dress'' that focuses on the self-consciousness of the central character, Mabel Waring.

Social and class discrimination . . . destroy emotional fulfilment in ''The New Dress,'' as seen in the character of Mabel Waring. Mabel is of the lower class, part of a family of ten 'never having money enough, always skimping and paring.' At Mrs. Dalloway's party, she thinks of 'her own drawing-room so shabby' and of her inability to dress fashionably because it is too costly. Mabel's anxiety about her appearance, her manners, and her values is provoked by her encounter with the society world of the Dalloways; however, her insecurity is more pervasive: 'At once the misery which she always tried to hide, the profound dissatisfaction—the sense that she had had, ever since she was a child, of being inferior to other people—set upon her, relentlessly, remorselessly, with an intensity which she could not beat off.' When she imagines that everyone is judging her appearance, Mabel's painful self-consciousness turns to self-hatred. Sensing her ineffectuality, she expresses her low self-esteem through an animal image, 'We are all like flies trying to crawl over the edge of the saucer'; she also expresses a similar sense of alienation from others: 'She was a fly—but the others were dragonflies, butterflies, beautiful insects.' Her need for assurance makes her attempt to communicate with another guest, Robert Haydon, whose polite but insincere comments leave her even more disillusioned and unhappy with herself and her social interactions.

Virginia Woolf suggests that society's conventions destroy Mabel's inner resources, since she implies that there are moments when Mabel has self-confidence and experiences pleasure.

Mabel's sense of alienation also exists because her insecurity makes her self-centered and unable to respond to others. She sees herself and another guest, Mrs Holman, as a yellow dot and a black dot, both detached; therefore, 'it was impossible that the black dot . . . should make the yellow dot, sitting solitary, self-centred, feel what the black dot was

feeling, yet they pretended!' Neither Mabel nor Mrs Holman understands what the other feels, because each demands sympathy for herself: 'Ah, it was tragic, this greed, this clamour of human beings . . . for sympathy—it was tragic, could one have felt it and not merely pretended to feel it!' To Mabel, and to Virginia Woolf, who presumably uses the above comment by the narrator to imply her own view, pretence and lies are more despicable and more destructive to interpersonal communication than a self-centred demand for sympathy.

Woolf does suggest positive values in this story. Again, although Mabel feels only distress from social interactions, she can at least remember moments of spontaneous joy, either in nature, where social competition and alienation do not exist, or in everyday activities. . . . Mabel's sense of the meaning and peace of life gives her a momentary determination to reject dissatisfying social relationships and strive for a way of life which provides 'divine moments.' She decides to leave Mrs Dalloway's party, but she is again caught in the trap of social intercourse. Exclaiming, 'I have enjoyed myself' to Mr and Mrs Dalloway, she realises that she is back 'right in the saucer.' Her struggle to rise above superficial social amenities and painful social interactions is thus largely unsuccessful. Mabel cannot develop a consistently independent sense of values necessary for security. Instead, she is vulnerable to social status and social pretences.

Source: Selma Meyerowitz, ''What Is to Console Us? The Politics of Deception in Woolf's Short Stories,'' in *New Feminist Essays on Virginia Woolf,* edited by Jane Marcus, University of Nebraska Press, 1981, pp. 238–52.

Stella McNichol

In the following excerpt, McNichol notes the interrelated nature of the stories she has collected and published as Mrs. Dalloway's Party: A Short Story Sequence, *to one another and to the novel* Mrs Dalloway.

''The New Dress'' was written in 1924 when Virginia Woolf was revising *Mrs Dalloway* for publication. In a pencil note to the manuscript opening of the story Virginia Woolf states:

> The New Dress At Mrs D's party She got it on this theory the theory of clothes but very little money this brings in the relation with sex; her estimate of herself.

''Mrs Dalloway in Bond Street'' and ''The New Dress'' are both connected with the genesis of the novel *Mrs Dalloway;* the other five stories written consecutively and probably not later than

May 1925 form a kind of epilogue to it. Though the party goes on after the novel is finished Mrs Dalloway's is no longer its central consciousness. The focus now shifts from guest to guest revealing their reflections and insights. It is the other side of Mrs Dalloway's party. The seven stories or chapters, therefore, besides being all centred on Mrs Dalloway were also all written more or less at the same time as the novel.

The Mrs Dalloway stories, then, do form a related group in that they relate to each other thematically: the social theme and subject of the party and the actual or implied presence of Mrs Dalloway give a unity to them.

Source: Stella McNichol, in an introduction to *Mrs Dalloway's Party: A Short Story Sequence,* by Virginia Woolf, edited by Stella McNichol, Hogarth Press, 1973, pp. 9–17.

Jean Guiguet

In the following excerpt, Guiguet discusses the relationship between the short story "The New Dress" and the novel Mrs. Dalloway's Party. *He identifies prominent themes, main characters, significant action, and satirical elements of the story and praises the story as a self-contained narrative.*

With "The New Dress" we come to the stories which form part of what one might call the *Mrs Dalloway* saga, which comprises also "The Man Who Loved His Kind," "Together and Apart" and "The Summing Up." In this group, "The New Dress" stands apart. From its date, 1927, as well as from several pieces of internal evidence, it seems to be a reject left over from the novel. We see the famous party through the eyes of Mabel, a humble acquaintance of the Dalloways. Like the other guests in the novel, she is greeted in the cloakroom by Mrs Barnet, who sizes up each visitor's class and dress. The perspicacity of the old servant . . . lies at the root of Mabel's misfortunes; Mrs Barnet's attitude makes her aware of the unsuitability of her dress, and this feeling isolates her during the whole party, making her conscious, amidst all these rich people, of her own poverty, then of the failure of her life, and revealing to her, moreover, the vanity and sterility of such social contacts. After having endured the hypocrisy, indifference and selfishness of others and her own humiliation, she makes her retreat with a polite lie: "I have enjoyed myself enormously." This lie synthesizes all the lies, all the treacheries not merely of these few hours but of the whole of existence. We see from this that its setting is not the only factor that connects "The New

Dress" with *Mrs Dalloway*. The satirical implications of the story are akin to those of the novel; at an even deeper level, through her pessimism, Mabel recalls Septimus, while like him she is connected with Clarissa by "a divine moment" of sea and sand and sun. Apart from the recurrence of this theme we may note also, as though referring to Peter Walsh and his life-story, Mabel's youthful daydream: she had pictured herself living in India, married to a hero, whereas Hubert, her husband, has a dreary subordinate job in the Law Courts. Finally, perhaps she was intended to form a parallel to Ellie Henderson, or else to take her place at the party. Like Ellie, in fact, Mabel is an outsider, reluctantly invited at the last minute, and is too poor to spend money on her dress. The distance that divides her from this world allows it to be seen, through her, from a different angle to that of the other characters. Nevertheless, Mabel's viewpoint is as unlike Ellie's as is their way of dressing: Ellie is natural and sweet-tempered, whereas Mabel is timid and embittered. Perhaps Virginia Woolf was rightly reluctant to alter the atmosphere of the closing pages of her novel by this corrosive ingredient, and therefore relegated this character into the drawer where she kept her rough sketches.

In spite of all the links that can be found between the short story and the novel, "The New Dress" is none the less a perfectly self-contained narrative, with its own progress and peripeteia. Mabel, having gone through the hell of her shame and loneliness, reaches the safe shore of happy memories, which reconcile her to herself and her life; she acquires new strength and resolution; but is it through having looked in the mirror, having once again encountered the same Mabel that the others see? She can merely mumble a conventional falsehood, and goes back to her own truth.

Source: Jean Guiguet, "Synthesis and Fiction: *Mrs. Dalloway,* Stories and Sketches," in *Virginia Woolf and Her Works,* translated by Jean Stewart, Harcourt, Brace, 1965, pp. 329–43.

Sources

Brace, Marjorie. "Worshipping Sold Objects: The Pagan World of Virginia Woolf," In *Accent Anthology: Selections from Accent, A Quarterly of New Literature,* edited by Kerker Quinn and Charles Shattuck, pp. 489-95. New York: Harcourt, Brace, and Co., 1946.

Woolf, Virginia. "Modern Fiction." In her *The Common Reader,* New York: Harcourt, Brace and Co., 1925.

Further Reading

Baldwin, Dean R. *Virginia Woolf: A Study of the Short Fiction,* Twayne, 1989, pp. 1-76.

A book-length analysis of Woolf's short stories which places them in a largely biographical context. Also contains short critical essays on selected stories.

Chapman, R. T. "'The Lady in the Looking-Glass': Modes of Perception in a Short Story by Virginia Woolf," *Modern Fiction Studies,* Vol. 18, No. 3, Autumn, 1972, pp. 331- 37.

Explains that Woolf's stories are fillled with the minute details of life. The way characters perceive these details constantly changes and drives the narratives forward to well- structured totalities that serve a greater function than the constituent parts.

Hussey, Mark. *Virginia Woolf A-Z: The Essential Reference to Her Life and Writings,* Oxford University Press, 1995, pp. 169-79.

An indispensable reference tool that provides lengthy historical and critical entries on Woolf's fiction, diaries, letters, and essays. It also offers listings for notable figures in Woolf's culture.

Mott, Frank Luther. "The Forum," in his *A History of American Magazines, 1885-1905,* Vol. 4, Harvard University Press, 1957, pp. 511-23.

Five-volume history of the rise of the American magazine industry. Provides detailed historical and contextual information for all major magazines published in the United States. Offers editorial, circulation, and subscription information for each publication.

Rice, Thomas Jackson. "Studies of the Short Stories," in his *Virginia Woolf: A Guide to Research,* Garland, 1984, pp. 163-67.

A short, now-dated annotated bibliography of essays and books written about Woolf's work. Organized by genre.

Roberts, Clayton, and David Roberts. "Britain between the Wars," in their *A History of England, 1688 to the Present,* Prentice-Hall, 1991, pp. 748-78.

An accessible and interesting textbook of English history. Follows the traditional periodization of British history and provides a useful overview of the social and cultural trends of each period. Offers helpful suggestions for further reading.

Woolf, Leonard. "Foreword," in *A Haunted House,* by Virginia Woolf, Harcourt, Brace, and Company, 1944, pp. v-vi.

Places Virginia Woolf's short story writing in the context of her other work and suggests that she used this genre as an interlude between the novels.

The Open Boat

Stephen Crane
1897

Published in 1897, "The Open Boat" is based on an actual incident from Stephen Crane's life in January of that year. While traveling to Cuba to work as a newspaper correspondent during the Cuban insurrection against Spain, Crane was stranded at sea for thirty hours after his ship, the *Commodore,* sank off the coast of Florida. Crane and three other men were forced to navigate their way to shore in a small boat. One of the men, an oiler named Billy Higgins, drowned while trying to swim to shore. Crane wrote the story "The Open Boat" soon afterward. The story tells of the travails of four men shipwrecked at sea who must make their way to shore in a dinghy. Crane's grippingly realistic depiction of their life-threatening ordeal captures the sensations and emotions of struggle for survival against the forces of nature. Because of the work's philosophical speculations, it is often classified as a work of Naturalism, a literary offshoot of the Realist movement. "The Open Boat" has proved an enduring classic that speaks to the timeless experience of suffering a close call with death.

Author Biography

Stephen Crane enjoyed both popular success and critical acclaim as a leading American author of the Realist school. Born in Newark, New Jersey in 1871, Crane was the youngest of fourteen children

born to Jonathan Townley Crane and Mary Helen Peck Crane. His father was a Methodist minister and his mother a devout social activist. Crane was raised in the idealistic atmosphere of evangelical reformism. Crane's father died in 1880 and his mother had to support the family by doing church work and writing for religious journals. Death became a familiar event in the Crane household; by 1892 only seven of the fourteen children were still living.

Crane attended military school at Claverack College, where he pursued an interest in Civil War studies. He later spent some semesters at Lafayette College and then Syracuse University, though during these years he was mainly concerned with freelance writing and the prospect of becoming a novelist. In 1891, Crane moved to New York City, where he supported himself by writing for the *New York Tribune.* His first-hand observations of the gritty life in the Bowery inspired his first novel *Maggie: A Girl of the Streets,* published in 1893 under the pseudonym ''Johnston Smith.'' Its frank portrayal of the sordid lives of the urban poor caused many publishers to reject the manuscript, requiring Crane to publish it on his own. Although *Maggie* received critical praise from prominent literary Realists, including Hamlin Garland and William Dean Howells, it was not widely read until its second printing in 1896 after Crane's reputation was established. In 1895, Crane achieved international fame with his second novel, *The Red Badge of Courage,* which told the story of a young Henry Fleming's experiences in the Civil War. This unsentimental account vividly captured the sensations of the battlefield as well as the emotions of the young soldier whose romantic illusions about warfare are shattered by his encounter with the real thing. Crane also published a collection of poetry in 1895 titled *The Black Riders and Other Lines.*

In 1897 Crane decided to leave New York to become a war correspondent. While covering the Cuban Revolution, Crane met Cora Taylor, the proprietor of a Florida hotel and brothel. The couple would eventually move to England as common-law husband and wife. While still covering the war in Cuba in 1897, Crane was shipwrecked at sea off the Florida coast. He was stranded at sea for thirty hours with three other men, who eventually rowed to shore in a small life raft. One of the men, an oiler named Billy Higgins, drowned in the surf while trying to swim to shore. Crane later turned the experience into what many consider his greatest short story, ''The Open Boat'' (1897). For the rest

of his life, he continued to work as a journalist and war correspondent, using his experiences as the basis for his fiction. Unable to return to New York because of his conflict with police, Crane spent most of his last years in England, where he lived beyond his means. His reputation as a leading author of the Realist school led him to form close friendships with other major writers, including Joseph Conrad, Henry James, and H. G. Wells. Crane's later works, including *The Third Violet* (1897) and *Active Service* (1899), were not considered up to the level of his earlier successes. In 1899 Crane's health began to deteriorate and he found himself plagued with financial troubles. While working on a new novel in 1900, Crane succumbed to tuberculosis and died at the age of twenty-eight.

Plot Summary

''The Open Boat'' begins with a description of men aboard a small boat on a rough sea. Details begin to emerge. They are four survivors of a shipwreck: the cook, overweight and sloppily dressed, who is bailing water out of the bottom of the boat; the oiler, a physically powerful man named Billie who is rowing with one oar; the unnamed correspondent, who is rowing with the other oar; and the captain, who lies injured in the bottom of the boat. Each man stares intently at the waves which threaten to swamp the boat. A few characteristics become evident about each man: the cook is the most talkative of the four; the oiler, taciturn and an adept seaman. The captain is profoundly sorrowful at the loss of his ship and the potential loss of life along with it. The correspondent remains less well defined. The reader does learn that he engages in rather pointless discussion with the cook about the liklihood of being seen by rescuers or of finding a house of refuge on shore. They debate the points until the oiler has twice repeated that they are ''not there yet.''

This section features further character development and superb descriptive passages depicting the tiny boat's course across the rough waves. The captain briefly expresses doubt about their chances of survival, but then reassures the men that ''we'll get ashore all right.'' The captain is the first to spot a barely visible lighthouse and they know they are approaching shore.

The captain improvises a sail using his overcoat and an oar to give the oiler and correspondent a chance to rest, but when the wind dies they resume rowing. The exhausted correspondent thinks of the absurdity—from his current point of view—of people chosing to row a boat for pleasure. He shares this thought with the other men, and the oiler smiles in sympathy. Unwilling to risk running the boat ashore in the rough surf, the men smoke cigars, drink from their water supply, and wait to be spotted by the lighthouse rescue crew.

The lighthouse appears deserted. The men discuss rowing toward land and swimming through the surf once the boat inevitably capsizes in the rougher water closer to shore. They know that they will only grow weaker with the passage of time. They exchange ''addresses and admonitions'' in case they do not all live through the ordeal. The narrator offers some musings—not attributed to any of the men in particular—about how unjust it would be to die after coming so far. When the oiler takes the boat toward shore, it quickly become apparent that the rougher waves will capsize their vessel when they are still much too far out to swim. They return to deeper but safer offshore water. A current takes them away from the lighthouse, and they row toward ''little dots which seemed to indicate a city on the shore.'' The correspondent and the oiler now take turns rowing so that each can spend some time at rest.

Someone is seen on the shore waving to them. Soon a crowd gathers, disembarking from a bus. Despite their efforts to communicate distress, the men realize that the people on shore are tourists who think they are fishermen or pleasure boaters. No help is coming.

The four men spend a cold night rowing steadily toward distant lights. While the correspondent is rowing alone, a large shark cruises in the vicinity of the boat. The predator is never named, but is described in terms of its shape, size, speed, and the sound of the dorsal fin slicing through the water. This eerie scene is powerfully depicted.

Thoughts of drowning plague the crew. They agonize privately over the injustice of their situation: ''If I am going to be drowned . . . why . . . was I allowed to come thus far?'' The repeated phrase is never attributed; it may be their collective inner refrain. The correspondent silently recalls—incorrectly—a poem he learned as a schoolboy and never before truly understood, about a soldier who dies lamenting that he will never again see his native land.

Stephen Crane

At dawn, the men decide that their only chance is to row toward the distant shore again and swim when the boat capsizes. The narrative stays primarily with the correspondent's inner thoughts during this passage. He reflects that nature—previously personified as malicious, desiring his death—is in fact perfectly indifferent to his fate. On the captain's order, the oiler rows the boat directly toward shore. Waves crash into the boat as it enters the breakers. The cook briefly bails out water, and then the men abandon the foundering craft. The oiler swims strongly and steadily toward the shore. The cook, in his lifejacket and clutching an oar, bobs along until the captain calls to him to turn over on his back; in that position he rows himself as if his large, bouyant body were a canoe. The correspondent clings to a piece of a lifejacket and paddles slowly, thinking of the vast distance he has yet to cross. The injured captain clings to the stern of the overturned boat, which is pushed toward the beach by the strong surf. A wave tosses the correspondent over the boat and into waist-deep water, but he is too weak to even stand up. Suddenly, a man appears on shore, stripping off his clothes and running into the water. The rescuer drags the cook to safety and then approaches the captain, who waves him away to help the correspondent first. Billie, the oiler, is face-down in the shallow water, dead. The three living men are fed and tended. That night they listen to the sound of the waves against the shore ''and they felt that they could then be interpreters.''

Characters

Billie
See Oiler

Captain
The injured captain is unable to help row the lifeboat. Having lost his ship, the captain is more forlorn and dejected than the other characters, but he feels that it is his duty to guide the men to safety. He makes the decisions for the crew, and he provides words of encouragement to the men rowing. At one point, the captain seems the least optimistic about the possibility of survival. However, he only once allows himself to express such pessimism, and he quickly reverses himself, speaking as if he is ''soothing his children,'' saying that ''we'll get ashore all right.'' in the end he survives by clinging to the overturned boat as it is washed into shallow water by the surf. Even then, he waves away a rescuer and points to the correspondent, indicating that he should be helped ashore first.

Cook
The cook is described as fat and untidily dressed. He does not help row, but he does work steadily bailing seawater out of the boat. He is the most talkative of the four men, and remains unshakably certain that they will be rescued. When they finally sight shore, and a building, he keeps commenting on how strange it is that the ''crew'' of what he imagines is a life-saving station has not spotted them and sent out a rescue boat yet. He repeats this long after it becomes apparent that the building is vacant and no one has seen them. He is the only one of the four men in the boat who wears a life jacket. Underscoring the randomness of the natural disaster that has befallen the four very different men, the unfit cook is one of the three who survives, while the oiler, a strong and capable seaman, drowns in the surf just off shore.

Correspondent
The character of the correspondent is autobiographical in nature. Crane was himself shipwrecked off the Florida coast while working as a war correspondent. The correspondent is the only character in the story to whose thoughts the reader is given direct access. As the story progresses, the absurdity of the situation impresses itself deeply on the correspondent's mind. He recognizes that he might drown despite all of his efforts to survive, which causes him to consider the disheartening possibility that nature is indifferent to his fate. His melancholy leads him to imagine his own death as like that of a French soldier in a poem who dies, unmourned, far from his homeland. In the end, the correspondent survives, largely due to sheer luck: a large wave that carries him into shallow water near land.

Oiler
The oiler, Billie, is the only character in the story whose name is given. This fact has often been remarked upon by critics. He is also the only character in the open boat who does not survive the ordeal. He is the most physically able of the four characters and seems the most determined to survive. The strongest rower, the oiler also makes the strongest effort to swim ashore when the boat capsizes in the surf. Yet his efforts come to nothing—he drowns in the shallow water just off shore while the other characters are saved by what appears to be random chance.

Themes

Individual vs. Nature
During the late nineteenth century, Americans had come to expect that they could control and conquer their environment. With the technological breakthroughs of the Industrial Revolution, humankind appeared to have demonstrated its ability to both understand and to dominate the forces of nature. In ''The Open Boat,'' Crane questions these self-confident assumptions by describing the precarious situation of four shipwrecked men as they are tossed about on the sea. The men seem to recognize that they are helpless in the face of nature. Their lives could be lost at any moment by the most common of natural phenomena: a wave, a current, the wind, a shark, or even simple starvation and exposure. The men are at the mercy of mere chance. This realization profoundly affects the correspondent, who is angered that he might be drowned despite all of his efforts to save himself. In a passage that drips with irony, Crane writes of the correspondent: ''He thought: 'Am I going to drown? Can it be possible? Can it be possible? Can it be possible?' Perhaps an individual must consider his own death

to be the final phenomenon of nature.'' This passage suggests the absurdity of an individual's sense of self-importance against the mindless power of nature.

Perspective

One of the main themes of the story concerns the limitations of any one perspective, or point of view. Crane's famous first sentence of the story presents this theme immediately: ''None of them knew the color of the sky.'' The men in the boat are so focused on the danger presented to them by the waves that they are oblivious to all else. The story continually emphasizes the limitations of a single perspective. When the shipwrecked men are first spotted from the shore, they are mistaken for fishermen. The people on shore do not perceive their distress and only wave cheerfully to the men. Crane writes of the men in the boat that if they were viewed ''from a balcony, the whole thing would doubtless have been weirdly picturesque.'' This serene perspective contrasts markedly with the frightening and violent reality the men in the boat are experiencing. Crane's point seems to be that humans can never fully comprehend the true quality of reality, but only their own limited view of it. Throughout the story, the situation of the men in the boat seems to them ''absurd,'' ''preposterous,'' and without any underlying reason or meaning. Yet once the three survivors are safely on shore at the end of the story, they believe that they can look back and ''interpret'' the import or meaning of what has happened to them. The reader is left to wonder whether anything can ever be truly understood, or if all understanding is simply an agreed-upon, limited perspective that provides the illusion of unity to the chaos of lived events.

Death

The drama of the story comes from the men's realization that they are likely to drown. Having to confront the probability of their own imminent death, each of the characters accepts what Crane calls a ''new ignorance of the grave-edge.'' It is interesting that Crane refers to this understanding as ''ignorance'' rather than ''knowledge.'' Being at the mercy of fate has demonstrated to them how wrong their previous beliefs about their own importance had been. The correspondent, in particular, is troubled by the senselessness of his predicament, and he thinks about a poem in which a French soldier dies, unceremoniously, far from his home

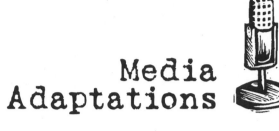

Media Adaptations

- ''The Open Boat'' is available on video from Film Video Library. Produced by the University of Michigan, this 29-minute black-and-white film was created in 1965 as part of the ''American Story Classics'' series.

and family. Facing senseless death, the universe suddenly seems deprived of the meaning he had previously attached to it. Thus, he is overtaken by a new ''ignorance'' about life, rather than a new ''knowledge.'' Crane seems to endorse the idea that nature is random and senseless by having the oiler drown in the surf. Of all the men, the oiler seemed the most likely to survive, being the most physically fit. His death implies that the others' survival was merely the result of good fortune. Once the survivors are safe from danger, however, death's senselessness is quickly forgotten.

Free Will

Crane was regarded as a leading member of the Realist or Naturalist movement in his time. One of the main concerns of the Naturalists involved the dilemma of whether human beings could exercise control over their fate or whether their fate was predetermined by their environment. To state it differently, they asked whether humans possess a free will or were powerless to shape external events. Drawing upon deterministic philosophies such as those of Charles Darwin, Auguste Comte, or Karl Marx, the Naturalists analyzed the various natural forces that effected the ''struggle for life.'' These concerns are evident in ''The Open Boat.'' Although the four men are clearly making the best effort to get to shore, it is never certain until the end whether they will drown. Their fate seems to rest mostly in the hands of forces beyond their control. A prime example of this comes when the correspondent gets caught in a current while trying to swim to the shore. He is trapped by an invisible force—an underwater current—which he can neither under-

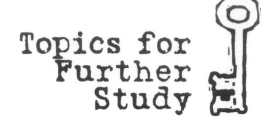

Topics for Further Study

- What philosophical values, if any, are presented or advocated by Crane in "The Open Boat"? Explain.

- How are heroism and courage defined in "The Open Boat"?

- Explain how the narrator's concentration on his senses, such as seeing, hearing, feeling, tasting, touching, smelling, create the feeling of immediacy in "The Open Boat"

- Like "The Open Boat," Winslow Homer's painting "The Gulf Stream" treats the theme of survival at sea. Compare Homer's treatment of this theme with Crane's treatment.

stand nor escape. For unknown reasons, the current suddenly frees him and he is washed ashore by a giant wave. It seems clear that Crane attributes the correspondent's survival more to uncontrollable forces than to his own efforts.

Style

Point of View

Perhaps the literary technique most remarked upon by critics of "The Open Boat" is Crane's unusual use of a shifting point of view. The story is told alternatively from the perspective of each of the crew members, as well as from the vantage point of an objective observer. Often, it is not clear whose viewpoint is predominant at a given time. There are passages of dialogue, too, in which the different speakers are never identified. In these ways, the reader is given the sense that all of the crew members share similar feelings about their predicament. There is also the suggestion that their reactions are archetypal and universal; that is, that anyone would respond the same way to what they are going

through. The correspondent is the only character whose inner thoughts are clearly identified—perhaps because he, being a writer, has the ability to articulate their experience best. Some critics have viewed Crane's shifting perspectives as a flaw, because it hinders independent character development. But, arguably, the story does not need its characters to develop as much as to experience the same fear and anger. Crane captures the sights, sounds, and emotions of a near-death experience so powerful that is denies the characters the ability to comprehend. For each of the characters the possibility of death seems unjust and senseless. Only in the end can they begin to "interpret" their experience, yet the reader is not privy to their conclusions. Thus, the shifting point of view appears to emphasize the failure of interpretation by all of the characters, rather than the knowledge that each has gained.

Realism

Stephen Crane is considered one of the foremost American authors of the Realistic and Naturalistic movements of the late nineteenth century. The Realists shared a mission to banish sentimentality and genteel conventions from their fiction. They sought to depict life as it is by constructing a "photographically" vivid description of familiar or harsh circumstances. Crane's precise rendering of the sea-tossed men in "The Open Boat" is a prime example of realist technique. He succeeds in making the reader feel as though he or she could understand exactly what it was like to live the experience. The Realists often shocked their readers with "objective" depictions of sexual indiscretion, brutality, vulgarity, and unredeemed injustice. Their fiction deliberately dispensed with the tone of moral condemnation that characterized most nineteenth-century fiction that addressed such themes.

Crane is usually associated with a particular brand of Realists known as the "Naturalists." In addition to the issue of objective treatment, the Naturalists were also intensely concerned with the question of whether human beings could exercise control over their fate or whether their fate was determined by their environment. Influenced by deterministic philosophies such as those of Charles Darwin or Karl Marx, the Naturalists analyzed the omnipotent, "natural" forces that effected the "struggle for life." These concerns are evident in "The Open Boat." The fate of the four men seems to rest mostly in the hands of forces beyond their control. A prime example of this comes when the correspondent gets caught in a current while trying to swim to the shore. He is trapped by an invisible force—an underwater current—which he can neither understand nor escape. For unknown reasons, the current suddenly frees him and he is washed ashore by a giant wave. Crane attributes the correspondent's survival to the uncontrollable forces of nature, not to his own efforts.

Setting

Since "The Open Boat" is the fictional treatment of a real-life experience that befell Crane off the coast of Florida, the setting of the story would seem determined by the actual event. However, there is good reason to question what the setting conveys about the themes and symbolic meanings of the story. Even though such an event actually happened, it was still Crane's choice as an artist to write about it. For Crane, the event must have held some deep meaning that was inseparable from the setting, or else he might have transformed it into a fictional account of a near-death experience in some other context. The experience of being in an open boat, adrift on the rough sea, seems to have communicated to Crane a sense of helplessness in the face of nature's indifference. Symbolically, nature is perfectly represented by the sea, the wind, the cold, and even the shark that periodically swims near the boat. These elements pose a great danger to the men, who have little they can do to protect themselves beyond rowing toward the shore and hoping for assistance. The nearly helpless men in the boat can been seen as a metaphor for all people before the forces of nature. Their power to act on their own behalf is small indeed when compared against the natural forces that allow them to exist, yet could strike them down at any moment.

Historical Context

Social Darwinism

Every field of thought in the late nineteenth-century was impacted by the theories of Charles Darwin. Although Darwin's *On the Origin of Species* was published in 1859, its influence was felt most strongly in the United States in the 1880s and 1890s. A variety of thinkers in the social sciences began to apply Darwin's evolutionary theories to explain the development of human societies. Known as the "Social Darwinists," these thinkers posited the existence of a process of evolution based on hereditary traits that predetermined the behavior of human beings. The most famous of these thinkers, an English social scientist named Herbert Spencer, popularized the phrase "survival of the fittest" to describe the omnipotent law of "natural selection" which determines the natural evolution of society. Most Social Darwinists adapted the idea of natural selection to existing racial theories, using this hereditary or evolutionary reasoning to explain the condition of the different races in their own time. The Social Darwinists were divided over the issue of whether humans could shape the direction of their own evolution for the better, or if they were powerless to influence the process of natural selection. While many resisted the arguments of all other Social Darwinists, their highly-publicized controversies led to the subtle spread and popularity of evolutionary reasoning in society at large.

Realism and Naturalism

The pervasiveness of Darwinism in the late nineteenth century was related to a trend in social thought away from abstract idealism toward the investigation of concrete reality. With the technological breakthroughs of the Industrial Revolution, the prestige of science and the experimental method had reached an all-time high. In literature, this cultural context was reflected in a new literary movement called Realism, which sought to construct a "photographically" vivid depiction of life as it is. Their preference for "hard facts" mimicked the scientific method. The Realists shared a mission to banish sentimentality and genteel conventions from their fiction. William Dean Howells preached the doctrine of Realism which gained the support of such authors as Mark Twain and Henry James. As the movement spread, Realism became more controversial when some practitioners began to shock their readers with "objective" depictions of sexuality, brutality, vulgarity, and unredeemed injustice. They deliberately dispensed with the tone of moral condemnation that characterized most nineteenth-century fiction dealing with such themes. In the 1890s, Realism took on a newly philosophical character in the writings of the Naturalists. Influenced by French novelist Emile Zola, the leading Naturalist, some American authors sought to integrate deterministic philosophies into their literature. The Naturalists were intensely concerned with the question of whether human beings could exercise control over their fate or whether their fate was

Compare
&
Contrast

- **1890s:** The Cuban struggle for independence from Spain becomes a unified political movement under the leadership of Jose Marti, following unsuccessful, small-scale revolts. American intervention in the war is followed by Cuba's independence from Spain and a period of U.S. occupation.

  1997: Cuba is now a communist nation under the leadership of Fidel Castro. In October, Cuba receives the remains of Castro's fellow revolutionary, Ernesto "Che" Guevara. Guevara had been killed in Bolivia thirty years earlier.

- **1896:** The United States's foreign policy is marked by aggressive imperialism, an approach advocated by the Republicans and the newly elected president, William McKinley. Alaska is purchased by the government in 1867, and Hawaii is annexed in 1898. Following the Spanish-American War in 1898–1899, the United States extends its influence to Cuba, Puerto Rico, the Philippines, and Guam.

  1990s: U.S. foreign policy is characterized as interventionist. As a member of the North Atlantic Treaty Organization (NATO), the United States helps to mediate conflicts around the world, including the Middle East and Bosnia. The Persian Gulf War in 1991 is fought by the United States to prevent Iraq from invading Kuwait.

---

determined by their environment. Influenced by deterministic philosophies such as those of Darwin or Marx, the Naturalists analyzed the "natural" forces or "scientific" laws that affected the "struggle for life." One of the most successful Naturalists, Stephen Crane, said that we live in "a world full of fists" in which the survivors are not necessarily the most "fit" but only the most fortunate.

The Spanish-American War

When Cuban revolutionaries began a war for independence against Spain in 1895, the United States lent financial and moral support to the uprising. American newspapers covered the rebellion closely and ran anti-Spanish stories on a daily basis. Crane, in fact, was employed as a newspaper correspondent on an assignment covering the uprising when the ship he was traveling on, carrying a cargo of arms for the revolutionaries, sank off the coast of Florida. The experience led him soon afterward to pen the story "The Open Boat." In February 1898, Spanish forces sank the American battleship *Maine* in Havana Harbor, killing 260 American seamen. On April 24, the United States declared war on Spain with the overwhelming support of the American people. The Spanish-American War was an extremely popular war that tapped into a glorification of masculine bravado that dominated society at the turn of the century. Theodore Roosevelt's "Rough Riders," who led the attack on San Juan Hill, became one of the most enduring symbols of courage and masculinity of the times. The reporting of the Spanish-American War reflected a dominant preoccupation with the human struggle to survive amid brutal circumstances.

Critical Overview

"The Open Boat" is widely considered to be a technical masterpiece of the modern short story. As far as artistry is concerned, the story's excellence in realism and dramatic execution have never been questioned. As Bettina Kapp wrote in *Stephen Crane,* "Crane's sensual images of man struggling against the sea remain vivid long after the reading of 'The Open Boat.' The salt spray and deafening roar of the waves pounding against the dinghy can almost be tasted and heard.'' Many critics have dissected the technical aspects of this story's Realism and plot construction. John Berryman has composed a nearly line-by-line close reading of the story, demonstrating its tight movement from the opening line to the last word.

On the surface, the meaning of ''The Open Boat'' would seem rather straightforward. Most contemporary readers of the story recognized the realism in Crane's approach, but few remarked on its deeper philosophical meanings. It has subsequently become clear, however, how much Crane shared with the more pessimistic Naturalists. Indeed, the most common understanding of the story would point out how it demonstrates that human fate is determined by the forces of nature. But, how does Crane characterize the meaning of nature? The way in which critics answer this question largely determines how they interpret the story. In ''The Essentials of Life: 'The Open Boat' as Existentialist Fiction,'' Peter Buitenhuis argues that, in fact, the story is not Naturalistic but Existential. To support this assertion, Buitenhuis points out that nature is not governed by any discernible natural laws in the story—Darwinian, Marxist, or otherwise. Instead, the story is about the correspondent's realization of the absurdity of the human condition. The Existentialists were a school of philosophers in the 1940s who argued that the only possible meaning given to the universe is subjective, that is, a creation of each person's individual perspective. Donna Gerstenberger has expanded on this position in '''The Open Boat': Additional Perspective.'' She argues that the story is essentially an ironic statement about the disparity between man's belief in a just and meaningful universe and the reality of a world that is totally indifferent to man's concerns. In contrast to Buitenhuis, Gerstenberger points out that the correspondent never reaches any kind of ''heroic'' knowledge of man's condition, but continues to insist on his false ability to ''interpret'' his experience. Both of these interpretations suggest that Crane may not fit very neatly into the category of ''Naturalist.'' While he shared many of their same concerns, Crane seems profoundly pessimistic about the possibility of understanding nature, or the universe, whereas most of the Naturalists believed that nature's laws could be discerned and explained (if not controlled).

In a recent article, ''For the Record: Text and Picture in 'The Open Boat','' George Monteiro provides evidence that suggests the story should not be too narrowly viewed as a retelling of personal experience. Monteiro demonstrates that Crane's descriptions closely resemble episodes from other sources, including an illustration, a poem, and a textbook. By drawing these parallels, he shows Crane's artistry in choosing particularly telling images and episodes to create his fiction rather than simply reconstructing actual events. Finally, James Nagel in *Stephen Crane and Literary Impressionism,* suggests that Crane's fiction mimicked the concepts of the Impressionists in painting. By emphasizing the flawed perspective of individuals, Crane did not simply attempt to reconstruct ''reality,'' but rather showed that reality cannot be reduced to a single viewpoint. The Impressionists believed that a truly realistic painting should depict the subjective and distorted impression that an image inscribes upon the mind. Nagel argues that in ''The Open Boat'' the characters are able to transcend this weakness by accepting the inadequacies of their own perspective.

Criticism

Mark Elliot

Elliot is a Ph.D student in history at New York University. With a strong background in American literature, he is a former editor of ''New England Puritan Literature'' for The Cambridge History of American Literature. *In the essay that follows, Elliot examines the way Crane transformed the raw material of his firsthand experience as a shipwreck survivor into a short story, ''The Open Boat,'' which ''explores the mysteries of nature and human life on many levels.''*

Ever since it was first published in 1897, ''The Open Boat'' has widely been considered a masterpiece of literary realism. All of the most recognizable elements of Realism are present within the story. In its graphic probing of events and in its objective description of the characters' psychological state, the story successfully presents a realistic sensation of the characters' experience without any of the false heroism or romantic plots that characterized other contemporary fiction. ''The Open Boat'' has no plot in the traditional sense; it is almost a mere description of thoughts and events. In fact, since author Stephen Crane actually experienced the events related in the story when he was ship-

"The Gulf Stream," a painting by American artist Winslow Homer (1836–1910), treats the theme of sea travel and the struggle to survive at sea that is also a feature of Crane's story "The Open Boat."

wrecked with the crew of the *Commodore,* one might suspect that the story is not fiction at all. Indeed, the story's subtitle, "A Tale Intended to be After the Fact, Being the Experience of Four Men From the Sunk Steamer Commodore," presents the story as if it were a journalistic account. Yet, despite its appearance as an objective narrative, "The Open Boat" raises deeply philosophical issues and is rife with symbolism. When analyzed closely, it becomes clear that a simplistic categorization of the story as "realistic" fiction fails to do justice to the multi-dimensional qualities of "The Open Boat."

A few days after Crane survived a shipwreck off the Florida coast, he published an account of his experience in a newspaper story entitled "Stephen Crane's Own Story." It is interesting to compare this non-fictional account with the short story "The Open Boat," which appeared six months later. In this first account, Crane relates only the events of the *Commodore*'s sinking, without either the descriptive quality or the access to inner thoughts that characterize the later fictional story. In addition, Crane deliberately leaves out any description of his experience on the life raft, commenting that "the history of life in an open boat for thirty hours would

no doubt be very instructive for the young, but none is to be told here now. For my part I would prefer to tell the story at once, because from it would shine the splendid manhood of Captain Edward Murphy and of William Higgins, the oiler." In this statement, the theme and purpose of "The Open Boat" can be discerned. Despite the unsentimental realism of the story, Crane sought to portray his idea of the true meaning of heroism. His remark that such a story would be "instructive for the young" is particularly revealing because it links the purpose of "The Open Boat" with that of Crane's most famous novel, *The Red Badge of Courage,* in which a young man's romantic dreams about courage and heroism are shattered by his encounter with a real war. Henry Fleming, the young soldier, learns that battle is chaotic and meaningless and that heroism has nothing to do with extraordinary acts, but more with the mere luck of survival. Similarly, after Crane reflected upon the events of his shipwreck, he tailored his fictional account of it to the theme of heroism in the face of imminent death. In a perfect metaphor of the forces of nature versus the struggles of man, Crane makes the men on the boat a symbol of the heroism of simple human endurance against an indifferent universe.

What Do I Read Next?

- In *The Red Badge of Courage* (1895) Stephen Crane explores the nature of courage and heroism through the eyes of Henry Fleming, a youth full of romantic dreams of war. Henry is rudely disillusioned when he enlists in the Union Army and discovers what real war is about on the battlefields of the American Civil War.

- Ernest Hemingway's *The Old Man and the Sea* (1952) tells the tragic yet triumphant story of an old fisherman's relentless battle with a giant marlin far out in the Gulf Stream off the coast of Cuba. The ordeal pushes the old man to the limits of human endurance in his determination to triumph over nature.

- Jack London's ''To Build a Fire'' (1902) is another naturalistic story of human struggle against nature. In this tale, a man's life depends on his ability to build a fire in the freezing wilderness.

- *Facing Facts: Realism in American Thought and Culture, 1850-1920* (1995) by David E. Shi provides a highly accessible survey of the Realistic movement in the arts in the late 19th and early 20th centuries. This book is valuable for any student studying the history, literature, art, or architecture of those years.

- Theodore Dreiser's *Sister Carrie* (1900) is a masterpiece of literary Naturalism. Dreiser's novel graphically depicts life in New York and Chicago at the turn of the century through the parallel stories of Carrie's fortuitous rise from a penniless farm girl to famous actress, and Hurstwood's dramatic fall from respectable tavern manager to homeless drifter.

- William Graham Sumner's *What the Social Classes Owe to Each Other* (1883) is a classic statement of Darwinian principles applied to human society. The work posits the omnipotent beneficial law of ''survival of the fittest'' which determines the state of all existing social conditions. The answer to the question posed in the book's title: nothing.

Each of the men in the dinghy is faced with the likelihood of his own death. While they row and wait to be rescued, the realization sets in that they are largely helpless in the face of nature's awesome power. The sea serves as a powerful reminder of the forces of nature: their lives could be lost at any moment by the most common of natural phenomena, such as a large wave, a strong current, an ill wind, or most ominously, a hungry shark. This profoundly affects the men, who feel that it would be unjust to be drowned after all their best efforts to save themselves. In a passage that drips with irony, Crane writes of the correspondent: ''He thought: 'Am I going to drown? Can it be possible? Can it be possible? Can it be possible?' Perhaps an individual must consider his own death to be the final phenomenon of nature.'' This passage suggests the absurdity of an individual's sense of self-importance against the mindless power of nature.

The heroism of the individuals in the story comes from their grim determination and human camaraderie in trying to overcome their situation. Crane creates a kind of collective consciousness for the crew by alternating the perspective from which the story is told, which includes each of the crew members as well as the vantage point of an objective observer. Often, it is not clear whose point of view is predominant at a given time. In this way, the reader is given the sense that all of the crew members share similar feelings about their predicament. In addition, each character contributes to the effort to save the group: the injured captain navigates, the correspondent and oiler take turns rowing, and the cook maintains lookout. None of them complain about the division of tasks, or betray any wish to improve their own chances of survival over the others. In a striking passage, the depth of their camaraderie is revealed: ''[T]hey were friends, friends in a more

> Crane creates a kind of collective consciousness for the crew by alternating the perspective from which the story is told."

curiously ironbound degree than may be common. . . . [T]here was this comradeship that the correspondent, for instance, who had been taught to be cynical of men, knew even at the time was the best experience of his life. But no one said that it was so. No one mentioned it." Paradoxically, the harrowing hours on the rough sea is both terrifying and "the best experience" of their lives. Comprehending the cold indifference of the universe to their plight, the men rely on each other in the understanding that—if nothing else—they share the same predicament and are not alone in the world. In a strangely Darwinian scene, their return to a primitive state of nature in the "struggle for life" does not reduce the men to savages but rather affirms their humanity.

The Darwinian implications of "The Open Boat" demonstrate Crane's interest in the philosophical ideas of the literary Naturalists. A European variant of the Realist movement, the Naturalists sought to integrate deterministic philosophies such as Darwinism or Marxism into their literature. The Naturalists emphasized the hidden forces or "natural" laws that affected what Darwin called the "struggle for life." They were intensely concerned with the question of whether human beings could exercise control over their fate, or whether their fate was entirely determined by their environment. In "The Open Boat," the fate of the four men would seem to rest mostly in the hands of forces beyond their control. For instance, when the correspondent makes his attempt to swim ashore he gets caught in a underwater current that prevents his progress. Literally and symbolically, he is trapped by an invisible force—a current—which he can neither understand nor escape. For unknown reasons, the current suddenly frees him and he is washed ashore by a giant wave. In this description, it would seem that Crane attributes the correspondent's survival more to uncontrollable forces than to his own efforts.

Crane departs from the Naturalists, however, in that he does not posit the existence of any discernible "laws of nature." Nature, in the story, is incomprehensible to man and probably without ultimate meaning or purpose. In an ironic reversal of the Darwinian rule of the "survival of the fittest," the only member of the crew to perish in the ordeal is the oiler, who had seemed the most physically "fit" to survive. While it is possible to interpret the oiler's death as a heroic sacrifice—suggesting that he exhausted himself rowing the boat for the others—it seems more in keeping with the theme of the story that the oiler was simply unlucky. For Crane, nature is chaotic and takes no account of human struggles. In the most famous passage from the story, the correspondent imagines that a tall windmill on shore with its back to the men is the personification of nature: "It represented to a degree, to the correspondent, the serenity of nature amid the struggles of the individual—nature in the wind, and nature in the vision of men. She did not seem cruel to him then, nor beneficent, nor treacherous, nor wise. But, she was indifferent, flatly indifferent." This realization haunts the men as they attempt to save themselves. Their heroism comes from their desire to live, and from their human dignity and camaraderie regardless of nature's indifference.

The suggestion that the perilous hours on the open boat constituted "the best time of their lives" presents the idea that their understanding of the human condition can only come when confronted with the probability of imminent death. Each of the characters acquires what Crane calls a "new ignorance of the grave-edge." It is interesting that Crane refers to this understanding as "ignorance" rather than "knowledge." Being at the mercy of fate has demonstrated to them how wrong their previous beliefs about their own importance had been—they revert to a kind of primitive innocence. The correspondent thinks about a poem in which a French soldier dies, unceremoniously, far from his home and family. Realizing that he faces a similarly senseless death, he finds the true meaning of courage and heroism in the simple will to survive. Once the survivors are safe from danger, however, death's senselessness is quickly forgotten. The last line of the story has the men looking out upon the sea once again deluded into believing they can make sense of it: "When it came night, the white waves paced to and fro in the moonlight, and the wind brought the sound of the great sea's voice to the men on shore, and they felt that they could then be interpreters."

With the death of the oiler and the rescue of the others, the bond between the men is broken and each is left to believe that his experience and particular reason for survival has some larger meaning. Their brief moment of human brotherhood and understanding ends with their rescue.

Compared to his journalistic account of the *Commodore*'s shipwreck in "Stephen Crane's Own Story," Crane's fictional account, "The Open Boat," possesses a depth of philosophical meditation and symbolic meaning that raises it far above simple Realism. While the descriptive quality of the story is vivid and evocative, it is more than a straightforward realistic telling of an actual event. Crane uses the incident to question the possibility of human understanding of nature, and to pose a definition of heroism constituting a selfless brotherhood in the struggle for life. Under adverse circumstances, the men experience a rare connection as fellow beings united in their helplessness before the power of nature, and in their silent recognition of its indifference to their struggles. This moment of heroic transcendence is fleeting, however, as the men return to the false security of human society in the end. A triumph of short fiction, Crane's "The Open Boat" explores the mysteries of nature and human life on many levels.

Source: Mark Elliot, "'Interpreting' the Uninterpretable: Unreasoning Nature and Heroic Endurance in Crane's 'The Open Boat'," in *Short Stories for Students,* Gale, 1998.

Bettina L. Knapp

In the following excerpt, Knapp commends "The Open Boat" as a great piece of short fiction and a compelling narrative of struggle between individuals and the indifferent, vast natural world

"The Open Boat" (1898), one of America's finest short stories, describes the adventure that satisfied Crane perhaps most fully. He said once that he wanted to go "to some quarter of the world where mail is uncertain." He did just that when he accepted Bacheller's assignment in November, 1896 to cover the Cuban Revolution. Thick fog enshrouded the St. Johns River as the Commodore set sail from Jacksonville with Crane aboard. Although Captain Edward Murphy had taken the precaution of hiring a local pilot to help the vessel out of the harbor, it struck a sand bar. The following morning, the Commodore was towed free, but Murphy neglected to review the damage done the ship, which continued on into deeper waters. By the time the leak was discovered, there was no hope of saving the ship.

Although the Captain tried to steer it back to the harbor, the pumps and engines gave out and it foundered. Passengers and crew were ordered into the lifeboats. Crane's conduct during this harrowing ordeal was superb: he soothed frightened men, helped bail out water, and acted like a born sailor. After the crew was in the lifeboats, Crane, the Captain, the cook and the oiler climbed into a ten-foot-long dinghy.

Although the boat managed to stay afloat on the high seas, Crane's harrowing experience was far from over. The mate's lifeboat capsized and the men on it drowned. Crane was deeply moved by the courage of the sailors who drowned: no shrieks, no groans, only silence.

The remaining lifeboats reached land the following day. The dinghy, however, could not get ashore because of the rough surf and so remained out at sea. No one on shore could see or hear the men in the dinghy. The captain fired his pistol but to no avail, and the men were forced to spend another night in the dinghy, rowing frantically to prevent being swallowed up by the rough seas. They then decided to row to Daytona Beach and try to make it through the breakers there. But the boat overturned, and they had to swim. A man on the beach saw what happened and ran for help. All but the oiler were saved.

"None of them knew the color of the sky," is perhaps one of the most celebrated opening lines of any short story. The opening line conveys the fierce struggle between finite man and the infinitude that engulfs him—as in Melville's *Moby-Dick.* The sea for Crane, as it is for Melville, is "the image of the ungraspable phantom of life."

The men's agony at not knowing their fate is underscored by the power of those surging waters— waves that could sweep the men under at any moment. "The horizon narrowed and widened, and dipped and rose, at all times its edge was jagged with waves that seemed thrust up in points like rocks."

Man, like the helpless survivors in the boat, is thrust here and there and floats about in utter helplessness. No matter how hard people try to fix and direct themselves, they are castaways. Salvation—if there is one—lies in the bonds between men that assuage their implacable solitude.

> The craft pranced and reared, and plunged like an animal. As each wave came, and she rose for it, she seemed like a horse making at a fence outrageously high. The manner of her scramble over these walls of

water is a mystic thing, and moreover, at the top of them were ordinarily these problems in white water, the foam racing down from the summit of each wave, requiring a new leap, and a leap from the air.

Crane's use of changing rhythms throughout the tale points up the terror of the dinghy's passengers and exemplifies the utter senselessness of existence itself.

Crane suggests that if an observer were to look upon the events objectively, viewing them "from a balcony, the whole thing would doubtless have been weirdly picturesque. But the men in the boat had no time to see it, and even if they had had leisure, there were other things to occupy their minds." Values of virtue, bravery, integrity were once of importance, but now are meaningless in a godless universe where nature observes impassively human despair and frustration. Yet, the harrowing sea journey creates a new morality, which gives fresh meaning to life: "the brotherhood of men . . . was established on the seas. No one said that it was so. No one mentioned it. But it dwelt in the boat, and each man felt it warm him." Comfort and feelings of well-being emerge as each helps the other assuage his growing terror.

In the midst of fear and harrowing terror, there is also irony and humor:

> If I am going to be drowned—if I am going to be drowned—if I am going to be drowned, why, in the name of the seven mad gods who rule the sea, was I allowed to come thus far and contemplate sand and trees? Was I brought here merely to have my nose dragged away as I was about to nibble the sacred cheese of life? It is preposterous. If this old ninny-woman, Fate, cannot do better than this, she should be deprived of the management of men's fortunes. She is an old hen who knows not her intention. If she has decided to drown me, why did she not do it in the beginning and save me all this trouble. The whole affair is absurd. . . . But, no, she cannot mean to drown me. Not after all this work.

A mystical relationship exists between the men in the dinghy—and the sea and heavens. Crane feels compelled to point out man's smallness, to set him back into nature and reduce him to size.

Conversations between the oiler and the cook, seemingly trivial, since they revolve around food— "What kind of pie do you like best?"—serve in reality to point out the absurdity of humankind's preoccupations. They also act as a way of dispelling progressive terror. As for the captain, he is ridiculed; the men laugh at him, again distracting themselves from their great fear of death.

The sight of a shark heightens the men's dreadful tension. Crane does not mention the shark by name, but the reader can almost hear the shark's fin cut the water's surface and see its phosphorescent gleaming body. Like the survivors of "Raft of the Medusa," whose harrowing episode is famous in French maritime history, the men in the dinghy do not know there is a lifesaving station twenty miles away.

When the ordeal is over, the men, safely on land, look back at the water: "white waves paced to and fro in the moonlight, and the wind brought the sound of the great sea's voice to the men on shore, and they felt that they could then be interpreters." The narrator's voice withdraws, as it were, from the chaotic drama, introducing a sense of spatial and temporal distance. Comfortable on land, the narrator can indulge in the luxury of waxing poetic and thus transform subjective emotions into a work of art.

Its poetry and rhythmic schemes make "The Open Boat" the match of Melville's "White Jacket" and the best of Jack London and Joseph Conrad. This tale's unusually punctuated sentences of contrasting length simulate the heart beat of man under extreme stress, producing an incantatory quality. Crane's sensual images of man struggling against the sea remain vivid long after the reading of "The Open Boat." The salt spray and deafening roar of the waves pounding against the dinghy can almost be tasted and heard. . . .

Source: Bettina L. Knapp, "Tales of Adventure," in *Stephen Crane,* Ungar Publishing Company, 1987, pp. 145–62.

George Monteiro

In the following excerpt, Monteiro asserts that "The Open Boat" derives not only from Crane's personal experience, but from his creative response to literary and other artistic sources as well.

Only the most primitive critical response would insist that Crane's fictional treatment of his experience of shipwreck off the Florida coast on New Year's Day 1897 could have been drawn directly and transparently from immediate life, that the author, moreover, had only to recall the details of existence aboard the small open boat, along with his moment-by-moment reactions to his plight and situation, to produce his "tale intended to be after the fact," as he described the story. In this note I shall attempt to show how in two key instances in "The Open Boat" Crane drew upon memories of his reactions to three texts: one poetic, one expository, and one visual.

Poetic and Visual

In an early review of *The Open Boat and Other Stories,* the London *Academy* called Stephen Crane "an analyst of the subconscious." To give "a faint notion of the curious and convincing scrutiny to which, through some forty pages, the minds of the crew are subjected" in the book's title story, the anonymous reviewer quotes two passages: the first is the "If I am going to be drowned—if I am going to be drowned" question that the correspondent poses to himself at various moments; the second is the correspondent's meditation on the "soldier of the Legion" dying in Algiers. It is the second instance that interests us here.

Having long since enlisted in what he called the beautiful war for realism, the young author nevertheless had reached back for a schoolboy's memory of Mrs. Caroline E. S. Norton's poem, "Bingen." "A verse mysteriously entered the correspondent's head," writes Crane; "he had even forgotten that he had forgotten this verse, but it suddenly was in his mind":

> A soldier of the Legion lay dying in Algiers,
> There was lack of woman's nursing, there was
>   dearth of woman's tears;
> But a comrade stood beside him, and he took that
>   comrade's hand,
> And he said: "I never more shall see my own, my
>   native land."

These, the opening lines of Mrs. Norton's poem, with some twenty words silently omitted at the very middle of the verse, Crane drew upon to render the emotional state of his castaway narrator. It was the pathos of the soldier, dying far from his homeland, in the throes of defining his hopeless situation and his unavoidable fate that came suitably to the writer's hand. Crane tells us that the correspondent "had been made acquainted" with the soldier dying in Algiers "in his childhood," even as Crane had probably discovered Mrs. Norton's poem, its title expanded to "Bingen on the Rhine," in his grade-school reader. (Over the years at random I have picked up copies of three such readers—*National Fifth Reader* (1870), *Lippincott's Fifth Reader* (1881), and *Swinton's Fifth Reader* (1883)—and in what must be a measure of the poem's popularity, each one of them prints "Bingen on the Rhine.") It is equally clear, however, that Crane's knowledge of Mrs. Norton's poem went beyond the unadorned reprintings in grade-school texts, for his description

> "Crane saw the events aboard the 'open boat' and subsequently out of it and in the ocean as ironically bringing to question the tenets of Christian consolation."

of the dying soldier and the setting for his death elaborate on Mrs. Norton's text. Crane expands,

> The correspondent plainly saw the soldier. He lay on the sand with his feet out straight and still. While his pale left hand was upon his chest in an attempt to thwart the going of his life, the blood came between his fingers. In the far Algerian distance, a city of low square forms was set against a sky that was faint with the last sunset hues.

There is nothing in the lines Crane quotes to validate the correspondent's view of the dying soldier, though the clause "the blood came between his fingers" expresses concretely what the poem, in a clause omitted by the correspondent, states more abstractly as "while his life-blood ebb'd away." It could be argued, of course, that in having the correspondent elaborate on the original lines of "Bingen," Crane was merely exercising a writer's legitimate license. It is more likely, however, that Crane was also familiar with a particular reprinting of Mrs. Norton's poem, an edition in 1883 featuring illustrations by William T. Smedley, Frederic B. Schell, Alfred Fredericks, Granville Perkins, J. D. Woodward, and Edmund H. Garrett. Published in Philadelphia by Porter and Coates, this edition appeared more than three decades after the first publication of the poem and six years after the poet's death. Crane's paragraph of "elaboration," it seems likely, draws directly on two illustrations by Smedley keyed into the lines "a Soldier of the Legion lay dying in Algiers" and "His voice grew faint and hoarser." Since the soldier does not hold his hand over his heart, as Crane has it, it is unlikely that Crane had Smedley's illustration before him as he wrote—though it is possible, one should note, that the "light" patch just below the soldier's throat might well have been remembered by Crane as the soldier's "pale left hand." But the soldier's feet, both in story and illustration (if not in the poem), are "out straight and still." And the soldier's death in both story and illustration (though not in the poem) plays itself out against "the Far Algerian distance, a city of low square forms. . . . set against a sky that was faint with the last sunset hues." It should surprise no one that we have here still another instance of Crane's translation of visual experience into the stuff of fiction.

Expository

The major lines of Crane's imagination were set by his familial concerns with matters of religion and warfare, particularly as that imagination shaped his early work. Indeed, ... Crane saw the events aboard the "open boat" and subsequently out of it and in the ocean as ironically bringing to question the tenets of Christian consolation. This he did in the broadest context, playing off the configuration of events against the trope of the Pilot-God and his Ship-World. Parables of man (a pilgrim) sailing in a lifeboat (belief in Christianity) on the rough seas (life in the world), dating from the Middle Ages, were abundant in Crane's time in religious tracts and emblem books. Such parables also appeared in textbooks used in the public school system. These later, however, were demythologized. There were no longer any Christian referents in stories of shipwreck in the grade-school readers issued by Lippincott's and Swinton's. Typical of these is the following excerpt, the concluding paragraphs of an account entitled "A Ship in a Storm," taken from a typical grade-school reader:

> On the dangerous points along our sea-coast are light-houses, which can be seen far out at sea, and serve as guides to ships. Sometimes the fog is so dense that these lights can not be seen, but most light-houses have great fog-bells or fog-horns; some of the latter are made to sound by steam, and can be heard for a long distance. These bells and horns are kept sounding as long as the fog lasts.

> There are also many life-saving stations along the coast where trained men are ready with life-boats. When a ship is driven ashore they at once go to the rescue of those on board, and thus many valuable lives are saved.

This account stresses not loss of life, but the saving of it. The efficacy of strategically placed light-houses and life-saving stations is indicated, the implication being that man is capable of mitigating and diminishing the dangers posed for him by a destructive sea. Many valuable lives are otherwise saved because of man's foresight in creating and skillfully deploying life-saving stations. This is the lesson of this grade-school account, and it is a lesson remembered (and subsequently tested) by the correspondent and his companions—babes in the wood—in the open boat.

> "There's a house of refuge just north of the Mosquito Inlet Light, and as soon as they see us, they'll come off in their boat and pick us up."

> "As soon as who see us?" said the correspondent.

> "The crew," said the cook.

> "Houses of refuge don't have crews," said the correspondent. "As I understand them, they are only places where clothes and grub are stored for the benefit of shipwrecked people. They don't carry crews."

> "Oh, yes, they do," said the cook.

> "No, they don't," said the correspondent.

> "Well, we're not there yet, anyhow," said the oiler, in the stern.

> "Well," said the cook, "perhaps it's not a house of refuge that I'm thinking of as being near Mosquito Inlet Light. Perhaps it's a lifesaving station."

> "We're not there yet," said the oiler, in the stern.

Nor would they ever get to it if they were thinking of a life-saving station, for there was not a one on that coast of Florida. (And if they returned their thoughts to houses of refuge, there was none within twenty to thirty miles in either direction, north or south.) Since there were no life-saving stations on the entire Florida coast, what prompted the cook and the correspondent to think that they might be close to one? And on what basis would the cook later say, "We must be about opposite New Smyrna. . . . Captain, by the way, I believe they abandoned that lifesaving station there about a year ago." To which assertion the captain answers only, "Did they?"

It is possible, of course, that the author of "The Open Boat" did not know, just as his cook did not and just as, possibly, the oiler and the captain did not, that there were no life-saving stations off the coast of Florida. It is further possible that the notion that there would be such stations, even to the extent of the cook's "remembering" the existence of one at New Smyrna, did not derive from personal experience but was the legacy of an elementary-school textbook. It is no wonder that they argue over the very existence and the probable location of those stations whose crews will save them, elation and despair following one another as they become sure and less than sure about the accuracy of their senses and the soundness of their information. Ultimately, of course, they will have to jettison their hopes for rescue by those who man such stations because there are no such stations anywhere near them. They will brave the unpredictable waves and the surf as each man is forced to strike out for himself.

A concluding point. The grade-school account had begun with the observation that the sea can have two opposing appearances: it can be blue and calm, the setting for joyous peace; and it can be turbulently destructive to human life. Something like this notion had impressed Crane. In a little poem collected in *War Is Kind* he wrote,

> To the maiden
> The sea was blue meadow
> Alive with little froth-people
> Singing.
> To the sailor, wrecked,
> The sea was dead grey walls
> Superlative in vacancy
> Upon which nevertheless at fateful time,
> Was written
> The grim hatred of nature.

In "The Open Boat" Crane had written wryly of those on shore who, certain of the nature of sport in a boat, waved gaily at the men in the dinghy in false recognition of their playful holiday at sea.

For Stephen Crane the task of the literary realist called for creative response to experience in all modes, including those that are literary and visual.

Source: George Monteiro, "For the Record: Text and Picture in 'The Open Boat'," in *Journal of Modern Literature,* Vol. 11, No. 2, July, 1984, pp. 307–11.

Donna Gerstenberger

In the following excerpt, Gerstenberger studies the epistemological aspect of "The Open Boat," which deals with the human limitations of knowing anything with objective certainty. She also examines Crane's choice to divide his point of view among the various characters in the story, with particular emphasis on the character of the correspondent.

Stephen Crane's "The Open Boat" is generally acknowledged to be among the masterpieces of the modern short story. The question of the story's excellence has never been debated; the only questions have been the proper means of defining the story's modernity and of accounting for what appear to be certain awkwardnesses of style, tone, and point of view.

"The Open Boat" has been hailed as an example of naturalistic fiction at its best until recent years, when the automatic and somewhat naive tendency to equate naturalism and modernity has been called into question in all the arts. Thus Peter

> **The implication of 'The Open Boat' is that the vision of any human being must, of necessity, be false, even if that vision be a knowledge of the absurdity of the universe."**

Buitenhuis asserts in a recent study ["'The Essentials of Life: 'The Open Boat' as Existentialist Fiction," *Modern Fiction Studies,* 3, 1959, 243–250], "'The Open Boat' is not a naturalistic story," and he confronts the story as "existentialist fiction," concentrating on Crane's ironic presentation and the story's demonstration of the absurdity of the human condition. While Mr. Buitenhuis does not address himself to the question of "The Open Boat" as a *modern* short story, the implicit assumption is that use of the term *existential* automatically confers the status of modernity, as well it may. Yet such a reading leaves its author troubled by the same kinds of questions that troubled those who saw the story as naturalistic fiction—questions about Crane's style and about the story's protagonist. The answers to such questions come into focus when "The Open Boat" is viewed as a story with an emphasis on the epistemological aspect of the existential crisis.

The epistemological question about the problems of knowing and the limitations of man's ability to see and to know has become both subject and style in modern art from Conrad to Joyce, Picasso to Faulkner, Pirandello to Beckett. So persistent and pervasive has been the preoccupation with epistemological questions in modern art that it might almost be said to constitute a way of defining one aspect of modernity. Conversely, it might be said that the somewhat naive and programmatic view of reality held by the naturalists gives their work a certain old-fashioned quality, which Crane's story, demonstrably, does not share. "The Open Boat" calls equally into question the assumptions of photographic reality as well as those of idealized, romantic views of the universe.

With his opening sentence, "None of them knew the colour of the sky," Crane makes clear a major concern of "The Open Boat." The word *knew* in this famous first sentence is the key word, for the story which follows is about man's limited capacities for knowing reality. This opening sentence leads the reader toward the concluding line of the story, "... and the wind brought the sound of the great sea's voice to the men on the shore, and they felt that they could then be interpreters"—a conclusion which, when the special emphasis of the story is acknowledged, is a good deal more complex than has generally been thought.

Crane's irony in "The Open Boat" grows out of the epistemological direction of the story. It is invested in the language and in the authorial point of view as well as in tone. This irony, based on Crane's perception of the disparity between man's vision of a just and meaningful universe and a world totally indifferent to such unrealistic notions, acknowledges the absurdity at the heart of the existentialist vision. Yet Crane, through his ironic treatment of his material, moves one step further: the implication of "The Open Boat" is that the vision of any human being must, of necessity, be false, *even if* that vision be a knowledge of the absurdity of the universe.

This extension of the epistemological question makes it clear that Crane intentionally divides his points of view among the various characters, and it is difficult to accept Peter Buitenhuis's conclusion that

> Unfortunately, instead of confining these attitudes to a single character, the protagonist Crane shifts at times to the points of view of the oiler, the cook, and the captain as well. He was probably trying to emphasize through this device that the experience was deeply shared by the four men, a point essential to the story's conclusion. However, in attributing to the four not only similar emotions but also similar formulations about the nature of existence, he presumes too much on the reader's willing suspension of disbelief. Crane also unnecessarily seeks to make his point by using the omniscient point of view.

To conclude, as Buitenhuis has, that Crane is mistaken in his failure to present his story from a single point of view, is to assert that Crane intended his story to be something other than it is, to assume that the sole aim of the story is a demonstration of the absurdity of the universe. I would suggest, on the contrary, that while the shared experience of absurdity is an aspect of the story, Crane's intention includes a demonstration of the impossibility of knowing anything with objective certainty, given the subjective, human instrument for perception.

The kind of authorial intrusion represented by the famous passage, "Viewed from a balcony, the whole thing would doubtless have been weirdly picturesque," can be accepted within the framework of Crane's intention when it is understood that, although the man on the balcony would have a distancing perspective not available to the men in the boat, he would be wrong about what he would be seeing. The human need to translate the open boat into the landscape terms of "picturesque" immediately falsifies at the same time that it represents a truth of human perception. The reader is reminded once again, by a passage like this, that a part of the injustice, the absurdity of the universe, is man's inability ever to know anything about the complex whole of experience.

In a similar kind of response, the correspondent, looking shoreward, contemplates the tall white windmill amidst the deserted cottages, which, in an echo of Goldsmith's formalized landscape, "might have formed a deserted village" and picturesquely sees it as "a giant, standing with its back to the plight of the ants." To see the wind tower is to translate it into something else, into a reality invested with subjective meaning, even though that meaning be a statement about the objectivity of nature. For the tower "represented in a degree, to the correspondent, the serenity of nature amid the struggles of the individual—nature in the wind, and nature in the vision of man."

In much of modern literature, there is a sense in which existential man sometimes seems to achieve a modicum of heroic stature when he apprehends and accepts the absurd universe, for he has done what man can do, and insofar as he has done what all men are not able to do, he stands apart from the common run of men. Crane, however, is not willing to grant to his correspondent an heroic moment as a result of the "right" kind of perception (which in itself, in existential terms, often becomes a kind of absolute), for as the correspondent contemplates the flat indifference of nature, "a distinction between right and wrong seems absurdly clear to him, then, in this new ignorance of the grave-edge, and he understands that if he were given another opportunity he would mend his conduct and his words, and be better and brighter during an introduction or at a tea."

One might expect Crane to speak of the man's "new *knowledge* of the grave-edge," but his insistence upon *ignorance* denies the correspondent the absolute sanction so often bestowed as a result of confronting hard reality. Further, the conclusion of the passage, "he would mend his conduct and his words, and be better and brighter during an introduction or at a tea'' has the same kind of anti-heroic effect worked so neatly upon Eliot's Prufrock, who can hardly be expected to force any moment to its crisis within the context of ''tea and cakes and ices.'' Crane refuses to permit his reader comfort of the kind involved in the equation that when the man who suffers becomes the man who *knows,* something of absolute value, however depressing, has been achieved.

Crane's practice of using apparently inappropriate or consciously awkward metaphors, analogies, or descriptive adjectives, which appear to devalue or overvalue in specific passages, challenges the reader's too-easy assumptions about what may be defined as heroic within the context of experiential stress. Several examples from the opening pages of the story may suggest the achievement of this general technique: ''By the very last star of truth, it is easier to steal eggs from under a hen than it was to change seats in the dinghy.'' The linking of absolute abstraction (''the very last star of truth'') with the homely, agrarian observation about the difficulty of stealing eggs from under a hen seems as inappropriate to the act of changing rowers as do the parts to each other. But the purpose of heroic deflation, of irony, is served, as it is in the serviceable awkwardness of the following: ''In a ten-foot dinghy one can get an idea of the resources of the sea in the line of waves that is not probable to the average experience, which is never at sea in a dinghy.'' Crane refuses to romanticize the absurdity of experience, and the reader is constantly reminded that experience, like perception, is betrayed by the language by which it is conceptualized.

Not only does Crane constantly deny by stylistic devices the heroism of action or even of enduring necessity, but he also denies the heroism of knowledge in the context discussed above. Crane's extensive use of the subjunctive mood is a part of his statement that even a tough-minded view of the universe involves man in an uncertain questioning of the conditions within which his responses, even to absurdity, must be framed.

Examples of this kind all bear on the claim that ''The Open Boat'' may best be viewed as a story with an epistemological emphasis, one which constantly reminds its reader of the impossibility of man's *knowing* anything, even that which he experiences. The reaction of the correspondent, near the close of the story, to his fight for life against a hostile current is of interest because of its reminders of earlier passages central to an understanding of the story. He sees the shore, the white beach, and ''green bluff topped with little silent cottages . . . spread like a picture before him.'' The shore, in fact, is very close at this point, but ''he was impressed as one who, in a gallery, looks at a scene from Brittany or Algiers.'' The immanence of death, the difficulty of achieving the shore, formalizes experience once again into landscape, reminding the reader of the necessarily false perception of the earlier hypothetical view of the open boat from a balcony. (The use of the word *gallery,* a term also meaning *balcony,* reinforces the relationship of the two passages.) The locating of the landscape in ''Brittany or Algiers'' inevitably calls up a vision of the soldier of the Legion dying in Algiers, both in the romanticized picture of Lady Carolyn Bingen's lines and also in terms of the moment of understanding and fellow feeling that the correspondent experiences as he pictures the soldier lying ''on the sand with his feet out straight and still.'' ''It was no longer merely a picture of a few throes in the breast of a poet, meanwhile drinking tea and warming his feet at the grate; it was an actuality—stern, mournful, and fine.''

It has generally been assumed that the soldier dying in Algiers is important to Crane's intentions in ''The Open Boat'' because he provides the opportunity for a clear example of the kind of understanding, of human sympathy, of the valuable kind of knowledge which comes from experiential stress. In this respect, ''The Open Boat'' has been viewed as an ''initiation'' story, pre-figuring Hemingway's use of experiential stress as a key to knowledge. But it is important to bear in mind that the correspondent's new attitude toward the soldier falsifies, as do all the ''pictures'' or ''landscapes'' by which man seeks a delineated context for knowledge. The story in its totality makes it perfectly clear (as do Crane's other tales) that there is nothing ''stern, mournful, and fine'' in death, and this incident, which has generally been read as indicative of the correspondent's growth in knowing, may well serve as an example of the impossibility of untainted knowledge. To *know* the soldier in Algiers without a self-pitying desire to find something ''stern, mournful, and fine'' in death is not possible. The death of Billie, the oiler, contrasts with the picture of the soldier's death, and it certainly is indicative of the indifference of nature, for the arbitrary absurdity of his death is underlined by the fact that he is the strongest and the most realistic of the men aboard the dinghy. Crane's description of his death is presented more starkly than anything else in the story: ''In the shallows, face downward lay the oiler. His forehead touched sand that was periodically, between each wave, clear of the sea.'' No pictures, no objectifying landscapes, no stylistic ironies. The question of human perception is no longer a problem that applies to the oiler.

Within the epistemological context discussed in his paper, it would seem necessary, finally, to raise a question about the concluding lines of Crane's story: ''the wind brought the sound of the great sea's voice to the men on the shore, and they felt that they could then be interpreters.'' The story has clearly shown the final absurdity to be the falsification of man's attempts to ''interpret,'' an act in which he is betrayed by the very language he must use to conceptualize, by the narrowness of vision, and by the further limitation of his need to frame, to formalize his apprehensions in a landscape, a poem, an irony, or a subjunctive statement of conditions that never were on land or sea. To ''interpret'' is not to be equated with knowing, and perhaps the final irony is in the community of shared experience which these final lines seem to suggest, for however communal the interpretation of the ''great sea's voice,'' nothing in the story suggests that any one of the three men remaining can conceptualize the death of the oiler without, perhaps, falsely transfiguring him into a figure like the soldier of the Legion, whose death was ''an actuality—stern, mournful, and fine.''

Source: Donna Gerstenberger, '''The Open Boat': Additional Perspective,'' in *Modern Fiction Studies,* Vol. XVII, No. 4, Winter, 1971, pp. 557–61.

Sources

Berryman, John. ''Stephen Crane: 'The Open Boat'.'' In *The Freedom of the Poet,* pp. 168-84. New York: Farrar, Straus and Giroux, 1976.

Buitenhuis, Peter. ''The Essentials of Life: 'The Open Boat' as Existentialist Fiction,'' *Modern Fiction Studies* Vol. 3, 1959, pp. 243-50.

Crane, Stephen. ''Stephen Crane's Own Story.'' In *American Literature: A Prentice Hall Anthology,* Elliott, Emory, editor, Prentice Hall, 1991.

Further Reading

Halliburton, David. *The Color of the Sky: A Study of Stephen Crane,* Cambridge University Press, 1989.
    Provocative study of Crane's entire body of work which emphasizes its philosophical aspects and is organized by themes rather than chronology or works. The title is taken from the opening line of ''The Open Boat.''

Nagel, James. *Stephen Crane and Literary Impressionism,* Pennsylvania State University Press, 1980.
    Fascinating study which suggests that Crane applied concepts derived from the impressionist school of painting to his fiction.

Pierre Menard, Author of the Quixote

Jorge Luis Borges
1939

Jorge Luis Borges wrote the story "Pierre Menard, Author of the Quixote" in 1939, soon after suffering a serious accident. Borges had until then been primarily a poet and the author of journalistic and critical articles, with little experience in writing short stories. However, after a fall on a staircase that resulted in a head injury, Borges attempted to reassure himself that the accident had not caused the loss of his writing ability, later telling an interviewer, "I thought I'd try my hand at something I hadn't done." "Pierre Menard" appeared in the spring 1939 issue of the magazine *Sur*. With it Borges commenced his production of the stories, or "fictions" as he called them, which influenced much twentieth-century fiction.

"Pierre Menard, Author of Don Quixote," like the other "fictions" "The Aleph," and "Tlon, Uqbar, Orbis Tertius," utilizes the voice of an academic narrator, well-versed in the discussion of obscure details of the literary life of many nations. The story is written in the style of a literary article in an academic French journal. The narrator purports to rectify a number of errors committed by another academic in recording the career of the writer Pierre Menard. According to the narrative, Menard had resolved to write *Don Quixote:* not to copy the story down as it exists in the version by Miguel de Cervantes, but to arrive at the conditions necessary to write exactly the *same* story through his own experiences. The narrator compares identical passages from Menard's *Quixote* and that of Cervantes,

concluding that Menard's is far superior. Borges's story, similarly, is doubled: although Borges is clearly interested in the ways in which history and context will always change a text's meaning, he is just as interested in satirizing pompous conventions of academia and in caricaturing the petty conflicts of the literary world.

Author Biography

Born in 1899 in Buenos Aires, Argentina, to a middle-class family with some English heritage, Jorge Luis Borges grew up among books, libraries, and languages—all of which would figure significantly in his writings. In 1901 the Borges family moved to the Palermo suburb of Buenos Aires, which Borges described as an area of "shabby, genteel people as well as more undesirable sorts." From 1914 to 1921 the family lived in Europe, and while at school in Geneva, Switzerland, Borges mastered French and Latin to go with the Spanish and English in which he was already fluent. Moving to Spain in 1919, Borges fell in with the avant-garde literary group known as the *ultraistas* that flourished in Seville and Madrid, and found his calling as a writer.

Returning to Buenos Aires in 1921, Borges founded a literary magazine and a literary review, and began to write poetry heavily influenced by avant-garde thinking in the Hispanic world. He was also employed in public and college libraries. At the outset of the 1930s Borges set a new task for himself: to renew prose fiction in an entirely new, innovative fashion. In 1939 Borges published "Pierre Menard, Author of Don Quixote" and his project, it seemed, was finally realized. With such collections as *Universal History of Infamy, Fictions, Labyrinths,* and *Dreamtigers,* Borges transformed the path of twentieth-century fiction. At the same time, he continued to work in libraries and colleges, a career that was detoured in 1946 with the accession of Juan Peron to power in Argentina. Because Borges had sympathized with the Allies in World War II, he was stripped of his library position and "promoted" to the position of head poultry inspector for Buenos Aires' local markets. Later, though, he regained his earlier position, and became in 1955 Director of the Argentine National Library.

Although he inspired the remarkable Latin American "boom" of writing talent in the post-World War II period, Borges was not seen as an important precursor by many of the "boom's" leading figures, who disapproved of Borges' lack of political engagement. Borges was most influential in the United States. During the 1960s, such eminent writers as John Updike and John Barth cited Borges as the very writer whose revolutionary insights and approaches could save American literature from its inertia. Borges, although nearly blind for much of the last part of his life, continued to write stories and poetry until his death in 1986.

Plot Summary

The first part of "Pierre Menard, Author of the Quixote" introduces the reader to both the tone and the narrator, both of which are scholarly. The narrator, a French academic, seeks to correct the erroneous and incomplete catalog of the work of an author named Pierre Menard that had been compiled by a Madame Henri Bachelier. The narrator proceeds to enumerate a list of Menard's "*visible*" works, which include poems, a number of scholarly works on philosophical and literary topics, a translation, a catalog preface, and other minor academic works.

The narrator then shifts to his primary topic: Menard's "subterranean, interminably heroic, and unequalled" work, which the narrator feels is "possibly the most significant of our time." This work consists of "the ninth and thirty-eighth chapters of Part One of *Don Quixote* and a fragment of the twenty-second chapter." Justifying the apparent "absurdity" of this statement, the narrator explains, is the purpose of this "note." Menard did not want to produce another *Don Quixote,* but *the Don Quixote,* the narrator stresses. At first, Menard considered recreating the events, circumstances, and cultural surroundings of Miguel de Cervantes's life in order to "become" the author and therefore be able to create the *Quixote* again; later, he abandoned this approach as "too easy." He decided that to remain Menard and still compose the *Quixote* would be a more arduous and therefore more rewarding undertaking.

The narrator never explains exactly how Menard succeeds in composing these fragments, and instead analyzes Menard's text. The narrator quotes at length from a letter of Menard's in which he explains that he chose the *Quixote* because, as a Frenchman, the book was not prominent in his literary education. The project of rewriting the *Quixote* is "considerably more difficult" than was the project of writing the novel in the first place, for in Cervantes' time the work was "perhaps inevitable," but in Menard's time it is "almost impossible."

The majority of the last half of the section is taken up with an explanation of why the Menard *Quixote* is "more subtle than that of Cervantes." Where Quixote simply "indulges in a rather coarse opposition" between chivalry stories and realistic descriptions of seventeenth-century Spain, Menard sets his story in the distant past, yet avoids describing his fictional setting with trite, stereotypical details of gypsies and the Inquisition. A discourse delivered by Don Quixote holding that arms were superior to letters is explicable in the Cervantes text by the fact that Cervantes himself was a soldier, but in the Menard *Quixote* the idea is distinctly more subtle and ironic. Cervantes' meditation on history is mere rhetoric while Menard's is clearly a reaction to the ideas of William James. The narrator concludes by evaluating the impact of Menard. His *Quixote* has enriched contemporary literature by its technique of "deliberate anachronism and erroncous attributions," and the narrator recommends applying Menard's technique in order to "improve" many classic works of literature.

Jorge Luis Borges

Characters

Henri Bachelier

Madame Henri Bachelier writes a preliminary catalog of Menard's works. The narrator of the story mistrusts her scholarship, and feels that it is especially suspect because it appeared in a newspaper with "Protestant leanings."

Madame Bachelier

See Henri Bachelier.

Baroness de Bacourt

The Baroness de Bacourt is one of the narrator's patronesses. She holds Friday salons for writers, which both the narrator and Menard attended, and sees in Menard's work the influence of Friedrich Nietzsche.

Countess de Bagnoregio

The Countess de Bagnoregio is another of the narrator's patronesses. Although she used to live in France, she married the international philanthropist Simon Kautsch and moved to Pittsburgh, Pennsylvania.

Pierre Menard

Although he is dead when the story opens, Pierre Menard is the protagonist of the story. Menard was a minor writer in France in the early part of the 1900s, a symbolist poet and scholar of philosophy. In 1934, Menard decided to write *Don Quixote:* not to copy the work down, or to write a modern-day *Don Quixote,* but to actually compose the work as if it had never been written before.

Narrator

The narrator of this story is never named, but readers learn a number of important things about him. He is probably French, because the story is set is the world of French literary scholarship of the 1930s. He has profitable relationships with at least two patronesses, the Baroness of Bacourt and the Countess de Bagnoregio. He is caught up in the academic world, and sees its small disagreements as very important. In addition, he is willing to draw extended conclusions from seemingly nonsensical data. As a result, he comes across as pretentious, perhaps even silly.

Themes

Absurdity

At first reading, "Pierre Menard" gives off an aura of absurdity. Both Menard and the narrator himself are absurd; the first for his inexplicable desire to write something that has already been written, and the second for his bizarre explanations of how two absolutely identical texts can mean completely different things. With these two characters, Borges is trying, among other things, to point out the absurdity of two groups of which he is a member: experimental (or "avant-garde") artists and scholars. Menard represents the avant-garde artists who flourished in Europe during the 1910s and 1920s, a time in which Borges lived in Switzerland and Spain. Borges knew many of the important figures in these movements.

The character of the narrator represents Borges in his identities as a scholar and librarian. The narrator's vindictive attitude towards Madame Bachelier mark him as a man obsessed with petty concerns, and his obsequiousness towards his wealthy patronesses demonstrate that he does not have the control over his own career that he craves. By having the narrator explain his own points without any other commentary on them, Borges emphasizes the absurd and nonsensical nature of the narrator's conclusions. Finally, a close reading of the story indicates the crowning absurdity, that there is no evidence that Menard ever wrote anything. The narrator seems to have inferred that Menard wrote the chapters he discusses based on Menard's letters proposing to accomplish this and the narrator's own "discovery" of Menard's themes in *Don Quixote*.

Artists and Society

Menard is the epitome of the over-intellectual experimental artist. His works, as listed by the narrator, are minor, arcane, and aimed at a tiny audience of his own contemporaries. He has only published one original poem (which appeared twice, "with minor variations," in the same magazine in

the same year. The only other creative works he produced are "a cycle of admirable sonnets for the Baroness de Bacourt" and "a transposition into Alexandrines" of a poem by Paul Valery.

According to the narrator, however, Menard's greatest work, and "possibly one of the most significant of our time," is his composition of *Don Quixote*. By foregrounding the narrator's apparently nonsensical praise of a work of Menard's that no one has ever seen, Borges seems to be criticizing the absurdity and valuelessness of art that is aimed only at a greatly limited audience of fellow-artists and intellectuals. Borges reinforces this criticism by the fact that the narrator is so clearly and so eagerly cut off from society, that he is more eager for the approval and support of the Countess and the Baroness than for the appreciation of a larger audience.

Language and Meaning

Borges subscribed to a philosophical view of language sometimes known as formalism. This view holds that language is not necessarily directly related to reality and that words have a sometimes misleading relationship with the things or actions that they name. However, in this story Borges makes fun of his own beliefs a little. The narrator's clearly silly explanation of how Menard's text is more meaningful and complex than Cervantes' original points out the ways that the "formalist" point of view can be absurd and self-contradictory at times.

Yet there is also a serious side to the narrator's explanation. The reader, Borges points out, is very concerned with *who* is speaking, and will grant more or less credence to a text depending on the reputation of the writer. The very same sentence certainly can mean different things, depending on who says it; a child's complaint about how hard life is, for instance, is much easier to reckon with than that of a philosopher. The narrator of the story is especially concerned with the ways that art depicts the past. The Spain of Cervantes's work was his own world, and little of his effort went into constructing a fantastic or fictional world. In the "Menard *Quixote*," the setting is the Spain of long ago, a place that has become almost a cliche after three hundred years of trite and stereotypical portrayals of it in plays, books, and paintings. Menard's accomplishment, the narrator feels, is to be a revolutionary artist, ignoring or rejecting the three centuries of tradition of what 1600s Spain "should" look like. Although Borges certainly points out the absurdity of the ''formalist'' view taken to an extreme, he also suggests that it can be a very valid way to look at writing.

Style

Point of View and Narration

The narrator of ''Pierre Menard'' is the driving force both of the themes of the story and of what action there is. Borges uses the first person, but it is not a traditional first-person narration, for the whole story is a parody of a scholarly article, one that might have appeared in a French journal in the 1930s. Like a good writer of a scholarly article, the narrator tries to avoid using ''I'' as the subject of his sentences. Nonetheless, the narrator's voice is precisely that of the cloistered ''egghead.'' He is a pretentious and obsequious intellectual, very concerned with petty academic conflicts and willing to make conclusions that seem very absurd. By using this person's voice, Borges makes points about how intellectuals and academics tend to shut themselves up in insular disciplines, and how their isolation can lead them to often sound simply silly.

Parody and Satire

''Pierre Menard, Author of the Quixote'' is a parody of a scholarly article. Borges employs many of the standard features of academic writing of the 1930s. The narrator, who seems to be a minor literary scholar, begins his article with a criticism of Madame Bachelier, a fellow scholar who has published an ''incomplete'' catalog of the writings of Pierre Menard, and then continues with a note of gratitude to his patronesses. Borges makes special fun of petty literary squabbles in heavily Catholic France by having the narrator comment that Madame Bachelier's article appeared in ''a certain newspaper, whose Protestant tendencies are no secret.''

The great majority of the parody, though, is of the narrator's great credulousness and seriousness in analyzing the Menard *Quixote*. He even says that he is ''reading *Don Quixote* —the entire work—as if Menard had conceived it,'' and finds everywhere the mark of Menard's genius. Through these details, Borges points out the tendency of academics to

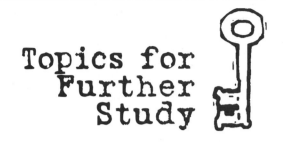

Topics for Further Study

- Why might a story mean something different in one time than it means in another time? Why does the narrator of ''Pierre Menard'' think that Menard's story of Don Quixote is better, more complicated, or more difficult to produce than that written by Cervantes?

- Look at some of the other writers of the Latin American ''boom.'' What are some of the countries that produced important writers after World War II? What political or social changes happened in those countries that these writers comment on in their works?

- Why is *Don Quixote* such an important book in Spanish and Latin American literature? Investigate some of the things people have said about this book from the time it was written until now.

- Borges lived during a very tumultuous time in Argentine history. What were the important political events in Argentina from 1900 to 1986? What happened in the 1970s and 1980s? Why do you think many of the Latin American writers who were influenced by Borges criticized his refusal to write about politics?

make often silly and insufficiently substantiated pronouncements and to go to great and torturous lengths in defending those pronouncements.

Allusion

Although the work makes fun of academics and intellectuals, Borges still is very academic in his composition of this story. Borges includes a number of tantalizing allusions, or references, to real writers and concepts that are closely related to Menard and his *Quixote*. Menard's name, for example, is very similar to the name of the French symbolist poet Louis Menard. The magazine in which Pierre Menard publishes his ''symbolist sonnet,'' *La Conque,* was a real French journal in which such writers as Paul Valery and Andre Gide published their work. The scholarly works of Menard—his monographs on

Boole and Leibnitz, his "examination of metric laws essential to French prose," and his discussions of logic problems—are all compatible with many scholarly works of the time. Finally, the story's most important allusion, to Cervantes's *Don Quixote*, thrusts Borges' story into a three-hundred-year old scholarly discourse about the novel—even though Borges, with his usual irony, has his narrator deny that this *Quixote* is at all compatible with Cervantes'.

Historical Context

Borges' Argentina

Argentina is a remarkably diverse country, and its citizens, like those of the United States, hail from any number of European countries. Borges himself was of both Spanish and English ancestry. When Borges was born in 1899, Argentina was governed by a conservative regime, allied with business and cattle ranching industries. Politicians of the conservative persuasion were forced, during the first years of Borges' life, to make alliances with so-called "Radicals," who wanted to reform the country. In 1916, the Radicals gained control of the government in the first truly popular vote the country had ever experienced, and ruled until 1930.

In that year, the military overthrew the civilian government and installed General Uriburu in the presidency. During the period 1930-43, the military held an uneasy balance of power with civilian governments. Argentina remained neutral during World War II. In 1945, Colonel Juan Peron ascended to power in Argentina, and remained in power until 1955, strengthened by the support of the generals and of the Argentine masses, who felt an affinity with Peron's wife, Eva. Although many Argentines supported Peron, he was an authoritarian leader with little tolerance for dissent. Although he lost power over the state in 1955, Peron retained a great deal of influence in Argentina through his Peronista party and through his pull in the labor unions. Throughout the 1960s and 1970s, Argentina was in a state of upheaval, with Peronistas, generals, and reformers fighting for power.

In March 1976, military officers again took over the government and ruled until after Borges' death. Their regime was marked by repression, an undeclared "civil war" in which they had tens of thousands of dissenters killed, and a short war with England. In that war, known at the Falkland Islands War, Argentina was forced to give up its claim on the Falklands. Argentina's history throughout Borges' life was tumultuous, complicated, and often violent. The fact that Borges, in his writing, rarely addressed these issues made many of his fellow writers resent him a great deal.

European Art 1890-1940

One of the most fervent periods of artistic innovation the world has ever known took place in Europe between 1890 and 1940. In music, painting, sculpture, theater, and literature, dozens of revolutionary movements were born, flourished, scandalized the public, and died, all with a period of months. London and Paris were the centers of all of this experimentation. In painting, the Impressionist movement gave way to the Post-Impressionists, the Primitives, the Fauvists, the Dadaists and the Surrealists; in literature, some of the important movements that made Paris or London their home were the Decadents, the Symbolists, the Imagists, the Vorticists, the Futurists, and the Lost Generation. Although Borges did not live in Paris or London, the spirit of experimentation flooded the continent's artists, and both in Geneva, where he attended school, and later in Spain, where he fell in with the "Ultraist" movement, Borges absorbed the artistic ferment and brought it back with him to Buenos Aires. Partly as a result of Borges' importation and dissemination of the European spirit of innovation, the countries of Latin America experienced what became known as the "boom"—an artistic revolution of similar proportions.

Critical Overview

When "Pierre Menard, Author of the Quixote" appeared in 1939, the story marked a turning-point for the career of Jorge Luis Borges, a little-known Argentine writer and librarian who had, up to then, concentrated his efforts on Symbolist poetry, critical essays, and short fictional sketches. He had, however, tried his hand at the parodic critical articles of which "Pierre Menard" is such a masterful examples. "Pierre Menard," Borges noted in 1968, "was still a halfway house between the essay and the true tale." After "Menard," Borges' achieve-

Compare & Contrast

- **1939:** France, the country in which "Pierre Menard, Author of the Quixote" takes place, is on the brink of war with Adolf Hitler's Germany. However, feeling secure behind their Maginot Line of defenses along the border with Germany, many French people are unaware of the danger posed by Hitler.

  1990s: France and Germany, along with most of the countries of Western Europe, form an alliance known as the European Union. Plans are in place for all EU countries to switch to a common currency by the year 2000.

- **1930s:** Before World War II, academics and intellectuals in Europe and America are largely drawn from the upper and upper-middle classes, since few members of the working class are able to afford a college education, both because of tuition and of young peoples' responsibility to provide for their families. Borges' narrator refers numerous times to his patronesses, the rich women who presumably sponsor his academic and scholarly work.

  1990s: Today, higher education is much more widespread. Most European public universities charge no tuition at all, and in the United States, despite the high cost of college, a larger percentage of young people than ever attend college.

- **1939:** James Joyce publishes his final work, *Finnegans Wake*. The work is in many ways the culmination of the "modernist" movement in art and literature that has been flourishing in Europe since before World War I, and that was an inspiration to many of the writers—including Borges—of the Latin American "boom."

  1990s: Today, much of the experimental work in the arts is done not in writing or painting but in the so-called "new media"—video, electronic music, performance art, and spoken-word performances.

---

ments multiplied, and building on the strikingly original techniques of that story, he wrote some of the most memorable pieces of short fiction of the twentieth century.

Ironically, although he was a father-figure for the great Latin American "boom" in literature after World War II, Borges was not admired by many of the writers he inspired. His lack of political commitment and his own cultural background, which he felt to be as much English as Argentine, caused writers such as Gabriel Garcia Marquez to feel much devotion to Borges. Mario Vargas Llosa said in 1967 that "I have always had a problem justifying my admiration for Borges," and Marquez remarked that "I have a great admiration for him. I read him every night. He is a writer I detest. His is a literature of evasion." His unwillingness to engage in political activity might have sprung from the day, in 1946, when the new Argentine dictator Juan Peron took Borges' job from him; at any rate,

Borges opposed the student movements of the late 1960s that were the touchstone for so much of the "boom" writing.

Consequently, it was the critics and writers of the Anglo-American world who most eagerly promoted Borges' work. Such American writers as John Updike and John Barth admired his experimentation, seeing in it a way out of the stagnation in current American writing. In his essay "The Literature of Exhaustion," Barth specifies just where the most important paradox and irony of the story lies, and feels that this seeming dead end is where the work is most triumphant: in "Pierre Menard," Borges "writes a remarkable and original work of literature, the implicit theme of which is the difficulty, perhaps the unnecessity, of writing original works of literature. His artistic victory is that he confronts an intellectual dead end and employs it against itself to accomplish new human work." Martin Stabb, though, disagrees, and writes in his book on Borges that ''Pierre Menard'' is primarily ''a masterful parody of the critical establishment'' and that the ''narrator's comment on Menard's principal achievement occupies that tenuous middle ground between high-powered critical intelligence and rampant sophisticated lunacy.''

Most of the commentary on ''Pierre Menard'' focuses on the story's treatment of the question of language and of relationships between works of literature. The Belgian-American critic Paul de Man, in his essay ''A Modern Master,'' points out ''Pierre Menard's'' roots in duplicity and misleading the reader, commenting that the knowledgeable reader will first think that Menard is meant to represent Paul Valery, then has this notion demolished when he reads that Menard has written an anti-Valery polemic. For de Man, the story is ''such a complex set of ironies, parodies, reflections, and issues that no brief commentary can begin to do them justice.'' Pierre Machery, in ''Borges and the Fictive Narrative,'' sees Borges as proposing that reading can never exhaust all of the meanings of a work. ''The book is incomplete because it harbours the promise of an inexhaustible variety,'' he points out, referring to the narrator's diverse readings of the identical passage from Cervantes and from Menard. Part of this incompletion or inexhaustibility results from the fact that Borges will always grant that the reverse of any idea he asserts might be as valid as his own idea.

Margaret Boegeman, writing on ''The Swerve from Kafka by Borges,'' argues that Borges always inserts a degree of uncertainty and contradiction into his stories. ''I think one should work into a story the idea of not being sure of all things, because that's the way reality is.'' Similarly, the narrator of ''Pierre Menard'' describes Menard's ''resigned or ironical habit of propagating ideas which are the strict reverse of those he preferred.''

Robert Scholes writes in ''The Reality of Borges'' that Pierre Menard is ''in one sense Borges' greatest hero and in another his greatest fool.'' After trying his hand at original writing, Menard has despaired of the possibility of literary creation. His way out of the futilities of his time is to become another, to live in another period entirely and to write the masterpiece of another era. Tying this to the philosophy of ''formalism,'' Scholes asserts that ''Borges is reminding us in this tale that there is no meaning without a meaner. Language always

assumes a larger context.'' Where all of these critics agree, though, is that this story brings out some extremely interesting questions about the relationship between writers, the works they produce, and the readers that read those works. How and where the last group should find the meaning of those works, Borges points out, is a much more complicated question than it first seems.

Criticism

Greg Barnhisel

Barnhisel is a Ph.D. candidate at the University of Texas at Austin. He also has published articles on Ezra Pound in academic journals and critical anthologies. In the following essay, he describes ''Pierre Menard'' as a story of ideas rather than of human relationships.

Jorge Luis Borges, the courtly blind Argentine, became in the 1960s probably the best-known and most respected foreign writer in the English-speaking world. Before the other writers of the Latin American ''boom'' had gained any fame, Borges was lecturing around the world and holding visiting professorships at prestigious American universities. In America, Borges was held up by such leading literary figures as John Updike, Paul de Man, and John Barth as the best hope modern fiction had to get beyond what they felt was its stagnation. Today in North America and to a growing extent in Latin America, Borges has passed into the realm of ''classic'' writers to become a figure of unquestioned achievement and importance. However, in Latin America Borges' place was much more precarious. His refusal to speak out against the repressive Argentine government earned him the enmity of such younger writers as Gabriel Garcia Marquez.

''Pierre Menard'' is an excellent example of Borges' unwillingness to address political issues. In 1939, when the story was written, the world was careening rapidly towards war, and France, where Borges set his story, was soon to be invaded and occupied. However, Borges ignores all of this and chooses to write a satire on intellectual and academic pretensions and petty disagreements. Borges endured the savagery of the Peron government and,

What Do I Read Next?

- Borges' most important collection in English, *Labyrinths*, contains most of his best-known "fictions," including "Pierre Menard," "The Lottery in Babylon," "The Garden of Forking Paths," "Emma Zunz," and "Funes the Memorious." The work is essential for anyone with an interest in Borges.

- Miguel de Cervantes' *Don Quixote* is the inspiration for Borges' story and the most important work of fiction in the Spanish language. Although long, this novel about the adventures of an old man, deluded into thinking he is a knight, and his "squire" Sancho Panza retains its ability to amuse, move, and even shock readers, almost four hundred years after its first appearance.

- *The Complete Stories 1883-1924*, by Franz Kafka. Kafka, a Jewish writer from Prague in Central Europe, composed dozens of short stories and "parables" that, in their surrealism and concern with questioning the limits of what fiction should be, are often compared with Borges' "fictions." Especially interesting are "The Metamorphosis," "In the Penal Colony," "The Hunger Artist," and "Give It Up!"

- Perhaps the best-known writer of the Latin American "boom" of which Borges was a founder is Colombia's Gabriel Garcia Marquez, winner of the Nobel Prize for Literature. Marquez's *One Hundred Years of Solitude* is his most classic work, and recounts the saga of the Buendia family, patriarchs of a small village.

- Another Latin American short story writer who, like Borges, has been called a practitioner of the "postmodern" is Clarice Lispector. This Brazilian author's collection *Soulstorm* (1989) anthologizes a number of her short, astringent pieces.

- One of Lispector's most important American admirers is the New York short story writer Grace Paley. Her *Collected Stories* (1994) exhibits much the same terseness and dislocation that Borges' stories engender in the reader.

- Vladimir Nabokov, a Russian expatriate who lived in the United States, Germany, and France, among other places, wrote stories that are reminiscent of Borges' works in that they plunge the reader, without introduction, deep into the mind and concerns of a character who is, more often than not, of an academic or scholarly bent. In 1995, *The Stories of Vladimir Nabokov* made available all of his brilliant and lapidary pieces.

- In *Stories and Texts for Nothing*, Samuel Beckett experiments with the short story form in much the same way that Borges does. Beckett's novel *Murphy* also uses many of Borges' techniques, especially the incorporation of various types of arcane knowledge as an essential element of the story.

---

later, of the military junta and their "dirty war" against dissenters, but did not acknowledge the horrors. Other writers in Latin American countries suffering under dictatorships considered the refusal of a public intellectual like Borges to address these issues reprehensible. Borges' whole career was characterized by this, and exemplifies the willful refusal to recognize and protest against repression in favor of a purely artistic accomplishment.

Yet, for those readers who do not subscribe to the idea that art must address social and political issues, Borges' work is of unquestioned mastery. In his essay for the *Dictionary of Literary Biography*, Alberto Julian Perez remarks that Borges' two most lasting contributions to literature are his "creation of stories whose principal objective is to deal with critical, literary, or aesthetic problems" and his "development of plots that communicate elaborate

> The narrator's explanation of how Menard's text is more meaningful and complex than Cervantes' original indicates the ways that the 'formalist' point of view can be absurd and self-contradictory at times."

and complex ideas that are transformed into the main thematic base of the story, provoking the action and relegating the characters—who appear as passive subjects in this inhuman, nightmarish world—to a secondary plane.'' Borges is not a writer who is particularly concerned with the details of human interaction. He is a writer of ideas, and it is ideas that drive his ''fictions.'' Perez even states that Borges treats these ideas as characters in themselves, ''exaggerat[ing] characteristics, deforming them and provoking a comic response in the reader who identifies with the critical point of view of the satirist.'' In his book *Paper Tigers,* John Sturrock argues that Borges ''writes as bookishly as he lived, refusing to play the game which writers of fiction habitually play of making us think they write not out of books but out of their deep, direct experience of human life. They forget to what a high degree their experience of life is interpreted for them by their experience of reading.''

Borges is an important precursor of the ''postmodern'' movement. The notion that books influence the way we experience life just as much as life influences the way we read books is an essential component of the ''postmodern.'' ''Borges uses metalanguages, quotations, intertextuality, parody and imitation,'' Perez explains in the *Dictionary of Literary Biography.* ''The real being of characters and objects do not necessarily coincide with their appearance.'' In ''Pierre Menard,'' Borges accomplishes both of these aims of the postmodern. By writing a story that masquerades as a scholarly article, Borges causes us to think about what makes a ''real'' short story, and also about the conventions of the scholarly article. Many of Borges' stories,

especially those he wrote in the late 1930s and early 1940s, use these same techniques.

With his extensive experience as a librarian and an academic, Borges was well aware of the idea of ''intertextuality,'' or how all books form a sort of interconnected net, each referring to other books and no book able to stake out a place entirely of its own. ''Pierre Menard, Author of Don Quixote'' satirizes scholarly writing and the classic novel, as well as pointing out the parasitic manner in which scholarship relies on creative work and current writing relies on older writing. The article is not only dependent on Menard's text for its own existence, it needed Madame Bachelier's ''erroneous'' article in order to come into being. Pierre Menard's project is another logical conclusion of that realization: for if one's book is necessarily going to refer to other books, why not make it simply an extended reference to another book?

Although the work is certainly a parody, there are a number of very serious issues relating to language and meaning that Borges addresses. Borges subscribed to a philosophical view of language sometimes known as ''formalism'' that says that language has no direct relation to reality and that words have a sometimes misleading relationship with the things or actions that they name. In this story Borges makes fun of his own beliefs a little. The narrator's explanation of how Menard's text is more meaningful and complex than Cervantes' original indicates the ways that the ''formalist'' point of view can be absurd and self-contradictory at times.

Yet Borges is not entirely facetious about formalism. In reading, Borges points out, we are very concerned with who is speaking, and we will grant more or less intelligence to a text depending on what we think of a writer. When Cervantes wrote *Don Quixote,* many of the philosophical ideas common in intellectual discourse today had not yet been developed. For this reason, the narrator finds the passage in ''Menard's'' *Quixote* to be much more complex and profound than the passage in the original—for after all, he is telling us, Cervantes could not have known of these concepts, and therefore could not have embedded them in his novel. Menard, an intellectual and avant-garde artist, was certainly familiar with these ideas, and consequently they must be in the text.

The underlying issue, then, is to what degree we must know something about how, when, and by whom a work of literature was composed in order to know what it means. While the narrator thinks that these conditions—which we might call a work's "circumstances of composition"—entirely determine what a work means, Borges' view is more difficult to identify. He probably does not agree wholly with the narrator, since so much of the story is devoted to making fun of this narrator for his isolation in the world of academia. Yet once we learn something about Borges, then we learn that it would make no sense for him to believe that literary works somehow exist out of time, and that (for example) we could read Aristotle as if his works contained references to quantum physics or Soviet Communism.

"Pierre Menard" makes fun of the very kind of scholarly discussion that it invites. By alluding to the very difficult and complicated philosophical issues that Menard wrote on during his lifetime, the narrator makes it necessary for himself to discuss these kinds of issues, and by extension we, also, need to address them in any reading of this story. However, as Martin Stabb points out in his book on Borges, "anyone who has the temerity to write about Borges' 'Pierre Menard' will, of course, run the risk of doing just what the story's pompous, self-important narrator attempted, namely, to seek fame and recognition vicariously through association with 'the great man.'" The equations recede before us: Menard seeks his fame by latching onto Cervantes, the narrator seeks his through Menard, Borges the author makes his name through characters like this narrator, and critics will attempt to make their fortunes by writing on Borges. It begins to seem nihilistic, to say the least.

However, Borges is not so nihilistic and absurd as all this. While he certainly wants to point out how all written works "piggyback," to some extent, on other works, he also appreciates the separate world created by just this web of intertextuality. Borges' formalist beliefs will not allow him to grant any claim of "truth" to any written text, but one gets the impression that "truth" is not of primary importance to Borges. Borges, the librarian, the child whose memories of childhood center on books and languages, prefers to live in that entirely interconnected web of books. Another of Borges' most famous stories, "The Library of Babel," describes an almost infinite library in which all possible combinations of letters, spaces, words, sentences, and chapters exist, and where people wander endlessly, searching for the volume that will explain their lives to them. Whether Borges sees this universe of texts as a dream or a nightmare is lost

somewhere in the web of references and allusions that make up his fictions.

Source: Greg Barnhisel, for *Short Stories for Students*, Gale, 1998.

Aburawi A. Elmajdoub and Mary K. Miller

In the following excerpt from a longer essay, the authors discuss challenges presented by the narratives of both "Garden of Forking Paths" and "Pierre Menard."

For Borges, the world is a book always being written. "Pierre Menard" centers upon such writing. In this case, Menard begins to write *Don Quixote*. In order to get past commonplaces of fiction and everyday reality, Borges constructs this story to appear illogical, irrational, and devoid of meaning. It is made of fragments, and it is totally unconcerned with the daily world. The reader has to fall into this labyrinthine reality and to thread his way out.

Pierre Menard, to begin, filters to us through a narrating critic of sorts. This critic considers himself a reliable connection between Menard and his audience. He rests his qualifications upon a correspondence-based friendship with Menard. He also alleges approval of his remarks from two of Menard's supporters: The Baroness de Bacourt and the Countess de Bagnoregio. A list of Menard's visible works comes to us through this narrator. We see the writer's vita, as it were: sonnets; alexandrines; a proposal for measuring French prose; translations of two Spanish works; discourses on philosophy, logic, and chess; a work in two editions centering upon Achilles and the tortoise called *Les Problemes d'un Problem;* journal articles concerning Valery; plus evidence of literary homage to his supporters.

Menard sounds precise, metered, structured, rational, calculating, and tenured. The narrator-critic sounds nervous, possessive, sentimental—actually, reminiscent of the glimpses that he gives us of the Countess de Bagnoregio. Early on, he has told us with regard to Menard that "Error is trying to tarnish his Memory." "Decidedly," he states, "a brief rectification is inevitable." He fears that the errant bibliographer Madame Henri Bachelier is corroding the dead Menard's image; he shall, on the other hand, restore the author to a livelier state. The narrator then passes from the required, expected, conventional works of Menard to a literary coup: Menard, enjoying the ongoing presence given him by Borges and his readers, perpetuates the earth-swallowed Cervantes, dead since 1616. We have the words of our narrator, excerpts of letters from Menard, and Menard's creation of Chapters Nine, Thirty-eight, and portions of Twenty-two *Don Quixote*. Part One, from which to construct our assessment of his effort.

We learn that Menard did not wish to compose another *Don Quixote,* nor did he wish to copy the original one. *Don Quixote* exists because Cervantes, his publisher, and his readers created it. Menard, taking up a favorite Borgian theme, assumes that his creation of *Quixote* is just as possible as our daily creations of external world, God, chance, time and space. Menard tells the narrator in a letter that the only difference in his creation and the philosophic creations of God, Chance, and Space is that he did not choose to "publish in pleasant volumes the intermediary stages of . . . work." Debating how best to accomplish his creative breakthrough, Menard—so the narrator tells us—prefers remaining Menard while arriving at *Quixote* rather than attempting to be Cervantes. Our critic leads us to a keener appreciation of Menard's choice:

> The fragmentary *Don Quixote* of Menard is more subtle than that of Cervantes. The latter indulges in a rather coarse opposition between tales of knighthood and the meager, provincial reality of his country; Menard chooses as "reality" the land of Carmen during the century of Lepanto and Lope . . . In his work there are neither bands of gypsies, conquistadors, mystics, Philip and Seconds, nor autos-da-fe. He disregards or proscribes local color. This disdain indicates a new approach to the historical novel.

Also, in this complex story (novel) by Borges (Menard), we learn that part of Menard's success in recreating the *Quixote,* at least Chapter Thirty-eight, lies in Menard's unquixotic habit "of propounding ideas which were the strict reverse of those he preferred." The author of the Cervantes-*Quixote,* having fought for Spain much of his life, allows his hero honestly to lament the disappearance of the horse and the lance in individual tests of courage and zeal. The Menard-*Quixote,* written by a French contemporary of Bertrand Russell, speaks up for arms because irony rules in modern literary circles while massive, impersonal arms rule the secular day.

When Menard coincides with Cervantes in Chapter Nine of *Quixote,* however, he means what he is saying about history. Cervantes conceives history quite differently, perhaps, although the words are identical in both the Cervantes and the Menard *Quixotes:*

> . . . la verdad, cuya madre es la historia, emula del tiempo, deposito de las acciones, testigo de lo pasado, ejemplo y aviso de lo presente, advertencia de lo por venir.
>
> [. . . truth, whose mother is history, who is the rival of time, depository of deeds, witness of the past, example and lesson to the present, and warning to the future.]

Where Cervantes is conceivably lauding history and truth as fixed, reliable entities—the former leading to the latter—Menard is focusing upon history's inventiveness, its persuasiveness which leads its believers to derive certainty from illusion. In lieu of striving for a historical truth, Menard's invention takes the vintage words of Cervantes (words which have an appearance of fixity, of historical character) and demonstrates their effervescence and fluidity. For Cervantes, a Spanish exponent of valor, history could offer temporal assurance and attractiveness, but historical truth, for France's Menard "is what we think took place." As Borges has stated elsewhere, "It is what we judge to have happened." History is one of our most ingenious inventions, surpassed only perhaps by Menard's *Quixote.*

These two stories "The Garden of Forking Paths" and "Pierre Menard, Author of *Don Quixote*" weave varying configurations of inventiveness. Cervantes and Borges existed in the realm of daily fiction—that time-encased capsule often called "external reality." Because these authors got beyond the strictures of time in their fiction, adventurous readers can travel labyrinths that circle and wind beyond daily, sensory illusion. Borges creates a Menard who perpetuates the spirit of the old don. Literature impels. As John Sturrock declares, Menard "shows an advanced understanding of what the Borgesian literary man should be expected to understand, that to criticize is to create." Squired by a nervous narrator, Menard is a worthy candidate for the Quixotic succession. Tilting on the Cervantian plain, Menard coaxed an ink-stained Rocinante past Chapters Nine, Thirty-eight, and Part or Twenty-two of the *Quixote* One. His discovery of ambiguous, evolving language has Dulcineic overtones. Created, creative Quixote and Menard expand time through an ongoing combustion with readers. This conflagration explodes reality as an old fiction needing new quests.

Like Ts'ui Pen, Stephen Albert, Menard, and the Borgian reader can flow, suspend, and proliferate in everwidening circles, fusing past and future to make an ongoing "now" in a challenging, reader-impelled, assimilative fiction.

Source: Aburawi A. Elmajdoub and Mary K. Miller, "The 'Eternal Now' in Borges' 'The Garden of Forking Paths' and 'Pierre Menard, Author of Don Quixote'," in *The Durham University Journal,* Vol. LXXXIII, No. 2, July, 1991, pp. 249–51.

Gene H. Bell-Villada

In the following excerpt from a longer essay, Bell-Villada discusses the theme of intellectual absurdity in "Pierre Menard."

"Pierre Menard, Author of the *Quixote*" similarly deals with an invented intellectual, a minor symbolist poet who, standing at the end of a tradition, also hits upon an elaborate and striking notion, one as novel as it is useless. As happens with Runeberg in his later years, Menard is totally taken up by his project, an obsession that might suggest madness were Menard depicted at closer quarters. Despite their differences—Runeberg is a somberly respectable academic, Menard a precious, turn-of-the-century decadent—both live single-mindedly for their manias: "writing" the *Quixote* in one instance, "rehabilitating" Judas in the other.

In format the story is a postmortem literary appreciation, an apology for Menard's life written shortly after his funeral. The unnamed narrator who looks back upon Menard is a snobbish reactionary (his initial paragraph flaunts his aristocratic ties and snipes at Protestants, Masons, and Jews), a very French type of polemicist still found in the pages of the right-wing *Action Française.* The catalog he gives of Menard's published works (each item of which is a delight) furnishes what Borges called "a diagram of [Menard's] mental history." Menard's mental space is conspicuously narrow, his subjects completely self-contained—pure poetry, symbolic logic (item *f* in the catalog), metrics (*i, j*), chess (*e, g*), even a project for an artificial poetic language (*b*). This introversion inevitably turns self-reflexive; for instance, the apocryphal retranslation into French of Quevedo's translation into Spanish of a devotional work originally in French (Borges's footnote), the study of metric patterns in French prose as evidenced in the prose of an author who had denied such patterns (*j*) and, of course, the revealing title *Les problèmes d'un problème* (*m*).

Indeed, much of Menard's work is so minute as to be pointless, for example, transposing Valery's greatest poem into a different metre (*o*) or improving the game of chess by eliminating one pawn (*e*)

> **At work in Borges's story is the thorny question of how much there remains to 'say' in literature and how much material there is left with which to say it."**

and then rejecting the proposal! Menard's "obstinate analysis" of poetry, his fascination with syntax (item *n*) and punctuation (*s*), and his concomitant belief that "censuring and praising" are merely "sentimental operations" that have "nothing to do with criticism" (*n*) all suggest a lifeless formalism, an effete nihilism in which basic questions of meaning and of value have lost their place. The one exception to this fine-grained claustrophobia is Menard's attack on his friend Valery, a piece expressing the exact opposite of Menard's feelings; this rather primitive incursion into irony later becomes a key to explicating and evaluating Menard's unpublished masterpiece.

The latter work happens to consist of two chapters from *Don Quixote,* Menard's texts being identical to those of Cervantes, yet with not one copied word in them. The narrator now recalls the steps by which Menard arrived at this undertaking. Inspired by a casual idea of Novalis about achieving total identification with an author, Menard first considers reliving Cervantes's life and forgetting three hundred years of European history. This project he discards as too easy because his aim is to create his own *Quixote,* not as Cervantes but as Pierre Menard. He also contemplates the possibility of immortality, a situation that would inevitably result in his writing of the *Quixote* (another "Borgesian" play on that old fancy about monkeys, typewriters, and *Hamlet*). Menard eventually realizes that, having gone through *Don Quixote* at age twelve and knowing Cervantes's other works from more recent reading, his own mind perceives the *Quixote* in the same dim way that any author senses within himself a book yet to be written. This is Menard's point of departure; after thousands of drafts, most of them put to flames before the narrator's eyes, Pierre accomplishes a tiny fraction of his self-appointed task.

The narrator now builds a cunning edifice of evaluation. As he sees it, the *Quixote* is an achievement surpassing that of Cervantes. Unlike the latter, a Spaniard who simply relied on his national experience and native tongue, Menard was a twentieth-century Frenchman faced with an array of deceptively quaint stereotypes (conquistadors, gypsies, Carmen) and a seventeenth-century foreign language. Yet another difficulty overcome by Menard was the portrayal of the knight debating the question of arms versus letters. The original Don Quixote came down on the side of arms, an obvious and easy recourse for Cervantes, a seasoned ex-soldier. On the other hand, for a bookish man of letters like Menard to have so convincingly defended arms is (according to the narrator) an awe-inspiring feat. Menard's capacity for transcending personal limits and praising soldierly values has been attributed, among other things, to the influence of Nietzsche and especially to the penchant for stating opinions contrary to his own—the precedent of course being his "attack" on Valery.

Now comes what may be Borges's most notorious conceit. The narrator quotes two long passages dealing with Truth and History, one by Cervantes, another "by" Menard. These two passages are absolutely identical. Not so, this is but apparent, says the narrator, who dismisses Cervantes's words as empty rhetoric but extols Menard's as contemporary in their outlook and Jamesian in their pragmatism; he therefore judges Menard superior! (On the other hand, he praises Cervantes's prose style as natural and direct, but faults Menard's language as "affected" and "archaic!") After some further reminiscing on Menard's speculations, the narrator finishes his account by pondering a new technique of reading, one that employs "deliberate anachronism" and "erroneous attribution"—that is, disregarding history, conceiving the *Aeneid* as pre-Homeric and the *Imitation of Christ* as if written by Celine or Joyce.

This literary mock-memoir was Borges's first major story; with its wealth of ideas and wit, it stands among his liveliest and best pieces. On one level, "Pierre Menard" is a clever parody of literary criticism and its sectarian debates, philosophical battles, and ardent attacks and vindications; Borges himself, with his own aesthetic to uphold, was often a willing participant in such critical activity. Borges's unnamed narrator, an amateur critic, puts to work many forensic tools—learned allusion, sly sophistry, sarcasm, nostalgia—all with a view to explicating and indeed justifying the monumental but futile product of an eccentric precieux. . . .

Also at work in Borges's story is the thorny question of how much there remains to "say" in literature and how much material there is left with which to say it. Though Borges himself has never expressed doubts about the infinite possibilities of language and the imagination, his character Pierre Menard stands within a set of circumstances hardly favorable to newness and originality. As Borges observed over French radio, Menard suffers from "an excess of intelligence, a sense of the uselessness of literature, as well as the idea that there are too many books." Coming as he does at the end of a literary period, Menard is weighed down by tiredness and scepticism. This is perfectly illustrated by Pierre's literary methods: his writings, which show no hint of any larger theme of his own, build exclusively upon the achievements of others. The *Quixote* project simply pushes his derivative tendencies to their ultimate conclusion. . . .

One of the most striking instances of the "Pierre Menard effect" can be found in Woody Allen's *Play It Again, Sam,* which opens by showing in its entirety the closing scene from *Casablanca.* The relationship of that emotionally charged episode to Woody Allen's comic plot completely alters the meaning of the original Moroccan airport melodrama. The culminating point of a familiar Bogart-Bergman love-and-war saga is thereby transformed into the wistful and jocose opening scene of Woody's bittersweet schlemiel satire.

In Borges's story, however, such practices and notions are carried to their ultimate and absurd extreme: the complete and unmodified re-production of an earlier work. The idea is intriguing, though of course unrealizable in practice. To present as new art a moustachioed Mona Lisa or a giant soup can—artifacts which at least differ somewhat from their originals and whose natures are immediately evident to the naked eye—is one thing, but to pass off an entire preexisting novel as one's own requires an added measure of brazenness or naivete. Borges, on the other hand, writes *about* someone actually doing this, comments on it with an implied aesthetic resembling the one formulated above, and, to cap the whole joke, defends an act of creation that is as admirable as it is useless. Although Pierre's own grandiose project is by itself a dead end (a fact aptly symbolized by the thousands of preliminary drafts he brought out and burnt), "his" *Quixote* raises countless questions about the relationship between art, history, and originality, between received tradition and individual talent.

The arguments set forth by Menard's unnamed encomiast are a mixture of sound thinking and sophistry, but then, Borges's story is an extended satire of the intellectual patterns, formal subtypes, and sophistries of the genre of literary criticism. The opening paragraph, with its reactionary mumblings, captures the passions of ideologically motivated aesthetics. The narrator's personal praise for Menard is in the tradition of the posthumous literary eulogy often printed in small literary journals. The list of Menard's visible works recalls many a philological enumeration or catalogue raisonne. The account of how Menard came to write *Don Quixote* is a genetic explanation usually found in literary biographies. The suggestion that Menard glorifies war under the "influence" of Nietzsche is a recognizable critical commonplace. On the other hand, the assertion that Menard's pro-war statements are ironic is itself an ironic imitation of a ruse by which a critic might justify works whose social doctrines make him uncomfortable (for example, Celine's anti-Semitic *Bagatelles pour un massacre* or Michael Cimino's anti-Asian *The Deer Hunter*). In the manner of historicist scholarship, the narrator finds in both Cervantes and Menard the philosophical ideas of their respective times. Last but not least, in his final paragraphs Borges prophetically satirizes the ahistorical structuralists of the future, with their synchronic and reversible perceptions of the entirety of world literature, their emphasis on reader rather than author and their attraction for words like "palimpsest." (Critics like Gerard Genette, in apparent disregard of Borges's general spirit of humor and parody, have built entire theories on the fanciful notions played with in "Pierre Menard.")

Borges's utilization of the *Quixote* in this context is by no means accidental. Cervantes's masterpiece, itself one of the great parodies, has been called the "Rohrschach blot" of art criticism, a work in which readers see what they want to see or what history conditions them to see. Literary commentators over the years have repeatedly read into *Don Quixote* the chief preoccupations of their own time and culture. Hence, eighteenth-century rationalists thought of Cervantes's would-be knight as an insensate fool; romantics esteemed him as a noble idealist fighting against an imperfect world; a religiously inclined Dostoevski saw in Don Quixote a figure of Christian purity and goodness; Marxists and other sociological critics see the knight as a representative of a decaying aristocracy clinging to superannuated feudal-chivalric values; Americo Castro, in his existentialist phase, saw Don Quixote as the individual who consciously and actively chooses to define himself and become a knight; and American interpreters, living in a world of uncertainty and flux, comb Cervantes's text for the finer ironies, the nuanced interplay between deceptive appearance and illusive reality. When Menard's commentator detects Jamesian pragmatism in Cervantes, he unwittingly falls in with a venerable old critical tradition.

Source: Gene H. Bell-Villada, in his *Borges and His Fiction: A Guide to His Mind and Art,* University of North Carolina Press, Chapel Hill, 1981, pp. 122–28.

Sources

Barnstone, Willis, editor. *Borges at Eighty: Conversations.* Bloomington: Indiana University Press, 1982.

Barth, John. "The Literature of Exhaustion." In *Critical Essays on Jorge Luis Borges,* ed. Jaime Alazraki. Boston: G.K. Hall and Co., 1987.

Doegeman, Margaret. "From Amhorctz to Exegete: The Swerve from Kafka to Borges." In *Critical Essays on Jorge Luis Borges,* ed. Jaime Alazraki. Boston: G.K. Hall and Co., 1987.

de Man, Paul. "A Modern Master." In *Critical Essays on Jorge Luis Borges,* ed. Jaime Alazraki. Boston: G.K. Hall and Co., 1987.

Macherey, Pierre. "Borges and the Fictive Narrative." In *Critical Essays on Jorge Luis Borges,* ed. Jaime Alazraki. Boston: G.K. Hall and Co., 1987.

Perez, Alberto Julian. "Jorge Luis Borges." In *Dictionary of Literary Biography* Vol. 113. Detroit: Gale Research Co., 1992.

Scholes, Robert. "The Reality of Borges." In *Critical Essays on Jorge Luis Borges,* ed. Jaime Alazraki. Boston: G.K. Hall and Co., 1987.

Sturrock, John. *Paper Tigers: The Ideal Fictions of Jorge Luis Borges.* Oxford: Clarendon Press, 1987.

Further Reading

Alazraki, Jaime. *Critical Essays on Jorge Luis Borges.* Boston: G.K. Hall and Co., 1987.
An excellent collection of primarily Anglo-American essays on Borges, from a number of perspectives. Alazraki also edited a Spanish-language collection on Borges with different critical essays included.

Stabb, Martin S. *Borges Revisited.* Boston: Twayne Publishers, 1991.

    Stabb provides a brief overview of Borges career and short discussions of his important works. A good introduction to Borges' place in the Latin American ''boom.''

The Revolt of 'Mother'

Mary E. Wilkins Freeman

1890

First published in 1890 in *Harper's Bazaar,* "The Revolt of 'Mother'" then appeared the following year, with only a few textual changes, in Mary E. Wilkins Freeman's second short story collection, *A New England Nun and Other Stories.*

Freeman is best known for her local color stories that portrayed rural life in small New England towns at the end of the nineteenth century, which was a time of great change. While her use of these elements contributes to her effective picture of the village community, in "The Revolt of 'Mother'" her emphasis lies more with the oppression and rebellion of women, a theme that she deals with in other stories written during the same period, notably "A New England Nun." In portraying a main character insistent on receiving fair treatment from her husband, both for herself and her family, Freeman conveys women's lack of power. At the same time, she puts forth one way to get around such inequality. Freeman also demonstrates other features of the New England village in the late nineteenth century, such as the lessening of importance of the once all-powerful minister and a closely knit community that is fascinated by the transgressive actions of others. All of these characteristics found in "The Revolt of 'Mother'" further an understanding of New England and the United States' history.

Author Biography

Mary E. Wilkins was born on October 31, 1852, in the small town of Randolph, Massachusetts, and moved with her family to Brattleboro, Vermont, when she was fifteen. After the deaths of both her parents, she returned to Randolph and lived the rest of her life there. To help support her family, Freeman taught at a girls' school and published poetry and stories, primarily in children's magazines, in the 1870s. In 1882, she won a cash prize for her first story for adults, and became a full-time writer. She set many of her stories in small New England towns like Randolph and Brattleboro, and wrote knowledgeably about the lives of the people who remained in these Eastern villages while much of the nation's vigorous youth were in the forefront of Western expansion. In 1891, Freeman published her second story collection, *A New England Nun and Other Stories*. This collection included ''The Revolt of 'Mother'''

Freeman wrote novels, plays, and poetry as well as short fiction, but found that only short story sales to magazines guaranteed her an income. She was self-supporting and helped to support various family members for most of her life on her proceeds from her published stories.

She married Dr. Charles Freeman in 1902. Both she and her husband developed addictions to drugs and alcohol that interfered with their lives, and her husband eventually died in a mental hospital. Her fiction from this period was never as popular or critically acclaimed as her early short stories from the 1880s anbd 1890s. Commentators generally agree that is was on the strength of these early works that the American Academy of Letters awarded Freeman the Howells Medal for distinction in fiction in 1925. The following year she was one of the first four American women—along with Edith Wharton—to be elected to the National Institute of Arts and Letters. Freeman died on March 15, 1930.

Plot Summary

As the story opens Sarah Penn asks her husband why men are digging in a nearby field. Adoniram Penn tries to avoid answering. Sarah compels her husband to reveal that the men are digging a cellar for a new barn on the very spot where Adoniram had promised to build a new house for the family.

Sarah goes back into her house, which is much smaller than the barn that already stands on the property. She learns from her son, Sam, that Adoniram is building the new, larger barn to house more livestock which he plans to buy. As they wash and dry dishes, her engaged daughter, Nanny, says that it's ''too bad'' that her father is building a new barn when the family needs a decent house. Sarah tells Nanny that the ways of ''men-folks'' differ greatly from those of women and are beyond understanding. When Nanny goes on to wish for a parlor in which to entertain guests, her mother insists that there is nothing wrong with receiving visitors in a nice clean kitchen, and reminds her daughter that many people live in worse circumstances.

Sarah confronts her husband with her belief that their house is inadequate. She reminds Adoniram that when they were married, forty years earlier, he promised her a fine new house on the very site where the new barn is under construction. And despite her defense of her ''nice clean kitchen,'' she echoes Nanny's wish for a parlor for the upcoming wedding. Adoniram refuses to discuss the matter with her, and Sarah declares that it is because he cannot speak without acknowledging that she is in the right.

Later, as Nanny sits in the kitchen sewing, she tells her mother she will be ashamed and embarrassed to have the wedding in their small, shabby kitchen. Her mother tries to console her with the thought that she may be able to put up new wallpaper by then. Nanny, half-jokingly and half-angrily, suggests that they hold the wedding in the new barn. Sarah Penn receives the comment thoughtfully.

Throughout the spring, the barn steadily goes up. The week before Adoniram plans to move the livestock into it, he leaves home for three or four days to look into the purchase of a new horse. All that morning, Sarah is preoccupied—her eyes are doubtful and her forehead is puckered. She talks to herself, working out some problem, and then suddenly announces that her husband's absense from home just then ''look like a providence,'' that is, a beneficent act of God.

When men deliver a load of hay ordered for the new barn, Sarah instructs them to put it in the old barn instead. After the midday meal, Sarah has her children pack up their belongings as she loads the contents of the kitchen into a basket. She oversees the move of all the furniture, the stove, and their belongings of the house, across the field, and into the new barn. She hangs quilts in front of the box stalls to make bedrooms, and the harness room, ''with its chimney and shelves,'' becomes ''the kitchen of her dreams.''

News of the unusual move spreads through town. Neighbors speculate that Sarah Penn is either mad or ''lawless and rebellious.'' The minister pays an ineffectual visit: she insists to him that the doings in her household are between herself, the Lord and her husband. On the day that Adoniram is due home, many of the townspeople gather on the road to witness his homecoming. Adoniram goes first to the house, then the shed—which now houses one of the new cows that the old barn cannot accomodate. He leads his horse to the new barn. And when he opens the doors, he finds his family inside.

Adoniram is very surprised. Sarah takes him aside and tells him calmly that the family has come to live in the barn. She says he must put in some windows and partitions and buy some new furniture. Adoniram seems to be in shock, barely responding as his wife helps him take off his jacket and urges him to wash up for dinner while their son leads the new horse to the old barn. After dinner, Sarah finds Adoniram crying. He promises to make any improvements to the barn that Sarah has asked for. He tells her that he had no idea she was so set on a new house.

Mary E. Wilkins Freeman

to having his way. He expects his wife and family to accept his decisions. When his wife finally speaks up on behalf of herself and her family in their need for a new house, Adoniram maintains his silence, declining to address her concerns and instead talks of the work he must do that day. But by the end of the story it is revealed that Adoniram is not so much uncommunicative as unable to hear and understand the needs of his wife. When he finally realizes to what lengths Sarah will go to in order to obtain a new house, he agrees to convert the new barn with windows and internal walls to suit the family's needs for a more expansive dwelling.

Characters

Father

See Adoniram Penn

Minister Hersey

Minister Hersey visits Sarah Penn after she has moved her family into the new barn. The narrative recounts little of what he actually says, but he is presented as an unimaginative and ineffectual man who does not know how to address this determined woman.

Mother

See Sarah Penn

Adoniram Penn

At the start of the story, Adoniram Penn is presented as an uncommunicative man who is used

Nanny Penn

Nanny Penn is the engaged daughter of Adoniram and Sarah. She is described as ''large'' and ''soft,'' not strong, and her mother worries about her ability to maintain her own household after her marriage. The mild-mannered, slow-moving Nanny shows one flash of impatience: she complains to her mother about her father building a new barn when his family does not have a decent house. Nanny makes the humorous remark that she might celebrate her wedding in the new barn, and it is evidently this that gives her mother the idea to move the household into that structure.

An American farm family circa 1890.

Sammy Penn

Sammy is the son of Adoniram and Sarah. He is fairly inarticulate, like his father. Sammy helps his father on the farm while attending school. Sammy has known about the new barn for several months before Sarah finds out about it, and it is he who gives his mother the news that Adoniram is buying more cows.

Sarah Penn

Sarah Penn is a strong-willed, patient, and hard-working woman. She has been married to Adoniram Penn for forty years and has had four children, two of whom survived and are living with their parents. When they were first married, her husband identified the location on their property where he promised to build her a new house; at the start of the story, she learns that workmen are breaking ground there for a new barn instead. She speaks forcefully to her husband of the forty years in which she has lived and worked uncomplainingly in the tiny, inadequate house while he has added to his farm's outbuildings, but he does not respond. Although Sarah will not allow their engaged daughter Nanny to complain about the shortcoming of their "box of a house," she argues on Nanny's behalf when she tells Adoniram that the young woman deserves an attractive setting in which to court and marry. Sarah remains composed and even-tempered after her husband refuses to discuss building a new house instead of a barn. When her husband is called away on business just as the new barn in completed and before the feed and livestock are delivered, she sees it as a "providential" sign and moves her entire household's contents into the magnificent new structure, commenting that it will only need a few windows and internal partitions to make it perfect.

Themes

Gender Roles

One of the most important themes in "The Revolt of 'Mother'" is the distinction and reversal of traditional gender roles. Sarah's initial acceptance of Adoniram's building of the barn, despite his 40-year-old promise of building her a house on that spot, shows the prevalent belief that her duty is to follow her husband. Though Sarah does express her feelings to her husband, when he refuses to speak about the matter, she lets the subject drop, and the barn goes up. Adoniram's refusal to truly listen to Sarah's concerns throughout the story are clearly shown in his last words: "Why, mother, I hadn't no idee you was so set on't as all this comes to." Throughout the story, Sarah has tried to explain her feelings but, Adoniram is not accustomed to listening to his wife.

One of Sarah's most important roles, in addition to cooking her husband's favorite meals and sewing shirts for him, is teaching Nanny these sex roles, and thus reinforcing them. When Nanny questions why her father would refuse to build his family a better house, Sarah explains that the ways of men are incomprehensible. When Nanny claims that her fiance would never act in a manner like her father, Sarah asserts that indeed he will one day. Sarah also defends Adoniram, pointing out that many other people do not live as well as the Penn family. In his instance, Sarah is fulfilling what she believes to be an important duty: engendering complete respect for the head of the household among her children.

Adoniram, for the great majority of the story, is as firmly entrenched in his role as his wife is in hers. He makes decisions for the family without consulting Sarah, even those that adversely affect her. For instance, he arranges for the purchase of more cows

without letting her know, although this will mean more work for her.

The reaction of the townspeople to Sarah's move into the barn further reinforces the importance of gender roles in the community. The hired man who first sees the transformation openly gapes and spreads the news to the rest of the village before the next morning. The neighbors talk about Sarah's action, even speculating that she is insane or somehow breaking the law.

God and Religion

Calvinist religious beliefs, including a strong belief in the will of God, play an important role in "The Revolt of 'Mother.'" Sarah equates the actions of men with Providence because it is so difficult to predict or understand either. Early in the story, she explains this to Nanny, wanting her daughter to have this knowledge before she marries and experiences it firsthand. She also says that it does no more good to complain about men's actions than to complain about the weather.

More importantly, Sarah's deeply religious nature actually encourages her move into the new barn. Because Providence is God's way of guiding Christians, Sarah can profit from circumstances. In fact, she must be alert to signs indicating what the Lord expects of her and be ready to do His will. The letter that removed Adoniram from the house can been seen " as a "guide-post" from God that He means for her to follow. She uses her strong belief as rebuttal to Minister Hersey, explaining that she made her radical decision with the help of prayer, and that her household concerns are strictly between her, the Lord, and her husband. Ironically, the man who is supposed to be God's representative on Earth is unable to understand her sincere spirituality. His concerns are more temporal–"he wondered more how Adoniram Penn would deal with his wife than how the Lord would."

Style

In medias res

"The Revolt of 'Mother'" begins *in medias res,* literally "in the midst of things." In this case it is a conversation between a long-married couple. This conversation hearkens back in time forty years, to the day that Adoniram and Sarah married and he promised her a new house. The reader is quickly apprised of the present situation—the fact that there

Topics for Further Study

- Investigate the events that took place after 1890 that led women in the United States to win the right to vote. Who were key figures in the women's suffrage movement? Did the majority of American women agree with the causes of the suffragists?

- Investigate what kinds of jobs were available for women in the late 1800s. Did women have equal educational opportunities that would allow them to get good jobs? Find out how women went about breaking down barriers that would not allow them to work and become educated in professions such as medicine and law.

- What kinds of technological innovations were taking place in the 1800s that made it less profitable for individuals to own and operate small farms? What happened to small farmers and small towns as this method of making a living became harder and less profitable?

- Freeman repudiated the actions of her protagonist in "The Revolt of 'Mother'," saying that no New England farm wife would have done what Sarah Penn does in the story. How believable do you find Sarah's actions? Can you imagine something similar that a wife and mother might do today that would shock her husband and neighbors as much as Sarah's behavior?

---

has been no house but that workers are breaking ground for a new barn—and that the Penns now have an engaged daughter who wants a more impressive dwelling for her wedding.

"The Revolt of 'Mother'" was originally written as piece of magazine fiction, and the technique of *in media res* effectively draws the reader quickly into the story. The provocative title also serves to entice readers immediately. They are forewarned of an unexpected "revolt" that will seem at odds with the behavior of the characters at the beginning of the story.

Point of View and Narration

"The Revolt of 'Mother'" is narrated in the third person omniscient point of view, which allows the narrator to present the thoughts or feelings of any or all of the characters. Most of the story, however, concerns Sarah Penn and her inner struggle to do what she believes is right. The narrator rarely chooses to directly relate what a character sees or feels. Instead, most of the story is told through a detached, objective point of view, which provides more information to the reader. This technique is used to full advantage to present a full picture of Sarah's life—her relationship with her husband, her desire to help her daughter, the lives and concerns of her fellow villagers, and the social mores of the late nineteenth-century New England community.

The detached narrator exerts a strong authority in relating the story, and the objective tone influences the reader to accept the opinions of this authorial voice. For instance, to show the eloquence of the arguments for a new house that Sarah presents to Adoniram, the narrator refers to her as "a Webster," referring to the renowned, influential public speaker Daniel Webster. Because the narrator has proven to be knowledgeable about other things, the reader is more likely to believe the narrator's analysis. The narrator also rarely delves into the characters' interior thoughts, so when such thoughts are actually expressed, like Adoniram's perception of his wife as "immovable" or the children's feelings of being "overawed," the reader is likely to notice these characterizations.

Setting

"The Revolt of 'Mother'" is set in a New England farming village. This location is meaningful because it is far from the city and the reforms and modernizations that take place there. It also has a great significance in the story because Sarah's conflict is dual; it exists between herself and her husband and between herself and the townspeople. The townspeople represent the societal norm, and when Sarah moves her household into the barn, her fellow villagers are astounded. They find the spirit of rebellion that Sarah embodies to be so unsettling that some speculate about her very sanity. Others think her a ''lawless and rebellious,'' although just what law she is trangressing is uncertain even to the minister, who calls on her formally to address her unorthodox action. Thus, the New England village takes on an important role as both a location and a state of mind.

Symbolism

While ''The Revolt of 'Mother''' derives most of its power from the events that take place and from the strength of Sarah's personality, it does rely on the use of several symbols. The barn is important to Adoniram's self-perception; it show he is a successful farmer. The new barn represents Adoniram's ability to make money, and Adoniram's decision to build a new barn while refusing to build a better home for his family shows his interest in earning and acquiring money for its own sake, not for the comforts it can buy.

The use of symbols also reinforces the gender roles of the characters. For instance, Adoniram's control over household matters manifests itself in the opening paragraphs of the story. While Sarah is pressing him about the construction, he harnesses his mare by roughly putting a collar around her neck and slapping the saddle on her back. He uses the living beings around him, and he does not use them gently. Although she has no reason to believe that she will ever get the new house long promised to her, Sarah does not react with hostility. She continues to sew, cook, and clean with the same scrupulous attention to detail that has characterized all of her actions for the forty years she has lived in the cramped, graceless house. Her tidiness and precision, even to the savory meals that appear promptly on her kitchen table every mealtime, will carry over when she sets up housekeeping in the spacious barn.

Historical Context

The New England Town

Freeman grew up in a small New England town at a time when the region was undergoing what

Mary Wilkins Freeman.

many social and cultural historians have viewed as an enervating change. Many of the area's vigorous youth, including a large percentage of men, had abandoned the settled communities of the East to pursue the country's westward expansion. The Civil War had also decimated the population of young men. The New England of Freeman's experience seemed overwhelmingly peopled by single women and old men. New England townspeople were similar racially and culturally, church-based, and strongly agricultural. Women usually did not work in the fields, but instead took on responsibility for the many tasks required to run a farm, such as making basic foodstuffs and clothing. The town itself was frequently made up of several villages along with the countryside in between, all of which were under the same government.

New England towns typically presented a close-knit community, which led to a pervasive interest in the affairs of one's neighbors as well as a concern for what others might think. Such a situation could make it extremely difficult for a person who chose to flaunt or break the accepted rules of the community. But while the gossip of neighbors often traveled quickly through the village, there was also a certain amount of respect for those who defied gossip to be true to themselves.

Compare
&
Contrast

- **1880s:** By the end of the 1880s, one-third of the population of the United States lived in towns. In the decade from 1880 to 1890, the number of U.S. cities of 45,000-75,000 increased from 23 to 39.

  1990s: By the 1990s, the majority of Americans—over 75 percent—live in urban areas. More than half of Americans live in cities with populations of at least one million. In 1990, the 100 largest cities in the United States all have populations of greater than 170,000.

- **1880s:** The United States has about 800 high schools in 1880 and 2,500 by 1890.

  1990s: In the 1990s, the United States has more than 30,000 public and private high schools.

- **1890s:** In 1890, Wyoming is the first government in the world and the only U.S. state to give women full suffrage. That year, two prominent women's suffrage organizations—the National Woman Suffrage Association and the American Woman Suffrage Association—joined to form the National American Woman Suffrage Association.

  1990s: All women in the United States have the right to vote. Women in some countries still do not have this right. In 1984, Geraldine Ferraro was the first woman to run for the office of vice president on a major ticket.

- **1900:** In the United States, only 21 percent of all women worked outside of the home.

  1990s: In the mid-1990s, around 55 percent of all women in the United States worked outside of the home. Women make up almost half of total work force, but constitute only around 20 percent of those in medicine, business, and law.

Calvinism

A secular government, made up of all voting citizens, and a group of pastors and deacons, chosen by the congregation, ruled over the religious, intellectual, and political life. As such, the churches had a strong influence on the development of the values of each child who lived in the town. Many of the New England churches followed Calvinism, a particularly austere version of Christianity that teaches, among other things, that humans are filled with sin. Many New Englanders grew up under the direction of this patriarchal, strict religion.

The descendants of the Puritans who had first settled New England maintained a stubborn religious faith. Their belief that they were probably among God's chosen people helped them to persevere in circumstances—like farming the hilly, rocky New England soil—that might cause others to give up. They believed that their own human will, when it coincided with God's, made them invincible.

By the mid-nineteenth century, Calvinism's hold on the community had begun to wane. In many communities, including Freeman's hometown of Randolph, liberal pastors preached a watered-down version of the original Calvinist message. Yet even the more moderate churches condemned such activities as dancing, insisted upon the key importance of the Ten Commandments, and placed emphasis on denial. Many pastors continued to preach old-time religion, steeped in doggedness and a capacity for suffering, handed down from their Puritan forefathers.

Change Comes to New England

By the late 1800s, the world familiar to New Englanders was radically changing. Economic depression came on the heels of the Civil War. Like Randolph, many small mill towns that carried out production of crafts in small factories and even sheds had become filled with deserted factories instead. Many men from these towns found that their small farms or craft work could not compete in the national farm industry or factory systems, and they left their small towns for cities or the West.

The homogeneity of the New England town also became diluted as new immigrants arrived in the United States. They brought with them new customs and outlooks to this region of the country that had been so similar for centuries. In some ways, this threatened the security of many New Englanders, who shared dialects, ancestors, and histories.

The Roles of Women and Women Writers

Women in the nineteenth century were often unskilled and uneducated. Single woman often had difficulties supporting themselves, as few occupations were open to them. But after the Civil War, women found it increasingly difficult to wed. This was caused not only by the departure of men from the New England towns, but the death and destruction brought on by the war. When husbands left the towns to earn a better living, many families lived in poverty. Many women ended up raising their children alone. A new female consciousness, one that maintained that the woman's sphere was not merely the home, began emerging in the late 1880s, however.

The roles of women with regards to their writing also began to rapidly change during the late nineteenth-century period. Freeman and her contemporaries were part of the so-called second generation of women writers. The first generation, including novelists such as Catharine Sedgwick and Augusta Evans, dominated the literary market in the United States from around 1820 through 1870. These works of these writers fell in the category of sentimental or domestic writings and generally ended with either the marriage or death of the heroine.

Freeman, however, was a part of a new school of writing known as realism. Freeman and her contemporaries wrote much of their work in reaction to this earlier romantic wok. These writers wanted the plots of stories read by women to more accurately reflect the lives of real women. They often questioned the institution of marriage as satisfying or fulfilling and presented the single life as viable and sometimes even preferable.

One element of this new realistic style was termed "local color" and used to describe realistic fiction concentrating on regional detail, authentic characterization, and the correct use of indigenous dialect. This term was used for the first time in a review appearing in the *Atlantic Monthly* in 1864. Soon, competing magazines also began to embrace realistic and local color stories, thus providing many new outlets for the short fiction of young writers interested, as was Freeman, in writing about what they knew best: their particular locale and its unique inhabitants.

Critical Overview

"The Revolt of 'Mother'" first appeared in *Harper's Bazaar* in 1890, and the following year was published with very little changes in Freeman's second short story collection, *A New England Nun and Other Stories*. A reviewer in *The Critic* in 1891 wrote about this collection, "Here are twenty-four stories so complete in form, so exquisite in texture, so fine that to single out any one, such as "The New England Nun," "Calla Lilies and Hannah," or "The Revolt of 'Mother'" for special praise means simply that there are times when the author has surpassed the even beauty of her literary style."

Reviewers have lauded the story subsequently. Charles Miner Thompson saw it as a comic tale, writing in the *Atlantic Monthly* that it was "the most distinctly humorous of [Freeman's] stories." Other reviewers looked at the story in a more serious light. In her 1903 essay concerning Freeman's art, Julia R. Tutwiler wrote, that "The Revolt of 'Mother'" "has the qualities of the classic."

In 1917 Freeman expressed in an essay that appeared in *The Saturday Evening Post* her own criticism of "The Revolt of 'Mother'," stating that it "was an evil day I wrote that tale." Freeman condemned her own story primarily on the basis that "all fiction ought to be true"; "The Revolt of 'Mother'" was not only false, Freeman wrote, but she asserted that the actions taken by Sarah Penn were "impossible." No New England farm wife, Freeman maintained, would have acted as Sarah Penn does in the story, and she regretted deviating from what she believed to be the truth about human nature for the sake of a piece of fiction. But that same year, when the *Independent* reprinted the story, Frederick Houk Law emphasized the literary appeal and pointed out some of these very truthful qualities of "The Revolt of 'Mother'" in his introduction: "The plot is simple but powerful; the atmospheric effects are given with the least possible amounts of description; the characters stand out sharply, vividly, presented without sentimentality or over-emphasis; the conversation is quick and pointed; the appeal is universal—felt wherever selfishness and inconsiderateness exist.''

Scholarly critics have generally assessed Freeman narrowly as a local-color writer. In 1915, the influential scholar Fred Lewis Pattee summed up Freeman as standing for ''short stories of the grim and bare New England social system.'' By the time of Freeman's death, many of her accomplishments had been forgotten; *Publishers Weekly,* for instance, reported erroneously that her first book was a novel instead of a collection of short stories. Freeman came to be seen as a reporter of the society in which she lived, rather than a writer who creates a convincing world filled with individual characters.

''The Revolt of 'Mother''' never completely disappeared from the view of the American public since its first publication, but for a time after Freeman's death in 1930, less attention was paid to it and Freeman's other work. The first biography about Freeman, written by Edward Foster in 1956, helped to create a new interest in Freeman's work. By the mid-1960s, a critical reassessment of Freeman's work began, much of it from a feminist perspective. Feminist critics tend to see certain of her female characters, particularly Sarah Penn, as heroic rebels. Some find in this story a woman's struggle to redefine a system of language that has not allowed her to speak, and they see Sarah Penn as a sort of premodern feminist heroine whose experiences raise issues important to all women.

Criticism

Rena Korb

Korb has a master's degree in English literature and creative writing and has written for a wide variety of educational publishers. In the following essay, she discusses the Freeman's reversal of gender roles in ''The Revolt of 'Mother.'''

Freeman's short story ''The Revolt of 'Mother''' reached such fame that it is reported that Theodore Roosevelt, who at the time was the governor of New York, recommended that mothers read it ''for its strong moral lesson.'' Freeman herself hardly approved of the attention the story drew; in 1917, more than 25 years after its original publication, she made a public statement in the *Saturday Evening Post* about what was and still remains one of her most widely read stories: ''It was an evil day I wrote that tale.'' She went on to explain, ''In the

first place all fiction ought to be true, and 'The Revolt of ''Mother''' is not in the least true. . . . There never was in New England a woman like Mother. If there had been she most certainly would not have moved into the palatial barn. . . . She simply would have lacked the nerve. She would also have lacked the imagination.''

Such statements, and those made in the rest of Freeman's essay, have puzzled critics for years, especially those readers who see in Freeman a sort of model of a prefeminist, a woman who chose a career before she chose marriage, a woman who was able to support herself financially. However, the debates and hypotheses put forth on Freeman's reasonings for writing this essay have led to numerous and valuable interpretations of both the story itself and Freeman's other work. For in her writings, Freeman consistently explores what it meant to be a New England woman of the late nineteenth century, paying particular attention to the internal struggles of woman torn between duty and justice; often Freeman's women actively rebel against the limits of their patriarchal society.

In ''The Revolt of 'Mother,''' Freeman presents Sarah Penn, a New England farm woman, one long accustomed to obeying her husband and who accepts the capricious nature of men. Sarah reaches her limit when her husband Adoniram builds a new, spacious barn on the very spot where he had for decades promised to build her a new house. Taking advantage of Adoniram's fortuitous absence, and realizing he will never honor his promise, Sarah decides to move her household into the barn, an action that shocks her husband, the neighbors, and the village minister. Freeman's statements about her story are particularly of interest because, while her words deny the truth of Sarah's actions, Freeman herself had enough imagination to create the story of this extreme rebellion.

Freeman grew up in an environment where such actions were rare, if not as she claims impossible, but New England villagers did indeed maintain a strong streak of individualism. As Perry D. Westbrook points out, one of the values people of this region held was that of self-reliance. He further points to an area of conflict: ''[i]f one is not independent in thought and action, the community frowns; if one's independence leads to a flaunting of other established values, the community disapproves.'' These dual attributes are clearly apparent in Sarah Penn's character, whose independence is evident before she takes her life-altering action of moving

What Do I Read Next?

- *Their Eyes Were Watching God* (1937) by Zora Neale Hurston. *Their Eyes Were Watching God* tells the story of Janie, an independent-minded young black woman, and her life with the free-spirited Tea Cake. Hurston paints a vivid portrait of the small African American towns of the deep South.

- *The Scarlet Letter* (1850) by Nathaniel Hawthorne. Hester Prynne lives in a repressive, Puritan town that has condemned her as an adulteress. Hawthorne dissects the hypocrisy behind the Puritan mindset and attempts to put forth an explanation for the New England way of thinking prevalent in the nineteenth century.

- *Pembroke* (1894), by Mary E. Wilkins Freeman. In *Pembroke*, Freeman tells a story based on an incident that happened in her mother's family. The fathers of two people about to marry get into an argument. The young man is ordered from his fiancee's house, and her father orders the engagement broken. The young suitor is a portrait in New England obstinance as well as a character so steeped in the fatalism of his Calvinist faith that he can make no move to win back the woman he loves.

- *The Country of the Pointed Firs* (1896), by Sarah Orne Jewett. This short story collection resonates with the author's understanding of the ways of life in a small New England community.

- *The Custom of the Country* (1913), by Edith Wharton. In this novel, Wharton portrays the efforts undertaken by an aggressively ambitious young woman to reach the heights of New York and Paris society. Through ruthless determination and an ability to take actions that went against the social mores of her time, Undine Spragg succeeds at achieving wealth and material comfort at the expense of almost everyone with whom she comes into contact.

- *Main-Travelled Roads* (1891), by Hamlin Garland. This collection of short stories pessimistically and unsentimentally details the lives of Midwestern farmers and their wives. In portraying the daily lives and meager existences of these farm families, Garland also campaigns for a more humane economic system that, he believes, would make these lives more fruitful and loving.

- ''The Yellow Wallpaper'' (1892), by Charlotte Perkins Gilman. In this story, an unnamed narrator has been confined to bed rest by her husband and doctor. The woman suffers depression after the birth of her baby, but the two men, believing her nervous disorder to be aggravated by thinking and writing, forbid her to do intellectual ''work'' of any kind. In the face of such inactivity, the woman plunges deep into mental derangement.

- ''A Jury of Her Peers'' (1917), by Susan Glaspell. Minnie Foster Wright is suspected of murdering her husband. When neighbor women accompany their husbands—one of whom is the sheriff—to search the Wright house for evidence, they find indications among common household objects that implicate her. As they discuss the details of the suspect's isolated, poverty-stricken life with a violent husband, they implicitly agree to withhold what they have discerned from their husbands—who have commented that the women would not recognize a clue if they stumbled across it anyway.

---

her home into the barn. She teaches her daughter Nanny that ''we'd ought to reckon men-folks in with Providence, an' not complain of what they do any more than we do of the weather'' but then proceeds to ''talk plain'' to Adoniram about the inadequacies of their home.

Interestingly, many early critics and readers found ''The Revolt of 'Mother''' a comic folk tale,

> " Sarah's revolt against the will of her husband and the will of her entire town and region touches on very serious issues of female identity and the relationship between the sexes."

particularly because of its magnification of Sarah's revolt, the portrait Freeman draws of the provincialism of the village, and Adoniram's sudden and unexpected reversal at the end of the story. But many later critics, particularly women, claim that these earlier and primarily masculine readers wanted to label the story as "comic fantasy" in order to deny a frightening picture—that of a woman who defies gender roles. Indeed, Sarah's revolt against the will of her husband and the will of her entire town and region touches on very serious issues of female identity and the relationship between the sexes.

At the start of the story, it is clear that Adoniram and Sarah closely adhere to their gender roles. Adoniram has complete charge of the farm and any business dealings, while Sarah's domain is the home. Though the home life was deemed as less significant than the world outside of the home—the world of business and commerce, which belonged to men—the narrator clearly invests a greater meaning to Sarah's work, proclaiming her to "a masterly keeper of her box of a house" and likening her to "an artist so perfect that he has apparently no art." Sarah's revolt itself, while shocking to the community, is undertaken in her role as the keeper of the family and the home. One of her primary reasons for usurping Adoniram's barn stems from her concern for her daughter's health. As Sarah tells Adoniram, because of the smallness of the house, "Nanny she can't live with us after she's married. She'll have to go somewheres else to live away from us. . . . She wa'n't ever strong . . . 'an she ain't fit to keep house an' do everything herself. She'll be all worn out inside of a year." And only after spending the morning watching Nanny, "pale and thin with her steady sewing," does Sarah make up her mind definitively.

In convincing Adoniram to allow the Penn family to keep the new barn as their new house instead, Sarah must learn and make known a new way of communication. Throughout the course of the story, Adoniram steadfastly holds on to his silence as a way of avoiding responsibility for his family. That he has used this tactic for their entire marriage is quite clear, for his speech, which is "almost inarticulate as a growl," had become for Sarah "her most native tongue." Yet, when she speaks with Adoniram about building the family a house instead of a new barn, she has no recourse because Adoniram refuses to utter any words on the subject, even such noncommunicative ones. After maintaining that will say nothing about the subject, he further confirms his feelings by "shut[ting] his mouth tight."

Faced with such obstinance, Sarah has no choice but to develop a new language. Instead of relying on words, Sarah creates a system of signs and uses actions to speak for her. By placing all the family's "little household goods into the new barn," Sarah gives the barn all the value of a home. Her action also indicates to her husband, in such a strong fashion that he can no longer ignore her feelings, that the "Home" is more important than the "Barn." Because of her ability to see in the barn a new home—the box-stalls as bedrooms, the harness-room as a kitchen—Sarah has finally found a way to make Adoniram share her vision. He understands the redesignation, for "after supper he went out, and sat down on the step of the smaller door at the right of the barn, through which he had meant his Jerseys to pass in stately file, but which Sarah designed for her front house door, and he leaned his head on his hands." By Sarah's imposition of a new reality on the barn, she forces Adoniram to at long last understand what she wants, and he stammers his acquiescence: "I'll—put up the—partitions, an'—everything you—want, mother."

"The Revolt of 'Mother'" succeeds so well because of Freeman's ability to show such real truths about the lives of women from her time period. But it also succeeds narratively because Freeman never sacrifices the structural features of a good short story. She effectively uses symbolism in Adoniram's promise of a new house, which dates back 40 years—Freeman's Bible-literate readers would easily recognize 40 years as the length of time in the Bible is consistently related to periods of tribulation and sacrifice, followed by deliverance. Many of the characters' names derive from the Bible as well, and the Biblical Sarah bore a child at the age of 90, an act of physical transgression that metaphorically equals Sarah Penn's transgression of the laws that govern her society. Another name that stands out in the story is that of George Eastman, Nanny's fiance, who never appears but whose full name is mentioned, rather awkwardly, twice. At the time Freeman was writing "The Revolt of 'Mother'" another George Eastman, the inventor of the Kodak camera, headed a company worth one million dollars. Through the fictional Eastman's marriage to Nanny, whose frailty makes her unfit for the harsh farm life, Freeman shows the turn that Americans were making towards urbanity and materialism. On a different note, Joseph R. McElrath, Jr., points out Freeman's artistry in piling crisis upon crisis yet still managing to manufacture a believable but unexpected happy ending. He calls Freeman' conclusion "one of the most complicated trick-endings in all of nineteenth-century American short fiction."

Freeman was recognized by contemporary readers as a writer of brilliant short stories of New England village life. Such a widespread perception, along with the support of such influential literary figures as William Dean Howells, who defended the supposed "sameness" of her writings, helped lead to the labeling of Freeman as a writer of "local color"—a term that describes realistic fiction concentrating on regional details, true-to-life characters, and the correct us of dialect. These elements are certainly present in "The Revolt of 'Mother'," from the ineffectiveness of the minister, who "was competent to grasp the Pilgrim Fathers and all historical innovators" but who could not comprehend Sarah because he knew of no precedent for such behavior, to the narrator's keen observation that "[A]ny deviation from the ordinary course of life in quiet town was enough to stop all progress in it," to the almost constant use of regional speech. But to categorize it simply as a "local-color" story does it a large injustice.

Freeman's writings have graver implications than merely as chronicles of the centuries-old New England way of life that was coming to an end. In "The Revolt of 'Mother'" she actually, and by her own admission, writes about what is not a feasible action for the time in which she lives. Much can be made of Sarah's act of rebellion, whether or not it is possible or impossible: if it is possible that a woman of Sarah's position would do what was worse than disagreeing with her husband—openly defying him—then Freeman has presented a feasible option, perhaps even a secret desire, to women living

in a strictly patriarchal society; if it is not possible than any New England woman would take such an action, then Freeman has written a prefeminist text, one that could give impetus to and support such future actions on the part of real women. It is no wonder that this story of a woman who forces her reluctant husband to recognize what is just and decent was embraced by many Americans as a serious tract on women's rights. No matter what claims Freeman herself might make about it, the truth and poignancy of her words has lasted throughout the twentieth century.

Source: Rena Korb, "One Woman's Independence," for *Short Stories for Students,* Gale, 1998.

Joseph R. McElrath, Jr.

In the following essay, McElrath praises the construction of "The Revolt of 'Mother'" for the author's deft handling of plot, suspense, and climax. He also states that the character of Sarah Penn is a classic liberated woman over whom there is "no need to quibble [with] feminists' characteristic distortions and general hobby-horse riding."

Mary E. Wilkins Freeman's "The Revolt of Mother" is a short story which is now receiving a good deal of attention because of its relevance to the history of American feminism. The mother in revolt is one of those tough-minded, self-aware, and determined females that began to appear at the close of the nineteenth century when the so-called "New Woman" was assuming clear definition. And there's no need to quibble over feminists' characteristic distortions and general hobby-horse riding: Sarah Penn *is* the real thing, a female who successfully revolts against and liberates herself from a familial situation of pernicious male dominance. There is, however, a more important reason for modern readers to focus upon this particular Freeman tale. It is one of her best. Artistically, it transcends the many, many similar pieces that Freeman produced for the American magazine and book reading public of the 1880s and '90s.

It should be stressed here that "The Revolt of Mother" is magazine fiction, first published in *Harper's Monthly* (1890) and then reprinted (with few, and no truly significant, textual alterations) in *A New England Nun* (1891). The reason for this emphasis is that in a collection of Freeman's stories—and this applies to all of them—the quality of individual stories is frequently overlooked or blurred as one finishes a tale and then quickly moves on to the next. In the collections there is a quality of

> " Forewarned of a revolt because of the title, the reader begins the story with the expectation of a crisis which will soon develop."

sameness which cannot be denied. Freeman worked with regional types, and by the time one finishes a collection of ten tales he usually knows all he wants to, thank you, about the New England spinster, the New England widow, the New England old folks, and the New England schoolmistress. Freeman's contemporaneous popularity and claim to attention in literary history cannot be fully understood until one forces himself to read her works as they first appeared. Freeman initially drew attention to herself as the author of individual tales which were published in individual issues of magazines. They were originally designed to be read in this manner, and they appear at their best when considered thus.

Magazine fiction, of then and now, must create certain immediate effects upon its reader which are not so sternly required in book publications. The cash investment in a book—versus the usually forgotten cost of a magazine subscription—insures a degree of patience on the part of the book reader. The magazine reader, on the other hand, may pick up an issue to pass a few idle moments, unmindful of his cash investment of several months previous. He is a bit more fickle, more easily distracted; if he is to be engaged the writer must stimulate his interest within the first few sentences—and thus the snappy-opener gimmicks now commonly associated with "pulp fiction." Once initial interest is stimulated, the magazine story-teller must continue to manipulate his readership so as to counter the distractions of the family parlor which vie with the writer's own demand upon the reader. Moreover, it does not hurt if the writer provides an unexpected "kick" or "twist" at the conclusion of the story, so as to leave the reader in a state of delighted surprise. (There's always that subsequent issue in which the writer will want to round-up his audience once again.)

Poe cannily understood the situation earlier in the century. In tales such as "The Pit and the Pendulum" and "The Tell-Tale Heart" he began in the most sensational fashion and structured from that with a series of crescendo effects. Freeman employs the same technique in "The Revolt of Mother": she abruptly seduces the reader into her fictional world and deliberately arranges her tensely emotional material in a series of crises, each of which seems to momentarily function as a climactic conclusion. With a rapid pace she seems to resolve the central conflict of the story, only to renew the same conflict. Then she quickly moves to another apparent resolution, whereupon that "resolution" complicates matters further. When the actual conclusion finally does occur—providing the most surprising and unexpectedly emotional resolution of all—the sympathetic reader who delights in complication piled upon complication receives a rich reward: a happy ending totally unanticipated by the crisis-ridden and foreboding events that led up to it. If masterful artistry involves the writer's ability to manipulate the reader's mind and emotions to the point of self-forgetfulness and total immersion in the workings of a tale, "The Revolt of Mother" is a masterwork. At the least, it is a classic example of the artful use of anticlimax as a deliberate narrative device.

Forewarned of a revolt because of the title, the reader begins the story with the expectation of a crisis which will soon develop. If one thought through his expectations before actually commencing the tale, he would hazard the guess that Freeman will fashion her materials toward the mid-story crisis/climax typical to the narrative structure of the conventional short story. Freeman, however, seems to second-guess her readership, aiming at the provision of a unique reading event for an experienced and possibly jaded magazine audience. Without even the "exposition of background data" one expects to find attending the introduction of the principal characters, Freeman immediately proceeds to dramatize the story's emotional conflict and to build toward the first (apparent) resolution.

"The Revolt" begins *in media res,* with the two main characters assuming definition through their actions and the imagery assigned by Freeman to them:

"Father!"

"What is it?"

"What are them men diggin' over there in the field for?"

There was a sudden dropping and enlarging of the lower part of the old man's face, as if some heavy weight had settled therein; he shut his mouth tight, and went on harnessing the great bay mare. He hustled the collar on to her neck with a jerk.

"Father!"

The old man slapped the saddle upon the mare's back.

Freeman's technique looks forward to the similar exposition of character through the silent and controlled violence of Ab Snopes in "Barn Burning." Father—Adoniram Penn—is thus introduced as the unsavory villain of the piece, a defiant man who will have his way and who will brook no opposition to his plans. He finally replies, roughly telling Mother to go into the house and mind her own affairs. "He ran his words together, and his speech was almost as inarticulate as a growl."

The sensationality of the opening is enhanced when the reader is allowed a view of the personality questioning Adoniram. It seems as though the sparks will fly, for she does not immediately go into the house; and Freeman provides the first indication of the fiercely independent person with whom Adoniram has to deal. Mother appears the "meek housewife"; but "her eyes, fixed upon the old man, looked as if the meekness had been the result of her own will, never the will of another." As we glance again at her, we are made to see someone who looks "as immovable . . . as one of the rocks in [Adoniram's] pastureland, bound to the earth with generations of blackberry vines." At this point, Adoniram is compelled by her presence of character to reveal to Mother that he is building a barn.

It is Adoniram who then retreats, although he does not change his mind about the barn. He temporarily defuses the situation by his withdrawal; and Freeman then turns to the Mother, explaining through dialogue that Adoniram has conspired to build the barn without her consent and against her known desires. By the time son Sammy reveals to Mother that Father also intends to buy four more cows, the first "act" of the story with its crisis/climax is complete. A stiff-necked Adoniram and equally willful Mother have completed their initial confrontation, and Adoniram has won the contest. Mother does silently return to her kitchen, where we soon discover that she is in no way as sinister as her husband seems and that, while she is strong-willed, she is clearly a sympathetically conceived victim of her husband's obstinate nature.

This constitutes the first resolution of conflict in "The Revolt of Mother," and hence the usefulness of a dramatic term such as "act" in explaining the short story. The first section of the story functions as a one-act play: a conflict was introduced; it moved toward a muted but real climax; and the conflict was resolved by the withdrawal of Adoniram and the capitulation of Mother.

But, the story, and the conflict, as it turns out, have only begun. The second act opens with Mother, saying "nothing more," entering her pantry. As Adoniram expressed his emotionality by roughly handling the mare, Mother likewise employs the means at hand: "a clatter of dishes" is heard. She attempts to resign herself to the situation in dutiful, housewifely fashion. But as she begins washing dishes with her daughter Nanny, the attempt seems to be failing. Her behavior bristles with suppressed rage. Mother "plunged her hands vigorously into the water" as Nanny identifies the cause of the conflict initiated in act one: "'don't you think it's too bad father's going to build that barn, much as we need a decent house to live in?'" That this is the root of resentment is confirmed by Mother who then "scrubbed a dish fiercely." Her anger is finally articulated: "'You ain't found out yet we're women-folks, Nanny Penn'."

Nanny goes on to lament the fact that her impending wedding will take place in their ill-decorated "box of a house." She is not exaggerating about the house. We may recall that in act one we were off-handedly told something about their dwelling. The details now assume a larger significance: "The house, standing at right angles with the great barn and a long reach of sheds and outbuildings, was infinitesimal compared to them. It was scarcely as commodious for people as the little boxes under the barn eaves were for doves." Nanny is upset; Mother is upset. But then Mother goes on to display the nobility of character which makes her such a positively fashioned heroine in the eyes of the reader and which, by way of contrast, makes Adoniram seem an even blacker villain. For forty years Adoniram has promised a decent house but has built only the structures he felt he needed for his business. Mother has just passed through the most recent and greatest betrayal of that promise. Yet she has strength of character enough not to exact revenge by turning Nanny against her father. She attempts to appreciate the finer points of her situation, reminding Nanny that "a good many girls don't have as good a place as this." Then she notes what a blessing it is that Adoniram built a cooking shed for them so that they would not have to bake in the house during hot weather.

A few hours later, with both of the children out of the way, a second crisis is initiated by Mother.

She calls Adoniram from his work, sits him down, reminds him that she has never complained before, and begins to complain at length about his placing barns and cows above familial obligations. She delivers a brilliantly passionate monologue, clearly vindicating her claim that she and her children have been wronged. ''Mrs. Penn's face was burning; her mild eyes gleamed. She had pleaded her little cause like a Webster,'' hearing in response only Adoniram's blunt reply, '''I ain't got nothin' to say'.'' That resolves the crisis. Adoniram shuffles out; Mother goes to the bedroom, and later comes back to the kitchen with reddened eyes. Renewed conflict—crisis—resolution.

A third act begins with Nanny returning to the kitchen miffed, sarcastically suggesting that her wedding might better be held in the new barn which will undoubtedly be nicer than the house. Nanny notes her mother's peculiar expression when she completes this pettish suggestion. It will become clear to the reader several hundred words later that this constitutes actual ''crisis'' moment of the narrative structure (determining the outcome of the tale): it is here that Mother decides to make the barn their new home should the opportunity afford itself. At present, though, Freeman withholds this information and runs the risk of maintaining reader interest with a peculiar kind of suspense. The question that comes to mind at this point is, where can the story possibly be going? In view of the many paragraphs remaining, *something* is certainly about to happen. But it is simply unthinkable, given the information Freeman has fed the reader, that Adoniram will change his mind.

The story leaps ahead through the spring months during which the barn is being constructed, and Freeman relates that Mother no longer speaks of the matter. We are duped into thinking that Mother has, indeed, resigned herself to the egotism of her husband—that the conflict of acts one and two has been truly resolved. Freeman now elaborates upon Adoniram's villainy, once again confirming the belief that Mother's situation is a hopeless one. While he claims he cannot afford to build the promised house and is insensitive to Nanny's having to be married in an old ''box,'' he makes plans to go to Vermont to buy ''jest the kind of a horse,'' he has long wanted. As he departs on the buying-trip, a hiss is the audience response that has been engineered by Freeman.

A maxim occurs to Mother after Adoniram's departure: '''Unsolicited opportunities are the guide-posts of the Lord to the new roads of life.''' To Mother, the opportunity ''looks like providence.'' She forthwith gives directions to the help: move all of the household belongings to the barn. The event is a grandly liberating and heroic one, even if it does seem destined to produce an unhappy outcome. ''During the next few hours a feat was performed by this simple, pious New England mother which was equal in its way to Wolfe's storming of the Heights of Abraham,'' Freeman tells us. But, we should recall that General Wolfe was mortally wounded during that conflict.

Most of the fourth act is given to the rising action leading to the true ''climax'' of the narrative structure and its rapidly executed denouement and conclusion. What *will* Adoniram do when he returns? We know only the most negative things about his character: he has seemed violent; he has acted in the most egotistical and pig-headed ways; he has been curt with Mother beyond the point of simple rudeness; and he expects no one to cross him, least of all Mother. We are free to imagine only dire consequences.

Reader interest is heightened through more suspense. The local characters begin ruminating over the probable outcome of this revolt; they loiter about the neighborhood on the day of Adoniram's return to see what will happen. We know that Mother is not going to back down. When the local minister comes to reason with her, she is shelling peas ''as if they were bullets,'' and when she looks at him there is in her eyes ''the spirit that her meek front had covered for a lifetime.'' Suspense is further increased when Sammy excitedly announces Adoniram's arrival and Nanny finds ''a hysterical sob in her throat.'' The reader is thus prepared for a stormy conclusion, possibly of blood and thunder.

What the reader does not except after all that has occurred is a comic reversal. But Freeman does end this tale of impending tragedy with a startling turn to a tragicomic resolution. And the truly amazing thing is that she turns the tables on the reader as convincingly as she does. Adoniram shows none of the anger that seemed to be so great a part of his nature at the story's beginning. Adoniram shows no anger at all. Rather, he is totally bewildered, able only to say '''Why, mother!''' again and again as he tries to grasp the change that has taken place. What are the cows doing in the house, and why is the house in the new barn? Mother leads him to the supper table and they eat in silence. Afterward, Mother touches his shoulder, breaking into his state of distraction, and he begins—weeping. He totally capitulates, promising to finish the new barn as a house. There is no resentment. Instead there is the first show of his love for Mother in the whole tale: "'Why, mother,' he said, hoarsely, 'I hadn't no idee you was so set on't as all this comes to'." He is telling the truth, oddly enough. Freeman had withheld the fact that Adoniram's could be, and was, a sensitive and loving nature—albeit an extraordinarily dense one. It is one of the most complicated trick-endings in all of nineteenth-century American short fiction. Freeman did all that she could to suppress suspicion that such an ending could be even remotely possible. Her mastery is especially made manifest when we think back over the story and note how she developed the scenes to obscure positive personality traits in Adoniram which were actually there all the time.

It should therefore appear as no mystery that William Dean Howells celebrated Freeman's technique and vision of life. When Howells reviewed *Main Travelled Roads,* he chided Hamlin Garland for his preoccupation with the grimmer, darker aspects of life. Howells suggested that in every field there were roses as well as thistles and that a truly representative picture of American life should note the beautiful as well as the ugly. The reassuring testimony to the admixture of good and evil in human nature with which Freeman startles the reader at the conclusion of "The Revolt" is vintage Howellsian realism at its enduring best. "The Revolt" is also, to speak more plainly, literary gimmickry at its best. It is so well executed that, while some readers may resent the withholding of *the* fact about Adoniram that changes everything, the rest of us can enjoy the notion that love can sometimes conquer all, in 1890 and even in the 1980s.

Source: Joseph R. McElrath, Jr., "The Artistry of Mary E. Wilkins Freeman's 'The Revolt'," in *Studies in Short Fiction,* Vol. 17, No. 3, Summer, 1980, pp. 255–61.

Edward J. Gallagher

In the following brief essay, Gallagher discusses the symbolism of names in Freeman's story.

"The Revolt of 'Mother'" is one of Mary E. Wilkins Freeman's most frequently anthologized stories, and, as an exemplary member of the local-color genre, its action is both poignant and culturally revealing. In this note I would like to call attention to a hitherto unnoticed aspect of Mrs. Freeman's art, that is, the way in which her names blend realistically with the story, while, at the same time, subtly enriching it.

The prominence of Biblical given names (Adoniram, Sarah, Samuel, Anna, Hiram, Rufus) in "The Revolt of 'Mother'," particularly names from the Old Testament, reflects a common rural Puritan practice. In Adoniram and Sarah, however, we can also *uncover* what must be a conscious correspondence between the fictional and the Biblical characters. The Biblical Adoniram was the overseer for King Solomon who managed the tribute and organized an important levy during the building of the Temple (*I Kings,* IV, 6; V, 14). The husbandry evinced by his New England namesake is certainly a worthy reflection on his name. The Biblical Sarah bore a child at the age of ninety (*Genesis,* XVII). It is only a metaphorical step from this suspension of physical law to the rebellious moral feat of her namesake. Mrs. Penn, therefore, carries within her, implicitly and symbolically, the great action which she will perform in her old age. These meaningful Biblical associations also account for the specific use of forty years (reiterated nine times) as the period of Sarah's repression. In the Bible, this number is consistently related to trial, tribulation, and sacrifice, which is followed by deliverance (e.g., *Exodus,* XVI, 35; *Judges* XIII, 1).

Given the above correspondences, it is also possible to posit a specific reason for naming Nanny Penn's suitor "George Eastman." George does not actually appear as a character in the story; he is mentioned but three times in the dialogue. One wonders, then, why it was necessary to give the suitor a full name, and even more, why Sarah would twice use the full name, rather awkwardly, in referring to him. The reason lies in the contemporary significance "George Eastman" would have for Mrs. Freeman, and in the symbolic value this name would lend to the story.

At the time "The Revolt of 'Mother'" was being written a real George Eastman was making social history in the United States. Rising from a modest background, Eastman had his own substantial photography business by the time he was thirty years old in 1884. By 1888 the first low-priced *Kodak* camera was on the market, and by 1890 the Eastman Company was worth one million dollars. Obviously, then, the "George Eastman" of Mrs. Freeman's story is meant to represent the urban, business, and materialistic society toward which America was turning. For Mrs. Freeman, the marriage of the frail Nanny Penn, unfit for the harshness of farm life, with George Eastman indicated the new trend in American social life. Sarah Penn was no longer willing to endure in primitive simplicity, and the embarrassment envisioned in the forthcoming marriage of her daughter is a prime cause of her ''revolt.''

The subtle submergence of art to action in ''The Revolt of 'Mother','' exemplified here in the choice of names, renders this story a very effective member of the local-color genre. The reader does not sense the mediation of the author; the objectivity necessary to ''capture'' a particular geographical region is preserved. In the simple, and often overlooked, art of naming, however, one can detect the sure and conscious hand of the author.

Source: Edward J. Gallagher, ''Freeman's 'The Revolt of ''Mother''','' in *The Explicator,* Vol. XXVII, No. 7, March, 1969, item 48.

Sources

Cutter, Martha. ''Frontier of Language: Engendering Discourse in ''The Revolt of 'Mother','' in *American Literature* Vol. 63, No. 2, 1991, pp. 279-91.

Freeman, Mary E. Wilkins. ''Who's Who—and Why: Mary E. Wilkins Freeman, an Autobiography,'' in *The Saturday Evening Post,* Vol. 190, No. 23, December 8, 1917, pp. 25, 75.

Marchalonis, Shirley, ed. An introduction to *Critical Essays on Mary Wilkins Freeman,* G.K. Hall & Co., 1991.

Meese, Elizabeth. ''Signs of Undecidability: Reconsidering the Stories of Mary Wilkins Freeman,'' in *Critical Essays on Mary Wilkins Freeman,* edited by Shirley Marchalonis, G.K. Hall & Co., 1991.

Reviews of *A New England Nun, and Other Stories,* in *Critical Essays on Mary Wilkins Freeman,* edited by Shirley Marchalonis, G.K. Hall & Co., 1991.

Reichardt, Mary R. *A Web of Relationship: Women in the Short Stories of Mary Wilkins Freeman,* University Press of Mississippi, 1992.

Tutwiler, Julia R. ''Two New England Writers—In Relation to Their Art and to Each Other,'' in *Critical Essays on Mary Wilkins Freeman,* edited by Shirley Marchalonis, G.K. Hall & Co., 1991.

Westbrook, Perry D. *Mary Wilkins Freeman,* G.K. Hall & Co., 1988.

Further Reading

Glaser, Leah Blatt. *In a Closet Hidden: The Life and Work of Mary E. Wilkins Freeman,* University of Massachusetts Press, 1996.
    A detailed biography of Freeman and analysis of her major works.

Shooting an Elephant

George Orwell's "Shooting an Elephant" first appeared in 1936. The British public already knew Orwell as the socially conscious author of *Down and Out in London and Paris* (1933), a nonfiction study of poverty, homelessness, unemployment, and subsistence living on poorly-paying menial jobs, and *Burmese Days* (1934), a novel of British colonialism. "Shooting an Elephant" functions as an addendum to *Burmese Days*. The story and novel share the same setting, and draw on Orwell's experience as a colonial official in India and Burma, two regions of the British Empire, in the middle of the century between the two world wars. The story (which some critics consider an essay) concerns a colonial officer's obligation to shoot a rogue elephant. The narrator does not want to shoot the elephant, but feels compelled to by a crowd of indigenous residents, before whom he does not wish to appear indecisive or cowardly. The situation and events that Orwell describes underscores the hostility between the administrators of the British Empire and their "native" subjects. Both sides feel hatred, distrust, and resentment. The situation is universally degrading. The shooting itself involves enormous pathos conveyed economically in a few words.

"Shooting an Elephant" is a central text in modern British literature and has generated perhaps more criticism than any other comparable short piece. In the politicized atmosphere of contemporary criticism, commentators are especially drawn into debate about whether Orwell apologizes for or

George Orwell

1936

condemns imperialism. Left-wing critics see insufficient condemnation; conservative critics point out that it is the narrator, an agent of empire, who explicitly denounces the British presence as pervasively corrupting to both sides. The story is one of the most widely anthologized and studied items of the modern English-language canon.

Author Biography

George Orwell was born Eric Blair on June 25, 1903, in Motihari, Bengal, which was then a province of India under British rule. Richard Blair, Orwell's father, was a British government official. Sent back to England for his education, Orwell attended St. Cyprians, Wellington College, and then Eton. After graduating, Orwell joined the Indian Imperial Police, from which he resigned in 1927, having in the meantime settled on writing as a career.

Interested in the life of the lower classes and the poor, Orwell lived in working-class neighborhoods in Paris and London in 1928 and 1929, collecting material that he would eventually publish, after many rejections (including one from T. S. Eliot), as *Down and Out in Paris and London,* under the pen-name George Orwell, in 1933. In the interval, Blair wrote essays, poetry, and journalism, including the drafts of *Burmese Days,* which also appeared in 1933. A series of novels followed, all under his new pen-name, with which he increasingly identified himself. He published *A Clergyman's Daughter* in 1935, *Keep the Aspidistra Flying* in 1936, *The Road to Wigan Pier* in 1937, and *Coming up for Air* in 1939, just before the outbreak of the war that the book predicted. Orwell fought in the Spanish Civil War on the Republican side. His motive was to fight against Fascism, represented by Franco's anti-Republican Falange Party. Orwell soon became disillusioned with the Republican side, however, seeing the hand of Stalin's KGB everywhere in its increasingly corrupt and ineffective policies. He published an account of his Spanish experience in the booklength essay *Homage to Catalonia* in 1938.

Orwell worked for the British Broadcasting Corporation (BBC) during World War II while working on the two novels for which he remains best known, *Animal Farm* (1944), a satire of Stalinism and of coercive collectivism in general, and *1984,* published in 1949, a bleak depiction of a world entirely subjugated to a totalitarian regime. In addition, he wrote essays and journalistic and broadcast pieces, and was active throughout the war on behalf of the Allied military effort.

Orwell had contracted tuberculosis in the 1920s. Overwork during the war years exacerbated his condition, and he became ill shortly after completing the manuscript of *1984*. He married his second wife while in the hospital, and was planning a trip to Switzerland to recuperate when he died of pulmonary edema on January 26, 1950.

Plot Summary

''Shooting an Elephant'' begins with a meditative prelude to the action in which the narrator, who may be presumed to be Orwell, comments on being a colonial policeman in British Burma in the middle of the twentieth century. ''I was hated by large numbers of people,''he says, and ''anti-European feeling was very bitter.'' A European woman crossing the market would likely be spat upon and a subdivisional police officer made an even more inviting target. Once, at a soccer match, a Burmese player deliberately fouled the narrator while the Burmese umpire conveniently looked the other direction and the largely Burmese crowd ''yelled with hideous laughter.'' The narrator understands such hatred and even thinks it justified, but he also confesses that his ''greatest joy'' at the time would have been to bayonet one of his tormenters.

The action of ''Shooting an Elephant'' begins when the narrator receives a telephone report of an elephant ''ravaging the bazaar.'' He takes his inadequate hunting rifle and rides on horseback to the area where the animal allegedly lurks. The narrator remarks on the squalor and poverty of the neighborhood, with its palm-leaf thatch on the huts and unplanned scattering of houses over a hillside. The narrator asks about the elephant and receives a vague answer. Suddenly an old woman comes into view shooing away a group of children. She is trying to prevent them seeing a corpse, a Burmese man crushed by the elephant. With a death confirmed, the situation has escalated. The narrator still hopes not to have to shoot the elephant. Nevertheless, he sends for an elephant rifle and five cartridges.

The narrator locates the now-calm elephant in a field. The crowd has followed him. He suddenly understands that, although the elephant no longer poses a threat, the crowd's expectation of the killing will force his to do it. Here Orwell suspends the narrative to insert a continuation of the story's opening meditation. The narrator speculates on the role-playing doom of the imperialist, who becomes so committed to his having to play the part of the colonial overlord that he also becomes a grotesque caricature of that role. He becomes the very thing that his critics claim him to be, a tyrant operating outside the normal code of ethics. He must kill the elephant because the crowd will otherwise laugh at him and the laughter of the "natives" is intolerable to the notion of empire.

"There was only one alternative," the narrator says. He loads the cartridges into the gun ("a beautiful German thing with cross-hair sights") and pulls the trigger. A compressed paragraph describes the elephant's death. The animal, Orwell writes, suddenly looked terribly aged, as if transformed from a lively youth to an old sick man in a single second; the creature staggers pathetically as it collapses to its knees, and saliva pours from its mouth. The narrator shoots again. The animal staggers but attempts in an agony to rise. The narrator fires a third time, and now the animal is down to stay. Its crash shakes the ground under the narrator's feet. The three bullets have not killed the elephant, however, which continues to gasp in pain as it lies in the field. The narrator now takes up his small-calibre hunting rifle and fires into the animal's heart. Still it does not die. Too shaken to remain, the narrator departs, adding that he afterwards learned that it took the elephant a half-hour to die.

The denouement concerns legalistic quibbling over the deed. The elephant had an owner, which might have complicated matters, but since it had killed a man, it qualified as a rogue and the law required that it be dispatched. These circumstances vindicate the narrator's action technically. "I was very glad," he says, "that the coolie had been killed; it put me legally in the right."

Characters

The Crowd

The crowd makes itself known through "hideous laughter," the cackling that accompanies the petty acts of revenge which the Burmese inflict on their foreign rulers. This same laughter coercively implies a choice which the narrator cannot escape— the choice between becoming the object of the

George Orwell

mob's disappointment and ire, or shooting the elephant, a creature which he knows ought to be left alone. The crowd is not a "Burmese crowd," or even vaguely an "Asian" as opposed to a "European crowd"; it is a generic crowd, behaving as all crowds do, with less and less reason the larger it grows and with an increasing taste for for venting its collective resentment against some arbitrary victim, here either the narrator himself, conspicuous because of his office, or the elephant, a convenient substitute and safer because, as a non-human, its victimage entails less possibility of reprisal.

The Elephant

The elephant acquires a character during the course of Orwell's narrative, so that even though he is not human, he deserves to be mentioned. The narrator describes him as a rogue who has escaped his mahout (driver). Indian, Burmese, and Thai elephants are working animals, used for lifting and hauling. The elephant therefore has something analogous to a social station—he is a "worker"—and resembles, in his servant-to-master relation the native Burmese, who have been enrolled without veto into the service of the British Empire. In its final moments, the elephant very much resembles a human victim, which is no doubt what drives the narrator to flee before the agonized animal has died.

Handlers with a tranquilized elephant in Kruger National Park, South Africa.

The Narrator

The anonymous narrator of "Shooting an Elephant," shares biographical details with Orwell himself. A British police official in Burma, the narrator is a questioning colonialist. He perfectly understands the Burmese resentment of the British, while at the same time he hates the petty harassments that the natives inflict on him and his compatriots. As an ostensible agent of control, he understands that the will of the crowd demands the death of the elephant despite his unwillingness to shoot the animal.

Themes

Conscience

The narrator's mental division points to conscience as one of the underlying themes of "Shooting an Elephant." The narrator must do his duty as a colonial policeman. He despises the native Burmese for loathing and tormenting him as their foreign oppressor; yet he also perfectly well understands their loathing and tormenting; he even takes their side privately. His official position, rather than his moral disposition, compels the narrator to act in the way that he does, so as to uphold his office precisely by keeping the native Burmese in their subordinate and dependent place. As a colonial official, the narrator must not let himself become a spectacle before the native crowds. Not shooting the elephant would make him seem like a coward, so he shoots the elephant. The narrator's moral conscience appears in the moment when the corpse of the Burmese crushed by the elephant comes to his attention; the narrator says that the man lay sprawled in a "crucified" posture, invoking all of the poignant and rich symbolism that the term "crucified" offers. The elephant, too, especially in its pain-wracked death, evokes in the narrator feelings of terrible pity, not soothed by his knowledge that he acted within the law. Law, indeed, opposes conscience in "Shooting an Elephant." The brute fact of Empire, thoroughly institutionalized, is irreconcilable with the individual's moral analysis of the situation.

Culture Clash

The obvious culture clash in "Shooting an Elephant" is that between the colonizers and the colonized, the British and the Burmese. The British represent the industrial West with its notions of civic administration and its technological excellence; the Burmese represent a powerless pre-industrial society set upon by an industrial superpower looking beyond its own borders for a field of action.

Topics for Further Study

- The theme of sacrifice in "Shooting an Elephant" is also evident in Orwell's essay "A Hanging." Read "A Hanging" and compare it with "Shooting an Elephant." What elements do the two pieces have in common? What fundamental human traits do they explore?

- The narrator of "Shooting an Elephant" is an agent of the British Empire and is thus implicated in the "dirty business" of British imperial affairs. He is also a man of conscience. Discuss the narrator's guilt. To what extent should he be condemned for participating in the shooting of the elephant? To what extent should he be vindicated for identifying the intricacies of the situation?

- Despite being an agent of the British Empire, the narrator of "Shooting an Elephant" deplores his role in the business of imperial colonization. Contrast this attitude with that of the character of Kurtz in Joseph Conrad's *Heart of Darkness*. Is it possibly to theorize about the respective attitudes of the two authors toward colonization from their literary works?

- "Shooting an Elephant" concerns mob behavior. Think of some other instances of mob behavior, either from real-life stories or works of fiction. Are the actions of the mob similar to those in Orwell's account? Discuss the human tendency for people to resent the differences of others. How does this resentment lead to conflict and violence?

The Burmese despise the British; the British condescend to the Burmese. Less obvious, but far more important, are two other culture clashes. The first is the ethical difference setting the narrator, as a representative of the West, apart from the native Burmese, who belong to the local village-culture and live in a pre-industrial world from which the West itself has long since emerged. The narrator does not want to kill the elephant; the crowd does. The narrator personifies the animal and feels the pathos of its painful death at his own hands; the crowd strip it bare of its flesh within a few hours of its having fallen to the ground. The dead Burmese seems far more important to the narrator than to the crowd who is following him around. The mob's thirst for violence is very different from the narrator's hope of avoiding it. The second less obvious culture clash takes place within the narrator himself. Here the personal culture of an ethical Western individual is at odds with his institutional culture; the narrator's personal values—his sense that the dead Burmese has been, in some manner, crucified, and that the elephant is a victim pure and simple—clash with his duty as a colonial policeman.

Order and Disorder

Order prevails when the mahout (elephant handler) ties up the elephant and keeps him under control; disorder prevails when the elephant slips his keeper and ravages the bazaar. A policeman, too, is a keeper of order, which is why Orwell's narrator cannot avoid the unpleasant duty of shooting the elephant. Not to do so would be to condone disorder and provoke it even further, by appearing to be unwilling to carry out official violence against the disruption of daily affairs. Disorder is a type of violence within the daily round, dissolving the habitual peace. Disorder-as-violence can only be halted by a supplementary administration of violence, and even the narrator admits that this supplement is morally dubious, no matter how practical or necessary it might be. Disorder-as-violence appears on many occasions directed against the British, as when random Burmese spit betel juice on passing European women, as when Buddhist priests laugh spitefully at the narrator, as when the umpire on the playing field looks conveniently the other way while a Burmese player fouls the very same narrator. But this disorder also quells a possibly greater disorder, that of general rebellion against the British. Order, it appears, calls for a strange and paradoxical use of disorder to satisfy rebellious urges which would otherwise grow strong and run amok like a rogue elephant.

Prejudice and Tolerance

The narrator explains how one falls into prejudice, a state of mind in which expediency suppresses conscience: One finds oneself in a role, like that of a colonial policeman; one's personal judgments, which run to sympathy with the native people, necessarily must give way to duty towards the job, towards the empire, and this in turn requires treating the locals as inferiors. Organizationally and technically, the locals are inferior, in the purely Darwinian sense that their society cannot prevail over the society that has colonized them; thus, out of habit, they concede the role of overlord to the colonists, and this too conspires to make the agent of empire act out of prejudgment in a type of imposed role. All acts, by everyone, in this context, are prejudged and stereotyped. On the other hand, both sides tolerate each other, in the neutral rather than in the morally exemplary sense, conceding to each other their complementary roles and biding their time.

Style

Point of View

In "Shooting an Elephant," Orwell employs a casually assumed first-person point of view; what readers know of the event described in the story, they know primarily from the narrator's direct and apparently candid divulgence. Couching the tale in the first person enables Orwell to engage in the rhythm of meditation and action without it seeming forced; because the narrator is reminiscing about the event, which occurred some time in the past, his interweaving of essayistic reflections with the main action strikes the reader as quite natural. The use of reminiscence has a further consequence, that of the splitting off of the narrator as narrator from the narrator as agent of an action. The narrator not only directly reports the impressions and thoughts that he experienced at the time of the elephant episode; he also imposes his present, removed, retrospective analysis on the impressions and thoughts of that time. (This is one of the ways in which readers know

that the narrator is a man of conscience.) Despite the first-person point of view, the perspectives of others—the Burmese—also come through, since the narrators reports them frankly.

Setting

The setting is colonial Burma, part of the British Empire, sometime in the late 1920s or early 1930s; specifically, Orwell sets the story in a district town called Moulmein. Few British are present compared to the numerous local people, yet the British rule, and the narrator, as sub-divisional police officer, is an agent of that rule. This paradox, that a few succeed in governing a great mass, is part of the setting, as is the local resentment against the British presence. As the narrator says, the local people hate him, and manifest this hatred by subterfuge rather than directly. Burma is a remote outpost of the Empire, and Moulmein is very poor, with its palm-thatched huts and rice paddys. In the rice-farming economy, an elephant corresponds to heavy capital, and only the comparatively wealthy own one. The elephant is a working animal in the Burmese context, performing heavy labor. Readers may glean some sense of the poverty of the people from the fact that they stand ready to strip the dead elephant of its flesh and indeed do so as soon as the narrator has used up his ammunition and departed.

Structure

The narrative, while broken up by the narrator's reflections on the events he is recalling, is essentially straightforward and makes use of two motifs, inevitability and augmentation. As soon as the narrator receives the telephone report of the rogue elephant, it becomes inevitable that he will have to kill the animal; merely going out to see what is happening insures this, as does the discovery of the trampled Burmese man, and the narrator's sending for the elephant gun and cartridges. The increasingly agitated crowd (augmentation) also militates against sparing the animal. The increasing size and unanimity of the crowd thus also functions as part of the story, the mob itself becoming something ever more enormous and dangerous, like a rogue elephant, whose danger the narrator avert only through offering it what it wants, namely the death of the creature (and the subsequent boon of its flesh). The story exhibits a certain rhythm, already remarked, that of meditation and action; it starts with reflection, tells part of the story, reflects further, offers its climax, and then ends with a final reflection.

Symbols and Imagery

The narrator himself is a symbol for the people over whom, as a colonial policeman, he holds authority: He is, for them, an image of foreign and arbitrary rule and the object of their resentment and hatred. Signs of his having been reduced by them to a symbol include his being mocked by the young Buddhists and being tripped on the soccer field by a Burmese to the sound of the crowd's laughter. What of the elephant itself? A captive laborer who, in his animal fashion, resents his subjugation, he breaks loose, exercises his freedom, tramples one of his tormentors, and finally parks himself peacefully enough in a field. Yet rebellion requires chastisement and he must die. The narrator personifies the elephant, whose death-agonies take on extraordinary pathos. The personified elephant becomes a walking symbol of human nature put upon and deformed and finally sacrificed for something inhuman, but also sacrificed for the sake of the mob's anger and appetite, so that he becomes the innocent victim of all parties, not merely of the colonial "oppressors."

Historical Context

The British Empire and Nationalism

"The City of London," writes Paul Johnson in *Modern Times,* "was incapable of planning anything, let alone a world-wide conspiracy; it simply followed what it imagined (often wrongly) to be its short-term interests, on a day-to-day basis." Johnson refers to the British Empire, with its far-flung dominions, and to the widespread contemporary idea that the age of imperialism resulted from the malicious foresight of evil powers. Johnson argues instead the great empires of Britain, France, and the Netherlands expanded through a series of unplanned acquisitions, burdening the home country with moral guilt and monetary debt, and dissolving as spontaneously as they formed. Something of Johnson's analysis seems to inform "Shooting an Elephant," with its air of absurdity and directionlessness. If anyone knew about the tedious minutiae of imperial administration, it was George Orwell, who had been born in India and who served in Burma (1922-27) as a colonial policeman.

Orwell arrived at a time when Burmese native interests began to assert themselves against British rule (the British had been in Burma since 1824, when they defeated a Burmese warlord, Maha Bandula, who aggressively opposed British interests in Bengal). Strikes organized by the Young Buddhists paralyzed the administrative center of Rangoon; the antimodern Sayan San movement gained strength in the countryside (and would foment a full-scale rebellion in 1932, a few years after Orwell's departure). Indeed, one of the chief consequences of Western imperial expansion in Asia (as in Africa) was that it brought industrialized and non-industrialized societies forcibly together in a world made ever smaller by technological progress and so provoked resentment between the "haves" and "have-nots." The resentment persisted, moreover, even where the colonized society benefited materially from the imperial presence. Burma was one of the few arms of the British Empire that actually produced a profit, through rice exports, in the period between the two world wars. Nationalism is the political expression of the spontaneous resentment against the foreigners recorded by Orwell in his story.

Western Self-Doubt after World War One

"Shooting an Elephant" takes place in an exotic setting, but it is a Britisher's story and tells us at least as much about Europe between the wars as it does about colonial Burma in the same period. The story's narrator above all doubts his own legitimacy, and this self-doubt characterizes much of European life in the aftermath of World War I. That war shattered the confidence of the proverbial Good European; it seemed to prove that civilization was a kind of delusion always ready to collapse into the fraternal violence of international conflict. World War One vindicated the West's pursuit of technological excellence: aviation and broadcasting, for example—features of modern life—emerged from the war; but Western nations came to question their moral capacities after participation in the bloodbath of the war. One response to the horror of the war was the escapist enthusiasm of "the Roaring Twenties," but, for intellectuals, this offered little consolation, precisely because it was so obviously escapist. Much thoughtful literature of the 1920s is full of bewilderment and pessimism, with works like T. S. Eliot's *The Waste Land* and Franz Kafka's *The Trial* suggesting the intellectual temper of the times.

Close-up of a scoline tranquilizer dart in an African elephant.

The American stock-market crash in 1929, and subsequent worldwide economic depression, provoked an even greater depth of crisis. European nations, not yet fully recovered economically from the war, plunged into catastrophic non-production, inflation, and unemployment.

The response to crisis is often to look for scapegoats. The 1930s, the decade when "Shooting an Elephant" appeared, was already the decade of persecution in the service of nationalism. The Hitler regime had ascended to power on its anti-semitic platform in 1933, and Stalin had been persecuting (and murdering) so-called counter-revolutionaries in Soviet Russia for ten years. Spain erupted into a ferociously recriminating civil war in 1936, in which Orwell fought on the Republican side, but with decreasing commitment to any politicized cause.

Critical Overview

At the very beginning of "Shooting an Elephant," Orwell notes that during his tenure as a colonial policeman in Burma many people hated him. Furthermore, as a writer of nonpartisan political criticism (paying equal attention to the strengths and weaknesses of all sides), Orwell attracted, and still attracts, his share of personal attacks. As Paul Johnson notes in *Intellectuals* (1988), "Orwell had always put experience before theory," and when experience showed that the political Left, with which he had previously identified himself, was just as capable of error as the Right, he said so. Thus the critical tradition concerning Orwell's work generally and his politically charged writings, including "Shooting an Elephant," is controversial.

Readers can glean a sense of how those who favor Orwell tend to treat him from Paul Johnson's remark that, for Orwell, "human beings mattered more than abstract ideas." The general position of those who denounce Orwell shows up in Terry Eagleton's pronouncement about *Burmese Days:* that it "is less a considered critique of imperialism than an exploration of private guilt," an offense in Eagleton's eyes. If the reader accepts Eagleton's premise that political concerns should outweigh personal ones, then the final sentence of the story: "I often wondered whether any of the others grasped that I had done it solely to avoid looking a fool" is unacceptable. In a recent article in the journal *Academic Questions,* Steve Kogan has tallied recent criticism of Orwell and finds it to be overwhelmingly in the Eagletonian vein.

Compare & Contrast

- **1930s:** High-water mark of the British Empire. Burma is one of the Empire's most productive colonies. Also an important decade for incipient independence movements, like those of Nehru's Congress Party in India and the various anti-British movements in Burma itself.

  1990s: Burma achieved independence in 1948 and almost immediately fell into a succession of internal rebellions. In the 1990s the Socialist Republic of the Union of Burma is ruled by a repressive military dictatorship.

- **1930s:** Spain breaks out in civil war in 1936 (Orwell fights); Germany and Austria very nearly go to war in the same year. Japan continues its campaign in China, where it invaded, with the aim of establishing colonies, in 1931. Show-trials begin in the Soviet Union.

  1990s. The disappearance of European empires, all of them dissolved in the decade after World War Two, neither leads to prosperity in former colonies nor insures against the oppression of ethnic or other minorities, as the continuing plight of the Third World demonstrates. Ethnic disputes abound in all regions of the world in the last decade of the twentieth century.

- **1930s:** British writer Rudyard Kipling, known for his poems and stories of colonial India and Burma, dies. Kipling's stories in many ways defined the "conservative" attitude toward empire, that the overseas colonies were Britain's obligatory burden and that they constituted a civilizing mission. Orwell wrote an obituary essay on the occasion of Kipling's death. While critical of Kipling's jingoism, Orwell defends him against the charge of "fascism," saying that Kipling's denouncers tend far more toward totalitarianism than Kipling ever did.

  1990s: It a critical commonplace to denounce Kipling as both a fascist and a racist, and Orwell is regularly described as an apologist for the British Empire and a racist. The tendency to politicize letters, which Orwell diagnosed and strove to quell, results in Orwell himself becoming a target and makes him a still-relevant analyst of the intellectual scene.

An interesting aspect of commentary on "Shooting an Elephant" is whether it is a story or an autobiographical essay. In favor of the latter, Peter Davison points out, in his *George Orwell* (1996), Orwell indeed shot an elephant while serving on police duty in Burma: "He shot the creature but then was in considerable trouble because the elephant, which was valuable, belonged to one of the influential European timber companies." Accepting that the piece stems from experience—as is so often the case with Orwell—and remembering that the action ceases on a number of occasions so as to permit discussion of the events, the designation of "essay" seems plausible. On the other hand, Orwell made many alterations to the actual case on which the finished item was based, effectively rendering "Shooting an Elephant" fictional. Of course, the problem is merely technical and by no means irresolvable, and the mixture of genres even amounts to an added strength. Orwell himself classified the piece as an essay, including it in a collection of his essays as late as 1949.

Criticism

Thomas Bertonneau

Bertonneau holds a Ph.D. in Comparative Literature from UCLA and is the author of nearly forty scholarly articles exploring the anthropological aspects of American, European, and Classical poetry and prose. In the following essay, he tries to

What Do I Read Next?

- The essay "Such, Such were the Joys . . ." is an autobiographical account of Orwell's years in the bleak and unsympathetic environment of an English boarding school. This essay is included in *George Orwell: A Collection of Essays,* New York: Harcourt Brace, 1981.

- Orwell's essay "England Your England," written during the Blitz (the German saturation bombing campaign of London in 1941), is an assessment of British character in its moment of greatest trial. See *George Orwell: A Collection of Essays,* New York: Harcourt Brace, 1981.

- In 1939, Orwell wrote an essay called "Boy's Weeklies," which devotes itself with gusto and approval to the slew of pulp magazines which, in the first half of the twentieth century, especially catered to an audience of literate adolescent males. Orwell had himself been a reader of the weeklies. See *George Orwell: A Collection of Essays,* New York: Harcourt Brace, 1981.

- In "Reflections on Gandhi" (1949), another essay, Orwell returns to the topic of the British Empire, which he earlier treated in "Shooting an Elephant," to which the meditation on Gandhi is therefore an important companion piece. See *George Orwell: A Collection of Essays,* New York: Harcourt Brace, 1981.

- Michael Shelden's *Orwell: The Authorized Biography* is an extremely well researched and lively account of Orwell's life and career. Shelden devotes much interesting discussion to the India-Burma period. New York: Harper Collins. 1991.

- *A Passage to India* (1924) by E. M. Forster is often considered the preeminent novel of English colonialism in India. It is commended for a greater degree of insight into Indian culture than is usually attained by English writers.

- The 1975 novel *Heat and Dust,* by Ruth Prawer Jhabvala, also deals with the experiences of the English in India. In the first part of this narrative, the lonely wife of an English colonial officer enters into an affair with a wealthy Indian man. Two generations later, her granddaughter travels to India and retraces her ancestor's steps.

- "The Short Happy Life of Francis Macomber," by Ernest Hemingway. This 1936 short story is set in Africa and deals with a wealthy couple on safari. Francis Macomber panics during a lion hunt, and his contemptuous wife spends the night with their paid guide. The next day Macomber stands his ground while shooting at a charging buffalo, but is shot and killed by his wife.

---

understand "Shooting an Elephant" in an anthropological and non-political way.

The proper question to pose regarding George Orwell's "Shooting an Elephant" is not: what does it tell us about the British Empire or the politics of imperialism? (That, in any case, is always a rhetorical question.) The question is, rather, what does Orwell's compact masterpiece tell us about human nature, and therefore about the universal morality which grows from an awareness of that nature? In answering this question, the critic might well stumble on some replies to the other, the usual, and by

implication the misleading, question. For it is possible that the most important phenomenon of empire is simply the most important phenomenon of humanity, the one around which every ethical system effectively or ineffectively revolves: Resentment, that invidious sense of difference as an intolerable contrast, and the violence that it always and everywhere portends.

Resentment of various types pervades "Shooting an Elephant," from the beginning to the end. As a conspicuous agent of the foreign presence, a stranger-master, the narrator finds himself, "for the only time in [his] life,'' automatically "hated by large numbers of people.'' This hatred takes the form, in its non-crisis mode, of "an aimless, petty ... anti-European feeling ... very bitter,'' expressed in opportunistic acts like spitting betel juice on the dress of a European woman crossing the bazaar, or deliberately fouling a European player during a British-Burmese soccer-match, while the referee (a Burman) conveniently turns his back. The fouled player is the narrator himself, whose misfortune on the playing-field occasions what he calls the "hideous laughter'' of the crowd. This laughter recurs at important junctures of the narrative. Note that such laughter constitutes the unanimous vocalization of a crowd polarized around a unique, if momentary, victim, who serves as an individual, actual, and arbitrary, token of the foreign power in the abstract. The structure of this laughter is unanimity-minus-one. (The "British Empire'' is never present in and of itself, because it is an abstraction, a system; it only appears through its agents.) Resentment being a mimetic, or imitative, phenomenon (you punch me, I punch you back), the narrator naturally experiences a gut-level response of his own. Despite that fact that he regards the Empire that he serves as "evil'' and proposes to throw off his job as soon as the first chance offers, the narrator would nevertheless fondly like to "drive a bayonet into a Buddhist priest's guts'' on account of the fact "the young Buddhist priests were the worst of all ... none of them seemed to have anything to do except stand on street corners and jeer at Europeans.'' Spitting, laughing, hooting and jeering are, in this context, related gestures. They designate a convenient scapegoat for the expression of pent-up and dangerous resentment. (Too severe a provocation will entail a punitive response, so the practical spite must be held in check at the level of annoyance.)

Enter the elephant. Orwell as author, his protagonist as narrator, and indeed the crowd all anthropomorphize, attribute human characteristics, to the elephant. But the elephant, of course, is well-known for its high level of intelligence, a fact which raises it out of the merely animal category; and the social structure of Burmese society under the British tends to underscore such quasi-human status. The animal is a working animal and to do work is to engage in a recognizably social activity; the animal belongs, as Orwell later discloses, to an Indian, a person below the British in the local hierarchy but above the Burmese, a person of some wealth, for the elephant is the equivalent of "a huge and costly piece of machinery'' in the local economy. The

> "Orwell as author, his protagonist as narrator, and indeed the crowd all anthropomorphize, attribute human characteristics, to the elephant."

elephant, like the human overlords of the place, can therefore function as an object of resentment, a safer one (in fact) than any actual person, because offending him entails little chance of official reprisal. Moreover, the elephant has "destroyed somebody's bamboo hut, killed a cow, and raided some fruit-stalls,'' and he has trampled to death "a black, Dravidian coolie.'' The quasi-human animal has committed a quasi-criminal act, one involving deadly violence, which places him in jeopardy of a quasi-legal and fully lethal response. The ambiant resentment of Moulmein, the town where the action occurs, suddenly possesses a center around which it can safely polarize, around which a fierce unanimity-minus-one can abruptly form and find satisfaction for its hitherto blocked resentment.

Orwell carefully recounts the coalescence of the crowd's Dionysiac passion; at the same time, he gives us a sharp-eyed description of generic crowd-behavior, which is inevitably persecutorial, focused on a victim. As the narrator brandishes his elephant gun, "practically the whole population of the quarter flocked out of the houses'' to follow him. Previously, they showed only a lethargic interest in the career of the rogue animal, but now, with an execution in the offing, everyone sharpens his appetite for the event. The narrator too, despite his conscience, will be swept into the lethal consensus: "I had no intention of shooting the elephant,'' he says; "I knew with perfect certainty that I ought not to shoot him''; "I did not in the least want to shoot him.'' Yet "it is always unnerving to have a crowd following you,'' for the crowd, in its collective presence, exerts a coercive influence. After all, the narrator knows that the crowd expects him to kill the elephant, and that the people have suspended their usual annoyance against him only because the elephant has transiently assumed his place as the object of their invidious animation. Disappointing the crowd would cancel the suspension of its ire against him, with the potential result of a lynching. (In the midst of a mob, with no hostile witnesses, the urge to gain revenge on one of the foreign masters would be hard to restrain.) When the narrator sees the ''sea of yellow faces'' concentrating on him and feels ''two thousand wills pressing [him] forward,'' he understands that he will ''have to shoot the elephant.''

This scene resembles certain other scenes central to the Western tradition, specifically to the Judaeo-Christian strain of that tradition, which Orwell has earlier evoked by describing the trampled Dravidian as ''crucified.'' Pilate does not want to execute Jesus, but the crowd does, and Pilate bows to the will of the crowd. Captain Vere, in Herman Melville's *Billy Budd,* does not want to execute Billy, but must bow to the imagined pressure of British naval law and carry out the death sentence which the situation technically, if not morally, demands. Human beings are imitative creatures—this is their glory and their damnation—who follow the examples set, often quite accidentally, by others, or by tradition accepted without criticism. Orwell's narrator can no more resist the crowd than Pilate can; he can no more resist the tradition of lynching than Captain Vere can. ''A sahib has got to act like a sahib.'' But the narrator knows that, in this case, he is not a ''sahib,'' a foreign overlord; he is, rather, ''an absurd puppet'' assimilated to the crowd against his will, imitating its convergent desire—that the elephant should die—without the power to resist. To spare the creature would be ''impossible,'' as ''the crowd would laugh at me.'' Orwell has already exhibited the sinister conjunction of mocking laughter and scapegoating violence. It is no coincidence, then, that *hooting* and *shooting* should turn out to be stages in the same escalation, like *laughter* and *slaughter.*.

Should he merely test the elephant to confirm his sense that it has passed its ''must'' and is now in a peaceable mood, and should the elephant against his expectation charge him, ''those two thousand Burmans would see me pursued, caught, trampled and reduced to a grinning corpse like that Indian up the hill.'' Whereupon he, too, would be humiliated and crucified.

The narrator now becomes the designated executioner on behalf of the crowd. When he pulls the trigger, the crowd's vocal approval, earlier a mere ''aimless'' *Schadenfreude,* now becomes a single ''devilish roar of glee.'' A parallel incident from a

literary tradition might be the cry of *''Hic est nostri contemptor!''* or ''There is the one who mocks us!'' uttered by the Bacchantes just before they converge on, murder, and dismember Orpheus, who has trespassed into their territory. The ''devilish roar of glee'' is the lynching cry. As for the victim of this paradigmatic victimary scene, the poor elephant, in death he becomes more human than ever: ''He looked suddenly stricken, shrunken, immensely old . . . he sagged flabbily to his knees . . . You could see the agony of it jolt his body.'' Not yet dead— ''he was dying very slowly and in great agony''— the elephant lies in a panting mound, his breath ''very rhythmical with long rattling gasps.'' The narrator tries to end the creature's suffering with his sport rifle (having used all of his elephant cartridges), but to no avail. ''I could not stand it any longer and went away.''

To complete the sacrificial ritual which this crowd-scene comprises, the narrator records how the crowd were closing in on the moribund beast ''bringing dahs and baskets even before I left, and I was told they had stripped his body almost to the bones by the afternoon.'' As in the murder of Orpheus, the scene concludes with a *sparagmos,* the frenzied dismemberment and consumption of the victim.

''Shooting an Elephant'' depicts a cycle of resentment and violence, in part obvious, in part subtle. Obvious is the fact that, in oppressing the Burmese, the British incur their righteous wrath. Orwell spares little in his picture of the imperial order. A colonial policeman sees ''the dirty work of Empire at close quarters. The wretched prisoners huddling in the stinking cages of the lock-ups, the grey, cowed faces of the long-term convicts, the scarred buttocks of the men who have been flogged with bamboos.'' The Empire has ''clamped down . . . upon the will of prostrate peoples.'' A humiliated people understandably hates its *contemptor* and seeks the means to return the disfavor of conquest; absent a direct means, indirect means must suffice, as when the anger that the crowd feels towards the narrator as an agent of empire gets deflected to the elephant. But is Orwell condoning the crowd's behavior, or his own, pressured by the crowd?

No, no more than he condones the British Empire's behavior in its Asian dominions, or his own behavior in the service of the Empire. If the British presence, enforcing itself by violence against the Burmese, is unjust, violating the intuitive rules of universal humanity, then the Burmese persecution of individual Europeans is no less unjust according to the same criterion. The most that one can say in mitigation of Burmese cruelty is that it is a response to British cruelty, but cruelty is never, under any circumstances, just. Justice consists in the opposite of imitative violence: It consists in restraint, consideration, compassion, and tolerance, none of which is exhibited by either side in the British-Burmese conflict.

The key to the moral content of "Shooting an Elephant" lies in a chain of identifications made by the narrator, beginning with his identification of the trampled Dravidian with the victim of the crucifixion. The dead man is truly an innocent victim whom the elephant, in his rogue career, has charged and trampled; he has humiliated the man in the root-sense of the word by grinding him into the *humus* or mud. It is a senseless, undeserved death. When the narrator pulls the trigger, the elephant collapses into the mud, making the image of him congruent with the image of the dead Dravidian. Overcome by the wounded animal's suffering, the narrator identifies, empathizes, with it, and having authored the creature's misery, he tries to end it. All of these identifications (Dravidian with Jesus, elephant with Dravidian, narrator with elephant) come together with an earlier image, that of the humiliated Burmese in the Imperial jail, the "prostrate peoples" victimized by Empire. Readers should not forget that the narrator, too, has been humiliated, tripped up on the soccer-field and made the focus of cackling scorn. No group in "Shooting an Elephant" holds the monopoly on victimhood; every group is capable of persecution.

This is to say that all groups are human and prove their humanity by displaying the same propensity to focus their "aimless" resentment by imitating such actions of others as tend (perhaps quite accidentally, perhaps by a prior meditation) to designate a victim, whereupon, unconstrained by effective (i.e., moral) order, they converge on the victim and immolate him. The narrator's disgust is thus not simply with an unjust British Empire, but with "the younger empires that are going to supplant it," a calculatedly ambiguous phrase which suggests that humanity will remain perennially liable to its own basest motives, empire succeeding empire, world without end. The only exit from this eternal cycle of resentment and violence, followed by counter-resentment and counter-violence, is a type of consciousness which can turn its back on the fascination of such things and assimilate the knowledge about what human beings are, at base, and how

their worst proclivities might be curbed. Significantly, in introducing his story, the narrator says that, before he killed the elephant, he "could get nothing into perspective." Afterwards, he understands that his own vanity caused his assimilation to the crowd and made him the instrument of its blood-lust. "I had done it," he says, "solely to avoid looking a fool." He has crossed from the unconsciousness of being the puppet of a spontaneous collective killing to the consciousness of his own vulnerability to senseless imitation and participation mystique. One does not achieve such consciousness without an accompanying guilt.

Source: Thomas Bertonneau, for *Short Stories for Students*, Gale, 1998.

Peter Marks

In the following essay, Marks discusses Orwell's literary reputation and discusses "Shooting an Elephant" as an example of "eye-witness" literature, in which Orwell, as narrator and witness, should be considered unreliable.

The resilient myth of George Orwell as a blunt, contentious, but fundamentally honest writer draws much of its force from Orwell's position as an eye-witness to crucial events or significant situations. Whether as down-and-outer in London, imperial policeman in Burma, militia man in Spain, or investigative reporter in northern England, Orwell had seen for himself many of the things he would later describe. This fact, coupled with a spare prose style—a style too readily accepted as guileless—gave to much of Orwell's writing the quality of reality, faithfully captured. Modern critical debate, however, has called into question the capacity of the author to depict reality, objectively or otherwise; the terms themselves—'author', 'depiction', 'reality' and 'objectivity', are viewed with varying degrees of scepticism. The role and status of the eye-witness, the 'I' in literature, are under scrutiny.

This has always been true in the proper arena for the eye-witness, the court of law. In court, the eye-witness is not to be trusted. Or, at very least, not to be trusted completely, or immediately. Although the claim to have seen an event, to be in possession of evidence, suggests a grasp of reality, the inherent subjectivity of the first-hand account is manifest. In a court of law the eye-witness is liable to rigorous questioning. Both the bona fides, the 'character', of the eye-witness, and the validity of the account itself must be established. And there is always the threat of other evidence, other eye-witnesses.

> 'Shooting an Elephant' occupies the ambiguous space at the intersection of fiction and non-fiction."

In literature the situation is different. Since the narrator, the 'I' of the work, exists only as words on paper, the establishing of the 'character' of the eye-witness must itself be confined to the text. More importantly, all the 'evidence' presented has been selected and arranged by the author with a particular verdict in mind. The trial, it would seem, is rigged. Yet, in terms of the courtroom analogy, the reader operates as a jury, weighing evidence, accepting and rejecting as seems fit. Literature fundamentally differs from law in that, potentially, there are as many verdicts as there are readers.

The role and status of the eye-witness have a particular relevance for Orwell criticism. A recurring element in analyses of his work is the conflation of the writer and his writings. Bernard Crick has noted 'astonishing agreement . . . that [Orwell's] work can only be understood by characterizing the man'. The confusion of writer and writings is heightened in those works purporting to give first-hand accounts of events or situations. Is the narrator of such pieces, the 'I' from whose viewpoint the narrative unfolds, to be taken as Orwell? If so, what effect might this have on any interpretation of the 'evidence' put forward? This problem is especially important in Orwell's case, for he is one of those intriguing writers able to draw vilification or praise from either political wing. To compound these difficulties, before the publication of *Animal Farm* in 1945, only five years before his death, Orwell was a well-considered but relatively minor writer. The received Orwell is a multifaceted, and in many ways posthumous, creation. Nevertheless, the problem of disentangling Orwell from his work remains; the writer may be 'dead', in Barthes' terms, but is still capable of haunting the text. Examining two short, early pieces by Orwell allows for the consideration of these questions and problems.

'A Hanging' and 'Shooting an Elephant' occupy the ambiguous space at the intersection of fiction and non-fiction. Both can operate successfully as fictional short stories. Nevertheless, in the index to *The Collected Essays, Journalism and Letters of George Orwell*, both are categorized as 'non-literary' events in Orwell's life; 'shoots an elephant' and 'participates in hanging' are given equivalent status with 'street fighting in Barcelona' and the rather less momentous 'buys chessmen and mends a fuse'. There is no corroborating evidence that these events occurred, the respective index references pointing solely to these works. Clearly, the editors of the collection accept Orwell's role in these events, and consequently consider 'A Hanging' and 'Shooting an Elephant' to be first-hand accounts. Analysis of each piece questions this simplistic assumption. Orwell uses the perspective and persona of the eye-witness, the 'I', as a rhetorical device, both for structural and ideological purposes. . . .

If the narrator in 'A Hanging' is primarily a spectator, that of 'Shooting an Elephant' is the focal point. Though, again, a middle-ranking imperial official, the narrator of the second piece is a far more complex character and central to the situation he describes. 'Shooting an Elephant' begins: 'In Moulmein, in Lower Burma, I was hated by large numbers of people—the only time in my life that I have been important enough for this to happen to me'. He is the target of physical and verbal abuse for the native population. A pivotal opposition, between individual and group, is established immediately, one that will reverberate through the narrative. The narrator's position is complicated by the fact that he is antagonistic to the system he ostensibly represents: 'Theoretically—and secretly, of course—I was all for the Burmese and all against their oppressors, the British'. Further oppositions are established, between British and Burmese, colonizer and colonized, the powerful and the powerless. Yet while the narrator's relationship to the group, the large numbers who hate him, is clear, he stands in an ambiguous position as regards the other divisions; he is an anti-British Briton, an anti-Empire imperialist, and a figure of power put upon by those he has nominal power over.

The complexity of both situation and character is heightened by the fact that the narrator's condemnation of imperialism is equivocal. He states that he 'did not even know that the British Empire is dying, still less did I know that it is a great deal better than the younger empires that are going to supplant it'. The confused sense of time is important. The narrator confesses not to have known of something happening at the time of writing (that the British Empire *is* dying) or of something that will happen in the future (that the empires *that are going* to supplant it will be worse). In the latter case he has no logical way of knowing how the (unspecified) younger empires will operate. This confusion nevertheless strongly suggests that while all empires are evil, some are more evil than others.

The narrator's apparent inconsistencies threaten his role as a credible eye-witness. His 'character' is in doubt. This problem is overcome in paradoxical fashion by the self-revelation of racist and sadistic leanings. The narrator portrays the native population as laughing 'hideously', of possessing 'sneering little yellow faces', of being 'evil-spirited little beasts'. With one part of his mind he recognizes the British Raj as a tyranny, but with another part the narrator confesses 'that the greatest joy in the world would be normal by-products of imperialism; ask any Anglo-Indian official, if you catch him off duty'. This shocking revelation functions in two ways. Acknowledgement of the brutalizing effect of imperialism on its own functionaries reinforces the attack on the system. More subtly, however, the narrator is shown to be acutely self-aware and disarmingly honest about his prejudices. The reader's trust in the 'character' of the narrator, with the consequent willingness to accept the perspective presented, is achieved by the revelation of alarming tendencies.

The construction of a self-revelatory narrator is a preamble to the central narrative, the shooting itself. Called upon as the local representative of imperial power, to put down what supposedly is a rampaging elephant, the narrator, on sighting the animal, recognizes that in the interim it has become harmless. Yet the huge crowd of Burmese that have followed him force the narrator to a moment of crisis:

> I realized that I should have to shoot the elephant after all. The people expected it of me and I had to do it . . . I was only an absurd puppet pushed to and fro by the will of those yellow faces behind. I perceived in this moment that when the white man turns tyrant it is his own freedom that he destroys.

. . .

The narrator's function as the personification of imperialism is seen clearly in the revelatory claim that 'when the white man turns tyrant it is his own freedom that he destroys'. This appears to indict imperialism, to provide an index of its dehumanizing impact. The stunningly myopic statement in fact blatantly ignores the effect of imperialism on the local population. Emphasis on, and a consequent empathy with, the white man's loss of freedom leaves that of the Burmese unconsidered. This one-sidedness is founded on the opposition of individual and group. The narrator, the solitary, vulnerable individual, is exposed as essentially powerless. In contrast, the Burmese are viewed as a largely undifferentiated, depersonalized, mass. Their very amorphousness suggests an ability to resist imposed pressures, to survive the impact of imperialism. The concentration on the narrator's individual crisis undermines a thorough-going critique of imperialism.

The eye-witness perspective would seem to imply an exploration of the self by the narrator, and to an extent this occurs in both 'A Hanging' and 'Shooting an Elephant'. In neither case, however, is self-definition or self-examination of prime importance. Instead, what analysis of both pieces foregrounds is the ideological and structural functions of the eye-witness, and the degree to which these two elements interact. The narrator, by defining and validating certain groups in 'A Hanging', and by remaining largely ill-defined, universalizes the attack upon capital punishment. Yet, consequently, this diverts attention from the realities of imperialism. In 'Shooting an Elephant', the juxtaposition of impotent individual and powerful, amorphous mass, functions to the same purpose. . . .

Orwell's use of the persona of the eye-witness, then, has importance both in terms of the narrative and ideology. At the same time it seems clear that it is unnecessary to situate Orwell within either piece to validate interpretation. An understanding of the symbolic importance of the dog, and its role in the construction of the narrative of 'A Hanging', leads to the reconsideration of the narrator as himself a narrative component, rather than a narrative constructor. The invocation of Orwell as narrator is superfluous to an understanding of that tale. The same is true in 'Shooting an Elephant'. In terms of an eye-witness account it suffers from the fact that it was written at least eight years after Orwell had left Burma. His 'evidence' would hardly be credible in a court of law, nor can it be more so in a purported eye-witness prose work. Orwell considered writing the piece only after a request for contributions to John Lehmann's periodical, *New Writing*. Without this prompt it might never have been written. Despite Orwell's avowed hatred of imperialism, it is an ideological position complicated by the fact that 'Orwell'—as a narrative construct—does not speak with the vehemence of the recent exposure to events that characterize and invigorate *The Road To Wigan Pier* or *Homage To Catalonia,* which were to appear within two years of the publication of 'Shooting an Elephant'.

Mention of these later works invites a parting shot at the Orwell myth. Orwell is far too readily accepted in holistic terms, as a unified and consistent writer. His prose style is partly to blame, suggesting by its apparent simplicity a clear, coherent vision. And the various hagiographic characterizations of the man tend to draw attention away from his writings. These, in turn, are often read 'backwards', interpretations of Orwell's later and more famous works, *Animal Farm* and *Nineteen Eighty-Four,* being taken as keys to all Orwell's work. The examination of texts like 'A Hanging' and 'Shooting an Elephant', however, suggests a more complex picture of a writer sometimes sure-footed, sometimes stumbling in his efforts to accommodate the demands of politics and literature. Moreover, by allowing the 'eye-witness' to recoil upon itself as a textual component, the boundaries between language and reference, fiction and auto-biography, become problematic. This is especially true of those early works like 'A Hanging' and 'Shooting an Elephant',, written before Orwell (or even Blair) had become what we now accept as 'Orwell'.

Source: Peter Marks, ''The Ideological Eye-witness: An Examination of the Eye-witness in Two Works by George Orwell,'' in *Subjectivity and Literature from the Romantics to the Present Day,* edited by Philip Shaw and Peter Stockwell, Pinter Publishers, 1991, pp. 85–92.

D. H. Stewart

In the following essay, Stewart compares Orwell to another Indian-born English writer, Rudyard Kipling. Both wrote essays on killing elephants, though Kipling used more humor in his account. In contrast, Orwell often took himself too seriously, according to Stewart, and thereby jeopardized his credibility.

Malcolm Muggeridge called attention to the affinity between Orwell and Kipling: ''When I used sometimes to say to Orwell that he and Kipling had a great deal in common, he would laugh that curious rusty laugh of his and change the subject. When Kipling died in 1936, Orwell wanted to offer some kind of tribute—a salute of guns, if such a thing were available—to the story teller who was so important in my youth.''

Similarities and differences are so numerous that one requires a specific point of departure to avoid bare catalogues. My point of departure is a coincidence: both Kipling and Orwell described the shooting of an elephant. Kipling's story, ''The Killing of *Hatim Tai*,'' is a trifle. He wrote it for *The*

Civil and Military Gazette, Lahore (May 12, 1888), and signed it ''Din,'' perhaps signaling that it was not his own but borrowed from a story printed sixty years earlier in Hone's *Every-Day Book* (March 9, 1826). It is interesting first because of the accidental connection with Orwell, and second because it is always printed (certainly in any edition that Orwell possibly read) immediately after a series of six brief stories about one Smith Sahib, whose management of his household compound symbolizes British rule of India. All of the stories are humorous, but they relate a sequence of misadventures analogous to the one monumental misadventure of Orwell's story. . . .

''The Killing of *Hatim Tai''* tells of an elephant in *musth* (rut) who has killed his *mahout* and misbehaved generally. Awkward to execute because of his size, he is turned over to three doctors who give him arsenic, strychnine, opium and then an assortment of other lethal concoctions. In pain, he struggles against his fetters but finally seems unfazed. At day's end, a young subaltern, contemptuous of the bungling doctors, kills him with one perfectly placed shot.

There is no evidence that Kipling witnessed such a killing, but he knew William Hone's account of a caged elephant's destruction at Exeter Change, London, in March, 1826. When arsenic failed and the animal threatened to smash his pen, keepers fired over 120 rifle rounds at a range of twelve feet and stabbed him with spears and a sword before he died. It is a gruesome story, the more so because Hone expresses little sympathy for the animal but great concern for endangered property; and he concludes that within a day ''the menagerie was destitute of offensive smell, and, in every respect, preserved its usual appearance of order and cleanliness.''

It is unclear from Bernard Crick's biography whether Orwell personally shot or witnessed the shooting of an elephant. His account of the incident is stunning both because of his style and because it occurs within the intensely moral context of its narrator's quest for virtue. The story radiates the moral earnestness that is thought to be an indispensable ingredient in serious English writing. Explicit as he is about the divided loyalties and moral ambiguities of his position, the narrator establishes an unwarranted personal superiority—unwarranted because it depends on paranoid assumptions that all ''natives'' loathe white men and that all white men are (or should be) guilt-stricken for imperial sin. Like other white men managing an empire, ''he wears a mask, and his face grows to fit it''; but unlike other whites, the narrator sees behind both mask and face and is sickened by the aggression he finds there.

The major difference between Orwell's and Kipling's stories is that Orwell is humorless. He seems to say, "one dare not laugh about such dirty business." But Kipling does laugh. His narrator, perhaps semi-autobiographical, is amusing. The pomposity and arrogance that the mask imposes and that Orwell deplores become comical in Kipling. Smith's opening statement reveals this fully:

> How does a King feel when he has kept peace in his borders by skillfully playing off people, sect against sect, and kin against kin? Does he go out into the back verandah, take off his terai-crown, and rub his hands softly, chuckling the while—as I do now? Does he pat himself on the back and hum merry little tunes as he walks up and down his garden? A man who takes no delight in ruling men—dozens of them—is no man. Behold! India has been squabbling over the Great Cow Question any time these four hundred years, to the certain knowledge of history and successive governments. I, Smith, have settled it. That is all!

He is a silly fellow, the epitome of Orwell's masked white. Does he deserve to be laughed at by the natives? He does indeed. They laugh at him, and so does the reader. But Orwell's poor narrator, as full of rectitude and outrage as a young missionary from Indiana, cannot abide the thought of being laughed at because he cannot imagine laughing at himself.

If it is true that "Shooting an Elephant" was written or drafted while Orwell worked on *Burmese Days* (1934), perhaps even as an episode in the novel, then the lack of authorial detachment is easily explained. The novel's hero, Flory, with a large blue birthmark blemishing half his face, kills himself in part because he and Orwell refuse to laugh at a world populated by stereotypes. Kipling, on the other hand, often saw life as a Punch and Judy show full of clownish administrators, shrewd women and cocky subalterns, all dancing their way to oblivion but accomplishing more good than evil insofar as they behaved responsibly toward other people.

Orwell shared with Hone a certain righteous detachment which enables them to tell stories of incompetence complacently. To be sure, Hone's concern is the commercial interest of the menagerie owner, while Orwell sympathizes with colonial "natives" and condones his schlemiel narrator. Kipling never spares incompetence. He scorns it because it is a fault that hard work, intelligence and discipline can correct. Stupidity can be pitied. In-

> The story radiates the moral earnestness that is thought to be an indispensable ingredient in serious English writing."

competence cannot. At times, Kipling became enamored of a Wellsian "technological elite," the kind of managerial class that Shaw pilloried in *Man and Superman,* but often the poet and humorist in him countered this mistake. Thirty-eight years his junior, Orwell knew better than to trust engineers, especially engineers of the soul. But then he slips in the opposite direction, embracing the contumacious boy from St. Cyprian's and Eton—the Eric Blair whom George Orwell never entirely overcame.

By 1942 when he wrote an article on Kipling, Orwell had partially outgrown his lopsided vision, and the article contains a remark that sheds light on both authors. He says we derive a "shameful pleasure" from Kipling because we have the "sense of being seduced by something spurious." If this is true of Kipling, it is no less true of Orwell because he deliberately misrepresents and falsifies his own experience. *Homage to Catalonia* (1937) may be an exception, but in his "documentary tales" about his school days, experiences in Burma, or vagabonding in the slums, his preoccupation with "higher" political and ideological truth often betrays him. When he sets up as a "civilized" person looking down on vulgar Kipling (as well as "the pansy Left"); when he uses the word "civilized" five times in a brief essay, always to Kipling's disadvantage, one may conclude that he protests too much—and that he violates his own injunctions in "Politics and the English Language" (1946).

Orwell seems not to have learned at Eton what Kipling learned at Westward Ho! where the headmaster, Cormell Price, "always told us that there was not much justice in the world, and that we had better accustom ourselves to the lack of it early" ("An English School," 1893).

Orwell accepted the grand twentieth-century delusion that capitalist imperialism and class conflict produce injustice, when in fact they are only modern expressions of an eternal problem. Kipling would no doubt have accepted Plato's idea that justice is the product of temperance, courage and wisdom, which occur together randomly, rarely and briefly—on occasion even in the Raj, as Kipling witnessed or imagined it. Smith's administration, however clumsy and ludicrous, is just—which may explain why India and Burma have retained British administrative forms.

Possibly one needs to have bungled killing a large animal to appreciate Orwell's perfect description of the elephant at the moment of the bullet's impact, "suddenly stricken, shrunken, immensely old." He might have added the grisly detail of the dust cloud that accompanies a bullet's impact. What Orwell does not explain is the wave of guilt that comes with bad shooting, the sense of inflicting pain through incompetence. His narrator had the right tools but did not know how to use them. This is partly what caused his discomfiture, in addition to his awareness of playing a marginal role in imperial administration.

His efforts to befriend the "common man" notwithstanding, Orwell identified with the intelligentsia. It is improbable that he understood the article of Kipling's creed that unites him permanently with people outside the intelligentsia: a writer "must recognize the gulf that separates even the least of those who do things worthy to be written about from even the best of those who have written things worthy of being talked about" ("Literature," 1906). That opinion sets Kipling apart from post-Romantic idolators of artists and intellectuals generally, but it puts him in the company of bards since Homer. It also led him to respect expert craftsmen of any trade or profession. He knew that everything in the world breaks sooner or later and that expert repairmen keep things running better than amateurs do. It vexed him that societies, the human equivalent to nature's order, are usually managed by amateurs whose competence rarely matches their responsibilities. The incongruity creates humor as well as grief, and Kipling registers both while Orwell misses the fun. Together with most English writers of the twentieth century, he could have learned more from Kipling than he did.

Like cattle breaking down the fence into a green pasture, people have a lark when they break out of history's routine and go conquesting. The brave ones are willing to pay a high price for it—as both Kipling and Orwell learned, but Kipling at a younger age. Perhaps everyone dreams of crusading

with Alexander the Great, fewer with Napoleon or Lenin or Hitler. Some marched for Franco; some against him. Whether for fraud, as Orwell believed, or glory, as Kipling hoped, the British empire was one of the most successful larks in history. On balance, it provided more pleasure and less pain to more people than any comparable adventure—even in the Raj. Certainly, as Orwell claimed, the British empire was a "great deal better than the younger empires that are going to supplant it."

Might we infer that Kipling's lighthearted portraits of the vain administrator and decisive subaltern provide more serviceable models for decent behavior than Orwell's solemn portraits of "civilized" reformers? Say what we will, it is the dutiful expert who manages and repairs everything, whatever the ruling political or ideological form.

It is not necessary to conclude, on the basis of a comparison between the two men, that one is praiseworthy, the other not. Their respect for the integrity of their calling as writers finally makes them equal and enables both to transcend the limits of politics, to perfect styles of writing comparably succinct and vivid, and to create visions of modernity that are complementary. Nor may we dismiss this as a case of overlapping between ultra-Right and -Left. Theirs is the voice of free individuals sounding the alarm at the advent of the Massman, the Group-Thinker, the apotheosized Liar. By 1947, a mature Orwell said emphatically in "Why I Write" that the novel "is a product of the free mind, of the autonomous individual"; it is written "by people who are *not frightened*." Kipling insisted that only the "masterless man" could convert deeds into words that "became alive and walked up and down in the hearts of all his hearers." Both writers knew that the magic is in the words, not the man. This is why they agree that the writer, as Orwell put it, "struggles constantly to efface one's own personality," so that the "demon" that drives him can find expression. Kipling had to "drift, wait, obey" when his "Daemon" possessed him.

The voice of the "demon" is a bond that unites people of good will throughout history because it is the voice of each person proclaiming a unique identity within the social mass, however defined. Republic—empire; socialist—capitalist; despotic—democratic: whatever the name for mass-life, all forms threaten "the masterless man with the magic words." Because they assented to this, Kipling's and Orwell's political differences finally seem unimportant. To be sure, fanatics of the Right and

Left will conclude that the two men are "unreliable," perhaps traitors to the Cause with which each identified. A wiser interpretation suggests that art, even in our partisan times, reaches beyond the relativity of each moment and invites judgment by the eternal standard of good sense.

Source: D. H. Stewart, "Shooting Elephants Right," in *The Southern Review,* Vol. 22, No. 1, Winter, 1986, pp. 86–92.

Kenneth Keskinen

In the following essay, Keskinen examines Orwell's style and structure in "Shooting an Elephant," which he states is an exemplary and effective essay.

As teachers of writing, we are concerned with teaching our students how to communicate thoughts and feelings clearly, effectively, and responsibly. Naturally we feel most comfortable and competent in teaching expository writing in which such matters as organization and paragraph development seem to be most apparent, and therefore most teachable. Furthermore, we find our best teaching models in expository essays that have a recognizable structure and a discernible progression of ideas. But we ask more than easy-to-outline mechanical exposition in our models; we want more than physics reports or journalism. We want the vivifying touch of the creative writer whose imagination is at work in matters of selection and structure, of style, and tone.

George Orwell is such a writer. His essays are such models, worth study and imitation. Not only is he a competent and creative writer, but he is, as well, a man who has much to say about the world around him—our world. Specifically, I should like to consider in this paper one of the better essays of our time, "Shooting an Elephant." It is perhaps Orwell's finest essay. For those readers, unfamiliar with Orwell, or only familiar with *1984* or *Animal Farm,* it should serve as an introduction to his other essays. Indeed, all the writings of Orwell deserve the thoughtful attention of the modern reader. . . .

Orwell's essay defies any easy classification. Is it an essay? If so, what "type"? We agree, first of all, that it fits the definition of an essay: it is the conscious attempt of a writer to share his thoughts, feelings, and impressions with his reader on a subject that can be satisfactorily considered in a limited space. What type? We try to distinguish— too often and too mechanically perhaps—between types of writing: the expository, the argumentative, the descriptive, the narrative, and the impressionis-

> **"** Orwell wants to persuade us of something; he wants us to adopt his point of view, accept his conclusions.**"**

tic. Which of these types of writing is "Shooting an Elephant" ? It is all of these. Basically, it is an expository essay—an essay to explain. But, as are most essays, either explicitly or implicitly, it is an "argumentative" essay. After all, Orwell wants to persuade us of something; he wants us to adopt his point of view, accept his conclusions. It is a descriptive essay insofar as descriptive detail supports the argument. It is narrative, for it recounts an incident. It is impressionistic, for Orwell's creative mind is at work with the selection and presentation of vivid detail—those images that will have a powerful effect on the feelings of the reader. This essay, then, is no mechanical type—or combination of types— but a dynamically developed relationship between idea and feeling and words. . . .

In structure, tone, selection . . . word choice— all those matters we unfortunately tend to lump under the one word *style*—in all these the essay reveals a powerful talent combined with imagination and insight.

Let us consider now, in some detail, the entire essay, from the "details out"—from the use of words to the structure of the sentences and paragraphs and of the essay as a whole, ending with a brief look at the essay as a relevant and significant statement of our time. . . .

We are struck immediately by the urgent, even emotional tone of the opening of the essay. The emotionally charged words reflect the intensity of Orwell's feelings, such expressions as "sneering" and "hideous laughter." In the second paragraph he uses "guilt," "hatred," and "evil-spirited little beasts." These words, along with his use of the personal pronouns, make us aware that here is a writer who is personally and deeply concerned, a writer whose concern gives immediacy and power to his account. This is evident from the very first sentence in which he states that ". . .I was hated by large numbers of people. . . ." Indeed, most of Orwell's essays begin with such compelling sentences; consider the following opening sentences from several other essays:

From ''Such, Such Were the Joys. . . .''

Soon after I arrived at Crossgates (not immediately, but after a week or two, just when I seemed to be settling into the routine of school life) I began wetting my bed.

From ''Marrakech''

As the corpse went past the flies left the restaurant table in a cloud and rushed after it, but they came back a few minutes later.

From ''England Your England''

As I write, highly civilised human beings are flying overhead, trying to kill me.

The intensely personal responses and attitudes, however, are not the rantings of an overwrought author. They are given substance and support—and proof—by the descriptive details, the images that prove that the writer is someone ''who was there,'' who saw and heard and felt.

A useful device to show the effective use of images is to re-write any one of the many vivid and concrete sentences in more abstract terms. For example, sentence three of paragraph one might be re-written thus: ''No one had the courage to cause trouble, but if a European woman went out alone, she would probably be insulted.'' Compare it to the original:

No one had the guts to raise a riot, but if a European woman went through the bazaars alone somebody would probably spit betel juice over her dress.

For those of us teachers whose perennial plea to students is ''Support your generalizations,'' Orwell's essay is an admirable example of how it should be done. Orwell knows the power of descriptive detail, the observable evidence that gives his account its validity. Consider these sentences from later paragraphs:

The people said that the elephant had come suddenly upon him round the corner of the hut, caught him with its trunk, put its foot on his back and ground him into the earth. This was the rainy season and the ground was soft, and his face had scored a trench a foot deep and a couple of yards long.

He was tearing up bunches of grass, beating them against his knees to clean them and stuffing them into his mouth.

When the straight, factual description cannot adequately convey the impression, Orwell looks for an effective comparison. The figure of speech for Orwell, as it should be for all writers, is not merely decorative or clever—it serves a vital descriptive function.

The friction of the great beast's foot had stripped the skin from his back as neatly as one skins a rabbit.

I watched him beating his bunch of grass against his knees, with that preoccupied grandmotherly air that elephants have.

His mouth was open—I could see down into caverns of pale pink throat.

The thick blood welled out of him like red velvet.

The crowd grew very still, and a deep, low, happy sigh, as of people who see the theatre curtain go up at last, breathed from innumerable throats.

Through the comparisons we have clearer pictures. However, the figures of speech also convey other feelings and suggest other relationships. Through the first four examples above, we sense Orwell's own sensitivity—in contrast to that of the Burmese—toward the killing of the elephant. It is no dumb beast; it is made not only human, but regal. The last example gives us the expectant quality of the theater—strengthening the irony in the essay, the irony of circumstance in which the white ''leader'' must ''play a part,'' and must soon become a ''puppet,'' a ''hollow, posing dummy.''

Some of the purists among us would find objection, in some instances, to Orwell's use of words. There are such phrases as ''pack of lies,'' ''had the guts,'' ''got on my nerves,'' and ''took to his heels.'' Indeed, were we to find them on student papers, we would put ''tr'' in the margin and ask the student to find a ''fresh original image'' for the trite one. Similarly, some of us might question Orwell's use of colloquialisms, such as ''guts,'' ''chucked up,'' and ''dirty work.'' However, in the sweep of Orwell's narrative, they go unnoticed, for they are consistent with the direct, personal tone that gives the essay its immediacy. Here is a man who has something to say, writing directly and vividly, concerned more with communication than with English teachers with red pencils.

The use of words, then, is unpretentious, yet powerful. The simplicity of language makes for forceful, immediate communication of thoughts and feelings. The simple but effective vocabulary is reinforced with figures of speech that give us—who find such Burmese experiences remote—a means to experience Orwell's sensations through images familiar to us.

It might be useful to present Orwell's own "rules" on the use of words as presented in his essay, "Politics and the English Language":

(i) Never use a metaphor, simile, or other figure of speech which you are used to seeing in print.

(ii) Never use a long word where a short one will do.

(iii) If it is possible to cut a word out, always cut it out.

(iv) Never use the passive where you can use the active.

(v) Never use a foreign phrase, a scientific word, or a jargon word if you can think of an everyday English equivalent.

(vi) Break any of these rules sooner than say anything outright barbarous.

Like his choice of words, the structure of Orwell's sentences is natural and vigorous, reflecting a writer whose thoughts and feelings find their expression in the rhythms of the English language. The sentences vary in length and complexity. The sentences are from three to 52 words long, but most sentences are between 20 and 30 words long. Short sentences reflect the rapid movement of the narrative or the crisp quality of Orwell's thinking. A few examples will illustrate: "I had halted on the road." "But I did not want to shoot the elephant." "I got up." "All this was perplexing and upsetting." Longer sentences develop or contrast ideas. When a sentence is complex, it is so because the clear working out of the relationship of ideas requires that it be.

Structure and rhythm also reinforce the effectiveness of many sentences. Consider, for example, this sentence from paragraph 11, showing the impact of the first shot on the elephant: "He looked suddenly stricken, shrunken, immensely old, as though the frightful impact of the bullet had paralyzed him without knocking him down." The comma pauses after the predicate adjectives are not simply conventions of the mechanics of writing; they reflect the physical condition of the elephant— the physiological jerks of a being that senses its mortal agony, a being that then slowly begins to feel the vitality slipping away; and this "slipping away" is suggested by the run-on quality of the concluding dependent clause of the sentence. Here, as in the entire essay, sentence structure—or perhaps we should say sentence rhythm—enhances meaning and feeling.

Paragraph 11, from which the quoted sentence is taken, follows now in its entirety, to illustrate the relationship between sentence structure and rhythm of meaning.

> When I pulled the trigger I did not hear the bang or feel the kick—one never does when a shot goes home—but I heard the devilish roar of glee that went up from the crowd. In that instant, in too short a time, one would have thought, even for the bullet to get there, a mysterious, terrible change had come over the elephant. He neither stirred nor fell, but every line of his body had altered. He looked suddenly stricken, shrunken, immensely old, as though the frightful impact of the bullet had paralyzed him without knocking him down. At last, after what seemed a long time—it might have been five seconds, I dare say— he sagged flabbily to his knees. His mouth slobbered. An enormous senility seemed to have settled upon him. One could have imagined him thousands of years old. I fired again into the same spot. At the second shot he did not collapse but climbed with desperate slowness to his feet and stood weakly upright, with legs sagging and head drooping. I fired a third time. That was the shot that did for him. You could see the agony of it jolt his whole body and knock the last remnant of strength from his legs. But in falling he seemed to tower upward like a huge rock toppling, his trunk reaching skywards like a tree. He trumpeted, for the first and only time. And then down he came, his belly towards me, with a crash that seemed to shake the ground even where I lay.

The paragraph is narrative, and it recounts the shooting and falling of the elephant. In the opening sentence we read that the first shot is fired. The collapse of the beast is described in the last sentence. In between, we have the description of the slow, ponderous, terrible dying of a magnificent beast. The beast—like an empire (and we must never forget this essential metaphor)—is slow to die. The paragraph has its own climax; the tension is developed and heightened as we wait for the elephant to die; we feel the terribleness of his death. The action, deliberate and detailed, is dramatically interrupted with short sentences: "I fired again in the same spot." "I fired a third time."

Just as the sentences and paragraphs have their own appropriate structure and rhythm, so too the essay as a whole has a natural and logical structure. In studying the structure of an essay, we often talk of the "order of support," with facts supporting an assertion which, in turn, supports a more abstract statement which, in its turn, helps substantiate the general thesis of the paper. This "order" we perceive most often in argumentative essays. We talk too of the "order of climax" in narrative writing in which the tension of the essential conflict is heightened until it is resolved at the climax of the action. . . .

The paragraphs are in themselves well-structured, organized "units" in the larger narrative. Each paragraph has a well-supported topic sentence, and each topic sentence clearly advances the narrative. A useful device here, in giving students an idea of the overall structure, is to ask them to find and write down all topic sentences. It is not a difficult task. Furthermore, they will see that the entire narrative can be effectively summarized in 17 sentences from the text. Thirteen of them can be clearly labeled "topic sentences," and 12 of them are opening sentences in paragraphs.

In the beginning, as we have seen, Orwell uses action and detail to get and maintain interest. After two introductory paragraphs, the action of the narrative begins; and from this point, the essay is sustained narrative with relevant descriptive detail with only one significant break in the "rising action." This break occurs just before the climax, just before the actual shooting of the elephant when the reader's attention is securely held. At this point, about two-thirds of the way through the narrative, the narrator's inner conflict and its resolution bring about his most meaningful reflection on the position of the white man in the East, and of an individual man trying to maintain his dignity. After this reflection, the actual shooting of the elephant has even more significance; and the reader returns to the narrative not only for the "story," but with the full realization of what the shooting "means," both for Orwell and for all men who are concerned with the conflicts between man and man and between man and himself. It is indeed a significant reflection, and it comes at precisely the right moment in the essay.

In a sense, there are really two "conflicts" in the essay that develop their tensions simultaneously. One is Orwell's inner conflict, of which we are aware from the essay's opening sentence. The other is the outer conflict represented in the action which we become aware of when the wild elephant is reported. Both conflicts can be stated as questions: for the inner conflict it is, "Why must I shoot the elephant?" For the outer, it is, "When will Orwell shoot the elephant and what will happen when he does?" Through the inner conflict we experience Orwell's dilemma as our own. With the outer conflict, however, we are removed, watching the action. The elements of catharsis—terror and pity, empathy and aloofness—are here. The resolution of the inner conflict, of course, leads inevitably to the resolution of the action. The shooting that follows is simply the manifestation of Orwell's state of mind. The internal conflict, in other words, brings on his "epiphany," which is, after all, the important matter. Structurally, the important thing to note is that the climaxes occur where they should—near the end of the story.

The elephant is shot. The dead beast is stripped of its hide and flesh. Other British officials and Indians have a bit to say "afterwards." But the tension has been released, and the narrative must end quickly, as it does. The essay, then, is a skillful creative interweaving of commentary and interesting detail, of developing tensions and releases, and of swift-moving narrative. The structure of the essay reveals the hand and mind of a master storyteller and teacher.

What, after all, does the essay say? We have seen that it is the work of an intelligent and honest man who comments on his experiences with unpretentious candor. He is, to be sure, a worthy model for all writers. We can also try to look at our world as clearly and directly as Orwell does, and, in writing about it, we can let our words serve their primary function—to communicate our thoughts and feelings as exactly and simply as possible. We have seen that this essay is an example of organized, vivid, and effective communication. But what does it "communicate"?

We are aware today of the political and human dilemmas that confront man everywhere, from Africa and Viet Nam to Mississippi. Colonialism, like the great elephant with its royal blood, "like velvet," is dying. Trusteeships are created. Individuals seize power. Political structures are made, altered, replaced. The nature of the world situation indeed demands consideration of man as a political being, for through political activity he can find the means to self-expression; there are natural and civil rights to be achieved. However, it is not simply that the British, the Belgian, the Yankee should "go home;" but those who help and lead, those who are helped and led, must recognize the individual human being, with feelings and dignity, as well as the political being seeking civil rights. What can happen to the human being in the structured society is important to Orwell, whether the society is benevolent imperialism, a republic, a democracy, or the tight caste system of an English public school. Orwell's own abhorrence of the "unfree" society that does not let the individual be his human "off-duty" self is present in ''Shooting an Elephant.'' It is an abhorrence that would lead to his denunciation of communism in his best-known works, *1984* and *Animal Farm.* Orwell seems always to be asking basic questions: How free can man be? What are the masks—in the name of progress, of tradition, of duty, of civilization, or of the *status quo* —that men try to wear as they deal with other men? Ultimately, Orwell decries the wearing of any mask that keeps us from recognizing that there are human needs, human strengths, human failings and feelings that we all share ''off duty'' in a world where the white and colored, the Negro, the African, and the Burmese are not political entities but human beings.

Source: Kenneth Keskinen, '''Shooting an Elephant'—An Essay to Teach,'' in *English Journal,* Vol. 55, No. 6, September, 1966, pp. 669–75

Sources

Davison, Peter. *George Orwell: A Literary Life.* New York: St. Martin's, 1996.

Eagleton, Terry. ''Orwell and the Lower Middle Class Novel.'' In Bernard Oldsey and Joseph Browne, editors, *Critical Essays on George Orwell.* Boston: G.K. Hall & Co., 1986.

Johnson, Paul. *Intellectuals.* New York: Harper and Row, 1988.

Johnson, Paul. *Modern Times: The World from the Twenties to the Eighties (Revised Edition).* New York: Harper & Row, 1991. 153, 154-55.

Kogan, Steve. ''In Celebration of George Orwell.'' *Academic Questions.* Vol. 10, No. 1. 13-30.

Muggeridge, Malcolm. *Burmese Days.* In Harold Bloom, editor, *George Orwell: Modern Critical Views,* New York: Chelsea House, 1987. 23.

Further Reading

Hitchens, Christopher, and Norman Podhoretz. ''An Exchange on Orwell.'' *Harper's* Vol. 266, No 1593, February 1983, pp. 56–8.
    Hitchens responds to an earlier essay by Podhoretz (see below) speculating that had he lived, Orwell would have become a political neoconservative. Hitchens questions several of Podhoretz's contentions regarding Orwell's political attitudes. He especially attacks Podhoretz's contention that Owell maintained a Leftist stance primarily to give weight to his criticism of left-wing politics. Podhoretz responds with selected quotations from Orwell's works to support his contentions.

Hunter, Lynette. *George Orwell: The Search for a Voice.* Stony Stratford, England: Open University Press, 1984, 242 p.
    An examination of Orwell's narrative voice in all of his major works.

Meyers, Jeffrey. *A Reader's Guide to George Orwell.* London: Thames and Hudson, 1975, 192 p.
    Concise and accessible, yet thorough and scholarly, introduction to Orwell's works.

Podhoretz, Norman. ''If Orwell were Alive Today.'' *Harper's* Vol. 266, No. 1592, January 1983, pp. 30–2, 34–7.
    Speculates that had he lived into the 1980s, Orwell's political views would have shifted from democratic socialism to neoconservatism.

Slave on the Block

Langston Hughes

1933

"Slave on the Block," by Langston Hughes, is the story of a well-meaning but patronizing white couple's interactions with their young black employee. With cutting irony, Hughes dramatizes the tension that arises when the couple takes the young black man into their home in order use him as a source of artistic inspiration. Hughes presents the psychological dynamics between black and white characters in order to criticize the limitations of a racially divided society and to illustrate the subtle as well as overt forms racism can take.

"Slave on the Block," was first published in *Scribner's* magazine in September, 1933, when Hughes was 31. It also appeared in a collection of short stories entitled *The Ways of White Folks,* which came out the following year. Hughes had already established his reputation as a major voice of the literary movement known as the Harlem Renaissance, but *The Ways of White Folks* was his first collection of short stories. Best known as a blues poet, Hughes devoted the main part of his career to writing about the experiences and expressions of ordinary, urban black people. *The Ways of White Folks* marks a temporary departure from this topic, focusing instead on the strange and contradictory racial attitudes of white people as seen from a black point of view.

Though *The Ways of White Folks* received favorable reviews when it came out, praised for its assured ironic voice and incisive understanding of human psychology, some critics found Hughes's portrayal of white characters unfair. Since then, scholars have responded that Hughes's critical portrayal of whites is a mark of maturity and an important step in the development of African-American literature.

Author Biography

Langston Hughes was born in Joplin, Missouri, in 1902. His parents divorced, and he grew up with his mother and grandmother, moving frequently around the South and Midwest. Hughes first went to New York at age nineteen in order to attend Columbia University. He soon dropped out of college, but stayed in New York where he met the group of writers and intellectuals with whom he was to socialize and collaborate over the next decade. Together they forged the literary movement known as the Harlem Renaissance. When Hughes published his first book of poetry, *The Weary Blues,* in 1926, he was immediately recognized as a significant literary talent. That year he enrolled at Lincoln University, sponsored by a wealthy white patron, Mrs. Osgood Mason, a woman to whom Hughes referred as "godmother." With her pressure and encouragement, Hughes continued to write as he earned his degree. But in 1930 he broke off his emotional and financial relationship with Mrs. Mason and with several of his Harlem Renaissance peers.

Hans Ostrom writes, "*The Ways of White Folks* closes an early phase of Hughes's life and literary career and opens a new, more sober one." It was Hughes's first book after breaking with his patron, and it displays his growing radical political consciousness. While traveling in the Soviet Union in 1932, Hughes read British modernist D. H. Lawrence's "The Lovely Lady." Its main character reminded him of Mrs. Mason, and its direct style of psychological and social criticism inspired him to write short stories.

Over the next decades Hughes became more involved in leftist politics, both through his participation in the radical Black Aesthetic movement and through his political activism. Most of his fiction and poetry shows a desire to represent the experiences of working-class, urban African Americans. Hughes was a cosmopolitan man who was acquainted with many of the most important artists and thinkers of the twentieth century. He was, at once, an observer and a champion of the common person,

Langston Hughes

a man who devoted his career to making great art out of humble folk forms.

In his preface to *Langston Hughes: Critical Perspectives Past and Present,* Henry Louis Gates, Jr., describes Hughes as a man who was as lonely as he was gregarious. Hughes never married or had children. Although he is thought to have been homosexual, some friends described him as asexual. "Hughes knew *everybody,*" Gates writes, "but almost no one knew him, or was able to penetrate the veils and masks the truly vulnerable fabricate to present public personae to the world." Hughes lived in Europe most of his adult life, but frequently visited New York. He died there in 1967 from complications following surgery.

Plot Summary

The story opens with a description of Michael and Anne Carraway, a well-to-do white couple living in Greenwich Village who "went in for Negroes." "The Village" is considered liberal and bohemian, and the Carraways think of themselves as liberal and bohemian as well as artistic: Michael composes piano music and Anne paints. They "adore" and collect African-American art and music and attempt to cultivate friendships with blacks—whom they consider ''a race too charming and naive and lovely for words.'' The Carraways are unable to sustain ongoing interracial relationships, although they do have a live-in black cook and maid, ''dear Emma.''

After Emma ''took sick and died in her room in their basement,'' the Carraways hire a new black maid, Mattie, and then meet Emma's nephew, Luther, ''the most marvellous ebony boy.'' Anne longs to paint him, so they hire him to maintain the ''garden,'' a tiny space behind the house. Mattie introduces Luther to Harlem nightlife, keeping him out late so that he falls asleep as Anne paints him. Staring at the sleeping youth, she decides that she should paint him half nude, posed as a slave on an auction block. Michael uses Luther's slave pose as an inspiration for a piece of music he calls ''a modern slave plaint.''

Luther becomes a familiar part of the household. The Carraways display him to friends and have him sing ''southern worksongs and reels . . . spirituals and ballads.'' Eventually the Carraways find both Luther and Mattie ''a bit difficult to handle.'' Luther does less and less work, helps himself to their cigarettes and wine, and joins their guests uninvited. The Carraways find Luther and Mattie in bed together. They cannot allow themselves to disapprove because of their vaunted liberality and open-mindedness—which they are convinced stems from their artistic genius. However, when they hear Mattie and Luther argue, they feel that the angry atmosphere inhibits their creativity. Anne wants to finish her ''Boy on the Block'' slave painting, but Michael hints that he is ''a little bored with the same Negro always in the way.''

Michael's imperious mother, Mrs. Carraway, comes for a visit. Luther is deliberately over-familiar with her, and during an angry exchange between them she screams ''a short loud, dignified scream'' of outrage at his ''impudence.'' She demands that Michael fire Luther; although Anne protests that she has not finished her slave painting, Michael sides with his mother. Luther seems more amused than distressed about his abrupt dismissal. Mattie joins him, saying that she and Luther have ''stood enough'' from the Carraways. Michael and Anne have no idea what she is talking about. As they leave, Anne moans in distress at the loss of her 'Boy on the Block'.''

Characters

Anne Carraway

Anne Carraway lives with her husband Michael in Greenwich Village. They are wealthy white patrons of black art and culture. The two of them consider themselves liberal, open-minded, artistic geniuses. Anne is a painter, and her enthusiasm for ''things Negro'' extends to using her black servants as models for her paintings.

When Luther appears, he appeals to her on what she describes as a visual level: ''He *is* the jungle,'' she says. Her first picture of Luther is called ''The Sleeping Negro.'' It reflects her vision of blacks as ''dear, natural, childlike people.'' She decides to paint another picture of him, ''nude, or at least half nude.'' Anne admires Luther's physical beauty, but her way of looking at him is possessive and objectifying. She is, like her husband, portrayed as a caricature of the condescending, unwittingly offensive white thrillseeker dabbling in what she considers a ''primitive'' culture.

Michael Carraway

Michael Carraway lives with his wife Anne in Greenwich Village. They are wealthy white patrons of black art and culture. The two of them consider themselves liberal, open-minded, artistic geniuses. Michael is a composer for piano, and he draws from black musical traditions for inspiration. The single one of his compositions described in the story sounds unpleasant and cacaphonous. Like Anne, he is portrayed as a charicature of the condescending, unwittingly offensive white thrillseeker dabbling in black culture. There are also overtones of sexual jealousy in his reaction to his wife's enthusiastic appreciation of Luther's physicality. When his visiting mother has an angry confrontation with Luther, Michael takes his mother's side and fires Luther. He had grown ''a little bored with the same Negro always in the way.''

Mrs. Carraway

Mrs. Carraway, Michael's mother, comes from Kansas City to visit the couple in New York. She has a rigid sense of racial and class divisions, saying ''I never play with servants,'' an implicit criticism of Anne and Michael's interactions with Luther. When she reprimands Luther for being too familiar, he calls her ''poor white'' and she calls him a ''nigger servant.'' She insists that Michael choose between Luther's presence in the house and her own, leading to Luther's dismissal.

Emma

Emma is Luther's aunt, who is deceased at the time the story takes place. Emma had been the Carraways' cook and Anne had painted a number of portraits of her. They meet Luther when he comes to pick up her belongings.

Luther

Luther is a young black man who, when the story begins, has recently moved from the South to live with relatives in New Jersey. The action of the story begins with his introduction to the Carraway household and ends with his departure. The story circles around various characters' response to Luther's presence. The liberal Carraways stereotype and objectify Luther as the essense of blackness and the jungle, and assign him nominal work in the household while Anne paints pictures of him and Michael is inspired to compose a "modern slave plaint." They display him to guests and have him sing spirituals and work songs. Their cook and maid, Mattie, introduces him to Harlem nightlife, begins a sexual relationship with him, and spends money on clothing for him. Mattie and Luther agree that they are treated and paid well, but that the Carraways are "funny" and make them uncomfortable. There is a suggestion in the text that Luther exploits the Carraways' narrow ideas about blacks as simple, childlike people by living up to all their preconceived notions: shirking his work and indulging himself sensually.

Mattie

Mattie is Anne and Michael Carraway's black maid. She is living at their house when Luther arrives. She is suspicious of the Carraways' fascination with blacks and, unlike Luther, keeps her distance from them. She sees it as her job to cook for them, not to pose for pictures or to inspire them. Mattie likes to get out of the Carraways' house in the evenings and to stay out late in the clubs of Harlem. She introduces Luther to Harlem nightlife and enters into a sexual relationship with him. The Carraways suspect that she is in love with Luther because she buys him gifts and gives him money. When Luther is fired, Mattie tells the Carraways that she and he have both both "stood enough foolery from you white folks" and leaves her job as well.

Themes

Freedom and Slavery

The very title "Slave on the Block" calls immediate attention to the theme of freedom and slavery. Just as slaves were displayed to prospective buyers, the Carraways put Luther on display in their household. Anne's great inspiration is to paint Luther as a slave, and Michael is moved to compose "a modern slave plaint" when he sees the young man posing. One day, when called to pose, he reluctantly appears, singing "Before I'd be a slave / I'd be buried in ma grave / And go home to my Jesus / And be free." That same afternoon he almost lets the furnace go out. Slaves often sang spirituals about freedom as a masked form of rebellion. This song can be seen as Luther's criticism of his status in the Carraway household.

Race and Racism

For all their enthusiasm for "things Negro," the Carraways do not acknowledge Luther, or indeed any black person, as an individual. In fact, they hold firmly to grotesquely racist opinions about blacks as a simple, childlike race, "charming and naive and lovely," who should be left "unspoiled" and simply enjoyed. Unfortunately for the Carraways, the individual blacks whom they meet persist in being individual people with their own ideas of how they would prefer to live. It is clear throughout the story—and particularly at its end—that the Carraways will never overcome their own lack of comprehension. Luther shuns the nominal "work" he has been hired to perform, begins a sexual affair with Mattie, takes things from the household, and avoids posing for Anne for days at a time, perhaps exploiting the Carraways stereotypes to his own advantage. The story implies that it is not despite but *because* of their fascination with certain stereotyped concepts of blackness that the Carraways are racist.

Class Conflict

Issues of economic class form an underlying theme of the story. Despite the fact that the Carraways think of their interest in black culture as part of a radical artistic project, their only actual relationships with black people are the essentially economic ones they have with their servants. The third-person narrator of the story reports that the occasional "furtive Negro" or "lesser Harlem celebrity or two" who attends one of their "rather slow parties . . . seldom came back for more," perhaps because

Topics for Further Study

- Think of some examples of times when you have heard irony used in informal contexts, such as conversation. What are some of the differences and similarities between the kinds of irony you find in literature and in casual speech? What is so powerful about irony? As a writing exercise, identify an issue you feel strongly about and try to make your point by using irony.

- Hughes is known primarily as a blues poet. Much of his poetry based is on blues rhythms and themes, and he incorporates the lyrics of several songs into ''Slave on the Block.'' Listen to some blues music and do some research about the history of this musical form. How do blues themes reflect on the conflicts and issues that Hughes raises in the story?

- Identify some white artists, writers, or musicians who draw on African-American culture for their inspiration, either from Hughes's generation or

from your own. With Hughes's criticism of the Carraways in mind, analyze the work of these artists in terms of the way they represent black people and culture. Can you see any of the same stereotypes described in the story at work, such as exoticism, simplicity, or sexuality? What are some of the other conclusions about race relations you can draw from the work of these artists?

- Despite the fact that Hughes is extremely critical of the Carraways' racial attitude in the story, he portrays them as human and their prejudice as a form of weakness. Find some psychological studies of prejudice and racism. What are the existing theories, and which do you find most useful or convincing? Do any of these theories seem to pertain the interpersonal dynamics described in the story or give you a new way of understanding the characters?

---

the Carraways live in an exclusive, well-to-do and hard-to-find little enclave in the city.

Sex and Sexuality

The narrative avoids any overt discussion of the Carraways' sexuality. However, Anne Carraway's response to Luther carries erotic overtones. She admires his physical appearance, stares at him while he is sleeping, and decides she wants to paint him nude—quickly emended to ''or at least half nude.'' When she finds out that Luther and Mattie are having sex, she contends that it is ''simple and natural for Negroes to make love.'' The narrative makes plain, however, that the Carraways give a great deal of thought to Luther's sexuality: Anne in particular blaming the older Mattie for ''spoiling a nice simple young boy.'' She notes that Luther is wearing increasingly nice clothing bought by Mattie and going out with her nightly. At no point does the narrator comment on these intrusions into Luther and Mattie's privacy; they are simply noted.

While Michael Carraway initially shares his wife's enthusiasm for Luther's inspiring presence, when Luther becomes more ''familiar,'' Michael's enthusiasm wanes. Anne wants to keep Luther on so she finish her painting, and because he is teaching her the dances he has learned at the Harlem nightclubs that he frequents with Mattie. When Luther antagonizes Michael's visiting mother, he is again shirtless because he expects to pose for Anne; Anne is described as moaning ''Oh!'' repeatedly—no less than four times—and gazing at his shirtless body as Luther leaves for good.

Style

Point of View and Irony

Hughes tells the story of Luther's interactions with the Carraways by using a third-person narrator, meaning that the events in ''Slave on the

Block'' are described from the position of an outside observer. This third-person narrator is omniscient, having access to the characters' private thoughts. For example, the narrator is in a position to report, ''They didn't understand the vagaries of white folks, neither Luther nor Mattie, and they didn't want to be bothered trying.'' Most often however, third-person narration assumes an objective presentation of facts and events. For example, the narrator does not comment on the fact that the Carraways considered Luther ''so charming and naive to ask right away for what he wanted'' when he comes to them looking for work, but instead presents the information in a straightforward and neutral manner. However, Hughes does not intend for this information to evoke a neutral response, for he has already established that the Carraways believe that all blacks are charming and naive, and thus this information is an indictment of their use of stereotype. When there is an imbalance between what is presented and what is felt, the effect created is one of irony. Throughout the story, Hughes's narration is highly ironic. He criticizes the Carraways' attitudes and beliefs about race through describing their narrow ideas about black people in a distant and objective manner, offering a bitter and precise portrait of their particular brand of racism. The story's ironic narration is perhaps its most striking stylistic feature. Hughes's use of irony suggests the influence of both modernist writing and traditional African and African-American storytelling.

Setting

When Hughes sets out to define ''the ways of white folks'' he carefully delineates the social milieu he is addressing and the attitudes specific to a particular time and place. The story opens with a description of the type of white folks the Carraways are. They are part of a New York intellectual and artistic clique that embraces black culture, lives in an exclusive and expensive area of Greenwich Village, and frequents the upscale clubs and bars of Harlem that cater specifically to white sensation-seekers.

Although the larger context of a modern, segregated New York City is carefully defined, all of the action in the story takes place within the Carraways' household. Their home is the only scene of contact between the Carraways and their domestic servants. Although both enjoy Harlem nightlife, it is noted that the Carraways favor ''the ritzy joints where Negroes couldn't go themselves'' other than to work and perform. The action of the story is initiated when Luther arrives at their door and the story ends when he leaves. The plot builds from the tense series of actions and reactions between the Carraways and Luther within the domestic setting.

Symbolism

Hughes carefully weaves symbolism into the texture of a realistically represented social setting. For example, Anne's portrait of Luther as a slave on the block fits in with Anne's role as an artist in the social context of Greenwich Village. However, the symbolic significance of the painting is profound. Through the symbol of the painting, Hughes suggests that the Luther's relationship to the Carraways echoes slavery, despite the fact that the Carraways think of themselves as liberals and free-thinkers who ''love Negroes.'' Anne poses Luther on a box in the same way that a slave trader would place a slave on the block, displaying him for sale. Anne's social status gives her the power to represent him as a slave, and thus contributes to the production of the kind of stereotypes that oppress Luther in her household.

The roses that Luther carries into the library on the day he has the confrontation with Mrs. Carraway also have symbolic meaning. The roses add to the visual impact of the scene. Shirtless, Luther is a decorative object in the household, not unlike the roses. Luther's sensual appearance is part of what disturbs Mrs. Carraway and part of what pleases Anne. When Luther is fired, he tells Anne to arrange the flowers in the vases. To Luther, the roses represent work. He hands the roses to Anne in what can be seen as the inversion of a romantic gesture. Thus the roses symbolizes Anne's misguided, romanticized vision of Luther.

Satire

In literature, satire is the art of using ridicule, humor, and wit to criticize human nature and institutions. The white liberal couple the Carraways are clearly satirized in ''Slave on the Block''. They represent a type of patronizing, unconsciously offensive white patron of black arts in the 1920s and 30s. Although such individuals certainly did exist, the Carraways are portrayed nearly as caricatures, with their unpleasant characteristics exaggerated to underscore the themes of the story. The black characters similarly convey little depth: the reader learns little of their inner lives or private thoughts, although they are not as harshly presented as are the Carraways.

Historical Context

The Great Migration

The early twentieth century was a period of increasing urbanization in America. In 1920 the census showed that for the first time in U.S. history the majority of Americans lived in cities. However, while white Americans had been gradually moving into urban areas over the course of a century, black Americans became city-dwellers much more suddenly. Vast numbers of African Americans moved to northern cities between the 1910s and 1940s in a population shift known as the Great Migration (or the Great Black Migration).

In 1910 about 90 percent of the African American population of the United States lived in the South, with 78 percent living in rural areas. Economic factors such as crop failures in the South, the labor vacuum created by World War I, and the stemming of European immigrants after 1914, plus political factors such as segregation, discrimination, and lynching in the South, led to a huge influx of blacks into northern cities. Between 1910 and 1930, the black population in New York City tripled.

The Harlem Renaissance

Hughes is one of the authors most closely associated with the literary and cultural movement known as the Harlem Renaissance. Like many African Americans of his generation, Hughes was born in the South and found his way to Harlem, a neighborhood in New York City. A group of white artistic and financial mentors interested in African-American culture whmo Hughes met in New York shaped his impression of "the ways of white folks" as characterized in the story.

The Harlem Renaissance began around 1917, with the huge increase of blacks living in New York. About two-thirds of all black New Yorkers resided in Harlem. A thriving community and cultural center for blacks, Harlem was referred to as "the Negro capital of America." Concurrent with this population shift arose a new interest among white artists and intellectuals in black culture. New York's Greenwich Village was the center for a group of bohemian whites much like the Carraways, who were critical of mainstream society and tended to see African Americans as a primitive force of innocence and regeneration. Harlem became a popular entertainment spot for whites as well as blacks, famous for its clubs and cabarets. Bessie Smith and Paul Robeson, whose records the Carraways collect, are black singers who performed in Harlem. Countee Cullen, whose manuscript the Carraways own, is a black Harlem Renaissance poet. W. E. B. DuBois is a black leader, and Carl Van Vechten is a white Renaissance writer and patron of the arts. White artists fascinated with blacks and interested in writing about them dominated the early phase of the Harlem Renaissance.

Within a few years, starting around 1923, a small group of talented and well-educated African Americans living in Harlem became visible as they began to publish literature about their own experiences. Hughes was part of a group of writers who drew on black folk culture to create great art. These black artists saw artistic achievement as an important way for African Americans to overcome racism and win civil rights in the United States. They were promoted and financially supported by a group of wealthy and sympathetic whites. For several years, Hughes and a few of his peers were supported by an elderly white woman, Mrs. Osgood Mason, to whom they referred as their "godmother."

The Harlem Renaissance ended around 1935. In the last part of the Renaissance, young black artists became more rebellious and more critical of their white mentors, whom they accused of reducing them to stereotypes. By the time Hughes wrote "Slave on the Block," he had broken off his relationship with Mrs. Mason. Many of the Harlem Renaissance writers, including Hughes, had begun to question the earlier goal of assimilation and strove for a racially distinct style. Harlem Renaissance writing also became more explicitly political, sometimes influenced by Marxist theories of class division and economic exploitation. This position was shaped, in part, by the increasing economic divide between blacksf and whites as a result of the Great Depression. By 1935 several of the talented young writers of the Renaissance had died and many more had left Harlem.

The Great Depression

The Great Depression, initiated by the stock market crash of 1929, was a period of great economic hardship across the nation, but the troubled economy hurt African Americans disproportionately. Despite the artistic achievements and visibility of blacks in this period, they remained economically powerless. Harlem families, for example, paid twice as much of their income in rent as did white families in 1931, and by the end of 1932 almost half of Harlemites were unemployed. The median family income in Harlem dropped approximately 44%

Compare
&
Contrast

- **1930s:** White mob violence and economic depression in the south, and higher-paying industrial jobs in the north, encourage African-Americans to move to northern cities in a vast relocation known as The Great Migration.

  1990s: The trend of "white flight" from the cities to the suburbs, which began in the 1970s, remains evident, with blacks making up the majority in most urban centers. Since the 1970s, southern as well as northern cities have become a common destination for African-Americans.

- **1930s:** In the 1930s, public schools, public transportation, and other public places are legally segregated by race throughout the South. A 1935 survey of southern schools finds that an average of $17.04 is spent on each black student as compared to $49.30 for each white student. The NAACP (National Association for the Advancement of Colored People) begins a series of lawsuits in accordance with the Supreme Court's provision that facilities may separate but must be of equal quality, eventually culminating in the Civil Rights Movement of the 1960s. Only about 5 percent of eligible blacks in the South are registered to vote. Arthur W. Mitchell of Chicago is the first African American elected to the House of Representatives. Over the course of the decade, there are 111 recorded lynchings. Anti-lynching legislation is introduced.

  1990s: A Harvard University study shows that racial segregation is rising to levels not seen since 1968. It finds that 66 percent of African-American students attend predominantly minority schools. A record number of 40 members of the U.S. Congress are black. The Supreme Court sets limits on the 1965 Voting Rights Act.

- **1939:** *Gone with the Wind,* a heroic portrayal of a white southern family's struggle during and after the Civil War, is a hit movie. Hattie McDaniel, who plays a loyal slave and servant, becomes the first African-American woman to win an Academy Award. Boxer Joe Louis becomes world champion. Undefeated until his 1949 retirement, he remains a symbol of black power and achievement among African Americans.

  1990s: Television talk-show host Oprah Winfrey is one of the top-ten wealthiest entertainers in the United States. She is the only African-American named as one of the ten most admired women in a national poll.

---

between 1930 and 1932. The Harlem artists were dependent on the support of white patrons, publishers, audiences and readers. As the economy foundered, financial support dried up and white interest in African-American art and culture also subsided.

Critical Overview

Hughes was surprised when his story "Slave on the Block" was accepted for publication in the distinguished and well-established magazine *Scribner's.* Other mainstream magazines hesitated to publish the stories he wrote in this period, particularly those referring to interracial sexual relationships. In 1934 Hughes collected the stories and published them a volume called *The Ways of White Folks,* his first book of short fiction. Its title is a reference to W. E. B. DuBois's influential 1903 book *The Souls of Black Folk,* famous for its claim that "the problem of the twentieth century is the problem of the color line"—that is, the problem of the division between the black and white races. As a group, Hughes's stories address the new complications in interactions between the races in the early twentieth century, largely drawing from his own experiences with liberal whites, and in particular, with the white patron from whom he broke early in his career.

In *The Life of Langston Hughes,* biographer Arnold Rampersad describes the critical response to *The Ways of White Folks* as generally very favorable. He reports that at the time it was published, reviewers considered it not only his finest work to date, but some of the best writing to have appeared in the country in years. However, the book was not without its critics. Negative responses to the collection centered around Hughes's apparent anger and bitterness toward white people. Rampersad quotes one of the leading voices of the Harlem Renaissance, Alain Locke, saying that "greater artistry, deeper sympathy, and less resentment would have made it a book for all times." Sherwood Anderson, a white writer who moved in Hughes's circle, wrote in a review for the *Nation,* "The Negro people in these stories of his are so alive, warm, and real, and the whites are all caricatures. . . . Mr. Hughes, my hat is off to you in relation to your own race but not to mine." According to Rampersad, prominent white liberal Martha Greuning had a similar criticism, reproaching Hughes for representing white people as "either sordid and cruel, or silly and sentimental."

In "The Practice of a Social Art," Maryemma Graham quotes Hughes in an interview given thirty years after the publication of *The Ways of White Folks.* Responding to criticisms of his representation of whites, Hughes explains his intentions: "Through at least one (maybe only one) white character in each story, I try to indicate that they are human, too. . . . What I try to indicate is that circumstances and conditions make it very hard for whites, in interracial relationships, each to his own self be true.'"

With the advantage of historical hindsight, recent scholars have been able to argue that the direct and angry portraits of race relations in *The Ways of White Folks* anticipated the cultural changes of the 1960s, including both the Civil Rights Movement and the development of the more radical style of Black Aesthetics. Rampersad says that *The Ways of White Folks* "set a new standard for excellence for black writers" and describes it as "a striking original, daring to say what had never been said so definitively before." Rampersad describes Hughes's writing in this collection, compared to his earlier work, as "far more adult and neurotic, more militant and defensive, and thus more modern and accurate as a description of the Afro-American temper as it was emerging." In his *Langston Hughes: A Study of the Short Fiction,* Hans Ostrom writes that the lack of uniform critical praise for *The Ways of White Folks* is largely due to the fact that "it

addresses questions of racial, class and sexual conflict so directly, uses fierce, even bitter, irony, and reflects Hughes's notions about short fiction, which were not altogether mainstream." Thus such criticism, Ostrom writes, "is in a sense only another measure of the book's distinctiveness."

Criticism

Sarah Madsen Hardy

Sarah Madsen Hardy holds a Ph.D. in English Language and Literature. In the following essay, she analyzes Hughes's choice to focus on white characters in "Slave on the Block."

One can see Langston Hughes's choice to write a collection of stories focusing on the "ways of white folks" as a curious one. For he was part of a vanguard of young black writers who set out to prove not only that African Americans had the talent to write literature, but that black people's experiences were as valid a subject for great art as those of whites. Earlier in his career, Hughes had transformed the black musical folk tradition of the blues into powerful poetry about the African American urban experience. Furthermore, for Hughes, representing African-American experiences had political implications as well as artistic ones. As an important voice in the literary movement known as the Harlem Renaissance, Hughes believed that the artistic representation of blacks' complex humanity could be an instrument for gaining civil rights and a weapon against racism. Last but not least, Hughes was well educated and could see that the great majority of American literature was written by white people and preoccupied with their experiences. Why should a black writer spend his time representing the attitudes and habits of whites?

Hughes's unflinching portrayal of race relations in "Slave on the Block," one of the stories in the collection, offers an avenue for exploring this question. Hughes is explicit about the fact that Luther and Mattie, two African-American domestic servants, would prefer not to think about their white employers, the Carraways, or their fascination with all things black. He writes, "They didn't understand the vagaries of white people, neither Luther nor Mattie, and they didn't want to be bothered trying." However, what Luther and Mattie want is not the only factor to consider. Hughes places the black characters in a position of econom-

What Do I Read Next?

- *Montage of a Dream Deferred* (1951), a collection of Hughes's poetry dealing with the pleasures and disappointments of Harlem's urban world. In this book, as in much of his poetry, Hughes refers to the rhythms and themes of the African-American musical tradition of the blues.

- *The Best of Simple* (1961), a compilation of tales that Hughes wrote featuring the urban folk hero Jesse B. Simple, a character he invented for a column in the *Chicago Defender* in the 1940s. Hughes uses oral story-telling methods in these witty, comic, ironic sketches about everyday people.

- *The Collected Stories* by D. H. Lawrence, a British modernist whose work greatly influenced Hughes. Hughes admired Lawrence's bold, direct style of psychological analysis and social critique. One story in this collection, "The Lovely Lady," which is about a controlling elderly woman who reminded Hughes of his mentor Mrs. Mason, directly inspired him to write *The Ways of White Folks*.

- *Dubliners* (1914) by James Joyce, who is considered one of the most important and influential modernist writers. This early collection of short stories forms a scrupulously realistic group portrait of the way of life in the city of Dublin. Critics have pointed out that *The Ways of White Folks* is comparable to *Dubliners* in that they both assemble stories about different characters who live in the same city to create a complex vision of a particular time and place.

- *Home to Harlem* (1928) by Caribbean emigre and Harlem Renaissance writer Claude McKay. Concerning the colorful adventures and exploits of black citizens of Harlem, this novel was important in defining the Harlem style and was the only Harlem Renaissance novel published in the 1920s to become a best-seller.

- *Quicksand and Passing* (1929), a set of two novellas by Nella Larsen, another Harlem Renaissance writer. Both novellas center on mixed-race characters who struggle to find their place in a racially segregated society. The narratives deal with the assumptions that blacks and whites have about each other, with emphasis on how women experience race and racism.

- *Black No More* (1931) by George Schuyler, a satirical novel about the obsession with skin color in the United States. The plot revolves around a young black man who becomes white thanks to a scientific discovery, and the trouble that ensues.

- *Black Like Me* (1960) by John Howard Griffin, a nonfiction account of a white man who alters his appearance, and travels through the United States passing for black. The book describes trials of racism against blacks from a white point of view, painting a grim picture of American race relations.

---

ic dependence and close personal vicinity in which they have no choice but to deal with the Carraways' thoughts, feelings, and fantasies about their race. This is exacerbated in Luther's case, because the Carraways have hired him specifically to serve as a muse for their racially inspired artwork. By placing his characters in this context, Hughes suggests how continually African Americans must contend with white people's distorted images of them. Thus white attitudes become an intrinsic part of the black experience, an experience Hughes and his peers were committed to representing in all of its complexity. In Hughes's own personal experience, whites fascinated with the perceived vitality and simplicity of African-American art and artists were a formative part of his struggle to establish himself as an artist and a constant element of his social life in Harlem. In order to represent this reality, he needed to delve into the realm of white folks and their strange and contradictory ways.

> By placing his characters in this context, Hughes suggests how continually African Americans must contend with white people's distorted images of them."

The title that Hughes chose for the collection, *The Ways of White Folks,* reflects on its subject matter in a manner more subtle than may first be apparent. The title is not only a description of the stories' content, it is also an allusion to an influential collection of essays on black culture and spirit called *The Souls of Black Folk,* written by W. E. B. DuBois in 1903. DuBois was an important black intellectual, and his writing inspired many artists and thinkers in the younger Harlem Renaissance generation of which Hughes was part. One of the most powerful concepts DuBois puts forth in *The Souls of Black Folk* is his description the psychological effect of racism on African Americans, an effect he calls "double consciousness." DuBois argues that American blacks constantly have to think of themselves in relation to the racial stereotypes that they regularly confront in various aspects of daily life. He contends that African Americans see things from their own unique cultural perspective, but that they are, at once, perpetually aware of the negative ways in which their race is *seen* in the wider mainstream culture. The consciousness of blacks is "double" because on the one hand, blacks internalize these derogatory images, incorporating them into their sense of identity, and on the other they struggle against them. In other words, the ways of white folks play a central if unwelcome role within the divided souls of black folk. Hughes's stories refer to DuBois's theory and reflect the condition he describes, dramatizing the pervasive influence of stereotype as it affects interracial perceptions and dynamics.

DuBois says that American blacks are "born with a veil." He suggests that while blacks can—and, indeed, must—understand and participate in the perspectives of the white dominant culture,

whites can only see things from their own racial point of view. Whites create their own images of blackness and are blind to how different these images are from the reality of black life, which remains figuratively invisible to them behind its veil. "Slave on the Block" embroiders on this visual metaphor. Hughes's ironic narration—the gap between what he says and what he means—is built in order to reveal to his readers just how blind the Carraways are in their perceptions of Luther. When Luther first enters their house, the Carraways almost miss him: "They could hardly see the boy, it being dark in the hall, and he being dark, too." This failure to see has symbolic meaning. Because he is "dark," they focus on his racial appearance and the stereotypical associations it calls up for them. When they see Luther, all they see is that he looks "as black as all the Negroes they'd ever known put together." Hughes has already established the fact that the Carraways don't have African-American friends. Their idea of Luther is determined by the generalized image of blacks they have absorbed through popular and literary representations, images for the most part created in the white imagination.

Looking more closely at one particular stereotype, the figure of the "Uncle Tom," provides an additional context for understanding the significance of racial representation in "Slave on the Block." An "Uncle Tom" is a black man who is more loyal to whites than he is to his own people. He is happy to serve whites and to fulfill their wishes because he sees the role of the slave as befitting his simple, humble race. The term derives from *Uncle Tom's Cabin,* an anti-slavery novel Harriet Beecher Stowe wrote on the eve of the Civil War. Stowe, like the Carraways, certainly meant well when she created the character of Uncle Tom. Her book was meant to convince people that slavery was un-Christian. However, she accomplished this through relying on narrow ideas about racial differences. This story of a humble and simple slave, ever loyal to his white owners, formed one of the most enduring stereotypes for black men.

In "Slave on the Block" Hughes creates in Luther a black male character who does not conform to the image of a simple and contented servant who knows his place in the tradition of *Uncle Tom's Cabin.* One can glean from Luther's impudent smile a repudiation of one of the most powerful stereotypes of black men. Also, and perhaps more importantly, the story illustrates how stereotypes distort the racial attitudes of well-meaning whites like the

Carraways. The Carraways don't recognize that their admiration of Luther as "childlike" and "simple" can be traced back to the negative stereotype for the "Uncle Tom," and neither do they recognize how inaccurate these terms are for describing Luther, whom Hughes portrays as sardonic and rebellious.

The "Uncle Tom" is only one of the stereotypes in play in the story. Not only do the Carraways wish to see Luther as a childlike and naive "boy," they also wish to see him as "fervent" and sexual, a creature of the jungle—a stereotype with a different derivation. However, thinking about "Slave on the Block" as a response to *Uncle Tom's Cabin* is particularly helpful in understanding Hughes's choice to write a collection of stories portraying the ways of whites. *Uncle Tom's Cabin* was the first novel published in the United States that had an African American as a main character. It was also the first best-seller in American history. The novel as well as its many stage adaptations were wildly popular for over fifty years, rendering the story familiar to the great majority of Americans. The success of *Uncle Tom's Cabin* illustrates how thoroughly white representations of black people permeated American culture.

Like Stowe, the Carraways are artists interested in portraying blacks. "Slave on the Block" can be interpreted as a commentary on the power that white artists have to create and circulate images of black people—images that reflect a view of the race more closely related to other images created by whites than to black ways or souls. The story can at once be interpreted as an intervention, in which Hughes seizes some of this representational power in order to create an opposing set of images. Because Anne is a painter, she is in a position to create an image of Luther that places him in the position of a slave. By writing stories like "Slave on the Block," Hughes assumes control of how blacks and whites are represented, and creates and alternate image of freedom and slavery. In Hughes's story, Luther rebels against the Carraways, rejects their influence, and walks away free. The Carraways perpetuate their view of blacks as naive and simple through their artistic representations. In his story, Hughes shows how simple and limited the Carraways' views are. In many places in the story, the Carraways come across as naive, especially in regard to how they interact with Luther and Mattie. For example, near the conclusion of the story, when Mattie quits in solidarity with Luther, she tells the Carraways that they'd "stood enough foolery from you white

folks!" Because the Carraways cannot see how their stereotypes are harmful, they fail to understand what Mattie means. "What could she mean, 'stood enough'? What had they done to them, Anne and Michael wondered. They had tried to be kind." It is not enough for Hughes to refute negative stereotypes of blacks. With fierce, unblinking portrayals of white ways, he also shows the havoc that stereotypes wreak on interracial interactions, compromising even whites with the best of intentions.

Describing the state of mind of blacks living in a culture in which representations like the "Uncle Tom" circulate freely, DuBois writes, "It is a peculiar sensation, this double consciousness, this sense of always looking at one's self through the eyes of others, of measuring one's soul by the tape of a world that looks on in amused contempt and pity." In writing "Slave on the Block," Hughes turns the tables, representing the Carraways with considerable contempt and pity. This ought not be understood as merely vengeful—a second wrong that can't make a right. DuBois shows how the peculiar sensation of seeing yourself as other sees you is a constitutive part of the black American experience, but not of the white one. In *The Ways of White Folks* Hughes offers white readers a rare opportunity to see themselves and to measure their souls from a point of view on the other side of the color line.

Source: Sarah Madsen Hardy, "White Ways and Black Souls," for *Short Stories for Students,* Gale, 1998.

Carl Mowery

Mowery has a doctorate in rhetoric/composition and literature from Southern Illinois University. He has taught there and Murray State University. In the following essay he examines the theme of unintended, or "benign" racism.

Overt racism—insults, threats, violence and discrimination—is not the only problem faced by African Americans. There is a more insidious kind that is more difficult to confront: unintended racism. In the short story "Slave on the Block," Langston Hughes addressed this type of bigotry. The characters in the tale are well-meaning people who are unaware of the effect their behavior has on people around them.

The Carraways are introduced as "people who went in for Negroes." But their attitude toward the blacks they meet is patronizing and condescending. In trying to express appreciation, they actually depreciate blacks with their insensitive remarks. When they first meet Luther, Anne says, "He is the jungle." Michael continues with "He's so utterly Negro." In both statements they fail to acknowledge Luther as a human being. When Michael accidentally finds Luther and Mattie in bed together, Anne's remark is again condescending. "It's so simple and natural for Negroes to make love." After Mattie and Luther begin spending time together, the Carraways worry that "she [is] spoiling a nice simple young boy." Their selfish concern is based on the belief that Mattie is "old enough to know better" than to interfere in the "delightful simplicity" of Luther.

These comments reduce Luther and Mattie to the level of children. Anne calls them "dear, natural childlike people." They treat Luther more as a house pet than as a servant with chores to do. He is asked to sing and dance for assembled guests. He is made to pose for Anne's paintings. He teaches Anne some of the dances he learns at clubs in Harlem. But he is never treated like a young adult.

The Carraways like to have parties to which "occasionally, a furtive Negro" or "sometimes a lesser Harlem celebrity" might come. Those who do attend seldom come back because the Carraways "tried too hard to make friends" and the blacks become suspicious of their motives. Symbolically, the Carraways are as far from a meaningful interaction with blacks as their secluded house is from Harlem.

Another aspect of the Carraways' naive indulgence of blacks can be found in their penchant for collecting art works by and about blacks. They are artists themselves, but "they never tried to influence that art, they only bought it and raved over it, and copied it." In their zeal to add to their collection of African-American art, they included the work of the Mexican artist Covarrubias, because "he caught the darky spirit!" Covarrubias is known primarily as an illustrator. Many of his works included caricatures of blacks that would be insulting and unacceptable in the 1990s. The couple reduces black artists and their work to a non-black representative, whose fame rested on unflattering caricatures of blacks. By fawning over these works, they expose their complete lack of sensitivity to what it means to be African American or an African-American artist.

They collect the recordings of Paul Robeson, a prominent black entertainer and singer whose creative life was spent in Europe because he was not accepted by American audiences, an indignity which does not concern the Carraways. They want to leave them "unspoiled and just enjoy them," as if such artists existed merely for their entertainment. "They knew Harlem like their own backyard," which was only "about as big as Michael's grand piano." They attended black clubs, for which they had to top the head man heavily, and "ritzy joints," where blacks could not get in. This is yet another example of how they reduce all things black to small collectible items.

The underlying theme here is a racism which seems to be benign on the surface. There is no confrontation or deliberate belittling of Negroes, no name calling, no threats of violence. Their effusive adulation of blacks is similar to the way the Kittridges treat Paul in the opening scenes of the movie *Six Degrees of Separation*.

This is quite different from the elder Mrs. Carraway's nasty attitude seen at the end of the story. She snaps at Luther, commenting on his race and saying, "Never, never, never have I suffered such impudence from servants . . . in my own son's house." In this one, intense, emotionally charged scene she shows the face of an overt racist. She reveals her contempt for black servants, especially if they talk back to her. This kind of behavior is easily identified and therefore more easily confronted than Anne's and Michael's behavior.

In the commencement address for Washington University's class of 1992, Marian Wright Edelman, president of the Children's Defense Fund, said that in order to combat racism, people should never accept racist remarks in their presence. In the context of a social conversation, one person can make others aware of the unacceptableness of racism. A reader of Hughes's story is immediately aware of Mrs. Carraway's attitude and, were it possible, might make a comment to her about it.

But in the case of Anne and Michael, their behavior seems polite and supportive. A comment about their behaviors might seem to be insensitive toward the Carraways themselves. They support minority artists by attending their theaters and clubs and by inviting them into their home. But these acts are selfishly motivated by their desire to collect "things black." This phony support is the kind of unintentional racism that is difficult to confront.

Anne and Michael are selfish. When they first hire Luther "to look after the garden," it seems that they are doing him a favor. But "they had to have some excuse to hire him," and soon Luther is only posing for Anne's paintings. They both indulge Luther, letting him wander about the house without a shirt. He "had grown a bit familiar" too, drinking their wine and smoking their cigarettes. Luther even came upstairs when they "had guests who didn't share their enthusiasm for Negroes." The Carraways react as they would to an unruly pet that disturbs the company.

But since Anne's picture is not finished, "they kept him," even though "Michael said he was getting a little bored with the same Negro always in the way." But after Mrs. Carraway insists that they fire him, and they do so without protest. Anne's only concern at this point is for "her Boy on the block," her "black boy." Luther says, "Don't worry bout me," a sentiment that is not a concern for the Carraways. They only worry about themselves.

Hughes has addressed this theme in other short stories. In the opening paragraphs of the short story "Who's Passing for Who?" Hughes says that people like the Carraways are little more than "kind-hearted and well-meaning bores." One can only guess what the parties at the Carraways' house were like, but since few of the invited guests ever returned, it might be assumed that these "rather slow parties" were populated by the "well-meaning bores" Hughes has identified. The whites in "Who's Passing," are identified as "overearnest uplifters" who patronize clubs in Harlem and buy drinks for black artists. They are the guests of a black man, Caleb, who bore their newfound black audience with their stuffy attitudes and effusive comments about having "never met" black artists before. Despite the fact that they usually "gather around to help" blacks, they have little to offer "except their company—which is often appallingly dull."

The Carraways, in the other tale, also seem to bore others whenever they are present. At parties that include blacks, "they gushed over them." But the "Negroes didn't seem to love Michael and Anne" as much as they loved the black folks. Michael and Anne do not recognize the impact they have had on those they have met. Instead, they see what they want to see: idealized figures who represent "the jungle," and who are "utterly Negro."

It was not widely accepted in the United States in the 1920s and 1930s for African Americans to speak out about racial and social injustice. Therefore, Hughes took a low-key approach to this touchy issue. When he attended Columbia University in 1924, he faced racism in very personal ways. In the poem, "Theme for English B" he addressed

> " Symbolically, the Carraways are as far from a meaningful interaction with blacks as their secluded house is from Harlem."

the situation. An instructor's assignment was an essay for English class, which Hughes wrote in the form of a poem. In it, Hughes said that the instructor (who was white) was as much a part of him (a black student) as he was a part of the instructor, because they interacted with each other regardless of their intentions.

> Sometimes perhaps you don't want to be a part of me. / Nor do I often want to be a part of you. / But we are, That's true! / As I learn from you, / I guess you learn from me— / although you're older—and white— / and somewhat more free.

These simple lines revealed Hughes's desire to raise the issue of race with his professor without creating a potentially inflammatory situation. He did not call for confrontation nor did he make demands. His poem quietly asked to be recognized as an individual human being.

That is also the point of his short story. He created whites in "Slave" who were patronizing and condescending in their attempts to keep blacks in a subservient position. In "Who's Passing" he cast the whites as overbearing and well-meaning, without real substance to their desires to "help." In both cases he called for understanding and acceptance of the individual as a human, not part of a collective, and not because of skin color. He did not preach in the stories or the poem; rather he held up a mirror for the white society to see what it was doing. Although Hughes never said that individual acceptance is the key to the solution of this troublesome issue, that message is there. It is up to the reader to find it.

Source: Carl Mowery, for *Short Stories for Students*, Gale, 1998.

Robert Bone

Bone is an American critic and educator who specializes in African-American literature as well as Shakespeare. In the excerpt below, he gives an analysis of Hughes's short fiction.

Pastoral, whose source is disillusionment with courtly life, contains within itself the seeds of satire. The higher the degree of alienation from the life-style of courtiers and kings, the greater the tendency toward satire. Langston Hughes is essentially a satirist, at least in the short-story form. His first book of stories, *The Ways of White Folks,* might well have been subtitled "In Dispraise of Courtly Life." The pride and pretentiousness, arrogance and hypocrisy, boorishness and inhumanity of white folks are the targets of his caustic prose. The genius of Langston Hughes, which is a gift for comedy and satire, is thus displayed within the broad outlines of the pastoral tradition.

Within the context of its times, however, *The Ways of White Folks* functioned as antipastoral. The early, or ascending phase of the Harlem Renaissance was dominated by the myth of primitivism. Hughes himself, during what may be described as the undergraduate phase of his career, conformed substantially to the requirements of the myth. The late, or declining phase of the Renaissance, however, was increasingly antagonistic to the stereotype of the Negro as primitive. Finely tuned as always to the climate of the times, Hughes joined forces with such authors as Wallace Thurman and Sterling Brown to discredit the myth and challenge its pastoral assumptions. . . .

It is against this background that we must seek to comprehend Hughes' career as a short-story writer. After a brief experimental period in 1927–1928, he turned to serious professional work in 1933. During that year he wrote fourteen stories, all of which were published in *The Ways of White Folks.* Retaining this momentum, in 1934 he wrote eleven more, most of which were collected some years later in *Laughing to Keep from Crying.* From 1935 to 1939 there was a tapering off (only five stories), as he turned from fiction to drama. A year at Hollow Hills Farm in 1941 produced a cluster of four stories. In 1943 the first Simple sketch appeared, and from that date until his death in 1967 Hughes wrote only seven tales. . . .

An end to white paternalism was one of the things that the Renaissance was all about. Hughes' literary manifesto, ["The Negro Artist and the Racial Mountain"], in the *Nation* was nothing if not a declaration of independence. Yet paradoxically, it was promulgated by a writer who depended on a series of white patrons for his daily bread. The stark reality of the New Negro movement was that Hughes and his contemporaries were dependent in many ways on white patrons, impresarios, editors, agents, critics, and ordinary members of the reading public. It was an agonizing dilemma, which neither Hughes nor the generation of which he was a leading spokesman was able to resolve.

The Ways of White Folks was at bottom an attempt to come to grips with this dilemma. Hughes' solution was to strike a satirical stance toward his former patron and the world that she represents. In this way, he was able to preserve an essential dignity and self-respect, even while living rent-free in Noel Sullivan's cottage at Carmel. His experience with Mrs. Mason had left him in a satirical frame of mind. He was more than ready for a caustic treatment of white folks, rich folks, or pompous and pretentious folks of any hue. This turn to satire, moreover, involved a momentary shift from poetry to prose. For a brief period, the short-story form became the growing edge of his career.

The unmasking of hypocrisy became his central theme. The emotional source of this impulse was of course his father, who made a show of fatherly concern which in fact he didn't feel. By a process of transference, Hughes attributed the sins of his delinquent father to the patrons of the Harlem Renaissance. They too, he had come to feel, were lacking in a genuine commitment to the cause that they espoused. This is the burden of several stories in *The Ways of White Folks.*

Eleven of [this book's] . . . fourteen tales are satires, and the rest contain satiric elements. The book was born in a sense of personal affront. Wounded by his former patron, Hughes lashes back at white paternalism in all its forms. His objects of attack include delinquent parents, domineering patrons, unscrupulous employers, and self-appointed missionaries in whatever guise. In the caustic language of H. L. Mencken (it is no accident that two of these stories first appeared in the *American Mercury*), Hughes excoriates the guile and mendacity, self-deception and equivocation, insincerity and sanctimoniousness, sham, humbug, and sheer fakery of white America in all its dealings with the black minority.

The author's personal pique is obvious enough, and to lift the curse of his vindictiveness toward Mrs. Mason, Hughes assumes a mask of genial humor. His comic muse is most apparent in such light satires as "Slave on the Block," "A Good Job

Gone,'' and ''Rejuvenation Through Joy.'' Hughes is a gifted humorist, but it would be an error to construe this gift in narrow literary terms. Rather it constitutes a lusty adaptation to his life circumstances. Nourished by the boundless absurdities of American racism, this humor is, by the author's own account, a matter of ''laughing to keep from crying.'' But ''laughing to keep from hating'' may be closer to the mark. In any case, a humor of diverse tonalities is an essential feature of Hughes' satiric mask.

Irony . . . is the satirist's linguistic mode. Hughes is a resourceful ironist whose verbal indirections often saturate his tales. Among his favorite rhetorical devices are ironic understatement (to intensify, while seeming to diminish, the satirical attack); ironic inversion (to apportion praise or blame by indirection); ironic reversal (to add an element of shock or surprise to the attack); and ironic repetition or refrain (to create a cumulative tension that is finally discharged against the satiric victim). These are but a few of the devices by which Hughes is able to control his anger and simulate the coolness and detachment of effective satire.

Two standards of morality are juxtaposed in Hughes' satiric fiction: a white and Negro code. This division is the basis of the bipartite structure of his tales. He begins with the arraignment of a white society which constantly betrays its own professed ideals. But at some point a Negro character is introduced who embodies a different and more authentic moral code. This character—whether maid-of-all-work, kitchen boy, janitor, or jazz musician—provides the low norm by which the conduct of the whites is judged and found wanting. For the whites, despite their wealth and power, are failures as human beings, while the blacks, despite their poverty and vulnerability, are tough and resourceful and certain to survive. . . .

Source: Robert Bone, ''Langston Hughes,'' in his *Down Home: Origins of the Afro-American Short Story,* Columbia University Press, 1988, pp. 239–71.

Peter Bruck

In the following excerpt from a longer essay, Bruck provides a social, literary, and historical perspective on Hughes's short fiction, concentrating on the collection The Ways of White Folks.

Langston Hughes (1902–1967), according to many critics ''poet laureate of Harlem'' and ''Dean of American Negro Writers,'' began his literary career by winning a poetry contest sponsored by the black magazine *Opportunity* in 1925. ''The Weary Blues'' was noted by Carl Van Vechten, through whose sponsorship Hughes was able to get his first contract with the noted publisher Alfred Knopf. Van Vechten, who acted as a main ambassadorial advisor and patron of black literature to white publishing firms during the 1920's, not only paved the way for Hughes' literary career but also became the ''chief architect of his early success.'' Just as with [Paul Laurence] Dunbar and [Charles Waddell] Chesnutt, white patronage played a decisive role in the literary emergence of Langston Hughes. The omnipresence of the white patron with his significant socio-literary influence on the black author was a discovery that the young Hughes was still to make; his gradual and painstaking emancipation from the grip of such white patrons was to become the major concern of his early phase and to play a dominant theme in his short fiction. . . .

Although his first stories, all reflecting the author's experiences as a seaman on a voyage along the West coast of Africa, were already published in Harlem's literary magazine *The Messenger* in 1927, it took another six years before Hughes really devoted himself to writing short fiction. From the spring of 1932 to the fall of 1933 he visited the Soviet Union and the Far East. It was during his stay in Moscow that he had a decisive reading experience [having read D. H. Lawrence's collection *The Lovely Lady*] which prompted him to devote himself to the short story. . . . The years to come were to see amazing results from this literary initiation. Between 1933 and 1934 he devoted himself exclusively to this genre.

[*The Ways of White Folks,*] which received rather favorable reviews, presents, thematically, a close examination of black-white relationships. Mostly satirical in tone, the stories try to unmask several manifestations of the Harlem Renaissance. Specifically, the theme of white patronage, as displayed in ''Slave on the Block,'' ''Poor Little Black Fellow,'' and ''The Blues I'm Playing,'' is used to demonstrate the dishonesty of whites and the absurd notion of their paternalistic philanthropy. In this context, it is of particular socio-literary interest to note that Hughes' fictional treatment of the incipient dissociation from white predominance caused him no setback in magazine publication. Instead, his new literary efforts soon found their way into leading periodicals. Whereas Hughes' poetry was usually printed in such black journals as *Opportunity* and *The Crisis* (he had complained in 1929 that ''maga-

> The theme of white patronage, as displayed in 'Slave on the Block' is used to demonstrate the dishonesty of whites and the absurd notion of their paternalistic philanthropy."

zines used very few stories with Negro themes, since Negro themes were considered exotic, in a class with Chinese or East Indian features), four out of his five stories written in Moscow were now accepted and published by such noted periodicals as *The American Mercury, Scribner's Magazine* and *Esquire.* This major breakthrough provided him with a nation-wide, non-parochial platform, allowing him to escape from his predicament, and opened up the opportunity of gaining a primarily white reading audience. . . .

Despite favorable reviews, the first issue of *The Ways of White Folk* sold only 2500 copies. This meagre success may be accounted for not only by the fact that Hughes had not yet gained, as he was to do later with his "Simple Tales," a genuine black reading audience; the commercial failure also seems to demonstrate that with the end of the Harlem Renaissance the potential white audience no longer shared a larger enthusiasm in black literary products. From a historical and socio-literary perspective, however, the stories of *The Ways of White Folk* caused a major breakthrough in paving the way for a racially unrestricted audience. By re-examining the black-white relationships of the 1920's and by unmasking the falseness of the enthusiasm of whites for the 'New Negro,' [Donald C. Dickinson states that] Hughes "clarified for the Negro audience their own strength and dignity and . . . supplied the white audience with an explanation of how the Negro feels and what he wants." Six years after the publication of this collection, Richard Wright, in a review of Hughes' autobiography *The Big Sea,* perhaps summed up the importance of the early works of Hughes best. In his eyes, Hughes, on account of his extensive publications, had served as a "cultural ambassador for the case of the blacks."

Source: Peter Bruck, "Langston Hughes: 'The Blues I'm Playing' (1934)," in *The Black American Short Story in the 20th Century: A Collection of Critical Essays,* edited by Peter Bruck, B. R. Gruner Publishing Co., 1977, pp. 71–84.

Waters E. Turpin

Turpin was an American novelist, dramatist, and editor. In the excerpt below, he presents "Slave on the Block" as an example of Hughes's successful use of satire.

Langston Hughes's "Slave on the Block" is a penetrating, satirical portraiture of arty, "liberal" whites, represented by Michael and Anne Carraway in this short story. Ostensibly it is the story of a young Negro migrated to New Jersey from the deep South, who has come to retrieve the belongings of his Aunt Emma, lately deceased in the employ of the Carraways, residents of Greenwich Village. However, the story becomes a vehicle for the author to reveal certain absurdities in the behavior of white employers toward their Negro domestics, and at the same time pungently scathe the stereotypes of Negroes held by certain strata of white America, particularly phony liberals. The ironic twist of the narrative is that the Carraways lose their domestics by the very tactics and attitudes with which they had hoped to retain them.

The first . . . paragraphs of "Slave on the Block" set the tone and prepare the way for what is to happen:

> They were people who went in for Negroes—Michael and Anne—the Carraways. But not in the social-service, philanthropic sort of way, no. They saw no use in helping a race that was already too charming and naive and lovely for words. Leave them unspoiled and just enjoy them, Michael and Anne felt. So they went in for the Art of Negroes— the dancing that had such jungle life about it, the songs that were so simple and fervent, the poetry that was so direct, so real. They never tried to influence that art, they only bought it and raved over it, and copied it. For they were artists, too. (pp. 64–5)

> They were acquainted with lots of Negroes, too—but somehow the Negroes didn't seem to like them very much. Maybe the Carraways gushed over them too soon. Or maybe they looked a little like poor white folks, although they were really quite well off. . . . As much as they loved Negroes, Negroes didn't seem to love Michael and Anne. But they were blessed with a wonderful colored cook and maid—until she took sick and died in her room in their basement. . . .

And the place of their maid's abode and death tells the reader something very pertinent about Michael and Anne.

Into these circumstances comes young Luther, "as black as all the Negroes they'd ever known put together." Anne describes Luther: "He *is* the jungle. . . ." Michael describes him as "He's 'I Couldn't Hear Nobody Pray. . . .'" Each adheres to the terms of the Carraway art interest—Anne's in painting, Michael's in music. And Hughes, no doubt at this point, was having a chuckling good time all by himself.

Luther becomes a combination houseboy, model for Anne, and purveyor of Negro music for Michael. They inform him that they "loved your aunt so much. She was the best cook we ever had."

The redoubtable foil of the Carraways, however, is Mattie, their fortyish but still sexually active replacement for Luther's lately mourned aunt. She proceeds to enlighten the young man about the ways of his new environment, downtown and uptown, and especially her favorite Harlem haunts. Soon they are sleeping together, to the momentary shock of the Carraways but without their disapproval. "It's so simple and natural for Negroes to make love," is Anne's blithe comment. And when Luther, as a result of his nocturnal forays to Harlem night-spots with Mattie, culminating in carnal calisthenics during the wee hours, poses somnolently for Anne, she decides to do a painting of him, entitled "The Sleeping Negro." Following this, she asks him to pose in the half-nude for her painting dubbed "The Boy on the Block," with a New Orleans slave auction background. Michael, not to be outdone by his wife,

> . . . went to the piano and began to play something that sounded like "Deep River" in the jaws of a dog, but . . . said it was a modern slave plaint, 1850 in terms of 1933. Vieux Carre remembered on 135th Street. Slavery in the Cotton Club.

As a consequence of these contretemps, the servant-master-mistress relationships in the Carraway establishment becomes strained, if not dissipated, since the "boy" from the South no longer is the likeable, "child-like creature he first appeared to be by Carraway standards. He takes all sort of liberties, strolling about in the half-nude, availing himself of Carraway potables and cigaretts. The breaking point is reached upon the appearance of Michael's Kansas City mother—the apotheosis of Philip Wiley's "Mom," who, after an affront by Luther, gets her son to dismiss both servants summarily. Mattie's reaction to this is Hughes' final thrust at the phony white type he is satirizing:

> "Yes, we'll go," boomed Mattie from the doorway, who had come up from below, fat and belligerent.

"We've stood enough foolery from you white folks! Yes, we'll go. Come on, Luther." What could she mean, "stood enough?" What had they done to them, Anne and Michael wondered. They had tried to be kind. "Oh!" "Sneaking around knocking on our door at night," Mattie went on. "Yes, we'll go. Pay us! Pay us!" So she remembered the time they had come for Luther at night. That was it.

And to complete the Carraway's bouleversement, Luther hands the roses he has gathered from the small garden he had nurtured to Anne, saying:

> "Good-bye. . . . You fix the vases." He handed her his armful of roses, glanced impudently at old Mrs. Carraway and grinned—grinned that wide, beautiful white-toothed grin that made Anne say when she first saw him, "He looks like the jungle." Grinned and disappeared in the dark hall, with no shirt on his back. "Oh," moaned Anne distressfully, "my 'Boy on the Block'!" "Huh!" snorted Mrs. Carraway.

In his "Slave on the Block," it is obvious that Hughes is having a gleeful time stilettoing his satirical prey. Yet, the ring of truth chimes from the piece. He has caught with eye and ear the totality of his subject. At the same time we can see here the piercing of the stereotype image which still haunts the white mind in many quarters.

Source: Waters E. Turpin, "Four Short Fiction Writers of the Harlem Renaissance—Their Legacy of Achievement," in *CLA Journal*, Vol. XI, No. 1, September, 1967, pp. 59–72.

Sources

Anderson, Sherwood. A review of *The Ways of White Folks* in *The Nation*, July 11, 1934. Reprinted in *Langston Hughes: Critical Perspectives Past and Present*, edited by Henry Louis Gates, Jr., and K. A. Appiah, New York, Amistad Books, 1993, p. 18.

DuBois, W. E. B. *The Souls of Black Folks*, New York, Bantam Books, 1989.

Gates, Henry Louis, Jr. Preface to *Langston Hughes: Critical Perspectives Past and Present*, edited by Henry Louis Gates, Jr., and K. A. Appiah, New York, Amistad Books, 1993, pp. ix-xii.

Graham, Maryemma. "The Practice of a Social Art," in *Langston Hughes: Critical Perspectives Past and Present*, edited by Henry Louis Gates, Jr., and K. A. Appiah, New York, Amistad Books, 1993, p. 213-36.

Ostrom, Hans. *Langston Hughes: A Study of the Short Fiction*, New York, Twayne Publishers, 1993.

Rampersad, Arnold. *The Life of Langston Hughes*, Vol. 1, New York, Oxford University Press, 1986.

Further Reading

Anderson, Jervis. *This Was Harlem.* New York: Farrar, Straus & Giroux, 1981.
    A lively account of life in Harlem during the Renaissance era, focusing on the black entertainment scene.

Hughes, Langston. *The Big Sea: An Autobiography.* New York: Hill and Wang, 1940.
    Hughes's autobiographical account of his life as a young writer, up until shortly before the time he wrote *The Ways of White Folks.*

Lewis, David Levering. *When Harlem Was in Vogue.* New York: Oxford University Press, 1981.
    A thorough and readable analysis of the historical and cultural factors behind the Harlem Renaissance.

Ostrom, Hans. *Langston Hughes: A Study of the Short Fiction.* New York: Twayne, 1993.
    Provides a clear and in-depth critical interpretation of Hughes's short stories and also reprints a series of contemporaneous reviews of this material.

Sophistication

Sherwood Anderson
1919

Sherwood Anderson wrote "Sophistication" as part of his novel *Winesburg, Ohio,* which was first published in 1919. For four years, living alone in an apartment in Chicago, he had worked steadily on the stories comprising the longer work, having been inspired by Edgar Lee Masters's *Spoon River Anthology* and Gertrude Stein's *Three Lives.* "Sophistication," one of the final three chapters of *Winesburg, Ohio,* though part of a larger work, has often been interpreted by critics and readers as an independent story. Early reviewers said that the story reveals the secrets and hopes of George Willard and Helen White through its use of clear, conversational diction and graphic description of setting. Critics also noted that the character of George was a not-well-disguised portrait of Anderson himself. In the story, George hopes to fulfill his dream of becoming a thoughtful writer, not a "mere peddler of words," as one of his teachers puts it. Back home during a summer festival, George visits Helen White again. With her encouragement, he seeks to escape peer pressure from old and young citizens of the town by undertaking the rites of passage that every young person must endure. From initial praise by reviewers in the early 1920s, through a lapse of attention through the 1930s and on to the present day, both the short story and the novel of which it is a part have become minor American classics that evoke the stifling nature of small-town life in the early twentieth century.

Author Biography

Sherwood Anderson was born the third of seven children in Camden, Ohio, on September 13, 1876. His father was locally renowned as a storyteller, and his brother Karl achieved success as a painter. Thus, from an early age Anderson was exposed to the arts. His father's changing financial fortunes caused the family to move several times; they finally settled in the village of Clyde, Ohio, which is the model for the village in *Winesburg, Ohio.* Anderson's education was sporadic and erratic. His formal education ended after one year at Wittenberg Academy, but his many jobs as newsboy, farmhand, and laborer gave him a lively awareness of small-town life and served as an inspiration for his fiction. He served for one year in the U.S. Army during the Spanish-American War, after which he began writing advertising copy in Chicago, which helped him to launch a successful business career as the owner of a paint factory, the Anderson Manufacturing Company. However, he suffered a nervous breakdown in 1912 and walked away from his paint factory, never again to return. His first marriage—the first of four—ended shortly after his collapse.

Moving back to Chicago, he began writing stories and novels, one of which was ''Sophistication.'' With *Winesburg, Ohio,* Anderson greatly influenced a later generation of writers, including Ernest Hemingway, through his simple style and straightforward sentences, whether describing situations and persons, or writing dialogue between characters. In addition, novelists such as John Steinbeck and William Faulkner learned from Anderson the importance of regional emphasis and local color.

Anderson lived from 1927 until his death in 1941 in the small town of Marion in southwestern Virginia, where for a time he edited and published two local newspapers. He also published numerous articles, short stories, memoirs, and novels. Perhaps the most distinguished of his later works are the novels *Dark Laughter* and *Poor White,* along with the short stories collected in *The Triumph of the Egg, Horses and Men,* and *Death in the Woods.* For a while, during the 1930s, he became a fellow traveler with communists and socialists. His died in South America from peritonitis, which developed after he swallowed a broken toothpick while eating hors d'oeuvres.

Plot Summary

It is important to note that although the plot of ''Sophistication'' is self-contained, it also relies heavily on the events that precede it in *Winesburg, Ohio.* Furthermore, the story is more a moment in George Willard's and Helen White's shared life than it is a story with a typical plot. It is late fall. George is pushing his way through the crowded streets of his hometown, and he hides in the doorway of Dr. Reefy's office so that he can observe the ebb and flow of the children and farmers, the buggies and wagons, the wives and grandmothers, the dogs and horses. The Winesburg County Fair has brought almost everyone to town, and George, a young man with high hopes but vague plans, seeks to separate himself from these townspeople, who seem vulgar to him. He feels lonely and old; he is still mourning the death of his mother and he longs to find Helen White, whose respect and affection he yearns for.

George is agitated that Helen has come home from college in Cleveland with a young college instructor. George finds the crowd distracting and boorish, especially a group of men listening to Wesley Moyer coarsely bragging about the victory of his stallion in a race at the fair ground earlier in the day. George vows to go straight to Helen's house to see her, so that his moment of sophisticated sadness might not destroy him.

In the story's second part, the narrator describes Helen's restlessness with the college instructor, who bores her with his belittling remarks about the town as they sit on the veranda of her house. To her ears he sounds ''pompous and heavy.''

Helen leaves the veranda and goes to the garden in the back of the house. In the same way that George finds communication with others impossible, she thinks that ''the world [is] full of meaningless people saying words.'' Crude farm language or highborn college talk cause both Helen and George to seek ''sophistication'' with each other. As she cries to herself, ''George, where are you?,'' George stumbles into her, still muttering, ''I'll go to Helen White's house. . . . I'll walk right in.'' He takes her hand, and they walk off to the Winesburg fair ground. The final part of the story depicts the simultaneously sad and joyous moment that they share together.

At the empty fairground, George and Helen climb the bleachers and sit beside each other. Just a few hours earlier, the town and the fair ground had been filled with life; people had poured into Winesburg from outlying farms, but now the fair is over and the people, like ghosts from the past, have departed. George's loneliness is "both broken and intensified" and "what he felt was reflected in her."

Remembering the ghosts of the past, revering the multitudes of the present, they experience a moment of depth. He takes her hand, and as she leans closer, he holds her shoulder. After shuddering at the meaninglessness of life earlier in the evening, George now shares understanding caresses with Helen, who has been frustrated by the patronizing college instructor. "In the mind of each was the same thought. 'I have come to this lonely place and here is this other.'"

For a moment they are embarrassed by what they have experienced, and they begin to tease and chase each other, laughing and shouting like children. This mood passes quickly, and though they cannot understand it or explain it, they have shared "the thing needed."

Sherwood Anderson

Characters

College instructor

This ambitious young man is Helen's pompous, vain instructor at college. Though Helen's mother believes the professor is a better match for her daughter than any of the men in the town, the professor makes George and Helen appear "sophisticated" in comparison.

Wesley Moyer

Wesley Moyer is a farmer and owner of a livery stable in Winesburg who brags about winning a horse race with his stallion, Tony Tip, at the Winesburg County Fair. When George overhears Wesley's boasting, he becomes inflamed with anger at the small-mindedness of the townspeople and decides to find Helen—the one person he feels he can identify with.

Helen White

Helen White is the daughter of the only banker in the town of Winesburg. She has a certain elegance that causes George to distinguish her from others. In fact, "When the moment of sophistication came to George Willard his mind turned to Helen White, the Winesburg banker's daughter." Helen is a college girl who is home for the county fair. Her mother has invited Helen's college instructor along with her for a visit, and she says to him, "There is no one here fit to associate with a girl of Helen's breeding." Helen is vain enough to want to be seen in public with the professor because he is a well-dressed stranger. However, in a short time she finds him to be empty and conceited. Thus, like George Willard, she too is caught between her past and her future; between people she perceives as country bumpkins and a professor whom she initially admired but has found to be flawed, between her girlish vanity and developing grace. In the midst of this conflict, she seeks out George, and together in the grandstand at the empty fairground, a moment of understanding—at once sad and fulfilling—passes between them.

George Willard

George Willard is an eighteen-year-old newspaper writer in the small town of Winesburg, Ohio, who seeks to rise above the constraints of his unsophisticated background. However, his distaste of small-town life does not prevent many people around town from seeking his company and advice, because they see in him hope and possibility. While examining his life after forming goals for his future, the dissonance between who he is and who he wants to become forms the basis for his moment of ''sophistication'' with Helen. This discomfort with his past leads George on the journey to adulthood as he reacts to his upbringing, finally rejecting most of it—except for what he has found with Helen, another soul also on the brink of maturity, who understands him.

George is angry because of the lack of culture among the adults in the community. He is saddened by the unfulfilled lives he has seen and heard of; he is frightened at the loneliness he feels: ''He knows that in spite of all the stout talk of his fellows he must live and die in uncertainty, a thing blown by the winds, a thing destined like corn to wilt in the sun.''

Themes

American Dream

George and Helen, both seeking to escape from the restrictions of small-town life, find in each other a moment of sophistication, or wisdom, as they sit in the empty grandstand together. Part of their wisdom is gained from their disillusionment with the American Dream. The idea that anyone can succeed through hard work and determination is a lie—as George realizes from listening to the townsfolk, and Helen learns from suffering the pomposity of the college professor. None of the many people who come and go around the fair ground is a success; they work hard and hope hard, but they are doomed to being lost in the crowd. The melancholy mood arising from this realization, and their separateness from society because of it, draws them together in a moment of mutual understanding. Their sophistication results from rejecting the deceit of the American Dream in favor of the realization that a true connection with another human being is a greater reward than the American Dream.

Art and Experience

George hopes to be a writer. On the day of the fair, he is planning to leave Winesburg and go away to a city where he hopes to work for a newspaper. This decision makes him feel grown up. He wants to put into words the depth and sadness of human beings, most of whom live lives ''of quiet desperation,'' as Henry David Thoreau had put it. And so George ''began to think of the people in the town where he had always lived with something like reverence.'' Indeed, George's plan to be a writer reflects Anderson's own struggle to become a writer. In ''Sophistication,'' Anderson transforms a simple moment of mutual recognition in the lives of two young people into a work of literature, thus bridging the chasm between art and experience.

Sex

George has changed from an adolescent boy with sexual impulses into a thoughtful young man. As he confronts Helen, ''He wanted to love and to be loved by her, but he did not want at the moment to be confused by her womanhood.'' As they embrace and kiss, their moment of sophistication deepens, and they become ''Not man and woman, not boy and girl, but excited little animals.'' This is followed by a moment of respect, when ''she took his arm and walked beside him in dignified silence.'' Though George and Helen have not been physically intimate, what passes between them is a moment of sexual awareness that transcends the body. Sexuality, far from being ignored, becomes only one component of their relationship, which has been cemented by a bond of unspoken understanding about their place in the world.

Growth and Development

At eighteen, George has reached a point in his life at which he feels ready to leave Winesburg, Ohio, to pursue ''the dreams of his manhood.'' In the stories that precede ''Sophistication,'' namely, ''Hands,'' ''The Thinker,'' and ''An Awakening,'' the process of George's maturation is outlined. George, through conversations with town drunks, barbers, religious fanatics, failed farmers, and older and wiser women, grows to this moment of sophistication, where he sees and reflects upon his place within the confines of small-town life. In ''Sophistication,'' both George and Helen see the difference between the townspeople and themselves, and their resulting loneliness causes them to seek each other out. They are not shallow; they know that they, too, will be bruised by life. George ''already . . . hears death calling''; which makes all the more precious his moment of wisdom with Helen. The moment when each of them seeks out another to help fill the emptiness inside of them is the moment in which their development into mature adults is complete.

Topics for Further Study

- Research psychologist Erik Erikson's theory of psychological development. To what extent does "Sophistication" explore the stages of development known as Identity versus Identity Confusion and Intimacy versus Isolation?

- Read Anderson's *Winesburg, Ohio* , which ends with George's departure from town several months after his moment with Helen White. Does "Sophistication" need to be read as part of the novel, or does it have its own meaning without the novel? Also, does the novel need this story to make sense? What is missing from the novel without "Sophistication?"

- As he sits beside Helen in the empty grandstand, George thinks that he "wanted to love and be loved by her, but he did not want at the moment to be confused by her womanhood." Examine two current books on adolescent sexual relationships and compare contemporary depictions of such relationships to the relationship between George and Helen. Have things changed in the years since Anderson wrote "Sophistication"?

- Modern feminists have sought to reinterpret traditional texts such as "Sophistication." How does Helen represent feminism? In what ways does she not represent feminism? Analyze some of the other female characters in *Winesburg, Ohio,* in a feminist light.

Style

Point of View

"Sophistication" is told in the third person omniscient, meaning that readers have access to the thoughts of both George and Helen. The narrator, who is not to be confused with the author, succeeds in moving readers into George's mind for the purpose of identification with a young man on the brink of maturity. In the same way, the narrator explains how Helen feels: "What George felt, she in her young woman's way felt also. She was no longer a girl and hungered to reach into the grace and beauty of womanhood." At the same time, the narrator remains somewhat distant. The distance created by a third-person point of view helps instill a tone of wistfulness to the moment of discovery between the young couple.

Setting

The setting for "Sophistication" is the small midwestern town of Winesburg, Ohio. More specifically, the social hubbub created by the county fair creates a contrast for the tale of loneliness and connection between two people. The action and words of the townspeople, which George takes to be coarse, create the scene from which his understanding of self arises. Both George and Helen share a magical moment in the bleachers of the empty fair ground, the silence even more striking after a day of carefree fun by others, but fun that neither of them felt or enjoyed themselves.

Descriptive Language

The language of "Sophistication" is simple, and the narrator carefully paints a colorful portrait of a town during its county fair, using many adjectives and metaphors: "People surged up and down like cattle confined in a pen." "Young men with shining red faces walked awkwardly about with girls on their arms." There are "murmurs of voices and the loud blare of horns." Other metaphors include the description of "little flames of the fire [that] danced crazily about," and "the wind [that] whispered among the dry corn blades." Through the description of so much action, all happily attributed to the social event of the fair, George's bad mood and Helen's longing appears all the more out of sync with the setting. Through these descriptive contrasts Anderson gives more power to the very understated plot of his story.

Historical Context

History Frozen in Time

Anderson's "Sophistication" reflects almost none of the modern culture into which the United States was moving during the time of the story—the 1890s. During this time, the nation's cities were rapidly industrializing—railroads and steel mills dominated the landscape of the Eastern United States. In a few years, automobiles would begin to irrevocably fracture community life by allowing people to live and work in vastly wider areas. But in Winesburg, Ohio, modeled on the town of Clyde, Ohio, where Anderson lived as a child, life had not yet succumbed wholly to the modern age. Nevertheless, young people of the day, like George and Helen, felt the pull of the cities and longed to break free of the "old-fashioned" world of their parents, in which county fairs and horse races figured prominently. George longs for city life, where he can immerse himself in the frenetic pace of a daily newspaper, making an impact in a realm larger than his own small town. Likewise, Helen is attending college in the city of Cleveland—still an unusual move for a young woman of the time. Though she invites a professor home with her, his trite attempts at urbanity bore her. She urges George to follow his dream to the city, in a scene that was undoubtedly played out by millions of young people at the turn of the century as the United States became increasingly urbanized. As an exercise in bittersweet nostalgia, Anderson ignores the era in which he was writing. In 1919, the world had just waged the deadliest war in history, and technologies like airplanes, automobiles, telephones, and modern weaponry were transforming the world, both for better and for worse. During this time of chaos and immense growth, Anderson recalls an earlier time, evoking vivid memories of small-town life—both the joyousness of a county fair and the restlessness of the young generation who felt the urge to participate in the urban turmoil of modern life, forsaking the things they grew up with as being old-fashioned and "unsophisticated."

Critical Overview

Published as one of the final chapters of *Winesburg, Ohio*, "Sophistication" received positive criticism when it first appeared in 1919. In the *New Republic*, Maxwell Anderson remarked, "As a challenge to the snappy short story form, with its planned proportions of flippant philosophy, epigrammatic conversation and sex danger, nothing better has come out of America than *Winesburg, Ohio*. . . . It was set down by a patient and loving craftsman; it is in a new mood, and one not easily forgotten." The acerbic critic H. L. Mencken, whom Anderson himself criticized for making fun of small-town folks, nevertheless declared that "What remains is pure representation—and it is representation so vivid, so full of insight, so shiningly life-like and glowing, that the book is lifted into a category all its own. Nothing quite like it has ever been done in America. It is a book that, at one stroke, turns depression into enthusiasm." The author Rebecca West in 1922 called it "an extraordinarily good book."

As the twentieth century advanced, Anderson lost his initial critical acclaim; he was satirized as "Sherwood Lawrence" (a reference to D. H. Lawrence) because a dark sexuality seemed to be the primary motivation of many of his characters. When Anderson died in 1941, Waldo Frank paid critical homage to the novel twenty years after it first appeared, calling *Winesburg, Ohio* "a classic." Ten years later, Irving Howe contended, "The ultimate unity of the book is a unity of feeling, a sureness of warmth, and a readiness to accept Winesburg's lost grotesques with the embrace of humility. Many American writers have taken as their theme the loss of love in the modern world, but few, if any at all, have so thoroughly realized it in the accents of love." In 1962 Walter Rideout, Anderson's biographer, agreed that *Winesburg, Ohio* is "a kind of American classic." Among other Anderson critics, Malcolm Cowley has stated about that "There are moments in American life to which [Anderson] gave not only the first but the final expression."

Criticism

John S. Reist Jr.

Reist is a Christian clergyman and Professor of Christianity and Literature at Hillsdale College in Michigan. His 1993 essay on the unity of Winesburg, Ohio *was included in a recent critical edition of that work. In the following essay, he attempts "to show how Anderson's descriptive power, haunting language, simple dialogue, and carefully arranged series of events all come together to form an artis-*

Compare & Contrast

- **1890s:** In "Sophistication," the town's residents "work terribly at the task of amusing itself." Entertainment of the day takes a variety of forms. Drinking occupies many men, but it is unacceptable for a woman to appear drunk. Socializing is a favorite activity of women, and they frequently gather for meals, or in parlors to talk, sing, play games, or have afternoon tea. Dances are popular, and more physical activities such as roller-skating and bicycling are gaining in popularity.

  1919: Movies are a primary source of entertainment, though they remain silent until 1927. At 10 cents a ticket, however, it is an affordable way for many people to spend a weekend afternoon. By 1916, comedic actor Charlie Chaplin was well-known around the world. In 1918, Chaplin and another popular movie star, Mary Pickford, each signed contracts with film studios for more than $1 million. Other forms of entertainment include burlesque and vaudeville shows.

  1990s: New technologies, including television, VCRs, cable television, and computers expand possibilities for in-home entertainment. Popular social activities include movies, sporting events, and theater. Admission to movies may cost $7.00 or more.

- **1900s:** The Winesburg County Fair is responsible for bringing crowds of "country people" into town. County fairs have been in existence in Ohio since the mid 1800s and are promoted by the Ohio Agriculture Department, organized in 1846. The fair brings people together to celebrate the state's farming industry. Livestock and other farm products are judged and awarded prizes.

  1990s: Farmers comprise about 2 percent of Ohio's population in 1996, but agriculture remains the state's largest single industry, and county fairs are still popular. Modern county fairs are promoted on the World Wide Web and livestock are tested for illegal drugs that may be used to enhance the appearance of champion animals. Of Ohio's 88 counties, 87 have county fairs. While fairs are still designed to showcase local agriculture, additional attractions often include carnival rides, political booths, and variety of merchants and entertainment.

---

tic and moral whole" in Winesburg, Ohio, *with "Sophistication" being "a fundamental part of the novel."*

Ever since "Sophistication" appeared in 1919 as part of the ending of *Winesburg, Ohio*, critics have been unable to account for the continuing hold it has on the literary world. Even though we live in a highly technological, industrialized world, the cluster of stories which make up the novel still provides a telling account of human life trapped in community—the same community in which each townsperson, druggist, grocer, parson, and farmer searches for lasting communion. The purpose of this essay is to show how Anderson's descriptive power, haunting language, simple dialogue, and carefully arranged series of events all come together to form an artistic and moral whole. "Sophistication" is a fundamental part of the novel, and in this essay it will be treated as such, instead of as a short story on its own.

Irving Howe has commented that "*Winesburg* is an excellently formed piece of fiction, each of its stories following a parabola of movement which abstractly graphs the book's meaning." However, he concludes that "The ultimate unity of the book is a unity of feeling, a sureness of warmth, and a readiness to accept Winesburg's lost grotesques with the embrace of humility. Many American writers have taken as their theme the loss of love in the modern world, but few, if any at all, have so thoroughly realized it in the accents of love." The accents of love ebb and flow in the novel as each of the characters in each of the stories reaches out for

What Do I Read Next?

- *A Story-Teller's Story* (1924) by Sherwood Anderson is a semi-autobiographical work in which the author outlines his journey as a writer and artist in the early twentieth century.

- James Joyce's *A Portrait Of The Artist as A Young Man* (1916) portrays the development of Stephen Dedalus, an Irish man, from childhood to his leaving a Roman Catholic seminary. Stephen is a writer, as George is, and this novel depicts Stephen's departure for the larger world.

- Ernest Hemingway's *The Torrents of Spring* (1926) is a satirical novel which ridicules Anderson's simple, small-town prose, as well as his focus on common folk.

- William Graham Sumner's *Folkways* (1907) is a sociological study which argues that all ethics and customs begin with intuition and instinctive responses to hunger, sex, vanity, and fear.

- Edgar Lee Master's *Spoon River Anthology* (1915) is a series of stories told from beyond the grave by small-town midwesterners. The stories reveal candid, bitter, and cynical portraits of small town and rural life. Anderson was influenced by Masters.

- Robert S. and Helen M. Lynd's *Middletown* (1929) is a sociological study of small-town life, tracing the development of a midwestern town of grocers and farmers from 1890 through its growth to a center of industry by 1924.

---

acceptance and fulfillment. However, these absorbing, moving, sometimes terrifying searches for acceptance come to a climax in "Sophistication" as the ebb and flow of emotion is realized in a dramatic merger of the feeling of "mutual respect" that envelopes George and Helen. This wisdom, this insight, as momentary as it is, nonetheless prepares George to leave Winesburg to search for his own identity, freed from the trap of the small town, but also educated by the relationships he has experienced with various lost and searching souls.

Waldo Frank, who first published some of the episodes of the novel in the journal *Seven Arts,* of which he was managing editor, has argued that the power of the novel is lyrical: "For an analogy to the aesthetic of the Winesburg tales, one must go to music, perhaps to the songs that Schubert wove from old refrains; or to the lyric art of the Old Testament psalmists and prophets to whom the literary medium was so allied to music that their texts have always been sung in the synagogues. The Winesburg design is quite uniform: a theme-statement of a character with his mood, followed by a recounting of actions that are merely variations on

the theme." He goes on to say "These variations make incarnate what has already been revealed to the reader; they weave the theme into life by the always subordinate confrontation of other characters (usually one) and by an evocation of landscape and village." But the confrontation of characters is not subordinate to the theme; it *is* the theme, for the novel weaves its magic into a web of social encounters that constitute finally a total moral, social and artistic unity that is unforgettable.

For example, Helen White is not the only woman with whom and by whom George is shaped. Similarly, Kate Swift, George's school teacher, realizes his literary potential: "Kate's mind was ablaze with thoughts of George Willard. In something he had written as a schoolboy she thought she had recognized the spark of genius and wanted to blow on the spark." She has been unable to express her inner passionate nature, and like Dr. Parcival, she hopes that George might become her surrogate. And after his rendezvous with Louise Trunnion, George sneaks back to town muttering, "nobody knows." Continuing to seek his identity through sexual encounters, George ultimately fails with

Kate Swift because he is younger than she, and because he has not gained enough discipline with the words that he speaks.

It is not only sexual encounters with women (for which Anderson was criticized as immoral and lascivious) that shape George. The novel is also about writing—its importance and effects. George is a younger newspaper reporter, and the villagers seek out George for his power with words, for they—many of them quite older than he—have never been able to say what they mean. For example, Dr. Parcival, who is a failed medical doctor, is writing a novel which almost certainly will never be published. So he declares to George: ''You must pay attention to me. . . . If something happens perhaps you will be able to write the book that I may never get written. The idea is very simple, so simple that if you are not careful you will forget it. It is this—that everyone in the world is Christ and they are all crucified.'' The doctor is rather excessive in his reference to Christ; but if that crucifixion was for all humankind, it is not difficult to see that all pain, all suffering, all hope and hopelessness are gathered up into one aching whole, the town of Winesburg, which is a local manifestation of the entire human race.

Anderson in the section called ''Godliness'' provides the religious context for the townspeople. Jesse Bentley is an old man who thinks he is a failed prophet of Yahweh. ''There were two influences at work in Jesse Bentley and all his life his mind had been a battleground for these influences. First there was the old thing in him. He wanted to be a man of God and a leader among men of God. His walking in the fields and through forests at night had brought him close to nature and there were forces in the passionately religious man that ran out to the forces in nature.'' It is in his cultural insecurity that Bentley's religion also fails, for modern life has produced an almost entirely new world in which ''Jesse formed the habit of reading newspapers and magazines. He invented a machine for the making of fence out of wire. Faintly he realized that the atmosphere of old times and places that he had always cultivated in his own mind was strange and foreign to the thing that was growing up in the minds of others. The beginning of the most materialistic age in the history of the world, when wars would be fought without patriotism, when men would forget God and only pay attention to moral standards, when the will to power would replace the will to serve and beauty would be well-nigh forgotten in the terrible headlong rush of mankind toward

> ''The accents of love ebb and flow in the novel as each of the characters in each of the stories reaches out for acceptance and fulfillment.''

the acquiring of possessions, was telling its story to Jesse, the man of God as it was to the men about him.'' So, the older gods of the harvest, the supernatural God of the heavens, has begun to die, or at least to disappear, and thus Jesse is losing his grip: ''when night came on and the stars came out it was harder to get back the old feeling of a close and personal God who lived in the sky overhead and who might at any moment reach out his hand, touch him on the shoulder, and appoint for him some heroic task to be done.'' His failure as a lost leftover from the 1890s (the time of the novel) obstructs achievement of the religious sophistication or wisdom which the ancestors of Winesburg achieved. This makes all the more profound George's and Helen's moment of sophistication at the end of the novel. Emptied of supernatural power, loosened from Bentley's God, George and Helen show that modern community, though momentary, is still deep and moving.

Anderson combines the themes of sexuality and verbal power in George's humiliation with Belle Carpenter, in the story ''An Awakening'' : for ''an hour Belle Carpenter and the young reporter walked about under the trees in the sweet night air. George Willard was full of big words. The sense of power that had come to him during the hour of darkness in the alleyway remained with him and he talked boldly, swaggering and swinging his arms about.'' His silly preening, ranting and whispering to Belle lead to his embarrassment, for Ed Hanby, Belle's real lover, arrives and makes a fool of George. ''Three times the young reporter sprang at Ed Hanby and each time the bartender, catching him by the shoulder, hurled him back into the bushes. The older man seemed prepared to keep the exercise going indefinitely but George Willard's head struck the root of a tree and he lay still.''

What an immense difference between these encounters and the final sophistication, or achievement of communion, between George and Helen at the end! George seeks another of like mind; Anderson puts it this way: "With all his heart he wants to come close to some other human, touch someone with his hands, be touched by the hand of another. If he prefers that the other be a woman, that is because he believes that a woman will be gentle, that she will understand. He wants, most of all, understanding." This moment of sophistication is sad and bitter-sweet, but not cynical and bitter and dark, as some critics have said. For example, Lionel Trilling re-marks: "his people have passion without body, and sexuality without gaiety and joy, although it is often through sex that they are supposed to find their salvation." He further contends, "Anderson liked to catch people with their single human secret, their essence, but the more he looks for their essence the more his characters vanish into the vast limbo of meaningless life, the less they are human beings. . . . Certainly the precious essence of personality to which Anderson was so much committed could not be preserved by any of the people or any of the deeds his own books delight in." Although these judgements come from one of the finest literary and cultural critics the United States has produced, they are wrong, especially as they might apply to "So-phistication" and all of *Winesburg, Ohio.*

Better to listen to another great American nov-elist, William Faulkner, who contended that Ander-son "was sometimes a sentimentalist in his writing (so was Shakespeare sometimes) but he was never impure in it. He never scanted it, cheapened it, took the easy way; never failed to approach writing except with humility and an almost religious, al-most abject faith and patience and willingness to surrender, relinquish himself to it and into it." Such was the writer Sherwood Anderson, about whom Faulkner also wrote these lines after having seen him at a cocktail party for the first time in a long while, because Anderson had been affronted by an unpublished satire on him which Faulkner had done: "Then I remembered *Winesburg, Ohio* and *The Triumph of The Egg* and some of the pieces in *Horses and Men* and I knew that I had seen, was looking at, a giant in an earth populated to a great—too great—extent by pygmies, even if he did make but the two or perhaps three gestures commensurate with gianthood."

"Sophistication" is one of the gestures, part of the greater gesture, *Winesburg, Ohio* which endures because it grips us as an artistic unity comprised of many shorter narratives. In "Sophistication" George and Helen attain "the thing needed"; and in "De-

parture," George prepares to leave the town on the morning train. "With the recollection of little things occupying his mind he closed his eyes and leaned back in the car seat. He stayed that way for a long time and when he aroused himself and again looked out of the car window the town of Winesburg had disappeared and his life there had become but a background on which to paint the dreams of his manhood."

Source: John S. Reist Jr., "Overview of 'Sophistication'," in *Short Stories for Students,* Gale, 1998.

J. A. Ward

In the following excerpt, Ward offers his inter-pretation of the role played by spoken language and silence in "Sophistication," especially in regard to how they relate to theme and characterization.

Anderson shows the impossibility of the honest communication of feeling by surrounding his gro-tesques [in *Winesburg, Ohio*] with a chorus of towns-people whose constant example reveals the meager possibilities of actual speech. The speech of the chorus is nothing but cliches and slogans, the language of the near-official American dogma of success and masculine bullying as it has filtered down to the small provincial town. Implicit in a number of the stories is the belief that most speech is mimicry, that most of the words that people say are imitations of what they have heard others say. Thus George reiterates the military officer's command and Elmer the idiot's foolish saying. The overheard loud chatter of the town is mostly boasting, the telling of lies that are regarded to be assertions of deeds that deserve society's approval. Anderson relates little of such discourse, but he refers to it as gossip, boasting, and joking—modes of speech essentially self-serving, as well as impersonal and unoriginal. Winesburg culture offers no acceptable mode of private communication. Dr. Reefy writes notes to himself, which he crumples in his pock-ets; other characters wave their arms, pace the streets, and get drunk—all improvised, inadequate substitutes for a speech that always fails them.

In several of the stories sexual contact is repre-sented as an easier form of communication between man and woman than conversation, and probably for that reason not as satisfying as the dreamed of conversation would be. In the fragile and rare mo-ments in which love is experienced in *Winesburg, Ohio* its expression is in silence. The main example is "Sophistication," the climactic story that con-cerns George Willard's final experience before his departure from Winesburg. In other ways as well, the story is the coda of the principal themes of the book and its most coherent resolution of the difficult problem of communicating for characters most comfortable with silence.

"Sophistication" is George Willard's story, and it shows his state of mind and feelings after his encounters with numerous lonely people and before his departure from Winesburg. The recent death of his mother has brought home to George a strong sense of his own mortality. "The sadness of sophistication has come to the boy. With a little gasp he sees himself as merely a leaf blown through the streets of his village. He knows that in spite of all the stout talk of his fellows he must live and die in uncertainty, a thing blown by the winds". He recalls with shame his own "stout talk" in his previous walk with Helen White, whom he desires to be with this night. On the previous summer evening he could speak to Helen only by boasting of his confident ambitions: "I'm going to be a big man, the biggest that ever lived here in Winesburg". The distasteful recollection makes addedly repugnant the overheard boasting of a man whose horse had just won the race at the country fair, to which George had responded: "Old windbag. . . . Why does he want to be bragging? Why don't he shut up?"

The important setting of "Sophistication" is the Winesburg County Fair, the day-long celebration in which "an American town worked terribly at the task of amusing itself". At first the "sense of crowding, moving that closed in about him" is oppressive to George, an intensification of the usual threat of the townspeople to his private self. But as in most of the stories the life of the town—even on its annual day of festivity—barely touches George, and in this story more than any we see Anderson's representation of community as a hollow fiction.

Helen's mother had invited an instructor from her daughter's college to stay with the family during the fair, and through the instructor and Helen's mother Anderson gratuitously introduces another instance of fraudulent speech—the language of class and intellectual pretension. When the instructor tells Helen, "Your life is still bound up with the life of this town" Helen thinks "his voice sounded pompous and heavy". She flees to the garden thinking "that the world was full of meaningless people saying words". In the garden she encounters George, who has impetuously decided to enter Helen's house to speak with her. Thus the meeting

> "Anderson does not further elaborate 'the thing they needed'; to do so would cheapen the various desperate efforts of the other characters to define the object of their desires."

is prepared by the separate repudiations of "bragging" and "words" by the young man and woman. When George finds Helen he wonders "what he had better do and say". In fact he says nothing, nor does Helen, as they walk to the grandstand in the fairground, where they sit for awhile, and then walk down the hill. For more than three pages the couple is together and Anderson includes not a word of dialogue. Earlier in the evening George had felt the need for Helen's understanding, and at the very end of the story, "for some reason they could not have explained they had both got from their silent evening together the thing they needed. Man or boy, woman or girl, they had for a moment taken hold of the thing that makes the mature life of men and women in the modern world possible".

Nearly as reticent as his characters, Anderson does not further elaborate "the thing they needed"; to do so would cheapen the various desperate efforts of the other characters to define the object of their desires. But in the course of the interlude shared by George and Helen, some striking feelings that affect George give substance and definition to that which makes maturity in the modern world possible. First, George experiences the strange silence of the fairground a few hours after it had been crowded with people: "The place has been filled to overflowing with life. It has itched and squirmed with life and now it is night and the life has all gone away. The silence is almost terrifying". This is a new and different silence for the Anderson character—the silence not of inarticulateness but of loss, negation, the absence of life. It is a silence external to oneself and therefore a mode of experiencing the relation of the world of nonself to the self, which is also silent. Explicitly George interprets the sensation as a reinforcement of his sense of "his own insignificance in the scheme of existence'', but the insignificance is a paradoxical kind of significance. Retaining the mood induced by the deserted fairground, he tightly holds Helen. The two share the same feeling and thus further enlarge their sense of identity as they experience its frailty: "In the mind of each was the same thought. 'I have come to this lonely place and here is this other,' was the substance of the thing felt''.

Helen and George remain silent. "They kissed but that impulse did not last.'' Slightly embarrassed, they "dropped into the animalism of youth. They laughed and began to pull and haul at each other. . . . they became, not man and woman, not boy and girl, but excited little animals''. They laugh again; George rolls down the hill; Helen runs after him. Then, with Helen holding George's arm, they walk away "in dignified silence''. Except for the momentary embarrassment after each rejects the tentative impulse to kiss, the entire episode is remarkably easy and spontaneous—certainly the only occasion in the book of such intensely felt companionship. The close emotional attention to external silence takes George and presumably Helen beyond the confines of self, and presents George for the first time with a consciousness of his neighbors as "his people,'' most vividly felt in their absence. The refusal of sex underscores the inadequacy of sexual relationships apparent in the several stories that deal with the subject. The recovery of the ability to play like children, even animals, is a physical expression of life and joy that is not sexual but is more satisfying than sexuality, perhaps because it is free of tension, aggression, and the awkward assumption of adult powers. Although George realizes that "there is no way of knowing what woman's thought went through her mind,'' he feels little need to know and is not once disturbed by his own silence during the entire episode.

The experiencing of love and friendship through silence is very much in accordance with Emerson's and Thoreau's prescriptions for "love'' and "friendship.'' But ideal silence in Anderson is no transcendence of materiality and mortality, rather an untroubled acquiescence in one's normal mode of being. Otherwise in *Winesburg, Ohio* silence is almost always a handicap, a terrible disability resulting from what the inarticulate characters mistakenly regard as a crippling affliction that prevents intercourse with others. In "Sophistication'' it is the opposite. Silence itself becomes the only and the essential mode in which love and understanding can be achieved.

Source: J. A. Ward, in *American Silences: The Realism of James Agee, Walker Evans, and Edward Hopper,* Louisiana State University Press, 1985, pp. 46–50.

Sister M. Joselyn

In the following excerpt, the critic offers her interpretation of Anderson's use of lyric and epic elements in "Sophistication."

At this date, not much remains to be done by way of appointing Sherwood Anderson a place among American writers; in fact he himself succinctly indicated his own position when he remarked in the *Memoirs* that "For all my egotism, I know I am but a minor figure.'' There is little disagreement, either, about the work on which Anderson's reputation rests—*Winesburg,* "Death in the Woods,'' a few stories from *The Triumph of the Egg.* When we come to estimate the accomplishment represented by *Winesburg,* however, things are not quite so clear. There are those who wish, still, to view the collection as a frame-story, but they then must reckon with the difficulty of seeming to reduce all the stories to the dead level of equivalent exhibits. Those on the other hand who want to read *Winesburg* as an initiation novel about George Willard have to face the problem of resting their case upon a character who in the end remains the thinnest figment. To choose to relegate Anderson and *Winesburg* to the limbo of regionalism is no longer acceptable.

Perhaps the sanest way is to view *Winesburg,* an uneven collection, as a special kind of amalgam of naturalism and lyricism. Every reader, whether approvingly or not, acknowledges the lyric intensity of the best Anderson stories. To Herbert Gold, Anderson is "one of the purest, most intense poets of loneliness,'' while Irving Howe (who has also called Anderson a "pre-poet'') holds that no other American writer "has yet been able to realize that strain of lyrical and nostalgic feeling which in Anderson's best work reminds one of another and greater poet of tenderness, Turgenev.'' Robert Gorham Davis ascribes the "great impression'' made by *Winesburg* to its "freshness and lyric intensity.'' It is Paul Rosenfeld, however, who has seen most clearly that Anderson's lyricism is a method as much as an effect, for to this reader, Anderson's narratives "really are lyrics with epic characteristics, lyrics narrative of event.''

In analyzing the elements that go into Anderson's lyricism, Rosenfeld notes the "legendary tone, the repetitions of slow rhythms and the loose joints'' of the American tale, as well as the personal feeling that rises from the region between Anderson's "conscious and unconscious minds." But Rosenfeld places greatest stress on the purely verbal aspects of Anderson's poetic quality, for

> Anderson's inclusion among the authors of the lyric story . . . flows first of all from the fact that, using the language of actuality, he nonetheless invariably wrings sonority and cadence from it; unobtrusively indeed, without transcending the easy pitch of familiar prose. . . . He sustains tones broadly with assonances and with repeated or echoing words and phrases. He creates accent-patterns and even stanza-like paragraphs with the periodic repetition or alternation of features such as syllables, sounds, words, phrases, entire periods. . . . (Introduction to *The Sherwood Anderson Reader,* pp. xiv–xv.)

Many readers of Anderson will see these assertions as a part of Rosenfeld's special pleading and will doubtless be more inclined to share Irving Howe's belief that amidst the " chaos of his creative life Anderson had to cast around for a device with which to establish some minimum of order in his work" and found it "in the undulations of his verbal rhythms. . . ." Indeed, it is precisely in those pieces where he was "most at sea imaginatively" that "the rhythm is most insistently established."

Rosenfeld, I think it can be shown, is on much stronger ground when contending that Anderson's stories are—in other ways—"lyrics with epic characteristics," and in holding that

> As for his own specimens of the lyric story-kind, they have 'inner form' like Gertrude Stein's, but their rhythms are livelier, longer, more self-completive than those of the somnolent lady-Buddha of the *rue de Fleurus.* While wanting the suavity of expression in Turgenev's lyric tales, Anderson's share the warmly singing tone of the Russian's, surpass them of course in point of tension, and have the Andersonian qualities of subtlety of attack and humorous and acute feeling, perceptions of the essential in the singular, glamour over the commonplace, boldness of image. . . . Wonderfully they 'stay by us.' (*Sherwood Anderson Reader,* p. xix.)

What, precisely, is the "inner form" of Anderson's stories and how can they be said to be "lyrics with epic characteristics"?

In the first place it must be noted that the best Anderson stories always contain and lead up to a *revelation,* epiphany, or state of realized experience. Robert Morss Lovett has said that Anderson's stories "reach outward into the unknown," while Granville Hicks asserts that "Surfaces, deeds, even words scarcely concern him; everything is bent to the task of revelation." To Herbert Gold, "The experience of epiphany is characteristic of great

> "Anderson demonstrates a high degree of cunning in not attempting any sort of philosophic resolution of George's dilemmas but by providing instead a rather quiet culminating scene in which all the contradictory aspects of George's and Helen's consciousness are caught up in a symbolic action."

literature, and the lyric tales of Anderson give this wonderful rapt coming-forth, time and time again." Irving Howe—uncomplimentarily—notes that Anderson "wrote best when he had no need to develop situations or show change and interaction—," but Anderson's own ideal of art is expressed precisely in his idealization of "the tale of perfect balance," with all its "elements . . . understood, an infinite number of minute adjustments perfectly made. . . ."

Summaries of Anderson stories reveal even less than is usually the case about the significance of the narratives; obviously in Anderson what is at stake is not histories, biographies, gossip, or even tales. From Anderson's best work one does derive an unmistakable sense of authentic experience being worked out from within, in the manner of the great Russians—Turgenev and Chekhov—with their unparalleled suggestiveness and extreme economy of means. Like the Russians, Anderson does not "import his poetry into the work—he allows only the poetry that is *there*" (Herbert Gold). The significance of an Anderson story has very little to do with the "facts" that are related but it has something to do with the arrangement of those facts and with the relationship of these "epic" elements to other, more properly poetic strains.

Anderson's abandonment of pure naturalism involved him in a movement away from structures dependent upon sequential action or gradually increased intensity and toward an arrangement of events which would better dramatize the centrifugal, diffused, resonant effect his materials called for. The halting, tentative, digressive style, and the circular, hovering or "Chinese box" approach to "what happened" thus do not so much demonstrate Anderson's affectation of the manner of oral tale-telling as they illustrate his understanding that the "epic" base of the story must be manipulated in such a way that weight is thrown upon the significance of the happenings as it reveals itself to the central consciousness and to the reader, rather than upon the events themselves. This is, of course, essentially a "poetic" strategy.

Moreover, as Jon Lawry has demonstrated in his reading of "Death in the Woods," the narrative strategy, by which the story is not really "told" to any assumed audience, makes it possible that "its process of growth and contact is discovered by the audience, through the act itself rather than through the narrator's relation of the act," for "The audience is invited to enter as individuals into a process almost identical with that of the narrator and to reach with him for contact with another life." This narrative method makes it possible for the "unacknowledged audience" to "share directly not only the narrator's responses but his act of discovering and creating those responses"—and this is precisely the "method" of the post-symbolist lyric. It is also the technique by which in Anderson fantasy is most controlled, or, "if not exactly controlled, simplified, given a single lyrical line," and ambivalent—if not contradictory—emotions enfolded within one action. . . .

In "Sophistication," the "epic" elements are arranged in such a way that George Willard's restlessness and puzzlement are dramatized—rather than merely reported—through the structure itself with its jerky, spasmodic focusing and refocusing. Anderson, moreover, demonstrates a high degree of cunning in not attempting any sort of philosophic resolution of George's dilemmas but by providing instead a rather quiet culminating scene in which all the contradictory aspects of George's and Helen's consciousness are caught up in a symbolic action (is it ludicrous to see a resemblance to Yeats' use of the great-rooted blossomer?):

> It was so they went down the hill. . . . Once, running swiftly forward, Helen tripped George and he fell. He squirmed and shouted. Shaking with laughter, he rolled down the hill. Helen ran after him. For just a moment she stopped in the darkness. . . . When the bottom of the hill was reached and she came up to the boy, she took his arm and walked beside him in dignified silence.

Other symbol-like devices appearing in the story are the cornfields, the dry leaves and trees, the stallion, and the grandstand. Anderson's conducting of the narrative is too loose and diffuse for these objects to form a genuine symbolic pattern, but their presence does add power to the lyric suggestiveness of the narrative. . . .

It is in the *Winesburg* stories such as "The Thinker," "Adventure," "Hands," "Sophistication," and "The Untold Lie" that Anderson manages to reinforce a certain surface fidelity with what Ernest Boyd has called the "deeper realism which sees beyond and beneath the exterior world to the hidden reality which is the essence of things." By combining in a special manner the story's "epic" elements with characteristic lyric devices, Anderson is able, at least on occasion, to reach the "something totally private, untouchable, beyond appearance and action, in all of us" and thus exemplifies his own belief that "To live is to create new forms: with the body in living children; in new and more beautiful forms carved out of materials; in the creation of a world of the fancy ; in scholarship; in clear and lucid thought. . . ."

Source: Sister M. Joselyn, "Sherwood Anderson and the Lyric Story," in *The Twenties: Poetry and Prose, 20 Critical Essays,* edited by Richard E. Langford and William E. Taylor, Everett Edwards, Inc., 1966, pp. 70–3.

Walter B. Rideout

Rideout has written a biography of Sherwood Anderson, scheduled for publication in 1998. In the following excerpt, he offers his interpretation of "Sophistication" as the climax of George's coming of age.

Where "An Awakening" records a defeat, "Sophistication" records in all ways a triumph. Though Anderson presents the moment in essay rather than dramatic form, there comes to George, as to "every boy," a flash of insight when "he stops under a tree and waits as for a voice calling his name." But this time "the voices outside himself" do not speak of the possibilities of universal order, nor do they speak of guilt. Instead they "whisper a message concerning the limitations of life," the brief light of human existence between two darks. The insight emphasizes the unity of all human beings in their necessary submission to death and their need for communication one with another. It is an insight that produces self-awareness but not self-centeredness, that produces, in short, the mature, "sophisticated" person.

The mind of such a person does not "run off into words." Hence Helen White, who has had an intuition similar to George's, runs away from the empty talk of her college instructor and her mother, and finds George, whose first and last words to her in the story, pronounced as they first meet, are "Come on." Together in the dimly-lit fair grounds on the hill over-looking the town of Winesburg, George and Helen share a brief hour of absolute awareness. Whereas his relationship with Belle Carpenter [in "An Awakening"] had produced in George self-centeredness, misunderstanding, hate, frustration, humiliation, that with Helen produces quite the opposite feelings. The feeling of oneness spreads outward, furthermore. Through his communication with Helen he begins "to think of the people in the town where he had lived with something like reverence." When he has come to this point, when he loves and respects the inhabitants of Winesburg, the "daylight" people as well as the "night" ones, the way of the artist lies clear before him. George Willard is ready for his "Departure."

Like Hart Crane, other readers will find the simplicity of *Winesburg, Ohio* "baffling"; but it is very probably this paradoxical quality which has attracted and will continue to attract admirers to a book that Anderson himself, with a mixture of amusement, deprecation, defensiveness, and satisfaction, quite accurately termed "a kind of American classic."

Source: Walter B. Rideout, "The Simplicity of *Winesburg, Ohio*," in *Shenandoah*, Vol. 13, no. 3, Spring, 1962, pp. 20–31.

Charles Child Walcutt

In the following excerpt, Walcutt offers his interpretation of the precise moment when George and Helen feel that they have reached mutual understanding and have undergone individual growth.

The climax (perhaps it should be called the high point in George's life until then) of [*Winesburg, Ohio*] occurs when George and Helen White reach a complete understanding one autumn evening, sitting up in the old grandstand on the fair grounds, rapt and wordless. "With all his strength he tried to hold and to understand the mood that had come upon him. In that high place in the darkness the two oddly sensitive human atoms held each other tightly and waited. In the mind of each was the same thought. 'I have come to this lonely place and here is this other,' was the substance of the thing felt." It is most significant that this experience is almost entirely wordless. The shared feeling, indeed, is of

seeking and wondering. It is inarticulate because it occurs in a world without meaning. Such incidents suggest that men's instincts are good but that conventional morality has warped and stifled them. Interpreted in terms of the divided stream of transcendentalism, they show that the spirit is misdirected because its physical house is mistreated. When Whitman wrote

> Logic and sermons never convince, The damp of the night drives deeper into my soul Only what proves itself to every man and woman is so.

he was making the same plea for the liberation of body and spirit together that we infer from *Winesburg, Ohio.* I say infer, because Anderson does not precisely say this; one might infer that he regards these repressions as inseparable from life—that he takes the tragic view of man—but I do not think entirely so. The pains of growth are probably inevitable, but the whole world is not as confining as Winesburg, and Anderson seems to say that people *should* be able to grow up less painfully to more abundant lives. His protagonist does, and gets away from Winesburg, though he endures torments and misunderstanding and unsatisfied love which cannot be laid to Winesburg so much as to the condition of youth in this world.

Source: Charles Child Walcutt, "Sherwood Anderson: Impressionism and the Buried Life," in *The Sewanee Review*, Vol. 60, no. 1, January-March, 1952, pp. 28–47.

Irving Howe

In the following excerpt, Howe offers his view on George Willard's relation to the other characters in Winesburg, Ohio, *as well as on the place of "Sophistication" in that story cycle.*

The burden which the grotesques would impose on George Willard is beyond his strength. He is not yet himself a grotesque mainly because he has not yet experienced very deeply, but for the role to which they would assign him he is too absorbed in his own ambition and restlessness. The grotesques see in his difference from them the possibility of saving themselves, but actually it is the barrier to an ultimate companionship. George Willard's adolescent receptivity to the grotesques can only give him the momentary emotional illumination described in that lovely story, "Sophistication." On the eve of his departure from Winesburg, George Willard reaches the point "when he for the first time takes the backward view of life. . . . With a little gasp he sees himself as merely a leaf blown by the wind through the streets of his village. He knows that in spite of all the stout talk of his fellows he must live and die in uncertainty, a thing blown by the winds, a thing destined like corn to wilt in the sun. . . . Already he hears death calling. With all his heart he wants to come close to some other human, touch someone with all his hands. . . .'' For George this illumination is enough, but it is not for the grotesques. They are a moment in his education, he a confirmation of their doom. ''I have missed something. I have missed something Kate Swift was trying to tell me,'' he says to himself one night as he falls asleep. He has missed the meaning of Kate Swift's life: it is not his fault: her salvation, like the salvation of the other grotesques, is beyond his capacities. . . .

Winesburg is an excellently formed piece of fiction, each of its stories following a parabola of movement which abstractly graphs the book's meaning. From a state of feeling rather than a dramatic conflict there develops in one of the grotesques a rising lyrical excitement, usually stimulated to intensity by the presence of George Willard. At the moment before reaching a climax, this excitement is frustrated by a fatal inability at communication and then it rapidly dissolves into its original diffuse base. This structural pattern is sometimes varied by an ironic turn, as in ''Nobody Knows'' and ''A Man of Ideas,'' but in only one story, ''Sophistication,'' is the emotional ascent allowed to move forward without interruption.

Source: Irving Howe, ''The Book of the Grotesque,'' in *Sherwood Anderson,* Stanford University Press, 1951, pp. 91–110.

Sources

Anderson, Maxwell. ''A Country Town.'' *The New Republic,* June 25, 1919, pp. 257, 260.

Cowley, Malcolm. Introduction to *Winesburg, Ohio,* by Sherwood Anderson, Viking Press, 1960, pp. 1–15.

Faulkner, William. ''A Note on Sherwood Anderson.'' In *Essays, Speeches & Public Letters,* edited by James B. Meriwether, Random House, 1965, pp. 3-10.

Frank, Waldo. ''*Winesburg, Ohio* after Twenty Years.'' *Story,* Vol. 29, no. 9, September-October, 1941, pp. 29-33.

Howe, Irving. *Sherwood Anderson: A Biographical and Critical Study,* William Sloane Associates, 1951, 271 p.

Mencken, H. L. ''Novels, Chiefly Bad—II.'' *The Smart Set,* Vol. 59, no. 4, August, 1919, pp. 140, 142.

Rideout, Walter. ''The Simplicity of *Winesburg, Ohio,*'' *Shenandoah,* Vol. 13, no. 3, Spring, 1962, pp. 20-31.

Trilling, Lionel. ''Sherwood Anderson.'' In *The Liberal Imagination,* Viking Press, 1947, pp. 22–33.

West, Rebecca. Review of *Winesburg, Ohio,* by Sherwood Anderson, in *The New Statesman,* Vol. 29, no. 484, July 22, 1922, pp. 443-44.

Further Reading

Abcarian, Richard. ''Innocence and Experience in *Winesburg, Ohio.*'' *University Review,* Vol. 35, Winter, 1968, pp. 95-105.
  Considers the wastefulness of human life to be the central focus of Anderson's novel.

Asselineau, Roger. ''Beyond Realism: Sherwood Anderson's Transcendalist Aesthetics,'' *The Transcendentalist Constant in American Literature,* New York University Press, 1980, pp. 124-36.
  Argues that each story in the novel is lyrical poetry.

Baker, Carlos. ''Sherwood Anderson's Winesburg: A Reprise,'' *The Virginia Quarterly Review,* Vol. 48, Autumn, 1972, pp. 568-79.
  States that the themes of quest and suppression, not sexuality, unite the stories.

Boyd, Ernest. Introduction to *Winesburg, Ohio,* Modern Library, 1919.
  Theorizes that the novel is a depiction of rebellion against American society.

Dewey, Joseph. ''No God in The Sky and No God in Myself: 'Godliness' and Anderson's *Winesburg, Ohio, Modern Fiction Studies,* Summer, 1981, pp. 251-59.
  Jesse Bentley unlocks the puritan vision of life for George Willard.

Gross, Barry. ''The Revolt That Wasn't: The Legacies of Critical Myopia,'' *CEA Critic,* Vol. 2, January, 1977, pp. 4-8.
  Gross states that the novel is a nostalgic memoir for rural America, not a critique of it.

White, Ray Lewis. ''Of Time and *Winesburg, Ohio.*'' *Modern Fiction Studies,* Vol. 25, Winter, 1979-80, pp. 658-66.
  Discusses the historical facts of the novel, stating that the action of the novel extends from July, 1894 to April, 1896.

Souvenir

Jayne Anne Phillips
1979

"Souvenir" is one of the twelve longer stories published in Jayne Anne Phillips's collection *Black Tickets*. The other fifteen stories in this collection are very short and are, appropriately, characterized as "short short stories." *Black Tickets* was published in 1979 to widespread critical acclaim.

The protagonist of "Souvenir" is the adult daughter of a fifty-five year old mother who is diagnosed with a potentially fatal brain tumor. Kate's mother is better able to face this terrible possibility with acceptance and calm than is Kate or her adult brother Robert. In this story, the younger woman struggles to come to terms with death, loss, and separation. Phillips presents Kate's special efforts to maintain a close contact with her mother, even though, as the conversations and scenes between them reveal, she and her mother sometimes disagree. The reader learns, for example, that Kate sends her mother a Valentine's Day card every year, except the year in which the events of this story take place, this year when her mother falls ill. By having Kate's failure to fulfill this special gesture coincide with the year that her mother falls ill, Phillips points to the inevitable failure of, or, at least, inadequacy of, our attempts to overcome or avoid the pain of life's separations.

Author Biography

Jayne Anne Phillips was born in Buckhannon, West Virginia, on July 19, 1952. She began to write at the age of nine as a way to entertain herself and her friends, and at the age of fifteen she became serious about herself as a writer and started to compose poetry. She received encouragement from her mother and a high school teacher, Irene McKinney, who was a poet in her own right. Phillips attended West Virginia University, and continued writing, publishing her work in small literary magazines.

Following her graduation from West Virginia University in 1974, Phillips hitchhiked with friends to California, lived in Oakland, California, for a time, and then moved to Colorado. She held various jobs to support herself during this period and gathered material that has sustained her writing ever since, although perhaps her short story collections most obviously record the lives she led, and the lives she witnessed, during her early adulthood. Eventually Phillips returned to West Virginia, later joining the prestigious Iowa writers' program.

In 1976 Phillips's collection of very short stories *Sweethearts,* was published. By the end of 1979, Phillips had completed the Iowa program, *Black Tickets* had been published to great acclaim, and she had given up a professorship at California State University at Humboldt in favor of a fellowship at Radcliffe College on the East coast. She also had begun work on her first novel, *Machine Dreams.* ''Souvenir,'' with its treatment of educated middle-class characters (a mother, a daughter, and a son), stands out in the collection *Black Tickets* as one of the longer stories and also as one of the few stories which is not about working-class Americans or more socially marginal characters. Phillips now lives near Boston, Massachusetts, with her husband and children, and she continues to write and publish novels and short stories.

Plot Summary

''Souvenir'' is related by an omniscient narrator. This narration is occasionally supplanted by dialogue between characters. The story begins with the information that the story's protagonist, Kate, has always sent her mother a Valentine's Day card,

timed to arrive precisely on the holiday. This year, however, Kate has forgotten until it is too late for a timely mailing. She waits until the evening of the holiday and telephones her mother instead. Their conversation provides insight into their professional lives and their relationship.

The next morning, Kate's brother Robert phones to tell her that her mother is in the hospital. Kate flies to the hometown that Robert and her mother never left and meets her brother at the hospital. He insists that they keep from their mother the truth about her condition: that she suffers from a possibly malignant brain tumor and that the surgery itself may prove debilitating or fatal. Kate dislikes the deception, but Robert points out that they will know nothing for certain until after the surgery, which may in fact be entirely successful.

Kate and Robert visit with her mother. Some tension is evident between them, which their mother skillfully diffuses by joking with them. Alone in the room after Robert leaves and her mother has been taken away for more medical testing, Kate finds that her mother has brought with her all of the Valentines that Kate has sent her over the years. She spends the night watching over her mother. The next morning they eat breakfast together and look out the hospital room window at a fair or carnival set up in a park across the highway. They reminisce about the county fairs and carnivals that Kate loved as a child, and Kate offers to ask her mother's doctor if they can walk over to the park.

The two women cross a pedestrian footbridge and approach the park and its amusement rides. They ride the Ferris wheel together, Kate holding her mother's hand at first and then grasping the metal safety bar. Her mother tells her calmly that she knows ''what you haven't told me'' about her condition. Mother and daughter gaze levelly at one another and the story ends.

Characters

Kate

The protagonist Kate is a graduate student whose mother objected to her move from her hometown a year before the action of the story. She applied herself obsessively as an undergraduate student after her brother's failure at a small junior college was upsetting to her mother. Kate has maintained contact with her mother and has sent her a card every Valentine's Day since her father's death because her parents always celebrated that day together.

Mother

Kate's mother is a school superintendent whose husband died six years before the events of the story. Her phone conversation with Kate at the beginning of the story reveals an intelligent and vital woman with a sense of humor and self-possession. She has diabetes, and she is diagnosed with a potentially malignant brain tumor. Kate and her brother agree not tell their mother the full truth about the seriousness of her condition, but she reveals that she knows.

Robert

Kate's brother Robert never left their hometown. As a young adult his failure at a small junior college was a source of great disappointment for their mother. The story implies that Kate felt driven to succeed as a student in compensation. He has since become a successful insurance salesman. He insists that he and Kate not tell their mother all the possible negative outcomes of her diagnosis and surgery because they will know nothing for certain until after the surgery and it is possible that she will make a good recovery.

Themes

Death

The inevitability of separation and loss is a major theme in "Souvenir". For the six years since her father's death, the protagonist has sent her mother a Valentine's Day card, to commemorate the day that her parents always celebrated together in some way. The day after the first Valentine's Day she forgets to send the card, she learns that her mother might die from a brain tumor. The rituals that serve to maintain human connections are inadequate in the face of inevitable loss.

Cycle of Life

The story ends with Kate and her mother at the top of a Ferris wheel. As the ride began, Kate asks her mother if she is "ready for the big sky,"

Jayne Anne Phillips

unwittingly voicing her concerns about her mother's now precarious hold on life. This unconscious reference suggests the ultimate separation of parent and child by death. Nevertheless, it is important that the scene is a Ferris wheel. This revolving ride suggests the cyclical natural routine of birth and death, degeneration and regeneration. The Ferris wheel's revolutions take riders on a circular ride through space; riders descend, only to be taken upwards once again. In this story about connections lost to death, this final image of endless revolution suggests that human death is but one stage in a cycle. Human birth, life, and death are all only parts of a ceaseless and larger natural cycle.

Alienation and Loneliness

Alienation and loneliness are themes closely related to that of death. To contemplate the death of a loved one leads to the contemplation of the individual's isolation as a discrete human consciousness. After Kate's brother has told her about her mother's tumor, Kate thinks about how she and her mother each eat many of their meals alone, separated by great distance. She is also stirred to remember an incident from her recent past when she spent a night with a strange man. This night which was supposed to amount to a connection between two individuals turned out to be the opposite. They

Media Adaptations

- "Souvenir" was recorded as an audiocassette in 1991, along with excerpts from *Machine Dreams*, read by Jayne Anne Phillips. Available from American Audio Prose Library.

---

failed to connect in any meaningful way and the memory is a dismal one.

Style

Point of View and Narration

"Souvenir" is narrated in the third person, a narrative form sometimes referred to as omniscient. The narrative voice does not always explicitly describe the thoughts or feelings of the characters; rather, the reader can often judge them by what the characters do or say. Instead of writing "Kate was upset," the narrator tells the reader that Kate sat "for a long time"over the same cup of coffee, remembering something unpleasant that seems to have no connection to her mother's illness. The reader surmises her feelings from what is described. On the other hand, when she talks with her mother in the hospital, the narrative recounts that Kate "felt her heart begin to open. . . ."

Foreshadowing

Kate's thoughts following the Valentine's Day telephone call to her mother offer instances of foreshadowing, or hints of what is to come in the story. She thinks about the curtains in her mother's house, all white and identical: "From the street it looked as if the house was always in order." Later in the story, the reader learns about familial conflicts, disappointments, and missed chances to "settle things." Other images of white objects, order, and precision are suggestive of the white institutional expanses found in hospitals. Kate muses about a

man she slept with whose name she can no longer remember; her mother wakes up in her hospital bed and does not know who Kate is.

Symbolism

The candlestick souvenirs which give this story its name are important symbols in the story. As the narrative progresses, the reader learns that Kate left her hometown only the year before, and against her mother's wishes. They argued about her leaving, but before her departure they went shopping together. Each bought the other a pewter candlestick as "a souvenir. A reminder. . . ." The word souvenir is taken from the French. In French, as in English, the word signifies an object that embodies special memories. In French it also means memory. Kate finds that her mother has brought other souvenirs with her to the hospital: all of the valentines from her father and from her, baby pictures of Kate and Robert. The actual photographs are indistinct; Kate's mother calls a childhood memory of Kate's "a pretty exaggerated picture."

Illness as Metaphor

The circumstance around which "Souvenir" revolves is the potentially life-threatening illness of the protagonist's mother. Immediately before this plot development the reader learns that Kate's mother is diabetic. The description of the mother's house, with its identical white curtains and its paraphernalia of a diabetic life, brings to mind a hospital room as living space. Or, conceivably, these identical fresh white curtains correspond to the "fleecy clouds" of heaven to which Kate's mother refers later in the story. These associations, along with Kate's own paranoid thoughts about an "agent" in her blood "making ready to work against her," make illness a central metaphor in the story. Illness in "Souvenir" functions as a metaphor for the fragility and mortality of the human being.

Historical Context

The 1970s: Youth Movements and Politics

Jayne Anne Phillips graduated from high school in 1970. This means that her teen years coincided

Topics for Further Study

- "Souvenir" is a story about a middle-class American family, all of whose members live separately. Research contemporary demographic patterns in the United States. How often do people move now as opposed to several generations ago? How far away do they typically move? How large is an average family today compared to fifty years ago? What do you think these demographic patterns tell us about society?

- "Souvenir" is a portrait of a family. The bond between mother and daughter is highlighted. There appears to be a certain degree of rivalry between sister and brother. Reread the story closely, paying special attention to the development of the children's relationship to their parents and to each other. To what extent have Kate and Robert become the adults that they are because of their responses to their parents' expectations and to each other? Imagine a conversation between Kate and Robert during the hours that their mother is undergoing surgery. What grudges or resentments might they hold against one another? Do you imagine that this crisis

would bring them closer or drive them further apart? Give reasons for your answer.

- Most hospitals employ medical ethicists to advise staff, patients, and family members facing the complex legal, moral, spiritual, and emotional dilemmas that modern medicine presents. These can include whether or not to perform surgery on a terminally ill person that may only add days or weeks of life; to offer or withhold artificial measures of sustaining life in comatose or brain-dead patients; and whether or not to use "heroic measures" to resuscitate a very old or terminally ill patient. Research the kinds of cases regularly faced by medical ethicists. Should family members have the right to withhold information from a competent person (as Kate and Robert do with their mother)? Why or why not? Would your answer be different if the patient were not mentally competent? To what extent should parents have the right to make all medical decisions regarding a minor child? Under what circumstances, if any, should parental wishes be overruled? Why?

---

with the last years of the 1960s. During this decade, youth culture became a dominant social force due to such phenomena as pop music, recreational drug use among the young, and such anti-establishment, unconventional youth groups identifying themselves in various ways: as hippies, yippies, or "Greens" for example. A prominent political position taken by many young people, and by many Americans of all ages, was opposition to the Vietnam War. The American public was deeply ambivalent about sacrificing young Americans in this conflict.

President Richard Nixon officially ended US involvement in the Vietnam War in 1973. That same year he was discovered to have engaged in illegal activities and in 1974 became the first president to resign from the office. This scandal, known as Watergate, undoubtedly produced a permanent

effect on the national consciousness, leaving Americans somewhat cynical regarding the honesty of public figures.

"Second Wave" Feminism

While the history of feminism in the western world is a long one, it was in first decades of the twentieth century that women's rights began to play an important role in United States' cultural and political life. The right to vote, attend institutes of higher learning, university, and work in all professions, were achieved by the "first wave" of twentieth century feminists. Feminism's "second wave," beginning in the 1970s, addressed such issues as negative attitudes toward and demeaning treatment of women as well as legal, professional, and political issues, rallying at one point under the slogan "The personal *is* the political."

Compare & Contrast

- **1970s:** The birth control pill abets the "sexual revolution," leading to widespread change in sexual mores.

  1990s: The sexual revolution is curtailed by the spread of incurable sexually transmitted diseases, including herpes and AIDS.

- **1970s:** A numerical decline in the number of two-parent families in the U.S. begins in this decade. The decrease continues at a rate of about 4% per year.

  1990s: The decline in the number of two-parent families stabilizes in mid-decade and slowly begins to reverse. there are about 25.1 million married couples with children in the U.S. in 1995—an increase of about 521,000 since 1990.

- **1970s:** Teenagers and young adults become a distinct demographic with enormous buying power and hence, the power to influence popular culture. The choices, beliefs, and icons of a youthful generation are seen as significant historically.

  1990s: Economists note that people born in the post-World-War-II years who came of age in the 1970s constitute the first generation of Americans who will enter middle age less well off financially than their parents were at that point in their lives.

Critical Overview

The short story collection *Black Tickets,* which contains "Souvenir," was Jayne Anne Phillips's first major publication. It appeared in 1979. Most commentary on the book discusses the collection as a whole.

Critical reviews of *Black Tickets* tend to make certain recurring points and distinctions. Commentators focus on the longer stories in the collection (of which "Souvenir" is one). Mary Peterson describes these stories in *The North American Review,* writing that they "have at their center a young woman who makes contact, or misses it, with one of her parents."

Peterson had called some of Phillips's shorter stories "flashy," and Doris Grumbach, in a review for *The Chronicle of Higher Education,* writes that they achieve their power from unnecessarily "ornate" language. In poetic prose, most of the stories in *Black Tickets* are about drug-addicts, pimps, prostitutes, and other marginal figures. They are shocking, then, not only because of how ornately and densely they are written, but also because the voices which speak come from outside the mainstream. Peterson considers that the longer stories "show more range, take bigger risks, and mostly succeed at what they try."

Criticism

Carol Dell'Amico

Carol Dell'Amico is a doctoral candidate in Literatures in English at the State University of New Jersey, Rutgers. Her primary field is twentieth-century literature. In the following essay, she discusses "Souvenir" within the context of literary realism, and Black Tickets *within the context of short short stories in contemporary prose fiction.*

This essay in criticism on Phillips is a genre study, so the notion of genre first will be defined. The word genre generally refers to two things. On the one hand, it refers to forms found in literature, such as the novel, the short story, the sonnet, the lyric, the essay, and so on. On the other hand, it is used to refer to styles within these genres, such as realism, science fiction, magic realism, gothic. Genre studies classify novels and look at the history of forms. When did realism begin; what is realism? When does science fiction take off as a highly popular sub-genre? "Souvenir" as a story, and *Black Tickets* as a collection of stories, are both interesting topics in genre. Stylistically, some of the longer short stories in *Black Tickets* such as "Souvenir" are treated in genre criticism as stories by American writers which evince a "return to realism" in contemporary letters. The significance of this critical claim will be explored, and "Souvenir" as an instance in realism will be addressed. Then, since *Black Tickets* contains fifteen stories out of twenty-seven which are four pages or less in length, and since other contemporary writers have written "short short stories," the generic phenomenon of the short short story in contemporary letters will be the final brief discussion in this essay on Phillips and genre.

Jayne Anne Phillips immediately comes to mind when reading recent critical studies announcing a return to realism on the part of writers. This resurgence tends to be dated from the 1970s. Realism in this sense is distinguished from prose fiction that departs from stable points of view or that tends to a greater artifice in plot or narrative construction. Stories told from multiple viewpoints that contest each other and thus make discovering a discrete story-line difficult, or stories which contain significant elements of dream or fantasy, or stories which depart from the process of story-telling to self-consciously comment upon what is being written about can be excluded from stories more properly described as realist stories. Realism proceeds around the minutiae of life. It is like a historical chronicle of the individual, her thoughts and activities, in her open-ended present. The bulk of nineteenth-century fiction is realist, and, beginning with writers such as Willa Cather and F. Scott Fitzgerald, realism in the novel and short story modified somewhat to suit the modern age. However, since twentieth-century fiction also witnessed significant developments in narrative quite different from this modified realism, much of the genre criticism on twentieth-century forms addresses itself to these developments. Some of these developments are modernist stream-of-consciousness writing, symbolic fiction, and so-called metafiction like self-reflexive writing or historiographic metafiction. Historiographic metafiction in some instances involves the meshing of real historical figures within an overarching fictional work and is a form of writing particularly widespread and popular in post-modern, or post-World War II, fiction (Michael Ondaatjie's *The English Patient,* for example). While prose fiction continues to change (witness developments in

What Do I Read Next?

- *Reasons to Live* (1985) by Amy Hempel is a collection of short short stories. Hempel's narrative voices offer wry, pithy observations that are both intriguing and disturbing.

- *Housekeeping* (1970), by Marilynne Robinson, is a novel about a family of four women. Robinson's prose captures the pace of rural life and of her characters' lives and thoughts.

- *White Noise* (1984) by Ron Delillo is a keen, funny satire and reflection on contemporary American life. In it, a blended family makes its way through surreal mutations in environment that characterize an age of malls, multiplexes, media, and technology.

cyberspace publishing), and while new twentieth-century forms must be generically addressed, nevertheless, realist prose never really stopped being written. This "return to realism" conversation most accurately points to how young writers coming of age from the mid-1960s on simply felt less pressured to try out non-realist forms in writing and felt freer to continue in the realist tradition. Thus, realism persists, and the "return" in this equation includes a return to paying attention to this tradition. Today, it seems best to acknowledge that the field of prose fiction is highly diverse, harboring everything from the realism found in some of Phillips's work, to the gothic supernaturalism of a writer like Anne Rice.

The question then becomes, if realist fiction resembles a historical chronicle of people's lives, then whose lives does Phillips chronicle in "Souvenir"? The story is about a middle-class family, and focuses on a young woman's relationship to especially her mother, but also to her father and brother as well. Kate, her mother, her dead father, and her brother, Robert, are the characters in "Souvenir." Given the story's focus on Kate and her mother, the story's realism could be said to provide us with a glimpse at the ways that mothers and daughters

> " Phillips writes about the changing status of women in culture, and the clash that resulted between an older more traditional generation and a younger, changing generation."

communicated and related in the 1970s. Kate and her mother are educated, and are tolerant of each other, this much we learn from the initial telephone conversation between them. We also detect in this conversation the generational divide, a major source of conflict between them. Kate, as the younger will do, urges her mother to live more recklessly than she does in her life as a school superintendent. For her part, Kate's mother encourages Kate to be careful in her dealings with men. What we glean from this conversation is a sense of a generational divide produced by a difference of mores, or values. This sense is confirmed in the portion of the story which is a sustained treatment of a scene from these two women's past.

In this scene, Kate and her mother are arguing bitterly, and both are upset. The dialogue reveals the source of the conflict:

> "But, hypothetically," Kate continued, her own voice unaccountably shaking, "if I'm willing to endure whatever I have to, do you have a right to object? You're my mother. You're supposed to defend my choices."
>
> "You'll have enough trouble without choosing more for yourself. Using birth control that'll ruin your insides, moving from one place to another. I can't defend your choices. I can't even defend myself against you." She wiped her eyes with a napkin.

The particular historical moment which Phillips captures here chronicles the changing sexual mores of a nation. Kate's free lifestyle and her use of birth control frighten her mother, but Kate desires approbation and support from her parent. No matter what happened and was not spoken about in middle-class homes before the 1960s, until the 1960s, the American middle-class woman remained celibate (or were supposed to) unless married. Here, Phillips writes about the changing status of women in cul-

ture, and the clash that resulted between an older more traditional generation and a younger, changing generation. As in "Home," another story in *Black Tickets,* Phillips's realism treats historically specific conflicts between mothers and daughters.

The second topic in genre this essay takes up is *Black Tickets* as a whole, that is, as a short story *collection.* Considering that most of the stories in *Black Tickets* are short short stories, we can take Phillips at her word and try to read this shortening of the short story as a deliberate attempt to modify the short story in terms of expectations of length. Since other contemporary writers have also written short short stories, this genre is deserving of mention as, at least, a phenomenon in contemporary letters. One wonders if *Black Tickets* could have made the impact it did if it were not in part because of these startling exercises in short short fiction. Critics who have attempted to theorize about this sub-generic efflorescence come up with different commentary. Perhaps it is a bit early to say. A critic like Miriam Marty Clark, for example, asks whether these fragments are not evidence of a weakening in the sense of history? "The stories I am interested in here," she writes in *Studies in Short Fiction,* "thematize *within* narrative the weakening of historicity." Is this inability to sustain a story a sign of the inability to place an individual within history, and project a coherent future for that individual? A possible criticism of this position is to note how a writer like Phillips can write this sort of fiction but then can write a historical novel as well (*Machine Dreams*). Another approach would be to note how these fragments capture slices of scenes and lives and voices that together add up to a sort of anthropological or ethnographic conglomeration of fragments which attest to an incredibly diverse world. In this case, a fascination with difference and the specificity of the local and particular can be seen to be urge behind this type of writing. In the short short stories of a writer like Amy Hempel, for example, the argot, cadences, and rhythms of contemporary urban Los Angeles are captured with documentary-like clarity, in one short burst of vision followed by another.

Genre studies make up one area of literary critical inquiry. Novels and short stories are a part of an intricate cultural web undergoing continuous change. Generic classifications keep track of the history of forms and trends in literatures and the arts. The longer short stories in *Black Tickets* like "Souvenir" correspond to a twentieth-century tradition of realist prose. But Phillips can not be too easily "pegged" as a writer. In her short short stories, her prose pushes the bounds of realism in its highly condensed temporal scope. Since the publication of *Black Tickets,* Phillips has published another collection of short stories, *Fast Lanes* (1987), and, besides *Machine Dreams* (1984), another novel entitled *Shelter* (1994).

Source: Carol Dell'Amico, "Topics in Genre in the Writing of Jayne Anne Phillips," for *Short Stories for Students,* Gale, 1998.

D. Mesher

Mesher is a professor of English and American Studies at San Jose State University. In the following essay, he discusses Jayne Anne Phillips use of characterization in "Souvenir."

"Souvenir," the one-word title of Jayne Anne Phillips' story about Kate, a woman who comes to terms with herself and her mother when the latter is diagnosed with terminal cancer, means "to remember" in French. A souvenir is a keepsake, a memento, something to serve as a reminder. Near the beginning of the story, Kate recalls a visit with her mother the previous summer, when "they bought each other pewter candle holders. 'A souvenir,' her mother said. 'A reminder to always be nice to yourself.'" But the visit begins much less pleasantly: Kate feels frustrated and betrayed by her mother's criticisms of her, while the mother predicts that Kate "may feel different later on," once the mother is dead and "floating around on a fleecy cloud." In the time-present of the story, Kate remembers that visit between receiving the telephone calls from her brother Robert, that inform her of her mother's hospitalization, first, and then of the diagnosis. The memory, a souvenir in itself, effectively portrays the tension, as well as the love, between mother and daughter, in a story in which characterization, and not plot, is the chief focus.

Someone reading only for plot might not find much in "Souvenir": Kate learns that her mother has cancer, and agrees to abide by her brother's decision not to tell her mother the truth; later, while she is visiting her mother in the hospital, the two women walk to a park and take a ride on a Ferris wheel. Her mother tells Kate, "I know what you haven't told me." Such a reading, however, would miss the rich texture of Kate's characterization, as well as Phillips' achievement in producing so complex a personality within the limitations of a short story. In "Souvenir," that texture is woven from strands of personality often only suggested or im-

> " In 'Souvenir,' texture is woven from strands of personality often only suggested or implied, producing what seem to be confused or contradictory impressions of the main character."

plied, producing what seem to be confused or contradictory impressions of the main character.

Consider the false impression created in the first lines of "Souvenir": "Kate always sent her mother a card on Valentine's Day," the story begins, conjuring up the image of a loving daughter in a cherished relationship with her mother. The rest of the story's opening, however, undermines that image. Kate's Valentine's Day tradition has only been going on six years, since her father's death, not "always"; and, rather than an act of love, Kate has sent the cards as—in the story's cold and impersonal phrase—"a gesture of compensatory remembrance." Further, there has been a decline in her effort over those six years, from hand-made cards to mass-produced "art reproductions . . . with blank insides" on which she has written short, almost trite sentiments. That decline culminates with the Valentine's Day on which the story begins. "This time, she forgot." And even the long-distance telephone call she makes to her mother, in place of the forgotten card, seems devalued, because Kate waits until "night when the rates were low."

Having reduced Kate in the reader's estimation, however, Phillips begins to rehabilitate her. Though the mother's voice grows "suddenly brighter" when she realizes it is her daughter calling, Kate recognizes in it "a tone reserved for welcome company"—as if family has always been of less importance to her mother and, worse yet, as if sometimes it takes her mother "a while to warm up" that welcoming tone in Kate's case. By the time her mother says, "this is costing you money," the reader may be wondering if Kate waited for the low rates before calling to save money or merely to please her mother.

But why begin with a false impression of Kate as the loving daughter, only to undercut the image and then blame the mother for the problem? In part, the answer has to do with narrative technique: the story is told in the third person, not from an omniscient point of view, but from Kate's "center of consciousness." All the thoughts and descriptions in the story are Kate's, and the narrative never leaves her presence, or her mind. The story's first line, "Kate always sent her mother a card on Valentine's Day," is therefore not a statement of fact, but Kate's own way of looking at herself, and the details that follow are her own recognition of the falseness of that image. Further, the reader cannot be sure that there is ever any "tone reserved for welcome company" in her mother's voice; what is certain, however, is that Kate thinks there is such a tone, since the description comes from her thoughts, as related by the narrator. Through the use of these apparently contradictory impressions, then, Phillips has involved the reader in a sense of the tensions that are at the core of Kate's characterization.

Those same tensions are also expressed in the story in other ways, including, on occasion, the incongruent pairings of Kate's thoughts. When, for example, her brother Robert phones early on the morning after Valentine's Day, with the news of her mother's hospitalization, Kate thinks of herself, "She would never make much money, and recently she had begun wearing make-up again, waking in smeared mascara as she had in high school." Sitting over a cup of coffee after speaking with Robert, Kate again reflects on herself: "She hadn't slept with anyone for five weeks, and the skin beneath her eyes had taken on a creamy darkness." The fact that Kate's thoughts turn inward, when her mother has fallen ill, is revealing in itself. But what is the connection between making money and wearing make-up, or having sex and having dark patches under one's eyes? The free associations underlying both pairings seem to offer a glimpse into Kate's troubled subconscious, and to suggest that she lacks a sense of fulfillment in her life. By leaving the exact terms of those associations undefined, Phillips adds to her portrait of an emotionally distraught young woman.

One of the most important strategies in Phillips' creation of Kate's characterization is her use of the double—a literary technique in which two characters share parallel (or opposing) attributes,

allowing elements of the minor character's personality to reflect directly on that of the major one. For all the tension between them, Kate and her mother are doubles in "Souvenir." They are both women, both teachers, both living alone. That Kate recognizes this part of their relationship is clear from the frequent comparisons she makes between herself and her mother. Sometimes, those comparison point out their differences, as when Kate makes a "cup of strong Chinese tea," and then thinks that "her mother kept no real tea in the house." But she is just as likely to focus on similarities: her mother is a diabetic, so Kate fears "a secret agent in her blood making ready to work against her." They both eat their meals alone, Kate thinks, at "similar times of day, hundreds of miles apart. Women by themselves."

After Robert's call, Kate remembers the curtains on her mother's windows: "all the same, white cotton hemmed with a ruffle, tiebacks blousing the cloth into identical shapes. From the street it looked as if the house was always in order." On one level, this suggests that her mother's house is not always in order. But whose house always is? Without any evidence as to the degree of disorder, it is unclear whether those curtains hide a mother who is too concerned with appearances, or reveal a daughter who unreasonably holds her mother responsible for the random nature of everyday life.

When Kate arrives at the hospital, however, her role has been reversed. Having acceded to Robert's demand that the diagnosis be kept secret from the patient, Kate finds herself in the uncomfortable position of putting up a false front. Yet her remark to Robert, that "we're lying to her, all of us, more and more," suggests that Kate now believes the current one to be only the latest in the succession of lies she has told her mother. The "succession of blocks tumbling over," which she sees when she closes her eyes, may represent the collapse of walls she has built from those lies to separate herself from her mother.

The role-reversal continues during their first visit, when her mother comforts Kate, instead of the other way around: "'You're not alone,' her mother said, 'I'm right here'." Again, Kate experiences an emotional change described in concrete terms: "She sat motionless and felt her heart begin to open like a box with a hinged lid. The fullness had no edges." But for all the emotional progress Kate has made during the story, she is still in denial, thinking mostly about herself. This is best illustrated when, looking for hand cream in her mother's suitcase, Kate finds "a stack of postmarked envelopes" her mother's keepsakes, "beginning with the first of the marriage" and including family photographs and "Kate's homemade Valentines." These are her mother's souvenirs, reminders of her own happiness. But Kate finds the love they suggest to be literally smothering: "Kate stared. *What will I do with these things? She wanted air; she needed to breathe.*" And when a few of the photographs fly out of an open window, Kate does not even try to reach them.

Kate would like to believe that, despite the "tension," there has always been "a trusted clarity," between her mother and herself—a clarity now "twisted," because she has gone along with Robert and hidden the truth of her mother's condition from her. Instead of revealing that truth, however, Kate takes her mother to the small amusement park near the hospital to ride the Ferris wheel. As they ascend on the ride, Kate finds herself again reassured by her dying mother, this time about an approaching storm, when her mother makes a comforting gesture, moving "her hand to Kate's knee and touch[ing] the cloth of her daughter's skirt." And once again she feels smothered, aware of "the immense weight of the air as they moved through it."

This time, however, something is different: her mother is close to death, which she once described as "floating around on a fleecy cloud." The description is recalled when, as they begin to ascend, Kate asks her mother, "Are you ready for the big sky?" Near the top of the Ferris wheel, literally suspended between heaven and earth and figuratively between life and death, her mother withdraws her hand and Kate, no longer smothered, feels "the absence of the warmth." It is at this climactic point that Kate's mother resolves the tensions between them. "I know all about it. . . . I know what you haven't told me," she says, apparently referring to a great deal more than the doctor's diagnosis. And the story ends, as Kate sees "herself in her mother's wide brown eyes" and feels she is "falling slowly into them"—an image of acceptance and harmony between mother and daughter at last.

Source: D. Mesher, for *Short Stories for Students,* Gale, 1998.

Jayne Anne Phillips with Celia Gilbert

Gilbert is an American poet, editor, and critic. Below, Phillips discusses her life and writing career.

Phillips, 31, slender and lovely with brown hair parted simply in the middle and huge, intelligent eyes, is also the author of *Black Tickets,* a collection of short stories published in 1979, which won her instant critical acclaim and a large readership when it was translated into 12 languages.

Many of those stories were set in fictional Bellington, a small town in West Virginia like the one Phillips herself grew up in. Readers of *Black Tickets* will find in [her novel] *Machine Dreams* themes and incidents they remember from the short stories. Phillips has always been obsessed by the rootlessness of her generation and the accommodations families have to make to changing times.

"I didn't start out to write a novel," she says. "I had been meditating, brooding over some of the characters in the family stories of *Black Tickets,* but I planned nothing until I got deeply into the book. I wanted to write a book that worked associatively, rather than a book that worked according to a story or that took place in three days. I wanted to give a sense of time going on and beyond for the characters. . . ."

Phillips would never define herself as a political writer, nor are her characters at all interested in politics, but, she says, "I think writing about so-called ordinary people is a political statement because it's talking about everyday life and why it's precious and why it's worth defending against whatever forces. It was only when politics filtered down to ordinary people like the people in the book [*Machine Dreams*] that anything changed. If you feel yourself or your family to be immediately imperiled, well—people will do anything to keep from losing their children. It really comes down to survival, and then people realize they have to survive, against their own governments in some cases."

Phillips values affection and family ties. She grew up in a small town (pop. 8000) in West Virginia, the middle child and only girl born to a father who was in the road construction business and a mother who was a schoolteacher.

"West Virginia is a strange state," says Phillips. "It's never belonged to the South or the North. The rural population is larger than the urban one. Family and tradition are what's important there. It's hemmed in by hills and valleys. People don't *leave* West Virginia."

Yet, as a child, Phillips dreamed of traveling. "I was never the kind of kid who said, I want to be a mommy when I grow up. I was a voracious reader;

I'd sit indoors all day in the summer reading a book. Not particularly good ones, but somehow very early I got the idea that language was some kind of private, secretive means of travel, a way of living beyond your own life.''

Her mother encouraged independence in her children. ''She wanted all her kids to be somebody,'' says Phillips. ''She wanted us to be proud, in the sense that we wouldn't be ground down by anybody, and she communicated that to me especially because I was the girl and I'd have to protect myself, not my physical self as much as my spiritual self.''

Her drive for independence and adventure is reflected in the material Phillips used in her short stories. She had jobs in amusement parks, motels, taught reading in a rural school and helped put herself through the University of West Virginia by working for a home improvements company.

It was at the University that she first began publishing her work, then poetry, in very small magazines. She liked that, she says, because it gave her a sense of privacy which she needed. ''It was like a guarantee that my identity as a writer and my identity as a person were entirely separate. Part of that need came from growing up in a small town where everyone knew everyone else. But part, too, came from my feeling that the writer in the family structure is the one who has been entrusted with the psyche of the family. Obsessed, that person will explore it, perhaps trying to save the family by making a new environment. The writer is caught by being charged with this responsibility and, at the same time, running great risk for herself and the others. Of course, in reality you are always writing about yourself, but when you start out, if you're writing about family members or characters based on them, it's good to have this guarantee of secrecy.''

Out of the school in 1974, she traveled across the country, lived in the black section of Oakland for a while, and then went on to Colorado, supporting herself by waitressing. Writing about drifters, stripteasers and addicts, people on the road and at loose ends, she reflected part of her generation's experience, the generation that was of college age in the '70s.

''Unlike the people of the '60s, we didn't have a strong sense of goals, nor the illusion we could make a difference. They were very organized and considered themselves a community. Their enemy was an obvious one. By the '70s, people began to experience a kind of massive ennui. People felt on their own. Kids dropping acid did it to obliterate themselves, not to have a religious experience. Only people with a strong sense of self came through.

''On the other hand,'' Phillips continues, ''we still thought of ourselves as outside the political system. The undergraduates I see today certainly don't; that's the last thing they want.''

Phillips has been teaching since 1982 in the Creative Writing Program at Boston University. ''Some of the undergraduates don't know if we fought North or South Vietnam. They don't have a sense of recent history at all. They feel they have no control over their government, and they're trying to make their personal situation as strong and protected as possible. They're concerned about money, and they want structures very much. In the '70s there was still enough security so that people felt they could be floaters. Now things are too shaky for that.''

In 1976 Phillips was accepted by the writing program at Iowa on the basis of poems and only two short stories. In the summer of that year, on her 24th birthday (''I'm superstitious, says Phillips), Truck Press, a small press, brought out an edition of 24 one-page prose pieces of hers in a collection called *Sweethearts*. The book has subsequently gone into three printings. Phillips, who had started out as a poet, was changing.

''I became more challenged by the difficulty of writing fiction; I was really attracted by the *subversive* look of the paragraph,'' she says. ''In a poem you're always having to confront the identity of the writer. In fiction the reader becomes less defended against that identity and more open to the text.''

Iowa was a new experience for Phillips. She had never had a writing course before. It was the first time she'd ever lived in a community of writers, and she enjoyed both that and her respite from waitressing jobs. Reflecting on creative writing programs in general, Phillips has very definite ideas. Writers shouldn't become involved in them until, in a personal sense at least, they have established their identities as writers and until they have lived on their own for a while.

She's very enthusiastic about the support of small presses. After *Sweethearts* appeared, she worked with Annabelle Levitt, who publishes Vehicles Editions, on a book called *Counting*, this year in September, Levitt will do a short story collection of hers, called *Fast Lanes*. ''It's nice now that I can support the small presses because I think it's important for those who've been helped early on to continue to publish with them,'' she says.

In 1978 Phillips attended the St. Lawrence writer's conference. There, meeting Seymour Lawrence, then an editor at Delacorte, she asked him if he was interested in publishing short stories. The answer was a firm no. Nothing daunted, she gave him a copy of *Sweethearts*. He asked to see her manuscript and, later that summer, at home, just as she was about to get into her car and set out to California to a job at Humboldt State University, the phone rang. Her mother rushed out of the house; Lawrence was on the phone and he was taking *Black Tickets*.

''Working with Sam has been a great experience,'' says Phillips with a smile. ''He's not an editor who edits your copy; he leaves you entirely alone on that, but once he decides to take on an author, he's really committed to that person's work. Since it's very hard to find long-range relationships in the publishing world today, it's great to know that you have someone to stand by you.

''It was also his brainstorm,'' she adds, ''to do a simultaneous quality trade paperback of *Black Tickets* in addition to the 2500 hardcovers they were bringing out. They did 10 or 15 thousand; for a first collection, that's an ideal way to publish.''

Today, Lawrence is reaping the benefits of his loyalty to his author, as foreign rights for *Machine Dreams* have been sold for record amounts in England and Germany, and at home Pocket Books outbid Dell for paperback rights. Both BOMC and its subsidiary, QPBC, have chosen the books as an alternate.

While she is pleased by all this, Phillips doesn't feel it puts pressure on her. She defines herself as a writer who is a seeker, ''a seeking consciousness, not even a person,'' in her phrase. ''I write for my own psychic survival,'' she explains, ''and that's why I never have considered the reader. Nor have I ever written with any kind of plan, because the whole point is to follow the story to its center, not to impose some point of view. I believe that you are led to discover what things mean and how things relate to each other through the process of doing the work. The real risk is to be strong enough to understand and accept what you're going to find out so that you are not destroyed by what you find. If there's a sense of surprise in the work, it's coming to grips with that risk that makes the revelation. That's the reason to do it.

''I'm the type of writer for whom writing is more painful than anything else, the kind of writer without the personal exuberance or ego orientation of those who are more like public performers. We are like acolytes, or novices, people who have put themselves at the mercy of something they surrender to completely.

''If I've had a good day, I feel that I've stumbled onto some kind of knowledge and I'm sort of wiped clean. I'm a little shell-shocked and awed, not at anything about myself, but at how things have ended up making sense.

''Once the book is done, I don't relate to it very personally because I feel that a work of art is completely separate from the personality that created it. It's on its own. There's much that the writer isn't even aware is there. The writer can take the credit for having seen it through, but not everything that came together in it.

''Of course, I care very deeply about what is in the book, so I hope that it's understood and valued, but I don't necessarily expect that it's going to be understood.

''I work very slowly,'' says Phillips. ''I don't write every day. Sometimes I go for months without writing. I work like a poet, really, one line at a time. . . . But the writers who've influenced me, not for their style but their subject matter, were Welty, Porter, Faulkner and Edgar Lee Masters, writers who wrote about materially disenfranchised people who had rich histories and myths, stories that were almost destinies in themselves.''

Source: Jayne Anne Phillips with Celia Gilbert, in an interview for *Publishers Weekly,* Vol. 225, No. 23, June 8, 1984, pp. 65–6.

Keith Cushman

Cushman offers a favorable review of Phillips's collection of stories.

Jayne Anne Phillips brings a new voice and talent to familiar literary terrain. *Black Tickets* will buy you admission to Flannery O'Connor and Eudora Welty country, where the people, mostly poor whites, are invalids and grotesques and where all are desperately lonely. Love is at best something that happened a long time ago.

Phillips tries her range with all sorts of characters, many of whom tell their own stories. She takes a virtuoso delight in trying to get under the skin of strippers, bar owners, delinquent teen-aged girls, even homicidal maniacs. She is most convincing though in the several stories which depict the homecoming of a woman in her middle twenties, at the end of an affair and uncertain where to turn. Home is the place where, when you have to go there, they have to take you in. But these young women discover that the parents are now just as adrift and emotionally needy as they are. Only memories of happier times remain, and the memories are not to be trusted.

Jayne Anne Phillips was a poet before she became a short story writer. The poet's feeling for language and habit of condensation are qualities that set this collection apart. Phillips captures her disturbed characters in prose that is disturbing. The writing is bright and bold and sometimes elliptical, stylized but authentic:

> We went to the movies every Friday and Sunday. On Friday nights the Colonial filled with an oily fragrance of teen-agers while we hid in the back row of the balcony. An aura of light from the projection booth curved across our shoulders, round under cotton sweaters. Sacred grunts rose in black corners. The screen was far away and spilling color—big men sweating on their horses and women with powdered breasts floating under satin. Near the end the film smelled hot and twisted as boys shuddered and girls sank down in their seats. We ran to the lobby before the lights came up to stand by the big ash can and watch them walk slowly downstairs. Mouths swollen and ripe, they drifted down like a sigh of steam. The boys held their arms tense and shuffled from one foot to the other while the girls sniffed and combed their hair in the big mirror. Outside the neon lights on Main Street flashed stripes across asphalt in the rain. They tossed their heads and shivered like ponies.

Sixteen of the twenty-seven stories are extremely brief, a paragraph or two in length, and these highly compressed pieces are less successful. The brief stories tend to be splashy and self-indulgent, but they display in concentrated form Phillips' heady delight in the sounds and rhythms of the American language.

Black Tickets reminds me of the work of Ann Beattie, a better-established young woman who also writes about lonely people coping, not very successfully, with their bleak lives. Like Beattie, Phillips knows that the chilliest scenes of winter are to be found inside us. At the same time the two authors relate to their damaged characters quite differently. Phillips treats hers not only with fascination but also with compassion. That compassion is to be preferred to Beattie's icy detachment.

Black Tickets won the 1980 Sue Kaufman Prize for First Fiction presented by the American Academy and Institute of Arts and Letters. These stories are the work of a young writer, still trying to find her legs, but they also add up to a notable debut. Though it seems heretical to say it in the pages of *Studies in Short Fiction,* I'm looking forward to the novel Phillips is inevitably writing now.

Source: Keith Cushman, a review of *Black Tickets,* in *Studies in Short Fiction,* Vol. 18, No. 1, Winter, 1981, 92–4.

Thomas R. Edwards

Edwards examines the tone of the stories in Black Tickets, *concluding that Phillips is at her best when portraying ordinary family life.*

When she cares to invoke it, Jayne Anne Phillips also has a strong sense of place (Appalachia, in her case), and she could never be accused of saying too much. More than half the stories in *Black Tickets* run to a page or less, and the longer ones have no fat on them. Compared with [Scott] Spencer and [Alice] Munro, who work coolly, well within the limits of their means, Phillips writes with noticeable power, even violence, so that her brevity seems more a matter of conscious self-discipline than of natural sensibility.

Her usual fictional material, as it happens, calls for self-discipline. Consider the remarkable "Under the Board Walk," a sketch of only five paragraphs. "Her name is Joyce Castro," it flatly begins, "and she rides our school bus. The Castros all look alike. Skinny, freckled, straw-haired." Her father is a fundamentalist preacher, and Joyce is never seen without her transistor radio: "Music is the work of a devil that licks at her legs. She stands, radio pressed to her face, lips working. Undah the boardwalk, down by the sea ee ee ye eh eh. Ona blanket with my baybeh's where I'll be." She is shy, stares at the floor, doesn't talk to the other kids. She is also pregnant, by her brother ("The Castros all look alike"), who's gone off to work in the steel mills.

The words of the song "Under the Boardwalk" come hideously true in the story's next to last paragraph, with perhaps a touch of overcalculation that yet doesn't spoil a brilliantly imagined moment:

> She disappears from school but comes back a month later, having had it in a bloody way. She rolled up a horse blanket and walked to the field. Daddy thundering I won't lay eyes on your sin and big brother in Youngstown, holding a thing that burns orange fire. She rolls yelping, dogs come close and sniff. They circle. The sky circles. Points of light up there that sting. Finally she sees that they are stars. Washing herself in the creek she remembers the scythe against the grass, its whispering rip.

Phillips finds a kind of beauty in this horror— the phallic suggestion in the red-hot steel the brother holds and its association with the stinging "points of light," her animal yelping that seems almost to create the ominously circling dogs, the suggestion, in her seeing the stars and remembering the sound of the scythe through the grass, that giving birth has been, even for her, a brief participation in natural order.

But the story's final sentences return bleakly to things as they are in Joyce's world. When she is alone in the house the next day, "The dogs come in with pieces in their mouths. She stands in the kitchen shaking while the Drifters do some easy moanin." Their simulated commercial moaning is indeed easy, and it seems appallingly possible that her "shaking" may be only her habitual, mindless reaction to the music and not a recognition of what the dogs have brought her. This is remarkably alert and resourceful writing.

But Phillips pays a price for her interest in human beings who are frozen into their worst possible cases. Most of the stories in *Black Tickets* examine the lives of people who are desperately poor, morally deadened, in some way denied comfort, beauty, and love. Girls tell each other dirty stories in a shack, while small boys listen avidly outside; a crazed black woman beats up drunken derelicts while policemen laugh, drug drops are made in porn movie lavatories; a rich old homosexual is cared for by a calculating male nurse who spends all his spare time in peep shows; a fourteen-year-old mute orphan girl sells dirty pictures and hustles her body for her drug-addict pimp; a Son of Sam type describes his quest for murderable girls; the sighted daughter of blind parents watches her nearly blind brother die of (apparently) a cerebral

> **Phillips wonderfully catches the tones and gestures in which familial love unexpectedly persists even after altered circumstances have made it impossible to express directly."**

hemorrhage; and so on. None of these alone, is an unworthy subject for art, and Phillips's interest is compassionate; but in such heavy concentration, horror begins to seem predictable, and then positively funny. So represented, the world in effect becomes a machine designed to do the worst things possible—sidewalks are for displaying dog-puke, delivery boys are for screwing suburban housewives while the prissy neighbors watch with binoculars through the curtains; public lavatories are for drunks and juveniles to throw up in.

Happily, a small group of these stories— and the best ones. I think—deals not with the lower depths but with more or less ordinary people in families, who are trying to love each other across a gap. Their common situation is the more or less reluctant return home of a young woman, usually a student or a teacher, who finds herself challenged or threatened by her parent's concern about what she's doing with her life. The parent, usually the mother, is invariably divorced or widowed, not at all ill-willed or obtuse, not very demanding but anxious to understand better what has replaced the old closeness they once had. These stories are full of beautiful touches that stand without need of explanation— a mother who leaves the house when she hears her daughter making love with her boyfriend, not out of offended assumptions about decency but because she fears getting interested again in sex, a father who touchingly deflects his worry about his daughter into an obsessive and annoying worry about the condition of her car.

Phillips wonderfully catches the tones and gestures in which familial love unexpectedly persists even after altered circumstances have made it impossible to express directly, the ways in which grown children, while cherishing even an unrewarding freedom, can be caught, and hurt, and consoled by their vestigial yearning for dependency, safety, a human closeness that usually seems forever lost. I don't of course mean that Phillips should devote her very promising talent to writing more stories about such parents and children, but I do think that her remarkable powers work best in the realm of the ordinary and the domestic.

Source: Thomas R. Edwards, ''It's Love!,'' in *The New York Review of Books,* Vol. XXVII, No. 3, March 6, 1980, pp. 43–5.

Joseph Brown

Brown is an American critic, journalist, and author of several children's books. Below, he commends Black Tickets *for its memorable surrealistic tone.*

The short stories, prose poems and surreal vignettes that comprise *Black Tickets* read like comments on life from one who has stood graveside with Samuel Beckett and nodded mournful agreement as he intoned, ''Astride of a grave and a difficult birth. Down in the hole lingeringly, the gravedigger puts on the forceps. We have time to grow old. The air is full of our cries.''

The 27 ''cries'' recorded by Jayne Ann Phillips in this her first publication, especially those of young women and teen-age girls, are reproduced with perfect pitch.

''Wedding Pictures,'' more a succinct three-paragraph poetic description than a story, introduces us, fugue-like, to the themes of emptiness, estrangement and despair which resonate through each succeeding page. From the incipient misery of children in ''Blind Girls,'' ''Lechery'' and ''Under the Boardwalk,'' to the drug-induced horrors of ''The Powder of the Angels and I'm Yours'' and ''Black Tickets,'' to the perversion and psychoses in ''Sweethearts,'' ''Satisfaction'' and ''1934,'' most of the stories are tickets by which we gain admission to watch Phillips present her characters in the fashion of the killer in the concluding story ''Gemcrack,'' who wants to ''crack . . . and expose their light in the dark Saturdays, the night.''

Black Tickets presents a creative variety of prose forms ranging from impressionistic essays and terse, cathartic outbursts to intimidatingly articulated nightmares. One of the most effectively innovative works is ''El Paso,'' The story is a series of monologues, each one as stark and searing as the Texas desert ''glaring as a lidless eye.'' The five speakers, life's detritus, are presented as they exist—separate, fragmented creatures who speak directly to the reader as if life mattered, but who know on the gut level that ''it's already over.''

Phillips's most successfully orchestrated and viable work is three stories that are stories in the modern recognizable sense of the word: ''Home,'' ''The Heavenly Animal'' and ''Souvenir.'' Each story sensitively enacts the moribund relations between daughters and mothers.

''Home'' verifies Thomas Wolfe's dictum, and whenever the daughter does return to visit her mother, an alien being glazed over with the monotonous routine of television and incessant knitting, each visit becomes less endurable and more oxymoronic. In the final scene, the mother washes and rewashes dishes, tormented by the sounds of her daughter's lovemaking during the previous night with one of her many lovers. The sounds (the ''cries'') have rendered her own life, as well as her daughter's, more unbearably inexplicable. ''I heard you, I heard it. Here in my own house. Please, how much can you expect me to take? I don't know what to do about anything. She looks into the water, keeps looking. And we stand here just like this.'' Standing there, endlessly peripheral to one another.

When the 25-year-old daughter in ''The Heavenly Animal'' returns for separate visits with her divorced parents, they all struggle awkwardly to prove that once they did exist as relevant family members in an irretrievable past. Neither whiskey nor dalmane will blot out the daughter's awareness of their pathetic sham, however, and she drives off fighting not to lose herself in remembrances of things past, when ''her father was driving. Her brothers had shining play pistols with leather holsters. Her mother wore clip-on earrings of tiny wreaths. They were all dressed in new clothes, and they moved down the road through the trees.''

In ''Souvenir,'' the mother, dying with a malignant brain tumor, whispers to her daughter that ''except for when the pain comes, it's all a show that goes on without me." This statement could have been made by every character in *Black Tickets*. These are the people Jayne Ann Phillips wants us to see, creatures who could have been sketched by Hogarth or Brueghel in their most hideous portrayals of life, creatures for whom life is only a show that goes on without them. Except, of course, when there's pain.

Quite possibly, much of this book will be forgotten in the weeks or months after it's been read, but I believe most readers will carry the stubs of Black Tickets around in their minds for years to come.

Source: Joseph Brown, in a review of *Black Tickets,* in *America,* Vol. 141, No. 18, December 8, 1979, p. 376.

Sources

Clark, Miriam Marty. "Contemporary Short Fiction and the Postmodern Condition," in *Studies in Short Fiction,* Spring, 1995, pp. 147-59.

Gorro, Michael. A review of *Machine Dreams,* in *Boston Review,* August, 1984, p. 27.

Grumbach, Doris. "Stories Caged in Glass," a review of *Black Tickets,* in *Books & Arts,* November 23, 1979, pp. 8-9.

Peterson, Mary. "Earned Praise," in *The North American Review,* Winter, 1979, pp. 77-8.

Tyler, Anne. "The Wounds of War," in *The New York Times Book Review,* July 1, 1984, p. 3.

Further Reading

Adams, Michael J. "Jayne Anne Phillips," in *Postmodern Fiction: A Bio-Bibliographic Guide,* edited by Larry McCaffery, Greenwood, 1986, pp. 481-83.
Useful reference guide.

Hill, Dorothy Combs. "Interview with Jayne Anne Phillips," in *South Carolina Review,* Fall, 1991, pp. 53-73.
Phillips discusses her life and career.

Lassner, Phyllis. "Women's Narration and the Recreation of History," in *American Women Writing Fiction,* edited by Mickey Perlman, University Press of Kentucky, 1989, pp. 193-206.
An exploration of the different narrative voices in *Machine Dreams* considered individually and as contributing to the overall effect of the novel.

Price, Joanna. "Remembering Vietnam: Subjectivity and Mourning in American New Realist Writing," in *Journal of American Studies,* August, 1993, pp. 173-86.
Besides touching on the question of "new realism," Price explores Phillips's treatment of character and the Vietnam war in the novel *Machine Dreams.*

The Star

Arthur C. Clarke

1955

Arthur C. Clarke's short story "The Star" appeared in the science fiction magazine *Infinity Science Fiction* in 1955. It was reprinted in a collection of Clarke's short stories called *The Other Side of the Sky* in 1958. In his introduction to this collection, Clarke noted that he wrote the story for a contest in the London *Observer* on the subject "2500 AD." "I realized that I had a theme already to hand. The story was written in a state of unusually intense emotion; needless to say, it wasn't even placed among the 'also rans.'" The story deals with themes treated in a work by H. G. Wells also titled "The Star" (1897). In Wells's story, a planetoid's collision with Jupiter and the destruction of that planet chillingly reminds the human race that it could just as easily have been destroyed. Clarke's story similarly places the human race in an intergalactic context that suggests that the planet Earth and its inhabitants may not be all that important in the cosmic scheme of things

Religion, and in particular religious faith, are central themes in "The Star." The narrative is the interior monologue of the central character, a Jesuit astrophysicist. He is aboard a starship on a mission to investigate the causes of a supernova in a distant galaxy. He and the rest of the crew discover the artifacts of a highly developed civilization, carefully preserved on the only planet that remains in orbit around the supernova. Knowing that all life would be wiped out when their sun flared into a supernova, this race of sentient beings left a record of who they

were and what they accomplished. The pictures, sculptures, music, and other relics of a very human-like race doomed to destruction depress the crew and investigating scientists, who are far from their own homes and lonely. What the narrator has learned but not yet communicated to the others is that the supernova that destroyed this civilization was the Star of Bethlehem, which burned brightly in the sky to herald the birth of Jesus Christ. His discovery has caused him to reexamine and to question his own faith.

Author Biography

Arthur C. Clarke was born on December 16, 1917, in Minehead, Somerset, England. He was brought up on a farm by his parents Charles Wright Clarke and Norah Mary Willis Clarke. Just before his ninth birthday, Clarke took his first airplane ride and was thrilled by air travel. He combined his interest in flying with rocketry and, by the time he entered his early teens, he was making homemade rockets, fireworks, and experimenting with communication devices. Clarke built his own refractor telescopes from old lenses, cardboard tubes, and miscellaneous spare parts. At age seventeen Clarke built a light-beam transmitter, which used light to transmit sound. It formed the basis for Clarke's later design for what became the communications satellite.

As a child, Clarke briefly attended an Anglican Church Sunday school. He later recalled that after a few months he concluded that it was "a bunch of nonsense" and refused to return. His rejection of religion and his interest in science and technology form the basis for much of his writing. Nearly all of his fiction involves underlying religious themes, with the spiritual evolution of humankind a particularly prominent theme.

There is speculation that the death of his father when Clarke was only thirteen was a great influence on his life. His writing reflects this loss and often features father figures and father-son relationships, perhaps most prominently in the novel *Childhood's End.* Another important influence on Clarke's later career as a writer was his discovery, at the age of twelve, of the magazine *Amazing Stories,* which features science fiction as well as fantasy tales.

Clarke was an early member of the British Interplanetary Society, a group of science fiction fans and writers. He began publishing science fiction stories in the 1930s and early 1940s—the beginning of the period known as "the Golden Age of Science Fiction," when most of the genre's acknowledged masters, including Isaac Asimov and Robert A. Heinlein, were beginning their careers. In 1941 he joined the British Air Force, becoming adept in radar applications, mathematics, and electronics. After World War II, he entered college and took degrees in physics and mathematics. By the early 1950s, with the publication of his first nonfiction book, *The Exploration of Space,* and the novel *Childhood's End,* Clarke became a full-time and very prolific writer. He continued to write both fiction and nonfiction works that draw from his extensive scientific background. He is acknowledged as the preeminent writer of "hard science fiction" that does not depart from known science or natural law or employ elements of the fantastic, and his nonfiction writings are praised for their ability to make scientific ideas understandable to a general readership.

Clarke first visited Sri Lanka (then Ceylon) in 1954 and established permanent residence there in 1975. He lived there part-time for twenty years, required by local laws to leave the country for at least six months a year. During the filming of *2001: A Space Odyssey,* he was in the United States for so long that he had to obtain a Resident Alien card. He joked that the card always made him "feel like a certified extraterrestrial." He was finally able to obtain legal "Resident Guest" status in Sri Lanka when that country passed what became known as "The Clarke Act" in 1974. He continues to live and write in Sri Lanka. Late in the twentieth century, Clarke has expressed optimism that he will live into the year 2001 and the new millennium.

Plot Summary

The story opens with the unnamed first-person narrator musing that at one time he had believed that his travels in outer space could not alter his faith in God. The reader learns that he is a Jesuit as well as an astrophysicist. He is aboard a starship returning from a scientific mission three thousand light-years from Earth. Something he learned on this mission, as yet unknown to the rest of the scientists and crew, has caused him to question his faith. He reflects

Arthur C. Clarke

regretfully that the data gathered on the mission will soon make the cause of his own doubt—"this ultimate irony"—known to everyone.

The narrator reflects on the "private, good-natured, but fundamentally serious war" that the largely irreligious crew has waged with him during the long mission. He thinks particularly of the ship's doctor, Dr. Chandler, who sometimes professes himself willing to believe that "*Something*" created the infinite vastness of space and everything in it, but cannot accept that a being so powerful could possibly care about "us and our miserable little world."

The narrative goes on to reveal more details about the mission. The ship had been sent to examine the aftermath of a supernova—the explosion of a star, during which it burns with an intensity and a luminosity that may be a billion times that of the Earth's sun. Following such an explosion, a star becomes a white dwarf, a body of very dense matter. These scientific details are imparted almost incidentally as the first-person narrative continues.

When the ship reaches the solar system surrounding the white dwarf, they are surprised to find that the outermost planet survived the force of the supernova explosion, and that it contains a clearly demarcated vault. Within it they find artifacts recording the accomplishments of a highly advanced civilization. The narrator reports that his colleagues have asked him how to reconcile the destruction of an entire civilization with a merciful and loving God. His answer: that "God has no need to justify His actions to man," is not accepted by the others, who say that the random destruction of worlds is further proof that there is no supreme being, that "the Universe has no purpose and no plan." The narrator has learned, but not yet revealed, that the supernova was the Star of Bethlehem, which heralded the birth of Christ.

Characters

Narrator

The entire story consists of the male narrator's reflections on what he has learned during a scientific mission to investigate a "white dwarf," a sun in a distant galaxy that became a supernova and burned itself out thousands of years earlier. The reader learns that he is a Jesuit priest and an astrophysicist aboard a starship, and that he has been fighting a "private, good-natured, but fundamentally serious war" against the atheism of the crew. The findings of the mission cause him to question the foundations of his faith.

Dr. Chandler

The ship's doctor is the only person's name the reader learns in the story. A conversation between the narrator and the doctor reveals the atheistic attitudes that the Jesuit astrophysicist encounters from the ship's crew and officers during the mission.

Themes

Religion and Science

The most important theme in "The Star" is the opposition of religion and science. The reader is presented with a very religious narrator who has his faith seriously shaken. The narrator has long attempted to show that science and religion are compatible. He believed that science affirms the existence of God and helps humanity to appreciate the dependence of science on the intricacies of God's ultimate plan. A large part of his faith was founded in the belief that humankind achieved redemption from sin through the birth, death, and resurrection of Jesus Christ. When the narrator calculates that the explosion of the supernova, wiping out an entire sentient, human-like race, was the star of Bethlehem, he is thrown into doubt. How can he reconcile his believe that God created all things with the knowledge that God annihilated this planet and its people in order to signal the redemption of the human race on Earth? Does it mean that the creator values certain of his creations over others? He fears that his findings will further convince a largely irreligious public that the universe is, in fact, random and not the work of an all-knowing, caring, and loving God.

Homocentrism

An important theme in "The Star" is the idea of homocentrism: that humankind is the center of the universe and the reason for all of creation. This concept embodies the idea that the universe revolves around the creation of humanity, and that everything that happens in the universe is directly related to the progress of humanity. The narrator, as

a Jesuit, has been taught by his Roman Catholic faith that God so loved humanity that He sent His only Son to save humans from their sins. He is confronted with the uncomfortable fact that in order to hold onto this belief, he must admit that his God was neither merciful nor loving toward this admirable alien race—or, in another scenario, that God did not create all things and the extinct alien race is not part of a divine scheme of creation.

Style

Point of View and Narration

"The Star" is a first person narration by an astrophysicist who is also a Jesuit. The narrative unfolds for the reader the emotions of this individual as he tries to comes to terms with the knowledge he has gained on a scientific mission to a distant galaxy—knowledge that has caused him for the first time to question his faith.

Foreshadowing and Irony

In the course of the story, the reader is given clues to the ironic outcome of the story. One of the first occurs in the opening paragraph when the narrator says, "*Once,* I believed that space could have no power over faith ... that the heavens declared the glory of God's handiwork" (emphasis added). He goes on to tell the reader that something has shaken that belief and left his faith "sorely troubled."

The narrative gradually reveals the information the narrator has gained and foreshadows the ultimate irony of the story's denouement, or final outcome. The story's irony is situational; that is, an event intended or presumed to have had one purpose or effect has also had a markedly different one. In this story, one result of the supernova's explosion is that an entire civilization was annihilated. However, the exploding star, burning brightly in the sky, also signaled the birth of the Christ child. The narrator even considers the name of the Nebula created by the supernova—the Phoenix Nebula—ironic. The phoenix is a mythological bird which creates new life through its own death, immolating itself every hundred years so that a new phoenix can rise from the ashes. It occurs to the narrator that whatever rises from the ashes of the dead civilization found

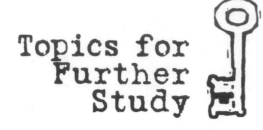

Topics for Further Study

- ''The Star'' is an example of an interior monologue. Do you think that the narrator's doubts heighten the suspense of the ending? Do his doubts detract from the suspense?

- The story looks at the idea that humanity is central to God's plan for the universe. Does this plan seem fair to other civilizations which may inhabit the universe?

- The narrator mentions that humans have found traces of other long-dead civilizations, but have never made contact with a living alien race. Does this make the story more believable? Less believable? Why? Would knowledge that other races of sentient beings exist in the universe tend to strengthen or weaken traditional Christian tenets of faith? Why?

- The story ends with reference to the star of Bethlehem. Is it necessary that the reader be Christian in order to feel the impact of the ending? Why or why not?

- Only one other character, Dr. Chandler, is heard from besides the narrator. The narrator considers the doctor a ''notorious atheist'' and suggests that most of the starship's other scientists and crew are too. How might a confirmed atheist react to the news that the supernova was the star of Bethlehem? What might be the response of a deeply religious person who is not a Christian— a Jew, a Muslem, or a Hindu? How might their reactions differ from that of the Jesuit narrator?

---

on a planet in the Phoenix Nebula is likely to supersede Christianity.

Quest and Hubris

The mission described in the story begins as a quest to find the cause of the supernova. It in some respects resembles such classic ''quest'' narratives as Arthurian legend or the Gilgamesh epic, in which a small-scale or personal quest turns out to have universal significance. The plot follows rather ordinary forms through exposition, rising action, and climax, but then does something unexpected– it does not provide a final resolution. The narrator's own feelings about what he has learned are revealed, as are his fears about how humankind will receive the information. But the reader is left to ponder how he or she imagines the human race will respond.

It is at this point that hubris is revealed. Hubris is a term derived from ancient Greek drama. It refers to the characteristic of excessive pride which leads to the misfortune of the protagonist in a tragedy. In ''The Star'', the entire human race has been guilty

of the ultimate hubris: believing themselves to be centrally important in the universe and the greatest creation of God. According to the events of the story, if humankind is the center, then God created the alien race only to be destroyed in the conflagration of the supernova. Conversely, if humans are to continue to accept an interpretation of God as loving and caring for all of His creations, how can they reconcile His destruction of the alien race? What the scientists have learned on the mission may require a wrenching re-thinking of many central religious principles.

Historical Context

The 1950s: U.S.-Soviet Rivalry and the ''Red Scare''

Arthur C. Clarke wrote ''The Star'' during a time of political and social unease. Both the ''space race'' and the ''arms race'' between the United States and the Soviet Union, were ongoing, fueled

Compare
&
Contrast

- **1954:** There are 32,501 Jesuit priests, brothers, and scholars in the world, with 7,630 in the United States.

  1990s: The number of Jesuits has declined to 22,000. There are fewer than 4,000 Jesuits in the U.S.

- **1950s:** The "space race" begins, with the worlds's two superpowers, the Soviet Union and the United States, separately developing space travel technology. The Soviet Union launches Sputnik I, the first manufactured satellite, and Sputnik II, carrying a live dog, into orbit around the earth in 1956.

  1990s: The lunar surface is littered with debris from 32 unmanned probes and nine manned missions to the moon. The U.S. space shuttles Atlantis, Discovery, and Endeavour regularly carry U.S. astronauts and scientists to work aboard the Russian space station MIR.

- **1950s:** The "arms race" between the U.S. and the U.S.S.R. parallels the space race between the two superpowers. In 1954, the U.S. Atomic Commission explodes a nuclear-fusion hydrogen bomb on Bikini Atoll in the South Pacific. The device is hundreds of times more powerful than the atomic bombs detonated over Hiroshima and Nagasaki.

  1990s: The U.S. and the former Soviet Union have signed numerous arms treaties and have committed to destroying their nuclear arsenals. Numerous smaller countries, however, have developed nuclear capabilities.

---

by cold war animosity between the two superpowers. Both countries were developing and testing newer and more destructive weapons, including the hydrogen bomb, in the aftermath of the atomic bombs used in 1945 against Japan.

Growing fear of Communism leads to the "red scare" in the U.S. A number of high-profile nuclear espionage cases, including that of the Rosenbergs in 1952, convince a portion of the American public and government that Communist infiltrators are potentially everywhere. Large numbers of writers and actors are blacklisted by publishers and Hollywood movie studios after being accused of Communist Party membership or merely having Communist sympathies. Even U.S. atomic scientist J. Robert Oppenheimer, who led the Manhattan Project that developed the atomic bomb, is considered a threat to American security because of his opposition to development of the hydrogen bomb. In 1954 the Atomic Energy Commission clears him of disloyalty charges but still revokes his security clearance. American Senator Joseph McCarthy (R-Wisconsin) conducts a campaign of accusations that the U.S. State Department is infiltrated by "card-carrying Communists." In hearings before the Senate Permanent Investigations Subcommittee, McCarthy charges that the Secretary of the Army is concealing evidence of a Soviet spy ring operating out of a U.S. Army Signal Corps installation in New Jersey.

The State of Science Fiction

The 1950s were also a period of change in science fiction. The careers of many notable science fiction writers, including Isaac Asimov and Robert Heinlein, began in the 1930s and 1940s—a period known as science fiction's "Golden Age." Numerous science fiction magazines began publishing in these years as well; they were called "pulps" because of the inexpensive paper on which they were printed. It was one such magazine, *Infinity Science Fiction,* that bought "The Star" in 1955 for $80. Much of what was written and published as science fiction in the early part of the twentieth century has been dismissed as "space opera": action-packed, improbable adventures involving steely-eyed astronaut heroes wielding ray guns against voracious tentacled aliens. The genre was expanding into more thoughtful and speculative realms when Clarke began publishing; however, he has always been considered the preeminent "hard science fiction" writer. He rarely departed from known science or natural law in his stories, and in fact he is often commended for his ability to make scientific ideas understandable to a general readership.

Science Fiction and Science Fact

Clarke is also the author of dozens of nonfiction books that are commended for their readily comprehensible presentation of complex scientific ideas involving two areas of great interest to him: space travel and undersea exploration. Because of his status as a well-known writer fascinated by the idea of interplanetary flight, Clarke was allowed to tour the White Sands Proving Grounds in 1952 and to witness tests of Honest John battlefield missiles. After seeing one of the missiles launched on a typical angle trajectory, Clarke remarked, "Why get excited about anything that doesn't go straight up?"

Critical Overview

"The Star" was first published in the United States in the magazine *Infinity Science Fiction* in early 1955. It went on to win the most prestigious science fiction writing award, the Hugo, in 1956 as the best short story of the previous year. It has consistently been regarded by genre fans and critics as one of the greatest science fiction stories of all time. From its first appearance in an anthology of Clarke's stories, it has been singled out for comment. In 1958, science fiction, fantasy, and horror writer Fritz Leiber identified "The Star" as "unusual and controversy–rousing." Subsequent criticism, however, has been almost unanimous in commending the story's complex ambiguities. By 1978 science fiction writer and literary critic Thomas M. Disch named "The Star" one of Clarke's "few undeniable classics." Genre critic George Edgar Slusser, focuses on the story's Odyssey-like circular structure. He notes that even though the reader does not see it through to the end, the voyage of discovery out does conclude with a return voyage home. He also comments on the paradox of a Jesuit finding what seems like proof of cosmic indifference together with proof of the existence of the Star of Bethlehem. In a comparison with the H. G. Wells story of the same title, John Hollow pronounces

"The Star" "anti-Christian," and focuses on the emotional torment of the Jesuit suddenly forced to reevaluate his Earth-centered view of Creation. Similarly, Patricia Ferrara views the story as a challenge to the morality of viewing the universe as human-centered. Daniel Born ranks "The Star" with other science fiction stories of a future in which "Christianity is tested . . . and found to be wanting."

In 1980 Alexander Nedelkovich found elements in the story of the same homocentrism that most commentators believe Clarke intended to criticize. He considers it an unfortunate choice for Clarke to have portrayed an alien race enough like humans to automatically elicit both sympathy and empathy: is the story's tragedy, he wonders, "only in the loss of a civilization *we like*?" He assesses it overall, however, as an excellent story that contributed to the development of science fiction from mere "space opera" to more thoughtful considerations.

Written early in his long and productive career, "The Star" evinces many of the qualities that critics have consistently noted in Clarke's fiction. His stories, here as elsewhere, seamlessly interweaves scientific facts in a way that has become his trademark: Clarke is universally acknowledged as a master of "hard" science fiction, rarely departing from known fact or reasonable extrapolation.

Criticism

Theresa M. Girard

Girard is finishing a Ph.D. in science fiction and feminist theory. She received her Master's degree by completing her essay on Arthur C. Clarke's Childhood's End. *In the following essay she discusses the religious beliefs that are central to "The Star" and many of Clarke's stories.*

At the age of eighty, Arthur C. Clarke has received every honor possible for his science fiction writing, including numerous Hugo Awards, Nebula Awards, John W. Campbell Awards, and Jupiter Awards. In addition, he has also received awards for his nonfiction writing, inventions, innovations, and service to humanity. Clarke received the 1982

What Do I Read Next?

- *The Nine Billion Names of God: The Best Short Stories of Arthur C. Clarke* (1967) by Arthur C. Clarke. This collection includes the title story "The Nine Billion Names of God." This story deals with a philosophical confrontation between Western scientists and the religious beliefs of Tibetan monks.

- *Childhood's End* (1953) by Arthur C. Clarke. This was the first of Clarke's major novels to win wide public acclaim. It deals with the evolution of utopia imposed on Earth by an alien race which confines humanity to its own planet by eliminating space travel.

- *2001: A Space Odyssey* (1968) derives from his short story "The Sentinel" and was written concurrently with the screenplay for the motion picture of the same name The novel is divided into sections. In the first section, a monolith appears on Earth and signals the dawn of man by nudging pre-homo-sapiens into learning about tools and taking a giant evolutionary step. In the next section, set in 2001, humans find a second monolith on the moon and set out to track the signal it is transmitting to a distant receiver. Clarke continued the saga in three further works: 2010: Odyssey Two (1982); 2061: Odyssey Three (1987), and 3001: The Final Odyssey (1997).

- "Nightfall" (1941) by Isaac Asimov. "Nightfall" has been voted the best science fiction short story of all time by the Science Fiction Writers of America. The story is about a world which has six suns, at least one of which is always shining. Once every two thousand years, however, the planet's alignment is such that the sky becomes dark and true night comes to the world. Because of the incredibly long periods between nightfalls, the idea of total darkness has become a disbelieved legend on the planet. The story revolves around the effect that nightfall has on that civilization.

- *Starship Troopers* (1959) by Robert Heinlein. This was one of Heinlein's line of "young adult" novels, but it is often considered overly violent and right-wing. It won a 1960 Hugo award, but earned Heinlein a reputation as a militarist or even fascist. The story revolves around a young man who joins the military as a professional soldier in the "Bug War" against insect-like aliens. It was released as a motion picture, carrying an "R" rating because of the violence, in 1997.

- *A Canticle for Leibowitz* (1960) by Walter M. Miller, Jr. Emphasizing the cyclical nature of history, Miller's Hugo Award-winning novel depicts the reestablishment of Western civilization following a nuclear catastrophe which has thrown the world into a new Dark Ages.

Marconi Fellowship Award, which is "granted to individuals who have made a significant contribution to the advancement of the technology of communications through discoveries, inventions or innovations in the physical or information sciences or engineering." In 1986, Clarke was awarded the Science Fiction Writers of America Grand Master Award for life achievement and, in 1989, was given the honor of Commander of the British Empire (CBE), by Queen Elizabeth, for service to British cultural interests in Sri Lanka.

Clarke received one of his first awards, the Hugo, for "The Star." The story is told in first-person narration by a narrator who only identifies himself as a Jesuit astrophysicist. A Jesuit is a Roman Catholic member of a religious order founded by Saint Ignatius of Loyola. The Jesuits are known for their missions of exploration and their scientific endeavors. On the North American continent, Jesuits were among the first to do missionary work among Native Americans. Several universities, including Notre Dame in Indiana, Loyola Uni-

> The reader is to assume that a man of God can also be a man of science and vice versa."

versity in Chicago, and the University of Detroit in Michigan were founded by the Jesuits. They were the first Europeans to establish trade relations with the Japanese.

It is with all of these influences in mind that Clarke made his narrator a Jesuit priest. This is obvious when the narrator refers to "tampering with the truth which often gave my order a bad name in the olden days." He wrestles with his conscience about what to tell the crew and when to tell them. On the one hand, he says that anyone can figure out what he knows because the "facts are there for all to read." However, on the other hand, he feels that the crew is "already sufficiently depressed." He doesn't have to tamper with the truth, but he can withhold his conclusion and, if questioned about it, he can simply say that he thought that they would know based on the information they had gathered. In that way, if they don't figure it out, he will not have to try to reconcile the facts with his beliefs in God and his religion. His faith has been shaken and he is not sure if he could take a full-fledged attack by the atheists armed with the new knowledge.

Clarke continues his assault on the beliefs of the Jesuit through the crew and, in particular, Dr. Chandler. The reader only knows that Dr. Chandler is a medical man. Clarke seems to impose his own beliefs on the doctor when he has the priest wonder why medical men are notorious atheists. The doctor, addressing the priest on the observation deck, talks about how the universe goes on forever and says that "perhaps Something made it." He continues by wondering how the priest can expect anyone to believe that, even if God made it, God would have any special interest in humanity. The narrator does not respond with theological arguments, but, instead, points out all of his scientific writing. The reader is to assume that, therefore, a man of God can also be a man of science and vice versa.

The introspection by the narrator serves a two-fold purpose. One purpose is to heighten the sus-

pense as to what he has discovered. The other purpose is to give background information so that the suspense will have some grounding in fact and history. For example, the narrator wonders what the founder of his order, Ignatius of Loyola, would do in a similar situation, if his faith would have risen to the challenge as the narrator feels his has not. The reader is also introduced to the motto of the Jesuits, *Ad Maiorem Dei Gloriam,* but is not, significantly, given the English translation "To the Greater Glory of God." This is what the narrator feels he can no longer believe. He cannot believe that the destruction of a civilization at its height contributes to the glory of God.

The nationalities of the narrator and the crew are never mentioned anywhere in the story. This lack of differentiation serves to unite humanity against the cosmos. Clearly, Clarke is saying that humanity can only achieve the stars through cooperation of all of the people of earth. Not only does he see unity in the people of earth, but he sees a similarity in people of the universe. Because the ancient civilization has been destroyed at its height, the narrator says that, "even if they had not been so disturbingly human," they would still have been upset and depressed. The fact that the crew was so far from home and lonely, they were more touched by the similarities between the two worlds. He talks about their music, their architecture, and even the children playing by the sea, much like earth children. He makes no distinction between nationalities or races, other than to compare their destruction to the rise and fall of nations and cultures on earth. The priest contrasts it by saying that he cannot understand how a merciful God could destroy a race "in the full flower of its achievement." The narrator even refers to ancient civilizations on other worlds which had run their course and left only their ruins behind. Those did not compare to the wholesale, mindless destruction incurred by the supernova. He fails to see how, at the risk of blasphemy, God could have signaled the birth of His Son through such wholesale slaughter.

The question of individual religions is not a question that Clarke raises directly in the story. However, he does imply that organized belief in a Godhead who cares for His "children" on earth, seems to be homocentric as well as extremely arrogant. Clarke is not simply addressing the religious belief of Roman Catholic by having a Catholic, Jesuit priest as narrator, but he is using the scientific religious man as a pawn to show how the two are not compatible. He sets up his story to reflect his own belief that religion is nonsense. Only science is fact and space travel will show humans the way, and achieving space travel requires the cooperation of all of humanity.

Source: Theresa M. Girard, for *Short Stories for Students*, Gale, 1998.

Patricia Ferrara

In the following excerpt, Ferrera suggests that "The Star" derives its themes from the William Wordsworth poem "Ode: Intimations." She concludes her analysis with an interpretation of the story as a challenge to the morality of viewing God and the universe as human-centered.

Much of Arthur C. Clarke's fiction is oriented towards rapid and simplistic plot development in the way that most pulp fiction is, frequently to the detriment of any other literary values; yet his fiction deserves more critical attention than its faults warrant. Noting this, Michael Thron has argued that we should judge the value of Clarke's fiction, not by literary standards, but by the value of the ideas it contains, and many of the other critics in Joseph Olander's collection of essays seem to agree implicitly with this judgment, mixing esthetics with scientific and philosophic appeal as criteria in applied criticism. But T. S. Eliot points out that great or even good fiction of any genre is not remarkable for the quality of the ideas embodied in it; *King Lear* and the *Divine Comedy,* he says, do not offer much in the realm of abstract thought, and their power does not come from the strength of the reader's shared belief in the social and religious philosophies presented in the works. Clarke varies only slightly from this norm in offering somewhat new scientific ideas as well as elaborating on old philosophical ones. Certainly, his value as a popular scientific thinker who can help the reader understand the implications of space travel and research is without question. His "Death and the Senator" (1961) is a good hypothetical scenario of what could happen if the United States did not continue its space research. It is one of his most reprinted stories largely because of this aspect of relevancy (or even propaganda). The scientific ideas in the story are significant enough for it to have been read before the U. S. House of Representatives Committee on Astronautics on March 14, 1972. But as literature, it is sentimental and predictable: a man finds that his imminent death can ennoble him. The theme is not new, nor is it particularly well-realized, and the

> The juxtaposition of the coldly beautiful objectivity of space with the intensely subjective vision of the narrator is powerful in a literary way, unrelated to the values of the ideas it embodies."

work suffers from a lack of character development and imagery.

The science fiction story's lack of traditional literary merit is often dismissed on the basis of generic criteria. Asimov's defense of the genre's poor characterization is typical:

> Science fiction stories are notoriously weak on characterization as compared with mainstream stories. At least, so the critics say.
>
> I am always struck with impatience at such cavils. Even if it be true, there happens to be a good reason for it. The characters are a smaller portion of science fiction than of the mainstream. . . .
>
> The double task of building the background society and developing the foreground plot is extremely difficult, and it requires an extraordinary amount of the writer's attention. There is that much less attention that is, or can be, paid to the characters. There is, physically less room in the story for character development.

. . . [More] than once Clarke has managed to make all the elements in his story work together, as he does in "The Star." This story brings up perhaps the trickiest and most important criterion to apply to Clarke: his intertextuality with other writers. If his novels and short stories are important as literature, they should somehow contain narrative patterns and literary tropes which form the basis of other important literature. Despite arguing for new criteria, Slusser's examination of the voyage pattern in the *Space Odysseys of Arthur C. Clarke* places Clarke clearly within a literary tradition. John Hollow has also noted Clarke's roots in such poets as Tennyson and Houseman, and Slusser has mentioned his similarity to Keats. However, we can go one step further and find a highly developed relationship between

Wordsworth's "Ode: Intimations" and Clarke's "The Star" which shows clearly the value of applying literary, rather than sociological, scientific, or philosophical criteria to Clarke's fiction. One of the central tropes of Clarke's work, that of children on a beach in juxtaposition with a vision of eternity, seems to come, not from Houseman or from H. G. Wells, or from Keats, but from Wordsworth's ode. The debt is particularly strong in "The Star," in which Clarke places his narrator in circumstances ironically parallel to those of Wordsworth's narrator, gives him a vision of children on the beach which is similar to Wordsworth's, yet turns Wordsworth's tropes inside out to defy and reverse Wordsworthian meaning. This parallel may seem extraordinary, simply because no one thinks of looking for such a connection between a mainstream work and science fiction. And this is probably why no critic has seen it previously. Yet given Clarke's education in English schools in the early part of the century, he must have read a considerable amount of Wordsworth, including this famous poem. This virtual certainty combined with strong textual parallels would make a convincing argument that one mainstream author was ringing changes on another mainstream author's score. And as Stanley Fish points out, to discover that a recognized work is better than anyone thought it was should be a sure way of gaining acceptance for one's view. The parallels between Clarke's story and Wordsworth's poem are strong enough to persuade the reader of the possibility that the two works interact in this fashion, and open the door to the consideration of other such parallels between science fiction and the mainstream.

For the Wordsworthian narrator, the child's "first affections" will allow the man he has become to transport himself metaphorically:

> Hence in a season of calm weather Though inland far we be, Our Souls have sight of that immortal sea Which brought us hither, Can in a moment travel thither, And see the Children sport upon the shore, And hear the mighty waters rolling evermore.

The similarity to Clarke's vision speaks for itself:

> One scene is still before my eyes—a group of children on a beach of strange blue sand, playing in the waves as children play on Earth. Curious whiplike trees line the shore, and some very large animal is wading in the shallows yet attracting no attention at all.

Many writers have described figures on a beach, but several key features point to a clearly Wordsworthian basis for Clarke's passage: the plural rather than singular number of figures; the circumstance of their being children rather than adults; the circumstance of both groups playing, rather than looking at the stars; and the narrator seeing them only once, and then remembering them in tranquility as he works out his spiritual difficulties. The achingly nostalgic context of the vision is much different from Keats or Houseman; and the lack of a progressive vision at different points in time eliminates Wells as a primary source. This vision and many other correlations between Wordsworth's poem and Clarke's story lay the groundwork for Clarke's final disruption of Wordsworth's metaphor.

Both works introduce us to troubled narrators, the source of whose mental turmoil is at first unclear, but becomes clear as the works progress. "Ode: Intimations" relates the narrator's subjective search for the faded glory of nature, which derives from "our life's Star," the soul. The narrator mourns that only the youth, "Nature's priest," has contact with the light of this Star, which has "elsewhere had its setting / And cometh from afar." Clarke literally sends "Nature's priest," a Jesuit-astrophysicist, off to look for a real star, turning Wordsworth's metaphors into plot realities. In the process of his investigation, he finds the vision of eternity, the filmstrip of the children on the beach, just as Wordsworth's narrator discovers the metaphor of the children during his progress. But this vision is not the end of the Jesuit's discoveries, any more than it is the end of Wordsworth's discoveries in his poem. Wordsworth's narrator finds new ways of placing himself within nature, as nature's center. Clarke's narrator finds unexpected confirmation of Wordsworth's anthropocentric universe which is morally insupportable: God did favor mankind above all races, blowing this star into destruction in order to signal to man the birth of the Christ child. "Our life's Star" did indeed "set" or die, taking with it an entire civilization, before it could shine briefly for man.

Wordsworth deliberately confuses nature-as-metaphor-for-self with nature and self as two separate entities. The poem's narrator makes a metaphorical search through his subjective universe for the light of "our life's Star." Clarke objects to such subjectivity because it assumes that man is the center of the universe. It is this pathetic fallacy turned into a principle of philosophy which Clarke turns topsy-turvy. The idea of anthropocentrism which is unquestioned and comforting in Wordsworth is questioned and discomfortable in its morality in Clarke.

Clarke's objective universe parallels Wordsworth's subjective one. This reversal of Wordsworth's tropes de-anthropocentrises nature without removing its wonder and emotional impact. Because Wordsworth's narrator searches for some way to *feel* immortal by regaining a state of mind, his vision of the seashore is undetailed and almost entirely metaphorical; there is no sense of a remembrance of an actual occurrence. In Clarke's story, the vision of the children on the seashore is detailed and concrete. Clarke's children, like the nature which surrounds them, cannot be appropriated as metaphors for the self. They are (or were) real, and the narrator remembers them only because he actually saw them on a filmstrip. Clarke underlines the otherness of the vision: these children are not human, and the concrete details of the "strange blue sand" and "curious whiplike trees" and the unknown "large animal" indicate the narrator's distance from the children and nature. Clarke's narrator empathizes with the dead race with painful acuity, but recognizes them as irretrievably alien. He is not even momentarily tempted to project his own changed view of nature onto the universe. The stars shine with "undiminished brilliance" throughout his spiritual difficulties. The glory remains in the flower. And despite his strongly emotional and subjective response to nature, no pansy will ever ask this man a question. Instead, he asks himself why a civilization had to be destroyed when it was in "full flower." In Wordsworth's universe nature creates questions, images, and metaphors; Clarke's Jesuit clearly recognizes that he invents the metaphor and the question. The universe cannot speak, yet continually demands to be recognized as the foundation of ideas about God and man. Both narrators struggle to resolve a newly felt estrangement from nature; the Jesuit leaves the question unresolved because he sees a comfortingly subjective nature as emotionally irreconcilable to morality, requiring a cold-hearted acceptance of man's right to primacy in the universe. Clarke implicitly rejects Wordsworth's metaphoric approach to nature as a philosophy, and hence he also rejects his resulting resolution, leaving instead an open ending. The Jesuit's painful moral paralysis is the result of realizing that these beings with whom he and the reader empathize will remain forever separate from us because our only way of retrieving unity with the cosmos requires us to assume a philosophical stance which rejects our brotherhood with the beings who inhabit it.

Clarke's overall strategy in "The Star" is intertextual. The method of its intertextuality is also clearly literary—a reversal of tropes—and it is extremely well done. In a very Bloomian manner, Clarke has disrupted Wordsworth's text with his own, thus moving into the mainstream of fiction. The story also has a definitely literary structure of some sophistication. It carefully embodies its stance in literary tropes, such as in the journey towards the star and the truly poignant, rather than merely sentimental, vision of the children on the beach. Other sheerly literary values abound. The juxtaposition of the coldly beautiful objectivity of space with the intensely subjective vision of the narrator is powerful in a literary way, unrelated to the values of the ideas it embodies. The first person narration vividly conveys the disembodied, alienated voice of the main character, the Jesuit; and in this story the cardboard nature of the other characters on the spaceship is a literary merit, since it enhances the intense subjectivity and isolation of the Jesuit, who feels closer to the cosmos and the dead civilization than to his own shipmates.

It could be argued that "The Star" is important because it presents Clarke's idea of God, and much attention has focussed on this aspect of the story and of Clarke's fiction in general. However, the story presents no definite image of God, but rather a challenge to the morality of viewing God and the universe as man-centered, a challenge to the Romantic view. Other critics interpret the work variously. Slusser and Hollow disagree entirely on the nature of the Jesuit's problem. Hollow thinks the supernova does not prove the Christian God's existence, while Slusser feels that proof of the existence of a Christian God coincides with proof of cosmic indifference. Roger Bozzetto suggests that science has taken on God's comforting and humanistic moral validity. The basic disagreement about Clarke's ideas result from literary ambiguity rather than philosophical brilliance. As the narrator points out, the problem of God's power and man's questions appears in the Book of Job. There is nothing philosophically new here. And Clarke himself had already treated the scientific aspect of the Star of Bethlehem in an essay entitled "The Star of the Magi" before he wrote the short story, making a second statement scientifically redundant. While the scientific bent of Clarke's imagination is a necessary element in his fiction, if he and other science fiction writers are going to receive serious critical attention, critics should judge the genre by accepted literary criteria. Being a science fiction writer does not entitle one to special nonliterary criteria. And despite Clarke's many failings, his work at its best has more than sufficient merit to warrant such attention.

Source: Patricia Ferrara, "Nature's Priest: Establishing Literary Criteria for Arthur C. Clarke's 'The Star'," in *Extrapolation,* Vol. 28, No. 2, Summer, 1987, pp. 148–58.

Daniel Born

In the following excerpt, Born considers that Clarke's characterization of the Jesuit astrophysicist in "The Star" renders the story superior to most antireligious science fiction.

[Two] stories serve as good examples of how Christianity is tested in a science fiction future and found to be wanting. However, in these stories, Harry Harrison's "The Streets of Ashkelon" and Clarke's "The Star," the anti-Christian rhetoric assumes more power in part because the men of faith have ceased to appear as ridiculous primitives. In Clarke's story, by far the most devastating in terms of casting doubt on Christianity's credibility, the priest is actually portrayed in a sympathetic light. Also, while the real purpose of the first three stories already examined is a glorification of scientific culture—to which the Christian merely serves as a foil—the attention of Harrison's and Clarke's stories is solidly upon the men of faith themselves. The scientific frames of reference in which Christianity is tested are not eulogized but rather simply assumed to be reliable. . . .

The Jesuit astrophysicist in Clarke's "The Star" poses, in several ways, a contrast to the four previous Christian protagonists [discussed in an unexcerpted portion of the essay]. Most noticeable is his first-person narration. We see the Christian's point of view through his own eyes rather than from the author's omniscient vantage point, and in this case that means the character is viewed with neither antagonism nor irony. And besides being a sympathetic character, the astrophysicist is an intellectual and a scientist. This further distinguishes "The Star" from the run-of-the-mill antireligious science fiction story—the Jesuit is evidence that one man can hold both religious and scientific attitudes. He cannot be written off as an intellectual dwarf because he establishes his credentials almost immediately: "It was, I think, the apparent incongruity of my position that caused most amusement to the crew. In vain I would point to my three papers in the *Astrophysical Journal,* my five in the *Monthly Notices of the Royal Astronomical Society.* I would remind them that my order has long been famous for its scientific works."

Besides describing his relationship to the other members of the crew, the Jesuit reveals himself further by providing details of the decor in his living quarters. On his wall hang a crucifix and a Rubens engraving of Loyola. These details taken together with his status on board ship all add up to the impression that piety and intellect can coexist, and the conjunction of these in the Jesuit is what makes his discovery of the supernova's date of explosion so dreadful and poignant. Gary Wolfe has commented that "though his [Clarke's] stories are weak in characterization and often crude in style, they occasionally attain a sort of science fiction version of the sublime—a vision at once humane and technological, personal and cosmic." It is Clarke's artistic choice and characterization of a Jesuit both religious and scientific that accounts for the "sublime" quality of "The Star." The story told from an agnostic or atheistic viewpoint would be ineffective since the problem of evil exists as a "problem" primarily for the theist—how can a just God allow evil? The Jesuit realizes that his problem is a unique one, a product of belief, because for the atheist "there is no divine justice, for there is no God."

At the same time, the Jesuit is capable of losing his faith because he, as a responsible scientist, takes scientific evidence seriously. His choices are three, in light of the evidence: (1) Accept a peculiarly perverse God who willfully destroyed a civilization while creating what appeared on Earth as the Star of Bethlehem; (2) Accept God's purposes in the universe as so incomprehensible to human understanding that they appear amoral and meaningless to a traditional Christian ethic; (3) Stop believing God exists. Although Roger Elwood remarks that among science fiction writers, scientists, and philosophers "it is generally agreed by all sides that . . . no scientific experiment can prove or disprove God's existence," Clarke postulates a situation where the evidence approaches such an experimental possibility. And it should be noted that 1955 was the year when Clarke not only published " The Star," but philosopher Antony Flew also asked his famous question, which still reverberates in college and seminary classrooms: "What would have to occur or to have occurred to constitute . . . a disproof of the love of, or of the existence of, God?" Clarke's story seems tailored to such a query.

If the Jesuit's God has not disappeared, then he has at least become unrecognizable in terms of the crucifix hanging on the wall. J. Norman King comments that man, who must think within categories of space and time, had, as we have seen, imaginatively visualized a God—symbol and basis of human value and meaning—as located just beyond the spheres, hovering concernedly—or even retributively—near to man. But as the distance, spatial and temporal, is indefinitely extended, the same image of God results in pushing that God farther and farther away until he virtually disappears from the galactic universe.

Whatever the differences among these five stories—the Christian's vision being alternately painted as superstitious and savage, naively destructive, or simply inadequate—they all posit an inherent antagonism between Christian and empirical weltanschauungen, and the Christian paradigm is found defective and/or outmoded every time. Their content and conclusions are dictated by the strict adherence to positivism, which Gunn argues is central to all science fiction about religion. However, as suggested earlier, science fiction bound to such positivistic dogma perhaps loses its speculative quality because the possibilities are narrowly limited a priori. This condition seems averse to the very nature of speculative fiction. . . .

Source: Daniel Born, ''Character as Perception: Science Fiction and the Christian Man of Faith,'' in *Extrapolation*, Vol. 24, No. 3, Fall, 1983, pp. 251–71.

Alexander Nedelkovich

The excerpt printed below is part of a longer essay comparing ''The Star,'' by Arthur C. Clarke, ''Neutron Star'' by Larry Niven, and ''To the Dark Star'' by Robert Silverberg. Nedelkovich identifies both strengths and shortcomings in Clarke's narrative. Nedelkovich concludes that this widely read story's focus on character contributed to the development of science fiction as a genre.

Clarke's story opens with the famous sentence (one of the best introductory sentences ever in the American science-fiction short story): ''It is three thousand light-years to the Vatican.'' The narrator is, curiously, a Jesuit priest who is also a practicing astronomer and a space-traveler, and he is a member (the chief astrophysicist) of a rather multitudinous expedition which surveys the remains of a supernova that exploded 6,000 years before. The story is set in the thirtieth century. (If it is true that one of the jobs of literary criticism is to *re-create* the work of art, then I should withhold the punch line from you and try to build suspense. But I will not.) The hero computes that the light of this supernova, which killed an entire race of people, was *the* star of Bethlehem; and the readers learn this only in

> **The story told from an agnostic or atheistic viewpoint would be ineffective since the problem of evil exists as a 'problem' primarily for the theist—how can a just God allow evil?''**

the last sentence of the story, which makes for one of the most famous, classical punch lines in the history of the science-fiction short story. As the ship, with its precious cargo of information, alien artifacts, and works of art, speeds back towards Earth, the Jesuit grieves over the theological and moral implications of his discovery.

In my opinion, Clarke errs against plausibility in one matter. He postulates that the destroyed civilization, in the years before its destruction, could reach its outermost planet, its equivalent of Pluto, with such huge machinery and so much cargo that a vast bunkered museum was built there and marked by a colossal stone pillar—''The pylon . . . a mile high when it was built''—but they did not put a colony of their people into that same shelter to survive. The Jesuit even says, ''It will take us generations to examine all the treasures that were placed in the Vault. They had plenty of time to prepare, for their sun must have given its first warnings many years before its final detonation.'' Is it credible that they would have such priorities, that they would build a titanic museum instead of a place where hundreds could live?. . .

There is one unpleasant matter. I have to say that in ''The Star,'' Clarke reveals an attitude toward aliens which is odd and, in my view, quite unacceptable. Of course, a narrator speaks in the story, not the author, but nevertheless, consider these three points. (1) There are no living aliens in the story even though there easily could have been. It is quite obvious and it really strikes us that there should have been a survival colony in the bunker, not the colossal museum. Perhaps the author went out of his way so that he would not have to deal with any aliens. (2) The preserved picture of the aliens show them to be ''disturbingly human'' in appearance—this should mean, very strongly anthropomorphic. (3) About two hundred words are spent insisting that the aliens were good according to Earth standards of goodness, even "musical" in speech. Is tragedy in the loss of a civilization or only in the loss of a civilization *we like*? "They could travel freely enough between the planets of their own sun, but they had not yet learned to cross the interstellar gulfs, and the nearest solar system was a hundred light-years away. Yet even had they possessed the secret of the Transfinite drive no more than a few millions could have been saved. Perhaps it was better thus."

Now imagine a mainstream writer, F. Scott Fitzgerald, for instance, writing something in this general vein and having his narrator, Nick Carraway, say:

> What a lovely, big heap of ruins I saw at West Egg! Gatsby's mansion had caved in, you see, roof and all, during a big party, and all doors were locked, so everybody was killed. Saw their pictures—they all looked like me. I think it is a tragedy because they weren't just any people, they looked disturbingly like me. Oh, and there was a vault there, uncollapsed, quite safe, within their reach, but they didn't go for shelter there, they all just flung their medallions and pocketwatches there, and a tape recorder. Thinking about those doors: even had the doors been wide open, only a few dozen people would have saved themselves. Perhaps it was better thus.

This may be painful to a science-fiction fan, but if science fiction is good literature, why not put its best writers and the best mainstream writers up against one another and just look at them? Perhaps it is better thus. . . .

In so many stories about space travel, the discovery of an alien civilization or some such thing is never reported, brought back only by the lonely ship, practically by word of mouth, in a somewhat medieval fashion. One example of this occurs in Clarke's story: if the ship with the Jesuit should crash, no one would ever know what was discovered, if anything. All-the-eggs-in-one-starship, then. . . .

"The Star" opens and closes with the Jesuit Father in his cell, thinking, contemplating, as the spacecraft is voyaging back to Earth. Inside that frame is the canvas itself: remembered discussions on board the ship before the arrival at the star and remembered images of the exploration itself. But there are also brief glimpses of the distant past of 6,000 years ago when the civilization in question still existed. And much is said about what will happen on Earth when the discovery is revealed.

This structure reminds me of a canvas in a solid, four-sided frame, with an attached piece of painting behind it and another in front of it. The reader has to change telescopes several times. But all of this is firmly integrated into the confessional monologue. The story strikes me as cold and sad, a monotone voice in a little room. Reading it, I seem to hear a clock tick. Clarke's is the only story I have ever read that detonates a supernova quietly. There is a good reason for the shortness of the story: this solitary contemplation could not go on much longer without, to put it bluntly, getting dull. . . .

Clarke's hero, the Jesuit, seems to be a very quiet and composed person. He is primarily concerned with the broad moral and theological implications of his discovery. That discovery he still does not share with anybody. (So, if anything should happen to him, the discovery could be buried forever; thus he increases and prolongs the danger to a piece of scientific knowledge.) Nonetheless, Clarke's excellent story, which appeared in 1955 and was widely read, probably has contributed to the development of the science-fiction genre by focusing so successfully on things other than space opera. The personality of the narrator must have been helpful. . . .

Source: Alexander Nedelkovich, "The Stellar Parallels: Robert Silverberg, Larry Niven, and Arthur C. Clarke," in *Extrapolation,* Vol. 21, No. 4, Winter, 1980, pp. 348–60.

John Hollow

In the following essay, Hollow discusses the theological philosophy espoused in "The Star," comparing the story to another story by the same title written by H. G. Wells in the nineteenth century.

Clarke's response to Wells' legacy can perhaps best be presented by comparing two of their stories, both of which happen to be entitled "The Star" (Wells, 1897; Clarke, 1955). Clarke's story does not seem, at least not consciously, to have been meant to allude to that of his predecessor, but both refer to the Star of Bethlehem, both contemplate the seemingly meaningless destruction of a civilization, and both finally are about whether the universe can be understood.

In Wells' story, a planetoid wanders into our solar system, where it collides with Neptune and ignites into a giant fireball, the new "star" of the title. As these interlocked bodies narrowly miss the Earth on their fall into the Sun, the result on our planet is terrible storms, earthquakes, and a flood almost as universal as that described in Genesis.

The theme is typically Wellsian: we humans, who thought ourselves the center of creation, suddenly realize that we are no more guaranteed survival than was Neptune. Our fate, for that matter, would be no more detectable over the vast distances of space than was that of whatever beings may have lived on that planet. A new star in the heavens, says the story, is much more likely to announce that the universe is a random and uncaring place than that a savior is born.

Clarke's story, in turn, is equally anti-Christian. A Jesuit priest, an astrophysicist, is returning to Earth from an expedition to investigate the remains of a supernova at the extreme edge of our galaxy. The investigators have found, buried on the planet which must have been the Pluto of the destroyed system, a time fault filled with the relics of a brilliant and beautiful civilization, destroyed when the star exploded. "It is one thing for a race to fail and die, as nations and cultures have done on Earth," the Jesuit says to himself; "but to be destroyed so completely in the full flower of its achievement, leaving no survivors—how can that be reconciled with the mercy of God?"

"I know in what year the light of this colossal conflagration reached our Earth," he says. "I know how brilliantly the supernova whose corpse now dwindles behind our speeding ship once shown in terrestrial skies. I know how it must have blazed low in the east before sunrise, like a beacon in the oriental dawn." "What was the need to give these people to the fire," he cries out; was it "that the symbol of their passing might shine above Bethlehem?"

It is not the ruin of civilizations that undermines the priest's faith. As he says, he and several other members of the expedition have "seen the ruins of ancient civilizations on other worlds." To such routine disasters he is able to answer, as the voice from the whirlwind answers Job, that "God has no need to justify His actions to man. He who built the Universe can destroy it when He chooses." The priest's real difficulty is the same as that of the people in Wells' story: his religion has claimed too much. The human assumption that this world is the center of the cosmos, which is exemplified in both stories by the Star of the Magi, is bound sooner or later to come up against the fact of other inhabited planets; perhaps in very dramatic fashion. Are we to believe, asks Clarke's story, that God so loved this world that He destroyed another for it? It would be better, the priest is close to deciding, if the crucifix

> **The universe may be indifferent, but the story offers intelligent life and beauty as contrary suggestions, as aspects of existence which make total pessimism uncertain."**

were to be seen as "an empty symbol," if humans were to admit that the Earth-centered view of the universe has difficulties which not even the great founder of his order, not even the far-seeing Loyola of the Rubens engraving, could foresee.

If the priest is to keep his intellectual honesty, he must do as the people in Wells' story do: he must give up the idea of divine favor. (It is even suggested, in Wells' story, that such a surrender would bring about a "new brotherhood" among men, would make of the world a more Christian place than Christianity managed to do.) The priest must realize that the state of human knowledge is as the ship's doctor describes it to him one day when the two of them are looking out from the ship's observation deck at the "stars and nebulae" swinging "in silent, endless arcs." "Well, Father," the doctor says, "it goes on forever and forever, and perhaps *something* made it. But how you can believe that something has a special interest in us and our miserable little world—that beats me." Or as Clarke has said in another context, in answer to the psalmist's "What is man that Thou art mindful of him?": "What indeed?" ("Of Space and Spirit," 1959).

The priest has to learn to see all peoples, his own and those of the destroyed civilization, as the latter present themselves in one of the "visual records" they left in the time vault: as children playing on a beach. The image does not favor one people over another; instead, it captures, as it always has, the poignant beauty of mortality, especially of mortality seen against the magnificent immensity of the universe. Some cultures may be swept away, as in Housman's "Smooth Between Sea and Land"; some cultures may learn to sail the sea, as in Clarke's "Transience." The point is that both are beautiful. The passing of culture is no worse than the passing of a generation, than the passing of an individual. We must concentrate, as does the art of the destroyed civilization, on the moment of youth against the sweep of time, on the moment of intelligent life against the background of death. From such a viewpoint, focused on such an image, it still might be possible for the Jesuit to hope that such beauty—simply because it is beautiful—is *Ad Majorem Dei Gloriam*. The universe and the existence of life in it still may testify to the glory of a creator.

The difference between Wells' "The Star" and Clarke's "The Star" is this faint hope still available to the priest. In Wells' story, the master mathematician, who has been staying up night and day calculating the path of the new "star," finally stands at his window and says, as if to the new star: "You may kill me. . . . But I can hold you—and all of the universe for that matter—in the grip of this little brain." What he means, of course, is that he has the words and the numbers to describe the catastrophe that is about to happen. He is able to conclude that the Earth is not the center of a planned universe, that the human race "has lived in vain." He can only stare his doom in the face, comfort himself that he has understanding, and say bravely: "I would not change. Even now."

For Clarke, as we have seen, the issue is not—at least not yet—so clear. The priest's too limited view of the universe is undermined by the timing of the supernova, but Clarke's story does not suggest that the destroyed civilization lived in vain, nor does it conclude that the universe was not made by *something*. George Edgar Slusser has said that, "paradoxically, the hero's perception of cosmic indifference coincides with clear proof of the Christian religion—the Biblical account was correct after all, there was a Star of Bethlehem" I am fairly certain that the supernova is *not* supposed to be a "clear proof of the Christian religion," but I do think Slusser is correct when he describes the story's "final juxtaposition" as "that of a lyrically heightened voice brooding on the spectacle of universal indifference." And I am sure that the story wants the outcome of such brooding to be open-ended, not to be simply the Wellsian conclusion that the cosmos is a random as well as a deadly place. The universe may be indifferent—that is certainly one of the conclusions the priest could come to—

but the story offers intelligent life and beauty as contrary suggestions, as aspects of existence which make total pessimism uncertain.

Source: John Hollow, in his *Against the Night, the Stars: The Science Fiction of Arthur C. Clarke,* Ohio University Press, 1976, pp. 14–8.

Sources

Clarke, Arthur C. *The Other Side of the Sky,* Signet, 1959, p. vi.

Hollow, John. *Against the Night, the Stars: The Science Fiction of Arthur C. Clarke* Harcourt Brace Jovanovich, 1983, 197 p.

Leiber, Fritz. "Engaging Adventure Tales," in *Chicago Sunday Tribune Magazine,* February 16, 1958, p. 7.

McAleer, Neil. *Arthur C. Clarke: The Authorized Biography,* Contemporary Books, 1992, pp. 44, 82-83, 114, 296.

Rabkin, Eric S. *Arthur C. Clarke: Starmont Reader's Guide 1,* Starmont House, 1980, p. 57.

Reid, Robin Anne. *Arthur C. Clarke: A Critical Companion,* Greenwood Press, 1997.

Slusser, George Edgar. *The Space Odysseys of Arthur C. Clarke,* Borgo Press, 1978, 64 p.

Further Reading

Aldiss, Brian W. *Trillion Year Spree,* Avon Books, 1986.
    A history of science fiction. Aldiss places the genesis of the genre in Gothic literature and traces it through late twentieth century literature and film.

Clute, John and Peter Nicholls, eds. *The Encyclopedia of Science Fiction.* New York: St. Martin's, 1995.
    A carefully compiled reference work.

Olander, Joseph D. Olander and Martin Harry Greenberg, eds. *Arthur C. Clarke.* New York: Taplinger Publishing Company, 1977.
    Nine critical essays by writers, critics, and academicians.

Reid, Robin Anne. *Arthur C. Clarke: A Critical Companion.* Westport, Conn.: Greenwood Press, 1997.
    Provides biographical information about Clarke, analytical readings of Clarke's works, and discusses his place as a preeminent writer of science fiction. Reid also includes an extensive bibliography of Clarke's work.

The Tell-Tale Heart

Edgar Allan Poe
1843

One of Edgar Allan Poe's most famous short stories, "The Tell-Tale Heart," was first published in the January, 1843 edition of James Russell Lowell's *The Pioneer* and was reprinted in the August 23, 1845 issue of *The Broadway Journal*. The story is a psychological portrait of a mad narrator who kills a man and afterward hears his victim's relentless heartbeat. While "The Tell-Tale Heart" and his other short stories were not critically acclaimed during his lifetime, Poe earned respect among his peers as a competent writer, insightful literary critic, and gifted poet, particularly after the publication of his famous poem, "The Raven," in 1845.

After Poe's death in 1849, some critics faulted his obsession with dark and depraved themes. Other critics, like George Woodberry in his 1885 study of Poe, considered "The Tell-Tale Heart" merely a "tale of conscience." But this simplistic view has changed over the years as more complex views of Poe and his works have emerged. Poe is now considered a forefather of two literary genres, detective stories and science fiction, and is regarded as an important writer of psychological thrillers and horror.

"The Tell-Tale Heart" is simultaneously a horror story and psychological thriller told from a first-person perspective. It is admired as an excellent example of how a short story can produce an effect on the reader. Poe believed that all good literature must create a unity of effect on the reader

and this effect must reveal truth or evoke emotions. "The Tell-Tale Heart" exemplifies Poe's ability to expose the dark side of humankind and is a harbinger of novels and films dealing with psychological realism. Poe's work has influenced genres as diverse as French symbolist poetry and Hollywood horror films, and writers as diverse as Ambrose Bierce and Sir Arthur Conan Doyle.

Author Biography

Edgar Allan Poe was born into a theatrical family on January 19, 1809. His father, David Poe, was a lawyer-turned-actor, and his mother, Elizabeth Arnold, was an English actress. Both his parents died before Poe turned three years old, and he was raised by John Allan, a rich businessman, in Richmond, Virginia. Allan never legally adopted Poe, and their relationship became a stormy one after Poe reached his teenage years.

Unlike the narrator in "The Tell-Tale Heart," who claims that he had no desires for the old man's gold, Poe was dependent on Allan for financial support. While Allan funded Poe's education at a private school in England for five years, he failed to support him when he attended the University of Virginia and the United States Military Academy at West Point. Aware that he would never inherit much from his prosperous foster father, Poe embarked on a literary career at the age of twenty-one.

In 1835, Poe secretly married his thirteen-year-old cousin, Virginia Clemm. For the next two years, he worked as an assistant editor for the *Southern Literary Messenger* while publishing fiction and book reviews. He was ill-suited for editorial work. Like his natural father, Poe was an alcoholic. Dismissed by his employer, Poe moved to New York City and later to Philadelphia. He published several works, including "The Narrative of Arthur Gordon Pym" in 1838, "The Fall of the House of Usher" in 1839, and "The Tell-Tale Heart" in 1843. While his writings were well regarded, his financial position was constantly precarious. Poe took on a series of editorial positions, but his alcoholism and contentious temper continued to plague him. In 1845 Poe published "The Raven," his most famous poem. Celebrated as a gifted poet, he failed to win many friends due to his unpleasant temperament. After his wife's death from tuberculosis in 1847, Poe became involved in a number of romances, including one with Elmira Royster that had been

interrupted in his youth. Now Elmira was the widowed Mrs. Shelton. It was during the time they were preparing for their marriage that Poe, for reasons unknown, arrived in Baltimore in late September of 1849. On October 3, he was discovered in a state of semiconsciousness. He died on October 7 without being able to explain what had happened during the last days of his life.

Upon Poe's death in 1849, his one-time friend and literary executor, R. W. Griswold, wrote a libelous obituary in the *New York Tribune* defaming Poe by attributing the psychological conditions of many of his literary characters to Poe's own state of mind. Most critics, however, contend that there is nothing to suggest that Poe psychologically resembled any of his emotionally and mentally unstable fictitious characters. Indeed, he took pride in demonstrating his keen intellect in his "tales of ratiocination."

Plot Summary

"The Tell-Tale Heart" begins with the famous line "True!—nervous—very, very nervous I had been and am; but why *will* you say that I am mad?" The narrator insists that his disease has sharpened, not dulled, his senses. He tells the tale of how an old man who lives in his house has never wronged him. For an unknown reason, the old man's cloudy, pale blue eye has incited madness in the narrator. Whenever the old man looks at him, his blood turns cold. Thus, he is determined to kill him to get rid of this curse.

Again, the narrator argues that he is not mad. He claims the fact that he has proceeded cautiously indicates that he is sane. For a whole week, he has snuck into the man's room every night, but the victim has been sound asleep with his eyes closed each time. The narrator cannot bring himself to kill the man without seeing his "Evil Eye." On the eighth night, however, the man springs up and cries "Who's there?" In the dark room, the narrator waits silently for an hour. The man does not go back to sleep; instead, he gives out a slight groan, realizing that "Death" is approaching. Eventually, the narrator shines his lamp on the old man's eye. The narrator immediately becomes furious at the "damned spot," but he soon hears the beating of a heart so loud that he fears the neighbors will hear it. With a yell, he leaps into the room and kills the old man. Despite the murder, he continues to hear the man's relentless heartbeat.

He dismembers the corpse and hides the body parts beneath the floorboards. There is a knock on the front door; the police have come to investigate a shriek the neighbors have reported. The narrator invites them to search the premises. He blames his scream on a bad dream and explains that the old man is not home. The officers are satisfied but refuse to leave. Soon the sound of the heartbeat resumes, growing more and more distinct. The narrator grows pale and raises his voice to muffle the sound. At last, unable to stand it any longer, the narrator screams: "I admit the deed!—tear up the planks!—here, here!—it is the beating of his hideous heart!"

Characters

Narrator

The narrator of "The Tell-Tale Heart" recounts his murder of an old man. Since he tells the story in first-person, the reader cannot determine how much of what he says is true; thus, he is an unreliable narrator. Though he repeatedly states that he is sane, the reader suspects otherwise from his bizarre reasoning, behavior, and speech. He speaks with trepidation from the famous first line of the story: "True—nervous—very, very dreadfully nervous I had been and am; but why *will* you say that I am mad?" The reader soon realizes through Poe's jolting description of the narrator's state of mind that the protagonist has in fact descended into madness. The narrator claims that he loves the old man and has no motive for the murder other than growing dislike of a cloudy film over one of the old man's eyes. Poe effectively conveys panic in the narrator's voice, and the reader senses uneasiness and growing tension in the narrative. Through the first-person narrative of a madman, Poe effectively creates a gothic tale full of horror and psychological torment, a style he termed "arabesque."

Old man

The old man is known to readers only through the narration of the insane protagonist. According to the narrator, the old man had never done anything to warrant his murder. However, the old man's cloudy, pale blue eye bothers the narrator tremendously. The narrator believes that only by killing the old man can he get rid of the eye's overpowering malignant force. The old man is apparently quite

Edgar Allan Poe

rich, for he possesses "treasures" and "gold" and he locks the window shutters in his room for fear of robbers. However, the narrator states that he has no desire for his gold. In fact, he claims that he loves the old man. Through the narrator, the reader understands the horror that the old man experiences as he realizes that his companion is about to kill him. The narrator claims that he too knows this horror very well. Some critics argue that the old man must have known about the narrator's violent tendencies, for he cries out in horror well before the narrator kills him. Other critics suggest that the old man may have been the narrator's guardian or even father. Still other critics believe that the old man is a doppelganger for the narrator, that is, he is his double, and the narrator's loathing for the man represents his own self-loathing.

Themes

Guilt and Innocence

The guilt of the narrator is a major theme in "The Tell-Tale Heart." The story is about a mad person who, after killing a companion for no apparent reason, hears an interminable heartbeat and releases his overwhelming sense of guilt by shout-

Media Adaptations

- *Listen & Read Edgar Allan Poe's "The Tell-Tale Heart" and Other Stories* is an audio-cassette recording packaged with a book. Produced by Dover Press, 1996.

- "The Tell-Tale Heart" was adapted into a black-and-white film starring Sam Jaffe in 1980. It is available on video from Facets Multimedia, Chicago.

- In 1934, "The Tell-Tale Heart" was made into a movie entitled *Bucket of Blood* starring John Kelt as The Old Man and Norman Dryden as the protagonist.

- In 1956 producer/director Lee W. Wilder loosely adapted two of Poe's stories, "The Gold Bug" and "The Tell-Tale Heart," in his movie *Manfish*.

- In 1962, "The Tell-Tale Heart" was made into a British movie by director Ernest Morris. Known as *The Tell-Tale Heart*, it also carries the alternate title *The Hidden Room of 1,000 Horrors*. It is available on video from Nostalgia Family Video.

- In 1969, "The Tell-Tale Heart" was made into an animated film narrated by actor James Mason. A Columbia Pictures release, it is also available on video.

- Another audio recording is available from Downsview of Ontario, Canada. *Tales of Mystery and Horror* features the voice of actor Christopher Lee. Produced in 1981.

---

ing his confession to the police. Indeed, some early critics saw the story as a straightforward parable about self-betrayal by the criminal's conscience.

The narrator never pretends to be innocent, fully admitting that he has killed the old man because of the victim's pale blue, film-covered eye which the narrator believes to be a malignant force. The narrator suggests that there are uncontrollable forces which can drive people to commit violent acts. In the end, however, Poe's skillful writing allows the reader to sympathize with the narrator's miserable state despite fully recognizing that he is guilty by reason of insanity.

Sanity and Insanity

Closely related to the theme of guilt and innocence is the issue of sanity. From the first line of the story—"True!—nervous—very, very dreadfully nervous I had been and am, but why *will* you say that I am mad?"—the reader recognizes that something strange has occurred. His obsession with conveying to his audience that he is sane only amplifies his lack of sanity. The first tangible sign that the narrator is indeed mad appears in the second paragraph, when he compares the old man's eye to a vulture's eye. He explains his decision to "take the life of the old man" in order to free himself from the curse of the eye. The narrator's argument that he is sane, calculating, and methodical is unconvincing, however, and his erratic and confused language suggests that he is disordered. Thus, what the narrator considers to be evidence of a sane person—the meticulous and thoughtful plans required to carry out a ghastly and unpleasant deed—are interpreted instead by the reader to be manifestations of insanity.

Time

A secondary theme in "The Tell-Tale Heart" is the role of time as a pervasive force throughout the story. Some critics note that the narrator is obsessed with time. While the entire narrative is told as one long flashback, the narrator is painfully aware of the agonizing effect on him of time. Although the action in this narrative occurs mainly during one long night, the numerous references the narrator makes to time show that the horror he experiences has been building over time. From the beginning, he explains that his obsession with ridding the curse of the eye has "haunted [him] day and night." For seven long nights the narrator waits for the right moment to murder his victim. When on the eighth night the old man realizes that someone is in his room, the narrator remains still for an entire hour. The old man's terror is also felt by the narrator, who had endured "night after night hearkening to the death watches in the wall." (Death watches are a type of small beetle that live in wood and make a ticking sound.)

For the narrator, death and time are closely linked. He explains that "the old man's hour had come," all the while painfully aware of the hours it takes to kill a victim and clean up the scene of the crime. What drives the narrator over the edge is hearing the overwhelming sound of a heartbeat, which he compares to "a low, dull, quick sound, such as a watch makes when enveloped in cotton." Yet after killing the old man, the narrator says that for "many minutes, the heart beat on." He repeats his comparison of the heartbeat to a ticking watch as the unrelenting sound drives him to confess to the police. The narrator's hour has also arrived.

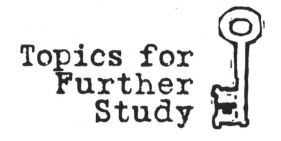

Topics for Further Study

- Research the illnesses of schizophrenia and paranoia. Do you think the protagonist suffers from either of these conditions? Why or why not?

- Research how Manifest Destiny was a pervasive ideology in mid-nineteenth century America. How does "The Tell-Tale Heart" challenge the rationalism and optimism of a young nation?

- "The Tell-Tale Heart" was written more than 150 years ago. Why do you think it is still widely read today? What are some elements of the story which make it timeless? What makes a classic literary or artistic work?

Style

Point of View

A notable aspect of "The Tell-Tale Heart" is that the story is told from the first-person point of view. The story is a monologue of a nervous narrator telling the reader how he murdered someone. He is eventually driven to confess to the police. The entire straightforward narrative is told from his point of view in a nervous tone. Through Poe's masterful and inventive writing, the narrator's twisted logic increasingly reveals that he is insane. By using a first-person narrative, Poe heightens the tension and fear running through the mind of the narrator. There is a clear connection between the language used by the narrator and his psychological state. The narrator switches between calm, logical statements and quick, irrational outbursts. His use of frequent exclamations reveals his extreme nervousness. The first-person point of view draws the reader into the mind of the insane narrator, enabling one to ironically sympathize with his wretched state of mind. Some critics suggest that the entire narrative represents a kind of confession, as at a trial or police station. Others consider the first-person point of view as a logical way to present a parable of self-

betrayal by the criminal's conscience—a remarkable record of the voice of a guilty mind.

Denouement

The denouement, or the resolution, of the narrative occurs in "The Tell-Tale Heart" when the narrator, prompted by the incessant sound of a beating heart, can no longer contain his ever-increasing sense of guilt. Poe is regarded by literary critics as having helped define the architecture of the modern short story, in which its brevity requires an economical use of sentences and paragraphs and the climactic ending often occurs in the last paragraph. The abrupt ending in this story is calculated to concentrate an effect on the reader. In "The Tell-Tale Heart" the crisis of conscience is resolved when the murderer shrieks the last lines of the story: "I admit the deed!—tear up the planks!—here, here!—it is the beating of his hideous heart!" This abrupt outburst is a shock to the reader, a sudden bursting of the tension that has filled the story, and it provides the dramatic, emotional conclusion to the story.

Aestheticism and Arabesque

Poe was a writer concerned more with style and mood than his American contemporaries were, like James Fenimore Cooper, whose fiction was often morally didactic. Poe believed that a story should create a mood in a reader, or evoke emotions in order to be successful, and that it should not try to teach the reader a lesson. He called his style ''arabesque,'' and it was notable for its ornate, intricate prose that sought to create a feeling of unsettlement in the reader. This arabesque prose became a primary component of the ''art for art's sake'' movement, known as Aestheticism, that began in France in the nineteenth century. Poe's works were highly esteemed by French writers, like the poet Charles Baudelaire, and their emulation of his style eventually influenced the Symbolists and helped bring an end to the Victorian age in literature. In ''The Tell-Tale Heart,'' an example of arabesque prose is when the narrator describes sneaking into the old man's room in the middle of the night: ''I heard a slight groan, and I knew it was the groan of mortal terror. It was not a groan of pain or of grief—oh no!—it was the low stifled sound that arises from the bottom of the soul when overcharged with awe.'' Instead of simply stating that he had heard a groan, the narrator describes the sound in detail, creating in the reader a sense of suspense and foreboding.

Doppelganger

In literature, a doppelganger is a character that functions as the main character's double in order to highlight the main character's personality or act as a foil to it. Some critics have maintained that in ''The Tell-Tale Heart,'' the old man functions as a doppelganger to the narrator. Thus, the narrator is truly mad, and he kills the old man because he cannot stand himself, perhaps fearing becoming old or disfigured like him. The narrator recounts evidence to support this idea: he does not hate the man, in fact, he professes to love him; on the eighth night when the narrator sneaks into his room, the old man awakens, sits bolt upright in bed and listens in silence for an hour in the darkness, as does the narrator. Most notably, when the old man begins to moan, the narrator admits that the same sound had ''welled up from my own bosom'' many nights. When he hears the man's heart quicken with terror, he admits that he is nervous, too. Other critics have maintained that the old man does not exist. After all, the narrator tells police that it was he who screamed, and it is not stated that the police actually found a body. According to this viewpoint, the old man's cloudy eye is nothing more than a twisted fixation of the narrator's own mind, and the relentless heartbeat is not the old man's, but the narrator's.

Historical Context

Literature in the 19th Century

Poe wrote at a time when the United States was experiencing rapid economical and geographical expansion. During the mid-nineteenth century, the most popular authors in the growing United States were those who wrote adventure fiction. American nautical explorations (particularly of the Pacific region) and westward expansion captured the imagination of the public. Such Poe stories as ''A Descent into the Maelstrom'' and ''The Gold Bug'' reflect the public's fascination with adventures at home and abroad. Poe's America was a vibrant and self-assured young nation with a firm belief in its manifest destiny. James Fenimore Cooper's *The Last of the Mohicans,* which outlined the moral struggles of an expanding country, was a moral tale that pitted the white man against Native Americans. Herman Melville was a favorite with readers, with his novels of sea-faring life, which often paled in comparison to the adventures of his own youth. Long, action-oriented novels such as these were a primary form of entertainment for many people. Washington Irving, who lived and wrote in the emerging metropolis of New York City, began to catalogue some of the arising American folklore in his tales and stories, although he frequently traveled in Europe to gather material for his writing and followed a tradition British format in his prose. Novels in this era typically imitated British literature until new themes arose from authors who were distinctly American. Poe was one of the first to create a distinctly American literature. In his short stories, particularly, he sought to fashion tales of terror based on mood and language. He also helped popularize the short story form, and soon many magazines were being published that provided their audiences with new stories every month. The magazines became an important part of popular life, and Poe published many stories in them, though few brought him solid popularity. Through his short stories, especially ''Murders in the Rue Morgue'' Poe became one of the first practitioners of the detective story, in which a mystery is presented that must be solved by an observant inspector, whose viewpoint is also that of the reader's.

Psychological Elements of Poe's Fiction

Historians note that Poe's writings emphasizing the dark side of humanity and nature challenged the optimistic and confident spirit of the American

Compare & Contrast

- **1840s:** Mental illness is thought to be related to immoral behavior or the physical degeneration of the central nervous system. Insanity is thought to be the result of such diseases as syphilis.

  1990s: After years of institutionalizing mentally ill patients and subjecting them to electroshock therapy, modern treatment of mental illness such as depression, bi-polar disorder, and schizophrenia include counseling and drug therapy.

- **1840s:** "The Tell-Tale Heart" is published in 1843. The story is a psychological thriller that invites the reader into the world of the narrator's insanity. Other examples of Poe's eerie, macabre

style include "The Pit and the Pendulum," written in 1842, which explores the dark side of human nature and features both cruelty and torture.

1990s: People continue to be fascinated by the dark side of humanity. The popular film *Silence of the Lambs* examines the psychological motivations of a serial killer. Best-selling author Stephen King, along with other horror writers, explores the supernatural, the paranormal, and the way in which seemingly ordinary events can suddenly turn into terrifying encounters with psychotic killers.

---

people during the nineteenth century. Scientific progress and rational thought were revolutionizing industry and agriculture. For example, such nineteenth-century creations as steamships expanded commerce, while steel plows and the McCormick reapers increased agricultural production manyfold. Poe, like other writers of his time, was influenced by the exaggerated emotions and sombre moods of Romanticism, but he differs from his contemporaries in a number of ways. While Poe does not reject rational science (his "tales of ratiocination" herald the triumph of the superior rational mind), he undermines the faith in rationality in some of his stories. "The Tell-Tale Heart" tells of a man who ironically (and perhaps also paradoxically) strongly believes in the need for making methodical and calculated decisions but is eventually overcome by inexplicable psychological forces that stem from his irrational, unstable nature. Thus, while Poe's works display a strong interest in rational science, his writings also explore the psychologically unfathomable aspects of the human condition and the inexplicable elements of the universe.

Poe differs from writers of his time in one other significant way. "The Tell-Tale Heart" is an example of how his writing produces a psychological effect. While his contemporaries generally re-

garded a story's moral or ideological position as paramount, Poe believed that the aim of literature is to reveal truth or elicit an emotional or psychological reaction. Poe also rejected the emphasis by his contemporaries on the utilitarian value of literature. He considered their ideological view a "heresy of the Didactic." Instead, Poe proposed an ideology of "art for art's sake," with style and aesthetics playing prominent roles. Literary critics and historians now consider Poe as one of the architects of the modern short story. Indeed, Poe proposes that a short literary work can use its brevity to concentrate a unified effect on the reader. Poe's precise and controlled language works to produce a particular effect on the reader. Writers of poetry and short fiction since Poe have generally acknowledged his maxim as fundamental. Poe's works have influenced many writers, including Baudelaire and Ambrose Bierce, and such literary movements as the French Symbolists and Surrealists.

Critical Overview

During his lifetime, Poe's greatest recognition came from France. Charles Baudelaire translated and commented on Poe's stories in the 1850s. Baudelaire was a famous French writer in his own right, and his translations are considered by a few critics to be superior to Poe's original prose. These translations popularized Poe in France, bringing him wide fame and influence. In the later half of the nineteenth century, the psychological aspects of Poe's writings influenced French Symbolist poets. In the United States, however, Poe was often criticized for his stories. Many writers thought that they were overly emotional and contained no good lessons or stories. Poe never made much money from his fiction, although he had limited success as a poet.

In the generations since his death, however, critics have come to fully appreciate Poe's works. His poetry continues to be popular, and he is now regarded as an early master of the short story, particularly for his contributions to the detective and horror genres, of which "The Tell-Tale Heart" is a prime example. One of the reasons why he is so highly regarded is because his stories are open to so many different interpretations, a factor that was not appreciated in his day. Contemporary critics acknowledge that "The Tell-Tale Heart" can be read as a classic example of American Gothicism, a morality tale, a supernatural story, a criticism of rationalism, and a multi-level psychological narrative. The full dimension and nuances of this tale are explored in James Gargano's "The Theme of Time in 'The Tell-Tale Heart'." Gargano proposes that "The Tell-Tale Heart" is more complicated than it might first appear because Poe laces the story with "internally consistent symbols that are charged with meaning" and because the narrator is unreliable, causing the reader to question the veracity of his story. E. Arthur Robinson explores the idea of the doppelganger in his essay "Poe's 'The Tell-Tale Heart'," claiming that the narrator and the old man identify closely with each other and arguing that beneath the flow of the narration, "the story illustrates the elaboration of design which Poe customarily sought."

While two of Poe's stories, "MS. Found in a Bottle" and "The Gold Bug" were critically well received, each winning a prize during Poe's lifetime, "The Tell-Tale Heart" obtained no special recognition. Poe's contemporaries accorded him respect as a talented poet, literary critic and fiction writer. Some of his works received a measure of popular success, particularly "The Raven," his most well known poem, which was first published in 1845. However, temperamentally unpleasant and a chronic alcoholic, Poe did not handle his success well, alienating some of his potential supporters.

Some early critics saw the psychologically unbalanced state of his fictional characters as an extension of Poe's own mental state. His literary executor, R. W. Griswold, wrote a libelous obituary in the *New York Tribune* vilifying him as mentally depraved. Even as late as 1924, critic Alfred C. Ward, writing about "The Tell-Tale Heart" in *Aspects of the Modern Short Story: English and American* argued that Poe "had ever before him the aberrations of his own troubled mind—doubtfully poised at all times, perhaps, and almost certainly subject to more or less frequent periods of disorder: consequently, it was probably more nearly normal, for him, to picture the abnormal than to depict the average." Other early critics considered stories such as "The Tell-Tale Heart" basically self-explanatory. One nineteenth century critic, George Woodberry, simply called it a "tale of conscience" in his 1885 study, *Edgar Allan Poe.*

Although "The Tell-Tale Heart" did not receive much recognition during the author's lifetime, its status has gained steadily since his death. Now among one of his most widely read works, the tale adds to Poe's reputation as an innovator of literary form, technique, and vision. Almost every important American writer since Poe shows signs of his influence, particularly those writing gothic fiction and grotesque satires and humor.

Criticism

John Chua

Chua is a multimedia associate with the National Council of Teachers of English. In the following essay, he examines the role of the twin and the doppelganger in "The Tell-Tale Heart."

A salient feature in many of Edgar Allan Poe's stories is the concept of a nemesis appearing as a *doppelganger.* A *doppelganger* is a double—an apparitional twin or counterpart to another living person. In Poe's stories involving a *doppelganger,* the protagonist identifies closely with the antagonist and vice versa. The double appears in such stories as "The Purloined Letter," "The Fall of the House of Usher," and "The Tell-Tale Heart." The idea of the protagonist fighting a counterpart occurs so often in Poe's works that critics often suggest that it indicates Poe's attempts to work out, through his writings, his own inner conflicts and psychological struggles.

What Do I Read Next?

- ''Young Goodman Brown'' (1835) by Nathaniel Hawthorne concerns a newly married man who must leave home on a short journey. While walking through the woods, he encounters the townspeople engaged in a satanic ritual. This vision destroys Goodman Brown, though it is never clear whether he actually saw the things he claimed, or just imagined them.

- ''The Monkey's Paw'' (1902) by W. W. Jacobs is the story about a Sergeant-Major who brings a monkey's paw back from his travels in India. He presents it to the White family, who joke about its supposed power to grant the owner three wishes. The Whites's careless wishes lead to tragedy and horror.

- ''The Secret Sharer'' (1909) by Joseph Conrad is the story of a young sea captain who knowingly harbors a stowaway on his ship. The man, who has been accused of murder, serves as a doppelganger for the young captain, and gives him the courage to stand up to his crew, even though the stowaway's life and character remain shrouded in mystery.

- Poe's short story ''The Fall of the House of Usher'' (1839) also explores the impulses of a deranged protagonist who entombs his sister only to find that she returns to destroy him.

- Poe's ''William Wilson'' also deals with the lifelong confrontation of a protagonist with a mysterious *doppelganger,* or double.

- *The Turn of the Screw* (1898), a novella by Henry James, tells the story of ghostly apparitions seen by an English governess in Victorian mansion. Some critics interpret the hallucinations as the manifestations of a repressed mind.

The identification of the narrator in ''The Tell-Tale Heart'' with the old man is a primary motif in the story. Many times throughout the story, the narrator says that he knows how the old man feels. He claims to know the groans of the old man, and that he too had experienced the same moans—not of pain or sadness but of mortal terror. It is a terror which ''arises from the bottom of the soul when overcharged with awe.'' The narrator says: ''I knew the sound well. Many a night, just at midnight, when all the world slept, it has welled up from my bosom, deepening, with its echo, the terrors that distracted me. I say I knew it well. I know what the old man felt. . . .'' The narrator knows such fearful restlessness first hand: ''He (the old man) was still sitting up in the bed, listening;—just as I have done, night after night, hearkening to the death watches in the wall.'' Thus the narrator and the old man are on such equal footing that they seem almost like the same person.

Ostensibly, the protagonist has no rational reason for wanting to kill the old man. Indeed, he claims the old man has never done him wrong and that he loves him and does not want his money. Why, then, is there a need for murder? ''Object there was none. Passion there was none,'' says the narrator. Neither does the narrator explain how or why exactly the old man's ''pale blue eye, with a film over it'' bothers him so greatly. In fact he only *thinks* it was the eye that first prompted him with murderous thoughts: ''I think it was his eye! yes, it was this!'' Critic Charles E. May, however, interprets the ''eye'' not as an organ of vision but as the homonym of ''I.'' Thus, what the narrator ultimately wants to destroy is the self, and he succumbs to this urge when he could no longer contain his overwhelming sense of guilt.

The idea of knowing the antagonist so well as to know his every move reappears in ''The Purloined Letter,'' a story about two long-time nemeses, Dupin and Minister D. In this story, Minister D. steals a compromising letter from the Queen, and Dupin attempts to recover the letter. Minister D. blackmails the Queen by threatening to divulge to

> " The narrator and the old man are on such equal footing that they seem almost like the same person."

the King the information gained from the letter. The Queen's agents are unable to find the letter because they assume that the Minister thinks like them. Dupin, however, finds the letter because he knows the Minister well enough to know how he thinks. He sets up his nemesis for a fall when he replaces the letter with a counterfeit one, thereby endangering the Minister's life when he attempts to blackmail the Queen with a worthless note. Dupin claims that he accomplishes all this because he shares the same intellect and interests as the Minister—they possess the same poetic yet mathematical mind. Dupin knows Minister D. so intimately that he knows how to hold his interest in a meeting while stealing back the letter from under his nose.

In Poe's works involving protagonists and *doppelgangers,* the characters exist in a moral vacuum. Poe's concerns with aesthetics, style, and effect on the reader override concerns with moral issues. In the struggle between Dupin and Minister D., the reader never knows whether Dupin is working for the "right" political cause. The reader assumes that the Queen has committed an imprudent deed and suspects that there is something very undemocratic about the police working directly for the Queen in what may be a partisan political struggle. But political positions are immaterial in Poe's morally ambiguous stories. The fact that Dupin could possibly be aiding a corrupt or undemocratic faction while Minister D. could be a rebellious politician and brave with anti-monarchical goals is not really an issue with Poe. He never advocates a political or moral position or suggests which is the "correct" one. Poe rejected the position of many of his contemporaries who valued the utilitarian nature of literature and who also believed that literature should be instructive and provide moral guidance. Poe called their ideological position "the heresy of the didactic." Poe's writing aims at a concentrated effect on or emotional response from the reader; the moral positions of the protagonist, antagonist, or other characters do not play a prominent role in

the stories. Morally, therefore, the protagonist and his double are identical. The elimination of the *doppelganger* becomes a destruction of a moral twin—sometimes a self-destructive act.

The idea of the nemesis as twin reappears in "The Fall of the House of Usher." Roderick Usher is so close to his twin sister, Madeline, that the two are said to share one consciousness. In this tale, the narrator is visiting Roderick, a childhood friend who has fallen on hard times. Roderick announces that his sister is dead and entombs her in a coffin in the basement. But the narrative hints that she is still alive, for she expresses "a faint blush" even as the narrator and Roderick close the lid to her coffin. She appears to be suffering from catalepsy, a condition which causes muscle rigidity and an appearance of death. When she mysteriously awakens from her catatonic state late one night, she walks to her terrified brother and falls on him. Roderick and his twin then collapse, both dead. Roderick understands exactly how Madeline feels and acts; there are strong psychological and sexual links between the two. The narrator implies that the Usher family survives only via incest; Roderick and Madeline are the last members of this accursed house. Some critics thus interpret Roderick's act of entombing Madeline alive as an attempt to end this curse. The similarities and links between Roderick and Madeline are too obvious to dismiss. One of Roderick Usher's paintings features a burial vault lit from within, as if he knows about a life-force emanating from inside a coffin. Roderick loves his sister like no other. Their birth and death occur at the same time. Both siblings emit feelings of gloom and doom. Madeline appears wraithlike, as if she is just an apparition. Roderick too appears deathlike and feels his sister's every move and presence; when he announces that she is outside the door and has come for him, she appears exactly as he predicts. The elimination of one sibling thus spells the end of the other. Indeed, after entombing his sister, Roderick becomes more agitated, wild, and fearful, realizing fully that his time too has arrived.

If the two siblings are in fact one in spirit, then their actions may also be interpreted as suicide rather than murder. Poe does not concern himself with the moral actions of the characters in "The Fall of the House of Usher"; the narrator feels no immediate guilt for having aided in the entombment of a person who may possibly be alive. The story seeks primarily to stir fear in the reader, with the issue of morality marginalized. The characters operate in an inscrutable universe where all of them, particularly the protagonist and the *doppelganger*, are equally amoral.

Returning to "The Tell-Tale Heart," one can thus argue that the murder becomes an act of suicide and that the protagonist and the antagonist are moral equals. Taking this argument one step further, one can suggest that the two characters could well be the same person. Ostensibly, the police find no trace of an old man in the house. The narrator has hidden him so well that the old man may exist only in the narrator's mind. Some critics imply that the beating heart is really the sound of the narrator's own heartbeat. As his excitement, nervousness, and guilt mount, his heartbeat seems to grow louder to his overly acute senses. In the end, the narrator tells the police that he was the one who shrieked, waking himself up from a nightmare and a dreamlike logic as well as destroying an enemy which might not have existed.

Critics who have studied Poe sometimes suggest that his characters resemble him both physically and temperamentally. Similarities can be seen between physical descriptions of Roderick Usher—particularly his pale face and large luminous eyes—and of photographs (daguerreotypes) of Poe. Parallels can also be drawn between the conflicts between the protagonists and antagonists in Poe's works and Poe's difficult financial and emotional relationship with his foster father, John Allan. Such conflicts in his writings as the struggles of the protagonist against the *doppelganger* and overwhelming inexplicable natural forces represent a therapeutic banishment of Poe's own inner demons and psychological struggles.

Source: John Chua, "Overview of 'The Tell-Tale Heart'," in *Short Stories for Students*, Gale, 1998.

E. Arthur Robinson

In the following essay, Robinson provides an overview of the style, themes, narrative technique, and multiple levels of meaning in "The Tell-Tale Heart."

Poe's "The Tell-Tale Heart" consists of a monologue in which an accused murderer protests his sanity rather than his innocence. The point of view is the criminal's, but the tone is ironic in that his protestation of sanity produces an opposite effect upon the reader. From these two premises stem multiple levels of action in the story. The criminal, for example, appears obsessed with defending his psychic self at whatever cost, but actually his drive is self-destructive since successful defense upon either implied charge—of murder or of criminal insanity—automatically involves admission of guilt upon the other.

Specifically, the narrator bases his plea upon the assumption that madness is incompatible with systematic action, and as evidence of his capacity for the latter he relates how he has executed a horrible crime with rational precision. He reiterates this argument until it falls into a pattern: "If still you think me mad, you will think so no longer when I describe the wise precautions I took for concealment of the body." At the same time he discloses a deep psychological confusion. Almost casually he admits lack of normal motivation: "Object there was none. Passion there was none. I loved the old man." Yet in spite of this affection he says that the idea of murder "haunted me day and night." Since such processes of reasoning tend to convict the speaker of madness, it does not seem out of keeping that he is driven to confession by "hearing" reverberations of the still-beating heart in the corpse he has dismembered, nor that he appears unaware of the irrationalities in his defense of rationality.

At first reading, the elements of "The Tell-Tale Heart" appear simple: the story itself is one of Poe's shortest; it contains only two main characters, both unnamed, and three indistinguishable police officers; even the setting of the narration is left unspecified. In the present study my object is to show that beneath its narrative flow the story illustrates the elaboration of design which Poe customarily sought, and also that it contains two of the major psychological themes dramatized in his longer works.

It is important to note that Poe's theory of art emphasizes development almost equally with unity of effect. There must be, he insists, "a repetition of purpose," a "dropping of the water upon the rock;" thus he calls heavily upon the artist's craftsmanship to devise thematic modifications of the "preconceived effect." A favorite image in his stories is that of arabesque ornamentation with repetitive design. In "The Tell-Tale Heart" one can distinguish several such recurring devices filling out the "design" of the tale, the most evident being what the narrator calls his "over acuteness of the senses." He incorporates this physical keenness into his plea of sanity: ". . . why *will* you say that I am mad? The disease had sharpened my senses—not destroyed, not dulled them. Above all was the sense of hearing acute." He likens the sound of the old man's heart to the ticking of a watch "enveloped in cotton" and then fancies that its terrified beating may arouse the neighbors. His sensitivity to sight is equally disturbing, for it is the old man's eye, "a pale blue eye, with a film over it," which first vexed him and which he seeks to destroy. Similar though less extreme powers are ascribed to the old man. For example, the murderer congratulates himself that not even his victim could have detected anything wrong with the floor which has been replaced over the body, and earlier he imagines the old man, awakened by "the first slight noise," listening to determine whether the sound has come from an intruder or "the wind in the chimney." Variations such as these give the sensory details a thematic significance similar to that of the "morbid acuteness of the senses" of Roderick Usher in "The Fall of the House of Usher" or the intensity with which the victim of the Inquisition hears, sees, and smells his approaching doom in "The Pit and the Pendulum."

These sensory data provide the foundation of an interesting psychological phenomenon in the story. As the characters listen in the darkness, intervals of strained attention are prolonged until the effect resembles that of slow motion. Thus for seven nights the madman enters the room so "very, very slowly" that it takes him an hour to get his head through the doorway; as he says, "a watch's minute-hand moves more quickly than did mine." When on the eighth night the old man is alarmed, "for a whole hour I did not move a muscle." Later he is roused to fury by the man's terror, but "even yet," he declares, "I refrained and kept still. I scarcely breathed." On different nights both men sit paralyzed in bed, listening for terrors real or imagined. After the murder is completed, "I placed my hand upon the heart and held it there many minutes." In the end it seems to his overstrained nerves that the police officers linger inordinately in the house, chatting and smiling, until he is driven frantic by their cheerful persistence.

This psychological process is important to "The Tell-Tale Heart" in two ways. First, reduplication of the device gives the story structural power. Poe here repeats a dominating impression at least seven times in a brief story. Several of the instances mentioned pertain to plot, but others function to emphasize the former and to provide aesthetic satisfaction. To use Poe's words, "by such means, with such care and skill, a picture is at length painted which leaves in the mind of him who contemplates it with a kindred art, a sense of the fullest satisfac-

tion. The idea of the tale, its thesis, has been presented unblemished. . . ." Here Poe is speaking specifically of "skilfully-constructed tales," and the complementary aspects of technique described are first to omit extraneous material and second to combine incidents, tone, and style to develop the "pre-established design." In this manner, form and "idea" become one. The thematic repetition and variation of incident in "The Tell-Tale Heart" offer one of the clearest examples of this architectural principle of Poe's at work.

Second, this slow-motion technique intensifies the subjectivity of "The Tell-Tale Heart" beyond that attained by mere use of a narrator. In the psychological triad of stimulus, internal response, and action, the first and third elements are slighted and the middle stage is given exaggerated attention. [In a footnote, the critic notes: Joseph Warren Beach in *The Twentieth-Century Novel* (New York, 1932), p. 407, describes a similar effect in stream-of-consciousness writing: "The subjective element becomes noticeable in fiction, as in everyday psychology, when an interval occurs between the stimulus to action and the resulting act." In extreme application of this technique, he declares, "there is a tendency to exhaust the content of the moment presented, there is *an infinite expansion of the moment,*" and he adds that the danger is that "there may come to pass a disintegration of the psychological complex, a divorce between motive and conduct" (p. 409). This is close to the state of Poe's narrator and murderer]. In "The Tell-Tale Heart," stimulus in objective sense scarcely exists at all. Only the man's eye motivates the murderer, and that almost wholly through his internal reaction to it. The action too, though decisive, is quickly over: "In an instant I dragged him to the floor, and pulled the heavy bed over him." In contrast, the intermediate, subjective experience is prolonged to a point where psychologically it is beyond objective measurement. At first the intervals receive conventional description—an "hour," or "many minutes"—but eventually such designations become meaningless and duration can be presented only in terms of the experience itself. Thus, in the conclusion of the story, the ringing in the madman's ears first is "fancied," then later becomes "distinct," then is discovered to be so "definite" that it is erroneously accorded external actuality, and finally grows to such obsessive proportions that it drives the criminal into an emotional and physical frenzy. Of the objective duration of these stages no information is given; the experience simply "continued" until "at length'' the narrator ''found'' that its quality had changed.

Through such psychological handling of time Poe achieves in several of his most effective stories, including ''The Tell-Tale Heart,'' two levels of chronological development which are at work simultaneously throughout the story. Typically, the action reaches its most intense point when the relation between the objective and subjective time sense falters or fails. At this point too the mental world of the subject is at its greatest danger of collapse. Thus we have the mental agony of the bound prisoner who loses all count of time as he alternately swoons and lives intensified existence while he observes the slowly descending pendulum. The narrator in ''The Pit and the Pendulum'' specifically refuses to accept responsibility for objective time-correlations: ''There was another interval of insensibility; it was brief; for, upon again lapsing into life, there had been no perceptible descent in the pendulum. But it might have been long; for I knew there were demons who took note of my swoon, and who could have arrested the vibration at pleasure.'' These demons are his Inquisitional persecutors, but more subjective ''demons'' are at work in the timeless terror and fascination of the mariner whirled around the abyss in ''The Descent into the Maelstrom,'' or the powerless waiting of Usher for days after he first hears his sister stirring within the tomb. In each instance the objective world has been reduced to the microcosm of an individual's experience; his time sense fades under the pressure of emotional stress and physical paralysis.

Even when not literally present, paralysis often may be regarded as symbolic in Poe's stories. In *The Narrative of Arthur Gordon Pym* (1838), Pym's terrifying dreams in the hold of the ship represent physical and mental paralysis: ''Had a thousand lives hung upon the movement of a limb or the utterance of a syllable, I could have neither stirred nor spoken. . . . I felt that my powers of body and mind were fast leaving me.'' Other examples are the ''convolutions'' of bonds about the narrator in ''The Pit and the Pendulum,'' the death-grasp on the ring-bolt in ''The Descent into the Maelstrom,'' the inaction of Roderick and (more literally) the catalepsy of Madeline Usher, and in part the supposed rationality of the madman in ''The Tell-Tale Heart,'' which turns out to be subservience of his mental to his emotional nature. In most applications of the slow-motion technique in ''The Tell-Tale Heart,'' three states of being are present concurrent-

> In 'The Tell-Tale Heart,' three states of being are present concurrently: emotional tension, loss of mental grasp upon the actualities of the situation, and inability to act or to act deliberately."

ly: emotional tension, loss of mental grasp upon the actualities of the situation, and inability to act or to act deliberately. Often these conditions both invite and postpone catastrophe, with the effect of focusing attention upon the intervening experience.

In the two years following publication of ''The Tell-Tale Heart,'' Poe extended this timeless paralysis to fantasies of hypnosis lasting beyond death. ''Mesmeric Revelation'' (1844) contains speculations about the relation between sensory experience and eternity. In ''The Facts in the Case of M. Valdemar'' (1845) the hypnotized subject is maintained for nearly seven months in a state of suspended ''death'' and undergoes instant dissolution when revived. His pleading for either life or death suggests that his internal condition had included awareness and suffering. Similarly the narrator in ''The Tell-Tale Heart'' records: ''Oh God! what *could* I do? I foamed—I raved—I swore!''—while all the time the police officers notice no foaming nor raving, for still they ''chatted pleasantly, and smiled.'' His reaction is still essentially subjective, although he paces the room and grates his chair upon the boards above the beating heart. All these experiences move toward ultimate collapse, which is reached in ''The Tell-Tale Heart'' as it is for Usher and the hypnotized victims, while a last-moment reprieve is granted in ''The Pit and the Pendulum'' and ''The Descent into the Maelstrom.''

A second major theme in ''The Tell-Tale Heart'' is the murderer's psychological identification with the man he kills. Similar sensory details connect the two men. The vulture eye which the subject casts upon the narrator is duplicated in the ''single dim ray'' of the lantern that falls upon his own eye; like the unshuttered lantern, it is always one eye that is mentioned, never two. One man hears the creaking of the lantern hinge, the other the slipping of a finger upon the fastening. Both lie awake at midnight "hearkening to the death-watches in the wall." The loud yell of the murderer is echoed in the old man's shriek, which the narrator, as though with increasing clairvoyance, later tells the police was his own. Most of all the identity is implied in the key psychological occurrence in the story—the madman's mistaking his own heartbeat for that of his victim, both before and after the murder.

These two psychological themes—the indefinite extension of subjective time and the psychic merging of killer and killed—are linked closely together in the story. This is illustrated in the narrator's commentary after he has awakened the old man by an incautious sound and each waits for the other to move:

> Presently I heard a slight groan, and I knew it was the groan of mortal terror. It was not a groan of pain or of grief—oh, no!—it was the low stifled sound that arises from the bottom of the soul when overcharged with awe. I knew the sound well. Many a night, just at midnight, when all the world slept, it has welled up from my own bosom, deepening, with its dreadful echo, the terrors that distracted me. I say I knew it well. I knew that he had been lying awake ever since the first slight noise, when he had turned in the bed. His fears had been ever since growing upon him. He had been trying to fancy them causeless, but could not. He had been saying to himself—"It is nothing but the wind in the chimney—it is only a mouse crossing the floor," or "it is merely a cricket which has made a single chirp." Yes, he had been trying to comfort himself with these suppositions: but he had found all in vain.

Here the slow-motion technique is applied to both characters, with emphasis upon first their subjective experience and second the essential identity of that experience. The madman feels compelled to delay the murder until his subject is overcome by the same nameless fears that have possessed his own soul. The groan is an "echo" of these terrors within. The speaker has attempted a kind of catharsis by forcing his own inner horror to arise in his companion and then feeding his self-pity upon it. This pity cannot prevent the murder, which is a further attempt at exorcism. The final two sentences of the paragraph quoted explain why he believes that destruction is inevitable:

> *All in vain;* because Death, in approaching him, had stalked with his black shadow before him, and enveloped the victim. And it was the mournful influence of the unperceived shadow that caused him to feel—

although he neither saw nor heard—to *feel* the presence of my head within the room.

The significance of these sentences becomes clearer when we consider how strikingly the overall effect of time-extension in "The Tell-Tale Heart" resembles that produced in Poe's "The Colloquy of Monos and Una," published two years earlier. In Monos's account of dying and passing into eternity, he prefaces his final experience with a sensory acuteness similar to that experienced by the narrator in "The Tell-Tale Heart." "The senses were unusually active," Monos reports, "though eccentrically so...." As the five senses fade in death, they are not utterly lost but merge into a sixth—of simple duration:

> Motion in the animal frame had fully ceased. No muscle quivered; no nerve thrilled; no artery throbbed. But there seems to have sprung up in the brain . . . a mental pendulous pulsation. . . . By its aid I measured the irregularities of the clock upon the mantel, and of the watches of the attendants. . . . And this—this keen, perfect, self-existing sentiment of *duration* . . . this sixth sense, upspringing from the ashes of the rest, was the first obvious and certain step of the intemporal soul upon the threshold of the temporal Eternity.

Likewise the old man in "The Tell-Tale Heart" listens as through paralyzed, unable either to move or to hear anything that will dissolve his fears. This resembles Monos' sensory intensity and the cessation of "motion in the animal frame." Also subjective time is prolonged, becomes partially divorced from objective measurement, and dominates it. The most significant similarity comes in the conclusion of the experience. The old man does not know it but he is undergoing the same dissolution as Monos. He waits in vain for his fear to subside because actually it is "Death" whose shadow is approaching him, and "it was the mournful influence of that shadow that caused him to feel" his destroyer within the room. Like Monos, beyond his normal senses he has arrived at a "sixth sense," which is at first duration and then death.

But if the old man is nearing death so too must be the narrator, who has felt the same "mortal terror" in his own bosom. This similarity serves to unify the story. In Poe's tales, extreme sensitivity of the senses usually signalizes approaching death, as in the case of Monos and of Roderick Usher. This "over acuteness" in "The Tell-Tale Heart" however, pertains chiefly to the murderer, while death comes to the man with the "vulture eye." By making the narrator dramatize his feelings in the old man, Poe draws these two motifs together. We must remember, writes one commentator upon the story, "that the criminal sought his own death in that of his victim, and that he had in effect become the man who now lies dead." [Patrick F. Quinn, *The French Face of Edgar Poe* (Carbondale, Illinois, 1957). p. 236. Quinn makes this identity the theme of the story, without describing the full sensory patterns upon which it is based.] Symbolically this is true. The resurgence of the beating heart shows that the horrors within himself, which the criminal attempted to identify with the old man and thus destroy, still live. In the death of the old man he sought to kill a part of himself, but his "demons" could not be exorcised through murder, for he himself is their destined victim.

From this point of view, the theme of "The Tell-Tale Heart" is self-destruction through extreme subjectivity marked paradoxically by both an excess of sensitivity and temporal solipsism. How seriously Poe could take this relativity of time and experience is evident in the poetic philosophy of his *Eureka* (1849). There time is extended almost infinitely into the life-cycle of the universe, but that cycle itself is only one heartbeat of God, who is the ultimate subjectivity. Romantically, indeed, Poe goes even further in the conclusion to *Eureka* and sees individual man becoming God, enclosing reality within himself, and acting as his own creative agent. In this state, distinction between subjective and objective fades: "the sense of individual identity will be gradually merged in the general consciousness." Destruction then becomes self-destruction, the madman and his victim being aspects of the same universal identity. Death not only is self-willed but takes on some of the sanctity of creative and hence destructive Deity. The heartbeat of the red slayer and the slain merge in Poe's metaphysical speculations as well as in the denouement of a horror story.

This extreme subjectivity, moreover, leaves the ethical problem of "The Tell-Tale Heart" unresolved. In the opening paragraph of the story is foreshadowed an issue of good and evil connected with the speaker's madness: "I heard all things in the heaven and in the earth. I heard many things in hell. How, then, am I mad?" To be dramatically functional such an issue must be related to the murder. The only outward motivation for the murder is irritation at the "vulture eye." It is the evil of the eye, not the old man (whom he "loved"), that the murderer can no longer live with, and to make sure that it is destroyed he will not kill the man while he is sleeping. What the "Evil Eye" represents that it so arouses the madman we do not know, but since

> The madman feels compelled to delay the murder until his subject is overcome by the same nameless fears that have possessed his own soul."

he sees himself in his companion the result is self-knowledge. Vision becomes insight, the "Evil Eye" an evil "I," and the murdered man a victim sacrificed to a self-constituted deity. In this story, we have undeveloped hints of the self-abhorrence uncovered in "William Wilson" and "The Imp of the Perverse."

Poe also has left unresolved the story's ultimate degree of subjectivity. No objective setting is provided; so completely subjective is the narration that few or no points of alignment with the external world remain. From internal evidence, we assume the speaker to be mad, but whether his words constitute a defense before some criminal tribunal or the complete fantasy of a madman there is no way of ascertaining. [The critic adds in a footnote that 'Despite lack of objective evidence, "The Tell-Tale Heart" bears much resemblance to a dream. The narrator acknowledges that the murdered man's shriek was such as occurs in dreams, and his memory of approaching the old man's bed upon eight successive midnights has the quality of a recurring nightmare. Poe frequently couples madness and dreaming, often with the variant "opium dreams," as in "Ligeia" and "The Fall of the House of Usher." "The Black Cat" a companion piece published the same year as "The Tell-Tale Heart" (1843), opens with an explicit denial of both madness and dreaming. The introductory paragraph of "Eleonora" (1842) runs the complete course of madness—dreams—death—good and evil: "Men have called me mad; but the question is not yet settled, whether madness is or is not the loftiest intelligence: whether much that is glorious, whether all that is profound, does not spring from disease of thought—from *moods* of mind exalted at the expense of the general intellect. They who dream by day are cognizant of many things which escape those who dream only by night. In their gray visions they obtain glimpses of eternity, and thrill, in awaking, to find that they have been upon the verge of the great secret. In snatches, they learn something of the wisdom which is of good, and more of the mere knowledge which is of evil''.'] The difference, however, is not material, for the subjective experience, however come by, *is* the story. Psychologically, the lengthening concentration upon internal states of being has divorced the murderer first from normal chronology and finally from relationship with the ''actual'' world. The result, in Beach's words, is ''disintegration of the psychological complex.'' The victim images himself as another and recoils from the vision. Seeing and seen eye become identical and must be destroyed.

Source: E. Arthur Robinson, ''Poe's 'The Tell-Tale Heart','' in *Nineteenth-Century Fiction,* Vol. 19, No. 4, March, 1965, pp. 369–78.

James W. Gargano

In the following excerpt, Gargano praises Poe's controlled presentation of an insane narrator in ''The Tell-Tale Heart.''

In ''The Tell-Tale Heart'' the cleavage between author and narrator is perfectly apparent. The sharp exclamations, nervous questions, and broken sentences almost too blatantly advertise Poe's conscious intention; the protagonist's painful insistence in ''proving'' himself sane only serves to intensify the idea of his madness. Once again Poe presides with precision of perception at the psychological drama he describes. He makes us understand that the voluble murderer has been tortured by the nightmarish terrors he attributes to his victim: ''He was sitting up in bed listening;—just as I have done, night after night, harkening to the death watches in the wall''; further, the narrator interprets the old man's groan in terms of his own persistent anguish: ''Many a night, just at midnight, when all the world slept, it has welled up from my own bosom, deepening, with its dreadful echo, the terrors that distracted me.'' Thus, Poe, in allowing his narrator to disburden himself of his tale, skillfully contrives to show also that he lives in a haunted and eerie world of his own demented making.

Poe assuredly knows what the narrator never suspects and what, by the controlled conditions of the tale, he is not meant to suspect—that the narrator is a victim of his own self-torturing obsessions. Poe so manipulates the action that the murder, instead of freeing the narrator, is shown to heighten his agony and intensify his delusions. The watches

in the wall become the ominously beating heart of the old man, and the narrator's vaunted self-control explodes into a frenzy that leads to self-betrayal. I find it almost impossible to believe that Poe has no serious artistic motive in ''The Tell-Tale Heart'' that he merely revels in horror and only inadvertently illuminates the depths of the human soul. I find it equally difficult to accept the view that Poe's style should be assailed because of the ejaculatory and crazy confession of his narrator.

Source: James W. Gargano, ''The Question of Poe's Narrators,'' in *College English,* Vol. 25, no. 3, December, 1963, pp. 177–81.

Alfred C. Ward

In the following excerpt, Ward notes with regard to ''The Tell-Tale Heart'' that Poe's short stories commonly deal with similar subject matter. He comments that Poe's narrative technique makes his stories powerful and effective, although his usual themes, such as madness, are unappealing.

''The Tell-Tale Heart'' is one of the most effective parables ever conceived. Shorn of its fantastic details regarding the murdered man's vulture-like eye, and the long-drawn-out detail concerning the murderer's slow entrance into his victim's room, the story stands as an unforgettable record of the voice of a guilty conscience.

Despite its merit as a parable, ''The Tell-Tale Heart'' is marred by the insanity of the chief character. From the very first sentence his madness is apparent through his desperate insistence upon his sanity; and the preliminaries of his crime go to prove that madness. The vital weakness of Poe's stories in this kind is his repeated use of the motive of mental abnormality. Psychological fiction (and Poe was among its earliest practitioners) depends for its effect upon the study of the human mind in its *conscious* state—whereas insanity is, to all intents and purposes, a condition of unconsciousness.

Is it not possible to contemplate a re-writing of ''The Tell-Tale Heart'' in a manner which would preserve its unique character as a parable of the self-betrayal of a criminal by his conscience, while at the same time vastly increasing its interest as a story of human action? As Poe writes the story, we have the spectacle of a demented creature smothering his helpless old victim without reason or provocation, other than the instigation of his own mad obsession: ''Object there was none. Passion there was none.'' This absence of motive robs the story of every vestige of dramatic interest, for it is an elementary axiom in criticism that what is motiveless is inadmissible in literary art. The provision of an adequate motive for the murder, and the subsequent commission of the murder by one who is otherwise sane, would bring the story on to the plane of credibility and dramatic interest. If the circumstances of the story were thus altered, the implacable workings of conscience and the portrayal of their cumulative influence upon the mind of the criminal, could scarcely fail to have a much more powerful effect upon the mind of the reader than is actually the case in the story as it stands.

Two things, at least, should be remembered, however, when we make these strictures in regard to Edgar Allan Poe's work. *First,* that he had ever before him the aberrations of his own troubled mind—doubtfully poised at all times, perhaps, and almost certainly subject to more or less frequent periods of disorder: consequently, it was probably more nearly normal, for him, to picture the abnormal than to depict the average. *Second,* that literary men in general, at the beginning of the nineteenth century, were still in the trough of the wave of German romanticism, which exalted extravagant and clamorous and stormy sentimentality above the quieter, deeper, truer moods of human feeling.

Considering, then, the temperamental drawbacks by which Poe was beset, and also that the naturalistic mode in literature is the fruitage of more recent times, he should be judged by standards different from those that serve for other writers. The wonder surely is that Poe should be able still to sway modern readers with such unprepossessing material.

Source: Alfred C. Ward, "Edgar Allan Poe: 'Tales of Mystery and Imagination'," in *Aspects of the Modern Short Story: English and American,* University of London Press, 1924, pp. 32–44.

Sources

Gargano, James W. "The Theme of Time in 'The Tell-Tale Heart'." *Studies in Short Fiction,* Vol. V, no. 1 (Fall 1967): 378-82.

> **The protagonist's painful insistence in 'proving' himself sane only serves to intensify the idea of his madness."**

Gargano, James W. "The Question of Poe's Narrators." *College English,* Vol. 25, no. 3 (December 1963): 177-81.

Robinson, E. Arthur. "Poe's 'The Tell-Tale Heart'." *Nineteenth-Century Fiction,* Vol. 19, no. 4 (March 1965): 369-78.

Ward, Alfred C. "Edgar Allan Poe: 'Tales of Mystery and Imagination'." *Aspects of the Modern Short Story: English and American,* University of London Press, 1924, pp. 32-44.

Further Reading

Lewis, R. W. B. *Edgar Allan Poe,* Chelsea House, 1997.
   A critical study of Poe's works.

Quinn, Arthur Hobsons, and Shawn J. Rosenheim. *Edgar Allan Poe: A Critical Biography,* Johns Hopkins University Press, 1997.
   Outlines Poe's life with special emphasis on his works.

Rosenheim, Shawn, and Stephen Rachman. *The American Face of Edgar Allan Poe,* Johns Hopkins University Press, 1995.
   Essays on Poe that compare his work to that of Jorge Borges and contemporaries Harriet Beecher Stowe and William Wordsworth. Other essays discuss themes such as psychoanalysis, literary nationalism, and authorial identity as it relates to his work.

A White Heron

Sarah Orne Jewett

1886

When "A White Heron" appeared in 1886 as the title story in Sarah Orne Jewett's collection *A White Heron and Other Stories,* the author was already established as one of the finest local color writers the United States had produced. This was Jewett's eighth published book, and she had enough influence with her publisher, Houghton, Mifflin, to open the book with the story, although it had already been rejected by the *Atlantic Monthly* magazine as too sentimental and romantic. Jewett's instincts, in this case, were right. The story of a young forest-dwelling girl who must choose whether or not to tell a handsome young hunter the secret of where the rare white heron has its nest was immediately recognized by critics as a treasure; it has since become the most admired and most widely anthologized of Jewett's nearly 150 short stories. While some critics have faulted the story for its shifts in narrative point of view which they saw as lack on control on the author's part, others have praised Jewett's narrative shifts, which they find add an important dimension to the narrator's role. Over the past century critics have explored themes of good versus evil, flesh versus spirit, nature versus civilization, feminine versus masculine world view, and innocence versus experience in "A White Heron." Mary E. Wilkins Freeman, another well-regarded nineteenth-century New England writer, praised the story. An anonymous 1886 reviewer in the *Overland Monthly* called it "a tiny classic," and noted that its themes "never were interpreted with more beauty and insight."

Author Biography

Known primarily as a regional writer, Sarah Orne Jewett spent most of her life on the rugged Maine coast that is the setting for much of her work. She was born in South Berwick, Maine, on September 3 1849, one of three daughters of an old and prosperous New England family. Both of her parents were readers, and they wanted their daughters to be well-educated—somewhat uncommon in the nineteenth century. For a time, Jewett even considered becoming a physician like her father; however, poor health made it impossible for her to complete rigorous medical training. Instead, she turned to her talent for writing.

Jewett often accompanied her father on his rounds and loved to hear him talk about books and ideas. At age eighteen she published her first short story, a melodramatic tale of love. This early success led to what would be her true calling: writing honestly and simply about the richness and poignancy of the common folk of Maine. From the beginning, her focus was on lonely, misunderstood people, particularly women, and their relationships; her stories often have little in the way of exciting or dramatic plot and action but are nonetheless powerfully moving.

In 1878 Jewett's father died, and Jewett was left without her dearest friend, whom she later described in the novel *A Country Doctor* (1884). Shortly after her father's death she began an intimate and lifelong relationship with Annie Fields, the wife of publisher James T. Fields. Through the Fieldses, Jewett became acquainted with many of the most noted writers of the day, including Celia Thaxter, George Eliot, Henry James, and Nathaniel Hawthorne. After James Fields's death, Jewett and Annie became closer, forming what was known as a ''Boston marriage;'' they did not always share a home, but they were treated as a couple by their friends.

Jewett continued writing, attracting a larger audience as her stories appeared in the *Atlantic Monthly* and *Harper's* magazines. ''A White Heron,'' rejected by the *Atlantic Monthly* as too sentimental, was published first in Jewett's collection *A White Heron and Other Stories*. She wrote novels in addition to short stories but they were not as successful, with the exception of her greatest work, *The Country of the Pointed Firs* (1896), a series of sketches about the residents of a fictional coastal village. This novel solidified her reputation as one of the century's greatest regional writers.

Jewett gave up writing after a 1902 carriage accident left her in disabling pain. She had published more than 150 stories and four novels. She devoted her remaining years to Annie Fields and other friends, including the young writer Willa Cather. Cather credited Jewett with influencing her to write about her home, Nebraska. Cather's first Nebraska novel, *O Pioneers!* (1913), was dedicated to Jewett, who had died in South Berwick on June 24, 1909.

Plot Summary

''A White Heron'' begins on a June evening near the Maine coast. As the sun sets, nine-year-old Sylvia drives home a cow, her ''valued companion.'' The child has no other playmates, and enjoys these evening walks with the cow, Mistress Moolly, and the hide-and-seek games the cow plays to escape being caught. It has taken an unusually long time to find the cow this night, and Sylvia hopes her grandmother, Mrs. Tilley, will not be worried. But Mrs. Tilley knows that Sylvia never hurries these walks, because she so loves wandering in the woods. After living her first eight years in a crowded and noisy city with her parents, Sylvia has found her true home with her grandmother in the country. Although she is afraid of people, ''there never was such a child for straying about out-of-doors since the world was made!''

As the two companions approach the farm, Sylvia listens to the birds and squirrels preparing for night, cools her tired feet in the brook, and thinks about how different her life is now from when she lived in the city. Just as she remembers uneasily a city boy who used to chase and frighten her, she is startled to hear whistling not far off. This is not the pleasant and friendly whistling of a bird, but the ''determined, and somewhat aggressive'' whistling of a boy. Before she can conceal herself in the woods, she encounters a tall young man with a gun, who asks her for directions to the road. He has been hunting for birds, and is lost.

Confused and frightened, Sylvia leads the hunter to the farm, where Mrs. Tilley offers him a bed for the night. The young man introduces himself as an

Sarah Orne Jewett

ornithologist gathering specimens for his collection. He is surprised to see how clean and cozy the homestead is, delights in his simple meal, and sits on the doorstep listening to the grandmother chatter about her home and family. Sylvia, she explains, most resembles her Uncle Dan, who knew the woods intimately and was a good enough hunter that Mrs. Tilley always had a bit of meat on the table. The hunter is excited to learn that Sylvia, sitting silently and sleepily through the conversation, knows the woods and knows about birds. He has spotted a rare white heron in the area, and would like to add it to his collection.

Sylvia is only half-listening to the man speak; she is more interested in watching a small toad hopping on the path. But when he describes the bird he is looking for, she recognizes it as one she has watched and dreamed about. Its home is near the salt marshes, near the sea, which she has never seen. He offers Sylvia ten dollars (a large sum for such a poor family in the nineteenth century) if she will show him the heron's nest.

The next morning, Sylvia and the hunter set out on a ramble through the woods. Gradually, she loses her fear of her new friend, although she recoils when he brings birds down with his gun. As they wander, he leads the way and does all the talking.

Although she knows the area and he is a stranger, she is content to follow and to listen. Her "woman's heart" is being vaguely awakened by the young man, and she begins to see what romantic love might be. Evening comes without the pair seeing the heron, and together they find the cow and drive her home.

Sylvia does not sleep that night, for she is making a plan to please her new friend. Before sunrise, she steals out of the house and runs to an old pine, the tallest tree in the forest. From the top of this tree, she has often thought, one could see the sea, and perhaps she can see the heron's nest from there. As she climbs, birds and squirrels scold her, and thorns grab at her. But she does not turn back.

She watches the sunrise from her perch, and at last sees what she is looking for: the white heron and its nest. But when she returns to the farm she does not reveal what she has seen. The hunter goes away, disappointed, and Sylvia loses her first human friend.

The story closes with the narrator addressing nature directly, asking it to bless this young girl—who has given up her chance to love the young man "as a dog loves"—and to share its "gifts and graces" with "this lonely country child."

Characters

Hunter

The hunter is heard before he is seen, whistling in a "determined, and somewhat aggressive" manner, in contrast to the birdsong that fills the air. He carries a gun and a heavy sack full of dead birds. He is an ornithologist proud of his collection of birds, "stuffed and preserved, dozens and dozens of them." Still, he is friendly and kind, if somewhat smug about his wealth and sophistication, and Sylvia is both attracted to and somewhat afraid of him. He is so eager to collect a white heron that he offers Sylvia ten dollars (a sum that means little to him but a great deal to her) if she will lead him to the bird. As they walk through the woods together, the two seem to take equal pleasure in the birds they see—Sylvia for their living beauty, and the hunter for their rarity and usefulness to him as trophies. Not much is known about the young man, who, appropriately, is never named. It is not his individuality, but what he represents: masculinity, acquisitiveness, romantic love—that matters.

Sylvia

Nine-year-old Sylvia is a true child of nature. Her name, "Sylvia," and her nickname, "Sylvy," come from the Latin *silva* meaning "wood" or "forest." She lives with her grandmother on an isolated farm in rural Maine, and she rarely sees other people. She remembers the early years of her life, when she lived in a noisy manufacturing town, as a frightening time, and she never wants to return. When a hunter comes looking for a white heron, she enjoys the company of another person for the first time and is puzzled by the conflicting emotions he stirs in her. He offers desperately needed money and also represents her first chance at friendship or romantic love. She alone can give him the bird he seeks. What she must decide is whether what he can give her is worth the betrayal of her relationship with nature. In the end, she does not reveal the heron's nesting place.

Mrs. Tilley

Mrs. Tilley is Sylvia's maternal grandmother. A year before the story opens, she traveled to the city to bring one of her daughter's children back to help her on the farm. That child was Sylvia, who has grown to love the forest. Mrs. Tilley has lost four children, and her two remaining adult children live far away. She appreciates Sylvia's help and company and lets her wander freely.

Themes

Flesh vs. Spirit

When an appealing ornithologist comes to the Maine woods, young Sylvia must decide whether to please her new friend by showing him the nesting place of the heron he wishes to kill for his collection, or remain loyal to her animal companions. Although the nine-year-old girl would never consider her situation in these terms, the decision Sylvia must make is the choice between flesh and spirit—between earthly human pleasures and the natural world. The narrator states the conflict in a sigh directed at the reader: "Alas, if the great wave of human interest which flooded for the first time this dull little life should sweep away the satisfaction of an existence heart to heart with nature and the dumb life of the forest!" The hunter's presence represents two aspects of fleshly desire. First, he offers Sylvia ten dollars if she will betray the heron. Although the sum seems to mean little to him, for Sylvia it is a great temptation: "He can make them

Media Adaptations

- *A White Heron* was adapted as a video for elementary and junior-high audiences, Learning Corporation of America, 1978; available in VHS, Beta and 3/4U formats from Modern Curriculum Press (MCP).

- The story has also been recorded as a book on tape; recorded by SoundWindow, the tape includes excerpts from Henry Beston's *The Outermost House,* distributed as *Christine Sweet Reads,* 1996.

rich with money; he has promised it, and they are poor now." When he first offers the money, her head swims in confusion as she thinks of all she might buy. She is dazed and confused for the rest of the story, until the moment she decides not to tell the secret. Secondly, the hunter represents—albeit in a subtle way for the young girl—the fleshly temptations of sex. It is his maleness she responds to, as "the woman's heart, asleep in the child, [is] vaguely thrilled by a dream of love." When Sylvia decides to keep her secret, she chooses grace over treasure, as the narrator's final plea to the natural world emphasizes: "Whatever treasures were lost to her . . . bring your gifts and graces . . . to this lonely country child!"

Rites of Passage

Sylvia's movement toward her decision follows the typical pattern of the hero story or the *Bildungsroman.* Before Sylvia can move from innocence to maturity, or from common mortal to hero, she must undergo a ritual test to prove her worthiness and strength. The girl feels at home in the forest—she does not wish to leave—and at times she feels as one with the natural world. But her relationship to nature has never been tested. Appropriately, her test takes the form of a literal climb to a higher place, from where she can see the world. When she approaches the highest tree where the land is highest, "the last of its generation," she does

Topics for Further Study

- The bird Jewett was thinking of when she wrote this story is more frequently called the snowy egret. Research the natural history of the snowy egret, especially its status at the beginning of the twentieth century, to see why Jewett was so concerned about this bird. Describe the reaction informed citizens of the 1890s might have had to the ornithologist's plan. What animals might be used in stories today to achieve a similar effect?

- Read an article or essay in a recent issue of a nature or conservation magazine (for example, *Audubon, National Wildlife* or *Sierra*). Compare and contrast the advantages and disadvantages of using fiction and nonfiction to argue for environmental protection.

- Visit a natural history museum, or another museum with a collection of "preserved and stuffed" animal specimens. Discuss with the curator or a guide the value of such collections. Report on what you learn.

- Research marriage in the United States at the end of the nineteenth century, focusing on the differing rights and responsibilities of husbands and wives. Compare your findings to the implications Jewett makes about marriage.

---

not know what she will do. She has often thought that from the top of this tree she might see the ocean, but she has never dared. Jewett presents this climb in the language of the hero myth: "What a spirit of adventure, what wild ambition! What fancied triumph and delight and glory." As Sylvia begins "with utmost bravery to mount to the top of it" the birds and squirrels scold her, the thorns and twigs seem to intentionally grab at her. But as she climbs on resolutely, the great tree itself assumes an active role in helping her, until at last she is at the top: "Sylvia's face was like a pale star, if one had seen it from the ground . . . and she stood trembling and tired and wholly triumphant." But the test is not yet over. Sylvia still thinks that what she has achieved,

she has achieved for the hunter. She expects to return to him, claim the money, claim his love and admiration. She is surprised to find (although the reader is not) that in the end she cannot reveal the heron's nesting place. She has completed the test and come out the other side a stronger, wiser, more mature person. Typical of the young hero, however, she has gone through the rites of passage though she does not yet know the extent of her own power.

Style

Set in an isolated portion of Maine, "A White Heron" tells of a lonely nine-year-old girl's decision not to reveal the location of a beautiful white heron and its nest to a visiting hunter. The hunter leaves, disappointed, and the girl, Sylvia, loses her first human friend.

Narrator/Point of View

Of all the technical aspects of this story, that of a young girl who must choose between revealing the location of a heron's nest to an appealing ornithologist and protecting the bird, none has proven more problematic to critics than point of view. Many readers have seen Jewett's abrupt and dramatic changes in point of view as a weakness and a sign of immature talent; however, more recently, readers have seen the shifts as intentional and effective. The story is told by an omniscient third-person narrator, that is, a narrator who is not present as a character in the story, but who looks out or down on the events and who can see more than the characters themselves see. This narrator sees more deeply into (or shows more interest in) Sylvia's thoughts and feelings than into the other characters'. Nothing is shown of the hunter's or Mrs. Tilley's thoughts beyond what they demonstrate through their words and actions. The narrator tells most of the story in the past tense, but three times shifts to present tense: when Sylvia first hears the hunter approaching ("this little woods-girl is horror-stricken"), when she has spotted the heron's nest ("she knows his secret now"), and when she finds that she cannot reveal the secret ("Sylvia does not speak after all"). These moments give an immediacy that is sharp but that does not last. Each time, the narrator backs up again and stands at a distance. At times detachment falls away completely, and the narrator addresses Sylvia ("look down again, Sylvia") or nature ("woodlands and summer-time, remember") directly; it feels as though the reader, too, were on the scene, watching and hoping. Gayle Smith finds in this mingling of past and present, of memory and experience, of detachment and involvement an example of Jewett's using language to show the transcendence of Sylvia's connection with nature.

Setting

Setting is important in "A White Heron," because it is Sylvia's close connection with nature that sets her apart from other people. Fittingly, the name "Sylvia" comes from the Latin *silva,* meaning "wood" or "forest," and the story takes place in the woods, far from the noisy city where Sylvia was born, and near the vast ocean that, until the story begins, she has never seen. "There ain't a foot o' ground she don't know her way over," and she knows the birds and animals, so she is the perfect guide for the hunter. However, when the two go out together, the young man leads the way. Here, the setting underscores the power differences between the two. The hunter chooses Sylvia specifically because she knows the scene, yet he guides her through it. The nearness of the coast is also important, because it is when the girl reaches the top of the old pine and can see the ocean and "the white sails of ships out at sea" that she realizes that this "vast and awesome world" is hers, and she has found it alone. She does not need the young man to show her the world; this "wonderful sight and pageant of the world" is before her. The time of the story is important as well. In the late nineteenth century, one could easily imagine a girl living in rural isolation, seeing few people other than her grandmother, and one could guess at how exciting and confusing a visitor offering money might be. Sylvia's innocence of the technological world is essential; she must be wholly in nature because that is where she belongs, yet it must seem unremarkable that she has never seen the sea.

Anthropomorphism

Throughout the first half of "A White Heron," the forest in which Sylvia lives is an ordinary forest, although her connection to it is clearly deeper than other people's. It contains trees and animals and bird songs of the expected kinds, and even the birds feeding out of her hands seem rare but not fantastic. But when she begins to climb the old pine tree, the tree is presented as an active, sentient being: "it must truly have been amazed that morning," "The old pine must have loved his new dependent." This anthropomorphism, or the attributing of human characteristics to nonhuman beings, is used to high-light Sylvia's extraordinary oneness with nature. Where at first the tree only seems "to lengthen itself out" as she climbs, by the time she reaches the top the tree's sentience is clear. The narrator does not say that the tree seems to hold the wind away from Sylvia, or that Sylvia imagines it holds back the wind; the bold statement is that "the tree stood still and held away the winds." The increasing anthropomorphism echoes Sylvia's increasing knowledge and power as she climbs.

Pathetic Fallacy

Closely related to anthropomorphism, the pathetic fallacy, or the assumption by the narrator that nature itself has human feeling and cares about human suffering, is used at the end of "A White Heron" when the narrator addresses nature directly on behalf of Sylvia. A direct address to "woodlands and summer-time" seems quaint to modern readers, but Jewett leads up to it by increasing the narrator's and the reader's involvement throughout the second half of the story. After the great tree has actively assisted Sylvia in her climb, and after her oneness with nature has been confirmed by her refusal to divulge the nesting place, it does not seem a great stretch of the imagination for the narrator to beg of nature itself: "Bring your gifts and graces and tell your secrets to this lonely country child!"

For early readers, the story was seen mostly as an admirable example of local color writing. The local color movement, which reached its peak in the United States in the 1880s, tried to capture the mannerisms, peculiar speech, dress, and customs of a particular region of the country. Some of its most successful proponents were Mark Twain, Joel Chandler Harris, Bret Harte, and Sarah Orne Jewett. Local color writing was thought to be less serious than other types of fiction, written primarily to be entertaining, even amusing. This is not to say that these writings were not of high quality, but readers did not generally look to them for deep issues and ideas.

By the 1920s, scholars began to take Jewett's work more seriously, following the lead of Willa Cather, who in her introduction to an edition of *The Best Short Stories of Sarah Orne Jewett* ranked Jewett with Nathaniel Hawthorne and Mark Twain. Commentators began to look again at the short stories and find in them issues of broad significance. While Jewett was still regarded as one of the greatest of the local color writers, she was also noted for the sophisticated way in which she dealt with the conflicts brought about by industrialization and capitalism. No important criticism of her work appeared in the 1930s or 1940s, but "A White Heron" continued to appear in anthologies and textbooks, and was often cited in literary histories as one of the finest examples of the American short story.

Historical Context

Advancements for Women

The end of the nineteenth century brought many new opportunities for women in the United States and other industrializing countries, and Sarah Orne Jewett took full advantage of them. In 1848, just one year before Jewett was born, Elizabeth Cady Stanton, Lucretia Mott and others had organized the famous Women's Rights Convention at Seneca Falls, New York. By the time Jewett graduated from Berwick Academy in 1866, women were being granted certificates to practice medicine (for a time, a dream of Jewett's), they were being admitted to universities, and led by Stanton, Mott, and Susan B. Anthony, they had formed the American Equal Rights Association dedicated to winning the vote for women and for African Americans. For the first time in American society, women were gradually and grudgingly allowed into full participation as citizens and as professionals.

Equally important for Jewett, women were beginning to enjoy a wider range of "acceptable" personal lifestyles. Married women could have careers, as in Louisa May Alcott's *Jo's Boys*, published in 1886, the same year as "A White Heron." But it was no longer taken for granted, at least among urban upper-class society, that every woman would marry as soon as she could and live out her life as an unequal partner to a man, with no property rights and no protection should the marriage prove unhappy. For Jewett and others, there was the possibility of living an independent life, outside the traditional patriarchal structure. Women could have careers and earn enough money to support themselves. And, although there were no public and political organizations for lesbians in the nineteenth century, many women like Jewett felt free to discreetly devote their emotional energy to other women. The idea of the "Boston marriage," or the intimate association of two women, was recognized and accepted, though not openly discussed.

All of this plays an important role in Jewett's writings, which tend to focus on independent-minded women struggling with or rejecting men. Jewett wrote several stories and novels about women doctors—impossible at an earlier time. And even many of her rural people, like Mrs. Tilley and Sylvia, live full lives without male associates. When Sylvia rejects the hunter, whom she perceives as a suitor, she is claiming her independence from male-dominated society, just as Jewett and many of her contemporaries were able to do. She "could have served and followed him and loved him as a dog loves," but in this new era she has other choices.

Industrialization

In large cities, manufacturing jobs were plentiful but dangerous, as corporate heads needed more and more cheap labor to keep the factories running. Laborers often went on strike to fight for better working conditions. In New York City, streetcar workers tied up the city for days in 1886 with a strike; finally they settled for a twelve-hour workday with a half-hour lunch break. New processes for working with metals were developed, the internal combustion engine was perfected, home products like Johnson's Wax and Avon cosmetics became available, and big department stores like Bloomingdale's opened their doors. It was still common in the countryside, however, for people to live simple lives of subsistence farming, without the benefits or hazards of industrial life.

The Growing Conservation Movement

By the late nineteenth century, what had once seemed a vast and limitless continent was now being recognized as fragile and in need of protection. Pollution in the cities like Sylvia's "crowded manufacturing town" was uncontrolled and much worse than it was a century later. The great buffalo herds had been greatly reduced, and their decimation was widely observed in popular songs and tales. Forests were being cut down at an alarming rate, bolstered by the Timber Culture Act of 1878 which permitted the clearing of public lands. A fledgling conservation movement had begun, targeting the preservation of forests and wildlife.

The woods where Sylvia lives are second-growth forest, but it is in the old-growth great pine, "the last of its generation," where she finds wisdom: "Whether it was left for a boundary mark, or for what reason, no one could say; the woodchoppers who had felled its mates were dead and gone long ago." Jewett uses a symbol, a rare old tree, to underscore the value of preserving the land.

The heron, too, is rare and in danger. According to George Held, the bird Jewett would have had in mind was the snowy egret, whose feathers were much in demand for trimming ladies' hats. It was nearly extinct by 1900, and federally protected in 1913.

A great white heron in a Florida swamp.

Critical Overview

In his 1962 *Sarah Orne Jewett,* the first book-length study devoted to the writer, Richard Cary identified Sylvia's rite of initiation as "an arduous journey of self-discovery and maturity." This theme of the rite of passage was explored by critics over the next three decades. Catherine B. Sherman read the story as a miniature *Bildungsroman,* a story of the development of a young person into adulthood, along the lines of Charles Dickens's *David Copperfield.* Kelley Griffith, Jr. took the theme one step further, and found in the story an echo of the archetypal myth of the hero. Sylvia, she wrote in the *Colby Library Quarterly* in 1985, "becomes a traditional hero who makes a quest after a much desired object." Elizabeth Ammons, also writing in the *Colby Library Quarterly,* compared the story's construction to that of a fairy tale.

Two issues have drawn the greatest attention from critics, and divided them the most sharply: the meaning of Sylvia's rejection of the hunter, and Jewett's shifts in narrative stance. Eugene Hillhouse Pool believed that Jewett's own refusal to marry stemmed from an immature attachment to her father, and considered her attachment to Annie Fields a poor second to marriage. Perhaps, he argued in the *Colby Library Quarterly* in 1967, the short story was so popular because "it is the expression of a situation closely paralleling her own personal problems, and thus contains her deepest feeling." By contrast, Ammons called the story "an anti-bildungsroman. It is a rite-of-passage story in which the heroine refuses to make the passage." For Ammons and other feminist critics (including George Held, whose 1982 *Colby Library Quarterly* article saw Sylvia growing into "a woman committed to values that will allow her to be her natural self"), refusal to marry was not a sign of immaturity but a mature choice. In Ammons words, Sylvia "chooses the world of her grandmother, a place defined as free, healthy and 'natural' in this story, over the world of heterosexual favor and violence represented by the hunter."

The matter of shifts in narrative stance has likewise been controversial. It was seen first as a weakness, by such critics as Cary, who commented that the story contains "too much jostling in the presentation to be worthy of the label 'perfect.'" More recently, the shifting has been regarded as an interesting and effective choice by critics including Michael Atkinson, who in a 1982 article in the *Colby Library Quarterly* found that the narrator's loss of detachment echoes the reader's own, and Gayle L. Smith, who described the high language as the "language of transcendence," also in the *Colby Library Quarterly,* in 1983.

Criticism

Cynthia Bily

Bily currently teaches at Adrian College. In the following essay, she examines the universal themes that Jewett uses in "A White Heron."

To her contemporaries, Sarah Orne Jewett was primarily a local color writer. Her stories and novels were peopled with typical villagers speaking in dialect, going about their daily work as country doctors or farmers or seafarers, moving about among

Compare
&
Contrast

- **1880s:** Concern for the environment becomes an issue in the United States in the years following the Civil War, when economic development increases rapidly at the expense of natural resources, such as timber. In 1891, President Harrison signs a proclamation that turns a million acres in Colorado into the nation's first forest preserve.

  1990s: Forest preservation threatens jobs in the Pacific Northwest, where loggers prohibited from destroying the habitat of the spotted owl face layoffs. Global concern for the environment results in conferences such as the 1992 Earth Summit, held in Brazil. Topics for discussion include global warming and the destruction of the rain forests.

- **1880s:** Naturalist John James Audubon (1785–1851) attains great wealth and fame from his paintings of birds. He works from dead models; disliking the stiffness of stuffed and mounted specimens, he requires many freshly killed birds for each painting.

1990s: The Audubon Society, founded in 1886 as the country's first bird preservation society, comprises 500 chapters, 9 regional, and 12 state offices.

- **1880s:** Many people move to crowded manufacturing towns, like the one in which Sylvia lives with her family, because of the availability of factory jobs. In the 1880s, the industrial sector grows rapidly as machine processes are standardized and new technologies, along with vast resources, make U.S. industries among the most productive in the world.

  1990s: Concerns regarding manufacturing industries are tied to environmental issues. Pollution from factory and automobile emissions is linked to global warming. While wealthier nations make some efforts to regulate emissions, developing countries dependent on industrialization to improve their economy lack the resources and desire to control pollution.

---

the flora and fauna and landscape of New England. As a young avid reader, Jewett had admired the work of Harriet Beecher Stowe, especially her depictions of the common folk of the South, with their strengths and short comings. One of Jewett's aims as a writer was to present the people of her native Maine in the same honest and respectful light. But if her characters' speech and dress and mannerisms were identifiably regional, their concerns and problems were not. Like all the best local color writing, Jewett's fiction uses regional settings, but explores themes that are universal.

Most of Jewett's central characters are women, and they usually operate to some extent out of the bustle of mainstream society: they are not young women having dramatic adventures and finding husbands, but spinsters and widows and children and professional women leading quiet, sometimes lonely, lives. Their conflicts are internal, their support is mainly from other women, their arena is domestic. It has often been observed that fiction with a male protagonist is considered suitable for all to read, but fiction about women is ''women's fiction.'' Perhaps this accounts in part for Jewett's having been treated as second-rate, although in the century since it was written *The Country of the Pointed Firs* has never been allowed to go out of print, and ''A White Heron'' has been anthologized dozens of times.

The story of ''A White Heron'' revolves around a conflict, a choice a young girl must make between listening to an external voice and heeding an internal one. It is the story of nine-year-old Sylvia, who lives in the Maine woods with her grandmother, Mrs. Tilley. The two women (if the word can be used to describe a nine-year-old) appear to have no

What Do I Read Next?

- *The Country of the Pointed Firs,* Jewett's 1896 novel, is often considered her greatest work and one of the nineteenth century's best pieces of regional fiction. Set in a New England coastal village and the surrounding countryside, and narrated in a strong female voice, it tells the stories of the typically eccentric people who shape the landscape, and are shaped by it.

- Sherwood Anderson's *Winesburg, Ohio* (1919) does for the American Midwest what Jewett's work does for New England: presents universally recognized characters in a highly localized setting. Anderson's male narrator observes life in his small town, recording the secret loneliness and pain of his neighbors.

- Mary Austin's 1903 *The Land of Little Rain* is an early work of Southwestern regional literature. It is nonfictional but very personal, a detailed look at the terrain, plants, animals, and Native Americans in the Sierras, presented by a woman who spent years living in the dry mountains and fighting to protect them from human exploitation.

- *Buffalo Gals and Other Animal Presences* is Ursula K. Le Guin's 1987 collection of short stories. Le Guin may be best known as a science fiction writer, but these stories explore the place of women and animals in a male-dominated culture. In "May's Lion" and other stories, she describes a world of women in which the earth's creatures are respected and welcomed.

- In one of the best-known works of American natural history, *Walden, or Life in the Woods* (1854), Henry David Thoreau abandons civilization for two years and attempts to live a life of self-sufficiency and exploration in a tiny cabin at the edge of Walden Pond.

---

near neighbors, and there is no family around. Sylvia's parents and siblings live in a "crowded manufacturing town" from which Mrs. Tilley rescued Sylvia a year before, and Sylvia has known from the day she arrived on the farm that "she never should wish to go home." Whatever men were once on the farm have wandered off or died. So the two women are alone, with only a cow, Mistress Moolly, for companionship. For Sylvia, the cow is a true "valued companion," giving "good milk and plenty of it," and offering an excuse for lingering walks through the woods between the pasture and home. Sylvia and her grandmother have plenty to eat and a "clean and comfortable little dwelling." They want for nothing. As Elizabeth Ammons describes it, it is a "rural paradise," a mythical woman-dominated Eden.

If the forest home has overtones of fantasy or myth, so too is Sylvia a most unnaturally natural child. Although born and raised in the city, her true home is in the forest (even her name is from the Latin for "wood"). Mrs. Tilley observes, "There ain't a foot o' ground she don't know her way over, and the wild creatur's counts her one o' themselves. Squer'ls she'll tame to come an' feed right out o' her hands, and all sorts o' birds." She is "afraid of folks," but she is not afraid to be in the woods after dark, even hearing the animals calling and rustling. Rather than causing fear, she listens to the bird calls "with a heart that beat fast with pleasure"; it makes her feel "as if she were a part of the gray shadows and moving leaves." Interestingly, the only thing that does disturb her in the forest is the memory from her city days of "the great red-faced boy who used to chase and frighten her."

Startling Sylvia out of this memory is the "determined, and somewhat aggressive" sound and then the appearance of another male, "the enemy," a handsome young man with a gun over his shoulder and a "heavy game bag." He is an ornithologist, a scientist who studies birds, and he is spending his vacation in the woods hunting for new specimens for his collection of "stuffed and preserved" birds. Sylvia responds to his friendliness

> If the forest home has overtones of fantasy or myth, so too is Sylvia a most unnaturally natural child."

by withdrawing. She can barely speak (she says only four words throughout the story), she does not "dare to look boldly" at him, she hangs her head "as if the stem of it were broken," she is "alarmed," "trembling." Mrs. Tilley, on the other hand, leaps to offer the guest a meal, his choice of bedding, and lively chatter about the farm, her lost family, and Sylvia. As the three "new friends" sit in the doorway after supper, Mrs. Tilley and the hunter chat. She tells him about her son Dan, who was so good with his gun that "I never wanted for pa'tridges or gray squer'ls while he was to home." The man talks about his own hunting, not for food, but for specimens for his collection. Mrs. Tilley is enjoying the man's company, but Sylvia avoids focusing on him, and pretends to be more interested in watching a hop-toad on the path.

The hunter is everything Sylvia is not. He is friendly and outgoing, while she is "afraid of folks." He has traveled freely, while Sylvia has "wondered and dreamed about" but never seen the ocean just a few miles away. (Mrs. Tilley, too, has always stayed close to home, but "I'd ha' seen the world myself if it had been I could.") He seems to have plenty of money, and offers ten dollars for the secret of where the white heron nests, but for Sylvia "no amount of thought ... could decide how many wished-for treasures then ten dollars, so lightly spoken of, would buy."

It is no wonder that Sylvia is confused. As her fear evaporates, she finds that he is "most kind and sympathetic." They walk through the woods together, watching the birds, listening to their songs. Her "woman's heart, asleep in the child, [is] vaguely thrilled by a dream of love." And yet there are uneasy moments. It does not trouble the girl, but the narrator notices that although they are in the woods Sylvia knows every foot of, the youngman always leads the way, and Sylvia follows. He does most of the talking; "The sound of her own unquestioned voice would have terrified her—it was hard enough to answer yes or know when there was need of that." Like the girl, the youngman admires birds, but he shows his admiration by killing them. The only times she is afraid with him now is when he kills "some unsuspecting creature." She is never one with the hunter, never on equal footing. Can the young child recognize that the hunter values Sylvia for the same reason he values the white heron: because in her special knowledge of the woods and the birds she is rare, and therefore useful?

The action of the story comes down to a choice for Sylvia. Having more knowledge than the hunter, she must choose whether to make him happy by telling him where the heron's nest is (and he "is so well worth making happy") or keep the secret to herself. Critics have offered many different interpretations about the meaning of this choice. The hunter offers a chance for money, for fulfilled womanhood, for human companionship, for sex. (Although Kelley Griffith, Jr. points out the inherent absurdity in assuming that this temporary partnership between the man and the child could become permanent.) Whatever he represents, it is clear that if Sylvia chooses him she will lose something of herself. She can remain a "lonely country child," or she can serve, follow, and love him "as a dog loves."

What Sylvia finds at the top of the tree is the world, and her place in it. George Held points out that the offer of money separates Sylvia for the first time from the natural world. As she climbs, the connection is restored. Watching the two hawks, "Sylvia felt as if she too could go flying away among the clouds." Back on the ground, when it is time to tell the secret, "she remembers how the white heron came flying through the golden air and how they watched the sea and the morning together." Sylvia knows where she belongs, she knows what she is complete with and whom she would always follow. And she has seen "the vast and awesome world" without anyone's help.

So Sylvia makes her choice. As Griffith explains, it is a limited triumph, "such a choice is fraught with risk—the risk of loneliness, isolation, disappointment, limited opportunity, and doubt." Having gone through this experience, Sylvia, who had seemed content to live without human companionship, is now a "lonely country child."

What is remarkable about "A White Heron" is how well it has spoken to readers of different generations. When Jewett wrote the story in the 1880s, she was concerned by the decimation of the

New England forests and the over-collecting of certain animals, including the heron. These concerns resurfaced in the United States in the 1970s, and gave readers an important look at environmental issues. Feminist concerns that faded from public consciousness after women's suffrage in the 1920s reappeared in the 1970s, and growing public discussion about sexual orientation gave critics new ways to look at the story and at Jewett's life. Of course, archetypal themes of good versus evil, flesh versus spirit, money versus grace, have always been with us. Jewett's great talent was in creating characters and relationships so rich that they have touched readers' hearts and minds for over a century.

Source: Cynthia Bily, ''Overview of 'A White Heron','' in *Short Stories for Students,* Gale, 1998.

Elizabeth Ammons

In the following excerpt, Ammons shares her interpretation of how natural images are used to develop the theme of feminism in Jewett's ''A White Heron.''

> Let us imagine that we live in a culture where time is a cycle, where the sand dollar lies beside its fossil (as it does). Where everything is seen to return, as the birds return to sight with the movement of the waves. As I return to the beach, again and again.
>
> Imagine that in that returning nothing stands outside; the bird is not separate from the wave but both are part of the same rhythm. Imagine that I know—not with my intellect but in my body, my heart—that I do not stand separate from the sand dollar or the fossil; that the slow forces that shaped the life of one and preserved the other under the deep pressure of settling mud for cycles upon cycles are the same forces that have formed my life; that when I hold the fossil in my hand I am looking into a mirror. . . . We are aware of the world as returning, the forms of our thoughts flow in circles, spirals, webs; they weave and dance, honoring the links, the connections, the patterns, the changes, so that nothing can be removed from its context (Starhawk, *Dreaming the Dark: Magic, Sex and Politics,* 1982, pp. 15–16).
>
> And now let us imagine that into this web—into this timeless cycle of birds and waves—walks a man with a gun.

I start with this quotation from the witch Starhawk because I want to suggest that ''A White Heron,'' on one level an interesting but ''easy'' story about the irreconcilable conflict between opposing sets of values: urban/rural, scientific/intuitional, civilized/natural, masculine/feminine, on a deeper level represents as radical—as sinister—a challenge to complacent heterosexual ideology as do the imaginings of a witch such as

> **Perhaps the most obvious meaning of 'A White Heron' comes from the female creation, or recreation, myth Jewett offers."**

Starhawk. Indeed, it will be my contention that the arguments of ''A White Heron'' and of Starhawk, ''birds'' separated by a century (Jewett's story was published in 1886, Starhawk's book in 1982), have things in common. Specifically, after talking briefly about ''A White Heron'' as creation myth and as historical commentary, I will be arguing three things: that ''A White Heron'' is a story about resistance to heterosexuality; that the form Jewett adopts to express her idea is, quite appropriately, the fairy tale; and that despite her protests to the contrary Jewett shows in this fiction her ability to create conventional ''plot''—that is, to use inherited masculine narrative shape—when she needs to.

Perhaps the most obvious meaning of ''A White Heron'' comes from the female creation, or recreation, myth Jewett offers. The story presents a little girl whose world is entirely female. No brother, father, uncle, or grandfather lives in it; the men have feuded and left or died. Only she and her grandmother inhabit the rural paradise to which the child was removed after spending the first eight years of her life in a noisy manmade mill-town, the strongest memory (and perfect symbol) of which is a ''great red-faced boy who used to chase and frighten her'' as she walked home through the streets at night. In the country with her grandmother she is safe. Named Sylvia (Latin for ''woods'') the girl feels that ''she never had been alive at all before she came to live on the farm.'' Her grandmother says: there ''never was such a child for straying out-of-doors since the world was made!'' Clearly Sylvia is nature's child, a pristine or first female, repelled by the city but so at home in the woods that the birds and animals share their secrets and the earth itself, her true grandmother, embraces her with gentle breezes and soft lullabies. Walking home through the woods one night (compare this with the experience she remembers from the city), she listens ''to the thrushes with a heart that beat fast with pleasure'' and senses "in the great boughs overhead . . . little birds and beasts . . . going about their world . . . [and] saying goodnight to each other in sleepy twitters. . . . It made her feel as if she were a part of the gray shadows and the moving leaves." As her grandmother boasts, "'the wild creatur's counts her one o' themselves'."

The whimsical and yet serious incarnation of this magical "natural" place to which the child has been restored, appropriately by her maternal grandmother, is a cow. Symbol of bountiful female nurture—a cow is a walking udder, a warm mobile milky mother (of a different species from us to be sure, but as this story shows, difference in species is not an important distinction to make in life)—the cow represents what the city is *not* and what the woods, healthy, wild, domestic, maternal, stands for in "A White Heron." In fact, Jewett opens the story by concentrating on the bond between this exaggeratedly female animal and her "little woodsgirl." The two of them, the mature female (Mistress Moolly the cow) and nine-year-old Sylvia, amble together through the woods away from the western light (which means toward the rising moon, the heavenly body associated with women) in a wending nightly ritual of hide-and-seek that is almost a dance, the two partners know their steps so well. Played with the wild but milky Mistress Moolly, this game of finding each other, situated as it is at the very opening of the story, serves as a metaphor for the whole realm of matrifocal happiness into which Jewett draws us. In this world females— human, bovine, it does not matter—*can* find each other. They can live together in fertile self-sufficiency and contentment, much as Jewett herself, of course, lived happily with her sisters and women friends within a complex and satisfying network of female support and intimacy into which men might wander, like the nameless intruder in this story, but always as strangers and never to stay.

Read historically, this Adamless Eden represents a response—mythic, spiritual—to the dramatic changes taking place in the lives of middle-class white American women toward the turn into the twentieth century. On the one hand, the middle-class nineteenth-century ideology of separate masculine and feminine spheres excluded women from competition and success in the public arena—medicine, commerce, high art, and the like. The ideology of separatism severely confined and limited women. At the same time, however, as Carroll Smith-Rosenberg points out in her classic study of middle-class, white, nineteenth-century female friendship in America (*Signs,* Autumn 1975, p. 9–10), separatism strengthened women by honoring female bonding and intimacy. As Smith-Rosenberg explains, "women . . . did not form an isolated and oppressed subcategory in male society. Their letters and diaries indicate that women's sphere had an essential integrity and dignity that grew out of women's shared experiences and mutual affection and that, despite the profound changes which affected American social structure and institutions between the 1760s and 1870s, retained a constancy and predictability" (Josephine Donovan, *New England Local Color Literature: A Women's Tradition,* 1983, p. 109).

Smith-Rosenberg's identification of the 1870s as the beginning of the end of this period of continuity for women highlights the fact that "A White Heron," written in 1881, celebrates the ideology of separatism at the time historically that it was beginning to fall apart. As Josephine Donovan notes, the story speaks to "the profound ambivalence women of the late nineteenth century felt as they were beginning to move out of the female-centered world of the home into male-centered institutions." Sylvia confronts and is tempted by the possibility of a new and traditionally masculine ethic for women. The hunter invites her to participate in his project. She can, like her sisters in the ranks of stenographers and typewriters smartly decking themselves out in shirtwaists and suit jackets to invade the nation's offices and boardrooms, bastions of male privilege and power previously off limits to women, identify with men. She can join the great masculine project of conquering and controlling ("harnessing") nature and agreeing on money as the best measure of worth and most effective medium of exchange between human beings. She can, in short, even though she is female, join in the great late nineteenth-century game of buying and selling the world.

She can—but she won't. Sylvia, and clearly Jewett as well, finds in the ideology of female separatism, despite its limitations, a better environment for women than that offered by the new ideology of integration, or identification with masculine values. The older ideology values compassion over profit and cooperation over competition. While the perfect bird for the ornithologist is a dead one, the perfect bird for the child is alive. Sylvia, choosing the past over the future, the bird over a ten dollar gold piece, says no to the temptation represented by the glamorous young scientist so eager to make a girl his partner. In the last paragraph the narrator concedes that the choice is not easy: "Were the birds better friends than their hunter might have been,—who can tell?". The young stranger with a gun is beautiful and powerful. "He can make them rich with money; he has promised it, and they are poor now. He is so well worth making happy." The stranger has great allure: the future is tempting. Indeed, Sylvia's grandmother is converted. But Sylvia is not. She may change when she is older; of that we cannot be certain. But the moment this story captures is the moment of her resistance. The moment of her saying no. . . .

Source: Elizabeth Ammons, "The Shape of Violence in Jewett's 'A White Heron'," in *Colby Library Quarterly,* Vol. XXII, No. 1, March, 1986, pp. 6–16.

Kelley Griffith, Jr.

In the following excerpt, Griffith examines some ways in which the character Sylvia from Jewett's "A White Heron" fits the archetype of a hero, with attention paid especially to the conflict of "man versus society."

"But what shall I do with my 'White Heron' now she is written? She isn't a very good magazine story, but I love her, and mean to keep her for the beginning of my next book." (Letters of Sarah Orne Jewett, ed. Annie Fields 1911, p. 60)

When Sarah Orne Jewett wrote these words to a friend, the *Atlantic Monthly* had rejected her story "A White Heron," and she was puzzled about its artistic merit. But after it appeared in a collection of her stories in 1886, it immediately attracted compliments from friends and fellow writers. Since then, it has become her most anthologized and best known story. I feel that the key to both the *Atlantic's* puzzlement and the story's wide appeal is its handling of the hero archetype. Sylvia, the protagonist, becomes a traditional hero who makes a quest after a much desired object. The *Atlantic* editors probably did not know what to make of this work of fantasy from a normally down-to-earth local color realist. But the story is much more than a simple fantasy. For Jewett, it seems to have been a personal "myth" that expressed her own experience and the experience of other women in the nineteenth century who had similar gifts, aspirations, and choices. And for modern readers its implications are even broader.

The hero archetype has been ably treated by a number of writers, but the definitive treatment is probably Joseph Campbell's *The Hero with a Thousand Faces* (1949). Campbell draws the hero's

> **"** Unconsciously she realizes that the white heron represents the essence of a mysterious new world, and she cannot betray it for a mere ten dollars."

basic story from his survey of myths, tales, rituals, and art from all over the world. The hero's career, he says, has three main parts. In the first, the "Departure," the hero receives a "call to adventure." By a seeming accident, someone or something invites the hero into "an unsuspected world," into "a relationship with forces that are not rightly understood" (Campbell, p. 51). Often he receives supernatural aid from a "protective figure" who helps him in his adventures (Campbell, p. 69). In the second part of the hero's story, the "Initiation," the hero crosses a dangerous "threshold" into a strange, fluid, dream-like world where he undergoes a succession of trials (Campbell, pp. 77, 97). The climax of these trials is the hero's victory over all opposition. Sometimes this victory is accompanied by a mystical vision that shows the hero something of the life-creating energy of all existence (Campbell, pp. 40–41). The third part of the hero's story is the "Return." Because of his victory, he now has a "boon" to bestow upon those he has left behind (Campbell, p. 30). The trip back to his homeland can be arduous, but once back he has a choice and a problem. He can withhold or bestow his boon, whatever he wants (Campbell, p. 193). And he must somehow integrate, if he can, his transcendental experience with the "banalities and noisy obscenities" of his old world (Campbell, p. 218).

This summary of Campbell's archetype fits "A White Heron" exactly. "A White Heron" is the story of Sylvia, a nine-year-old girl, who goes in quest of an exotic, almost miraculous bird. She herself has unusual gifts. Since coming from a "crowded manufacturing town" to live with her grandmother deep in the forest, she has become, as her name suggests, a "little woods-girl," a forest nymph. Her closeness to the forest and to the forest creatures is phenomenal. "There ain't a foot o' ground she don't know her way over," her grandmother says, "and the wild creatures counts her one o' themselves. Squer'ls she'll tame to come an' feed right out o' her hands, and all sorts o' birds." Her tale begins when the unexpected breaks into her life—a young hunter whistles and emerges from the shadows into her pathway. She is frightened but leads him home where her grandmother promises him a night's lodging. After supper, he explains that he collects birds—kills and stuffs them—and that he wants particularly to find a white heron, rare to the area, that he had glimpsed only a few miles away. He offers ten dollars to anyone who might help him find its nest. Sylvia's heart beats wildly, for not only would the ten dollars buy "many wished-for treasures," but she has herself seen the same white heron. This, to use Campbell's terms, is her "call to adventure." The next day she tags along behind the hunter, grows increasingly fond of him, and decides to find the heron's nest.

At this point, Jewett tells us that a "great pine tree, . . . the last of its generation," stands at the edge of the woods taller than any other tree around. This tree, we come to learn, has magical properties. Sylvia has often thought that from the top of this tree one could see the sea, something she dreams of doing. But now the tree means more. Not only could one see "all the world" from its top but the white heron's "hidden nest" as well. The next morning, the "Initiation" part of Campbell's archetype begins. She steals out of her house before daybreak and goes to the tree, "the monstrous ladder reaching up, up, almost to the sky itself." Her "threshold" is a white oak that just reaches the lowest branches of the pine tree: "When she made the dangerous pass from one tree to the other, the great enterprise would really begin."

Once on the pine tree she experiences the most difficult trials of her journey. The way is "harder than she thought; she must reach far and hold fast, the sharp dry twigs caught and held her and scratched her like angry talons, the pitch made her thin little fingers clumsy and stiff." But the tree itself now awakens to act as her supernatural guardian. It is "amazed" that "this determined spark of human spirit" is climbing it. It loves "the brave, beating heart of the solitary grey-eyed child," steadies its limbs for her, and frowns away the winds.

The climax of Sylvia's climb is a mystical experience corresponding to that in Campbell's archetype. For her, the pine tree becomes a tree of knowledge; it is, after all, like a "great main-mast to the voyaging earth." At the top, "wholly trium-

phant," she sees the sea for the first time, "with the dawning sun making a golden dazzle over it." She looks westward at the woods and farms and sees that "truly it was a vast and awesome world." And at the same time, she also sees the "solemn" white heron perched on a lower branch of her tree, and she sees it fly to its nest in "the green world beneath."

Now she "knows his secret" and begins the third part of the hero's journey, the "Return." The way down is "perilous" and "her fingers ache and her lamed feet slip." But she reaches home finally, where the hunter and her grandmother await her expectantly. All she has to do now is bestow her "boon." But although the hunter "can make them rich with money" and "is so well worth making happy," Sylvia at the last minute holds back her secret. Why? asks the author. Why, when "the great world for the first time puts out a hand to her," does she "thrust it aside for a bird's sake"? The answer is that Sylvia "remembers how the white heron came flying through the golden air and how they watched the sea and the morning together"; she cannot "give its life away." As in Campbell's archetype, Sylvia exercises her option to withhold her boon. She chooses to remain in the world of nature, the place of her adventures and the subject of her revelation. She will not—or cannot—integrate it with the materialistic world beyond the forest that now beckons to her.

The resemblance of Sylvia's experience to the hero archetype described by Campbell is probably not coincidental. Jewett was fond of the same kind of fantasy literature on which Campbell bases his archetype. It would not have been out of the way for her to write an adult fantasy of her own. But if Sylvia is a traditional hero, what is she a hero of? That is, what does she fight for? What does she fight against? What does she renounce? Had Jewett simply ended the story with Sylvia's refusal, the answers to these questions would be quickly forthcoming. Sylvia would be a heroic defender of pristine nature against those who would reduce it to a commercial value—ten dollars for the life of one heron. Sylvia, of course, refuses to betray nature, and in this way "A White Heron" is a "conservation" story. Most of the commentators on this story interpret it in exactly this way.

But Jewett does not end the story with Sylvia's refusal. She adds a paragraph that broadens the implication of the story and makes its meaning ambiguous. Here is the paragraph, the final one of the story:

Dear loyalty, that suffered a sharp pang as the guest went away disappointed later in the day, that would have served and followed him and loved him as a dog loves! Many a night Sylvia heard the echo of his whistle haunting the pasture path as she came home with the loitering cow. She forgot even her sorrow at the sharp report of his gun and the sight of thrushes and sparrows dropping silent to the ground, their songs hushed and their pretty feathers stained and wet with blood. Were the birds better friends than their hunter might have been,—who can tell? Whatever treasures were lost to her, woodlands and summertime, remember! Bring your gifts and graces and tell your secrets to this lonely country girl!

The story now no longer seems to be merely about a choice between nature and someone who would destroy it but between ''love''—a woman's love for a man—and loyalty to something else, something that inevitably leads to loneliness and isolation. Sylvia's attachment to the hunter, we learn earlier, is not just friendship or affection but romantic love. Although she cannot ''understand why he killed the very birds he seemed to like so much,'' she watches him ''with loving admiration'', ''her grey eyes dark with excitement.'' Her ''woman's heart,'' asleep until now, is ''vaguely thrilled by a dream of love,'' and the ''great power'' of love stirs and sways them both as they traverse ''the solemn woodlands with soft-footed silent care.'' Because of this new love, she makes her quest: ''What fancied triumph and delight and glory for the later morning,'' she thinks, ''when she could make known the secret! It was almost too real and too great for the childish heart to bear.''

Looked at realistically, this love motif makes little sense. Sylvia is only nine years old. Even if she told the hunter her secret, he would leave the area, probably never to return. Yet Jewett makes it seem as if Sylvia could have fulfilled a long-term commitment to the hunter, something akin to marriage. Jewett also indicates that the results of Sylvia's choice will be loneliness and lost ''treasures,'' even though Sylvia returns to the same idyllic conditions that existed before the hunter emerged. Finally, Jewett casts doubt upon the rightness of Sylvia's choice. . . .

Sylvia is a hero on several levels of meaning. On the literal level, she is a backwoods girl who quests for something that the man she ''loves'' wants, and at the climax of her quest she finds something much more valuable. She sees the sea, the morning sun, and the countryside—symbolically, the whole world—all at once. Unconsciously she realizes that the white heron represents the essence of this mysterious new world, and she

cannot betray it for a mere ten dollars. On another level, she is Jewett herself and other women like her who heroically reject the too-confining impositions of society for an independent, self-fulfilling life lived on their own terms. Sylvia's age underscores the abstract nature of that choice. She is not just rejecting one man; she is Jewett's surrogate, rejecting all men. But unlike the more polemical ''Farmer Finch'' and *A Country Doctor,* ''A White Heron'' qualifies the triumph of that choice. The final paragraph seems to suggest that such a choice is fraught with risk—the risk of loneliness, isolation, disappointment, limited opportunity, and doubt. On a third level the story achieves its most universal appeal. Sylvia is anyone who unselfishly quests for knowledge, receives a stunning revelation, and resists any cheapening of it. The hero, someone has said, does what normal people are not brave enough or strong enough to do. Most of us would have taken the ten dollars, if only to retain the warm approval and appreciation of those we love. But Sylvia does not, and she pays the penalty. This is her heroism. We admire her for it and would strive to do likewise.

Source: Kelley Griffith, Jr., ''Sylvia as Hero in Sarah Orne Jewett's 'A White Heron','' in *Colby Library Quarterly,* Vol. XXI, No. 1, March, 1985, pp. 22–7.

Michael Atkinson

Atkinson is Associate Professor of English at the University of Cincinnati. In the following excerpt, he offers his interpretation of the favorable impact varying narrative voices have on the conclusion of Jewett's ''A White Heron.''

''A White Heron'' seems a simple story of simple people, in a simple time. Seems. But if we look more closely, we see that Jewett has used diverse and unusual devices to give this much anthologized story the satisfying impact which puts us so at rest at its conclusion. In the next to last scene, for example, she uses authorial voice and privilege in genuinely extravagant ways: a tree's thoughts are reported and given weight, and the author not only urgently whispers counsel to the main character but later exhorts the very landscape and seasons of the year in pantheistic prayer. But these departures from ''common sense'' seem perfectly natural to us as we read the story, because they contribute so directly to the effect of the tale, the sense of which is a little uncommon. In fact, the work demands these extravagances.

''A White Heron'' is a story of innocence, a theme calculated to move us deeply, loss of inno-

> Sylvia's courage summons
> a response from the tree, a
> deep and intimate bond of
> trust in which nature rises to
> the needs of the girl without
> her asking."

cence being a mainstay of literature and myth from Genesis through Milton, Joyce, Salinger, and beyond—a theme of proven power. However, Jewett here writes not of innocence lost, but of innocence preserved, much rarer, yet in less obvious ways touching each of us in the corners of our lives where we remain uncalloused by experience, resignation, or cynicism. To make the story take, Jewett has to convince us emotionally that Sylvia's staying in the world of innocence is a positive step in her development as a person—not merely a cowering, a retreat, or a regression she must ultimately transcend. And it is to this end that she employs her extravagant means.

The world of innocence in which Sylvia lives is a frail one, lacking strength. Both the girl and her grandmother, innocents of youth and age, their cottage a virtual "hermitage," seem vulnerable in a number of ways, living in a balance that could be upset by Sylvia's return to the city or by the intrusion of even the genuinely nice young hunter/ornithologist who loves birds but kills what he loves, to preserve them, offering money to find the path to his prize. Our most immediate desire is that Sylvia remain in her innocent world, inviolate. But we also are made (by the impingement of threats from without) to want strength for her innocence that it might fend for itself—not a further retirement, but a compelling vision, an experience beside which anything promised by the thrill of infatuation for the hunter would pale.

And that vision is precisely what Jewett gives us in her management of the climactic scene, Sylvia's ascent of the great pine tree. As she climbs, our hopes and expectations are decidedly mixed: the climb is frightening, but the vision from the top tantalizing; the heron must be seen, but (contrary to Sylvia's conscious purpose in climbing) the hunter

must not be told. In short, we want for her a transforming vision, but fear she will fail to attain it or will squander it. Something more than a glimpse of the heron's nest is needed here—some transcendent way of seeing, beyond the capacity of Sylvia, or her grandmother, or the hunter, each of whom in turn has been a center of consciousness through which this story has been reflected so far. And it is to fulfill this precise need that Jewett gives us the following passage:

> The tree seemed to lengthen itself out as she went up, and to reach farther and farther upward. It was like a great mainmast to the voyaging earth; it must have been truly amazed that morning through all its ponderous frame as it felt this determined spark of human spirit creeping and climbing from higher branch to branch. Who knows how steadily the least twigs held themselves to advantage this light, weak creature on her way! The old pine must have loved its new dependent. More than all the hawks, and bats, and moths, and even the sweet voiced thrushes, was the brave, beating heart of the solitary gray-eyed child. And the tree stood still and held away the winds that June morning while the dawn grew bright in the east.

Sylvia's courage summons a response from the tree, a deep and intimate bond of trust in which nature rises to the needs of the girl without her asking, actively caring for the child and her birdlike soul, rare and wonderful, now hidden, like the heron, deeply and inaccessibly in nature itself.

Thus, it is not just that Sylvia has transcended her former viewpoint, symbolized (in the story's next paragraph) by her looking down upon the sea and the flying birds, but that the entire fiction has transcended its human limitations—and thus stepped outside the limits of human relationship which lured and threatened Sylvia. The validity of her remaining in nature and not forsaking its trust for human relationship is confirmed by the sentience of the tree, the towering and deeply rooted presence of nature embodied. Sylvia's final decision to keep her bond with nature inviolate is both anticipated and justified as we experience not just nature from her point of view, but her from nature's. She is its creature and child.

But another voice also makes itself heard in this scene, the voice of the tale's teller herself. Heretofore content to let the story tell itself by reflection through the consciousnesses of girl, grandmother, and hunter, and now tree, the narrator cannot keep silent at this crucial moment. She calls out to Sylvia silently, directly.

> There where you saw the white heron once you will see him again; look, look! a white spot of him like a

single floating feather.... And wait! wait! do not move a foot or finger, little girl, do not send an arrow of light and consciousness from your two eager eyes, for the heron has perched on a pine bough not far beyond yours.

The narrator's voice is given great power here, because as she directs, so Sylvia sees the long sought heron, the climactic moment of the climactic passage. The narrator's calling counsel is as unexpected as the articulated feelings of the tree. But it serves to confirm with human wisdom what the tree would show with natural intelligence. And like the consciousness of the tree, the voice of the narrator transcends other viewpoints in the story. She speaks from a wisdom greater than that possessed by the reader or any character in the tale. She is "older" and wiser than the grandmother, and sees what the old woman does not, representing a true maturity of innocence. She gives a voice to the reader's hopes, and in doing so extends and legitimates them—not by addressing *us* and telling *us* how it is, but by calling (as we in our wisest innocence might call out) to Sylvia.

This sudden cry of the narrator also prepares us for her speaking out in her own voice again at the end of the story. She addresses our uncertainties by articulating them herself: "Were the birds better friends than their hunter might have been,—who can tell?" And then, closing the circle between the points of nature's intelligence and human wisdom, she addresses nature itself: "Whatever treasures were lost to her, woodlands and summertime, remember! Bring your gifts and graces and tell your secrets to this lonely country child!" The hushed and urgent whisper of this conspiracy of wisdom confirms for us the value of Sylvia's experience and her decision not to tell of the white heron, transferring maturity from the social back to the natural realm—profounder, deeper, never to be betrayed. Her innocence is preserved, extended; her soul is larger and steadier; and our experience, complete.

Source: Michael Atkinson, "The Necessary Extravagance of Sarah Orne Jewett: Voices of Authority in 'A White Heron'," in *Studies in Short Fiction,* Vol. 19, No. 1, Winter, 1982, pp. 71–4.

Sources

Ammons, Elizabeth. "The Shape of Violence in Jewett's 'A White Heron.'" *Colby Library Quarterly,* 22, no. 1 (March 1986): 6-16.

Griffith, Jr., Kelley. "Sylvia as Hero in Sarah Orne Jewett's 'A White Heron.'" *Colby Library Quarterly,* 21, no. 1 (March 1985): 22-7.

Further Reading

Cary, Richard. *Sarah Orne Jewett.* Twayne, 1962.
  The first full-length critical review of Jewett's work. This book attempts to analyze all of Jewett's work. Cary finds "A White Heron" philosophically interesting but technically flawed.

Griffith, Jr., Kelley. "Sylvia as Hero in Sarah Orne Jewett's 'A White Heron.'" *Colby Library Quarterly,* Vol. 21, no. 1, March, 1985, pp. 22-7.
  Shows how Sylvia's story follows the archetypal pattern of a hero following a quest for a desired object, and suggests that Sylvia's independence mirrors Jewett's.

Held, George. "Heart to Heart with Nature: Ways of Looking at 'A White Heron.'" *Colby Library Quarterly,* 18 (1982): 55-65.
  Discusses his overall interpretation of Jewett's "A White Heron," paying particular attention to changes that occur in the character Sylvia's relationship with nature.

Johns, Barbara A. "'Mateless and Appealing': Growing into Spinsterhood in Sarah Orne Jewett," in *Critical Essays on Sarah Orne Jewett,* ed. Gwen L. Nagel, G. K. Hall, 1984, pp. 147-65.
  Explores a common theme of Jewett's works—the young woman who turns away from marriage and traditional female action once her view of the world is expanded—and examines Sylvia as an example of this.

Pool, Eugene Hillhouse. "The Child in Sarah Orne Jewett." *Colby Library Quarterly,* Vol. 7, September 1967, pp. 503-09.
  Reads Jewett's works as autobiography. Pool finds that Jewett herself wanted to remain a child and avoid adult relationships.

Smith, Gayle L. "The Language of Transcendence in Sarah Orne Jewett's 'A White Heron.'" *Colby Library Quarterly,* Vol. 19, 1983, pp. 37-44.
  Demonstrates the aptness of Jewett's use of these techniques in presenting a transcendental vision of reality, though some critics have found the shifting point of view and high language to be a weakness in the story.

Yellow Woman

Leslie Marmon Silko

1974

First published in 1974 in Kenneth Rosen's anthology, *The Man to Send Rain Clouds: Contemporary Stories By American Indians,* ''Yellow Woman'' has subsequently appeared in Leslie Marmon Silko's 1981 work, *Storyteller,* a collection of poems, stories and photographs. ''Yellow Woman'' tells the story of a young Laguna Pueblo woman who temporarily goes off with a strange man she meets on a walk along the river. The woman is swept up in the traditional Keresan myth of Kochininako, the Yellow Woman, who left her tribe and family to wander for years with the powerful ka'tsina, or spirit, Whirlwind Man. The story features a compelling blurring of the boundaries between myth and everyday experience, between contemporary Native American life and ancient myths.

In Kenneth Rosen's anthology, *The Man to Send Rain Clouds,* ''Yellow Woman'' was published to stand alone. In *Storyteller,* Silko surrounds ''Yellow Women'' with additional poems and stories that further elucidate Yellow Woman's relationship to the land, the spirits that pervade it and the stories that derive from it. Bernard Hirsch writes in *American Indian Quarterly* that ''this multigeneric work lovingly maps the fertile storytelling ground from which her art evolves and to which it is here returned—and offering to the oral tradition which nurtured it.'' In conjunction with the other works included in *Storyteller,* ''Yellow Woman'' manages to both recreate and comment upon the oral

traditions that have sustained the Laguna Pueblo community.

Author Biography

Born in 1948 in Albuquerque, New Mexico, Leslie Marmon Silko grew up on Laguna Pueblo, a Native American reservation fifty miles west of Albuquerque. The Laguna Pueblo is central to her sense of herself as a person and a writer. In *The Man to Send Rain Clouds,* she explains: "I grew up at Laguna Pueblo. I am of mixed-breed ancestry, but what I know is Laguna. This place I am from is everything I am as a writer and human being."

One of three sisters, Silko describes her childhood as "sheltered." Her parents valued education, and encouraged their daughters to succeed on many levels. In *Backtalk: Women Writers Speak Out,* Silko tells Donna Perry that her father, Lee Marmon, taught her to shoot a gun at age seven and let his daughters compete in contests against grown men: "My dad would say, 'Well, my girls can do anything your boys can do, and my girls can do it better.'" Silko describes her family as a "book family"; from a very early age, she was surrounded both by written words and the oral tradition of the Laguna Pueblo. Her family valued education so much that from the fifth grade on they sent her to a small private school in Albuquerque, fifty miles away when it became clear that the Laguna Day School, where she was not allowed to speak Keresan, the language spoken by the Laguna people, was providing an inferior education.

At the University of New Mexico, Silko majored in English. She published her first stories, "Tony's Story," and "The Man to Send Rain Clouds" before she graduated Phi Beta Kappa in 1969. While an undergraduate, she married her first husband and gave birth to her first son, Robert. Even though she had achieved critical success as a writer of fiction, she was determined to be a lawyer. She wanted to follow in the footsteps of her father, Lee Marmon, who had been a tribal officer and had successfully sued the State of New Mexico over six million acres of stolen land. While still in law school at the University of New Mexico, Silko received a National Endowment for the Arts Discovery Grant in 1971 for her short story "The Man

to Send Rain Clouds." After her second son, Casimir, was born, she decided that she would be a writer rather than a lawyer, and did not complete the program.

Silko was awarded the Pushcart Prize for poetry in 1973. Seven of her short stories (including "Yellow Woman") were anthologized in Kenneth Rosen's *The Man to Send Rain Clouds* (1974). In that same year, she published her volume of poetry, *Laguna Woman* to great critical acclaim. When she published her first novel, *Ceremony* in 1977, *The New York Times Book Review* called it "a splendid achievement," declaring, "Without question Leslie Silko is the most accomplished Indian writer of her generation." In her introduction to *Yellow Woman,* Melody Graulich writes that Silko's "early work focuses on growing up as an Indian and as mixed-breed, on young people who come to understand the 'I' in relation to their cultural practices and to the land, a significant theme in American Indian literature."

In 1981, Silko published *Storyteller,* in which she included "Yellow Woman" in a series of stories and poems. In *ARIEL,* Linda Krumholz explains: "*Storyteller* is a book of stories and a book about stories: it contains traditional Pueblo Indian stories, Silko's family stories, poems, conventional European style short stories, gossip stories and photographs, all woven together to create a self-reflexive text that examines the cyclical role of stories in recounting and generating meaning for individuals, communities and nations." That same year, Silko received a MacArthur Foundation fellowship, colloquially known as the "genius grant." The MacArthur Foundation fellowship allowed her to stop teaching and to devote all her time to her massive novel, *Almanac of the Dead* (1991). Eight hundred pages long, *Almanac of the Dead* is a departure from Silko's earlier work. Based on fragmentary Mayan almanacs, Silko spins dozens of interconnected tales to rewrite five hundred years of American history and envision a future where the tribal people of the Americas retake the land from the governments that stole it from them. Concludes Perry in *Backtalk,* "That Silko manages to pull off this tour de force is amazing; that she does it with humor is incredible." In 1985, she published a deeply moving collection of letters, *With the Delicacy and Strength of Lace.* In 1993, she told Perry that "*Almanac* spawned another novel about a woman who is a serial killer . . . [who] just kills policemen and politicians." Silko lives on a ranch outside Tucson, Arizona.

Leslie Marmon Silko

Plot Summary

The poem that prefaces "Yellow Woman" suggests that the story that follows is mythic. Whirlwind Man belongs "to the wind," and he and Kochininako, Yellow Woman, "travel swiftly / this whole world." At the story's opening, the unnamed female narrator awakens at dawn next to a man on a riverbank. She watches the sun rise, then gets up and walks south, following their footprints from the day before. She comes across their horses, and she looks for but cannot see her pueblo (a multi-storied dwelling built of adobe; capitalized, the word also means "people" in the sense of a tribal group).

She returns to the sleeping man to tell him she is leaving. He reminds her, smiling, that she must come with him. He calls her "Yellow Woman" and will not answer her questions about who he is, saying only that the night before she had guessed who he was and why he had come for her. The narrator insists she is *not* Yellow Woman ("I have my own name and I come from the pueblo on the other side of the mesa. Your name is Silva and you are a stranger I met by the river yesterday afternoon"). Laughing, he tells her that what happened yesterday has nothing to do with today. He calls her Yellow Woman again. The narrator evokes the Keresan myth explicitly, telling him that "the old stories about the ka'tsina spirit and Yellow Woman can't mean us."

The narrator recounts that in the old stories, Yellow Woman went away with a spirit from the North and lived with him for a long time. Eventually, she returned to her pueblo with twin sons. The narrator and the stranger make love in the river sand again, and she wonders if what she is currently experiencing "is what happens in the story." She speculates that the Yellow Woman of the ancient story may have been an ordinary woman with a family who did not realize, at first, that she was being taken by a mountain spirit. When Silva stands up, points to her clothes "tangled in the blanket" and says "Let's go," she walks off with him, but she hopes they will meet someone who will indicate that Silva is "only a man" and that she is just a woman and not Kochininako. They ride north, into the mountain foothills of black lava rock.

They arrive at Silva's house, and the narrator asks Silva if he often uses the story about Yellow Woman and the ka'tsina to lure women home with him. He does not answer her directly, but he says that "someday they will talk about us, and they will say, 'Those two lived long ago when things like that happened.'" Later she joins him on a ridge overlooking mesas, valleys, and plains. Although she cannot see her own pueblo, Silva tells her, "From here I can see the world." He indicates different areas of the landscape, pointing out ranches and pastureland owned by Texans and Mexicans. He reveals that he is a cattle rustler. The narrator asks if he is a Navajo, which he denies, implicitly insisting on his identity as the ka'tsina.

The narrator awakens alone the next morning in Silva's house. She thinks of her family, whom she imagines will report her missing. If her old grandpa were alive he would tell them that she'd been stolen by mountain spirit and would eventually come home "—they usually do." In the meantime, her mother and grandmother will raise her baby and her husband will find someone else. She imagines her family will continue as they have before but with a story about her disappearance. She decides to return home, and walks off, but returns to Silva's house at noon. When she sees the house, she remembers that she meant to go home, "But that didn't seem important any more." Silva is preparing a beef carcass, and he asks her to ride to Marquez with him to sell the meat.

As they are riding toward Marquez they encounter a fat white rancher who accuses Silva of rustling cattle. Silva tells the narrator to ride back up the mountain. As she urges her horse to run up the difficult mountain trail, she hears four shots and concludes that Silva has shot the rancher. Instead of continuing upward toward Silva's house, she rides into the valley and homeward. Near the place by the river where she first encountered Silva, she dismounts, and starts the horse off alone on the trail she has just traveled. She continues on foot in the opposite direction, sitting for a while by the river and thinking about Silva before walking the rest of the way to her pueblo. As she approaches, she can hear her mother, grandmother, husband, and baby. She decides to tell them she was kidnapped by a Navajo, and regrets that her old grandfather is not alive to hear her true story "because it was the Yellow woman stories he liked to tell best."

Characters

Kochininako
See Yellow Woman

Narrator

The main character of "Yellow Woman" is the narrator. The reader never learns her name. She is a Laguna Pueblo wife and mother. She has been to school and does not seem to relate her modern life with the myths of her people, but she heard "the old stories" from her grandfather before he died. She goes away with an appealing stranger whom she encounters on a riverbank, mildly surprised at the ease with which she walks away from her known life in the Pueblo. As she spends time with her mysterious lover, she begins to wonder if she is experiencing events identical to those that inspired the original Yellow Woman tales. After a violent encounter with a white rancher, she leaves her lover and returns home with a story to tell, adding to the Yellow Woman lore and interweaving her own tale and life with the traditions of her people.

Old Grandpa

The narrator's grandfather has died before "Yellow Woman" begins, but his presence informs the narrative. He was the person from whom the narrator heard the myths and legends of the Laguna, including the Yellow Woman stories, which were his favorites. The narrator thinks of her grandfatherseveral times during the course of the narrative. When she returns home, she wishes that he were alive to hear her new version of the Yellow Woman story. Old Grandpa represents the living history of the oral tradition.

The Rancher

The white rancher, a fat young man, precipitates the narrator's return to her community. He confronts Silva and the narrator as they ride to Marquez to sell stolen beef. The rancher represents the thievery of the Anglos who stole Indian lands, as well as hostility and racism.

Silva

The stranger whom the narrator encounters by the riverbank is called Silva. He is a cattle rustler who lives alone in the mountains and does not belong to any tribe that the narrator can ascertain. Silva repeatedly calls the narrator "Yellow Woman," and the narrator begins to identify herself with Yellow woman and Silva with Whirlwind Man, the ka'tsina who takes Yellow Woman to his House in the Sky in the myths. Silva says he can "see the whole world" from the prospect before his isolated mountain house, though the narrator cannot even see her home from that vantage point.

Silva tells the narrator that he steals cattle from the Texan and Mexican rancherss (who of course initially stole land from the Native people). Twice the narrator appears to be leaving him; once she returns to his mountain dwelling, but the second time she goes back to the spot where she first saw him by the riverbank. She wants to return to him then—"to kiss him and to touch him"—but the mountains seem very far away by then, and she continues to her own home, believing that one day she will find him again waiting for her by the river.

Yellow Woman

Yellow Woman, or Kochininako, is a central figure in Laguna oral tradition. Different Yellow Woman stories have various focal points—abduction, meeting with powerful spirits, getting power from the spirit world and returning it to the people, female sexuality, the birth of twins, the refusal to marry, weaving, grinding corn, getting water, outwitting evil spirits. Silko's story draws from a version in which Yellow Woman goes away with a ka'tsina or mountain spirit from the North and lives with him or a long time. Eventually, she returns to her pueblo with twin sons. Yellow Woman's nonconforming and often outrageous (by her community's standards) behavior often brings benefits to her people. She is seen less as a role model for Laguna women than as a remarkable avatar of the spirit of all womankind.

Themes

Ambiguity and Identity

Like many other contemporary Native American stories, "Yellow Woman" is concerned with liminality, which is a state of being between two worlds or two states of existance. In the Native American world view, "nature" includes the spirits as well as the animals and people who inhabit the land, and the land itself. The unnamed narrator of "Yellow Woman" finds herself between two worlds—that of her everyday life and that of the , mythic history of her people. It is also significant that from the bluff in front of Silva's house in the foothills, he can point out both Texan and Mexican lands to the narrator, underscoring that the story itself takes place in a borderland region.

That Silko never names the narrator of "Yellow Woman" adds to the story's ambiguity. The narrator and her companion potentially occupy several realms of reality at once. On one level she is a young Native American woman possessing a certain identity. She lives in real time, in a world dominated by automobiles and trains and the bustle of modern life. She has received a formal education; she is a wife, mother, daughter, and granddaughter. She is also identified with the Yellow Woman of Laguna folktale or legend. She meets and has a brief affair with a mysterious man and then returns home. He is seemingly a Navajo cattle rustler named Silva who has been sought by local Texan and Mexican ranchers for some time. On another level, he is closely identified with the mountain spirit or ka'tsina Whirlwind Man, who in the legend makes off with Kochininako, or Yellow Woman.

As "Yellow Woman" progresses, the narrator undertakes what Bernard Hirsch calls "a journey beyond the boundaries of time and place." She confuses her own identity with that of Kochininako, or Yellow Woman, and that of Silva with Whirlwind Man. By the time the story draws to a close, the reader sees her as both: a contemporary young woman who lives in real time with her ordinary family *and* as Yellow Woman, a living embodiment of Native American traditions and values. She now understands that her everyday experience and the timeless, all-inclusive mythic reality of her grandfather's stories are inextricably connected.

Storytelling, Transience, and Transcendence

Another important theme in "Yellow Woman" is the centrality of storytelling to a community's history and sense of itself. Native American cultures, including the Laguna, about whom Silko writes, have a rich oral tradition, in which favorite stories are repeated over and over again in family and ceremonial settings. Through the verbal retelling of ancient myths, the community is able to see the relationship of its presence to its past.But in the face of modern lifestyles, the oral tradition is dying; the narrator's grandfather, who loved the old stories, has passed away, and the narrator does not know anyone who can tell the ancient myths the way he did.

In "Yellow Woman," the narrator repeatedly insists that the story of Yellow Woman bears no meaning in her own life, that it could not happen in contemporary times. She suggests that the story is exists only in the past and that it has no relevance for her own life or for that of a late-twentieth-century Native American community: "The old stories about the ka'tsina spirit and Yellow Woman can't mean us," the narrator comments. "Those stories couldn't happen now."

As the narrative progresses, the narrator begins to realize that she, too, has a tale to share with her community: "I decided to tell them that some Navaho had kidnapped me." By contributing her own story to the community's rich oral traditions and by seeing the resemblance of her own experience to that of Yellow Woman, the narrator transcends her individual identity. True, she is a contemporary young mother who has been to school and has followed a strange man on an adventure, but she is also more than that. She is an incarnation of the mythic Yellow Woman. As the narrator's story is repeated among the people in her community, her individual narrative will become part of the larger narrative of the community and its history. As Silko says in Melody Graulich's book, *Yellow Woman: Women Writers: Texts and Contexts,* "Within one story there are many stories coming together."

Transgression, Sexuality, and Power

In many ways, "Yellow Woman" is a story about transgression and power through sexuality. The young narrator leaves her husband Al and her child to follow the mysterious Silva. Although she is a married woman with many responsibilities, the encounter by the the river leads her to leave her old life behind with scarcly a second thought. In an essay entitled "Yellow Woman and the Beauty of the Spirit," Silko writes: "Kochininako, Yellow Woman, represents all women in the old stories. Her deeds span the spectrum of human behavior and are mostly heroic. . . . Yellow Woman is my favorite because she dares to cross traditional boundaries of ordinary behavior during times of crisis to save the Pueblo; her power lies in her courage and in her uninhibited sexuality, which the old-time Pueblo stories celebrate again and again because fertility was so highly valued."

In *The Desert Is No Lady,* Patricia Clark Smith and Paula Gunn Allen explain that "the ultimate purpose of such ritual abductions and seductions is to transfer knowledge from the spirit world to the human sphere, and this transfer is not accomplished in an atmosphere of control or domination."

Nature

The theme of nature plays an important role in "Yellow Woman." Prior to her experience with Silva, the narrator has lived in a time-bound, historical world, in which she lives an ordinary life with her family. She has been to school, married, and given birth. Her grandfather's stories have given her a link to her past, but she, her mother, and grandmother live primarily in the present. The pueblo in which she has lived her whole life is her entire world.

In "Yellow Woman," nature seems mythic and timeless. When she is along with Silva in the mountains, there is nothing—no highways, cars, or people—to indicate the reality of the late twentieth century. (However, once she is making her way home again, she notices the trails of jets in the sky.) The world to which the narrator eventually returns may seem mundane—her mother and grandmother are making Jell-O, her husband is playing with their baby—but the narrator now knows these two worlds are inextricably connected.

Style

Setting

"Yellow Woman" is set along a river, on mountain trails, in Silva's mountain dwelling, and in the narrator's Laguna pueblo in Arizona. The

enclosed world of the pueblo, where the narrator lives with her family, suggests a limited and comfortable world. The world of the mountains, where Silva takes her, connotes timelessness and mythic knowledge. Although Silko's references to pick-up trucks, highways and Jell-O firmly place "Yellow Woman" in the later twentieth century, in one sense, the setting is timeless: myths cannot be contained by human conceptions of time and place. Since the narrator is simultaneously a modern young woman and Yellow Woman, living both in the late twentieth century and mythic time, it is important to consider that Silko employs a Native American understanding of time. In Native American philosophy, time is dynamic and achronous, or non-linear, meaning that the past and the future always exist in the present moment. Europeans conceptualize a "progressive" model of time, in which time "moves forward" or "advances." The Native American concept of time is circular; the past is never really past, it is always alive and informing the present. The circle or "sacred hoop" is a central image in many Native American belief systems.

Point of View and Narration

"Yellow Woman" is narrated in the first person by a young woman who remains unnamed throughout the story. First-person points of view limit the narrative to only what the narrator perceives. In "Yellow Woman," the entire narrative is filtered through the narrator's experiences, expectations and prior knowledge. In this instance, the first-person narrative contributes to the story's ambiguity, as the narrator has difficulty distinguishing whether her experience takes place in "real time" or in mythic time.

"Yellow Woman" is a self-reflexive story, meaning that the narrative refers to the process of composing the story itself. In "Yellow Woman," the narrator explicitly refers to the Yellow Woman story that her grandfather used to tell. She wonders if the original Yellow Woman knew that she was a character in a story. During her adventure with Silva, she repeatedly wonders if she has become the original Yellow Woman, or if she is reliving an episode similar to that actually experienced by a Laguna woman in "time immemorial" and will herself be the subject of a later tale.

Archetypes and the Oral Tradition

Although Silko's "Yellow Woman" does not assume that readers will be familiair with the original myth, it helps to be familiar with the concepts of archetypes and the ceremonial telling of stories in the Laguna Pueblo culture. Psychologist Carl Jung defined the archetype as the shared memories of the countless typical experiences of our ancestors, held in the "collective unconscious" of all humankind. In purely literary terms, an archetype is a universal type of recurring image, character, plot device, or action. Archetypes occur in myths, religion, and dreams as well as literature. That Yellow Woman represents all the women in the old stories, as Silko has suggests elsewhere, and that dozens of Yellow Woman stories exist in the oral tradition supports the interpretation of Yellow Woman as a cultural archetype. Additionally, through the identification of herself with Yellow Woman, the narrator experiences a deep connection with her culture, recognizing that the story that she will tell is part of the stories told by old Grandpa in the oral tradition.

Through the oral tradition, the passing down of tribal histories and myth in ceremonial fashion, each passing generation connects its present moment to that of the past. In its recounting of the Yellow Woman story that "old Grandpa" used to tell and in its suggestion that the written narrative presented to readers will also become part of an often-repeated story, Silko's "Yellow Woman" draws upon the significance of the oral tradition. Furthermore, Silko suggests that oral tradition, in which stories change with each teller in each new context, is the lifeblood of community because it connects who we once were to who we have become.

Historical Context

The Myth of Kochininako, Yellow Woman

In *The Sacred Hoop: Recovering the Feminine in American Indian Traditions,* Paula Gunn Allen observes that many different Kochininako, or Yellow Woman, stories circulate among the Laguna and Acoma Pueblos in New Mexico. The themes of these stories, she writes, are always female-centered and told from Yellow Woman's point of view. Allen notes that Yellow Woman stories concern many different things—abduction, meeting with powerful spirits, getting power from the spirit world and returning it to her people, the birth of twins, the refusal to marry, weaving, grinding corn, getting

water, outwitting evil spirits. Often, Yellow Woman stories highlight her alienation from her people. In some of the stories she is punished for her differences; others celebrate the ways in which her nonconformity helps the community. Kochininako might be seen as a role model for women, Allen suggests that she more accurately represents "the Spirit of Woman." In her essay, "Yellow Woman and a Beauty of the Spirit," Silko agrees: "Yellow Woman is my favorite because she dares to cross traditional boundaries of ordinary behavior during times of crisis in order to save the Pueblo; her power lies in her courage and in her uninhibited sexuality, which the old time Pueblo stories celebrate again and again because fertility was so highly valued. . . . In each story, the beauty that Yellow Woman possesses is the beauty of her passion, her daring, and her sheer strength to act when catastrophe is imminent."

Although Silko remembers looking at the traditional Native American tales collected in the 1920s by ethnologist Franz Boas and his protegee, Elsie Clews Parsons, she told Larry Evers and Denny Carr of *Sun Tracks* journal, "I've never sat down with them and said I'm going to make a poem or a story out of this." Furthermore, "the things in the anthropological reports looked dead and alien" to her, not part of a living language and culture. Indeed, the assumption behind Boas's and Parsons's ethnological project was that the Keresan language was dying out and needed to be preserved. Since the Keresan language is primarily an oral language and is actively spoken by the Laguna as well as other Pueblo peoples, such an assumption was not only inaccurate but offensive to many of them. Indeed, Silko's multiple and eclectic sources for "Yellow Woman" attest to the fact that the oral tradition is alive and well. In *Storyteller,* Silko explains: "I know Aunt Susie and Aunt Alice would tell me stories they had told me before but with changes in details and descriptions. The story was the important thing and little changes here and there were really part of the story. There were even stories about the different versions of the stories and how they imagined those differing versions came to be."

Native American Cosmology and World View

Balance and harmony are two primary assumptions of the Keres people who inhabit the Laguna and Acoma Pueblos of New Mexico. As Silko explains in *Yellow Woman and a Beauty of the*

Compare
&
Contrast

- **1970:** The publication of Dee Brown's *Bury My Heart at Wounded Knee* arouses widespread general interest in the history of Native American tribes.

    1990s: Native American studies have been integrated into many high school and college multicultural programs.

- **1973:** The Department of Education's Head Start Program begins operation in the Laguna Reservation, offering counselling and tutoring services to the schoolchildren of the reservation's six villages.

    1990s: The Laguna Head Start Program is con-

solidated at a central site, with 120 children enrolled in the program.

- **1974:** Laguna Pueblo residents begin producing their distinctive red, yellow, and orange pottery for sale. Painters and jewelry-makers recreate traditional tribal designs and market their works on a small scale to tourists.

    1990s: The Casa Blanca Village outside of Albuquerque is a shopping center that specializes in Pueblo handicrafts, providing a source of income for the Laguna Pueblo.

Spirit, the people and the land are inseparable: "In the old days there had been no boundaries between the people and the land; there had been mutual respect for the land that others were actively using. This respect extended to all living beings, especially the plants and animals." Everything in Keres culture—the human, the animal, the vegetative, the spirit world—is interconnected like the strands of a spider's web.

In Keres theology, the Great Creator is a woman, Thought Woman, or the Spider Woman. There is no time when Thought Woman did not exist. In *The Sacred Hoop,* Paula Gunn Allen explains that Thought Woman is the only creator of thought, and that thought precedes creation. With the help of her two sisters, Thought Woman created the entire universe. Her presence is felt everywhere—on the plains, in the forests, in the great canyons, on the mesas, beneath the seas. She is, writes Allen, "the Old Woman Spider who weaves us together in a fabric of interconnection."

Because everything is connected, the tribal concept of time is timelessness and the concept of space is multidimensional. As Silko's retelling of "Yellow Woman" makes clear, the world of the everyday incorporates the ceremonial or mythic,

and the mythic is present in ordinary experience. The past and the future dwell in the present moment. People cannot be separated from the landscape they inhabit. Every story contains every other story.

The Keres people are matrilineal, which means that women are central to their culture and descent is traced through the maternal rather than paternal line. Women are celebrated in social structures, architecture, law, custom and oral tradition. To address a person as "mother" is to pay the highest respect. In an interview with Kim Barnes in *MELUS,* Silko praises her Pueblo's fluid gender roles and matriarchal culture: "In the Pueblo, the lineage of the child is traced through the mother, so it's a matrilineal system. The houses are the property of the woman, not the man. The land is generally passed down through the female side because the houses belong to the women."

Because Native American communities value harmony between all living things, it is difficult for their belief system to remain intact in the late twentieth century. In her book *Song of the Turtle,* Paula Gunn Allen writes, "Legislation and local regulations concerning grazing, logging, fishing, hunting and particularly land, mineral, and water and power management have dramatically impaired not only the environment but the survival of Native peoples as communities and cultural entities in their own right.''

The Legacy of Manifest Destiny

Manifest Destiny was a nineteenth century doctrine that the United States had both the right and the moral imperative to expand throughout the North American continent, which was characterized as an uninhabited wilderness. The philosophy of Manifest Destiny enabled the genocide of the people who already inhabited the lands to which white Americans laid claim (genocide is the systematic destruction of an entire people or culture). In 1834, under President Andrew Jackson, Congress designated all lands west of the Mississippi ''and not within the States of Missouri and Louisiana and the Territory of Arkansas'' to be ''Indian Territory''; as Anglo-Americans traveled westward, however, the area designated ''Indian Territory'' grew smaller and smaller. During the 1838 Trail of Tears, in which the Cherokee Nation was forcibly moved from the Carolinas to ''Indian Territory'' (what is now Oklahoma), one out of every four Cherokees died from cold, hunger or disease. In *Bury My Heart at Wounded Knee,* historian Dee Brown writes that Manifest Destiny an ''era of violence, greed, audacity, sentimentality, undirected exuberance, and an almost reverential attitude toward the ideal of personal freedom for those who already had it.''

To fulfill its Manifest Destiny, the United States Government made many treaties with the various tribal nations and broke almost all of them. The stealing of their land is not ancient history to Native American tribes; Silko's father, Lee Marmon, was a tribal officer for the Laguna Pueblo people who successfully sued the State of New Mexico for six million acres that were improperly taken.

Critical Overview

''Yellow Woman'' is probably Silko's most famous story. After it first appeared in *The Man to Send Rain Clouds,* ''Yellow Woman'' received immediate attention and praise and was reprinted in a number of other collections. In the introduction to his anthology, *The Man to Send Rain Clouds,* Kenneth Rosen praises Silko's rich style and her explo-

ration of the intersection between traditional stories and individual voice: ''Using Indian lore and history as a kind of counterpoint to her special music, she writes with a depth and intensity that to my mind, set her work apart and mark her as a talent from whom we can expect new, important work.''

Some critics have felt that ''Yellow Woman'' is largely about cultural loss and the need to reconnect to an abandoned spiritual heritage. In *Spider Woman's Granddaughters,* Paula Gunn Allen observes that the narrator of ''Yellow Woman'' seems cut off from her culture. Allen writes that ''Silko's use of the Yellow Woman stories . . . leans more toward the isolation of her protagonist from her people rather than toward connectedness—though even here her sense of connection is of necessity through the stories by way of her family.'' In an early essay in *Multi-Ethnic Literatures of the United States* A. Lavonne Ruoff argues that in ''Yellow Woman,'' ''Silko emphasizes the need to return to the rituals and oral traditions of the past in order to rediscover the basis for one's cultural identity.'' Along with other critics, Ruoff and Allen have also paid particular attention to the ways in which ''Yellow Woman'' draws upon and revises the oral traditions and ceremonial practices of the Laguna Pueblo people. In an essay in *The Sacred Hoop,* Allen discusses the ways in which Silko draws upon the Laguna Pueblo people's ''gynocentric'' (or woman-centered) creation myth and subsequent understanding of the land as feminine in her celebration of female strength, courage, and sexuality.

Some feminists have voiced discomfort at Silko's treatment of female sexuality in ''Yellow Woman.'' Writing in *Modern Language Studies,* Victoria Boynton perceives sexual violence between Silva and the narrator, who knows that he can hurt her if he chooses. Nevertheless, in Silko's story, the narrator presents herself as a willing participant in the sexual encounters. Boynton acknowledges that Native American critics such as Allen understand the Yellow Woman stories to be celebrations of female sexuality. Nevertheless she is concerned that the ''rape fantasy'' represented in ''Yellow Woman'' is dangerous to women. In *The Desert Is No Lady,* Patricia Clark Smith and Paula Gunn Allen explain that ''the ultimate purpose of such ritual abductions and seductions is to transfer knowledge from the spirit world to the human sphere, and this transfer is not accomplished in an atmosphere of control or domination.''

Critics such as Bernard Hirsch in *American Indian Quarterly* and Tobey Langen in *Studies in American Indian Literatures* have focused on the design of *Storyteller,* which combines poems, fiction, autobiography and photographs to create a *written* representation of an *oral* storytelling. Hirsch comments upon the story's achronous representation of time, on how "successive narrative episodes cast long shadows both forward and back, lending different complementary shades of meaning to those preceding them." Langen argues that *Storyteller* produces for the reader the effect of participation in oral tradition, using repetition and interlocking clusters of poems, photographs and stories: "Leslie Silko has assembled the parts of *Storyteller* to distress and interrupt the activity of reading and to disown the authority of writing and authorship. . . . Reading a story takes less time than listening to one; a function of the photographs in *Storyteller* is to invite a more 'oral' tempo into our reading."

When considering "Yellow Woman," though, most critics discuss the theme of storytelling. Linda Danielson writes in *Studies in American Indian Literatures* that the structure of *Storyteller* resembles a spider's web: "While the radial strands provide the organizational pattern of the book, the web's lateral threads connect one thematic strand to another, suggesting a whole and woven fabric. . . .These pieces constantly guide the reader's attention back to the act of storytelling as creation, to the creative in all aspects of human interaction, to the female deities, and as well to the ordinary tribal women, Silko's most frequently selected narrators who carry on Thought Woman's function of speaking into being." Also focusing on the significance of storytelling, in *The CEA Critic,* Helen Jaskoski explores the ways in which *Storyteller* simultaneously addresses two different audiences, Laguna and non-Laguna, by translating oral story into written fiction and the role of the author into the performance of the storyteller.

Silko's use of Native American myths and celebration of female sexuality have led some critics to compare her work, including "Yellow Woman" to similar work by other contemporary women writers. For example, Catherine Lappas has compared Silko's compelling combination of myth and autobiography to that of Chinese-American writer Maxine Hong Kingston and Susan Castillo has compared treatments of gender and ethnicity in Silko's work to that of Louise Erdrich, who is of Chippewa descent.

Criticism

Cynthia Bily

Bily has a master's degree in English literature, and has written for a variety of educational publishers. In the following essay, she discusses "Yellow Woman" as a representation of the literature of ecofeminism.

Since the 1970s, many writers have explored the connections between human oppression and environmental abuse, and have developed a body of thought called *ecofeminism.* As explained by Carol J. Adams in the introduction to the anthology *Ecofeminism and the Sacred,* "Ecofeminism identifies the twin domination of women and the rest of nature. To the issues of sexism, racism, classicism, and heterosexism that concern feminists, ecofeminists add naturism—the oppression of the rest of nature. Ecofeminism argues that connections between the oppression of women and the rest of nature must be recognized to understand adequately both oppressions." This connection between the domination of women and the domination of nature is a strong thread running through much of Leslie Marmon Silko's work, including the novel *Ceremony* and the story "Yellow Woman."

The woman narrator of "Yellow Woman" does not reveal what she is running away from when she leaves her home and family. In fact, she does not seem to know what is wrong with her, or what the importance of the old stories might be in her life. Catherine Lappas explains in an essay excerpted in this volume, that "Hers is a condition born of cultural dislocation: She is an Indian woman living in a Western world that dismisses all stories as irrelevant. . . . In her Indian world, however, stories have an ongoing connection to people's lives." Or do they? This woman is constantly longing for her grandfather, the last member of her family to tell and understand the old stories, the old connections. According to Carol Lee Sanchez, a descendent like Silko of the Laguna Pueblo, "Native American Tribal histories and culture stories stress the idea of harmonious coexistence—providing both positive and negative examples, by consistently showing us how everything is related." I believe that the narrator of "Yellow Woman" is searching for a life of harmony, a way to escape the Western patriarchal structures that dominate her and dominate nature.

What Do I Read Next?

- *Ceremony* (1977), a novel by Silko. After fighting in World War II, a young Native American man, Tayo, finds health and new meaning by returning to traditional Native American practices. The novel also recounts the harsh realities of reservaton life.

- *Almanac of the Dead: A Novel* (1991), a novel by Silko. In what Silko calls "a 763-page indictment of the United States," she spins dozens of interconnected tales to rewrite five hundred years of American history and envision a future in which the aboriginal peoples of the North American continent take back their land.

- *Laguna Woman* (1974), a collection of poems by Silko. Poems included in this early volume received the 1973 Pushcart Prize for poetry. The poems contain themes that Silko later develops in her fiction.

- *Love Medicine* (1984), a novel by Louise Erdrich. The first book in Louise Erdrich's Native American series along with *The Beet Queen*, *Tracks* and *The Bingo Palace*, *Love Medicine* tells the stories of two Chippewa families in North Dakota.

- *The Woman Warrior: Memoirs of a Girlhood Among Ghosts* (1976), by Maxine Hong Kingston. Kingston combines myth, history and autobiography to explore a young Chinese-American womans exploration of her live, her relationship with her mother, and her cultural heritage. Winner of the 1976 National Book Critics Award for nonfiction.

- *The Broken Cord* (1989), an autobiographical work by Michael Dorris. In this deeply moving account, Dorris tells of his life with his adopted son, a Native American, who suffers from fetal alcohol syndrome.

- *House Made of Dawn* (1968), a novel by N. Scott Momaday. Awarded the Pulitzer Prize, this novel launched what Paula Gunn Allen calls the "second wave of American Indian Fiction." Like Silko's *Ceremony*, this novel also features a young Native American who returns from World War II to find himself and his community devastated and demoralized. On his recovery to health, the main character finds racism and brutality, but manages to survive through the rediscovery of the traditions and ceremonies of his peiople.

- *Bury My Heart At Wounded Knee: An Indian History of the American West* (1970), a history by Dee Brown. Brown reveals the dark side of Manifest Destiny—genocide of the Native Americans who occupied the land for which the United States Government hungered—and tells how they fought back.

- *Death Comes for the Archbishop* (1927), a novel by Willa Cather. In this gentle, meditative novel, set in the New Mexican desert in the 1850s, Cather writes about the encounters two Catholic priests have with the Native Americans who live there.

For a time, she believes that Silva can offer her that life.

The woman's inborn connection to nature is still alive in her. An important ecofeminist understanding is of the ways in which women of Western cultures are more closely connected to animals than men are. For the narrator of "Yellow Woman," the only connections that seem to resonate are to the animals around her; she does not reveal any deep feeling for or understanding of her husband or family, or the stranger Silva. She is not only more connected to animals than Silva is, she is more connected to animals than she is to men. In the story's second paragraph she walks over the where the horses are still lying down. They do not get up at her approach, and she speculates, "maybe it was because the corral was made out of thick cedar branches and the horses had not yet felt the sun like I had.'' In the first paragraph the man she has slept beside has felt the same sun she felt and has not gotten up, and she does not reveal the same curiosity about his motives. He is an enigma, and she never tries to understand him.

While she does not examine Silva closely (she doesn't mind that he is always watching her closely, but she does not often look at him), she is always aware of the sights and sounds of the natural world. She recognizes individual trees as tamaracks and willows and cedars and junipers, but she cannot tell what kind of man he is. As they travel to Silva's house she takes in her surroundings in great detail: ''I watched the change from the cottonwood trees along the river to the junipers that brushed past us in the foothills, and finally there were only piqons, and when I looked up at the rim of the mountain plateau I could see pine trees growing on the edge.'' From the corral at his house she can see ''faint mountain images in the distance miles across the vast spread of mesas and valleys and plains. I wondered who was over there to feel the mountain wind on those sheer blue edges—who walks on the pine needles in those blue mountains.'' As the two ride to Marqucz she stops looking into the distance because Silva questions her perceptions, but her close-up vision is just as acute: ''Only the waxy cactus flowers bloomed in the bright sun, and I saw every color that a cactus blossom can be; the white ones and the red ones were still buds, but the purple and the yellow were blossoms, open full and the most beautiful of all.''

Silva believes his vision is superior to hers: ''From here I can see the world.'' He frequently challenges her, telling her that she does not see what she thinks she sees, and does not understand what she thinks she understands. But what he sees is not the unity of nature, but man-made demarcations: ''The Navajo reservation begins over there. . . . The Pueblo boundaries are over here. . . .The Texans have their ranches over there, starting with that valley, the Concho Valley. The Mexicans run some cattle over there, too.'' He sees the land only in terms of territories, claims, property.

The woman is attracted to him in part because he lives outside the rules of the patriarchy. He does not recognize a husband's right to own or control a woman any more than he recognizes the cattle owners' rights to their cattle. For a time it seems to her that he offers an escape from ''highways and pickup trucks'' and the modern life that has separat-

> The woman is attracted to him in part because he lives outside the rules of the patriarchy."

ed her from her cultural connections to the Earth. But she comes to understand that his rejection of conventional rules is not an embracing of his place as a part of nature, or of her place as an equal. Although he rejects other men's rights to control his access to women and to animals, nevertheless he still claims his own right to power over them. He simply wants to control women and the rest of nature without interference from other men.

At the heart of the narrator's conflict with Silva is her respect for the animals around her and Silva's disregard for their spirits. For him, the horses and cattle are commodities: transportation, food, wealth. The woman has a closer relationship, feeling their warmth, listening to their breath just as she does with Silva's. When she returns to Silva's house after her walk, the narrator sees gray squirrels playing in the pines, the horses standing in the corral—and a beef carcass hanging from a tree. Some of the sharpest and most narrowly focused detail occurs in this scene: ''Flies buzzed around the clotted blood that hung from the carcass''; ''I looked into the bucket full of bloody water with brown-and-white animal hairs floating in it.'' In much of her writing, Silko insists that readers confront their fears of blood and death, and accept the giving up of life as part of the ritual of natural existence. In that regard, Silva is admirable. He does not flinch from what it means to take a life. But Silva again offers only a shadow of what the woman needs. When he lies to the white man he underscores the shallowness of his venture: he has not ''been hunting,'' as he claims, but only stealing domestic cattle from an enclosed area. He will not even close the circle and eat the flesh he has taken; he is on his way to sell it. He does not fear blood, but he sheds it for commerce, not for community.

The woman follows him for a time, across a ridge ''steep on both sides like an animal spine,'' until she sees in his eyes ''something ancient and dark'' just before he murders the white man. Early she had been afraid when she understood that "his strength could hurt me. . . . I knew he could destroy me." The white man's fear echoes her own. She flees on the horse, hearing but not seeing the four shots that "reminded me of deer hunting" but are instead another mockery of hunting. The last thing she sees as she turns the horse loose is the blood-soaked gunny sacks full of meat.

The narrator cannot rely on rationality to direct her decisions; her memory and thought patterns are clouded, unreliable. Instead, she follows natural instincts, seeking food and warmth as the animals do. Throughout the days of the story she is seen eating only potatoes and apricots—she eats no meat. She is frequently hungry, and her hunger directs her thoughts back to her family. The first time she feels hungry, at the beginning of the story, she starts to follow the river back the way she came after she met Silva. Memory of his warmth—her hunger for him sexually—send her back to him. As they approach Silva's house, "I felt hungry and wondered what they were doing at home now." The next morning, having decided again that she will leave him, she again thinks of food: "But first I had to eat, because I knew it would be a long walk home." Although she has not realized it, whenever she feels the call of the natural energy of hunger, she turns away from Silva.

The woman also follows the natural yearning for warmth. Different things make her warm: the sun's rays, the horse's body beneath her, Silva's body, the fire in the stove, the wind. Only three times does she find things chilling. After arguing with Silva about the meaning of the Yellow Woman story, she is pulled along beside him, "his hand around my wrist. I had stopped trying to pull away from him, because his hand felt cool and the sun was high." Later, when she first sees his house, she shivers, and when Silva reveals that he is a cattle thief she turns away from him, saying, "I'm cold. . . . I'm going inside." She does not seek warmth from him this time; she knows he cannot provide what she needs.

But the woman's spiritual home, her source of spiritual food and warmth, is not back with her family, either. They have become thorough Westernized. Pointedly, the narrator's mother is teaching the grandmother how to cook Jell-O, a packaged product made from the boiled tissues of animals, especially horses. The traditional order has been overturned. Daughter is passing knowledge on to mother, not the other way around, and the thing she

is teaching is a way of utilizing the bodies of animals without approaching their spirits. Old Grandpa would have listened to the woman's story and understood it—understood that it is a story of how Western patriarchal society distances people from nature and permits the destruction of Native cultures, and how modern Native American women have been cut off from their cultural connections to each other and to the Earth.

Source: Cynthia Bily, "Yellow Woman as Ecofeminist," for *Short Stories for Students,* Gale, 1998.

Catherine Lappas

In the following excerpt from a longer essay, Lappas discusses Silko's collection Storyteller *as a "polyphonic" autobiography, one that seeks to tell the story of not just one person, but also that person's community and historical traditions.*

Silko was born in 1948 of Laguna-Mexican-Anglo ancestry. Her work *Storyteller* was originally conceived not as an autobiography at all but as a multigenre form including poems, traditional tales, expository pieces on Laguna tradition, letters, even photographs. It was, in effect, an attempt to record an oral tradition that was in fear of disappearing, for, as Silko explains, "an entire history/an entire vision of the world" depended "upon memory/and retelling by subsequent generations." Such emphasis on community is not unusual coming from a person who is concerned primarily with relationships; after all, "that's all there really is."

"Polyphonic" autobiography, as Arnold Krupat and others have suggested, for many indigenous people and many women alike, establishes the self and maintains it through relationships that "bear witness." . . .

The Yellow Woman stories included in *Storyteller* are part of Cochiti and Laguna Pueblo oral tradition. Some of these stories were first collected by the famous anthropologist Franz Boas in the 1920s, but countless others exist unrecorded, in flux, reflecting the individual concerns of each teller and his or her community. In the first Yellow Woman story, a young woman awakens to find herself beside a stranger who has, we guess at first, abducted her from her village. As the story unfolds, the man's actions and the woman's responses seem to resemble those of lovers more than those of abductor/abductee.

Paula Gunn Allen explains that in Native American culture "the sacred and the ordinary are perceived as a seamless whole.'' Silko's modern-day Yellow Woman, in contrast, seems entirely incognizant of such perceptions. Hers is a condition born of cultural dislocation: She is an Indian woman living in a Western world that dismisses all stories as irrelevant and, in some cases, antithetical to lived life. In her Indian world, however, stories have an ongoing connection to people's lives. As a product of multiple cultures, like Silko herself, she experiences a kind of fracturing of her identity that mimics ''postmodern . . . schizophrenia.'' Dazed by her ''abduction,'' the protagonist desperately wonders ''if Yellow woman had known who she was—if she knew that she would become part of the stories.'' The boundaries between fact and fiction are thus problematized and grow increasingly so at the conclusion. There, three identities merge: Yellow Woman's, the protagonist's, and the narrator's. Returning home, her family is seemingly oblivious to her abduction—her mother and grandmother fixing ''Jell-O'' in the kitchen while her oblivious husband plays with the baby in an adjacent room. Throughout, she is a detached observer pondering a disappearance that may (or may not) have taken place. Unanswered, too, remains the question of which story is actually told to her family, thus leaving open the possibility for other tellings. Silko teases her audience further by not providing a traditional ending but instead playfully flaunting her ability to incorporate ''personal quirks and lapses of memory,'' those ''pluralistic voices of her autobiographical traditions, both oral and written, Indian and Anglo'' as aspects of her ''manifold identities'':

> I decided to tell them that
> some Navajo had kidnaped [sic] me, but I
>   was sorry
> that old Grandpa wasn't alive to hear my story
> because it was the Yellow Woman stories he
> liked to tell best. . . .

Source: Catherine Lappas, '''The way I heard it was . . .': Myth, Memory, and Autobiography in *Storyteller* and *The Woman Warrior*,'' in *CEA Critic,* Vol. 57, No. 1, Fall, 1994, pp. 57–67.

Linda Danielson

In the following essay, Danielson discusses the ''spiderweb structure'' of Silko's Storyteller, in which the Yellow Woman is a significant figure.

In American Indian traditional cultures, good songs and stories are useful, fostering the survival of the people and their culture. The verbal arts sustain cosmic relationships, testify to sources of creative energy, teach young people, heal the sick, bring lovers together, or reprimand the socially irresponsible. Leslie Silko's *Storyteller* is an heir of such tradition and a testimony to verbal art as a survival strategy. Moreover, the work takes its spiderweb-like structure from the Keresan mythologic traditions of female creative deities who think—or tell—the world into existence (Thought Woman) and who offer disciplined protection to the living beings (Grandmother Spider). When we read *Storyteller* bearing in mind the significance of both the spiderweb structure and the values underlying traditional verbal art, we realize that *Storyteller,* often dismissed as an oddly assorted album, is a coherent work about how tribal people survive. By making stories, people continue the tradition of Thought Woman and Grandmother Spider: they continuously create and protect themselves and their world. . . .

In *Storyteller,* thematic clusters constitute the radiating strands of the web. While the radial strands provide the organizational pattern of the book, the web's lateral threads connect one thematic strand to another, suggesting a whole and woven fabric. Throughout the book, Silko spins such a lateral thread of attention to storytellers and the art of storytelling. These pieces constantly guide the reader's attention back to the act of storytelling as creation, to the creative in all aspects of human interaction, to the female deities, and as well to the ordinary tribal women. Silko's most frequently selected narrators who carry on Thought Woman's function of speaking into being.

Grandmother Spider of course lives at the center of the web, giving *Storyteller* its authority. But Grandmother Spider, and thus the whole pantheon of protective, creative female deities, live also in the author and in all the aunts, grandmothers and other people from whom she heard these stories. . . .

The next radiating filament of *Storyteller*'s web structure involves stories of Kochininako, or Yellow Woman, which explore the creative power and survival value of this Everywoman figure among the Keresan holy people. Kochininako's power, Paula Gunn Allen observes, is that of an agent or catalyst. She enables the seasons to follow their appointed rounds, for example. Not only does she catalyze the seasonal progression, but, as A. Lavonne Ruoff points out, she renews tribal vitality through ''liaison with outside forces.''

> " As there is a bit of Grandmother Spider and Yellow Woman in all women, so there is a bit of Coyote in all people."

Her fictional character in ''Yellow Woman,'' Silko tells us, joins ''adolescent longings and the old stories, that plus the stories around Laguna at the time about people who did, in fact, just in recent times, use the river as a meeting place.'' Besides addressing an audience she assumes is sympathetic, this narrator is also telling herself the story she wants to hear, justifying herself, but with enough self-awareness and humor to recognize the doubtful elements in her story. She does bring renewal to her sense of mythic reality through her adventure with Silva, the ''outside force,'' as she almost convinces herself that she really is Yellow Woman. The proposition is not utterly unlikely. Yellow Woman exhibits the desires and weaknesses of ordinary women; why should the protagonist not be Yellow Woman? Through her adventure, at any rate, she livens up an apparently dull existence. She identifies with the freedom of Yellow Woman in her grandfather's stories, reminding us that modern women embody the potential of Yellow Woman, bring the vitality of imagination to everyday life. After all, the power to make a convincing excuse or to fool oneself is yet one more version of the power to create the universe.

Silko's story of a young woman going off with an attractive stranger whom she meets on a river-bank closely follows the beginning of a Laguna story published by Franz Boas under the title ''Cliff Dweller.'' The stranger, Silva, smilingly goes along with her suggestion that they may really be Yellow Woman and a Ka'tsina spirit. Eventually, the narrator makes her way back to the pueblo, reorienting herself to ordinary reality as she goes, speculating about what the family is doing in her absence.

In the course of the adventure she has renewed the power of the myth by imagining what Yellow Woman's life and state of mind would have been like:

I was wondering if Yellow Woman had known who she was—if she knew that she would become part of the stories. Maybe she'd had another name that her

husband and relatives called her so that only the ka'tsina from the north and the storytellers would know her as Yellow Woman.

Finally she sees her story as an artifact that only her grandfather could properly appreciate because the Yellow Woman stories were what he liked best. But it is not by chance that out of her grandfather's repertory the narrator recollects a Yellow Woman story involving a sexual encounter with Coyote. Silva, of course, is more opportunistic than evil, and thus more Coyote than Cliff Dweller. And the narrator shares the same appetite-driven opportunism. As there is a bit of Grandmother Spider and Yellow Woman in all women, so there is a bit of Coyote in all people. For storytellers are tricksters like Coyote as well as agents like Yellow Woman, or creator-deities, and this character certainly contains all three possibilities. . . .

Source: Linda Danielson, ''The Storytellers in *Storyteller,* in *Studies in American Indian Literatures,* Series 2, Vol. 1, No. 2, Fall, 1989, pp. 21–31.

Bernard A. Hirsch

In the following excerpt, Hirsch focuses on ''Yellow Woman'' and other pieces in Storyteller *as he examines how Native American oral traditions shape the structure and themes of her collection.*

Comprised of personal reminiscences and narratives, retellings of traditional Laguna stories, photographs, and a generous portion of her previously published short fiction and poetry, this multigeneric work [entitled Storyteller] lovingly maps the fertile storytelling ground from which her art evolves and to which it is here returned—an offering to the oral tradition which nurtured it.

Silko has acknowledged often and eloquently the importance of the oral tradition to her work and tries to embody its characteristics in her writing. This effort, as she well knows, is immensely difficult and potentially dangerous, and this awareness surfaces at several points in Storyteller. She recalls, for instance, talking with Nora, whose ''grandchildren had brought home / a . . . book that had my 'Laguna coyote' poem in it.''

''We all enjoyed it so much [says Nora] but I was telling the children the way my grandpa used to tell it is longer.''

''Yes, that's the trouble with writing,'' I said. You can't go on and on the way we do when we tell stories around here.

''The trouble with writing,'' in the context Silko here establishes for it is twofold: first, it is static; it freezes words in space and time. It does not allow the living story to change and grow, as does the old tradition. Second, though it potentially widens a story's audience, writing removes the story from its immediate context, from the place and people who nourished it in the telling, and thus robs it of much of its meaning. This absence of the story's dynamic context is why in writing "You can't go on the way we do / when we tell stories around. . . .

A photograph in what I will call the "Yellow Woman" section of Storyteller is of the Anaconda company's open-pit uranium mine. "This photograph," Silko tells us, "was made in the early 1960s. The mesas and hills that appear in the background and foreground are gone now, swallowed by the mine." This photograph deepens our understanding of many things in Storyteller: of the importance of the photographs to the stories, for one thing, and of Silko's father's love of photography for another. "He is still most at home in the canyons and sandrock," she says, "and most of his life regular jobs / have been a confinement he has avoided." Some might think less of him for this, but Silko stifles this tendency—first by the story of Reed Woman and Corn Woman that precedes the reminiscence about her father and second by his photographs themselves, one of which is that of the now vanished mesas and hills. Moreover, his photography intensified his love of the land and enabled him to relate to it in new and fulfilling ways. We learn, for instance, that

> His landscapes could not be done without certain kinds of clouds—some white and scattered like river rock and others mountains rolling into themselves swollen lavender before rainstorms

Clouds, as we know, are a source of life itself to the land, and for Lee H. Marmon they bring to it a profound and varied beauty as well. Essential to the continuity of physical life, the clouds are no less essential to his spirit in that they help him express through his art his particular vision of the land and by so doing, to define himself in terms of it. Equally important, in these times, is that his artistry can help others, be they Indians removed from the land or people who have never known it, to develop a richer, more meaningful sense of the land than is held by such as those who run Anaconda. It is precisely the development of such a relationship—to the land, to the spirits that pervade it, and to the stories that derive from it—that occupies the "Yellow Woman" section of Storyteller.

> **"** Like the prophets and visionaries of many cultures, Indian and non-Indian, the narrator travels to the mountain where she learns to see beyond the range of mundane experience."

The "Yellow Woman" section, comprising the short story "Yellow Woman," 4 poems, poetic retellings of two traditional stories, 4 reminiscences, 4 photographs, and 2 "gossip stories," is framed by "Yellow Woman" and "Storytelling," a poem consisting of six brief vignettes based on the abduction motif of the traditional Yellow Woman stories. As does "Storyteller" in the [earlier] "Survival" section, " Yellow Woman," and the traditional stories from which Silko's version evolves, establish the primary structural and thematic concerns of this section.

Based on the traditional stories in which Yellow Woman, on her way to draw water, is abducted by a mountain kachina, Silko's "Yellow Woman" concerns the development of the visionary character. This is hinted at in the story's epigram, "What Whirlwind Man Told Kochininako, Yellow Woman":

> I myself belong to the wind and so it is we will travel swiftly this whole world with dust and with windstorms.

Whirlwind Man will take her on a journey beyond the boundaries of time and place, a journey alive with sensation and danger which promises a perspective from which she can see the world new and entire. This in effect is what happens in the story. Like the prophets and visionaries of many cultures, Indian and non-Indian, the narrator travels to the mountain where she learns to see beyond the range of mundane experience. She recalls that, at Silva's mountain cabin.

> I was standing in the sky with nothing around me but the wind that came down from the blue mountain peak behind me. I could see faint mountain images in the distance miles across the vast spread of mesas and valleys and plains. I wondered who was over there to feel the mountain wind on those sheer blue edges—

who walks on the pine needles in those blue mountains. "Can you see the pueblo?" Silva was standing behind me. I shook my head, "We're too far, away." "From here I can see the world."

The pueblo, which comprised her whole world before, is, from the perspective of the mountain, but a barely discernible part of a much larger whole. With Silva, on the mountain, she has entered the more expansive and truer realm of imagination and myth.

When we can see imaginatively, William Blake has said, when we can see not merely with but through the eye, "the whole creation will appear infinite and holy whereas it now appears finite and corrupt. This will come to pass by an improvement of sensual enjoyment" (*The Marriage of Heaven and Hell*). This is the narrator's experience. She follows a strong impulse in running off with Silva; desire moves her to leave the familiar, secure world of the pueblo and her family to walk a new and daring road. She opens her story in the morning, after she and Silva first made love:

> My thigh clung to his with dampness, and I watched the sun rising up through the tamaracks and willows . . . I could hear the water, almost at our feet where the narrow fast channel bubbled and washed green ragged moss and fern leaves. I looked at him beside me, rolled in the red blanket on the white river sand.

She does not awaken to the proverbial harsh light of morning awash in guilt, but to a newly, more vibrantly alive world of sensation within and around her. But this is a world which, like Silva himself, is as frightening in its strength and intensity as it is seductive, and when Silva awakens she tells him she is leaving:

> He smiled now, eyes still closed. "You are coming with me, remember?" He sat up now with his bare dark chest and belly in the sun. "Where?" "To my place." "And will I come back?" He pulled his pants on. I walked away from him, feeling him behind me and smelling the willows. "Yellow Woman," he said. I turned to face him, "Who are you?" I asked.

Last night, he reminds her, "you guessed my name, and you knew why I had come." Their lovemaking made her intuitively aware of another, more vital level of being, one which had been within her all along, nurtured since childhood by her grandfather's Yellow Woman stories—and she knew she was Yellow Woman and her lover the dangerous mountain ka'tsina who carries her off.

But imaginative seeing on this morning after is threatening to the narrator, for seeing oneself whole demands eradication of those perceptual boundaries which offer the security of a readily discernible, if severely limited, sense of self. The narrator clings to that historical, time-bound sense of self like a child to her mother's skirts on the first day of school. "I'm not really her," she maintains, not really Yellow Woman. "I have my own name and I come from the pueblo on the other side of the mesa." It is not so much "confusion about what is dream and what is fact" that besets her here as it is the fear of losing that reality which has heretofore defined her—and him. As they walk she thinks to herself:

> I will see someone, eventually I will see someone, and then I will be certain that he [Silva] is only a man— some man from nearby—and I will be sure that I am not Yellow Woman. Because she is from out of time past and I live now and I've been to school and there are highways and pickup trucks that Yellow Woman never saw.

Jim Ruppert is right, I think, when he says that the narrator "struggles to . . . establish time boundaries and boundaries between objective reality and myths," and that struggle is part of the learning process she undergoes in the story. Newly awakened to her own imaginative potential, she has yet to discern the proper relationship between experiential reality and the timeless, all-inclusive mythic reality of her grandfather's stories.

Her desire, however, is stronger than her fear. After they reach his cabin, eat, and she looks out over the world from the mountain, Silva unrolls the bedroll and spreads the blankets. She hesitates, and he slowly undresses her. There is compulsion, this time, on his part, and fear on hers, but she is held to him more by her own passion than by his force. When she does leave, during their confrontation with a rancher who, rightly, accuses Silva of stealing cattle, it is at his command. "I felt sad at leaving him," she recalls, and considers going back, "but the mountains were too far away now. And I told myself, because I believe it, that he will come back sometime and be waiting again by the river."

She returns home. Yellow Woman stories usually end that way. And as she approaches her house, A. Lavonne Ruoff tells us, "she is brought back to the realities of her own life by the smell of supper cooking and the sight of her mother instructing her grandmother in the Anglo art of making Jell-O." The details here suggest a world governed more by routine than by passion, a world somewhat at odds with itself, as mother instructing grandmother suggests, and a world no longer receptive to the wonder and wisdom of the old stories. Having sensed this, she "decided to tell them that some Navajo had kidnapped me." But the unnamed narrator here, like the unnamed Eskimo girl in ''Storyteller,'' keeps the oral tradition alive by going on her own journey of self-discovery—a journey born of acknowledging the rightful demands of passion and imagination—and by intuitively accepting the guidance of her grandfather's stories. Her life itself has become part of a visionary drama to be completed by Silva's return, and within that context it has gained fullness and meaning. Her recognition, in the story's final sentence, that hers is a Yellow Woman story—and that she is Yellow Woman—reveals as much. She has come to see herself, in Momaday's words, ''whole and eternal'' and like Momaday when, on his journey, he came out upon the northern plains, she will ''never again . . . see things as [she] saw them yesterday or the day before.'' . . .

The context here established by the written word—Silko's short story—is essential in helping us to see Yellow Woman more completely than do the traditional stories alone, just as those stories in turn provide the necessary cultural context for ''Yellow Woman.'' Through the narrator's telling in Silko's story, the individual dimension predominates and personal longings are shown to be as powerful and worthwhile as communal needs. Silko well knows, as the *Cottonwood* poems make clear, that individual sacrifice is at times crucial to community survival. But, as ''Yellow Woman'' reveals, individual fulfillment can be equally important to a tribal community, especially in the modern world where acculturation pressures are perhaps greater than ever before. Silko shows us, in this opening sequence of the ''Yellow Woman'' section, that personal and communal fulfillment need not be mutually exclusive—that they in fact enhance each other. And, by extension, the same is true of oral tradition and the written word as ways of knowing and of expression. To attain this harmony requires a powerful and inclusive vision, one receptive both to internal and external demands and the diverse languages which give them meaning. The development of such a vision, and of the network of relationships to the land, the people, the stories, and oneself it fosters, is, as I have said, the controlling idea of what I have called the ''Yellow Woman'' section of *Storyteller,* and it is expressed in various ways in the narrative episodes that follow.

Silko alerts us as ''Storytelling'' begins that we ''should understand / the way it was / back then, / because it is the same / even now.'' The traditional stories, Silko is saying, both here and throughout *Storyteller,* offer profound and necessary insights into contemporary experiences. Specifically, the

''Yellow Woman'' stories, especially Silko's renderings of them, are among other things open, unqualified expressions of woman's sexuality. This is not to say that, because the traditional stories are abduction stories, Silko is dealing in rape fantasies. Quite the contrary. In her versions the coercive element, though present, is not the controlling one. Yellow Woman is at all times in charge of her own destiny. She understands and accepts her sexuality, expresses it honestly, and is guided by her own strong desire. We see this in Silko's short story, ''Yellow Woman,'' in the *Cottonwood* stories, and again in these two ''Storytelling'' vignettes. By focusing in these little narratives not on the lovemaking but on the prelude to it, Silko establishes the sexual integrity of both the mythic and contemporary Yellow Woman, and conveys with playful subtlety the charged eroticism between them and Buffalo Man and ''those / brown-eyed men from Cubero'' respectively.

Yellow Woman's sexual integrity gets a broadly comic touch in the fourth vignette, where Silko inverts the traditional abduction motif. The F.B.I. and state police in the summer of 1967 pursued a red '56 Ford with four Laguna women and three Navajo men inside. A kidnapping was involved, and the police followed a trail ''of wine bottles and / size 42 panties / hanging in bushes and trees / all along the road.'' When they were caught, one of the men explained: '''We couldn't escape them' . . . / 'We tried, but there were four of them and / only three of us'.''

But sexual honesty, especially a woman's, is, as we have seen, likely to be misunderstood. In the first *Cottonwood* poem, ''Story of Sun House,'' the Sun tells Yellow Woman that even though their union is necessary for the world to continue, ''the people may not understand''; and the narrator in ''Yellow Woman'' must make up a story for her family about being kidnapped by a Navajo. In fact, the abduction motif of the Yellow Woman stories proves useful, or almost so, in a number of situations. ''No! that gossip isn't true,'' says a distraught mother in the third ''Storytelling'' vignette: ''She didn't elope / She was *kidnapped* by / that Mexican / at Seama Feast. / You know / my daughter / isn't / *that* kind of girl.'' As was stated earlier, however, there cannot be a good story without a good storyteller, as the contemporary Yellow Woman of the sixth vignette learns, ''It was / that Navajo / from Alamo, / you know, / the tall / good-looking / one,'' she tells her husband. ''He told me / he'd kill me / if I didn't / go with him.'' That, rain, and muddy roads, she said, are why "it took me / so long / to get back home." When her husband leaves her, she blames herself: "I could have told / the story / better than I did."

In a *Sun-Tracks* interview, Silko said of "these gossip stories": "I don't look upon them as gossip. The connotation is all wrong. These stories about goings-on, about what people are up to, give identity to a place." What she argues for here is in effect what the "Yellow Woman" section is all about: a new way of seeing. Seen rightly, such stories are neither idle rumor nor trivial chatter, but are rather another mode of expression, a way in which people define themselves and declare who they are. Thus it is fitting that the "Yellow Woman" section, and this essay, conclude with a photograph taken of some of the houses in Laguna. Here, after all, is where the people live their lives and it is this sense of life being lived, of life timeless and ongoing, changing and evolving, contradictory and continuous, that Silko expresses with grace and power through her melding of oral tradition and the written word in *Storyteller*.

Source: Bernard A. Hirsch, "'The Telling Which Continues': Oral Tradition and the Written Word in Leslie Marmon Silko's 'Storyteller,'" in *American Indian Quarterly,* Vol. 12, No. 1, Winter, 1988, pp. 1–28.

Kim Barnes and Leslie Marmon Silko

In the following interview, Silko discusses her ideas on storytelling, the Laguna oral tradition, and the role of women in tribal culture.

[*Barnes*]: *The first question I want to ask you is, who do you consider to be your audience? Who are you writing for?*

[Silko]: I've never thought too much about an audience per se. When I first started writing, I wasn't sure that anyone would want to read or listen to the work that I did. I didn't think about it at first. In a way, it's good not to think about an audience. If you start thinking about the audience, it can inhibit what you do. When I was younger, there was concern about what will Grandma think, or what will Mama say or something like this, and that in a sense is being concerned about audience and can really inhibit a writer. Initially, I guess I assumed that I wouldn't have to worry about an audience because there would not be an audience. I didn't think about it, and I didn't even worry too much about what Mama would think or what Grandma would think or what Uncle So-and-So would think or what the people would think because at first I

didn't think that I would ever have to worry that they would see what I had written. Now, I'm working on this new novel which is long and complex to the point of being foolhardy. Who knows, a polite way would be to call it an ambitious project. But I'm so caught up in trying to see if I can make it happen. It's sort of a personal challenge, and again I'm not thinking about an audience. I've been quoted in other interviews as saying that I want this novel to be a novel that, when you shop at a Safeway store, it will be in the little wire racks at the check-out station and that I don't want to write something that the MLA will want. I want something that will horrify the people at the MLA. Mostly, I'm teasing, but in another way I'm not. I'm sad to see that so little serious fiction gets out into the world. I was amazed that Umberto Eco's *The Name of the Rose* and Mark Helprin's book *Winter's Tale* made it to the wire racks at the check-out stands in the United States. So I'm probably only part-way serious when I say that I don't think about an audience.

So you didn't write a book like Storyteller *for a particularly white or Indian audience.*

I don't think about Indian and white. What I wanted to do was clarify the interrelationship between the stories I had heard and my sense of storytelling and language that had been given to me by the old folks, the people back home. I gave examples of what I heard as best I could remember, and how I developed these elements into prose, into fiction and into poetry, moving from what was basically an oral tradition into a written tradition. The way I figured it, there would be some Native American people who would be interested in it and some Laguna Pueblo people who would be interested in it. There might be other people who are working out of a different cultural tradition but still working with oral material and working in their own art to bring the two together who would be interested. The book is for people who are interested in that relationship between the spoken and the written.

Do you consider yourself a storyteller in a traditional sense?

No, not at all. My friend Mei-mei Berssenbrugge, the poet, spent some time at Laguna Pueblo a few years ago, and she sat in on a kind of a session. I hesitate to call it a storytelling session because they're real spontaneous. It was at my uncle's house, and my uncle's wife Anita and her two sisters were there and some other people. It was in the evening and everyone was feeling jolly and talking. We might have started out with some kind of notorious incident that had happened recently, and pretty soon Mei-mei was sitting there listening to the way people would relate something that happened, and we'd all laugh and then one of Anita's sister's would say, ''Well, you remember the time,'' then the other sister would take over. When the whole session was over, we all went back over to my grandma's house where Mei-mei and I were staying, and Mei-mei said, ''They really have a way of telling these stories and incidents and kind of playing off one another.'' She was really impressed, and I said, ''See, I'm not in that class at all.'' I suppose if I didn't have the outlook of the writer, I might get better at storytelling, but I always say that I'm not good at giving off-the-cuff presentations. Oh, sometimes I have a fine moment. If you really want to hear people who can get rolling in telling, you have to do down to Laguna and kind of fall into the right situation, right feelings and right time.

Was a storyteller a spiritual leader? Was he or she someone who was born into or inherited that role?

It's not like that at all. There is a period of time at the winter solstice when people get together for four days and four nights, and they re-tell all the stories connected with the emergence and the migration of the People. There are people who have to learn and remember those stories and people who have to participate in that telling and re-telling once a year. Those people would probably be designated persons, but they would not be specially designated in any kind of ceremonial or religious way. They wouldn't be called storytellers; they would be called ceremonial religious leaders. The key to understanding storytellers and storytelling at Laguna Pueblo is to realize that you grow up not just being aware of narrative and making a story or seeing a story in what happens to you and what goes on around you all the time, but just being appreciative and delighted in narrative exchanges. When you meet somebody at a post office, he or she says, ''How are you, how are you doing?'' At Laguna, people will stand there and they'll tell you how they are doing. At Laguna, it's a way of interacting. It isn't like there's only one storyteller designated. That's not it at all. It's a whole way of being. When I say ''storytelling,'' I don't just mean sitting down and telling a once-upon-a-time kind of story. I mean a whole way of seeing yourself, the people around you, your life, the place of your life in the bigger context, not just in terms of nature and location, but in terms of what has gone on before, what's happened to other people. So it's a whole way of being, but there are some

people who are willing to be funnier or better storytellers than others, and some people because they are older or they remember better, have a larger repertoire of the *humma-hah* stories. It's not at all like the Irish idea of the bard or the chosen one.

Why are you writing these stories? Are you trying to put the oral tradition in a more stable or lasting form? Do you think anything is lost in the writing down of these stories?

Well, no, I'm not trying to save them, I'm not trying to put them in a stable or lasting form. I write them down because I like seeing how I can translate this sort of feeling or flavor or sense of a story that's told and heard onto the page. Obviously, some things will be lost because you're going from one medium to another. And I use *translate* in the broadest sense. I don't mean translate from the Laguna Pueblo language to English, I mean the feeling or the sense that language is being used orally. So I play with the page and things that you could do on the page, and repetitions. When you have an audience, when you're telling a story and people are listening, there's repetition of crucial points. That's something that on the printed page looks really crummy and is redundant and useless, but in the actual telling is necessary. So I play around with the page by using different kinds of spacing or indentations or even italics so that the reader can sense, say, that the tone of the voice has changed. If you were hearing a story, the speed would increase at certain points. I want to see how much I can make the page communicate those nuances and shifts to the reader. I'm intrigued with that. I recognize the inherent problem; there's no way that hearing a story and reading a story are the same thing; but that doesn't mean that everyone should throw up his hands and say it can't be done or say that what's done on the page isn't catching some of those senses. When I read off the page and read some of the *humma-hah* stories that I wrote down or go through some of the Aunt Susie material, then of course, I think it's more persuasive. In a way, that's not fair; because I'm reading it out loud, I've gone back again. But I think there are some instances where I've been successful so that the reader has a sense of how it might sound if I were reading it to him or her.

In a work like Storyteller, *are you actually creating something, or are you simply re-telling a myth?*

Every time a story is told, and this is one of the beauties of the oral tradition, each telling is a new and unique story, even if it's repeated word for word by the same teller sitting in the same chair. I work to try to help the reader have the sense of how it would sound if the reader could be hearing it. That's original. And no matter how carefully I remember, memory gets all mixed together with imagination. It does for everybody. But I don't change the spirit thing about the way she and I have gotten along, or how we related to one another? But, just remember what the position of the father and the mother would be in Pueblo society. If someone was going to thwart you or frighten you, it would tend to be a woman; you see it coming from your mother, or sent by your mother. . . .

I know that you have said in the past that the greatest influence on your writing has been your surroundings. Has there been a single novelist or poet whose work you find particularly inspirational or informational?

You mean working right now?

Not necessarily. I know you have talked about Milton and Shakespeare.

Well, lately, the one person that's meant a lot to me is Wittgenstein. I think his remarks on color turn into some of the most beautiful poetry I've ever read. People call Wittgenstein a philosopher and I call him a poet. I really like reading Wittgenstein right now.

How about influences on your style?

That is for style. You can see the clarity of his remarks on color in one of the last pieces he wrote before he died. With style, I'm like a sponge. I don't consciously look towards anyone. The poetry of my friend Mei-mei Berssenbrugge, I think, influences me. Her writing influences me, my ideas, and some of the things I write about influences her. And I think in terms of my prose style something of what she does with her poetry filters into me and has influenced me, but I couldn't say how exactly. What she does is real important, and so are some of her ideas about her connection with the so-called avant-garde in New York, and so forth. And the kinds of musicians, a lot of her interests have kind of filtered through to me, and I in turn have picked up and taken off with that in my own directions. My friend Larry McMurtry is a rare book dealer, and he comes across wonderful books in looking for rare expensive books. He's been breaking me out of the mold of just reading fiction or poetry. For example, H. D.'s tribute to Freud is wonderful. I like H.D.'s tribute to Freud about a million times more than I

like any of her damn poems. I would really not mind if some of H. D.'s magical prose rubbed off on mine; I would not mind that at all.

Paula Gunn Allen has said that reading Momaday's House Made of Dawn *was a turning point in her life. Has Momaday had the same effect on you as a writer?*

I'm trying to think. Turning point? Where was Paula headed before? I don't quite understand. No. I like *The Way to Rainy Mountain* very much, but I would have been doing what I was doing regardless of what Scott had done or not, written or not written.

Source: Leslie Marmon Silko and Kim Barnes, in an interview for *The Journal of Ethic Studies,* Vol. 13, No. 4, Winter, 1986, pp. 83–105.

Jim Ruppert

In the following essay, Ruppert discusses the mingling of reality and myth in Silko's collection of stories Ceremony.

Leslie Silko as a contemporary writer and a Laguna brings a new perception to the effort to topple [the boundaries of fiction], or rather an old one, older than American Literature. Her short fiction and her novel Ceremony are illuminated by the assumption that the story has a greater, truer reality than the objective reality of the world around us. In the story reality, the seeming simplicity and reality of objective actions and reinterpreted and woven into a larger scheme through which the actions take on a new and deeper meaning and their place in a mythic pattern emerges. The characters and the readers must believe as much as the author that the world exists in story which gives objective reality its meaning, or they are lost. Although the story may be stretched over eons, although it may move slowly and our understanding of it come only with great difficulty, we can understand it; we can enter into the story reality. Despite the hardships and the violent wrenchings of perspective required to do this, the attempt is necessary because it is only through entry into the story reality that each character is given his/her identity and perhaps ultimately so are we, the readers.

The "Yellow Woman" is an excellent example of the larger, all-encompassing reality of the story through which individual objective actions are reinterpreted and given new meaning. The contemporary girl by the river is incorporated into the traditional mythic Laguna story. In the Laguna story, Yellow Woman is near the river where she is surprised by a mountain spirit. The mountain spirit seduces her, and they go through a series of interesting adventures before she returns home, rather reluctantly to her husband and relatives. The original Yellow Woman of the Laguna tale is aware of the inevitability of her actions; it has been ordained since time immemorial. In Silko's story, a young girl is seduced by the river and swept away by someone who says he is a mountain spirit. She feels that an old Laguna story is patterning the encounter. The girl becomes confused and uncertain about her identity; is she the person she always thought she was, the one living in an objective mundane reality, or is she becoming Yellow Woman of the stories? She struggles to affirm that she is a girl with her own name and a family, to establish time boundaries and boundaries between objective reality and myths. ''I don't have to go,'' she says to the man. ''What they tell in stories was real only then, back in time immemorial, like they say.'' As she goes off with the mountain spirit man, she cries that if only she might see someone who knew her, who could place her in the objective reality, she would be sure of her identity. ''I will see someone, and then I will be certain that he is only a man—some man from nearby—and I will be sure I am not Yellow Woman.'' But the reality of the story triumphs and following the Laguna story, she runs off with the man. She is seduced into the story and goes off into the mountains where time seems to matter little and where she sees the larger pattern. When she leaves her husband, a new meaning is given it, and on the mountain she sees the larger patterns of living: in her own words, she can see ''the world.''

The girl's merging into the story seems to occur in part because it is ordained (a fortuitous collection of particulars), but more important the girl projects the proper psychic framework of a balanced being, while she is wondering if Yellow Woman herself had a sense of a separate identity or knew she was to become a story. The girl at this time is able to live totally in the present, in the story flow. ''This is the way it happens in the stories, I was thinking with no thought beyond the moment she meets the Ka'tsina spirit and they go.'' At this time, the girl is thinking about her identity, not about the past or the future, for identity, as all existentialists know, reveals a child of the present moment. As if understanding the girl's thoughts and anticipation of her words, the mountain spirit man says, ''What happened yesterday has nothing to do with what you will do today, Yellow Woman.'' Her description of her departure emphasizes the power of the story and her non-

> 'Yellow Woman' is an excellent example of the larger, all-encompassing reality of the story through which individual objective actions are reinterpreted and given new meaning."

willful entering into it. ''They the girl's family will go on like before, except there will be a story about the day I disappeared while I was walking along the river. Silva had come for me; he said he had. I did not decide to go. I just went. Moonflowers blossom in the sand hills before dawn, just as I followed him.'' When she finally returns home, according to the traditional story pattern, she speaks of ''my story'' and wishes that old grandpa was still alive because, as a storyteller, he would understand the identity the story gave her. In an interview in *Suntracks,* Silko explains this function of stories in oral traditions.

> That's how you know, that's how you belong, that's how you know you belong, if the stories incorporate you into them. There have to be stories. It's stories that make this a community. People tell those stories about you and your family or about others and they begin to create your identity. In a sense, you are told who you are, or you know who you are by the stories that are told about you. . . .

What I think we see in Silko's short fiction is that the story has a greater reality than objective reality, and that this story reality can be entered by placing ourselves in proximity to the story and acting with no thought beyond the moment so as to enter the story. In story reality, we assume an identity meaningful not only for ourselves, but also for the community that lives through the story. Perhaps this all becomes clearer if we turn now to Ceremony.

When Tayo returns from the war, he is sick, sick in much the same way his people are sick, and the world is sick through the influence of the manipulators. We are soon made to understand through old Betonie that ''his sickness was only part of something larger, and his cure would be found only in something greater and inclusive of everything.'' His cure will be long, slow and difficult like the telling of the story itself, but it can be of great benefit to the people, for his story will be merged with the larger one of the destroyers and the people. Or as Silko concludes, ''In the novel, it's the struggle between the force and the counter-force.''

If we agree that Tayo enters story reality in the novel, we may be tempted to say that it is through old Betonie's ceremony that he does so and hence the name of the novel. But near the end of the story, as the pattern and the proper ending is working itself out in the person of Tayo, Ts'eh, the mysterious mountain woman, observes that the Destroyers:

> Work to see how much can be lost, how much can be forgotten. They destroy the feeling people have for each other.

Tayo revives his hurt and the deaths of Rocky and Josiah, and she continues:

> Their highest ambition is to gut human beings while they are still breathing, to hold the heart still beating so the victim will never feel anything again. When they finish, you watch yourself from a distance and you can't even cry—not even for yourself.

This is the very sickness that has affected Tayo. His gutted feelings have been stimulated by Betonie, but it is not until the love of Ts'eh, the story woman of the mountains, that he is able to feel, to give himself to the flow of the story with no thought beyond the moment. At this point, he understands the larger story because he has entered it, as well as something of the false endings that the manipulators are trying to push on him. Through love, the boundaries dissolve between story-beings and real people, between the story as a true ongoing reality and our distinctions of time. As Leslie Silko puts it, ''One of the large battles Tayo begins to have to deal with is to keep the end of the story right. They're trying to manipulate him into doing something that would change the way the story has to go. It goes back to the ceremony thing that started long ago, and, of course, it does on and on.''

As Tayo struggles to conclude the story and the ceremony, the only honing device he has is the ''feeling of the story'' that he has received from Ts'eh and Betonie. With this to guide him, Tayo sees the world, its peoples and cultures as one huge swirling sandpainting and all the peoples of the world as one clan that must unite ceremonially to defeat the fate the destroyers have planned for mankind. ''Towards the end, everything Tayo sees is what Arrow Boy saw, but in a different century and a different form. It's there, it almost has to be. There's just no way around it.''

Tayo's identity comes from this understanding of the story's reality. He may be a savior or just a facilitator, but he must contribute his part to the ceremony. His strength at the end of the novel comes from this understanding. When he returns to the village, the old men understand the story. They want to know about the story woman he met in the mountains, and they conclude that they will be blessed again because he has seen her. His communal identity is secured because he is the one who has seen the woman in the mountains, who has brought the blessing, who has entered the story. They purify him, and the story has ended correctly. He is ready to gather the story-woman's seeds and to plant them as he promised. He has found himself.

However, when we put the book down, another important question can be asked. Has the reader understood the story? Has he entered the story reality? If the reader has, then he has an identity determined by the story either as a victim, a manipulator, or one of the aware people who must unite to defeat the destroyers. Let's hope we can all get the ending right.

It may be commonplace to say that Silko's work attempts to introduce dimensions of oral literature into written literature, and seeks a unification of the two in a new reality or a better explanation of the ordinary one, but her work at once stands out from modern fiction because of it and blends with it.

Of course, modern writers have injected and explored the mythic dimension in their works, but normally it has been in the creation of personal myths as with Yeats, the reemergence of mythic patterns as structural aides to meaning as in Joyce and Lawrence, or the expose and potential salvation of a disintegrated culture as with Eliot. In the development of contemporary fiction, ''self-conscious'' fiction struggles to incorporate the consciousness of the writer writing the story into the story, thus creating a myth of the writer. The result is that fiction and reality merge into one sphere. Silko, while having a different mission in inviting the story reality into what appears to be a non-story world, picks up the thrust of contemporary art toward an understanding of performance. The telling of the story creates a reality that merges with the non-story reality. The storyteller functions as a catalyst and an intersection for the merger of story reality and objective reality. The performance of the story becomes part of the story and though we do not feel the presence of Silko herself, the result is the same—a vision of the world as a unity of fiction and reality. More specifically in *Ceremony,* the unity is of the non-story world and the reality of the story-in-the-making. This is in effect a self-consciousness of oral literature. The story is being performed, and created. It is the material for future legends and the archetype for future tellings; the world and the story have been welded together.

Source: Jim Ruppert, ''Story Telling: The Fiction of Leslie Silko,'' in *The Journal of Ethnic Studies,* Vol. 9, No. 1, Spring, 1981, pp. 53–8.

Sources

Adams, Carol J. Introduction to *Ecofeminism and the Sacred,* Continuum, 1993.

Allen, Paula Gunn. *The Sacred Hoop: Recovering the Feminine in American Indian Traditions,* Beacon, 1986.

Allen, Paula Gunn. Introduction to *Song of the Turtle: American Indian Literature, 1974-1994,* Ballantine, 1996, pp. 3-17.

—*Spider Woman's Granddaughter,* Fawcett, 1989.

Barnes, Kim. In an interview in *The Journal of Ethnic Studies,* Vol. 13, No. 4, Winter 1986, pp. 83-105.

Boynton, Victoria. ''Desire's Revision: Feminist Appropriations of Native American Traditional Stories,'' in *Modern Language Studies,* Vol. 26, Nos. 2 and 3, Spring and Summer, 1996, pp. 53-72.

Brown, Dee. *Bury My Heart at Wounded Knee: An Indian History of the American West,* Bantam, 1970, pp. 1-13.

Castillo, Susan Perez. ''The Construction of Gender and Ethnicity in the Texts of Leslie Silko and Louise Erdrich,'' in *The Yearbook of English Studies,* Vol. 24, 1994, pp. 228-36.

Danielson, Linda. ''The Storytellers in *Storyteller,''* in *Studies in American Indian Literatures,* Series 2, Vol. 1, No. 2, Fall, 1989, pp. 21-31.

Evers, Larry and Denny Carr. Interview with Leslie Marmon Silko in *Sun Tracks,* Vol. 3, 1976, pp. 29-32.

Graulich, Melody, editor. Introduction to *Yellow Woman,* Rutgers University Press, 1993.

Hirsch, Bernard A. ''‘The Telling Which Continues’: Oral Tradition and the Written Word in Leslie Marmon Silko's *Storyteller,''* in *American Indian Quarterly,* Vol. 12, No. 1, Winter, 1988, pp. 1-28.

Jaskoski, Helen. ''Words Like Bones,'' in *CEA Critic,* Vol. 55, No. 1, Fall, 1992, pp. 70-84.

Krumholz, Linda J., in ''‘To Understand This World Differently’: Reading and Subversion in Leslie Marmon Silko's ''Storyteller,'' in *ARIEL: A Review of International English Literature,* Vol. 25, No. 1, January, 1994, pp. 89-113.

Lappas, Catherine. ''‘The Way I Heard It Was . . .’: Myth, Memory and Autobiography in *Storyteller* and *The Woman Warrior* in *CEA Critic,* Vol. 57, No. 1, Fall, 1994, pp. 57-67.

Perry, Donna. Interview with Leslie Marmon Silko in *Backtalk: Women Writers Speak Out,* Rutgers University Press, 1993, pp. 314-40.

Rosen, Kenneth, editor. Introduction to *The Man to Send Rain Clouds: Contemporary Stories by American Indians,* Viking, 1974.

Rubenstein, Roberta and Charles R. Larson. Interview with Leslie Marmon Silko in *Worlds of Fiction,* Macmillan, 1983, pp. 1086-87.

Ruoff, A. LaVonne. ''Ritual and Renewal: Keres Traditions in the Short Fiction of Leslie Silko,'' in *MELUS,* Vol. 5, 1979, pp. 1-15.

Ruppert, Jim. ''Story Telling: The Fiction of Leslie Silko,'' in *The Journal of Ethnic Studies,* Vol. 9, No. 1, Spring, 1981, pp. 53-8.

Sanchez, Carol Lee. ''Animal, Vegetable, and Mineral: The Sacred Connection,'' in *Ecofeminism and the Sacred,* edited by Carol J. Adams, Continuum, 1993, p. 211.

Silko, Leslie Marmon. ''Yellow Woman and a Beauty of the Spirit'' and ''The People and the Land ARE Inseparable'' in her collection, *Yellow Woman and a Beauty of the Spirit: Essays on Native American Life Today,* Simon & Schuster, 1996, pp. 60-72; 85-91.

Smith, Patricia Clark with Paula Gunn Allen. ''Earthly Relations, Carnal Knowledge: Southwestern American Indian Writers and Landscape,'' in *The Desert Is No Lady: Southwestern Landscapes in Women's Writing and Art,* edited by Vera Norwood and Janice Monk, Yale University Press, 1987, pp. 174-196

Further Reading

Black Elk. *Black Elk Speaks; Being the Life Story of a Holy Man of the Ogalala Sioux as told to John G. Neihardt,* Morrow, 1932.
　　The Memoirs of Black Elk, an Ogalala Sioux tribal leader who lived from 1863 until 1950.

Boas, Franz. *Keresan Texts,* American Ethnological Society, 1928.
　　An collection of oral stories of the Laguna and Acoma Pueblo gathered by the anthropologist Franz Boas in the early twentieth century in an attempt to make a written record of the Keresan language.

Zinn, Howard. *A People's History of the United States: 1492 to Present,* HarperPerennial, 1995.
　　This ambitious book recounts United States history from the perspective of underprivileged or powerless groups and includes several fine chapters that involve Native Americans.

Glossary of Literary Terms

A

Aestheticism: A literary and artistic movement of the nineteenth century. Followers of the movement believed that art should not be mixed with social, political, or moral teaching. The statement "art for art's sake" is a good summary of aestheticism. The movement had its roots in France, but it gained widespread importance in England in the last half of the nineteenth century, where it helped change the Victorian practice of including moral lessons in literature. Edgar Allan Poe is one of the best-known American "aesthetes."

Allegory: A narrative technique in which characters representing things or abstract ideas are used to convey a message or teach a lesson. Allegory is typically used to teach moral, ethical, or religious lessons but is sometimes used for satiric or political purposes. Many fairy tales are allegories.

Allusion: A reference to a familiar literary or historical person or event, used to make an idea more easily understood. Joyce Carol Oates's story "Where Are You Going, Where Have You Been?" exhibits several allusions to popular music.

Analogy: A comparison of two things made to explain something unfamiliar through its similarities to something familiar, or to prove one point based on the acceptance of another. Similes and metaphors are types of analogies.

Antagonist: The major character in a narrative or drama who works against the hero or protagonist. The Misfit in Flannery O'Connor's story "A Good Man Is Hard to Find" serves as the antagonist for the Grandmother.

Anthology: A collection of similar works of literature, art, or music. Zora Neale Hurston's "The Eatonville Anthology" is a collection of stories that take place in the same town.

Anthropomorphism: The presentation of animals or objects in human shape or with human characteristics. The term is derived from the Greek word for "human form." The fur necklet in Katherine Mansfield's story "Miss Brill" has anthropomorphic characteristics.

Anti-hero: A central character in a work of literature who lacks traditional heroic qualities such as courage, physical prowess, and fortitude. Anti-heroes typically distrust conventional values and are unable to commit themselves to any ideals. They generally feel helpless in a world over which they have no control. Anti-heroes usually accept, and often celebrate, their positions as social outcasts. A well-known anti-hero is Walter Mitty in James Thurber's story "The Secret Life of Walter Mitty."

Archetype: The word archetype is commonly used to describe an original pattern or model from which all other things of the same kind are made. Archetypes are the literary images that grow out of the "collective unconscious,'' a theory proposed by psychologist Carl Jung. They appear in literature as incidents and plots that repeat basic patterns of life. They may also appear as stereotyped characters. The ''schlemiel'' of Yiddish literature is an archetype.

Autobiography: A narrative in which an individual tells his or her life story. Examples include Benjamin Franklin's *Autobiography* and Amy Hempel's story ''In the Cemetery Where Al Jolson Is Buried,'' which has autobiographical characteristics even though it is a work of fiction.

Avant-garde: A literary term that describes new writing that rejects traditional approaches to literature in favor of innovations in style or content. Twentieth-century examples of the literary *avant-garde* include the modernists and the minimalists.

B

Belles-lettres: A French term meaning ''fine letters'' or ''beautiful writing.'' It is often used as a synonym for literature, typically referring to imaginative and artistic rather than scientific or expository writing. Current usage sometimes restricts the meaning to light or humorous writing and appreciative essays about literature. Lewis Carroll's *Alice in Wonderland* epitomizes the realm of belles-lettres.

Bildungsroman: A German word meaning ''novel of development.'' The *bildungsroman* is a study of the maturation of a youthful character, typically brought about through a series of social or sexual encounters that lead to self-awareness. J. D. Salinger's *Catcher in the Rye* is a *bildungsroman*, and Doris Lessing's story ''Through the Tunnel'' exhibits characteristics of a *bildungsroman* as well.

Black Aesthetic Movement: A period of artistic and literary development among African Americans in the 1960s and early 1970s. This was the first major African-American artistic movement since the Harlem Renaissance and was closely paralleled by the civil rights and black power movements. The black aesthetic writers attempted to produce works of art that would be meaningful to the black masses. Key figures in black aesthetics included one of its founders, poet and playwright Amiri Baraka, formerly known as LeRoi Jones; poet and essayist Haki R. Madhubuti, formerly Don L. Lee; poet and playwright Sonia Sanchez; and dramatist Ed Bullins. Works representative of the Black Aesthetic Movement include Amiri Baraka's play *Dutchman,* a 1964 Obie award-winner.

Black Humor: Writing that places grotesque elements side by side with humorous ones in an attempt to shock the reader, forcing him or her to laugh at the horrifying reality of a disordered world. ''Lamb to the Slaughter,'' by Roald Dahl, in which a placid housewife murders her husband and serves the murder weapon to the investigating policemen, is an example of black humor.

C

Catharsis: The release or purging of unwanted emotions—specifically fear and pity—brought about by exposure to art. The term was first used by the Greek philosopher Aristotle in his *Poetics* to refer to the desired effect of tragedy on spectators.

Character: Broadly speaking, a person in a literary work. The actions of characters are what constitute the plot of a story, novel, or poem. There are numerous types of characters, ranging from simple, stereotypical figures to intricate, multifaceted ones. ''Characterization'' is the process by which an author creates vivid, believable characters in a work of art. This may be done in a variety of ways, including (1) direct description of the character by the narrator; (2) the direct presentation of the speech, thoughts, or actions of the character; and (3) the responses of other characters to the character. The term ''character'' also refers to a form originated by the ancient Greek writer Theophrastus that later became popular in the seventeenth and eighteenth centuries. It is a short essay or sketch of a person who prominently displays a specific attribute or quality, such as miserliness or ambition. ''Miss Brill,'' a story by Katherine Mansfield, is an example of a character sketch.

Classical: In its strictest definition in literary criticism, classicism refers to works of ancient Greek or Roman literature. The term may also be used to describe a literary work of recognized importance (a ''classic'') from any time period or literature that exhibits the traits of classicism. Examples of later works and authors now described as classical include French literature of the seventeenth century, Western novels of the nineteenth century, and American fiction of the mid-nineteenth century such as that written by James Fenimore Cooper and Mark Twain.

Climax: The turning point in a narrative, the moment when the conflict is at its most intense. Typically, the structure of stories, novels, and plays is one of rising action, in which tension builds to the climax, followed by falling action, in which tension lessens as the story moves to its conclusion.

Comedy: One of two major types of drama, the other being tragedy. Its aim is to amuse, and it typically ends happily. Comedy assumes many forms, such as farce and burlesque, and uses a variety of techniques, from parody to satire. In a restricted sense the term comedy refers only to dramatic presentations, but in general usage it is commonly applied to nondramatic works as well.

Comic Relief: The use of humor to lighten the mood of a serious or tragic story, especially in plays. The technique is very common in Elizabethan works, and can be an integral part of the plot or simply a brief event designed to break the tension of the scene.

Conflict: The conflict in a work of fiction is the issue to be resolved in the story. It usually occurs between two characters, the protagonist and the antagonist, or between the protagonist and society or the protagonist and himself or herself. The conflict in Washington Irving's story "The Devil and Tom Walker" is that the Devil wants Tom Walker's soul, but Tom does not want to go to hell.

Criticism: The systematic study and evaluation of literary works, usually based on a specific method or set of principles. An important part of literary studies since ancient times, the practice of criticism has given rise to numerous theories, methods, and "schools," sometimes producing conflicting, even contradictory, interpretations of literature in general as well as of individual works. Even such basic issues as what constitutes a poem or a novel have been the subject of much criticism over the centuries. Seminal texts of literary criticism include Plato's *Republic,* Aristotle's *Poetics,* Sir Philip Sidney's *The Defence of Poesie,* and John Dryden's *Of Dramatic Poesie.* Contemporary schools of criticism include deconstruction, feminist, psychoanalytic, poststructuralist, new historicist, postcolonialist, and reader-response.

D

Deconstruction: A method of literary criticism characterized by multiple conflicting interpretations of a given work. Deconstructionists consider the impact of the language of a work and suggest that the true meaning of the work is not necessarily the meaning that the author intended.

Deduction: The process of reaching a conclusion through reasoning from general premises to a specific premise. Arthur Conan Doyle's character Sherlock Holmes often used deductive reasoning to solve mysteries.

Denotation: The definition of a word, apart from the impressions or feelings it creates in the reader. The word "apartheid" denotes a political and economic policy of segregation by race, but its connotations—oppression, slavery, inequality—are numerous.

Denouement: A French word meaning "the unknotting." In literature, it denotes the resolution of conflict in fiction or drama. The *denouement* follows the climax and provides an outcome to the primary plot situation as well as an explanation of secondary plot complications. A well-known example of *denouement* is the last scene of the play *As You Like It* by William Shakespeare, in which couples are married, an evil-doer repents, the identities of two disguised characters are revealed, and a ruler is restored to power. Also known as "falling action."

Detective Story: A narrative about the solution of a mystery or the identification of a criminal. The conventions of the detective story include the detective's scrupulous use of logic in solving the mystery; incompetent or ineffectual police; a suspect who appears guilty at first but is later proved innocent; and the detective's friend or confidant—often the narrator—whose slowness in interpreting clues emphasizes by contrast the detective's brilliance. Edgar Allan Poe's "Murders in the Rue Morgue" is commonly regarded as the earliest example of this type of story. Other practitioners are Arthur Conan Doyle, Dashiell Hammett, and Agatha Christie.

Dialogue: Dialogue is conversation between people in a literary work. In its most restricted sense, it refers specifically to the speech of characters in a drama. As a specific literary genre, a "dialogue" is a composition in which characters debate an issue or idea.

Didactic: A term used to describe works of literature that aim to teach a moral, religious, political, or practical lesson. Although didactic elements are often found inartistically pleasing works, the term "didactic" usually refers to literature in which the message is more important than the form. The term may also be used to criticize a work that the critic finds "overly didactic," that is, heavy-handed in its delivery of a lesson. An example of didactic literature is John Bunyan's *Pilgrim's Progress.*

Dramatic Irony: Occurs when the reader of a work of literature knows something that a character in the work itself does not know. The irony is in the contrast between the intended meaning of the statements or actions of a character and the additional information understood by the audience.

Dystopia: An imaginary place in a work of fiction where the characters lead dehumanized, fearful lives. George Orwell's *Nineteen Eighty-four,* and Margaret Atwood's *Handmaid's Tale* portray versions of dystopia.

E

Edwardian: Describes cultural conventions identified with the period of the reign of Edward VII of England (1901-1910). Writers of the Edwardian Age typically displayed a strong reaction against the propriety and conservatism of the Victorian Age. Their work often exhibits distrust of authority in religion, politics, and art and expresses strong doubts about the soundness of conventional values. Writers of this era include E. M. Forster, H. G. Wells, and Joseph Conrad.

Empathy: A sense of shared experience, including emotional and physical feelings, with someone or something other than oneself. Empathy is often used to describe the response of a reader to a literary character.

Epilogue: A concluding statement or section of a literary work. In dramas, particularly those of the seventeenth and eighteenth centuries, the epilogue is a closing speech, often in verse, delivered by an actor at the end of a play and spoken directly to the audience.

Epiphany: A sudden revelation of truth inspired by a seemingly trivial incident. The term was widely used by James Joyce in his critical writings, and the stories in Joyce's *Dubliners* are commonly called ''epiphanies.''

Epistolary Novel: A novel in the form of letters. The form was particularly popular in the eighteenth century. The form can also be applied to short stories, as in Edwidge Danticat's ''Children of the Sea.''

Epithet: A word or phrase, often disparaging or abusive, that expresses a character trait of someone or something. ''The Napoleon of crime'' is an epithet applied to Professor Moriarty, arch-rival of Sherlock Holmes in Arthur Conan Doyle's series of detective stories.

Existentialism: A predominantly twentieth-century philosophy concerned with the nature and perception of human existence. There are two major strains of existentialist thought: atheistic and Christian. Followers of atheistic existentialism believe that the individual is alone in a godless universe and that the basic human condition is one of suffering and loneliness. Nevertheless, because there are no fixed values, individuals can create their own characters—indeed, they can shape themselves—through the exercise of free will. The atheistic strain culminates in and is popularly associated with the works of Jean-Paul Sartre. The Christian existentialists, on the other hand, believe that only in God may people find freedom from life's anguish. The two strains hold certain beliefs in common: that existence cannot be fully understood or described through empirical effort; that anguish is a universal element of life; that individuals must bear responsibility for their actions; and that there is no common standard of behavior or perception for religious and ethical matters. Existentialist thought figures prominently in the works of such authors as Franz Kafka, Fyodor Dostoyevsky, and Albert Camus.

Expatriatism: The practice of leaving one's country to live for an extended period in another country. Literary expatriates include Irish author James Joyce who moved to Italy and France; American writers James Baldwin, Ernest Hemingway, Gertrude Stein, and F. Scott Fitzgerald who lived and wrote in Paris; and Polish novelist Joseph Conrad, who lived in England.

Exposition: Writing intended to explain the nature of an idea, thing, or theme. Expository writing is often combined with description, narration, or argument.

Expressionism: An indistinct literary term, originally used to describe an early twentieth-century school of German painting. The term applies to almost any mode of unconventional, highly subjective writing that distorts reality in some way. Advocates of Expressionism include Federico Garcia Lorca, Eugene O'Neill, Franz Kafka, and James Joyce.

F

Fable: A prose or verse narrative intended to convey a moral. Animals or inanimate objects with human characteristics often serve as characters in fables. A famous fable is Aesop's "The Tortoise and the Hare."

Fantasy: A literary form related to mythology and folklore. Fantasy literature is typically set in non-existent realms and features supernatural beings. Notable examples of literature with elements of fantasy are Gabriel Garcia Marquez's story "The Handsomest Drowned Man in the World" and Ursula K. LeGuin's "The Ones Who Walk Away from Omelas."

Farce: A type of comedy characterized by broad humor, outlandish incidents, and often vulgar subject matter. Much of the comedy in film and television could more accurately be described as farce.

Fiction: Any story that is the product of imagination rather than a documentation of fact. Characters and events in such narratives may be based in real life but their ultimate form and configuration is a creation of the author.

Figurative Language: A technique in which an author uses figures of speech such as hyperbole, irony, metaphor, or simile for a particular effect. Figurative language is the opposite of literal language, in which every word is truthful, accurate, and free of exaggeration or embellishment.

Flashback: A device used in literature to present action that occurred before the beginning of the story. Flashbacks are often introduced as the dreams or recollections of one or more characters.

Foil: A character in a work of literature whose physical or psychological qualities contrast strongly with, and therefore highlight, the corresponding qualities of another character. In his Sherlock Holmes stories, Arthur Conan Doyle portrayed Dr. Watson as a man of normal habits and intelligence, making him a foil for the eccentric and unusually perceptive Sherlock Holmes.

Folklore: Traditions and myths preserved in a culture or group of people. Typically, these are passed on by word of mouth in various forms—such as legends, songs, and proverbs—or preserved in customs and ceremonies. Washington Irving, in "The Devil and Tom Walker" and many of his other stories, incorporates many elements of the folklore of New England and Germany.

Folktale: A story originating in oral tradition. Folktales fall into a variety of categories, including legends, ghost stories, fairy tales, fables, and anecdotes based on historical figures and events.

Foreshadowing: A device used in literature to create expectation or to set up an explanation of later developments. Edgar Allan Poe uses foreshadowing to create suspense in "The Fall of the House of Usher" when the narrator comments on the crumbling state of disrepair in which he finds the house.

G

Genre: A category of literary work. Genre may refer to both the content of a given work—tragedy, comedy, horror, science fiction—and to its form, such as poetry, novel, or drama.

Gilded Age: A period in American history during the 1870s and after characterized by political corruption and materialism. A number of important novels of social and political criticism were written during this time. Henry James and Kate Chopin are two writers who were prominent during the Gilded Age.

Gothicism: In literature, works characterized by a taste for medieval or morbid characters and situations. A gothic novel prominently features elements of horror, the supernatural, gloom, and violence: clanking chains, terror, ghosts, medieval castles, and unexplained phenomena. The term "gothic novel" is also applied to novels that lack elements of the traditional gothic setting but that create a similar atmosphere of terror or dread. The term can also be applied to stories, plays, and poems. Mary Shelley's *Frankenstein* and Joyce Carol Oates's *Bellefleur* are both gothic novels.

Grotesque: In literature, a work that is characterized by exaggeration, deformity, freakishness, and disorder. The grotesque often includes an element of comic absurdity. Examples of the grotesque can be found in the works of Edgar Allan Poe, Flannery O'Connor, Joseph Heller, and Shirley Jackson.

H

Harlem Renaissance: The Harlem Renaissance of the 1920s is generally considered the first significant movement of black writers and artists in the United States. During this period, new and established black writers, many of whom lived in the region of New York City known as Harlem, published more fiction and poetry than ever before, the first influential black literary journals were established, and black authors and artists received their first widespread recognition and serious critical appraisal. Among the major writers associated with this period are Countee Cullen, Langston Hughes, Arna Bontemps, and Zora Neale Hurston.

Hero/Heroine: The principal sympathetic character in a literary work. Heroes and heroines typically exhibit admirable traits: idealism, courage, and integrity, for example. Famous heroes and heroines of literature include Charles Dickens's Oliver Twist, Margaret Mitchell's Scarlett O'Hara, and the anonymous narrator in Ralph Ellison's *Invisible Man*.

Hyperbole: Deliberate exaggeration used to achieve an effect. In William Shakespeare's *Macbeth,* Lady Macbeth hyperbolizes when she says, ''All the perfumes of Arabia could not sweeten this little hand.''

I

Image: A concrete representation of an object or sensory experience. Typically, such a representation helps evoke the feelings associated with the object or experience itself. Images are either ''literal'' or ''figurative.'' Literal images are especially concrete and involve little or no extension of the obvious meaning of the words used to express them. Figurative images do not follow the literal meaning of the words exactly. Images in literature are usually visual, but the term ''image'' can also refer to the representation of any sensory experience.

Imagery: The array of images in a literary work. Also used to convey the author's overall use of figurative language in a work.

In medias res: A Latin term meaning ''in the middle of things.'' It refers to the technique of beginning a story at its midpoint and then using various flashback devices to reveal previous action. This technique originated in such epics as Virgil's *Aeneid.*

Interior Monologue: A narrative technique in which characters' thoughts are revealed in a way that appears to be uncontrolled by the author. The interior monologue typically aims to reveal the inner self of a character. It portrays emotional experiences as they occur at both a conscious and unconscious level. One of the best-known interior monologues in English is the Molly Bloom section at the close of James Joyce's *Ulysses.* Katherine Anne Porter's ''The Jilting of Granny Weatherall'' is also told in the form of an interior monologue.

Irony: In literary criticism, the effect of language in which the intended meaning is the opposite of what is stated. The title of Jonathan Swift's ''A Modest Proposal'' is ironic because what Swift proposes in this essay is cannibalism—hardly ''modest.''

J

Jargon: Language that is used or understood only by a select group of people. Jargon may refer to terminology used in a certain profession, such as computer jargon, or it may refer to any nonsensical language that is not understood by most people. Anthony Burgess's *A Clockwork Orange* and James Thurber's ''The Secret Life of Walter Mitty'' both use jargon.

K

Knickerbocker Group: An indistinct group of New York writers of the first half of the nineteenth century. Members of the group were linked only by location and a common theme: New York life. Two famous members of the Knickerbocker Group were Washington Irving and William Cullen Bryant. The group's name derives from Irving's *Knickerbocker's History of New York.*

L

Literal Language: An author uses literal language when he or she writes without exaggerating or embellishing the subject matter and without any tools of figurative language. To say ''He ran very quickly down the street'' is to use literal language, whereas to say ''He ran like a hare down the street'' would be using figurative language.

Literature: Literature is broadly defined as any written or spoken material, but the term most often refers to creative works. Literature includes poetry, drama, fiction, and many kinds of nonfiction writing, as well as oral, dramatic, and broadcast compositions not necessarily preserved in a written format, such as films and television programs.

Lost Generation: A term first used by Gertrude Stein to describe the post-World War I generation of American writers: men and women haunted by a sense of betrayal and emptiness brought about by the destructiveness of the war. The term is commonly applied to Hart Crane, Ernest Hemingway, F. Scott Fitzgerald, and others.

M

Magic Realism: A form of literature that incorporates fantasy elements or supernatural occurrences into the narrative and accepts them as truth. Gabriel Garcia Marquez and Laura Esquivel are two writers known for their works of magic realism.

Metaphor: A figure of speech that expresses an idea through the image of another object. Metaphors suggest the essence of the first object by identifying it with certain qualities of the second object. An example is "But soft, what light through yonder window breaks? / It is the east, and Juliet is the sun" in William Shakespeare's *Romeo and Juliet.* Here, Juliet, the first object, is identified with qualities of the second object, the sun.

Minimalism: A literary style characterized by spare, simple prose with few elaborations. In minimalism, the main theme of the work is often never discussed directly. Amy Hempel and Ernest Hemingway are two writers known for their works of minimalism.

Modernism: Modern literary practices. Also, the principles of a literary school that lasted from roughly the beginning of the twentieth century until the end of World War II. Modernism is defined by its rejection of the literary conventions of the nineteenth century and by its opposition to conventional morality, taste, traditions, and economic values. Many writers are associated with the concepts of modernism, including Albert Camus, D. H. Lawrence, Ernest Hemingway, William Faulkner, Eugene O'Neill, and James Joyce.

Monologue: A composition, written or oral, by a single individual. More specifically, a speech given by a single individual in a drama or other public entertainment. It has no set length, although it is usually several or more lines long. "I Stand Here Ironing" by Tillie Olsen is an example of a story written in the form of a monologue.

Mood: The prevailing emotions of a work or of the author in his or her creation of the work. The mood of a work is not always what might be expected based on its subject matter.

Motif: A theme, character type, image, metaphor, or other verbal element that recurs throughout a single work of literature or occurs in a number of different works over a period of time. For example, the color white in Herman Melville's *Moby Dick* is a "specific" motif, while the trials of star-crossed lovers is a "conventional" motif from the literature of all periods.

N

Narration: The telling of a series of events, real or invented. A narration may be either a simple narrative, in which the events are recounted chronologically, or a narrative with a plot, in which the account is given in a style reflecting the author's artistic concept of the story. Narration is sometimes used as a synonym for "storyline."

Narrative: A verse or prose accounting of an event or sequence of events, real or invented. The term is also used as an adjective in the sense "method of narration." For example, in literary criticism, the expression "narrative technique" usually refers to the way the author structures and presents his or her story. Different narrative forms include diaries, travelogues, novels, ballads, epics, short stories, and other fictional forms.

Narrator: The teller of a story. The narrator may be the author or a character in the story through whom the author speaks. Huckleberry Finn is the narrator of Mark Twain's *The Adventures of Huckleberry Finn.*

Novella: An Italian term meaning "story." This term has been especially used to describe fourteenth-century Italian tales, but it also refers to modern short novels. Modern novellas include Leo Tolstoy's *The Death of Ivan Ilich,* Fyodor Dostoyevsky's *Notes from the Underground,* and Joseph Conrad's *Heart of Darkness.*

O

Oedipus Complex: A son's romantic obsession with his mother. The phrase is derived from the story of the ancient Theban hero Oedipus, who unknowingly killed his father and married his mother, and was popularized by Sigmund Freud's theory of psychoanalysis. Literary occurrences of the Oedipus complex include Sophocles' *Oedipus Rex* and D. H. Lawrence's "The Rocking-Horse Winner."

Onomatopoeia: The use of words whose sounds express or suggest their meaning. In its simplest sense, onomatopoeia may be represented by words that mimic the sounds they denote such as "hiss" or "meow." At a more subtle level, the pattern and rhythm of sounds and rhymes of a line or poem may be onomatopoeic.

Oral Tradition: A process by which songs, ballads, folklore, and other material are transmitted by word of mouth. The tradition of oral transmission predates the written record systems of literate society.

Oral transmission preserves material sometimes over generations, although often with variations. Memory plays a large part in the recitation and preservation of orally transmitted material. Native American myths and legends, and African folktales told by plantation slaves are examples of orally transmitted literature.

P

Parable: A story intended to teach a moral lesson or answer an ethical question. Examples of parables are the stories told by Jesus Christ in the New Testament, notably "The Prodigal Son," but parables also are used in Sufism, rabbinic literature, Hasidism, and Zen Buddhism. Isaac Bashevis Singer's story "Gimpel the Fool" exhibits characteristics of a parable.

Paradox: A statement that appears illogical or contradictory at first, but may actually point to an underlying truth. A literary example of a paradox is George Orwell's statement "All animals are equal, but some animals are more equal than others" in *Animal Farm.*

Parody: In literature, this term refers to an imitation of a serious literary work or the signature style of a particular author in a ridiculous manner. A typical parody adopts the style of the original and applies it to an inappropriate subject for humorous effect. Parody is a form of satire and could be considered the literary equivalent of a caricature or cartoon. Henry Fielding's *Shamela* is a parody of Samuel Richardson's *Pamela.*

Persona: A Latin term meaning "mask." Personae are the characters in a fictional work of literature. The persona generally functions as a mask through which the author tells a story in a voice other than his or her own. A persona is usually either a character in a story who acts as a narrator or an "implied author," a voice created by the author to act as the narrator for himself or herself. The persona in Charlotte Perkins Gilman's story "The Yellow Wallpaper" is the unnamed young mother experiencing a mental breakdown.

Personification: A figure of speech that gives human qualities to abstract ideas, animals, and inanimate objects. To say that "the sun is smiling" is to personify the sun.

Plot: The pattern of events in a narrative or drama. In its simplest sense, the plot guides the author in composing the work and helps the reader follow the work. Typically, plots exhibit causality and unity and have a beginning, a middle, and an end. Sometimes, however, a plot may consist of a series of disconnected events, in which case it is known as an "episodic plot."

Poetic Justice: An outcome in a literary work, not necessarily a poem, in which the good are rewarded and the evil are punished, especially in ways that particularly fit their virtues or crimes. For example, a murderer may himself be murdered, or a thief will find himself penniless.

Poetic License: Distortions of fact and literary convention made by a writer—not always a poet—for the sake of the effect gained. Poetic license is closely related to the concept of "artistic freedom." An author exercises poetic license by saying that a pile of money "reaches as high as a mountain" when the pile is actually only a foot or two high.

Point of View: The narrative perspective from which a literary work is presented to the reader. There are four traditional points of view. The "third-person omniscient" gives the reader a "godlike" perspective, unrestricted by time or place, from which to see actions and look into the minds of characters. This allows the author to comment openly on characters and events in the work. The "third person" point of view presents the events of the story from outside of any single character's perception, much like the omniscient point of view, but the reader must understand the action as it takes place and without any special insight into characters's minds or motivations. The "first person" or "personal" point of view relates events as they are perceived by a single character. The main character "tells" the story and may offer opinions about the action and characters which differ from those of the author. Much less common than omniscient, third person, and first person is the "second person" point of view, wherein the author tells the story as if it is happening to the reader. James Thurber employs the omniscient point of view in his short story "The Secret Life of Walter Mitty." Ernest Hemingway's "A Clean, Well-Lighted Place" is a short story told from the third-person point of view. Mark Twain's novel *Huckleberry Finn* is presented from the first-person viewpoint. Jay McInerney's *Bright Lights, Big City* is an example of a novel which uses the second person point of view.

Pornography: Writing intended to provoke feelings of lust in the reader. Such works are often condemned by critics and teachers, but those which can be shown to have literary value are viewed less harshly. Literary works that have been described as pornographic include D. H. Lawrence's *Lady Chatterley's Lover* and James Joyce's *Ulysses.*

Post-Aesthetic Movement: An artistic response made by African Americans to the black aesthetic movement of the 1960s and early 1970s. Writers since that time have adopted a somewhat different tone in their work, with less emphasis placed on the disparity between black and white in the United States. In the words of post-aesthetic authors such as Toni Morrison, John Edgar Wideman, and Kristin Hunter, African Americans are portrayed as looking inward for answers to their own questions, rather than always looking to the outside world. Two well-known examples of works produced as part of the post-aesthetic movement are the Pulitzer Prize-winning novels *The Color Purple* by Alice Walker and *Beloved* by Toni Morrison.

Postmodernism: Writing from the 1960s forward characterized by experimentation and application of modernist elements, which include existentialism and alienation. Postmodernists have gone a step further in the rejection of tradition begun with the modernists by also rejecting traditional forms, preferring the anti-novel over the novel and the anti-hero over the hero. Postmodern writers include Thomas Pynchon, Margaret Drabble, and Gabriel Garcia Marquez.

Prologue: An introductory section of a literary work. It often contains information establishing the situation of the characters or presents information about the setting, time period, or action. In drama, the prologue is spoken by a chorus or by one of the principal characters.

Prose: A literary medium that attempts to mirror the language of everyday speech. It is distinguished from poetry by its use of unmetered, unrhymed language consisting of logically related sentences. Prose is usually grouped into paragraphs that form a cohesive whole such as an essay or a novel. The term is sometimes used to mean an author's general writing.

Protagonist: The central character of a story who serves as a focus for its themes and incidents and as the principal rationale for its development. The protagonist is sometimes referred to in discussions of modern literature as the hero or anti-hero. Well-known protagonists are Hamlet in William Shakespeare's *Hamlet* and Jay Gatsby in F. Scott Fitzgerald's *The Great Gatsby.*

R

Realism: A nineteenth-century European literary movement that sought to portray familiar characters, situations, and settings in a realistic manner. This was done primarily by using an objective narrative point of view and through the buildup of accurate detail. The standard for success of any realistic work depends on how faithfully it transfers common experience into fictional forms. The realistic method may be altered or extended, as in stream of consciousness writing, to record highly subjective experience. Contemporary authors who often write in a realistic way include Nadine Gordimer and Grace Paley.

Resolution: The portion of a story following the climax, in which the conflict is resolved. The resolution of Jane Austen's *Northanger Abbey* is neatly summed up in the following sentence: "Henry and Catherine were married, the bells rang and everybody smiled."

Rising Action: The part of a drama where the plot becomes increasingly complicated. Rising action leads up to the climax, or turning point, of a drama. The final "chase scene" of an action film is generally the rising action which culminates in the film's climax.

Roman a clef: A French phrase meaning "novel with a key." It refers to a narrative in which real persons are portrayed under fictitious names. Jack Kerouac, for example, portrayed his various friends under fictitious names in the novel *On the Road.* D. H. Lawrence based "The Rocking-Horse Winner" on a family he knew.

Romanticism: This term has two widely accepted meanings. In historical criticism, it refers to a European intellectual and artistic movement of the late eighteenth and early nineteenth centuries that sought greater freedom of personal expression than that allowed by the strict rules of literary form and logic of the eighteenth-century neoclassicists. The Romantics preferred emotional and imaginative expression to rational analysis. They considered the individual to be at the center of all experience and so placed him or her at the center of their art. The Romantics believed that the creative imagination reveals nobler truths—unique feelings and attitudes—than those that could be discovered by logic or by scientific examination. "Romanticism" is also used as a general term to refer to a type of sensibility found in all periods of literary history and usually considered to be in opposition to the principles of classicism. In this sense, Romanticism signifies any work or philosophy in which the exotic or dreamlike figure strongly, or that is devoted to individualistic expression, self-analysis, or a pursuit of a higher realm of knowledge than can be discovered by human reason. Prominent Romantics include Jean-Jacques Rousseau, William Wordsworth, John Keats, Lord Byron, and Johann Wolfgang von Goethe.

S

Satire: A work that uses ridicule, humor, and wit to criticize and provoke change in human nature and institutions. Voltaire's novella *Candide* and Jonathan Swift's essay ''A Modest Proposal'' are both satires. Flannery O'Connor's portrayal of the family in ''A Good Man Is Hard to Find'' is a satire of a modern, Southern, American family.

Science Fiction: A type of narrative based upon real or imagined scientific theories and technology. Science fiction is often peopled with alien creatures and set on other planets or in different dimensions. Popular writers of science fiction are Isaac Asimov, Karel Capek, Ray Bradbury, and Ursula K. Le Guin.

Setting: The time, place, and culture in which the action of a narrative takes place. The elements of setting may include geographic location, characters's physical and mental environments, prevailing cultural attitudes, or the historical time in which the action takes place.

Short Story: A fictional prose narrative shorter and more focused than a novella. The short story usually deals with a single episode and often a single character. The ''tone,'' the author's attitude toward his or her subject and audience, is uniform throughout. The short story frequently also lacks *denouement*, ending instead at its climax.

Signifying Monkey: A popular trickster figure in black folklore, with hundreds of tales about this character documented since the 19th century. Henry Louis Gates Jr. examines the history of the signifying monkey in *The Signifying Monkey: Towards a Theory of Afro-American Literary Criticism,* published in 1988.

Simile: A comparison, usually using ''like'' or ''as,'' of two essentially dissimilar things, as in ''coffee as cold as ice'' or ''He sounded like a broken record.'' The title of Ernest Hemingway's ''Hills Like White Elephants'' contains a simile.

Socialist Realism: The Socialist Realism school of literary theory was proposed by Maxim Gorky and established as a dogma by the first Soviet Congress of Writers. It demanded adherence to a communist worldview in works of literature. Its doctrines required an objective viewpoint comprehensible to the working classes and themes of social struggle featuring strong proletarian heroes. Gabriel Garcia Marquez's stories exhibit some characteristics of Socialist Realism.

Stereotype: A stereotype was originally the name for a duplication made during the printing process; this led to its modern definition as a person or thing that is (or is assumed to be) the same as all others of its type. Common stereotypical characters include the absent-minded professor, the nagging wife, the troublemaking teenager, and the kindhearted grandmother.

Stream of Consciousness: A narrative technique for rendering the inward experience of a character. This technique is designed to give the impression of an ever-changing series of thoughts, emotions, images, and memories in the spontaneous and seemingly illogical order that they occur in life. The textbook example of stream of consciousness is the last section of James Joyce's *Ulysses*.

Structure: The form taken by a piece of literature. The structure may be made obvious for ease of understanding, as in nonfiction works, or may obscured for artistic purposes, as in some poetry or seemingly ''unstructured'' prose.

Style: A writer's distinctive manner of arranging words to suit his or her ideas and purpose in writing. The unique imprint of the author's personality upon his or her writing, style is the product of an author's way of arranging ideas and his or her use of diction, different sentence structures, rhythm, figures of speech, rhetorical principles, and other elements of composition.

Suspense: A literary device in which the author maintains the audience's attention through the build-up of events, the outcome of which will soon be revealed. Suspense in William Shakespeare's *Hamlet* is sustained throughout by the question of whether or not the Prince will achieve what he has been instructed to do.

Symbol: Something that suggests or stands for something else without losing its original identity. In literature, symbols combine their literal meaning with the suggestion of an abstract concept. Literary symbols are of two types: those that carry complex associations of meaning no matter what their contexts, and those that derive their suggestive meaning from their functions in specific literary works. Examples of symbols are sunshine suggesting happiness, rain suggesting sorrow, and storm clouds suggesting despair.

T

Tale: A story with a simple plot and little character development. Tales are usually relatively short and often carry a simple message. Examples of tales can be found in the works of Saki, Anton Chekhov, Guy de Maupassant, and O. Henry.

Tall Tale: A humorous tale told in a straightforward, credible tone but relating absolutely impossible events or feats of the characters. Such tales were commonly told of frontier adventures during the settlement of the West in the United States. Literary use of tall tales can be found in Washington Irving's *History of New York,* Mark Twain's *Life on the Mississippi,* and in the German R. F. Raspe's *Baron Munchausen's Narratives of His Marvellous Travels and Campaigns in Russia.*

Theme: The main point of a work of literature. The term is used interchangeably with thesis. Many works have multiple themes. One of the themes of Nathaniel Hawthorne's ''Young Goodman Brown'' is loss of faith.

Tone: The author's attitude toward his or her audience may be deduced from the tone of the work. A formal tone may create distance or convey politeness, while an informal tone may encourage a friendly, intimate, or intrusive feeling in the reader. The author's attitude toward his or her subject matter may also be deduced from the tone of the words he or she uses in discussing it. The tone of John F. Kennedy's speech which included the appeal to ''ask not what your country can do for you'' was intended to instill feelings of camaraderie and national pride in listeners.

Tragedy: A drama in prose or poetry about a noble, courageous hero of excellent character who, because of some tragic character flaw, brings ruin upon him or herself. Tragedy treats its subjects in a dignified and serious manner, using poetic language to help evoke pity and fear and bring about catharsis, a purging of these emotions. The tragic form was practiced extensively by the ancient Greeks. The classical form of tragedy was revived in the sixteenth century; it flourished especially on the Elizabethan stage. In modern times, dramatists have attempted to adapt the form to the needs of modern society by drawing their heroes from the ranks of ordinary men and women and defining the nobility of these heroes in terms of spirit rather than exalted social standing. Some contemporary works that are thought of as tragedies include *The Great Gatsby* by F. Scott Fitzgerald, and *The Sound and the Fury* by William Faulkner.

Tragic Flaw: In a tragedy, the quality within the hero or heroine which leads to his or her downfall. Examples of the tragic flaw include Othello's jealousy and Hamlet's indecisiveness, although most great tragedies defy such simple interpretation.

U

Utopia: A fictional perfect place, such as ''paradise'' or ''heaven.'' An early literary utopia was described in Plato's *Republic,* and in modern literature, Ursula K. Le Guin depicts a utopia in ''The Ones Who Walk Away from Omelas.''

V

Victorian: Refers broadly to the reign of Queen Victoria of England (1837-1901) and to anything with qualities typical of that era. For example, the qualities of smug narrow-mindedness, bourgeois materialism, faith in social progress, and priggish morality are often considered Victorian. In literature, the Victorian Period was the great age of the English novel, and the latter part of the era saw the rise of movements such as decadence and symbolism.

Cumulative Author/Title Index

Nationality/Ethnicity Index

Poe, Edgar Allan
  *The Fall of the House of
    Usher*: V2
  The Tell-Tale Heart: V4
Porter, Katherine Anne
  *The Jilting of Granny
    Weatherall*: V1
Silko, Leslie Marmon
  Yellow Woman: V4
Singer, Isaac Bashevis
  Gimpel the Fool: V2
Steinbeck, John
  Flight: V3
Stockton, Frank R.
  The Lady, or the Tiger?: V3
Thurber, James
  *The Secret Life of Walter
    Mitty*: V1
Twain, Mark
  *The Celebrated Jumping Frog of
    Calaveras County*: V1
Updike, John
  A & P: V3
Walker, Alice
  Everyday Use: V2
Welty, Eudora
  A Worn Path: V2
Wolff, Tobias
  *In the Garden of the North
    American Martyrs*: V4
Wright, Richard
  *The Man Who Lived
    Underground*: V3

Argentine

Borges, Jorge Luis
  *Pierre Menard, Author of the
    Quixote*: V4
Cortazar, Julio
  Axolotl: V3

Asian American

Kingston, Maxine Hong
  On Discovery: V3

Austrian

Kafka, Franz
  In the Penal Colony: V3

British

Carter, Angela
  The Bloody Chamber: V4
Clarke, Arthur C.
  The Star: V4
Conrad, Joseph
  The Secret Sharer: V1

Far, Sui Sin
  Mrs. Spring Fragrance: V4
Galsworthy, John
  The Japanese Quince: V3
Jacobs, W. W.
  The Monkey's Paw: V2
Lawrence, D. H.
  The Rocking-Horse Winner: V2
Lessing, Doris
  Through the Tunnel: V1
Orwell, George
  Shooting an Elephant: V4
Saki,
  The Open Window: V1
Wells, H. G.
  The Door in the Wall: V3
Woolf, Virginia
  The New Dress: V4

Canadian

Atwood, Margaret
  Rape Fantasies: V3

Chicano

Cisneros, Sandra
  Woman Hollering Creek: V3

Colombian

Marquez, Gabriel Garcia
  *The Handsomest Drowned Man in
    the World*: V1

Czech

Kafka, Franz
  In the Penal Colony: V3

Danish

Dinesen, Isak
  Sorrow-Acre: V3

Eurasian

Far, Sui Sin
  Mrs. Spring Fragrance: V4

French

Camus, Albert
  The Guest: V4
Maupassant, Guy de
  The Necklace: V4

German

Mann, Thomas
  Disorder and Early Sorrow: V4

Haitian

Danticat, Edwidge
  Children of the Sea: V1

Irish

Joyce, James
  Araby: V1

Jewish American

Ozick, Cynthia
  The Shawl: V3
Paley, Grace
  *A Conversation with My
    Father*: V3
Singer, Isaac Bashevis
  Gimpel the Fool: V2

Native American

Silko, Leslie Marmon
  Yellow Woman: V4

New Zealander

Mansfield, Katherine
  Miss Brill: V2

Nigerian

Achebe, Chinua
  Vengeful Creditor: V3

Polish

Conrad, Joseph
  The Secret Sharer: V1
Singer, Isaac Bashevis
  Gimpel the Fool: V2

Scottish

Doyle, Arthur Conan
  The Red-Headed League: V2

South African

Gordimer, Nadine
  The Train from Rhodesia: V2

Welsh

Dahl, Roald
  Lamb to the Slaughter: V4